PREFACE TO FIFTEENTH EDITION

For the first time this is a new Edition of Police Law without a preface by the author, Mr. Cecil Charles Hudson Moriarty, C.B.E., LL.D.

After distinguishing himself at Trinity College, Dublin, Mr. Moriarty joined the Royal Irish Constabulary in 1902. In 1918 he was appointed Assistant Chief Constable of Birmingham, becoming Chief Constable in 1935. In 1941 he retired from the police service but continued to take an active part in the revision of the police books he had written until he was taken ill shortly before his death in April, 1958.

The first edition of Police Law appeared in 1929 and was described by the late Sir Charles Rafter in his foreword as a book which went a long way in providing in a comprehensive form the knowledge which a constable finds difficult to obtain. During the following 30 years, Fourteen Editions and Seventeen Impressions of Police Law have been published. This proves that Mr. Moriarty in writing what has become the standard text-book of the policeman has ensured for himself the gratitude and esteem of generations of policemen.

Those who had the privilege of serving with Mr. Moriarty can testify to his gifts for hard work, clear thinking and his exceptional ability to condense abstruse legal phraseology into lucid and simple language.

Much of the revision necessary for the present edition had been approved by Mr. Moriarty before he was taken ill at the beginning of 1958, and the revision has been completed upon the lines which he himself laid down.

W. J. WILLIAMS.

CAERNARVON.
1st *January*, 1959.

POLICE LAW

An Arrangement of Law and Regulations for
the Use of Police Officers

FIFTEENTH EDITION

BY

THE LATE

CECIL C. H. MORIARTY
C.B.E., LL.D.

*Senior Moderator, Large Gold Medallist, and Prizeman, in History, Law and
Political Economy, Trinity College, Dublin*

SOMETIME CHIEF CONSTABLE OF BIRMINGHAM

AND

W. J. WILLIAMS
O.B.E., B.Sc., LL.B.

CHIEF CONSTABLE OF THE GWYNEDD CONSTABULARY

LONDON
BUTTERWORTH & CO. (PUBLISHERS) LTD

1959

a*

AFRICA: BUTTERWORTH & CO. (AFRICA) LTD.
                   DURBAN: 33/35 BEACH GROVE

AUSTRALIA: BUTTERWORTH & CO. (AUSTRALIA) LTD.
                   SYDNEY: 8 O'CONNELL STREET
                   MELBOURNE: 430 BOURKE STREET
                   BRISBANE: 240 QUEEN STREET

CANADA: BUTTERWORTH & CO. (CANADA) LTD.
                   TORONTO: 1367 DANFORTH AVENUE

NEW ZEALAND: BUTTERWORTH & CO. (NEW ZEALAND) LTD.
                   WELLINGTON: 49/51 BALLANCE STREET
                   AUCKLAND: 35 HIGH STREET

Printed in England by
PAGE BROS. (Norwich) LTD.

PREFACE TO FIRST EDITION

THE author has compiled this book with the view of assisting police officers in attaining a working knowledge of the law that they have to enforce.

The law dealing with each offence and with its kindred offences has been brought together under appropriate headings, and the chapters have been arranged in an order suitable for instructional purposes.

Legal principles and the more serious crimes are but briefly dealt with, and students would do well to study the law thereon as given in such standard text-books as Harris's Criminal Law and Archbold's Criminal Pleading, Evidence and Practice.

More prominence is given to the many Acts of Parliament and Statutory Orders and Regulations which should be known by the police, and which, of course, are to be found in Stone's Justices' Manual.

Particulars are given of the powers and duties entrusted to the police by law, and the book should prove useful in Police Training Schools, as in it a recruit may study police law and thus be able to follow his instructors when dealing with the steps to be taken for its practical enforcement.

It should also be useful to police officers desirous of refreshing their knowledge of police law, either preparatory to sitting for an examination, or with the object of becoming more proficient in their professional duties.

The author takes this opportunity of expressing his thanks to Mr. A. E. Field, of the Birmingham Prosecuting Solicitor's Staff, and to Superintendent B. D. Pinkerton, formerly Police Instructor in the Birmingham City Police Training School, for their assistance in revising the proofs.

C. C. H. MORIARTY.

BIRMINGHAM.
January 2, 1929.

TABLE OF CONTENTS

TABLE OF CONTENTS

NOTE AS TO ABBREVIATIONS

Some Statutes and Rules are frequently referred to, and their
descriptions are abbreviated as follows :

C.J.A. Act, 1914 = Criminal Justice Administration Act, 1914.
C.J. Act, 1925 = Criminal Justice Act, 1925.
R.T. Act, 1930 = Road Traffic Act, 1930.
C. and Y.P. Act, 1933 = Children and Young Persons Act, 1933.
R. and R.T. Act, 1933 = Road and Rail Traffic Act, 1933.
R.T. Act, 1934 = Road Traffic Act, 1934.
C.J. Act, 1948 = Criminal Justice Act, 1948.
M.C. Act, 1952 = Magistrates' Courts Act, 1952.
M.C. Rules, 1952 = Magistrates' Courts Rules, 1952.

FOREWORD TO FIRST EDITION

BY THE LATE SIR CHARLES HAUGHTON RAFTER, K.B.E.
CHIEF CONSTABLE OF THE BIRMINGHAM CITY POLICE FORCE

IN writing these remarks I feel impelled to make a few observations upon the police themselves.

After a long and varied experience of them and of the way in which they perform their various duties I must give unqualified testimony to my admiration and respect for the Police Forces of this country. Their fairness to and consideration for prisoners—as for any one in distress—their tact their courtesy, the many little acts of kindness that they do so quietly and unostentatiously from day to day, their great services to the public, have so endeared them to me that I am proud to reckon myself one of their number.

Only one closely associated with them can realise the immense knowledge possessed by the police of the intimate private lives and affairs of so many people. Yet never a hint of these matters is ever made public. The police force is, indeed, a silent service. What social mischief would ensue, were it otherwise, it is impossible to imagine. The public are justified in the confidence they place in their integrity and discretion.

In the course of his daily duties the constable must encounter many matters of much difficulty upon which he must decide on the instant—matters calling for tact, judgment, knowledge of the law and of his duties, and for decision of character.

To anyone responsible for the administration of a great police force one experience which recurs from time to time must make him think. It is the occasion of a great criminal trial, or perhaps a great criminal appeal. Ranged on each side are the best legal brains and the best legal knowledge in the country, and, on the Bench, some of our most learned and most distinguished judges.

Many conferences have been held, and great time and large fees have been spent in obtaining the best legal advice, and in putting the case forward in its best legal aspect, both by the prosecution and the defence. The Court—both bench and bar—is piled up with legal reference books. Case after case is quoted and debated. There is much discussion of the " Judges' Rules."

In the midst of all this there is a solitary police constable. He is the principal witness for the prosecution. He is in charge of the case. Naturally the question arises, " What's it all about ? " It is the conduct or the action of the constable that is being discussed.

Quite away from any help or legal advice, alone and un-assisted by books of reference, he has arrested a man for murder who is now on trial or appealing against his con-viction. The great question now is whether the constable has acted legally—in making the arrest, in cautioning his prisoner, in taking a voluntary statement from him which he now denies or alleges to have been extorted, in the method by which the prisoner has been identified, and in many other points which counsel, at their leisure, after consulting their clients and their books, most ingeniously devise. Clearly the constable is on his trial as well as the accused.

As he goes on his daily tour of duty he knows not what is in store for him, or what emergency he may encounter. It behoves him to adopt the Boy Scouts' motto and " Be Prepared " for any eventuality that may arise. He will have no time to consult musty reference books. The law and his knowledge of duty must be in his head, upon which he can alone rely to do the right thing at the right time ; so that he may emerge unscathed from the ordeal of legal criticism that he must encounter later on.

The constable suffers from many disabilities, not the least of which is the paucity of those books from which he may make himself master of his powers and duties.

Of these powers and duties that of arrest with all its con-
comitants is the greatest, as well as his greatest responsibility.

The Common Law with regard to arrests is very complicated,
depending as it does on abstruse definitions of various crimes,
and their division into felonies, misdemeanours, and minor
offences, or petty misdemeanours, the power of arrest varying
in each case.

In felonies and misdemeanours the power of arrest comes
from the Common Law and Statutes ; in case of minor offences
the police can only arrest where the statute creating the offence
gives that power.

In felonies and misdemeanours also the powers of arrest
vary in accordance with a variety of circumstances. The
Common Law of arrest is interpreted or amended also from
time to time by an immense number of judgments in what is
called " Case Law." These legal decisions are intended to
make the law clear for the guidance of the courts and for
lawyers.

There is no concise and easily understood direction for the
guidance of constables. The main books of reference also are
inaccessible to the ordinary constable.

At a meeting of the Chief Constables' Association on
May 30, 1918, in an address I said :

" Consider that most important subject, the powers and
duties of constables in making arrests. I do not know any
book published for the use of the English police forces which
gives full and adequate instruction on this subject. The best
instruction for police that I know is in the Irish Constables'
Guide, by the late Sir Andrew Reed, K.C.B., Inspector-General
of the Royal Irish Constabulary.

" In order to compile a complete and exhaustive instruction
on this point one has to consult many books. In none of the
ordinary law books available by the police can one find the
subject treated as a whole. For example, in Stone's Justices'
Manual it is dealt with in scraps in over fifty different places.
In Archbold's Pleading, Evidence and Practice in Criminal
Cases, in about twenty. The reason of this is that these books
are not written for police purposes. The most comprehensive

statement of the law on this subject, and the standard authority, is Burn's Justice of the Peace (now out of print) ; but, to complete it, one has to consult many others, including not only those above referred to, but Blackstone's Commentaries, Russell on Crimes, and other standard works.

" These books are not within reach of the ordinary police constable. How, then, is he to know the law, and his powers and duty under it, if this instruction is not collected from its various sources and put before him in the form of a comprehensive book ? "

These being my views on the subject of police instruction, I congratulate Mr. Moriarty on his meticulously careful preparation of this book of " Police Law," which goes a long way in providing in a comprehensive form that knowledge which the constable finds it difficult to obtain.

The book shows much evidence of careful research and co-ordination. I think it will supply a long-felt want to many members of the Police Service.

C. H. RAFTER.

BIRMINGHAM.
December 1928.

POLICE LAW

PART I.—LEGAL PRINCIPLES, PROCEDURE AND EVIDENCE

Chapter I

CRIME

Contents

Law.—A law is defined by the great lawyer Blackstone as a rule of action prescribed or dictated by some superior which an inferior is bound to obey. It also has been defined as a rule of action to which men are bound to make their conduct conform.

The word "law" implies obedience. When the laws of nature, of a country, of sport are referred to, it means those rules which people, citizens, sportsmen should obey.

The word law also implies penalty or sanction—namely, that if a law is broken some punishment ought to fall on the breaker, so as to prevent a repetition of the breach and to deter others from doing likewise.

The law of a country means the rules of conduct under which the people of that country live, and without which no person could hope to live peaceably and in safety as regards himself and his belongings. These rules either have gradually come into existence by the general agreement of the people or have been prescribed by those responsible for the government of the country.

Obedience to law must be enforced and the duty of enforcing the laws is assigned to the police, who are responsible to the State and to the people for the proper performance of their duty.

The law of England is composed of two kinds of laws, viz. :—

(1) **The Common Law,** which is made up of those general customs which have been regarded as laws in the land from time immemorial. By general agreement endorsed by the practice of the Courts certain rules of conduct have by custom become laws—and these laws are known as the Common Law. Breaches of these laws are termed common law offences—for example : affray, compounding a felony, conspiracy.

It is now much easier and speedier to create laws by written statute or order of the ruling authority, but it is still possible to deal with an act tending to the prejudice of the community, not especially provided for by the law, by bringing the offender before a judge and jury, who, by convicting him, will thus create another common law offence.

For example, see " Public Mischief," Chap. 21.

(2) **The Statute Law**—which includes all the laws made by direct order of the State and set out in Acts of Parliament or Statutes, which are ordinances made by the supreme power in this country, which is Parliament, consisting of the Sovereign, the House of Lords, and the House of Commons.

Such a law, in the form of a **Bill,** is usually proposed in the House of Commons. It is there discussed and if necessary amended, and if then approved it has to pass in the same manner through the House of Lords before it is presented to the Sovereign for his assent.

When a Bill has received the Royal Assent it becomes a **Statute** or **Act of Parliament,** and is known by a short name or title indicating its purport, and it may also be referred to by its chapter or number in the year of the reign of the Sovereign during whose reign it was passed.

Thus a Statute passed in the year 1933 dealing with the prevention of cruelty to children and other matters is known as the Children and Young Persons Act, 1933, and as 23 Geo. 5, c. 12. Usually several Statutes are enacted during each year of a Sovereign's reign, so they are numbered in the order of their passing as chapters in the complete law made during that year. Also each Statute or Act is subdivided into parts or sections to facilitate reference to the particular points dealt with.

Thus 23 Geo. 5, c. 12, s. 7, means the 7th section of the 12th Act of Parliament passed in the 23rd year of the reign of King George the Fifth—viz. 1933. Also Statutes may empower the making of Regulations or Statutory Orders or Rules all now termed "Statutory Instruments" (see "Statutory Instruments Act, 1946") which also have the force of law.

Many offences which were originally common law offences have been dealt with by Act of Parliament ; hence an offence may be both a common law offence and a statutory offence : for example, forgery is a misdemeanour at common law, and may be a felony under the Forgery Act, 1913.

Crime.—Stephen's Criminal Law defines a crime as an act of disobedience of the law forbidden under pain of punishment. Punishment in this criminal sense may be death or loss of liberty or (and) money penalty. There is however another kind of disobedience of law called a " civil injury," which is a wrongful act injuring some person or persons but which does not disturb the community in general. Eminent lawyers have framed definitions of the word " crime," designed to show the difference between a crime and a civil injury, but the difficulty is that both are breaches of law, and for some wrongful acts (such as assault) both civil and criminal remedies are available.

Generally speaking, a crime affects the interest of the community at large, while the effect of a civil injury is usually restricted to the injured person or persons. The criminal law is intended to secure public peace and order. The object of criminal proceedings is punishment, and the offender is punished as a warning to persons in general not to commit crime, but in civil proceedings the persons whose rights have been interfered with take action to obtain for themselves compensation or damages.

The practical test as to whether a particular act is a crime is whether it is punishable by the criminal law ; therefore any conduct punishable by the criminal law is a crime.

A crime consists of some wrongful act or conduct together with some guilty or blameable condition of mind. The criminal law does not punish illegal thoughts ; it waits until an unlawful thought is evidenced by some action or by neglect to take action. If an act, which by law should have been done, is not done, it is called an omission.

The guilty or blameable state of mind which is necessary to constitute a crime is known as **mens rea**, or the offender's mind. When a person of his own free will does an act he is said to do it wilfully. If an act is not freely willed by the doer, it is said to be involuntary.

Malice is the evil intent beforehand to do harm, intent being the person's intention or purpose. Malice is of two kinds, viz. :—

(1) Express malice, which is actual ill-will or intent to do harm to someone.

(2) Implied malice, which is the malice the law regards as existing when a wrongful act is done voluntarily and without excuse. The law presumes that a person intends the natural consequences of his acts, and if harmful consequences result from an act the law considers that the doer intended harm

Malice in respect to murder is dealt with in s. 1 of the Homicide Act, 1957, which abolished " constructive malice ".

As a general rule the law regards the criminal act itself as sufficient proof of the presence of malice, and it is for the accused to prove that he had no malice in his mind. However, in many cases the law fixes the state of mind or intention necessary before many acts can be regarded as criminal, when it lays down that such acts must have been done " maliciously," " knowingly," " fraudulently," " feloniously," or with some particular " intent." In such cases the prosecution has to prove by evidence that the accused was actuated by such a condition of mind.

Also in many offences the law definitely states that the mere doing of a certain act is an offence, even if the doer can prove he was not influenced by malice—for example, dangerous driving.

In certain offences the law directs that a person is responsible for certain acts done by his servants without his knowledge and even against his orders—for example, sale of drink to a drunken person. In these particular cases the law throws on the persons concerned the responsibility of taking effective care to prevent their commission.

Motive.—The motive for a crime is the condition of mind which leads the criminal to commit the crime : his reason for his conduct. " Motive " is not intention, for a person's intention is connected with the results or consequences of the act he intends to do. Thus a man may intend to go to an inn, his motive being to get a drink. In robbery the motive is usually need of money, and the intention will be to take money from the attacked person.

Motive, from the police point of view, is of the greatest importance. If the motive of a criminal be known, it will throw much light on the case and materially assist in the elucidation of the facts.

Crime and Offence.—The word " crime " is applied generally to any illegal act or conduct which entails criminal punishment, but it is usually applied in a narrower sense to an act which is punishable on indictment—that is, on a written charge put before a judge and jury, and therefore called indictable. See " Indictment," Chap. 5. The word " offence " also means an illegal action and, in a broad sense, may be applied to any illegal act or conduct which entails criminal punishment, but it usually refers to an act which is punishable on summary conviction by the magistrates.

The expression " criminal offence " is sometimes used and has the same meaning as " crime " or " offence," that is any illegal act or omission liable by law to punishment such as imprisonment or fine.

Thus " crimes " usually mean indictable offences or the more serious illegal and punishable acts, and " offences " usually indicate those minor illegal acts which are punishable by the magistrates in their courts.

For the purpose of dealing with persons who will not cease their criminal activities the expression " crime " is given a particular meaning in the Prevention of Crimes Act, 1871. See " Special Offenders," Chap. 28.

For the purposes of the Magistrates' Courts Act, 1952, the Act gives special meanings to " summary offences " and " indictable offences " (s. 125). See " A Magistrates' Court ", Chap. 4.

Classification of Crime.—Crimes may be arranged in two groups, viz :—

(1) Indictable Offences, which are the more serious breaches of the criminal law and for which an indictment lies which is a charge triable by a judge and jury.

(2) Summary Offences, which are less serious and are triable by justices without a jury and are termed non-indictable.

However this arrangement is merely a general classification. Many indictable offences may now, by Statute, be dealt with by justices without a jury. For instance the Magistrates' Courts Act, 1952, s. 19 allows a court of justices to deal summarily with a person of 17 or upwards for any of the indictable offences mentioned in the First Schedule to the Act if he consents to such a trial. A person accused of an indictable offence must be present at his trial.

Also under s. 25 of the same Act, a person aged 14 years or more charged before a summary court with a summary offence (which is not assault or offences under ss. 30, 31, 32 of the Sexual Offences Act, 1956) for which he is liable on conviction to imprisonment for more than 3 months, has the right, if present in person, to claim trial by jury, and should be told so before the charge is gone into. See " Progress of a Case,"Chap. 4.

If the law declares a particular offence to be punishable on conviction on indictment or on summary conviction, the offence should be regarded as an indictable offence. (See *R.* v. *Fussell* (1950)).

Any offence which could be tried on indictment may be regarded as indictable. (See *Hastings and Folkestone Glassworks, Ltd.* v. *Kalsan* (1948)).

The Director of Public Prosecutions should be informed of every prosecution of an indictable offence and of a summary offence which has been wholly withdrawn or was not proceeded with within a reasonable time. (See Appendix III.)

Indictable Offences comprise felonies (including treasons) and misdemeanours. Formerly certain illegal acts were singled out by the Common Law as so serious that persons convicted of them were usually sentenced to death and deprived of their property. These serious crimes were called felonies, and the term felony has been applied by Statutes to other serious crimes.

Felony therefore means a serious crime for which the law prescribes punishment such as death, imprisonment, fine, &c., and which it calls a felony—for example, treason, murder, manslaughter, rape, arson, burglary, sacrilege, robbery, larceny, bigamy. Unless the sentence is fixed by law, an offender convicted on indictment of felony, may be fined instead of or in addition to any other penalty (Criminal Justice Act, 1948, s. 13).

The term **misdemeanour,** meaning wrongdoing,· is specially applied to some other indictable offences, those crimes serious enough to be tried by a judge and jury but not declared by law to be felonies—for example, assault, false pretences, bribery, perjury, conspiracy, concealment of birth, blasphemy, libel, sedition, unlawful assembly, incest. However, any breach of the criminal law which is not a felony is a misdemeanour, but it is not usual to describe the minor summary offences as misdemeanours.

The description **offence** is usually restricted to those minor breaches of the law which may be dealt with summarily by magistrates without a jury. They have been created by Statutes which give the magistrates power to deal with them.

Crimes or breaches of the criminal law may therefore be classified as :—

1. Felonies, indicated by the letter F.
2. Misdemeanours, shown by the letter M.
3. Summary Offences, marked by the letter O.

It is of the utmost importance that a police officer should know whether any particular breach of the law is felony, misdemeanour, or summary offence, as the power to arrest without warrant may depend on the classification of the crime. In every case of felony he has power to arrest without a warrant or order from a magistrate. He has no power to arrest without warrant in a case of misdemeanour unless a breach of the peace is committed in his presence, or unless some Statute has specially given him the power to arrest without warrant for that particular misdemeanour. As regards a summary offence he has no power to arrest without warrant, unless the Statute which has created the offence has expressly given him such power of arrest. See " Arrest," Chap. 3.

Punishment for crime.—In early days such punishments included death by various painful methods, torture, loss of property, incarceration and fine, but as time went on most of these penalties fell into disuse, and now the Criminal Justice Act, 1948, has abolished penal servitude, imprisonment with hard labour or in a particular division of the prison (s. 1) and whipping by sentence of a court (s. 2). Convict prisons have ceased to exist.

The law now allows the following punishments. Sentence to death on conviction of treason, piracy with violence, arson of H.M. ships etc. and capital murder (with two exceptions as given in Chapter IX under " Legal Consequences of homicide and kindred offences ").

Imprisonment can be imposed for many crimes and offences, but not on an offender under 15 (not under 17 by a summary court, M. C. Act, 1952, s. 107) and on an offender under 21 only where no other method of dealing with him is appropriate (C.J. Act, 1948, s. 17), and a magistrates' court shall not pass a sentence of imprisonment on a first offender of or over the age of 21, unless the court is of opinion that no other method of dealing with him is appropriate (First Offenders Act, 1958, s. 1). Imprisonment in the form of corrective training or preventive detention can be imposed on persistent offenders (C.J. Act, 1948, s. 21) and certain discharged prisoners may be required to notify their address etc. (s. 22, C.J. Act, 1948, and s. 29, Prison Act, 1952). Instead of imprisonment an offender of unsound mind can be sent to a mental institution (M.C. Act, 1952, s. 30).

There is no limit to the imprisonment which can be inflicted for a common law misdemeanour (*R.* v. *Morris* (1950)).

The Criminal Justice Act, 1948, has also prescribed several kinds of milder imprisonment for youthful offenders such as detention in detention centres (s. 18), attendance centres (ss. 19, 48), remand centres (s. 27) and Borstal institutions (s. 20). The Children and Young Persons Act, 1933, established remand homes (ss. 77, 78), approved schools (ss. 79, 80, 81) and allowed youthful offenders to be entrusted to the care of fit persons (ss. 75, 85), or to be taken to places of safety (s. 107).

The C. and Y.P. (Amendment) Act, 1952, s. 3, arranged for special reception centres for the temporary reception of children under 12 in custody.

Fines can be imposed for many offences and for felony instead of or in addition to any other penalty (C.J. Act, 1948, s. 13).

Binding over to keep the peace and (or) to be of good behaviour is a precautionary measure.

Under the Criminal Justice Act, 1948, a convicted offender may be put on probation with additional requirements (s. 3), or he may be discharged either absolutely or conditionally that he commits no offence during a period (s. 7).

See also " Penalties," Chap. 28.

Excuses for Crime.—The law presumes that every person is sane and accountable for his actions, but it is open to an offender, when charged with an offence, to prove that he is not responsible in law for his illegal act because he had no intention or wish to do wrong, or to prove that he was justified in doing what he did. These defences or excuses are as follows :—

(1) **Insanity.** The accused may be an idiot or totally deranged in his mind or insane on some subject or subjects, and his insanity may be permanent or temporary. A person of unsound mind may be arrested and charged with an offence ; evidence may be given to prove he is insane and the decision rests with the court.

(2) **Drunkenness** as a rule is not an excuse for crime, except when it is involuntary—that is, contrived deliberately by other persons.

A person in a state of intoxication is *prima facie* liable for his acts, but he may plead his condition in mitigation of punishment. In a case where a particular intent is essential to make his conduct a crime, if he can prove that owing to his condition he had no such criminal intent, he may be acquitted.

If fraudulently made drunk by another an offender would not be accountable for his actions while under that influence.

(3) Ignorance or mistake. Ignorance of the law will not justify any breach of the law, even when committed by a foreigner. Aliens in our country are subject to our laws. An honest and reasonable mistake of fact may excuse a crime if the intention of the person committing the crime was not unlawful. However, the excuse of ignorance or mistake will not be of avail in the case of acts forbidden absolutely by law—for instance, the sale of intoxicants to a drunken person.

(4) Accident may be an excuse for an offence committed in the performance of a lawful act which is being done with proper caution.

(5) Compulsion. This excuse is also known as **coercion** or **duress** and would probably hold good in the case of a person compelled by direct physical compulsion to commit an offence. The compulsion of necessity will not justify the commission of a crime. Even threats to property or of future injury to the person will not excuse crime.

(6) Married women. The Common Law presumed that a crime, other than murder, committed by a wife in the presence of her husband, was committed under his coercion and therefore excused her from punishment. However, this presumption was abolished by the Criminal Justice Act, 1925, s. 47, which also directs that when a wife is charged with any offence except treason or murder, it shall be a good defence if she can prove that the offence was committed in the presence of, and under the coercion of, her husband.

Husband and wife may not alone be found guilty of conspiracy, being for some purposes considered in law as one person and therefore as having but one will.

(7) Justification. An act which ordinarily would be criminal may be authorised by law, as in the case of justifiable homicide, in which no guilt or fault attaches to the slayer, in his act.

An assault may be justified as committed in defence of person or property, or as committed in the process of reasonably correcting a child or scholar. Justification may be advanced as a defence in any prosecution, but its effect will depend on the facts of the case.

Exemptions from Liability for Crime.—The following are

more or less exempt from punishment for offences which they may commit :—

(1) The Sovereign. The maxim is that the Sovereign can do no wrong, and the Sovereign is beyond the reach of the law.

(2) Foreign Sovereigns and Ambassadors from foreign countries, while resident in this country, do not come under the jurisdiction of the English Courts. If they commit offences they may be requested by the State to leave the country. Diplomatic privileges have been extended to staffs and representatives of members of certain international organisations (as, for example, the United Nations) and to Commonwealth High Commissioners and their official and domestic staffs.

See the Diplomatic Privileges Act, 1708, the Diplomatic Privileges (Extension) Act, 1941, the International Organisations (Immunities and Privileges) Act, 1950, and the Diplomatic Immunities (Commonwealth Countries and Republic of Ireland) Act, 1952.

(3) A Corporation or Company composed of several persons obviously cannot be dealt with for crime as a human person, as it cannot be hanged or imprisoned ; but it can be prosecuted, as a Corporation, for all offences which may be punished by a fine. See Appendix IV re corporation offences.

Magistrates' Court Act, 1952, s. 36 and 2nd Sched. gives the procedure to be followed in the prosecution of a corporation for an indictable offence. If a crime is committed by the order of a corporation those concerned may be prosecuted individually and personally punished.

(4) Infants under the age of eight years are not punishable for any offence, as the law holds that under that age no child can be guilty of any offence (C. & Y.P. Act, 1933, s. 50). A child under eight, therefore, should not be arrested or charged with any offence, but if needing care or protection such a child may be taken to a place of safety and brought before a Court. See Chap. 12.

Children between the ages of eight and fourteen years are regarded as so wanting in discretion that they must not be punished for an offence unless it is proved that they knew quite well that they were doing wrong.

Offenders between eight and fourteen may therefore be arrested and tried for an offence, but may not be found guilty unless there is clear proof of their guilty knowledge.

A boy under fourteen years may not under any circumstances be convicted of rape or any offence of carnal knowledge.

Persons of fourteen years and upwards are considered to be of sufficient discretion to be liable for their illegal acts.

Offenders, therefore, of and above fourteen years of age may be arrested, tried, and found guilty of any offence against the criminal law.

Remission of Penalty.–The Crown has the right to remit punishment, by granting a pardon either with or without conditions, or by commuting the sentence.

By the Remission of Penalties Act, 1859, the Crown may remit in whole or in part any sum of money which under any Act may be imposed as a penalty or forfeiture on a convicted offender, although such money may be in whole or in part payable to some party other than the Crown.

The Sovereign may extend the Royal mercy to any person who may be imprisoned for non-payment of any sum of money so imposed, although it may be in whole or in part payable to some party other than the Crown.

Prison Act, 1952, s. 25, allows remission of part of a sentence of imprisonment on the ground of industry and good conduct, and allows the Prison Commissioners to release on licence under supervision a prisoner who was under the age of 21 at the commencement of his sentence.

S. 26 allows the release on licence with or without supervision of persons sentenced to corrective training or preventive detention.

S. 27 allows the Secretary of State to release on licence with conditions a person serving a sentence of imprisonment for life, and he may recall him to prison. See " Release on Licence and Supervision," Chap. 28.

Common Informers:—Under several Acts any person, as a common informer, could prosecute for the offences specified and recover the penalties for himself. The Common Informers Act, 1951 abolished these " common informer actions," but does not prevent proceedings for the offences and it substitutes penalties.

Chapter II

CRIMINALS

Contents

Criminals.—Strictly speaking a person who has committed a crime is a criminal, but the term is usually confined to a person who has been convicted of a crime. Although he may not have caused the commission of the intended crime, a person who incites another, conspires with another, or himself attempts to commit a crime is a criminal. Such intended crimes are called inchoate crimes to indicate—e.g. in the case of an attempt—that the intended crime has been begun but has not been completed. A person may also become a criminal by being unlawfully connected with a crime that has already been committed.

Incitement to Crime.—The inciting or urging some other person to commit a crime is a misdemeanour at common law. The offence is committed even though the other person does not commit the suggested crime.

Incitement to Mutiny Act, 1797, s. 1. It is a felony to incite any member of Her Majesty's Forces on sea or land to mutiny. See also " Sedition," Chap. 20, and " Incitement to Disaffection," Chap. 30.

Official Secrets Act, 1920, s. 7. It is felony, misdemeanour or a summary offence to incite another to commit any felony, misdemeanour, or summary offence against the Official Secrets Acts.

Offences against the Person Act, 1861, s. 4. Incitement to murder any other person is a misdemeanour.

Incitement of a woman to cause her own miscarriage would be felony under s. 58 of this Act.

Post Office Act, 1953, s. 68. It is a misdemeanour to incite any person to commit any offence indictable under this Act.

Betting and Loans (Infants) Act, 1892. Sending circulars, etc., inciting infants to bet or to borrow money is a misdemeanour. See " Advertising Betting," Chap. 36, and " Money-lenders," Chap. 31.

Accessories and Abettors Act, 1861, s. 2, provides that a person advising another to commit a felony may be dealt with as an accessory before the fact to the felony.

An attempt to incite to the commission of a crime is a mis-demeanour, and a conspiracy to incite a person to commit crime is also a misdemeanour.

When the incitement has caused the commission of the offence, the inciter is liable as an accessory before the fact in felony, and as a principal in misdemeanour and summary offence.

Magistrates' Courts Act, 1952, s. 19, permits that an adult (17 or over) if he consents may be dealt with summarily for any offence of inciting to commit a summary offence (and under s. 19 (8) the penalty cannot be greater than what is allowable for the summary offence) and for the offence of inciting to commit any indictable offence which may be dealt with summarily as given in the First Schedule to the Act.

Attempt to Commit Crime.—An attempt to commit a crime is any act done with intent to commit that crime and forming part of a series of acts which if not interrupted would result in the actual commission of the crime. An intention to commit an offence is not sufficient, as criminal liability does not commence until the offender takes some step towards the commission of a crime. Preparation for an intended crime will not amount to an " attempt "; for example, buying a box of matches will not be " attempted arson ".

The intent must be shown by some overt or open act con-nected with the commission of the intended crime.

A person indicted for a felony or misdemeanour may be con-victed of the attempt to commit that crime, if the jury is satisfied that he attempted to commit but did not complete the crime (Criminal Procedure Act, 1851, s. 9).

An attempt to commit a felony or a misdemeanour is a mis-demeanour at common law, and by statute the following attempts are felonies :—

Offences against the Person Act, 1861.

S.   15.   Attempt to commit murder. See also ss. 11 to 14.
S.   18.   Attempt to discharge loaded arms at any person with intent to maim or do some other grievous bodily harm or to prevent the arrest of any person.

Ss. 21, 22.   Attempt to choke, stupefy, etc., with intent to com-mit any indictable offence.
S.   29.   Attempt to injure persons by explosive or corrosive substances.
S.   30.   Attempt to do bodily injury to any person by placing explosives near buildings or ships.

Malicious Damage Act, 1861.

Ss.   8, 18.   Attempt to commit arson.
S.   10.   Attempt to blow up dwelling-houses, etc.

Larceny Act, 1916.

S.   23.   Attempt to rob, accompanied by assault.

Under the Magistrates' Courts Act, 1952, s. 19 and First Sched. any attempt by an adult to commit any indictable offence which may be dealt with summarily, may be dealt with summarily with the consent of the accused. This applies to an attempt to commit any offence which may be dealt with on indictment or summarily as such an offence is an indictable offence, and under s. 19 (9) of the Act a summary conviction for this last offence shall not entail any greater penalty than what summary conviction of the completed offence would have entailed.

Accomplice.—When two or more persons are concerned in the commission of an offence, each one is an accomplice of the other or others. An accomplice may give evidence on behalf of the prosecution, or, as it is sometimes called, give " Queen's Evidence," against his partners in the offence. Such evidence is usually given in the hope of escaping punishment and should be accepted with great caution. Naturally an accomplice will be able to give the facts of the crime, but his evidence will require corroboration (see " Corroborative Evidence," Chap. 7).

In practice a prisoner ought not to be convicted on the sole evidence of an accomplice, as other independent evidence implicating the prisoner will be required before the Court is satisfied (*R.* v. *Baskerville,* (1916)).

If an " accomplice " witness refuses to give evidence, it will be for the Court to decide whether the witness is in peril of prosecution (see " Privilege," Chap. 7), and whether he should or should not give evidence.

Accessories to a Crime.—There are four ways in which a person can be concerned in a felony.

(1) **Principal in the first degree,** who is the actual offender, and who in most cases has actually committed the felony with his own hands. There may be several principals in the first degree in a felony.

(2) **Principal in the second degree,** who helps the actual offender at the very time at which the felony is committed. He may be present at the commission of the felony (as in most cases), or he may be near at hand, watching or helping on in some way the commission of the felony.

(3) **Accessory before the fact,** who procures, advises, or aids another to commit a felony, but is not present at the time the felony is committed. If he were present, he would be a principal

(4) **Accessory after the fact,** who, knowing a felony has been committed, helps or assists the felon in such a way as might assist him to escape from justice.

Some active assistance to the felon is necessary ; mere knowledge that the person has committed a felony and allowing him to escape will not make an accessory. (Such inaction constitutes the misdemeanour of misprision of felony.)

A wife who assists her husband, knowing that he has committed a felony may not be an accessory after the fact. See C.J. Act, 1925, s. 47, under which a wife so accused may prove coercion by her husband. This is the only relationship that will excuse the act of assisting a felon, as a husband would be liable for assisting a wife who has committed a felony.

There are no " accessories " in treasons, misdemeanours, and summary offences, as all concerned are treated as principals.

The Accessories and Abettors Act, 1861, directs that an accessory before the fact may be indicted and punished as if he were the principal felon. It declares that an accessory to felony, either before the fact or after the fact, is guilty of felony and may be tried either with the principal felon or after his conviction, or for felony although the principal felon is not in custody or amenable to justice. It reaffirms the Common Law that any person who aids, abets, counsels, or procures the commission of any misdemeanour is liable to be punished as a principal.

The Magistrates' Courts Act, 1952, s. 35, enacts that a person who aids, abets, counsels or procures the commission by another person of a summary offence shall be guilty of the like offence and may be tried (whether or not he is charged as a principal) either by a court having jurisdiction to try that other person or by a Court having by virtue of his own offence jurisdiction to try him. The words "aid, abet, counsel, or procure " may be used to describe the offence (*Gough* v. *Rees* (1930)). The aider may be convicted even if the principal is acquitted. It should be proved that the aider knew the facts of the offence committed (*Thomas* v. *Lindop* (1950)).

M.C. Act, 1952, s. 19, and 1st Sched., allows an adult if he consents, to be dealt with summarily for aiding, abetting, counselling, or procuring the commission of any indictable offence which may be dealt with summarily. There is no provision in law for the Summary Trial of an accessory after the fact.

Compounding Offences.—The compounding of an offence is the agreeing not to prosecute the offender. The general principle is that any agreement to compound a criminal offence is not legal as a criminal prosecution is a proceeding for the benefit, not of an individual, but of the public, and the public have an interest in every guilty person being brought to justice.

Whether the compounding of any particular offence is an offence in itself or not depends on the nature of that particular offence, as will be seen by the following instances.

Compounding a Felony.—It is a misdemeanour at common law for a person, for any reward or advantage, to agree not to prosecute any person for felony. The taking back of stolen goods is no offence, but it is an offence to receive back stolen goods or some other amends on condition of not prosecuting.

A person who knows that a felony has been committed and

conceals it without being in any way a party to it commits the misdemeanour of misprision of felony. This does not apply to a misdemeanour.

Compounding a Misdemeanour.—Any agreement not to prosecute a misdemeanour is not legal, but such an agreement does not appear to be an offence unless it can be proved to amount to a conspiracy to defeat the ends of justice, which is a misdemeanour at common law.

Larceny Act, 1916, s. 34. It is a felony for any person to corruptly take any reward under pretence or upon account of helping any person to recover stolen property, unless he has used due diligence to cause the offender to be brought to trial.

Larceny Act, 1916, s. 5 (3). It is a misdemeanour for any person to corruptly take any reward under pretence or upon account of aiding any person to recover any stolen dog. See " Stealing Dogs," Chap. 35.

Larceny Act, 1861, s. 102. Any person who advertises a reward for the return of stolen or lost property, and in such advertisement uses words to the effect that " no questions will be asked " or no inquiry made, or that money lent or paid for such property will be repaid, is liable to summary conviction and fine. Under the Larceny Advertisements Act, 1870, no such action may be taken against the printer or publisher of a newspaper unless within six months of the publication and with the consent of the Attorney-General or Solicitor-General.

Extradition.—Extradition is the process by which a person who has committed a crime in this country and has fled abroad, or vice versa, is arrested and taken for trial to the country in which he had committed the crime.

The procedure as regards extradition to and from foreign countries is governed by the Extradition Acts and by the treaties in force with foreign countries, and extradition is possible only in the case of a person charged with any of the crimes mentioned in the treaty concerned.

The surrender of fugitive offenders to and from British Possessions is dealt with by the Fugitive Offenders Acts, 1881 and 1915, which also extend to cases affecting British subjects in certain foreign countries wherein British consular jurisdiction exists, and which cover all offences punishable in the place where committed by imprisonment with hard labour for twelve months or any greater punishment.

Cases under these Acts must be reported to the Director of Public Prosecutions (see Appendix III).

See Chap. XI on Extradition in Moriarty's Police Procedure and Administration.

Criminal Justice Act, 1948, s. 31, directs that any British subject employed under H.M. Government in the United Kingdom in the service of the Crown who commits, in a foreign country, in the course of his employment, any offence which would be indictable if committed in England, may be dealt with in any place in England in which he is arrested or in custody.

Visiting Forces Act, 1952.—This Act deals with the combatant forces of other countries while in the United Kingdom on the invitation of H.M. Government and they are termed "visiting forces". It repeals similar Acts of 1940 and 1942 and ss. 1. 2, 3, 5 (1) of the Act of 1933 (s. 18). The Act came into force on June 12, 1954 by virtue of the Visiting Forces Act 1952 (Commencement) Order, 1954.

It applies to the forces of the Commonwealth countries and of any country designated by order in Council (s. 1).

Orders in Council may apply to visiting forces any law relating to home forces, subject to any specified conditions (s. 8), and may extend the Act to colonies and dependencies (s. 15).

As regards inquests on persons connected with visiting forces see " Coroners," Chapter 39.

See Appendix V for further information.

Convicted Persons.—When a person is convicted of a crime or summary offence a record of the conviction is made by the Court which has convicted him.

Evidence Act, 1851, s. 13, allows the production in evidence, in any proceedings whatever, of a copy of the record of the trial and conviction, or acquittal, of a person charged with an indictable offence, provided it is certified by the officer having custody of the records of the Court of trial.

A previous conviction may be proved by producing a record or extract of such conviction signed by the Clerk of the Court of conviction, and giving proof of the identity of the person with the person shown by the extract to have been convicted (Prevention of Crimes Act, 1871, s. 18). The accused person should be present to be identified.

A summary conviction may be proved by producing a copy of the minute or memorandum of the conviction entered in the Court register, purporting to be signed by the Clerk of the Court by whom the register is kept, and by proving the identity of the person (Criminal Justice Administration Act, 1914, s. 28 (1)).

In any criminal proceedings a previous conviction may be proved against any person by finger-prints. A certificate from the Metropolitan Police that finger-prints are those of a person previously convicted, giving the conviction, with a certificate from the prison or remand centre in which the person was detained, that finger-prints are those of this person, together with a certificate from the Metropolitan Police that both these sets of finger-prints are finger-prints of the same person, shall be evidence of the fact (Criminal Justice Act, 1948, s. 39).

If a person admits the previous conviction, evidence of identity will not be necessary, but as a rule it is advisable to produce the record of the conviction.

An offender shall not be liable to be punished twice for the same offence (Interpretation Act, 1889, s. 33). If again charged with the identical offence or on the same acts or omissions on which he was previously convicted, he can effectively plead " Autrefois Convict."

Outstanding charges (previous offences not detected) which an accused admits after conviction for a later similar offence and asks should be taken into consideration before sentence, may be taken into consideration by the court, but any such previous offence which the court would not have had jurisdiction to try should be excluded (*R.* v. *Warn* (1937)).

However, where a person is convicted of an offence and other offences of his are taken into consideration before sentence, such taking into consideration does not amount to conviction on them (*R.* v. *Neal* (1949)).

When the Court announces conviction there is a conviction even if no sentence is pronounced and the case cannot be re-tried. (*R.* v. *Sheridan* (1937) and *R.* v. *Campbell, ex parte Haye* (1953)).

Apparently a magistrates' court has no power to alter its sentence once it is pronounced unless it does so at the same sitting of the court.

Chapter III

ARREST

Contents

ARREST is the taking or apprehending of a person and restraining him from his liberty. Arrest in a criminal sense is the apprehension or restraining of a person in order that he or she shall be forthcoming to answer an alleged or suspected offence.

The person making an arrest should give to his prisoner the reason for the arrest at the time of the arrest, though in law this requirement does not exist if the circumstances are such that the person arrested must know the general nature of the alleged offence for which he is detained (*Christie* v. *Leachinsky* (1947)). In this case the House of Lords on final appeal in 1947 declared that when a police officer arrests without warrant on reasonable suspicion he must normally inform his prisoner of the true ground of arrest. Precise or technical language need not be used but the prisoner should be told in substance the reason why he is being detained. If this is not done the officer may be liable for false imprisonment unless the prisoner has made it impossible to so inform him by running away or assaulting the officer, or unless the circumstances of the crime are so apparent that the prisoner must know the nature of the crime for which he is detained.

On arrest there is a right to search the prisoner for any article material to a criminal charge and the seizure of articles in possession or control of a person arrested is excused if later they are evidence of a crime committed by someone (*Elias* v. *Passmore* (1934)).

For procedure after arrest, see " Bail by Police," Chap. 5.

An arrest may be either without or with a warrant or written authority (see " Warrants," Chap. 5). Every police officer has certain powers of arrest either without warrant or with warrant. These powers are as follows :—

1. Arrest without Warrant at Common Law.—A constable's power of arrest without warrant under the Common Law may be classified according to the evidence available of the offence.

(1) On his own view. A constable may and should arrest any person whom he sees committing any treason or felony or inflicting any dangerous wound.

It is also his duty to interfere in the case of any riot, assault, or other breach of the peace, and to stop or prevent the same by arresting the persons he sees actually engaged therein.

A constable may arrest any person whom he sees threatening to commit treason, felony, or any breach of the peace, but if the threat is merely an idle one and there is no breach of the peace, an arrest would not be advisable.

He may arrest any person who assaults or obstructs him in the discharge of his duty.

He cannot, at common law, arrest without warrant for an ordinary assault not committed in his presence, nor ought he arrest without warrant after an affray is over and is not likely to be renewed.

He cannot arrest without warrant on a charge of misdemeanour unless express power to do so is given by statute; but he can, at common law, arrest without warrant a person attempting to commit a felony although such an attempt may be a misdemeanour at common law. He can, at common law, arrest without warrant when a breach of the peace is committed in his presence or when he has reasonable ground for believing it is about to be committed or renewed in his presence.

(2) On his own suspicion. A constable who knows that a felony has been committed and who has reasonable grounds to suspect a person of having committed it may arrest that person.

A constable who has reasonable cause to suspect that treason or felony has been committed by any person or that a dangerous wound has been given by any person may arrest such person. If it should afterwards appear that no such offence has been committed the arrest will be justified provided it was made on reasonable grounds of suspicion.

If it is established that the person so arrested is not concerned in a crime, he should be released.

Reasonable suspicion that a person has committed outside England what would be a felony here does not justify arrest without warrant. The Fugitive Offenders Act, 1881 (see Chap. 2) may apply to such cases (*Diamond* v. *Minter* (1941)).

(3) On the charge of a third person. When a person requests a constable to take another person into custody, alleging such other person is guilty of treason, or felony, or inflicting a grievous wound, the constable should, if the charge is reasonable, and made by a person deserving of credence, arrest the person so charged.

If the charge prove unfounded the person making it and not the constable will be responsible.

In such a case the constable, if he does not act, may render himself liable to punishment, but before taking action he should consider the repute of the person making the charge and also of the person accused, as well as the seriousness of the offence charged.

If no definite charge is made, but the information is merely given to the constable, leaving him to act or not act upon it as he may think right, the constable should make inquiry into the allegation and act very cautiously. If the offence alleged is a misdemeanour he has no power to arrest unless he procures a magistrate's warrant.

Felonies include treason and the more serious offences against person or property, such as murder, manslaughter, rape, robbery, wounding, assault with intent to rob, attempt to murder, causing injury by explosives, burglary, housebreaking, larceny, embezzlement, arson, attempted arson, piracy, making counterfeit coins, forgery, malicious damage to many things, sacrilege.

2. Arrest without Warrant by Statute.—Many Acts of Parliament contain provisions empowering a constable to arrest without warrant in specified cases of felonies, misdemeanours, and summary offences. See the following alphabetical list :—

Aliens Restriction Acts, 1914 and 1919. Aliens Order, 1953, Art 28. Any person who acts in contravention of this Order, or is reasonably suspected of having so acted may be arrested without warrant by any constable. See Chap. 29 for fuller description of this power.

Animals. Diseases of Animals Act, 1950, s. 71. A constable may stop and detain any person seen or found committing, or reasonably suspected of being engaged in committing, an offence against the Act (or orders or regulations made thereunder), and may arrest such person without warrant if his name and address are unknown and he fails to give them to the satisfaction of the constable. A constable may also without warrant arrest any person who obstructs or impedes him in the execution of his duty under the Act or the orders or regulations made thereunder. See Chap. 35.

Animals. Protection of Animals Act, 1911, s. 12. Any constable may arrest without warrant any person who he has reason to believe is guilty of an offence under this Act which is punishable by imprisonment without the option of a fine (cruelty to an animal), whether upon his own view thereof or upon the complaint and information of any other person who shall declare his name and place of abode to the constable. See Chap. 35.

Army Act, 1955, s. 186. On reasonable suspicion a deserter or absentee without leave may be arrested without warrant. See Chap. 30.

Army Act, 1955, s. 195 (3). A person who has in his possession, etc., without proper excuse any Army property, documents, etc., may be arrested without warrant. See Chap. 30.

Betting. Street Betting Act, 1906, s. 1. Any constable may arrest without warrant any person found committing an offence under this Act and may seize and detain any article liable to be forfeited under this Act. See Chap. 36.

Children and Young Persons Act, 1933, s. 13. For the commission of any offence given in the First Schedule to the Act (cruelty, injury, etc., as given in Chap. 12), a constable may arrest without warrant any person he sees committing same if he does not know and cannot ascertain the offender's name and residence, or any person who has committed or whom he has reason to believe has committed same if he believes such person will abscond, or if he does not know and cannot ascertain such person's name and address.

A constable may arrest without warrant a vagrant preventing a child from receiving education by habitually wandering with the child (s. 10).

A person who escapes or is absent from an approved school may be arrested without warrant (s. 82). A child or young person who runs away from the care of a fit person may be arrested without warrant (s. 85). See Chap. 12.

Coinage Offences Act, 1936, s. 11. Any person found committing any offence against this Act other than one against s. 8 (medals) may be arrested without warrant by any person. See Chap. 16.

Criminal Justice Act, 1948, s. 22 and **Prison Act,** 1952, First Sched. A previously convicted offender convicted on indictment and sentenced to 12 months imprisonment or more, who fails to comply with an order made under s. 29 of the Prison Act, 1952 to report his address, and does not register at a police station and (or) report once a month, commits a summary offence and may be arrested without warrant by any constable. See Chap. 28.

S. 65 (1). Any person sentenced to imprisonment, corrective training, preventive detention, or Borstal training or ordered to be detained in a detention centre or committed to a prison or remand centre, who is unlawfully at large may be arrested by a constable without warrant and taken to the place where he is to be detained (and s. 49 of the Prison Act, 1952). See Chap. 28.

S. 66. Any person required or authorised by the Act to be taken to any place or to be kept in custody, shall, while being so taken or kept, be deemed to be in legal custody and a constable while taking or keeping such person shall have all the powers, authorities, protection and privileges of a constable as well beyond his constablewick as within it. See Chap. 21.

Dangerous Drugs Act, 1951, s. 19. Any constable may arrest without warrant any person who has committed or attempted to commit, or is reasonably suspected by the constable of having committed or attempted to commit, an offence against the Act if he has reasonable ground for believing that that person will abscond unless arrested, or if the name and address of that person are unknown to and cannot be ascertained by him. See Chap. 39.

Drilling. Unlawful Drilling Act, 1819, s. 1. Any meeting for the purpose of its members being drilled without lawful authority may be dispersed by any constable and those present may be arrested. See Chap. 20.

Ecclesiastical Courts Jurisdiction Act, 1860, ss. 2 and 3. Any person molesting, etc., any authorised preacher or clergyman celebrating Divine Service, etc., or " brawling " in a place of religious worship or churchyard may be arrested by a constable or churchwarden. See Chaps. 20 and 29.

Explosives Act, 1875, s. 78. Any person found committing any act for which he is liable to a penalty under this Act or the bye-laws or rules made under it, and which tends to cause explosion or fire in or about any factory, magazine, store, railway, canal, harbour, wharf, carriage, ship, or boat, may be arrested without warrant by a constable. See Chap. 33.

Firearms Act, 1937, s. 6. A constable may demand from any person whom he believes to be in possession of a firearm or ammunition to which Part I of the Act applies (viz. any except smooth-bore guns of 20 inch or more barrel and airguns, etc.) the production of his firearm certificate. If he does not produce such certificate and allow it to be read, or does not show that he is exempt from the necessity of having a certificate, the constable may seize the firearm or ammunition and require the person to give his name and address. If any person refuses so to give his name and address, or is suspected of giving a false name or address, or of intending to abscond, the constable may arrest him without warrant. When executing a search warrant under the Act, a constable may arrest without warrant any person found on the premises whom he has reason to believe to be guilty of an offence under the Act (s. 26). See Chap. 34.

Gun Licence Act, 1870, s. 9. Any constable may demand from any person using or carrying a gun (unless exempt by law) the production of his licence under the Act. If such person does not produce such licence, or a licence to kill game, and permit it to be read the constable may require him to give his name and residence, and if he refuses he may be arrested. See Chap. 34.

Hawkers Act, 1888, s. 6. Any constable may arrest without warrant any person doing any act for which a hawker's licence is required by this Act, and who has no proper licence in force in that behalf or who does not immediately produce on demand a proper licence granted to him or his master and then in force, and bring him before a Justice to be summarily dealt with. See Chap. 31.

Highway Act, 1835, ss. 78 and 79. Any driver or unknown person offending against the Act may be arrested without warrant by any person who shall see such offence committed. See Chap. 24.

Indecent Advertisements Act, 1889, s. 6. Any constable may arrest without warrant any person whom he shall find committing any offence against this Act. See Chap. 11.

Larceny Act, 1861, s. 103. Larceny Act, 1916, s. 41. Any person found committing any offence under these Acts, except the offence of angling in the daytime (1861 Act, s. 24) and the misdemeanour of publishing or threatening to publish with intent to extort (1916 Act, s. 31), may be arrested without warrant by any person. Also any constable may arrest without warrant any person he finds lying or loitering in any highway, yard or other place during the night whom he shall have good cause to suspect of having committed or being about to commit any felony against the Act (s. 104, 1861 Act, and s. 41, 1916 Act). See Chaps. 14 and 28.

Licensing Act, 1872, s. 12. Any person who in any public place is drunk and disorderly, or drunk in charge of any carriage, horse, steam engine or cattle, or who (anywhere) is drunk in possession of loaded firearms may be arrested. See Chap. 38.

Licensing Act, 1902, ss. 1 and 2. Any person found in a public place or licensed premises, drunk and incapable, or drunk while in charge of a child apparently under the age of seven years may be arrested. See Chap. 38.

Licensing Act, 1953, s. 152. A constable executing a search warrant for intoxicants in unlicensed premises, when he has seized or removed liquor, may demand the name and address of any person found on the premises and if his answers are not satisfactory, he may arrest him without warrant. See Chap. 38.

Lunacy Act, 1890, s. 15. Every constable who has knowledge that any person wandering at large is deemed to be a person of unsound mind shall immediately arrest him and have him brought before a Justice. See Chap. 39.

Malicious Damage Act, 1861, s. 61. Any person found committing any offence punishable upon indictment or upon summary conviction under this Act may be arrested without warrant by any constable or by the owner of the property injured or his servants or any person authorised by him. See Chap. 15.

Mental Deficiency Act, 1913, s. 42. If a mental defective escapes, etc., from " his " institution he may be arrested without warrant by a constable. See Chap. 39.

Municipal Corporations Act, 1882, s. 193, and **Police Act,** 1946, s. 1 (4). A county borough constable may, while on duty, arrest any idle and disorderly person whom he finds disturbing the public peace or whom he has just cause to suspect of intention to commit a felony. See Chap. 28.

Musical Copyright Act, 1906, s. 1. On written authority from the owner to the Chief Officer of Police, a constable may arrest without warrant any person found in a street or public place selling pirated copies of such owner's musical works. See Chap. 17.

Official Secrets Act, 1911, s. 6. Any person who is found committing an offence under this Act, or who is reasonably suspected of having committed or having attempted to commit or being about to commit such an offence, may be arrested without warrant. See Chap. 20.

Pawnbrokers Act, 1872, s. 34. A pawnbroker may detain any person offering in pawn any article which he reasonably suspects to have been stolen or illegally or clandestinely obtained and hand him over to a constable. See Chap. 31.

Pedlars Act, 1871, s. 18. Any person acting as a pedlar, who refuses to produce to a constable his pedlar's certificate or who has none, or who refuses inspection of his pack, may be arrested without warrant by the constable. See Chap. 31,

Person and Property. Offences against the Person Act, 1861, s. 66, and Malicious Damage Act, 1861, s. 57. Any constable may arrest without warrant any person whom he shall find lying or loitering in any highway, yard or other place during the night and whom he shall have good cause to suspect of having committed or being about to commit any felony mentioned in these two Acts. See Chaps. 15 and 28 (night loitering).

Poaching. Night Poaching Act, 1828, s. 2. The owners or occupiers of the land, their gamekeepers and assistants, may arrest any persons found offending against the Act and deliver them to a constable. See Chap. 19.

Prevention of Crimes Act, 1871, s. 7. For arrest of a "special offender," see chap. 28.

Prevention of Crime Act, 1953. The power of arrest for without authority or reasonable excuse having an " offensive weapon " in a public place is given under " Robbery ", see Chap. 14.

Prevention of Offences Act, 1851, ss. 11 and 13. Any person found committing (that is in the act of committing) any indictable offence between the hours of 9 P.M. and 6 A.M. may be arrested without warrant by any person.

Prevention of Violence Act, 1939. See Chap. 22.

Prison Act, 1952, s. 49 gives a constable power to arrest without warrant any prisoner (as described in s. 65 (1) of the C.J. Act, 1948 given above) who is unlawfully at large. S. 8: Every prison officer while acting as such shall have all the powers, authority, protection and privileges of a constable. See Chap. 28.

Public Health Act, 1925, s. 74 (2). Any person riding or driving so as to endanger the life or limb of any person or to the common danger of the passengers in any street outside the Metropolitan Police District may be arrested without warrant by any constable who witnesses the occurrence. This section may be applied by Order to any rural district. Metropolitan Police Act, 1839, s. 54, gives the same power in that district. See Chap. 24.

Public Order Act, 1936, s. 7. A constable may without warrant arrest any person reasonably suspected by him to be committing an offence under s. 1 (political uniforms), s. 4 (offensive weapons) or s. 5 (offensive conduct) of the Act. By s. 6 he may also arrest without warrant for an offence under the added sub-section to s. 1 of the Public Meeting Act, 1908 (disorderly conduct). See Chap. 22.

Representation of the People Act, 1949.—Similar power of arrest for disorderly conduct at a political meeting is given by s. 84 of this Act. The 2nd Schedule gives power of arrest for misconduct or alleged personation in a polling station. See " Election Offences," Chap. 21.

Riot Act, 1714, s. 3. Persons to the number of twelve or more unlawfully, riotously, and tumultuously assembled together and not dispersing within one hour after proclamation of the " Riot Act " may be arrested without warrant. See Chap. 22.

Road Traffic Act, 1930. A constable may arrest without warrant any person driving a motor vehicle in a public place who is so under the influence of drink or a drug as to be incapable of having proper control of the vehicle (s. 15), as amended by Road Traffic Act, 1956, any person he sees recklessly or dangerously or carelessly driving a motor vehicle on a road unless such person gives his name and address or produces his licence (s. 20), and any person reasonably suspected of taking or attempting to take a motor vehicle without the owner's consent or other lawful authority (s. 28). See Chap. 24.

Sexual Offences Act, 1956. A constable may arrest without warrant in a case of procuration (s. 40), and anyone may arrest without warrant in a case of a man living on prostitution, or of a woman controlling a prostitute or of a man soliciting in a public place (s. 41). See Chap. 10.

Town Gardens Protection Act, 1863. A constable may

apprehend any person damaging, etc., any grounds in a city or borough set apart for the use of the inhabitants. See Chap. 15.

Town Police Clauses Act, 1847, s. 28. Any constable may arrest without warrant any person who within his view in any street (in an urban district where the Act is in force) commits any offence under s. 28 of the Act (various nuisances to the obstruction, annoyance, or danger of the residents or passengers). See Chap. 24.

Vagrancy Act, 1824, s. 6, and **Penal Servitude Act,** 1891, s. 7. Any person may arrest without warrant any suspected person or reputed thief loitering in any street, etc., with intent to commit a felony. See Chap. 28.

Vagrancy Act, 1824, s. 6. Any person found offending against the Act may be arrested without a warrant by any person and conveyed before a justice or delivered to a constable who is liable to a penalty if he refuses to take him into custody.

However by Criminal Justice Act, 1948, s. 68, a fortune teller, palmist, etc., can be so arrested only by a constable and not even by him unless he believes the offender will abscond or if he is not satisfied as to the identity or residence of the offender. See Chap. 27.

Note.—Fuller information regarding the various powers of arrest is given in the appropriate succeeding chapters.

Where a person is arrested without a warrant for an offence and retained in custody he should be brought before a Magistrates' Court as soon as practicable (M.C. Act, 1952, s. 38 (4)). After arrest without warrant the prisoner should be taken as soon as reasonably practicable (see *John Lewis and Co.* v. *Tims* (1952)) before a justice or to a police station (where the officer in charge has power to grant bail (see " Bail by Police " Chap. 5). He should not be taken to the scene of the crime. If after such an arrest the officer becomes satisfied that the prisoner is not guilty of the crime he should release him.

Unnecessary Arrests.—The main object of an arrest is that the person should be made amenable to the law, and a constable should be most careful to avoid unnecessary arrests. Arrests should not be made for minor offences when the offenders may be made amenable by summons. A constable has great powers of arrest, but he should exercise these powers with intelligence and discretion.

3. Arrest with Warrant.—A warrant to arrest is a written authority signed by a Justice directing the arrest of an offender so that he may be dealt with according to law.

A warrant to arrest should give the offence charged, the authority under which the arrest is to be made, the person or persons who are to execute it and the person who is to be arrested. It may contain a direction admitting the prisoner to bail. See " Warrants " and " Bail by Police," Chap. 5.

In cases in which immediate arrest is not necessary it is wiser to obtain a Justice's warrant authorising the arrest of the offender.

If there is power at Common Law or under any Act to arrest a person without warrant, a warrant for his arrest may be issued (C.J.A. Act, 1914, s. 27).

No action may be brought against a constable who has acted under a Justice's warrant until demand in writing for perusal and copy of the warrant has been made and refused or neglected for six days after such demand. If action is brought (and it must be brought within six months), on production and proof of the warrant, the jury must find for the constable notwithstanding any defect of jurisdiction in the Justice (Constables Protection Act, 1750).

4. Re-arrest.—If a person is arrested without warrant on a particular ground and later only a charge based on another ground is to be proceeded with, it seems that according to the case of *Christie* v. *Leachinsky* (1947) the prisoner should be discharged and re-arrested on the new charge.

Chapter IV

COURTS OF JUSTICE

Contents

Courts of Justice.—There are several courts before which criminal offences may come, as follows :—

1. The High Court of Parliament, or the **House of Lords.** This Court is composed of the Lords of Appeal, who are lawyers of eminence holding peerages and members of the House of Lords, and they will deal with points of law of great public interest brought before them on appeal from the Court of Criminal Appeal.

2. The Court of Criminal Appeal, which consists of the Lord Chief Justice of England and the Judges of the Queen's Bench Division of the High Court, and which may deal with criminal cases brought before it on appeal. See " Appeal," Chap. 5.

3. The High Court of Justice, of which the principal Courts for present purposes are :—

(1) The Queen's Bench Division of the High Court, which consists of the Lord Chief Justice, who is president, and other judges. One Judge, sitting and acting as a Judge of the High Court, has all the jurisdiction and powers of the High Court. Judges of the Queen's Bench Division sit in London and can deal with criminal cases and cases brought before the court by an order of certiorari or habeas corpus, or on a case stated, etc.

(2) Courts of Assize. England and Wales is divided into eight circuits or areas. Two Judges of the High Court of Justice visit each circuit at least twice a year to deal with all civil and criminal cases listed for hearing at these Assizes.

These Judges of Assize should try prisoners then awaiting trial in prison or on bail, so that prisoners may not be left too long untried. The Assize for London is held at least twelve times a year and is known as the **Central Criminal Court.**

4. The Quarter Sessions, or Sessions proper. These Courts deal with civil and criminal business and are of two kinds, viz. :—

(1) The General County Sessions of the Peace, held once in every quarter in every county. It consists of two or more Justices presided over by a Chairman, and with a jury it may deal with indictable offences, except certain serious ones such as treason, murder, bigamy, libel, incest (for list see Archbold), which must be tried at Assizes. However, certain serious offences as given in s. 2 of the Administration of Justice (Miscellaneous Provisions) Act, 1938, may be tried at Quarter Sessions. Its Appeal Committee may also deal with appeals against summary convictions. See " Appeal," Chap. 5.

(2) The Borough Quarter Sessions, held at least once in every quarter in many cities and towns. The Judge is called the **Recorder,** and with a jury he can try all criminal cases except those serious cases referred to above. This court also deals with appeals from magistrates' courts.

5. A Magistrates' Court.—The M.C. Act, 1952, has repealed much of the previous Acts which dealt with summary jurisdiction and it has 133 sections and 6 schedules dealing with the proceedings of Magistrates' Courts. The Act is supplemented by the Magistrates' Courts Rules, 1952. Both came into force on 1st June, 1953. The Act defines a " magistrates' court " as meaning any justice or justices of the peace acting under any enactment (including public and local Acts and orders and regulations made under them (s. 126) or by virtue of their commission or under the common law (s. 124).

The Justices of the Peace Act, 1949, s. 44, also defines a " magistrates' court " as a court of summary jurisdiction or examining justices and includes a single examining justice.

Such a court acts in a petty sessional court-house for a petty sessions area of a county and if the area is not a borough the justices may appoint another place (or places) as an occasional court-house (M.C. Act, 1952, s. 123).

At least two justices are necessary in a magistrates' court to try an information summarily or hear a complaint unless a single justice is allowed to do so by law in any particular case (M.C. Act, 1952, s. 98).

A magistrates' court to try summarily an indictable offence or hear a complaint must sit in a petty sessional court-house, but can try a non-indictable offence and impose imprisonment when sitting in an occasional court-house or a petty sessional court-house (s. 98).

Such courts are open to the public unless otherwise provided by law (s. 98). A court of a single justice or a court sitting in an occasional court-house cannot order more than 14 days imprisonment or 20 shillings fine (s. 98).

One justice sitting alone may deal with simple drunkenness (C.J.A. Act, 1914, s. 38), and any other offences definitely so allowed by some statutes.

A magistrates' court (which for conciseness is herein termed a summary court and it is a court of summary jurisdiction) can deal with summary offences, that is offences which by Statute can be disposed of then and there, and can, if it thinks fit and is so allowed by statute, deal with many indictable offences under circumstances laid down by statutes. It can also send an accused person to be dealt with by a higher court.

Under the 1952 Act, s. 2, such a court for a county or borough can try all summary offences committed within its county or borough. It has jurisdiction, when the magistrates are sitting as examining justices (see later), over any offence committed by a person who is before the court whether or not the offence was committed within the county or borough.

Where the magistrates are sitting as examining justices they can try summarily any indictable offence which they have power to try under ss. 18, 19, 20 or 21 of the Act (s. 2).

As far as this Act is concerned " summary offence " means an offence which if committed by an adult (17 years or over) is triable by a magistrates' court (whether or not it is also triable on indictment) except the 20 indictable offences which may be tried summarily with the consent of the accused under s. 19 of the Act (see " Progress of a Case " later) and libel published in a newspaper (s. 125).

In this 1952 Act " indictable offence " means an offence which if committed by an adult is triable on indictment (whether or not it is also triable by a summary court) except an offence otherwise triable only by a summary court but which under s. 25 of the Act (right to claim trial by jury) or any other Act is required to be tried on indictment by the accused or the prosecutor (s. 125).

A Juvenile Court under the Children and Young Persons Act, 1933, is a Court of Summary Jurisdiction (s. 45). It is composed of specially qualified justices (2nd Sched.) and deals with charges against and applications relating to children and young persons (s. 46). See the Summary Jurisdiction (Children and Young Persons) Rules, 1933, 1938, 1950, 1952, 1953.

The provisions of the M.C. Act, 1952 relating to the constitution, place of sitting and procedure of magistrates' courts have effect as regards juvenile courts subject to any special rules regarding such courts (s. 130).

It should deal with persons under seventeen (who are not jointly charged with adults), and in certain circumstances it may deal with persons over seventeen (s. 46 and s. 48 as amended by C.J. Act, 1948, 9th Sched.). It sits apart (different room or date) from other Courts, and is not an open Court (s. 47). See " Open Court," later and " Treatment of Youthful Offenders," Chap. 12.

It should consist of not more than three Justices, including one man, and one woman. A stipendiary magistrate may sit alone (Juvenile Courts Constitution Rules, 1954).

A Domestic Proceedings Court is somewhat similar to a juvenile court. It deals with guardianship of infants, separation and maintenance matters, family allowances and marriage under 21 and is not an open court. Newspaper reports of such proceedings are restricted to prescribed particulars and any contravention requires the consent of the Attorney-General before prosecution (M.C. Act, 1952, ss. 56 to 62).

The Coroner's Court deals with inquiries (inquests) as to the cause of the sudden or violent or unnatural death of any person, and also inquires into cases of treasure trove (valuables found concealed in the earth). The Coroner is in sole charge of this Court and may have the assistance of a jury. See " Coroners and Inquests," Chap. 39.

Justices of the Peace.—A Justice is a magistrate appointed by the Crown and commissioned to keep the peace, to receive complaints of offences, to deal with offences determinable in a summary way, and to commit offenders for trial by jury.

Justices are appointed for counties or boroughs. They receive no salary but may get travelling and lodging allowances. Before a Justice may act he must take the judicial oath and the oath of allegiance. His appointment is for life or until deprived of the Commission of the Peace but he may be placed on the supplemental list owing to age or for other reasons. See Justices of the Peace Act, 1949.

A Justice for a county may act as a Justice for any county or borough adjoining and in any detached part of a county which his county surrounds or adjoins, and a Justice for a borough may act as a Justice in any county or borough adjoining (M.C. Act, 1952, ss. 116, 117).

A Stipendiary Magistrate is a barrister or solicitor appointed to act as a paid magistrate. He is a Justice of the Peace and can do alone any act which by law requires two or more Justices (M.C. Act, 1952, s. 121).

Justices usually act as such sitting in courts or sessions.

The ordinary sittings or sessions in court of the Justices are termed Magistrates' Courts and take place in an open courthouse. These are Courts of Summary Jurisdiction.

This Court is often called the Police Court, as in it the Justices deal with persons who attend on summons or in custody charged with offences at the suit of the police.

County Justices may sit in the Court of County Quarter Sessions. Justices sit in Special Sessions for the discharge of certain administrative duties such as the granting of licences.

A single Justice sitting alone in a court-house may deal with a few summary offences (such as drunkenness) when the power to do so has been specially given by the Act of Parliament creating the offence.

A single Justice may receive informations and complaints, issue summonses and warrants, and under s. 4, M.C. Act, 1952, he can as an examining justice hold the preliminary inquiries into indictable offences which are known as "taking depositions," and discharge the prisoner or send him for trial on indictment.

"Examining justices" means the justices before whom a charge is made against a person for an indictable offence and the term includes a single examining justice (C.J. Act, 1925, s. 49 (2)).

A Justice who is a member of a local authority must not act in a court dealing with any proceedings by or against the local authority A Justice may be brought by a police officer to act in proceedings for an offence (Justices of the Peace Act, 1949, s. 3).

A single Justice has power, even when not sitting in a court, to bind over persons who quarrel or commit a breach of the peace in his presence and to deal with some statutory offences.

However, this power is seldom exercised, and a Justice as a rule does not act judicially unless as a Justice in a Court.

Justices were originally appointed for the conservation of the peace, but their jurisdiction and powers have been greatly extended by Acts of Parliament. They now have power to deal summarily with many offences, including a number of those indictable offences regarding which they formerly could hold only a preliminary inquiry to ascertain whether the case was one which ought to be sent for trial by a jury (see s. 19 M.C. Act, 1952, for list of such offences which is given later).

Proceedings before Justices.—The proceedings of magistrates' courts and examining justices are now regulated by the M.C. Acts, 1952 and 1957 and M.C. Rules, 1952 and 1957. (References in brackets are to the 1952 Act unless otherwise stated).

Magistrates' Courts. On the summary trial of an information the Court shall, if the accused appears, tell him the charge and ask him whether he pleads guilty or not. After hearing the evidence and the parties, the Court shall convict the accused or dismiss the information. If accused pleads guilty the court may convict him without hearing evidence (s. 13). The M.C. Act, 1957, as supplemented by the M.C. Rules, 1957, introduced a procedure for Magistrates' Courts, other than Juvenile Courts, which allows defendants, in certain circumstances, to plead guilty without appearing in Court, and also provided for the easier proof of previous convictions in the defendant's absence.

In cases which appear appropriate, it rests with the prosecution to initiate the new procedure, by serving with the summons a notice outlining the procedure and another notice giving a "Statement of Facts," which will be read to the Court. At the hearing the prosecution will not be allowed to add to the "Statement of Facts". After conviction, the Court may take into account any previous convictions if satisfied that the defendant has had 7 days' notice served upon him, in the prescribed manner,

CHAPTER IV.—COURTS OF JUSTICE

that the convictions would be brought to the notice of the Court. This procedure may not be used for an offence triable on indictment, nor for an offence punishable by more than 3 months' imprisonment. The Court may at any time adjourn the trial (s. 14). See " Remand " later.

If the prosecutor appears but the accused does not, the court, on proof of summons, may proceed in his absence or adjourn the hearing. If the conditions of this section and of s. 4, M.C. Act, 1957 are satisfied the court may issue a warrant to arrest him and bring him before the Court (s. 15).

If the accused appears but the prosecutor does not the Court may dismiss the case or if evidence had been previously received proceed in the absence of the prosecutor or adjourn the trial (s. 16).

If both prosecutor and accused do not appear the Court may dismiss the case or proceed in their absence if evidence had been received on a previous occasion (s. 17).

Subject to any law allowing unsworn evidence, evidence given before a court shall be on oath (s.78). A party to any proceedings before a Magistrates' Court may be represented by counsel or solicitor and an absent party so represented shall be deemed not to be absent except in cases where law or recognizance require his presence (s. 99).

A magistrates' court shall not impose imprisonment for less than 5 days and shall not order imprisonment on any person under 17 (s. 107). A magistrates' court, unless it is of opinion that no other method of dealing with him is appropriate, shall not pass sentence of imprisonment on an offender under 21 (C.J. Act, 1948, s. 17) nor on a first offender of or over the age of 21 (First Offenders Act, 1958, s. 1). Their power to order imprisonment is dealt with in s. 108 and to order detention in ss. 109 to 111.

On conviction for felony such a court may award compensation to any person aggrieved, on his application, for any loss of property through the felony, up to £100 (s. 34). See also s. 4, Forfeiture Act, 1870, later in Chap. XVIII.

Ss. 69 to 71 provide for the enforcement of fines, including the supervision of the offender until the fine is paid.

Justices sitting in a magistrates' court may, when necessary, act as examining justices.

Examining Justices.—The functions of examining justices may be discharged by a single Justice. They need not sit in open court. Evidence shall be given in the presence of the accused and the defence may question any witness (s. 4).

A witness's evidence shall be taken down in writing and his deposition shall be signed by the Justice. The accused can give evidence and call witnesses to give evidence and his counsel or solicitor shall be heard on his behalf (M.C. Rules, 1952, r. 5).

The justices shall bind each witness examined (except the accused and any witness merely to his character) by recognizance to attend and give evidence before the court of trial (see " Deposition " Chap. 6) and they shall bind the prosecutor to prosecute before that court, but the latter need not be so bound over in a case of the Director of Public Prosecutions (s. 5).

Where the attendance of a witness at the trial may not seem necessary because of any statement or admission of the accused or because his evidence is merely formal, he may be bound over conditionally, that is not to attend the trial unless given notice to do so by either party. If a witness refuses to be bound over the justices may commit him to custody until after the trial or until he sooner enters into the recognizance (s. 5).

The justices may at any time adjourn the hearing and remand the accused (s. 6) see " Remand " Chap. 5. Any statement by accused in answer to the charge should be taken down in writing and signed by one of the justices (M.C. Rules, 1952, r. 5) and may be given in evidence at his trial without further proof (C.J. Act, 1925, s. 12 as amended by 5th Sched., M.C. Act, 1952).

If satisfied that there is sufficient evidence to put the accused on trial for any indictable offence, the justices shall commit him in custody or on bail for trial by jury. If not so satisfied, if he is in custody for no other cause, they shall discharge him (s. 7). Provisions for committal for trial by Quarter Sessions or Assizes are given in ss. 9 to 12 of the M.C. Act, 1952.

Trial by Jury.—For criminal law purposes a jury is a body of persons called together to give a decision on a criminal matter.

It is the right of every adult to be tried for any serious crime by a jury of his fellow citizens and it is the duty of his fellow citizens to attend for the purpose when summoned to do so by the Sheriff. Men and women over twenty-one years of age may serve on a jury. Persons over sixty or engaged in various professions and occupations are exempted from jury service, and aliens, infamous criminals, and outlaws are disqualified (Juries Acts).

Persons, summoned to attend as jurors, who do not attend, may be fined by the Court.

There are two stages in a criminal trial by jury.

1. Preferring the Indictment. Before a criminal charge can be tried at Assizes or Quarter Sessions a written accusation of the crime, which is termed a bill of indictment, must be presented to the Court and approved by the proper authority. For many hundreds of years this " proper authority " was the Grand Jury, a body of not more than 23 nor less than 12 persons of good standing summoned to attend by the High Sheriff.

At the opening of the Assize or Quarter Sessions the members of the Grand Jury were sworn to inquire into the cases for trial, and the Judge, Chairman, or Recorder explained their nature and gave what instructions he considered necessary. Subsequently, in private, the Grand Jury considered these cases, heard the witnesses and decided by a majority (12 at least) whether there was sufficient ground to put the accused on trial. If they found the indictment was " a true bill," the accused was tried, and if they " ignored " the bill and marked it " no bill," the accused was discharged.

The Administration of Justice (Miscellaneous Provisions) Act, 1933, abolished grand juries and grand jurors in future were not to be summoned except for London and Middlesex, where grand juries could continue to deal in the manner described above with bills of indictment preferred under certain statutes which deal mainly with offences committed abroad

However this last function of a grand jury has been abolished by s. 31 of the C.J. Act, 1948, which provides for the trial of such offenders anywhere in England where they are arrested or in custody. See " Extradition," Chap. 2.

The Grand Jury has therefore disappeared, and the procedure as to indictments at Assizes and Quarter Sessions is as follows :

If a person has been committed for trial for an indictable offence (that is for trial by jury), or if a Judge of the High Court has consented to or directed such a trial, or if an order under s. 9 of the Perjury Act, 1911, has been made directing prosecution for perjury, a bill of indictment charging the accused with the crime, may be preferred by any person before a Court in which he may lawfully be indicted for that crime. If this has been correctly done in compliance with the Act or if the Judge or Chairman so directs, the bill of indictment shall be signed by the Clerk of Assize (at Assizes) or the Clerk of the Peace (at Quarter Sessions) and it shall thereupon become an indictment. The Indictments (Procedure) Rules, 1933, regulate the manner in which a Judge may direct a voluntary bill of indictment where the accused has not been committed for trial by Justices. See Administration of Justice (Misc. Provisions) Act 1933, s. 2.

Thus, where a person is sent for trial by the Justices or by a Judge, etc., and a bill of indictment against him is framed and handed in (by the prosecution), and is duly signed by the Clerk of the Court, the case is ready for trial by a jury.

2. Trial by Jury. A " panel " or list of persons summoned to attend at Assizes or Quarter Sessions as persons qualified and liable to serve as jurors (or " petty jurors," as they were formerly called to distinguish them from the " grand jurors " or members of the Grand Jury) is prepared and is in readiness in Court. A jury or petty jury consists of 12 persons, the first 12 names called at random from the list by the Clerk ot the Court. When the 12 jurors take their place in the jury box they are sworn to well and truly try the case and to give a true verdict according to the evidence.

The indictment against the prisoner is read, and the case proceeds. If a juror dies or has to be discharged through illness, if both sides assent in writing and if the number of jurors is not reduced below ten, the case can continue and a verdict may be given (C.J. Act, 1925, s. 15).

The duty of the jury is to listen to the evidence and to give their verdict whether the prisoner is innocent or guilty.

Before the 12 jurors are called to come to the jury box, the prisoner should be informed that he has a right to challenge (or object to) any or all of them before they are sworn.

The Crown or the prisoner may challenge the array, that is the whole panel or list of jurors summoned by the Sheriff, or may challenge the polls, that is individual jurors, and cause or good reason for every such objection must be shown.

A person charged on indictment for felony or misdemeanour may challenge peremptorily not more than 7 jurors without cause, and any juror or jurors for cause (C.J. Act, 1948, s. 35). The Crown has the right of calling on jurors to " stand by," that is, not to enter the jury box when called, but to remain in their places in the court as they are not wanted on that particular jury.

A jury must be unanimous in its verdict. It must not have any communication with the outside public, and a juror must not disclose what has occurred in the jury room.

The common law misdemeanour of embracery consists in attempting by any corrupt means to illegally influence jurors or incline them to favour one party in the case. It is also a common law misdemeanour to personate a juryman.

Progress of a Case.—As shown in Chapter 1, offences may be arranged in two groups, viz. Indictable Offences, which include felonies and misdemeanours, and Summary Offences, which are termed non-indictable. How a case may be dealt with will depend whether the offence is indictable or non-indictable.

(1) *Procedure in an indictable offence case :*—

The alleged offender (who must be present) is either arrested and brought before a summary court or examining justices or comes on summons before a summary court. If the case is dealt with as indictable to go before a higher court, the evidence is given and recorded in writing in the form of depositions (See Chap. 6) and the justices or court can discharge him or commit him (in custody or on bail) for trial at Quarter Sessions or Assizes.

At such a court an indictment is preferred, the witnesses give evidence (against him and for him) and a jury decides whether he is guilty or not guilty. If guilty, the Judge, Recorder or Chairman of the court pronounces sentence. If convicted, the offender may appeal to the Court of Criminal Appeal and may have a further appeal to the House of Lords. See " Appeal," Chap. 5.

However this procedure in indictable cases may not always be followed :—

(a) A child (under 14) charged before a summary court with an indictable offence other than homicide shall be tried summarily (and may be fined) provided that if charged jointly with a person of 14 or over both may be committed for trial on indictment (M.C. Act, 1952, s. 21).

(b) A young person (14-17) charged with any indictable offence other than homicide may consent to be dealt with summarily (M.C. Act, 1952, s. 20).

(c) Persons of 17 and over charged before summary courts with certain indictable offences may consent to be dealt with summarily (M.C. Act, 1952, s. 19).

These indictable offences are given in the First Schedule (s. 19) to this 1952 Act which includes offences under:—

(1) Larceny Act 1861, s. 27; (2) Malicious Damage Act, 1861, ss. 16, 20, 21, 51; (3) Offences against the Person Act, 1861, ss. 20, 47; (4) Telegraph Act, 1868, s. 20; (5) Debtors Act, 1869, s. 13 (1); (6) Falsification of Accounts Act, 1875; (7) Stamp Duties Management Act, 1891, s. 13; (8) Post Office Act, 1953, ss. 52 to 58; (9) Perjury Act, 1911, s. 5, *re* statutory declarations; (10) Forgery Act, 1913, ss. 2 (2) (*a*), 7 (*a*) where value of money or property does not exceed £20; (11) Larceny Act 1916 ss. 2, 4, 5, 8, 9, 10, 12, 13 (*a*), 14, 15 (1) (2), 16, 17 (1) (2), 18, 20 (value not exceeding £20), 32 (1), 33 (1) (2), 35 (aiding and abetting the aforesaid offences); (12) Criminal Justice Act, 1925, s. 36; (13) Agricultural Credits Act, 1928, s. 11; (14) Coinage Offences Act, 1936 (all misdemeanours); (15) Attempted Suicide; (16) Publishing, exhibiting or selling indecent or obscene matter; (17) Indecent assault on male or female under 16; (18) Offences *re* national insurance stamps; (19) Aiding, abetting, counselling or procuring the commission of any of the preceding offences, attempting to commit any such offence, and attempting to commit any offence which is both an indictable offence and a summary offence; (20) Any incitement to commit a summary offence or to commit any offence mentioned in paragraphs 1 to 18 of the Schedule.

Note: A person of 14 or upwards who is before a summary court charged with an offence (not an assault or an offence under ss. 30, 31 or 32 of the Sexual Offences Act, 1956) punishable with imprisonment exceeding 3 months, has the right to claim trial by jury and if he does the case will be dealt with as indictable (M.C. Act, 1952, s. 25).

(2) *Procedure in offences punishable summarily or on indictment* :—

The Magistrates Courts Act, 1952, s. 18, deals with such cases as follows:—

Where an information charges a person with such an offence the summary court shall, if the accused is 14 or over, proceed as if the case was indictable unless the court having jurisdiction to try the case summarily, determines to do so on the application of the prosecution made before any evidence is offered (sub-s. (1) and (2)).

Where the magistrates under sub-s. (1) have begun to try such a case summarily, they may, at any time before the conclusion of the evidence for the prosecution, discontinue the summary trial and proceed to inquire into the case as examining justices (sub-s. (5)). But, except as thus provided in sub-s. (5), a summary court, having begun to try an indictable case summarily, cannot afterwards deal with it as indictable (s. 24). Where the magistrates, under sub-s. (1), have begun to inquire into the case as examining justices then, at any time during the inquiry, on representations made by either party in the presence of the accused, they may proceed to try the case summarily but if the Director of Public Prosecutions is prosecuting his consent is necessary (sub-s. (3)). If such a summary trial is agreed on, any evidence already given before the examining justices shall be deemed to have been given to the court for the purposes of the summary trial (s. 23), but unless accused pleads guilty the court shall recall such previous witnesses for cross-examination except any not required for such purpose by the prosecutor or accused (M.C. Rules, 1952, r. 21).

This s. 18 does not affect any right given by law enabling the accused or the prosecutor to claim that a summary offence shall be tried by a jury (sub-s. (6)) and under s. 127 it applies to misdemeanours under s. 37 of the Malicious Damage Act, 1861. See "Telegraphs," Chap. 26.

A person of 17 or more charged with any of the indictable offences given in the First Schedule (see above) may be dealt with summarily. This can be done at any time during the inquiry, after representations made in the presence of the accused by either party, if the court considers it expedient and the accused consents. If the Director of Public Prosecutions is the prosecutor his consent is necessary as is the consent of the prosecutor in a case affecting the property or affairs of the Crown or of a public body (M.C. Act, 1952, s. 19).

The accused should be told of his right to be tried by a jury and should be asked whether he wished, instead of being tried summarily, to be tried by a jury, and should be told (as directed by s. 19), if the offence is triable by Quarter Sessions, that if convicted summarily, the court, on hearing his character and antecedents, may commit him under s. 29, M.C. Act, 1952 in custody to Quarter Sessions for heavier punishment in accordance with s. 29 of the C.J. Act, 1948. See " Previous Convictions," Chap. 7.

(3) *Procedure in a summary offence case.* The offender comes before a magistrates' court usually on summons but sometimes on arrest with or without warrant. The evidence is heard and the justices give their decision. A person thus convicted may appeal to Quarter Sessions, or may take a special case stated on a point of law to the Queen's Bench Division. The decision of Quarter Sessions on any question of fact is final, but that Court may state

a special case on a point of law for the opinion of the Queen's Bench Division. See " Case Stated," Chap. 5.

If a person of 14 or more is charged with a summary offence (which is not an assault nor an offence under ss. 30, 31 or 32 of the Sexual Offences Act, 1956) which is punishable by more than 3 months imprisonment or if a previous conviction of a like offence would justify like imprisonment, and if he appears in court in person and before he pleads to the charge, he should be informed by the court that he has the right to claim trial by jury. (M.C.Act, 1952, s. 25). If his right to so claim is based on the fact that he was previously convicted of a like offence, the Court should make enquiry to verify the fact of his previous conviction (M.C. Rules 1952, r. 23). Proper proof of such conviction seems advisable.

Where the prosecutor is entitled to claim trial by jury he must make his claim before the accused pleads to the charge.

If either party, being so entitled, makes such claim, the case has to be treated as indictable.

Where an accused of 17 or over is charged with a summary offence for which he may claim trial by jury and which is also triable on indictment by Quarter Sessions, if the court, having begun to inquire into it as an indictable offence then proceeds under s. 18 of the Act (see above) to deal with it summarily, the court shall, before asking the accused if he wishes to be tried by a jury, explain to him that if tried summarily and convicted he may be committed to Quarter Sessions (under s. 29) if his character and antecedents call for greater punishment than the summary court can inflict (M.C. Act, 1952, s. 25).

Open Court.—The general rule regarding the trial of an offence, whether indictable or summary, is that the trial should take place in open public court—that is, in a room or place to which the public generally may have access so far as the same may conveniently contain them (see M.C. Act, 1952, s. 98 (4)).

All evidence in a case must be given in Court in the presence of the accused or his advocate (*R.* v. *Bodmin Justices, Ex-parte McEwen* (1947)).

This " open court " rule does not apply to the taking of evidence by examining justices in indictable cases which are not being dealt with summarily (M.C. Act, 1952, s. 4) nor to applications for summonses or warrants, and such preliminary steps preceding actual trial may be taken privately.

Also it has been established by decided cases that a Court has an inherent power to exclude the public from a trial if it is necessary for the administration of justice, but such power should be exercised only for good reason (see 92 J.P.N. 79).

No person other than Court officials, persons concerned in the case, and press representatives, is allowed to attend in a Juvenile Court, except by leave of the Court (C. & Y.P. Act, 1933,

s. 47); and the same rule applies to Domestic Proceedings Courts (M.C. Act, 1952, s. 57).

The only persons prohibited by law from being present as spectators in court are children under fourteen years of age, not being infants in arms. If a child is present in court he shall be removed unless he is the accused or during such times as his presence is required as a witness or otherwise for the purposes of justice, but the prohibition does not apply to messengers, clerks, etc., required to attend at a court for purposes connected with their employment (C. & Y.P. Act, 1933, s. 36).

When a child or young person is to give evidence in relation to an offence or conduct contrary to decency or morality, the Court may order the court to be cleared and all persons who are not officers of the Court or connected with the case or pressmen shall be excluded from the court (C. & Y.P. Act, 1933, s. 37).

When a witness has to give evidence of indecent occurrences, for instance in cases of rape, sodomy, etc., it is customary for the Court to suggest that females should leave the court.

In any proceedings under the Official Secrets Acts, the Court on the application of the prosecution, may exclude the public during the hearing of the case (s. 8 (4), Official Secrets Act, 1920).

A Court has power to order the removal of persons who disturb the proceedings. See also " Contempt of Court," Chap. 21.

A Court has power to order witnesses out of court. See " Witnesses out of Court," Chap. 7. A witness who has given evidence should remain in court until permitted to leave.

Speeches in court.—Under the Magistrates' Courts Act, 1952, s. 13, on the summary trial of an information, the court will hear the parties in the case who, by s. 99, may be represented by counsel or solicitor.

On the summary trial of an information where the accused does not plead guilty the prosecutor calls evidence and before doing so may address the court. After the evidence for the prosecution the accused may address the court whether or not he calls evidence. After the evidence for the defence, if any, the prosecutor may call evidence to rebut that evidence. At the conclusion of the evidence if any for the defence, and the evidence in rebuttal, the accused may address the court if he has not previously done so, and if he has already done so, may do so again with the leave of the court if accused and any other witness on his behalf have given evidence. If the accused has addressed the court twice, the prosecutor may address the court in reply. (M.C. Rules 1952, r. 17).

M.C. Rules, 1952, r. 18, allows a similar procedure on the hearing of a complaint (civil proceedings) except where the court makes an order under s. 45 of the Act (civil debt, etc.) with the consent of the defendant without hearing evidence.

The " prosecutor " could be the person who, under M.C. Rule

4, laid the information or his counsel or solicitor or other person authorised in that behalf. See also " Lawyers," Chap. 29.

In cases of arrest without warrant the charge sheet would appear to be the " information " and " prosecutor " apparently would include the person who signs the charge sheet as well as the police officer who made the arrest.

Under the Costs in Criminal Cases Act 1952, s. 17, " prosecutor " includes any person at whose instance the prosecution has been instituted or who carries on the prosecution.

M.C. Rule 5 deals with the proceedings in a magistrates' court preliminary to the trial of an offence on indictment. After the evidence for the prosecution is taken down in depositions the accused shall be asked does he wish to say anything in reply to the charge. The accused can then make a statement. Counsel or solicitor for the accused shall be heard on his behalf.

If such counsel or solicitor has addressed the court both before and after the evidence is taken, counsel or solicitor for the prosecution shall be entitled to be heard in reply.

Chapter V
PROCEDURE
Contents

Information.—An information is a charge made before a justice (one justice is sufficient) to the effect that some person has or is suspected of having committed an offence. (M.C. Act, 1952, s. 1). (It is the preliminary step towards obtaining a summons or warrant. The accused person need not be present and, as a rule, is not present). An information need not be in writing or on oath unless some law directs it to be in writing or on oath and it can be made by the prosecutor or by his counsel or solicitor or other person authorised in that behalf (M.C. Rules, 1952, r. 4).

When a warrant to arrest is required the information should be written and on oath. A written sworn information is advisable in cases of indictable offences (M.C. Act, 1952, s. 1).

It should give the name, address, and occupation of the person charged and a brief outline of the offence or act alleged together with the time and place where it was committed. The offence should be described in ordinary language and reasonable information of the charge should be given. If the offence is one created by law there should be a reference to the law, giving the section. This applies to every information, summons, warrant or other document made for or in connection with any proceedings before a magistrates' court for any offence (M.C. Rules, 1952, r. 77).

An information should not charge more than one offence but two or more informations can be set out in one document (M.C. Rules, 1952, r. 14). Several offenders may be included in the same information provided it refers to the same act or offence committed at the same place and time.

A justice in his discretion on an information may grant a summons or warrant (M.C. Act, 1952, s. 1). Where any law gives power to a magistrates' court to deal with an offence or issue a summons or warrant against a person suspected of an offence on complaint of any person, for references to a complaint there shall be substituted references to an information (M.C. Act, 1952, s. 42).

Except as otherwise expressly provided by any enactment a magistrates' court shall not try an information unless the information was laid within six months from the time when the offence was committed but this does not restrict summary trial of an indictable offence which may be tried summarily with the consent of the accused but not otherwise (M.C. Act, 1952, s. 104).

No objection to defects in an information shall be allowed (M.C. Act, 1952, s. 100, but see under " Summons " later).

An informant in summary cases may conduct his case, examine and cross-examine witnesses and if necessary give evidence (*Duncan* v. *Toms* (1887)).

Affidavit.—An affidavit is a written statement upon oath taken before any person duly authorised to administer the oath. An affidavit may be made before a Justice or a Commissioner or other person empowered by law to administer an oath.

The knowingly and wilfully making of a false statement in an affidavit is punishable under the Perjury Act, 1911, and the forgery of an affidavit with intent to defraud or deceive is a felony under the Forgery Act, 1913.

The service of a summons may be proved by affidavit.

Summons.—A summons is a written order signed by a Justice directing the person named therein to appear at a given time in the court named with reference to a matter set out therein.

A summons should state shortly the matter of the information or complaint. If an offence is charged the offence should be described in ordinary language, and if the offence is one created by Statute or Regulation, etc., the section creating it should be given (M.C. Rules, 1952, r. 77). Where two or more informations (or complaints) are laid against the same person or persons a single summons may be issued against that person or each of those persons in respect of all the informations, provided that the matter of each information (or complaint) shall be separately stated in the summons. Any such summons shall be treated as if it were a separate summons in respect of each information (or complaint) (See M.C. Rules, 1952, r. 75).

Proceedings by summons is the usual method of making persons amenable for offences, and the issue of a summons rests in the discretion of the Justice to whom application is made.

Under the M.C. Act, 1952, s. 1, a justice on information before him that a person has or is suspected to have committed an offence, may issue a summons requiring him to appear before a magistrates' court in his county or borough. The issue of the summons is subject to the conditions laid down in the section and depends on the place of the offence and the whereabouts of the person (ss. 1 and 3).

If law requires the information to be laid before two or more justices one justice may issue the summons (or warrant) (M.C. Act, 1952, s. 1). A summons remains valid even if the justice who issued it has died or ceased to be a justice (M.C. Act, 1952, s. 101).

Although a summons for an indictable offence has been issued a warrant to arrest may afterwards be issued at any time (M.C. Act, 1952, s. 1).

Witness summonses direct persons to appear before a court and give evidence or produce documents or things.

Where a justice is satisfied that any person in England or Wales is likely to give material evidence or produce any document or thing as material evidence at any inquiry or trial or hearing by a magistrates' court for his area and that person will not voluntarily attend the court and give evidence etc., he shall issue a summons directing the person to attend and give evidence etc.

If a justice is satisfied by evidence on oath as above and it is probable such person will not attend on summons, he may, instead of summons, issue a warrant to arrest him and bring him before the court (but this cannot be done for the hearing of a complaint). If such person does not attend on summons without just excuse, the court, on evidence on oath, may issue a warrant to arrest him and bring him before the court.

If such a witness, in court, refuses without just excuse to be sworn or give evidence or produce any document or thing, the court may commit him in custody for up to seven days or until he sooner complies (M.C. Act 1952, s. 77). Conduct money should be paid or tendered with a witness' summons.

As regards civil jurisdiction and procedure, the issue of summons on complaint and the hearing of and dealing with complaints are dealt with in ss. 43 to 55 of the M.C. Act, 1952.

Under s. 43 a justice acting for a petty sessions area, when complaint is made to him upon which the local summary court has power to make an order against any person, may issue a summons requiring that person to appear before such court. Under s. 73 and M.C. Rules, 1952, r. 48, on default of payment of a sum enforceable as a civil debt, a justice, on complaint, may issue a judgment summons against the judgment debtor.

Under s. 100 of the M.C. Act, 1952, no objection shall be allowed to any information or complaint or to any summons, or warrant to procure the presence of a defendant, for any defect in substance or form or any variance between it and the evidence at the hearing, but if the court considers that any variance between a summons or warrant and the evidence at the hearing has misled the defendant, it shall, on the application of the defendant, adjourn the hearing.

A summons is made out in duplicate, the original may be

delivered to the person (personal service) or left for him with some person at his last known or usual place of abode or sent by registered letter addressed to him at his last known or usual place of abode.

" Place of abode " means place of residence, where a person lives or sleeps and does not include a shop where he does not reside. Last known or usual means the place where the person had his last known permanent address. Summons by post must not be used for the attendance of a person to give evidence or produce a document or thing or for service of summons outside England and Wales.

If a person fails to appear after service on him by post, the service is not effective unless it is proved that it came to his knowledge (any letter to that effect shall be admissible as evidence of this). Service of summons or other document issued by a justice on a Corporation may be effected by delivering or sending it by post to the clerk or secretary at the registered office in England or Wales or if no such office, to any place in England or Wales where it trades or carries on business (see M.C. Rules, 1952, r. 76 and M.C. Rules, 1957, r. 27).

If service by post is not effective and therefore the summons has not been served within the prescribed time after the commission of the offence, on proof of due posting, a second summons may be issued (M.C. Act, 1952, s. 37).

A summons for an indictable offence should be served by a constable and for a summary offence by a constable or other person to whom it shall be delivered.

The person who has served a summons should endorse his copy with the time, place and manner of service and may have to attend court to prove the service.

A summons should be served a reasonable time previous to the hearing of the case and it must be personally served when so directed by the Statute etc. under which proceedings are taken.

A summons, except in cases of treason, felony or breach of the peace should not be served on a Sunday (see " Sunday Process " later).

Summonses and warrants in criminal proceedings within the Metropolitan Police District should be served and executed by a constable of the Metropolitan Police and by none other (Metropolitan Police Act, 1839, s. 12, and M.C. Act, 1952, s. 119).

Process (including summons, warrants, etc.) issued by a summary court in England may be executed in Scotland and (by Order 1928) the Isle of Man if duly endorsed by a justice of the district in which it is to be executed (see Summary Jurisdiction (Process) Act, 1881.)

The service on any person of a summons or document required or authorised to be served in any proceedings before a magistrates' court and the handwriting or seal of a justice or other person on any summons, warrant or document issued or made in any such proceedings may be proved in any legal proceedings by a solemn declaration made under this Rule. The service of any document which should be served and the proper preparation and posting of a letter containing such a document may be proved in a summary court and at Quarter Sessions in appeal cases by a certificate signed by the person who effected the service or posted or registered the letter (M.C. Rules, 1952, r. 55).

Any statement false, in a material particular in any solemn declaration certificate or other writing made to be used as evidence of the service of any document or the handwriting or seal of any person is punishable summarily by up to 6 months' imprisonment or up to £100 fine or both (M.C. Act, 1952, s. 82).

Subpœna.—A subpœna is a writ or order commanding attendance in court on a certain day named therein under a penalty (*pœna*). A witness summons has much the same effect.

Subpœnas are issued either at the Crown Office, London. or by the Clerk of Assize or the Clerk of the Peace.

A person served with a subpœna may also be given a **reasonable** sum of money, sufficient to enable him to get to the **court.**

Subpœnas may be used to secure the attendance of witnesses. A subpœna may merely direct a witness to attend and give evidence, or it may direct him to attend, give evidence, and produce named documents in evidence.

Indictment.—An indictment is a written or printed **accusation** setting out the crime for which a person is to be tried by a **Court** of Assize or Quarter Sessions.

Hence the term " indictable offence " which is applied to all offences which may be tried at Assizes or Quarter Sessions.

More than one person may be charged with the crime in an indictment, as in the case of conspiracy.

Several crimes may be charged in an indictment, and each will be described in a separate paragraph, called a " count," but no one count should charge more than one offence. Each count should be put to the prisoner separately and he must be asked to plead to each count (*R* v. *Boyle* (1954)).

Before a prisoner can be tried for a crime at Assizes or Quarter Sessions, this written accusation, then called a " bill of indictment," must be given to the Clerk of the Court and it must be signed by him. Otherwise the case cannot be heard by the Court and Jury. When so signed the " bill " becomes an " indictment " (see " Trial by Jury," Chap. 4).

The Judge or Chairman, if satisfied that the requirements of the Act have been complied with, may, on the application of the prosecutor or on his own motion, direct the Clerk to sign the bill, and the Clerk shall do so (Administration of Justice (Misc. Prov.) Act, 1933).

Venue.—The venue is the place of trial.

A person charged with an indictable offence may be proceeded against, tried and punished by Quarter Sessions or Assizes in any county or place in which he was arrested or is in custody on a charge for the offence (C.J. Act, 1925, s. 11).

A magistrates' court may try all summary offences committed within its county or borough. It has jurisdiction as examining justices over any offence committed by a person who appears or is brought before the court whether or not the offence was committed within its county or borough, and in such cases it has jurisdiction to try summarily indictable offences where it has power to do so under ss. 18 (3), 19, 20 or 21 of the Act (M.C. Act, 1952, s. 2).

The jurisdiction of a summary court extends to offences committed on boundaries and on journeys begun in one jurisdiction and completed in another (M.C. Act, 1952, s. 3).

Accused or Defendant.—An " accused " is a person charged on information with an offence, summary or indictable and liable to be tried by a court (see M.C. Act, 1952, s. 1).

If he is arrested and appears before a court in custody he is " the prisoner ". At Assizes or Quarter Sessions he must take his place in the dock or place for prisoners and face the judge and jury being thus the prisoner at the bar of the court.

A " defendant " is a person ordered by legal process to appear before a court to defend what he has done or left undone.

A defendant is called to a magistrates' court by summons issued (on complaint) by a justice of the petty sessions area, who can do so when such court has power to make an order against any person upon such complaint (see M.C. Act, 1952, s. 43).

When his case is to be tried the accused's name is called. The charge against him is read and he is asked whether he is or is not guilty.

The burden of proving any excuse, exemption, &c. rests on the accused (M.C. Act, 1952, s. 81).

The trial will then proceed, unless an adjournment is allowed by the Court (M.C. Act, 1952, ss. 13, 14). See " Proceedings before Justices," Chap. 4 and " Remand," later.

Where a complaint is to be heard the court shall state the complaint to the defendant and hear evidence and make an order or dismiss the complaint or may adjourn the hearing (M.C. Act, 1952, ss. 45, 46).

The Criminal Justice Act, 1948, s. 30, abolished the privilege of peers in relation to criminal proceedings and now any peer who commits any offence is liable to the ordinary criminal procedure instead of being able to claim trial by his peers.

The Poor Prisoner's Defence Act, 1930, provides for the supplying of legal assistance at the cost of the local funds, to accused persons in criminal cases whose means are insufficient to enable them to obtain legal aid.

(1) The committing Justices or the Judge or Chairman of Assizes or Quarter Sessions may grant such a person, if committed for trial (or for sentence) for an indictable offence, a " defence certificate " entitling him to free legal aid, if it is considered desirable in the interests of justice. This should be done if such poor person is committed for trial for murder (s. 1).

(2) A court of summary jurisdiction or examining Justices may grant such person charged with any offence a " legal aid certificate " for free legal assistance, if it is considered desirable by reason of the gravity of the charge or of exceptional circumstances (s. 2).

(3) If the Judge or Chairman of Assizes or Quarter Sessions requests counsel to defend a prisoner to whom a defence certificate has not been granted, the fees of such counsel shall be included in any Court order for costs to be paid out of the local funds (s. 3).

See also the Legal Aid and Advice Act, 1949, at the end of this chapter.

Finger Prints.—Where any person not less than 14 years of age who has been taken into custody is charged with an offence before a magistrates' court the court may, on the application of a police officer not below the rank of inspector, order that his finger prints shall be taken by a constable. These may be taken by any reasonable force necessary, either at the court or at any place to which the person may be committed or remanded in custody. If the person is acquitted or discharged by the examining justices, the finger prints and all copies and records thereof shall be destroyed (M.C. Act, 1952, s. 40). See also " Convicted Persons," Chap. 2.

N.B.—The direction above as to destruction if prisoner is acquitted or discharged applies only to finger prints taken under this s. 40.

Warrants.—A warrant is a written authority, signed by a Justice, directing the person or persons to whom it is addressed, to arrest an offender to be dealt with according to law, to take a person to prison, to search premises, to levy distress for the non-payment of a legal penalty, etc.

Before a warrant to arrest may be granted it is necessary that a written sworn information should be made and the warrant may be issued by one justice notwithstanding any law requiring the information to be laid before two or more justices (M.C. Act, 1952, s.1). The known circumstances of the case should be placed before the Justice, as he has the responsibility for the issue of the warrant. When a warrant to arrest is required in a case depending on the evidence of a witness, it will sometimes be advisable to have a sworn information from the witness stating what he can prove, in support of the application for warrant.

CHAPTER V.—PROCEDURE 49

On application for a warrant to arrest for an indictable offence the justice may issue a summons and afterwards issue a warrant at any time. A justice has jurisdiction to issue a warrant to arrest for an offence similar to that allowing him to issue a summons for the offence (M.C. Act, 1952, s. 1). See " Summons," above.

If an offence which could be prosecuted on indictment in England or Wales has been committed outside England and Wales a warrant to arrest the alleged offender may be issued by a justice if such person resides or is, or is believed to reside or be, within his county or borough (M.C. Act, 1952, s. 1).

A warrant should contain a statement of the offence with which the accused is charged, and this should be set out in ordinary language. If the offence is one created by or under any written law, there should be a reference to the section of the Statute or Regulation etc. (M.C. Rules, 1952, r. 77).

The doing of the act directed in the warrant is called the execution of the warrant. The directions of a warrant should be strictly observed, otherwise the person executing it may not be justified in his acts. When a constable receives a warrant for execution he should read it over carefully, to see what it orders him to do and to see that the particulars in it are correct. If a mistake is found in a warrant it must not be altered, but the warrant should be returned without delay to the Clerk to the Justices.

A warrant remains valid even if the Justice who issued it dies or ceases to hold office (M.C. Act, 1952, s. 101).

A warrant of arrest, commitment, distress or search issued by a justice may be executed anywhere in England and Wales by any person to whom it is directed or by any constable acting within his police area. A warrant to arrest for an offence or a search warrant may be issued and executed on Sunday as on any other day (M.C. Act, 1952, s. 102). Such power of execution by any constable in any place does not extend to warrants issued elsewhere than in England or Wales (Criminal Justice Act, 1925, s. 49 (3)).

A warrant to arrest a person charged with an offence or an accused person or witness who after due process has not appeared in court or a commitment warrant, where the person has gone to Scotland, Isle of Man, the Channel Islands or Ireland, or *vice versa*, may be executed in the place where the person is if it is backed (endorsed) by a local magistrate who can do so if the warrant is accompanied by a sworn statement verifying the handwriting (signature) of the Justice who has issued the warrant (Indictable Offences Act, 1848, ss. 12 to 14, and M.C. Act, 1952, s. 103).

When a constable executing a warrant has it in his possession if asked he should show it and read it to the person concerned but should not allow it out of his possession.

All warrants executed or returned unexecuted should be endorsed by the constable concerned with the date, time and

manner of execution, or with the reason for failure to execute
or with date of attempt to execute, together with his signature and
the date.

Warrant to Arrest.—Every warrant to arrest should give the
offence charged, the authority under which the arrest is made,
the person or persons who are to execute it, and the person to
be arrested.

A warrant of arrest issued by a justice remains in force until it
is executed or withdrawn.

A warrant to arrest for an offence may be executed by a constable although it is not in his possession at the time, but on
demand of the prisoner it shall be shown to him as soon as practicable (M.C. Act, 1952, s. 102). In the execution of a felony
warrant a constable if refused admission may break doors to effect
the arrest, but not until after he has notified to those in the house
the cause of his coming and requested admittance. However the
breaking open of outer doors is so dangerous a proceeding that a
constable should not resort to it except on reasonable grounds of
suspicion and in extreme cases when an immediate arrest is
necessary.

Warrant to Remand or to Commit.—This warrant directs
that a person be taken to a specified place of detention, where he
is to be detained as set forth in the warrant. When the constable
delivers such a person at the place, he should hand in the warrant
with him and obtain a receipt for the person, which subsequently
should be handed in at his police station.

Warrant to Commit to Prison in Default.—Such a warrant
directs that the person be arrested and taken to H.M. Prison
unless he pays the amount shown on the warrant.

The person should be asked for the amount. If he pays it,
a receipt should be given him and the warrant should be endorsed
with the date and manner of execution.

The constable holding such a warrant of commitment may
receive part payment of the amount and shall note such payment
on the warrant. Such a payment will reduce the period of imprisonment (M.C. Act, 1952, s. 67 and M.C. Rules, 1952, r. 45). If
the person cannot or will not pay, he must be arrested and lodged
in prison. Such a warrant should not be executed on a Sunday. If
the person is arrested after the prison has closed or cannot be
brought to the prison before 10 p.m., he may be lodged in the
nearest police station until he can be received into prison.

Distress Warrant.—When default is made by a person in
paying a sum adjudged to be paid by a conviction or order of a
magistrates' court, the court may issue a warrant of distress for
levying the sum, or issue a commitment warrant if the distress
does not cover the sum or instead of a distress warrant (M.C. Act,
1952, s. 64). Under M.C. Rules, 1952, r. 43, a distress warrant

shall be issued to the police requiring them to levy the said sum by distress and sale of the goods belonging to the said person.

The warrant may be executed by any person under the direction of a constable. It will authorise the taking of any money as well as any goods of the person and require the person charged with the execution to pay the sum to be levied to the clerk of the court.

The wearing apparel or bedding of any person and his family or the tools and implements of his trade up to the value of five pounds must not be seized. The distress seized shall be sold within such period specified in the warrant not earlier than the 6th day after the making of the distress or if no period is specified within the period beginning on the 6th day and ending on the 14th day after the making of the distress. However the distress may be sold, with the written consent of the person before the beginning of the said period. The distress shall be sold by public auction or in such manner as the person may in writing allow.

There shall be no sale if the sum and the charges of taking and keeping are paid. If household goods are seized they shall not, without the person's written consent, be removed from the house until the day of sale.

A conspicuous mark shall be affixed on the articles impounded. The constable charged with the execution of the warrant shall cause the distress to be sold and may deduct out of the proceeds all costs and charges incurred and return to the owner any balance, retaining the sum payable with the proper costs and charges.

The constable executing the warrant shall as soon as practicable send a written account of the costs and charges incurred to the clerk of the court.

If the person pays the sum to the constable or produces a receipt for same from the clerk of the court and also pays the costs and charges incurred, the constable shall not execute the warrant or shall cease to execute as the case may be (M.C. Rules, 1952, r. 43). Any constable holding a warrant of distress or commitment in default of payment may receive a part payment (M.C. Rules, 1952, r. 45).

Any person who interferes with the mark or removes the marked goods is liable to fine up to £5, and if any person charged with the execution of a distress warrant wilfully retains or exacts excess charges or makes any improper charge he is liable to similar fine on summary conviction (M.C. Act, 1952, s. 66).

If there are no goods or no sufficient goods the constable should notify the clerk of the court. The warrant should not be executed between sunset and sunrise. Premises should not be broken into and excessive distraint should be avoided.

It is also the duty of the police to execute distress warrants for rates and it appears that any goods seized should not be left on the premises. See Stone " Rates General," and M.C. Act, 1952, s. 128.

The court may order a person adjudged to pay a sum by

conviction (or on an affiliation order) to be searched and any money so found or found on him when arrested or in prison, in default of payment or want of sufficient distress to satisfy such sum, may be applied towards payment of the sum adjudged, unless the court is satisfied that such money does not belong to him or that the loss of it would be more injurious to his family than his detention (M.C. Act, 1952, s. 68).

Search Warrant.—A warrant to search usually authorises the person to whom it is addressed and his assistants, to enter, by force if necessary, the place or premises named, to search every place and thing inside, to seize and take away any articles mentioned in the warrant, and to arrest the persons named in the warrant or the persons in whose possession the articles named are found. A search warrant remains in force until executed or when any limitation of time ends. It is usually " executed " when a search has been made, whether the articles named are found or not, but some search warrants authorize entry at any time or times.

A search warrant may be granted and executed on Sunday (M.C. Act, 1952, s. 102). The officer should have the warrant in his possession and produce it to be read if required.

Any special directions in a search warrant must be strictly observed. A search warrant may be granted at common law on sworn complaint alleging suspicion that larceny has been committed. It authorises search in any house, etc. in the daytime, and arrest of any person found in possession of the stolen goods.

Reasonable ground of suspicion is necessary before a search warrant is granted, as a Justice will not issue a warrant on bare surmise.

As the constable must strictly observe the directions of the warrant, he should not seize articles not mentioned in the warrant unless such unnamed articles are likely to furnish evidence of the identity of stolen articles or to substantiate the charge against the accused person.

A search warrant is really a warrant to search for evidence of a crime which is believed to have been committed.

A search warrant may be executed anywhere in England and Wales by the person to whom it is directed or by any constable within his area (M.C. Act, 1952, s. 102).

Search warrants may be granted on sworn informations under over fifty Acts of Parliament and in each case the directions given in the Act must be observed. For example :—

Larceny Acts, 1861, 1916.	For stolen property.
Coinage Offences Act, 1936.	For counterfeit coin, implements, etc.
Forgery Act, 1913.	For forged papers, etc.
Explosives Act, 1875.	For explosives.

Children and Young Persons Act, 1933.	For recovery of children or young persons cruelly treated.
Betting Act, 1853.	For betting houses.
Obscene Publications Act. 1857.	For obscene books, pictures, etc.
Sexual Offences Act, 1956	For man living on earnings of prostitution and for woman detained for immoral purposes.
Gaming Act, 1845.	For common gaming houses.
Licensing Act, 1953.	For intoxicating liquor or registered or unregistered clubs.
Offences against the Person Act, 1861.	For instruments, etc., for committing any felony under the Act.
Malicious Damage Act, 1861.	For instruments, etc., for committing any felony under the Act.

and other Acts such as the Official Secrets Act, 1911, Pawnbrokers Act, 1872, Old Metal Dealers Act, 1861, Petroleum Act, 1928, Cruelty to Animals Act, 1876, Customs and Excise Act, 1952.

Under section 42 of the Larceny Act, 1916, a search warrant to search and seize any property with respect to which any offence against the Act has been committed may be granted by a Justice. Also under the same section an authority to a constable to enter any premises and search for and seize any property he believes to have been stolen may be given in writing by a chief officer of police, if the premises to be searched:—

(a) are occupied by a person who has been convicted of any offence involving fraud or dishonesty and punishable with imprisonment, or

(b) are, or have been within the preceding twelve months, occupied by a person who has been convicted of receiving stolen property or harbouring thieves.

Any particular property need not be specified in such authority, which may be given if the chief officer of police has reason to believe generally that such premises are being made a receptacle for stolen goods. On arrest in private premises the premises may be searched if it seems likely that any material evidence (for or against the accused) might be obtained.

Under section 73 of the Explosives Act, 1875, on reasonable ground for believing that an offence has been or is being committed with respect to an explosive, and if the case is one of emergency and delay in obtaining a warrant would be likely to endanger life, a superintendent of police or other officer of equal or superior rank, may give a written order to enter at any time, if needs be by force, any place, and examine the same and search for explosives therein and take samples of any explosives or ingredients thereof found therein.

Under section 9 of the Official Secrets Act, 1911. in a case of great emergency, when in the interest of the State immediate action is necessary, a superintendent of police may by written order empower any constable to enter, at any time, any place named in the warrant, by force if necessary, and to search such place and every person found therein, and to seize anything which is evidence of an offence under the Official Secrets Act.

Commitment.—Commitment or committal in the legal sense means sending a person to prison or detention or for trial or sentence.

A warrant of commitment shall state the offence or other ground on which the person is committed. It is directed to the police of the area to arrest him and convey him to the place mentioned and to the keeper of the place of detention to keep him in his custody in accordance with the directions in the warrant. The police shall deliver him with the warrant and get the keeper's receipt for the person (M.C. Rules, 1952, r. 74).

A person by order of a court or by the warrant of a justice may be committed to prison. When a person has been convicted summarily and sentenced to imprisonment a commitment warrant is made out and on this warrant he is taken to prison to serve his sentence.

A warrant is not necessary in the case of a prisoner sentenced at Assizes or Quarter Sessions.

A committal or commitment to prison warrant may be issued in the case of non-payment of money. See " Warrants."

After the preliminary hearing (or examination) by a justice or justices a person accused of an indictable offence may be committed for trial by a judge, etc., and jury in a higher court. Such "committal for trial" means committed to prison but it also includes a person admitted to bail on recognizance to appear and stand his trial (Interpretation Act, 1889, s. 27).

Any commitment by a justice to any form of detention shall be by a warrant of commitment (M.C. Rules, 1952, r. 71).

The following are examples of commitment:

C.J. Act, 1948, s. 18, sending of person between 14 and 21 to a detention centre. See Chap. 12.

S. 27, sending person under 21 to remand home or remand centre for trial or sentence. See Chap. 12.

S. 75, sending young person (14–17) to a remand centre for inquiry into his mental or physical condition. See Chap. 12.

M.C. Act, 1952, s. 28, committing person (16–21) to Quarter Sessions for sentence to Borstal. See Chap. 28.

S. 29, committing person not less than 17 to Quarter Sessions for sentence. See Chap. 4.

S. 69, commitment for non-payment of a sum adjudged to be paid by a conviction.

C. and Y.P. Act, 1952, s.3, sending a child under 12 to a special reception centre. See Chap. 12.

Detention by Police.—Under the M.C. Act, 1952, a magistrates' court may order the detention of persons in police premises as follows:

Detention up to 4 days in police cells, etc., certified for the purpose by the Secretary of State instead of any imprisonment which the court has power to impose (s. 109). This must be by warrant of commitment (M.C. Rules, 1952, r. 71).

Detention up to 8 P.M. in the evening of the day on which the order is made, in a police station or court-house where the court has power to commit to prison a person convicted of an offence, but the order must not deprive the offender of a reasonable opportunity of returning to his abode on that day (s. 110). Such an order shall be in writing (M.C. Rules, 1952, r. 27).

Detention by warrant in a police station when the court has power to commit a person to prison in default of payment of a sum adjudged to be paid by a summary conviction.

This warrant, unless the sum is sooner paid, shall authorise any police constable to arrest the defaulter and take him to a police station where the officer in charge shall detain him until 8 A.M. in the morning of the day following that on which he is arrested, or if he is arrested between midnight and 8 A.M. in the morning until 8 A.M. in the morning of the day on which he was arrested. Provided that the officer may release him at any time within 4 hours before 8 A.M. in the morning if the officer thinks it is expedient to do so in order to enable him to go to his work or for any other reason appearing to the officer to be sufficient (s. 111).

If imprisonment for default of payment or sufficient distress is reduced by part payment to less than 5 days, the person may be committed either to prison or to a certified place (under s. 109 above) or if reduced to one day he may be detained in the court-house (under s. 110 above) (M.C. Rules, 1952, r. 45.)

If a magistrates' court has power to remand a person in custody, if the remand does not exceed 3 days, it may commit him to the custody of a constable (M.C. Act, 1952, s. 105).

Recognizance.—A recognizance is an obligation or bond under which a person acknowledges that he owes the Crown a certain sum of money if the condition or conditions specified in the recognizance are not carried out.

A person may be ordered to enter into a recognizance with or without sureties.

The recognizances of sureties may be taken separately and before or after the recognizance of the principal (C.J.A. Act, 1914, s. 24).

If sureties are required, the person who enters into the recognizance (the principal) and the sureties are liable to pay the amounts specified if the condition prescribed is not fulfilled.

Recognizances may be required for several purposes, such as to keep the peace or to be of good behaviour, to prosecute a particular person, to pursue an appeal, to appear and give evidence, to surrender to a court or when placed on probation.

If a surety makes complaint in writing and on oath to a justice for any county or borough that his principal has broken or is about to break the conditions of his recognizance to keep the peace or be of good behaviour, the justice if the principal is in such area or the recognizance was entered before a magistrates' court of such area, may issue a warrant to arrest the principal and bring him before a magistrates' court. If such complaint is not on oath the justice may issue a summons. (M.C. Act, 1952, s. 92).

If a recognizance to keep the peace or be of good behaviour or to appear before a magistrates' court or to do anything connected with a proceeding before the court appears to be forfeited, the court may declare it forfeited and adjudge the persons bound to pay the amounts or parts of them. Payment may be enforced as if the sum was a fine on summary conviction. However if the recognizance was to keep the peace or be of good behaviour, the court shall not declare it forfeited except by order made on complaint (M.C. Act, 1952, s. 96). See Chap. 22.

Breach of recognizance is not an offence so there is no appeal against the forfeiting of a recognizance (*R.* v. *Durham Justices, Ex-parte Laurent,* (1944)). Criminal Justice Act, 1948, ss. 14, 15, deal with the powers of Assizes and Quarter Sessions in relation to fines and forfeited recognizances.

A magistrates' court may fix the amounts of any recognizance which later may be taken by any justice or the clerk of any summary court or any police officer not below the rank of inspector or the officer in charge of any police station or the governor or keeper of the prison or place in which the person is detained.

A certificate from the clerk of the court giving particulars of the recognizance should be produced to any such person before he takes the recognizance and the recognizance should be sent to the clerk of the court (M.C. Act, 1952, s. 95, M.C. Rules, 1952, r. 68).

Bail.—Bail is a recognizance or bond taken by a duly authorised person to ensure the appearance of an accused person at an appointed place and time to answer to the charge made against him. See also " Recognizance," above.

It is based on the principle that an accused person should not be kept unnecessarily in custody, so whenever it is possible and can with safety be done, an untried prisoner should be released on bail.

Bail may be granted by a Court, by a Justice, and in some cases, as provided by Statute, by the officer in charge of a police station.

A person charged with treason shall not be admitted to bail except by order of a Judge of the High Court or the Secretary of State (M.C. Act, 1952, s. 8).

The object of bail being to secure the attendance of an accused person at the trial, the following points should be considered before bail is allowed :—

(1) The probability of accused's appearance at the trial.

(2) The nature and gravity of the charge.

(3) The nature and weight of evidence in support of the charge.

(4) The sufficiency of the sureties, if sureties are required.

A prisoner may be released on his own recognizance, or one or more sureties may be required in addition to his own bond. Such sureties are termed his bails or bailsmen, and they are responsible, in the amounts fixed, for the prisoner's attendance in court.

The amount of bail is discretionary and will depend on the nature of the charge and the quality of the prisoner. It is illegal to require excessive bail. Usually two householders are accepted as bails, provided the Justice or police officer is satisfied of their ability to answer the sums in which they are bound. Bail can be found after a Court has risen. See " Recognizance " above.

A bail recognizance may be conditioned for the appearance of the person at every hearing during the course of the proceedings, (M.C. Act, 1952, s. 105). This is termed " continuous bail ".

If a person charged with or convicted of an offence is released on bail to appear before a summary court and fails to appear, the court may issue a warrant for his arrest (M.C. Act, 1952, s. 97).

A person bailed to appear is by law in the custody of his sureties, and they may arrest him either with or without warrant if they fear his escape, and bring him before a Magistrate, thereby clearing themselves of their obligation.

If a person on bail fails to appear before the court the recognizance may be forfeited or estreated, and he and his sureties may be adjudged to pay the amounts in which they were bound (M.C. Act, 1952, s. 96 and see "Recognizance," above).

The officer in charge of a police station has power to admit to bail prisoners arrested without warrant, and he must, unless there are grave reasons to the contrary, admit to bail prisoners under seventeen years of age.

Bail by Police.—Certain Statutes authorise the police to admit prisoners to bail as follows :—

(1) Persons arrested without warrant.—When a person is arrested without warrant and brought to a police station a police officer not below the rank of inspector or the officer in charge of the station may, and if it will not be practicable to bring him before a summary court within 24 hours of the arrest, will inquire into the case and, unless the offence appears to be a serious one, release him on his entering into a recognizance with or without sureties, for a reasonable amount, to appear before a summary court at a named time and place (this does not affect prisoners under 17 for which see later).

If the inquiry into the case cannot be completed forthwith the officer may release the prisoner on recognizance with or without sureties for a reasonable amount, to appear at the police station at a fixed time unless he receives written notice that his attendance is not required. If the prisoner appears to be under 17, the recognizance conditioned for his appearance at the police station may be taken from his parent or guardian with or without sureties.

If such a prisoner is kept in custody he shall be brought before a summary court as soon as practicable (M.C. Act, 1952, s. 38).

(2) Persons arrested without warrant for offences against children and young persons. A person so arrested and brought to a police station shall be released on bail, with or without sureties to attend the hearing of the charge unless his release would tend to defeat the ends of justice or to cause injury or danger to the child or young person against whom the offence is alleged to have been committed (C. and Y.P. Act, 1933, s. 13). See " Cruelty to Children and Young Persons," Chap. 12.

(3) Prisoners under seventeen years of age. When a person apparently under seventeen is arrested with or without warrant and cannot be brought forthwith before a summary court, his case should be inquired into by the police and he may be released on bail but see " Treatment of Youthful Offenders," Chap. 12, and see above as regards a recognizance to appear at a police station.

(4) Persons arrested on warrant. If the warrant to arrest has been endorsed by the Justice issuing it with his consent to the prisoner, when arrested, being released on bail, the prisoner, when brought to a police station, should be released on bail in accordance with the directions in the endorsement (M.C. Act, 1952, s. 93).

(5) Persons arrested without warrant in County Boroughs. Any idle or disorderly person found disturbing the public peace or suspected on just cause of intention to commit a felony, may be arrested by a county borough constable and brought to a police station. Such a prisoner may, if it is thought fit, be released on bail to appear before a Justice (Municipal Corporations Act, 1882, ss. 193 and Police Act, 1946).

Remand.—Remand is the process of adjourning the hearing of the case against a person and taking precautions to ensure his presence at a future hearing.

CHAPTER V.—PROCEDURE 59

A remand is therefore an adjournment under which the Court puts back the person in custody or upon recognizance.

The M.C. Act, 1952, deals with remand as follows:

A magistrates' court may, before inquiring into an offence as examining justices or at any time during the inquiry adjourn the hearing and, if it does so, shall remand the accused (s. 6).

The court may at any time adjourn the trial of an information. The court, after convicting the accused and before sentence, may adjourn the case (up to three weeks at a time) for inquiries to be made or to decide the best method of dealing with it.

On adjourning a trial the court may remand the accused and shall do so if the accused is 17 or over and the offence is an indictable one or an indictable offence being tried summarily (s. 14).

If the court is satisfied that the accused has committed an offence punishable on summary conviction with imprisonment but considers inquiry should be made into his mental or physical condition it shall adjourn the case (up to three weeks at a time) so that the accused may be medically examined and remand him for that purpose as laid down in the section (s. 26).

A court may at any time adjourn the hearing of a complaint and remand the defendant (ss. 46, 47). A court, at common law, may adjourn for a reasonable time on reasonable grounds.

Where an accused has been convicted by a magistrates' court and the trial has been adjourned before sentence is given, he may be sentenced by a later court provided that if the later court is not composed of the same justices it must inquire into the facts and circumstances of the case before sentencing him (s. 98).

Where a magistrates' court has power to remand any person it may commit him to custody (prison or other detention, s. 126) or remand him on bail usually for eight clear days but it may be for longer periods as provided in the section, and if the remand in custody is for not more than three days it may commit him to the custody of a constable (s. 105).

S. 106 deals with further remands and also allows a court to further remand a person remanded to appear or be brought to court but unable to do so by reason of illness or accident, or to enlarge the recognizance of a person on bail in his absence.

" Clear days " means complete intervening days, excluding the day of remand and the day of appearing in court.

For remand of persons under 21 see " Treatment of Youthful Offenders," Chap. 12.

A summary court may adjourn the hearing of an information or complaint and fix a time for its resumption or, if it does not remand the accused or the defendant, it may leave the resumption to be decided later by the court (viz. adjournment *sine die*) (M.C. Act, 1952, ss. 14 and 46).

Acquittal.—When a person has been tried by a judge and jury for an indictable offence and the jury return a general verdict of " Not guilty," the prisoner is thereby acquitted or freed from the accusation and must be at once discharged, unless there is some other charge against him.

If his discharge was the result of some defect in the proceedings (e.g. the indictment was not sufficient so that he had not been in danger upon it), he may be detained and prosecuted afresh.

It is a rule at Common Law that a man may not be put twice in peril for the same offence. If a person is legally acquitted of an offence, he should not again be prosecuted for that offence.

If such a person is again prosecuted for the same offence he may, when asked to plead or reply to the charge against him, make the special plea of **autrefois acquit**, that is, that he had previously been acquitted of the same offence. If he effectively makes out this plea he will be discharged.

The fact that a person accused of an indictable offence has been discharged by the Court does not prevent his re-arrest, subsequent prosecution and conviction, if he had not been in danger of conviction on the first occasion.

If a person accused of an indictable offence is discharged by the examining Justices under s. 7 of the M.C. Act, 1952, he can again be brought before them if more evidence is forthcoming.

If a case has been tried on its merits and dismissed, the dismissal is a bar to subsequent proceedings for the same offence as the defendant was in danger and was acquitted.

Where on summary trial, under the provisions of the Act, of an offence which otherwise would have been punishable on indictment only, the court dismisses the information, this is equal to acquittal on indictment (M.C. Act, 1952, s. 22).

If the Justices dismiss a charge of assault under ss. 42 or 43 after a hearing upon the merits, they shall, if requested, give the defendant a certificate of dismissal which is a release from all further proceedings, civil or criminal, for the same cause (Offences against the Person Act, 1861, ss. 44 and 45).

Appeal.—Under the Magistrates' Courts Act, 1952, and Rules a person convicted by a magistrates' court may appeal to Quarter Sessions:

(1) If he pleaded guilty—against the sentence;

(2) If he did not plead guilty—against the conviction or sentence;

(3) If sentenced for the offence in respect of which he was *previously* put on probation or conditionally discharged—against the sentence.

In such cases " sentence " includes any order made on conviction by a summary court except:

(a) a probation order or an order for conditional discharge (see Chap. 28);

(b) an order for payment of costs;

(c) an order for the destruction of an animal under s. 2, Protection of Animals Act, 1911, or;

(d) an order made under any enactment which allows the court no discretion as to its making or terms (s. 83).

An appellant should give written notice of appeal (stating the grounds, M.C. Rule 59) within 14 days to the clerk of the summary court and to the other party. An extension of time may be allowed by Quarter Sessions on application to the Clerk of the Peace (s. 84). Such a notice can be sent by registered post to any person concerned (M.C. Rules, 1952, r. 59).

An appellant may abandon his appeal by giving notice in writing or by registered letter (M.C. Rules, 1952, r. 60), not later than the third day before the hearing, to the clerk of the summary court, and he may be ordered to pay costs (s. 85). Where appellant has given notice to abandon his appeal, any recognizances binding him to appear at the hearing of the appeal shall have effect to enforce his appearances before the summary court at a time and place to be notified to him by the clerk of the court (M.C. Rules, 1952, r. 60).

If the appellant is in custody, the summary court may release him on recognizance to appear at the hearing of the appeal, except in the case of committal to Quarter Sessions, under ss. 28 (Borstal) or s. 29 (for sentence on conviction for indictable offence (s. 89)).

There is an appeal to Quarter Sessions against an order binding over to be of good behaviour under 34 Edward III. See " Surety for Good Behaviour," Chap. 22.

There is no right of appeal to Quarter Sessions against the dismissal of a case except in bastardy cases (M.C. Act, 1952, s. 83) and excise cases (Customs and Excise Act, 1952, s. 283) but application may be made for case stated (see later).

The Summary Jurisdiction (Appeals) Act, 1933 deals with appeals from a summary court to Quarter Sessions. When notice to appeal has been given both parties, if poor, may be granted " Appeal Aid Certificates " entitling them to free legal aid (s. 2).

The decision of Quarter Sessions on an appeal against conviction or sentence is final on all points of fact but on a point of law the court may state a special case for the opinion of the Queen's Bench Division (C.J. Act, 1925, s. 20).

The C.J. Act, 1948, s. 37 gives the High Court power to grant bail to persons in custody who have appealed or asked for case stated or applied for an order of certiorari.

A person convicted on indictment or on Coroner's inquisition or at Quarter Sessions as an incorrigible rogue (see Chap. 27) may appeal to the Court of Criminal Appeal on a question of law or with leave on a question of fact or mixed law and fact or with leave against the sentence, subject to the provisions of the Criminal Appeal Act, 1907 and the Rules made thereunder.

The decision of the Court of Criminal Appeal is final except in any case in which the Attorney General (or Solicitor General—Law Officers Act, 1944) certifies that the decision involves a point of law of exceptional public importance and that it is desirable in the public interest that there should be a further appeal to the House of Lords.

Case stated.—Under the M.C. Act, 1952 ss. 87 to 90 and Rules, 1952, 61 to 64, any person who was a party to any proceeding before a Magistrates' Court (sitting as a Court of Summary Jurisdiction, see *Boulter* v. *Kent Justices* (1897) or is aggrieved by the conviction, order, determination or other proceeding of the court, may question it on the ground that it is wrong in law (a point of law of some substance) or is in excess of jurisdiction by applying within 14 days (in writing to the clerk of the court—Rule 61) to the court to state a case for the opinion of the High Court on the question of law or jurisdiction involved.

He cannot do so if it is a decision against which he has a right to appeal to the High Court or which, since 1879, is by law final. (s. 87).

The justices have three months within which to state the case (Rule 63).

If the justices consider the application is frivolous they may refuse to state a case and certify accordingly, and the High Court may make an order of mandamus requiring them to state a case.

The justices shall not refuse the Attorney General's application to state a case. If the application to state a case is in respect of a decision any right of the applicant to appeal to Quarter Sessions shall cease (s. 87).

The justices need not state a case until the applicant has entered into a recognizance, with or without sureties, to prosecute the matter without delay and submit to the judgment of the High Court and pay any costs awarded (s. 90). If the applicant is in custody the summary court may release him on recognizance, with or without sureties, to appear before the magistrates' court within 10 days after the judgment of the High Court, unless the decision has been reversed, but a person committed in custody under ss. 28 or 29 cannot be so released (s. 89).

The High Court has similar power to release the applicant on recognizance (C.J. Act, 1948, s. 37).

The Queen's Bench Division will hear and determine the question and its decision shall be final (S.J. Act, 1857, s. 6).

A case may be stated on behalf of the justices whose decision is questioned by any two or more of them (Rule 62). Examining justices have no power to state a case, it can only be done by a court of summary jurisdiction (*Card* v. *Salmon* (1953)).

Certiorari and Mandamus.—Certiorari is the name of an order of the Queen's Bench Division directing that the proceedings are to be removed from an inferior court and taken to the Queen's Bench Division to be there examined and if necessary quashed.

This order may be granted on proof that there has been some defect in the proceedings or excess of jurisdiction or that some difficult point of law is likely to arise on the trial, or that a fair and impartial trial cannot be had in the Court below, or that a conviction has been obtained fraudulently, etc., etc.

If the applicant is in custody, the High Court may release him on recognizance conditioned for his appearance as directed (C.J. Act, 1948, s. 37 (1)).

Evidence for and against the granting of the order will be heard and if the Queen's Bench Division thinks fit, the order of certiorari will be issued so that the case may be examined.

If a Justice (or Justices) does not perform any duty laid upon him, application by affidavit may be made to the Queen's Bench Division asking for leave to apply for an order of mandamus. If leave is granted the application is made after notice has been served on all persons directly affected, and the Court, if satisfied, may grant an order of mandamus, i.e. an order requiring the Justice or Justices to perform the duty.

Habeas Corpus.—This is the name given to a writ or order of the Queen's Bench Division, addressed to the person who holds another in custody, directing him to produce the body (corpus) of the prisoner and show the cause of his detention.

It came into existence as a remedy against illegal detention or undue detention without trial. A prisoner should be tried as soon as possible and must not be kept unduly in prison untried.

A writ of habeas corpus may now be used to investigate any alleged illegal action of Justices regarding an untried prisoner. It may also be used to bring a prisoner, who is in custody on one charge, before another Court to answer another charge. However, when the attendance of a person under legal detention is required at any place in the interests of justice or for any public inquiry or where such a person requires treatment in hospital, etc., the Secretary of State may direct him to be taken there (C.J. Act, 1948, s. 60 and Prison Act, 1952, s. 22).

Limitation of Proceedings.—The general principle is that there should be no delay in taking proceedings (that is, laying the information) after the discovery of the offender. In many cases a definite time limit is fixed by Statute and after the prescribed period has elapsed no proceedings may be taken.

Indictable offences. There is, at Common Law, no limit of time within which a prosecution for an offence must be commenced. No matter how long previous an indictable offence has been committed, proceedings may be taken against the offender unless some Act of Parliament or legal rule prevents such action by fixing a time limit to proceedings in the case of the particular offence. In the majority of indictable offences there is no such time limit.

Summary Offences. Under s. 104, M.C. Act, 1952, except as otherwise expressly provided by any enactment a magistrates' court shall not try an information or hear a complaint unless same was made within six months from the time when the offence was committed or the matter of complaint arose. But this section does not restrict any power to try summarily an indictable offence under ss. 19, 20 or 21 of this Act, or under any enactment under which an indictable offence may be tried summarily with the consent of the accused nor would it apply to a continuing offence.

Sunday Process.—Sunday Observance Act, 1677, s. 6, directs that no person upon the Lord's Day shall serve or execute any writ, process, warrant, order, judgment or decree (except in cases of treason, felony or breach of the peace) but the service of same shall be void. " Process " includes any summons or warrant or order of a summary court other than a warrant of arrestment (Summary Jurisdiction (Process) Act, 1881, s. 8). However the issue or execution of any warrant under the Act to arrest a person charged with an offence or of a search warrant shall be as effectual on Sunday as on any other day (M.C. Act, 1952, s. 102).

A police notice prior to proceedings to be taken would not appear to be " process " and therefore might be served on Sunday.

Costs in Criminal Cases Act, 1952.—This Act has repealed the similar Act of 1908 and sections of other Acts which dealt with costs in criminal cases and purport to deal with all such costs.

Generally speaking the Act allows payment of costs in indictable cases out of local funds by order of Assizes, Quarter Sessions, Magistrates' Courts and examining justices.

Assizes or Quarter Sessions may order payment of the reasonable costs of the prosecution and if accused is acquitted the costs of the defence or compensation for any witness (s. 1).

If accused is convicted Assizes or Quarter Sessions may order him to pay the costs of the prosecution but if he is acquitted on indictment the prosecution may be ordered to pay the costs of the defence if accused has not been in custody or bound by recognizance or if it is an offence under the Merchandise Marks Acts or a private prosecution for libel or corrupt election practice (s. 2).

Ss. 3 and 4 deal with the costs which may be awarded by the Court of Criminal Appeal and the House of Lords.

Magistrates dealing summarily with an indictable offence or inquiring as examining justices may order payment of the costs of the prosecution. If they dismiss such a case they may order payment of the costs of the defence or compensation to any witness (s. 5).

On summary trial of an information a magistrates' court may order payment of costs on conviction to be paid by accused to the prosecution but on dismissal of the case may order the costs to be paid by the prosecution to the accused. Only actual costs may be ordered; if an amount in excess is ordered it would be a penalty (*R.* v. *Highgate Justices* (1954)).

If examining justices determine not to commit the accused for trial considering that the evidence was not sufficient and that the charge was not made in good faith they may order the prosecution to pay the costs of the defence, but if the amount of such costs exceeds £25 the prosecutor may appeal to Quarter Sessions (s. 6).

The Witnesses' Allowances Regulations, 1955 and 1958 deal with the allowances payable to witnesses in criminal cases.

Director of Public Prosecutions.—The Director is the head of a legal Department in London. He is appointed under the Prosecution of Offences Act, 1908, and it is his duty, under the superintendence of the Attorney-General, to carry on such criminal proceedings and to give such advice and assistance to Chief Officers of Police, Clerks to Justices and other persons concerned in criminal proceedings as may be prescribed by regulations or as directed in any special case by the Attorney-General. Such regulations provide for the Director taking action in cases of importance or difficulty or which by statute require his action. He can undertake at any stage the conduct of any Criminal proceedings (s. 3). Normally he appears for the Crown in cases under the Criminal Appeal Act, 1907. The Regulations of 1946 are given in Appendix III at the end of the book.

Legal Aid and Advice Act, 1949.—Legal aid by solicitor and counsel may be given to a person who has reasonable grounds for taking, defending, etc., law proceedings in cases not excepted by the Act (s. 1), and whose disposable income does not exceed £420 per annum (s. 2) and he may be required to contribute to the cost (s. 3). Such person may select his legal aid from a local panel of lawyers (s. 6). The above provisions are in force for proceedings in the Supreme Court and the County Courts. The provisions affording legal aid in magistrates' courts are not yet in force.

In criminal proceedings where there is a right to free legal aid under older Acts, there is no prescribed income limit but if there is a doubt as to a person's sufficient means or as to the desirability of his having legal aid, he should be granted it (s. 18).

Application for free legal aid under the Poor Prisoner's Defence Act, 1930 (see " Accused or Defendant " above), may be made by letter to the clerk to the justices and a justice may grant a legal aid certificate (s. 19).

Making a false written statement to obtain legal aid will be a summary offence (s. 18).

Chapter VI

RECORD OF EVIDENCE

Contents

Statements by Persons suspected of Crime or by Prisoners in Police Custody.—In 1918 the Judges of the King's Bench Division approved a memorandum on the above subject, containing rules for the guidance of the police.

These rules were drawn up to ensure that any statement tendered in evidence should be a purely voluntary statement and therefore admissible in evidence. They explain the conditions under which the Courts would be likely to admit in evidence statements made by persons suspected of or charged with crime. They are not rules of law (see *R*. v. *Voisin* (1918), and *R*. v. *Wattam* (1952)) but are for the guidance of the police.

These rules are to the following effect :—

Persons suspected of crime.

(1) When a police officer is endeavouring to discover the author of a crime, there is no objection to his putting questions in respect thereof to any person or persons, whether suspected or not, from whom he thinks that useful information can be obtained.

(2) Whenever a police officer has made up his mind to charge a person with a crime, he should first caution such person before asking any questions or any further questions, as the case may be.

Prisoners.

(3) Persons in custody should not be questioned without the usual caution being first administered.

NOTE.—This rule was never intended to encourage or authorise the questioning or cross-examination of a person in custody after he has been cautioned, on the subject of the crime for which he is in custody.

But in some cases it may be proper and necessary to put questions to a person in custody after the caution has been administered, for instance, a person arrested for a burglary may, before he is formally charged, say " I have hidden or thrown the property away," and after caution he would properly be asked " Where have you hidden or thrown it ? " ; or a person, before he is formally charged as a habitual (persistent) criminal, is properly asked to give an account of what he has done since he last came out of prison.

Prima facie the expression " persons in custody " in this Rule (3) applies to persons arrested before they are confined in a police station or prison, but this rule equally applies to prisoners in the custody of the gaoler.

(4) If the prisoner wishes to volunteer any statement, the usual caution should be administered.

It is desirable that the last two words of the usual caution should be omitted, and that the caution should end with the words " be given in evidence."

(5) The caution to be administered to a prisoner, when he is *formally* charged, should therefore be in the following words : " Do you wish to say anything in answer to the charge ? You are not obliged to say anything unless you wish to do so, but whatever you say will be taken down in writing and may be given in evidence."

Care should be taken to avoid any suggestion that his answers can only be used in evidence against him, as this may prevent an innocent person making a statement which might assist to clear him of the charge.

NOTE.—With regard to the form of the caution it is obvious that the words in this Rule (5) are only applicable when the formal charge is made and can have no application when a violent or resisting prisoner is being taken to a police station. In any case before the formal charge is made, the usual caution is, or should be, " You are not obliged to say anything, but anything you say may be given in evidence."

This simple, emphatic and easily intelligible form of caution may be used at any time during the investigation of a crime at which it is necessary or right to administer a caution. For example, when a person is being questioned by a police officer under Rule (1) and a point is reached when the officer would not allow that person to depart until further inquiry has been made and any suspicion that may have been aroused had been cleared up, it is desirable that such a caution should be given before further questions are asked. When any form of restraint is actually imposed, such a caution should be given before further questions are asked.

When it comes to cautioning a prisoner immediately before or immediately after he is formally charged, the form prescribed in this Rule (5) should be used.

(6) A statement made by a prisoner before there is time to caution him is not rendered inadmissible in evidence merely

by reason of no caution having been given, but in such a case he should be cautioned as soon as possible.

(7) A prisoner making a voluntary statement must not be cross-examined, and no questions should be put to him about it except for the purpose of removing ambiguity in what he has actually said. For instance, if he has mentioned an hour without saying whether it was morning or evening, or has given a day of the week and day of the month which do not agree, or has not made it clear to what individual or what place he intended to refer in some part of his statement, he may be questioned sufficiently to clear up the point.

(8) When two or more persons are charged with the same offence and statements are taken separately from the persons charged, the police should not read these statements to the other persons charged, but each of such persons should be furnished by the police with a copy of such statements and nothing should be said or done by the police to invite a reply. If the person charged desires to make a statement in reply, the usual caution should be administered. (This rule should be carefully followed.) (See *R*. v. *Mills and Lemon* (1947)).

NOTE.—For the purpose of these Rules the words " crime " and " offence " are synonymous and include any offence for which a person may be apprehended or detained in custody.

(9) Any statement made in accordance with the above rules should, whenever possible, be taken down in writing and signed by the person making it after it has been read to him and he has been invited to make any corrections he may wish.

NOTE.—In giving evidence as to the circumstances in which any statement was made or taken down in writing, a police officer must be absolutely frank in describing to the Court exactly what occurred, and it will then be for the Court to decide whether or not the statement tendered should be admitted in evidence.

Admissions and Confessions.—A person summoned to a magistrates' court may in certain cases write pleading guilty and not attend (see " Proceedings before Justices," Chap. IV, *ante*). An admission made by a party in a case or made on his behalf is a disclosure of or an agreement with some fact which more or less tells against his case. An admission may be made in words or in writing or by mere silent conduct. If a statement is made in the presence of someone who would naturally contradict it if not true, but who nevertheless remains silent, he impliedly admits its truth unless he can show good cause for his silence.

A confession is a statement made by a person charged with a crime admitting that he committed the crime. A confession is an admission, but an admission may not amount to a confession of guilt.

All admissions and confessions in criminal cases, to be admissible in evidence, must be free and voluntary. It is the duty of the prosecution to prove that any confession produced in evidence has been given voluntarily.

If there has been any inducement or constraint from any person in authority over the accused, his resulting confession will not be admitted in evidence as it cannot be regarded as free and voluntary.

A police officer is a person in authority over a prisoner and he must be most careful in his conduct towards the prisoner so that he may be able to prove affirmatively that he held out no inducement or threat towards a prisoner who has made a confession or admission of any kind. An inducement or threat held out to a prisoner by a person not in authority over him does not prevent the giving in evidence of a resulting confession.

Any statement, admission, or confession, freely made without inducement or threat, to a police officer by a prisoner, is admissible in evidence. When a prisoner wishes to make a voluntary statement he should be cautioned that he is not obliged to say anything, but whatever he says will be taken down in writing and may be given in evidence.

The rule is that no person should be compelled to incriminate himself and the Judges' rules regarding statements from prisoners must be carefully observed. A prisoner's replies to questions may not, *prima facie*, be regarded as free and voluntary. The circumstances of the case must be taken into account and a police officer should not question his prisoner unless he can show good reason for doing so ; for example, a person who gives himself up for a crime may be asked questions necessary to elicit the facts.

Where a statement or complaint or charge is made in the presence of a person accusing him of a crime, his behaviour on the occasion may be given in evidence so that the jury may decide whether or not, at that time, he accepted or admitted the statement made against him.

Such a statement or charge is not evidence of the acts alleged therein, but the conduct of the accused when the statement was made may be equivalent to an admission of its correctness. However, a prisoner, when cautioned, may reply that he does not wish to say anything or he may remain silent.

Although a confession may not, for some reason, be admissible in evidence, yet anything discovered in consequence of what was stated in the confession will be admitted in evidence. Thus the finding of stolen goods as the result of an inadmissible confession may be proved.

Dying Declaration.—A dying declaration is a statement made by an injured and dying person as to the facts and circumstances which caused his injuries. It should give in the actual words of the injured person what has happened to him ; it should contain his opinion that he is dying and has no hope of recovery ; it need not be an oath ; it may be signed by the injured person if he is able to sign it ; the person charged with causing the injuries need not be present, though he may be ; and the person taking it should sign and date it and get it signed also by all the persons (if any) who have heard it being made by the injured person.

Any person may take a dying declaration.

The injured person should not be sworn, as it is considered that a person in such a serious position will feel bound to speak the truth.

There is no particular form of dying declaration, and if questions are put to the injured person the questions as well as the answers should be written down and will form part of the declaration.

If the person accused of causing the injuries be present, the injured person should be given the opportunity of identifying him, and everything said by both parties should be written down.

Dying declarations are admissible in evidence in cases where the death of the deceased person is the subject of the charge, that is, in trials for murder or manslaughter.

Before a Judge will receive a dying declaration in evidence he must be satisfied :—

(1) That at the time it was made the declarant was in actual danger of death.

(2) That he then realised his condition and had no hope of recovery.

(3) That he died and that the cause of death was the subject of the dying declaration.

However, if the accused person is available, and if it is at all possible, a Magistrate should be procured so that a deposition may be taken in the presence and hearing of the accused.

Deposition.—A deposition is a statement made on oath before a Justice, taken down in writing in the presence and hearing of the accused, and read over to the deponent or person making it, and by the Justice. It must be stated in the deposition that it was taken in the presence and hearing of the accused and he must be given an opportunity of cross-examining the deponent. It ought to be signed by the deponent.

When examining justices are inquiring into an offence the evidence of each witness shall be taken down in writing in the form of a deposition and read over to the accused (M.C. Rules, 1952, r. 5).

A deposition is a record of the evidence which a witness can give in a case and it should state in the words of the witness what the witness can testify. It is written down by the Magistrates' Clerk and remains in his custody until it is required at the Court where the trial of the accused person is to take place.

Persons committed for trial by a higher court are entitled to apply for and get copies of the depositions and if the information is in writing, of the information on reasonable payment (M.C. Rules, 1952, r. 13).

A person who thus makes a deposition in a case which is sent forward for trial by jury, is bound over by recognizance to attend and give evidence.

However, if the examining justices consider that the attendance of any witness at the trial is unnecessary by reason of any statement by the accused or plea of guilty by the accused or because his evidence is merely of a formal nature, they may bind him over to attend conditionally upon notice given to him and not otherwise. Such witness need not attend unless he gets notice to do so (M.C. Act, 1952, s. 5).

If a witness is dead or insane or too ill to travel, or kept away by the defence, or if his attendance is declared unnecessary by the Justices, his deposition may be read in evidence if the conditions of the section are satisfied (C.J. Act, 1925, s. 13).

Taking of Depositions of Persons dangerously ill.— Where a person is able and willing to give material information relating to an indictable offence or to anyone accused of an indictable offence, if a justice is satisfied by medical evidence that such person is dangerously ill and unlikely to recover and it is not practicable for examining justices to take his evidence in the normal manner, the justice may take in writing the deposition of the sick person on oath. Such a deposition may be given in evidence before examining justices and on the trial of the offender subject to the conditions laid down in s. 6 of the Criminal Law Amendment Act, 1867 (M.C. Act, 1952, s. 41).

The justice shall give reasonable notice of such taking to the person against whom it is to be used and allow full cross examination of the deponent. He shall sign the deposition and add a statement as to his reason for taking it, the day when and the place where it was taken and the names of any persons present when it was taken (M.C. Rules, 1952, r. 29).

The conditions prescribed by s. 6 of the C.L. Amendment Act, 1867, are that before being given in evidence the following must be complied with:

(a) Proof that the deponent is dead or that there is no reasonable probability that he will ever be able to travel or to give evidence;

(b) The deposition purports to be signed by the justice by or before it purports to have been taken;

(c) Proof that reasonable notice (in writing) of the intention to take such deposition had been given to the person against whom it was proposed to be read in evidence and that such person or his lawyer had, if present, full opportunity of cross-examining the deponent. S. 7 of this Act provides for the attendance of the accused when he is in custody at the time.

As regards a deposition taken from an injured child or young person see " Arrest, Search Warrant and Procedure," Chap. 12.

The above will apply in the case of a person seriously injured by another where his story should be placed on legal record as soon as possible. It also applies in the case of a necessary witness in an indictable case who is dangerously ill.

In such cases a statement should be taken from the person, his doctor should be interviewed and the facts laid before the clerk to the justice so that he and a justice should come and take the deposition.

If the injured person thinks he is going to die, and there is no hope of his recovery, his " dying declaration " should be taken, in case it is not possible to take his deposition as above.

See " Dying Declaration," above.

Chapter VII

EVIDENCE

Contents

Evidence.—The word evidence means that which makes evident or manifest or which supplies proof. In law the term " evidence " is used to indicate the means by which any fact or point in issue or question may be proved or disproved in a manner complying with the legal rules governing the subject.

A Court holds a judicial inquiry to ascertain whether a person is or is not guilty of some offence. The burden or task of proving that the accused is guilty rests on the prosecutor or person who asserts that he is guilty, as the law presumes a man to be innocent until the contrary is proved (*Woolmington* v. *Director of Public Prosecutions* (1935)). See " Onus of Proof," later.

The prosecutor, therefore, has to produce evidence, viz. a witness or witnesses who on oath relate the facts of the case and (or) produce any things necessary for that purpose. The accused person on his part may also tender witnesses to exonerate him from the charge and to prove that he had previously borne a good character. This tendering of evidence and the nature of the evidence so given are subject to legal rules, the rules of evidence. The object of these rules in criminal cases is to elicit the truth without causing undue prejudice to the prisoner.

To prove a particular fact the evidence must be **competent,** that is, it must be fit and appropriate proof of the fact alleged, and it should be **satisfactory,** that is, it must be sufficient to satisfy the Court beyond reasonable doubt. Facts are proved by persons testifying to their existence or occurrence, and the **credibility of a witness** depends on his knowledge of the facts, his impartiality, and his truthfulness.

When a witness comes before the Court to give evidence he is sworn to tell the truth, the whole truth, and nothing but the truth. Under the guidance of the party by whom he is called he gives his evidence and this is called his **examination in chief.** When this is finished he may be questioned or **cross-examined** by the opposing party, and when this is concluded, he may be **re-examined** by the side which has produced him to give evidence. Later he may be **recalled** by the Court to answer further questions.

Oath or Affirmation.—At Common Law the evidence of a witness was not admissible unless he had been sworn to tell the truth. Evidence given before a magistrates' court shall be given on oath except where unsworn evidence is authorised by law (M.C. Act, 1952, s. 78). The Oaths Act, 1909, prescribes the present form of oath. If a witness objects to being sworn on the grounds that the taking of an oath is contrary to his religious belief or that he has no religious belief, he may make a solemn affirmation, declaring that the evidence he is about to give is the truth (Oaths Act, 1888). Christians are sworn on the New Testament, with their hats off. Jews are sworn on the Old Testament, with their hats on. Mahommedans are sworn on the Koran. The general rule is that a witness may claim to be sworn in the manner prescribed by his religion or national law, and the oath should be such as the witness considers binding on his conscience, but if a witness objects to being sworn his solemn affirmation will be accepted. A child of tender years need not be sworn in offence cases (C. and Y.P. Act, 1933, s. 38). See " Children," Chap. 12.

Number of Witnesses.—The general rule is that the evidence of one witness may be sufficient to convict an accused person. However, at least two witnesses are required in the cases of treason, personation at an election, and blasphemy.

In a case of perjury the accused may not be convicted solely on the evidence of one witness as to the falsity of any statement alleged to be false. See " Perjury," Chap. 21.

In certain other cases as given below, corroboration of the evidence of only one witness is necessary before conviction.

Corroborative evidence means other independent evidence tending to support the truthfulness and accuracy of evidence already given. Corroboration of the evidence of one witness by other evidence connecting the accused with the offence is required by law in cases of perjury, procuration, of the unsworn evidence of children of tender years, and a motorist cannot be convicted for exceeding a speed limit merely on the opinion of one witness as to the rate of speed. See also Chap. 10 as to corroboration in sexual offence cases.

Also in practice, the evidence of the injured party in sexual cases (*R.* v. *Freebody* (1935)) and the evidence of an accomplice (*R.* v. *Baskerville*, (1916)) should be corroborated, but the jury, after warning by the Judge may convict without corroboration.

Evidence for the prosecution may be given by the prosecutor and any witnesses he may produce, but the wife of the accused cannot be required to give evidence for the prosecution except in the cases given below.

The husband or wife of the prosecutor is a competent witness for the prosecution or for the defence.

A confession of guilt which is proved to have been freely and voluntarily made by the defendant to anyone, may be given in evidence. See " Admissions and Confessions," Chap. 6.

Accused persons and their husbands or wives are entitled to give evidence on oath for the defence. An accused person can make a statement without being sworn. The accused is not a compellable witness, and should be told by the Court that he has a right to give evidence on his own behalf. He should not be called as a witness except on his own application. If he does not give evidence, his failure to do so must not be commented on by the prosecution. He is not obliged to provide evidence against himself.

An accused person who does give sworn evidence may be asked any question in cross-examination (even if the answer would incriminate him) as to the offence charged against him, but he may not be questioned as to any other offence he may have committed or as to his bad character, unless (1) he has given evidence of his good character or the defence has questioned the prosecution witnesses with a view to establish the good character of the accused or the defence has attacked the character of the prosecutor or of the witnesses for the prosecution, (see *R.* v. *Clark* (1955)) or unless (2) the fact that he has committed such other offence is admissible in evidence against him (see " Extent of Evidence"), or unless (3) he has given evidence against another person charged with the same offence (Criminal Evidence Act, 1898, s. 1). With these exceptions he may be asked any relevant question.

(*Stirland* v. *Director of Public Prosecutions* (1944), gives the rules regarding the cross-examination of an accused person who has given evidence.)

Generally speaking the wife or husband of the accused may not be called as a witness unless on accused's consent and application, provided that in the following cases the wife or husband of the accused may be called as a witness for the prosecution or for the defence and without the consent of the accused.

(1) By statute, in cases of rape, indecent assault, procuration, incest, bigamy, cruelty to children, etc., as given by s. 4 and the Schedule to the Criminal Evidence Act, 1898, and in later Acts. In cases under these statutes the husband or wife is competent to give evidence if willing to do so but is not compellable (*Leach* v. *R.* (1912)).

(2) At common law, where the one is charged with personal injury to the other, or the husband with forcible abduction followed by marriage, or perhaps in cases of treason. In such cases the husband or wife is a competent witness and is also a compellable witness, viz. can be ordered to give evidence (*R.* v. *Lapworth* (1930)).

Competency of Witnesses.—The question whether a person is competent or fit to give evidence is one to be determined by the Court. The general rule is that all persons are competent to give evidence in all cases. A Court may decide that a witness is not competent to give evidence because of want of discretion, as in the case of persons incapable of understanding the nature of an oath or of giving a rational answer to a sensible question. For example, an idiot, a lunatic, a drunken person. A child of tender years, who does not understand the nature of an oath, may give evidence in offence cases if the Court is satisfied that such child has sufficient intelligence and understands the duty of speaking the truth, but for a conviction there must be corroboration of such evidence (C. and Y.P. Act, 1933, s. 38). The husband or wife of the accused is not a competent witness for the prosecution, except in certain cases (see preceding paragraphs as to " Accused persons and their husbands or wives ").

The Evidence Act, 1843, provides that no person shall be excluded from giving evidence on account of incapacity from crime or interest. Accordingly persons who have been convicted of crime, or who stand to gain or lose by the result of the trial, cannot be prevented on those grounds from giving evidence.

An accomplice, an accessory, or a principal in the offence, may give evidence.

Witnesses out of Court.—At any period during a trial, the Court, at the request of either party, will usually order such witnesses of the opposite party as have not been examined to leave the Court until they are called in to give evidence. (See s. 57, M.C. Act, 1952) This is done so that each witness may be examined out of the hearing of other witnesses who are to be examined after him, the object being that the evidence of each witness should not be influenced by what he has heard previous witnesses testifying. Should a witness remain in Court after such order, the Court has no right to reject his evidence on this ground, but may punish him for contempt of Court.

Interference with Witnesses.—It is a misdemeanour, being an offence against the administration of justice, to dissuade, hinder, or prevent from attending Court any witness duly summoned or bound over by recognizance. It is also an offence to attempt in any way to keep witnesses away. Any interference with witnesses renders those concerned liable to committal for contempt of Court (see Chap. 21). A witness duly subpœnaed or summoned, or bound over by recognizance, is privileged from arrest on civil process whilst attending Court and for a reasonable time before and after the trial.

Where it becomes necessary to call as a witness a person under legal detention, application should be made to the Secretary of State for an order for him to be brought to the Court. See " Habeas Corpus," Chap. 5.

Nature of Evidence.—Evidence may be given in the following manner :—

(1) A relation of a fact or facts by a witness. Such verbal evidence is termed **parol or oral evidence.**

(2) A document being produced and the contents read to the Court. This is termed **documentary evidence.**

(3) An article connected with the circumstances of the case being produced by a witness (who usually gives parol evidence accounting for it). This may be called **real evidence.**

The rule is that the best evidence the nature of the case will admit should be produced at the trial, as its absence will tell against the party neglecting to produce it.

The best evidence is termed **primary evidence,** or evidence at first hand, and such evidence is also called **direct** or **positive evidence,** meaning that the evidence of any fact alleged to have been seen, heard, or perceived by the senses must be the evidence of a person who says he saw, heard, felt, etc., that fact. Primary or direct evidence of a document or thing is the production of the original document or actual thing. If primary evidence of a fact is not available, then the next best evidence of that fact, which is termed **secondary evidence,** may be offered. Thus secondary evidence of a person, document, or thing would be the production of a deposition or statement, a copy of the document, or a model of the thing. But before secondary evidence of a fact may be given it will be necessary to prove that primary evidence is not available ; for example, if a party wishes to put in evidence a particular document he should produce the original document (primary evidence), but if he can prove that the original document is destroyed, lost, in possession of the opposite party, or cannot be moved, he will be permitted to prove it by the secondary evidence of a true copy or of verbal evidence of its contents, but in the last case only if notice to produce it has been given to the party in whose possession it is or is supposed to be.

Parol or oral evidence given by a witness is admissible :—

(1) When it is the best evidence (primary evidence) of the fact which it is sought to establish.

(2) As secondary evidence of the contents of a document which cannot be produced in Court.

Oral evidence of a fact should be confined to direct evidence of that fact as within the personal knowledge of the witness, who should only relate facts which happened in his presence or within reach of his senses. To this rule there are some exceptions, such as hearsay evidence and the opinion or belief of a witness, which are dealt with in later paragraphs.

A confession of guilt by the accused or an admission that part of the evidence for the prosecution is correct, made by the accused or by some authorised person on his behalf, may be proved by the direct evidence of some person who has heard the confession or admission. As such evidence amounts to proof of a statement made by a person not called as a witness in the case, it is hearsay evidence to a certain extent, but as it comes, or is alleged to come, from the defendant or with his authority, confessions and admissions are not here included as hearsay but are dealt with separately in Chap. 6.

Documentary evidence.—Normally, a document produced before a Court has to be proved by a witness. A document 20 or more years old and produced from proper custody is admissible in evidence without further proof (Evidence Act, 1938, s. 4).

If an instrument (except a will) in any proceedings requires attestation, it may, instead of being proved by an attesting witness, be proved in the manner in which it might be proved if no attesting witness were alive (Evidence Act, 1938, s. 3).

In civil proceedings documentary evidence as to facts in issue will be admissible on the conditions prescribed in ss. 1 and 2 of the Evidence Act, 1938.

Evidence by Certificate.—The Criminal Justice Act, 1948, s. 41, provides as follows :—

In any criminal proceedings a certificate by a constable or person having qualifications as prescribed (by rules made by the Secretary of State) certifying that the plan or drawing exhibited is correctly made to scale by him, of the place or object specified, shall be evidence of the relative position of the things shown in the plan or drawing (s. 41 (1)). In any proceedings for an offence under the Road Traffic Acts or enactments (including orders, regulations, etc., s. 80) as to the use of vehicles on roads, a certificate in the prescribed form, signed by a constable, certifying that a person named stated to the constable that a particular motor vehicle :

(1) was being driven by or belonged to that person on a particular occasion, or

(2) belonged on a particular occasion to a firm in which that person also stated that he was, at the time of the statement, a partner, or

(3) belonged on a particular occasion to a corporation, of which that person also stated that he was, at the time of the statement, a director, officer or employee.

shall be evidence to show who was driving or to whom the vehicle belonged on that occasion (s. 41 (2)). Evidence by Certificate Rules, 1948, prescribe what is necessary.

In any proceedings for stealing railway or " transport " goods or receiving same or for stealing mail bags, postal packets, etc., or receiving same, a statutory declaration by any person that he sent, received or failed to receive any such articles, or that such articles when he sent or received them were in a particular state or condition, or that a vessel, vehicle or aircraft was at any time employed by the Post Office for transmission of postal packets, shall be admissible as evidence of the facts stated in the declaration (s. 41 (3)).

However such a certificate or declaration shall not be admissible in evidence unless oral evidence to the like effect would have been admissible and unless a copy has been served on the accused person not less than 7 days before the hearing or trial, or if the accused, not later than 3 days before the hearing or trial, serves notice on the prosecutor requiring the attendance at the trial, of the person who signed the certificate or declaration (s. 41 (5)).

A certificate from the clerk of a magistrates' court giving the court register or any extract from it shall be admissible in evidence in any legal proceedings (M.C. Rules, 1952, r. 56).

Evidence by certificate from the police can also be produced in some other cases. See " Summons," Chap. 5, " Notifying Address," Chap. 28, and " Deserters and Absentees," Chap. 30.

Hearsay evidence is evidence given by a witness of what he has heard another person (not the accused) say. Such evidence is not admissible unless what was said had been said in the presence and hearing of the accused. Hearsay is not admitted in evidence because what the other person said was not upon oath, and because the accused had no opportunity of contradicting or cross-examining him. There are some exceptions to this rule, and hearsay evidence may be admissible in certain cases, such as :—

(1) Dying declarations of persons whose death is the subject of the charge and whose declarations deal with the cause of death. (See " Dying Declaration," Chap. 6.)

(2) Rape, indecent assault on females and males and other similar offences. In such cases the fact that a complaint was

made by the injured person to some other person as soon as reasonably possible after the act alleged and the particulars of the complaint may be given in evidence by that other person not as proof or corroboration of the act alleged, but as evidence of the conduct of the injured person and of the fact that the act was not consented to (*R.* v. *Lillyman* (1896); and *R.* v. *Osborne* (1905)). See also *R.* v. *Camelleri* (1922), and *R.* v. *Cummings* (1948).

(3) Written records or statements made by deceased persons in the regular course of duty or business. For example, police reports, entries in official note-books, etc.

(4) Statements made by a person as to his bodily or mental feelings, if such feelings are material in the case. Thus in a poisoning case, the deceased's words as to his symptoms and feelings before death would be very material as part of the transaction on which the charge is made.

(5) When the hearsay comes in as part of the *res gestae* or things done or incidents relevant to the matter in issue, viz. where it is one of the facts which actually make up the occurence or transaction on which the charge is based. For example, in a case of manslaughter a statement made by the deceased immediately after he had been knocked down as to the cause of his injuries was admitted in evidence. However, it is extremely difficult to put in evidence hearsay as part of the matter which is the subject of the inquiry.

Opinion.—The rule is that a witness is permitted to give direct or primary evidence, and is not allowed to testify as to matters which he cannot himself prove. However, in some cases a witness may be allowed to give his opinion or belief regarding a fact in issue ; for instance :—

(1) In matters of science or trade, an expert or skilled person may be asked the probable result or consequence of certain facts which have already been proved by evidence. For example, the opinion of a doctor as to whether a wound was or was not self-inflicted, or as to whether a man has died from the results of a wound or from natural causes. The opinion of an expert on the facts as proved is admissible in evidence.

(2) In a question of the genuineness of handwriting, the opinion of an expert is admissible.

(3) When there is a dispute as to the identity of a particular person or thing, the belief of a person in a position to judge will be admitted.

(4) As to the good character of the accused, that is, his general reputation.

Handwriting.—The handwriting of a person may be proved by :—

(1) The evidence of the writer himself.

(2) A witness who actually saw the paper or signature written.

(3) A witness who has a knowledge of the person's writing, by having seen him write on other occasions.

(4) A witness who has seen in the ordinary course of business documents presumably written or signed by the person.

(5) Comparison of the disputed writing with any writing proved to be genuine, made by witnesses acquainted with the handwriting or by skilled witnesses who are experts in hand-writing.

The opinion of such a witness as in (3), (4) or (5), that the handwriting is or is not the handwriting of the person, is admissible.

Extent of Evidence.—Any matter which may lawfully be deposed to and which may contribute, however slightly, to the clearing up of any question in dispute in a Court may be tendered in evidence, if accepted by the Court as admissible.

Evidence may be given of any fact arising in or out of the case (facts in issue), and of any fact **relevant** to any fact in issue (that is, related to or connected with such fact in issue), subject to the decision of the Court as to whether the evidence offered is too remote to be material in the case, as the introduction of matter having no bearing on the case would unduly prolong the trial and confuse the issue.

The general rule is that the evidence in a case should be confined to evidence proving or disproving the matter in dispute.

The following facts would be regarded as relevant in a prosecution :—

(1) Facts showing a motive for the offence, preparation for its commission, and conduct after its commission.

(2) The conduct of the person against whom the offence was committed.

(3) Facts connected with the facts of the case, as being explanatory or introductory, fixing times or places, showing the relation of the parties concerned, establishing identity of persons or things, proving the genuineness of documents, or leading up to other facts which may be relevant.

The general rule given above would render inadmissible any evidence of things done or said by the accused in connection with other matters, which might have been similar to, but yet were not connected with the case under trial. Accordingly evidence that the accused had a bad character or had committed other offences would be excluded by this rule. However, in some cases the fact that the accused had said or done other things may assist the Court by throwing some light on the offence for which he is being tried. Accordingly evidence of other similar but unconnected transactions may be admissible in the following cases :—

(1) To prove intention or guilty knowledge on the part of the accused. In general a man is not held criminally responsible for his act unless he did it with some criminal intention. This intention or " malice " as a rule is displayed by the nature of the act committed, as the law presumes that a man intends the probable or natural results of his actions. Such proof of intention rebuts any suggestion or defence of accident or mistake. The question of intention or design is relevant in cases of murder, arson, rape, indecent exposure, forgery, coinage offences, conspiracy, embezzlement, false pretences, larceny, etc.

Under the Larceny Act, 1916, s. 43, special evidence of guilty knowledge (or *scienter*) may be given in cases of the possession or receiving of stolen property, as follows :—

(*a*) Evidence that other property, stolen within twelve months preceding the date of the offence, was found or had been in accused's possession.

(*b*) Evidence that within the five years preceding the date of the offence, accused was convicted of some offence involving fraud or dishonesty, but such fact may not be proved unless he has had seven days' notice in writing that proof of such conviction would be given, and unless evidence has been given that the property in respect of which he is being tried was found or has been in his possession.

Where a suspected person or reputed thief is charged with frequenting or loitering with intent to commit felony, evidence of his known character (including previous convictions) may be given as part of the evidence against him as it is a fact in issue. (Vagrancy Act, 1824, s. 4, supplemented by Prevention of Crimes Act, 1871, s. 15, and Penal Servitude Act, 1891, s. 7.)

See also " Loiterers and Suspected Persons," Chap. 28. For the special cases of a " persistent offender," see Chap. 28, and of a spy, see " Official Secrets Acts," Chap. 20.

(2) To prove system or course of conduct on the part of the accused, viz. that the act with which he is charged formed part of a number of similar acts in each of which he was concerned. This applies in arson, false pretences, poisoning and other cases.

(3) To prove character. An accused may call witnesses to prove that he has previously borne a good character (that is, a good reputation), and then the prosecution is at liberty to prove his previous convictions (if any), and to give evidence of bad character so as to rebut his evidence of good character.

(4) The accused may give in evidence anything which might justify or excuse his act. For example, he might in

sexual cases, produce evidence of the prosecutor's bad character as her character to some extent is in question, as she may have consented to the act.

Circumstantial evidence (see below) may be regarded also as an exception to the rule, as it does not directly or positively prove or disprove the matter in issue, although the facts it indirectly proves may be directly connected with the issue.

Circumstantial evidence means evidence, not of the actual fact to be proved, but of other facts from which that fact may be presumed with more or less certainty.

When there is a question of the past or present existence of a fact, direct evidence of that fact is the best evidence, but direct evidence of other relevant facts may enable the Court or jury to infer the past or present existence of the fact in question.

Circumstantial evidence may clearly establish guilt or innocence, and in any event it will usefully supplement direct evidence.

Presumptive evidence is the same as circumstantial evidence. When on the proof of some fact the existence of another fact may naturally be inferred, the fact thus inferred is said to be presumed—that is, taken for granted until the contrary is proved. These **presumptions of fact** stand good until proved incorrect. For example, if a man was stabbed in a field and the accused was seen standing beside him with a bloodstained pitchfork in his hands, these facts would raise a presumption that the accused had stabbed him.

Presumptions of law are certain directions that certain things are to be taken for granted. These directions are either conclusive, viz. they cannot be contradicted, or disputable, viz. they can be proved incorrect.

Conclusive presumptions cannot be challenged : for example, a child under eight is incapable of committing a crime ; a male under fourteen cannot commit rape.

Disputable presumptions can be overcome : for example, an accused person is presumed innocent ; every person is presumed sane until the contrary is proved ; every sane man is presumed to have intended the consequences of his own acts.

Circumstantial evidence indirectly establishes a fact by proving by direct or positive evidence certain facts from which the existence of the fact to be established may be reasonably inferred or presumed. Therefore, circumstantial evidence may be regarded as indirect evidence in its relation to the whole matter in issue.

Privilege is the right claimed by witnesses to decline to give evidence on certain matters. The general rule is that every person should testify as to what he knows, and it is for the Court to decide, subject to the practice as given below, whether any particular evidence need not be given on the ground that it is privileged,

(1) Husband and wife. The Evidence Amendment Act, 1853, and the Criminal Evidence Act, 1898, s. 1, enact that a husband cannot be compelled to disclose any communication made to him by his wife during their marriage, and that likewise a wife need not disclose anything told her by her husband during marriage.

(2) A witness is not bound to answer any question which might, in the opinion of the Court, expose him to the risk of any punishment, penalty, or forfeiture, but this does not apply to an accused giving evidence on his own behalf. (See " Accused persons and their husbands or wives," in this chapter.)

(3) Lawyer and client. Communications between a lawyer and his client for the purpose of the case are confidential and privileged.

(4) Priest and confessions. In practice a clergyman may not be required to give evidence of a confession made to him in his capacity as a priest, but he cannot claim privilege as of right.

(5) Public policy. If it would be contrary to the public interest or injurious to the public service to disclose a particular fact, the witness may claim privilege on the ground of public policy. The Court will then not compel the witness to disclose it. Official documents (with some exceptions) are privileged if their disclosure would be contrary to the public interest, and the witness, whenever necessary, should claim privilege and ask the Court for a direction on the matter. A police officer should not disclose the name of an informant unless ordered by the Judge to do so and the disclosure is material or is necessary in the interest of the accused.

Communications between a doctor and his patient, no matter how confidential, are not privileged.

Leading questions are questions which are so framed as to suggest to the witness the answer desired or which contain the answer desired. Generally speaking, they are questions which can be answered by " Yes " or " No."

The rule is that leading questions on material points must not be asked by the side which produces the witness, but for convenience a party is allowed to put leading questions to his witness in the following cases :—

(1) On all matters which are merely introductory and which do not form material part of the case.

(2) For the purpose of identifying persons or things.

(3) When a witness is called to contradict something to which another witness has sworn.

(4) Where a witness appears hostile to the party who has called him, provided the Court gives permission.

Where a witness's memory is defective or where the matter in question is complicated questions of such a nature as to lead the mind of the witness to the subject of the matter under inquiry may be allowed.

Refreshing Memory.—A witness in the witness-box is allowed to refresh his memory by referring to any entry in a book or paper made by himself or by someone in his presence, or seen and examined by him shortly after the occurrence of the fact to which the entry relates, provided that he can swear to the fact from his recollection.

Such entry must be produced and shown to the opposing side if so required, and the witness may be questioned on it. A witness cannot use a copy of an entry to refresh his memory, unless the copy was made by himself or in his presence and he knew it to be correct.

Hostile Witness.—When a witness shows himself adverse or opposed to the side which has called him he may be regarded as a " hostile witness." However, the fact that a witness's evidence is unfavourable to his side does not necessarily render him a hostile witness. It is for the Court to decide whether a witness should be treated as a " hostile witness."

If the Court gives permission, the side that has called a hostile witness may :—

(1) Put leading questions to him ;

(2) Cross-examine him ;

(3) Contradict him by other evidence ;

(4) Prove that he has made at other times a statement inconsistent with his present testimony, provided that before such proof is given, the circumstances of this previous statement must be mentioned to the witness and he must be asked whether he has or has not made such statement (Criminal Procedure Act, 1865, s. 3).

Unwilling Witness.—If a person attending or brought before a magistrates' court refuses without just excuse to be sworn or give evidence or to produce any document or thing, the Court may commit him in custody for up to 7 days or until he sooner gives evidence or produce the document or thing (M.C. Act, 1952, s. 77).

The Onus or Burden of Proof of any fact rests on the person who alleges it, therefore the task of proving an alleged offence rests on the prosecution, who have to satisfy the Court (and jury if there is one) beyond all reasonable doubt that the evidence proves the defendant guilty of the offence charged (*Woolmington* v. *Director of Public Prosecutions* (1935)). However, when the necessary facts are proved, the burden of proof is shifted to the accused, who has to prove his innocence or be convicted. In some cases Acts of Parliament place the burden of proof on the accused; for example, the person found in possession of coining implements or counterfeit coins must prove a lawful excuse, and in a customs case the accused has to prove that the duties have been paid or the goods were lawfully imported.

A Court should take **judicial notice**—that is, admit in evidence, without proof—certain facts of general knowledge, such as the laws of the country, the extent of the realm, the course of nature, etc.

In a criminal case all facts alleged should be proved and the accused's admissions will not enable the prosecution to dispense with proof though his confession may be proved against him.

Examination-in-chief.—This is the examination of a witness by the party who produces him, and it is also called his direct **examination,** of which the two main rules are :—

(1) The witness should be allowed to relate his story, and any questions asked should relate solely to the matter immediately in issue. No question should be asked if the probable answer would not have a tendency to prove the offence or the defence or other matter being tried. Questions must be relevant—that is, they should be such as are likely to elicit evidence of facts on which the Court may decide the guilt or innocence of the defendant.

(2) Leading questions on material points must not be asked. The few exceptions to this rule have been given above.

If an irrelevant or leading question is put, the opposing side may at once object, and if necessary appeal to the Court.

Cross-examination.—When the direct examination has finished the witness may be questioned or cross-examined by the other side. If the witness has told the whole truth, cross-examination of his evidence will render his story stronger and will impress the Court still more. In such a case cross-examination may be confined to questions attacking his credibility, by questioning his means of knowledge, his impartiality, or his character.

If the witness is not telling the truth, then he may be questioned as to his facts, as well as to his credibility, and the truth can later be proved by other witnesses.

In cross-examination a witness may be asked leading questions. In fact great latitude is allowed in cross-examination, though the rule is that questions should be relevant to the issue or calculated to bring out the witness's title to credit (or discredit).

Questions irrelevant to the issue may be put for the purpose of challenging his character or testing his credit, but the answers of the witness to such questions must be taken and cannot be contradicted by independent evidence except in the case where he denies that he has been previously convicted, as if so the conviction may be proved by production of certificate of conviction with proof of identity (Criminal Procedure Act, 1865 s. 6; Prevention of Crimes Act, 1871, s. 18).

If the questions put relate to relevant facts, the answers of the witness may be contradicted by independent evidence.

A witness can claim the right to refuse to answer certain questions, questions where the answers might expose him to any criminal charge, etc., as given more fully under the heading of " Privilege." He can appeal to the Court, which will decide whether he ought or ought not to answer such questions.

A witness can be cross-examined as to previous statements made by him in writing or reduced into writing relative to the case at trial, without such writing being shown to him.

If a witness, on cross-examination as to a former statement (written or verbal) made by him relative to the case and inconsistent with his present testimony, does not admit he made that statement, proof may be given that he did in fact make it, provided that he is first given the circumstances of the disputed statement and asked whether or not he did make it (Criminal Procedure Act, 1865, s. 4).

Accused persons giving evidence on their own behalf may be cross-examined subject to the restrictions given under " Accused persons and their husbands or wives."

Re-examination.—After a witness has been cross-examined the party who called him has a right to re-examine him upon any new facts which may have arisen out of the cross-examination, and may also ask questions necessary in order to explain any part of his cross-examination. He has no right to go further than this, and may not introduce matter new in itself and not necessary to explain any part of the cross-examination.

Recalling a Witness.—The Court may at any time recall a witness and ask him any questions. If something has been left out in the direct examination and cannot be brought in in re-examination because it was not referred to in the cross-examination, it is usual to ask the Court to make the inquiry of the witness, and the request is usually granted. If a witness for the prosecution is thus recalled, the accused is allowed to cross-examine him on the new evidence given.

When the magistrates begin to inquire into an indictable offence as examining justices and later proceed to deal summarily with the accused then, unless the accused pleads guilty, they shall recall for cross-examination any witnesses who have given evidence except any not required by the accused or prosecutor (M.C. Rules, 1952, r. 21).

Rebutting Evidence.—When the defence has produced evidence introducing new matter which the prosecution has not dealt with, the Court in its discretion may allow the prosecution to give evidence in reply to rebut or contradict it. When such rebutting evidence is given the defence is entitled to comment on it.

Thus evidence may be called to rebut or contradict an alibi. The Latin word " alibi " means " elsewhere," and **an alibi** is an effort to prove that the accused was elsewhere at the time of the alleged offence, and therefore could not have committed it. The prosecution also may call evidence to rebut evidence of good character given by the defence.

Character after Conviction.—When an accused person has been found guilty it is customary for the Court to inquire as to his previous character. It is the duty of the police to exercise the most scrupulous care in presenting to any Court the record of an accused person. Such evidence of character will consist of the record of any previous convictions (see Chap. 2), the result of any inquiries that may have been made, and what the officer testifying can depose to of his own personal knowledge. Nothing should be omitted that is in favour of the prisoner, and nothing should be said to his prejudice which the officer is not able to substantiate.

Previous Convictions. To prove a previous conviction strictly there should be documentary evidence from the convicting court and oral evidence of the identity of the person with the person referred to in such documentary evidence or the evidence of finger prints as mentioned under " Convicted Persons " in Chapter 2. Such strict proof is necessary if a previous conviction is used for any purpose before the conviction of an accused person unless the accused admits it. After conviction, any previous convictions as given in the accused's official record may be mentioned as part of his antecedents and character (*R.* v. *Van Pelz* (1943)).

The general rule is that information as to previous convictions, etc., should not be told to the Court until after conviction but

(1) If an adult (17 or over) is tried summarily for an indictable offence triable at Quarter Sessions and convicted, information as to his character and antecedents should then be given to the Court, including previous convictions if any. If the Court considers that greater punishment should be inflicted than the Court can inflict, the Court can commit the accused in custody to Quarter Sessions for sentence (C.J. Act, 1948, s. 29 and M.C. Act, 1952, s. 29). If a second summary conviction would entail an increased penalty the first one should be properly proved. See " Convicted Persons," Chap. 2. See s. 3, M.C. Act, 1957, as to proof of a previous summary conviction when a magistrates' court convicts a person of a summary offence, and M.C. Rules 1957 as to notice of it and service of summons.

(2) When considering bail the Court may consider any previous convictions of the accused (*R.* v. *Fletcher* (1949)).

The Judges of the High Court in January 1955, issued a statement as to the antecedent history of accused and convicted persons to the following effect:—

1. Details of previous convictions should, on request be supplied by the police to the defending lawyer so that the defence may be properly conducted as regards accused's character.

2. A prisoner's previous convictions will be given on the Confidential Calendar supplied to the Judge by the Governor of the prison. The police need not supply them to the Court before conviction but should give to the Governor any information he may require.

3. A police officer, for evidence, should prepare a statement containing a list of previous convictions with particulars of the accused's antecedents and circumstances.

   The prosecution should have this statement. If accused is convicted, the police officer should be sworn and the statement given to the Court and to the defence.

   If it is to be said that the accused associates with bad characters the officer saying so must be able to speak of this from his own knowledge.

The Perfect Witness.—He should relate in ordinary language the story he can tell of his own knowledge as to what he has seen, heard, etc. He should confine himself to facts, avoiding inferences and opinions or beliefs. He should tell his story in the natural order and sequence of events as they occurred. He should speak from memory, expressing himself clearly and accurately. He should not produce his notebook as a matter of course and read out all his evidence therefrom. If he finds it necessary to refresh his memory he may be allowed to consult his notes. When asked a question, he should listen carefully to the question, make sure that he understands it, and give an intelligent and proper anwers to the best of his ability. He should only answer the questions put to him, and then, in as few words as possible, promptly and frankly. He should never lose his temper under cross-examination, and should always reply politely and quietly to offensive questions.

He should not show partisanship or prejudice, and ought to give his evidence fairly and impartially, giving all the evidence in favour of the accused in addition to the evidence against him. If he does not know something asked he should say so. He is sworn to tell the whole truth, and nothing but the truth.

PART II.—OFFENCES AGAINST PERSONS

Chapter VIII

ASSAULT

Contents

Assault.—An assault is an attempt or offer by force or violence to do bodily injury to another. It is a misdemeanour at common law.

To constitute an assault it is not necessary that the other party should be touched or receive any injury. Some act accompanied by such circumstances as indicate an intention of using actual violence against the person of another will amount to an assault, provided that the attacker has the means of carrying out his intention.

A battery is the actual application of unlawful force to another, and any hostile touching, no matter how slight, is a battery.

Every battery includes an assault, as an assault becomes a battery when the party is touched or struck.

In practice the word " assault " is used to cover both the assault and the battery.

It is not necessary that the injury should be effected directly by the hand of the assailant, as, for example, there may be an assault by setting a dog at another person.

The intention is material, as an accidental injury does not amount to an " assault " in law. Where the act is done with the consent of the other party, it is not an "assault" unless such consent has been obtained through fraud or is the result of ignorance, or unless the act is attended with a breach of the peace or is in some way injurious to the public or unless there was such a degree of violence that bodily harm is a probable consequence. As regards consent, see *R.* v. *Donovan* (1934).

Thus a prize fight or a duel is unlawful, even though there is consent on both sides, as amounting to a breach of the peace. A challenge to fight or to fight a duel is also unlawful, being a misdemeanour, as likely to cause a breach of the peace. However, a prize fight properly conducted under rules indicating that the object is to win by skill, and not through exhaustion or injuries caused, is not illegal.

A parent or teacher or other person in lawful control or charge may administer reasonable and moderate chastisement to a child or young person (Children and Young Persons Act, 1933, s.1).

In some cases an assault may be justified at law, as in the case of a constable arresting his prisoner or of a person using necessary violence in self-defence or in defence of his wife (husband), parents, property, etc. However, in such cases the force used must be only so great as is necessary for effecting the object.

Insulting or provocative words do not make an assault and do not justify an assault.

Statutory Assaults.—Assaults can be dealt with summarily or on indictment, according to their nature, as follows :—

Offences against the Person Act, 1861.

S. 42: To unlawfully assault or beat any other person. This offence can be dealt with summarily when the information is made by the injured party or by someone on his behalf. Penalty, £5 fine or two months imprisonment or if dealt with on indictment imprisonment up to one year.

S. 43: An assault or battery of an aggravated nature upon any boy whose age does not exceed fourteen years or upon any female, on the information of the party aggrieved or other-wise, can be punished summarily by £50 fine or six months imprisonment (Criminal Justice Act, 1925, s. 39).

" Aggravated " here means made worse in respect of violence, but not in respect of indecency (*R.* v. *Baker* (1883)).

If a person charged under ss. 42 or 43 is convicted or acquitted with certificate of dismissal (s. 44), he is by s. 45 of the Act released from all other proceedings for the same cause. There-fore any future action to recover compensation cannot be taken against him.

The consent of a person under sixteen years of age to an indecent assault affords no defence to the charge as such a person cannot in law consent to it. See Sexual Offences Act, 1956, s. 15.

A charge of indecent assault on any person under the age of sixteeen years can be dealt with summarily provided the accused consents to be so dealt with (Magistrates' Courts Act, 1952, s. 19 and First Sched.). See also " Unnatural Crimes," Chap. 11.

S. 47: To assault any person, thereby occasioning actual bodily harm. M.

S. 20: To maliciously wound or inflict grievous bodily harm upon any person with or without any instrument. **M.**

These two misdemeanours (ss. 20 and 47) can be dealt with summarily if the accused consents (M.C. Act, 1952, s. 19 and First Sched.).

S. 38.   To assault any person with intent to commit felony. M.

In many other cases statutes provide penalties for assaults with intent to commit various offences. These assaults are mentioned with the offences with which they are connected. The right given to a defendant to claim trial by jury where the assault is punishable by more than 3 months imprisonment does not apply to an assault (M.C. Act, 1952, s. 25).

Offences against the Person Act, 1861, s. 46, provides that if a Summary Court finds that an assault was accompanied by an attempt to commit felony, or considers that the case should be dealt with on indictment, the Court should abstain from any adjudication thereon. It also declares that the Justices are not authorised to hear and determine any assault arising out of any question of the title to land or of any bankruptcy, insolvency, or execution under the process of any court of justice. This is termed " ouster of jurisdiction."

Assaulting, Obstructing or Resisting the Police :

Prevention of Crimes Act, 1871, s. 12.—Any person convicted of an assault on any constable when in the execution of his duty shall be guilty of an offence against this Act. Penalty, £20 fine or six months imprisonment, which may be increased to nine months if the accused has been convicted of a similar assault within the preceding two years.

Special Constables Act, 1831, s. 11.—It is a summary offence to assault or resist, or encourage any other person to assault or resist, any special constable whilst in the execution of his office, and by section 15, proceedings must be taken within two months after commission of the offence. Penalty, £20 fine.

The Municipal Corporations Act, 1882, s. 195, the Town Police Clauses Act, 1847, s. 20 (if applied by local Act), and the County Police Act, 1839, s. 8, also make it a summary offence to assault or resist a constable in the execution of his duty.

Offences against the Person Act, 1861, s. 38.—It is a misdemeanour to assault, resist or wilfully obstruct any police officer in the due execution of his duty or any person acting in aid of such officer, or to assault any person with intent to resist or prevent the lawful apprehension or detainer of himself or of any other person for any offence.

Prevention of Crimes Amendment Act, 1885. s. 2.—It is a summary offence to resist or wilfully obstruct any constable or police officer when in the execution of his duty. (See *Hinchliffe* v. *Sheldon* (1955)). Penalty, £5 fine.

An attempted rescue of a prisoner may be dealt with summarily as assaulting, obstructing or resisting the police.

Powers of Arrest.—A constable may arrest when an assault is committed in his presence. However, he should exercise this power with discretion, the main points to consider being the seriousness of any injury sustained and the likelihood of a repetition of the offence. In ordinary assaults the parties as a rule may be left to proceed by summons. A constable may also arrest a person who, in his view, threatens to commit an assault, except where the threat appears to be an empty one and there has been no breach of the peace.

A constable should arrest in cases where dangerous injuries have been inflicted, or are likely to be inflicted should the parties not be separated, or where the peace has been disturbed and the removal of the offender is necessary for its preservation.

If an interval has elapsed after the commission of a common assault, the constable should not arrest, except in the case of continued pursuit to arrest the person who has committed the assault.

Wounding and other Serious Assaults.—The Offences against the Person Act, 1861, provides severe punishment for these serious attacks on the person, which in some cases just fall short of homicide.

Wounding.—S. 18. Maliciously wounding or causing grievous bodily harm to any person or shooting at or attempting to discharge any loaded arms at any person, with intent to maim, disfigure, disable or do him grievous bodily harm, or with intent to prevent or resist the lawful apprehension of any person. F.

To constitute a " wounding " the whole skin must be broken. To " maim " is to injure any part of the body so as to render the person less capable of fighting. Grievous bodily harm includes any hurt or injury which seriously interferes with health or comfort.

S. 20: Maliciously wounding or inflicting any grievous bodily harm upon any person, either with or without any weapon or instrument. M. This can be dealt with summarily with accused's consent (M.C. Act, 1952, s. 19 and First Sched.).

Choking.—S. 21: Attempting to choke, suffocate, or strangle any person, or attempting to render any person insensible or incapable of resistance by any means calculated to choke, suffocate or strangle, with intent to commit an indictable offence. F. This crime is known as garrotting, and is usually committed by robbers who choke their victims into unconsciousness so as to take their property.

Drugging.—S. 22: Unlawfully administering or attempting to cause to be taken, any chloroform or other stupefying drug or thing with intent to enable the committing of an indictable offence. F. See also " Procuration," Chap. 10.

Poisoning.—S. 23: Maliciously administering any poison or other destructive or noxious thing so as thereby to endanger human life or cause grievous bodily harm. F.

S.24. Maliciously administering any poison or other destructive or noxious thing with intent to injure, aggrieve or annoy. M.

Burning, etc.—S. 29. Maliciously and with intent to burn, maim, disfigure, disable or cause grievous bodily harm, sending, placing, throwing or otherwise applying any corrosive fluid or any destructive or explosive substance, whether any bodily harm be effected or not. F. For the causing of grievous bodily harm by the unlawful use of explosives, see " Explosives," Chap. 33.

Threats and Menaces.—As it is possible that a person who has been threatened in any way may take such action as might lead to a breach of the peace, any person who makes any threats either verbally or by action or in writing is liable to be bound over to keep the peace and (or) be of good behaviour.

See " Breach of the Peace and Sureties," Chap. 22.

Threatening letters and certain threats and menaces affecting person, property or reputation are dealt with by statute as follows :

Offences against the Person Act, 1861, s. 16. It is a felony maliciously to send, deliver or utter or directly or indirectly cause to be received knowing the contents thereof, any letter or writing threatening to kill or murder any person.

Malicious Damage Act, 1861, s. 50. It is a felony to send, deliver or utter or directly or indirectly cause to be received knowing the contents thereof, any letter or writing threatening to burn or destroy any house, barn or other building, or any rick or stack of hay, grain or straw or other agricultural produce, or any agricultural produce in or under any building, or any ship or vessel, or to kill, maim or wound any cattle.

Larceny Act, 1916, s. 29. It is a felony :—

(1) To utter, knowing the contents thereof, any letter or writing demanding of any person with menaces and without any reasonable or probable cause, any property or valuable thing. " Menace " includes a threat of violence and also a threat of action unpleasant or harmful to the person and the prosecution should prove the absence of reasonable cause for the " menace " in any demand. (*Thorne* v. *Motor Trade Association* (1937)).

(2) To utter, knowing the contents thereof, any letter or writing accusing or threatening to accuse any other person (living or dead) of any crime punishable with death or seven years or more imprisonment, or of any assault with intent to commit rape or of any attempt to commit rape or of any attempt to induce any person to commit or permit the abominable crime of buggery, with intent to extort or gain any property or valuable thing from any person. (This is known as " **Blackmail**.")

(3) To accuse or threaten to accuse any person (living or dead) of any such crime, with intent to extort or gain any property or valuable thing from any person. (This is also " Blackmail.")

(4) To compel or induce any person to make, alter or destroy

any valuable security, or to attach any signature or seal to any document so as to render it a valuable security, when done with intent to defraud or injure any person and by any unlawful violence or restraint to the person of another or by accusing or threatening to accuse any person (living or dead) of any such crime or of any felony. (This too is " Blackmail.")

S. 31: It is a misdemeanour when done with intent either to extort any valuable thing from any person or to induce any person to confer or procure any post of profit or trust, for any person :—

(1) To publish or threaten to publish any libel upon any other person living or dead, or

(2) to threaten to publish, or to propose to abstain from publishing, or to offer to prevent the publishing of any matter or thing touching any other person living or dead. (This is also " Blackmail.") See " Libel," Chap. 23.

These blackmailing offences amount to attempts to extort money or property by threats to make public something seriously detrimental to the reputation of any person living or dead. In such cases the Court may request that the names of the persons concerned should not be made public.

S. 30: It is a felony to demand with menaces or by force of any person, anything capable of being stolen, with intent to steal the same.

S. 13: It is a felony for any person to steal in any dwelling-house any chattel, property or valuable security and by any menace or threat to put any person in such dwelling-house in bodily fear.

Sexual Offences Act, 1956, s. 2. It is an " offence " by threats or intimidation to procure or attempt to procure any woman or girl to have any unlawful sexual intercourse in any part of the world. See also " Procuration," Chap. 10.

For threats, etc., in labour disputes, see " Intimidation," Chap. 22.

Chapter IX

HOMICIDE

Contents

Homicide.—This is the killing of a human being by a human being.

Every case of " causing death " should be regarded as a possible murder (which is a felony at common law) unless there is evidence to show that it is not murder.

In all cases of homicide the prosecution should call as witnesses all persons present at the killing to give a full account of the circumstances. If there is evidence to indicate murder the accused, if he can, should produce evidence to prove that his action was justifiable or excusable or that it did not amount to felony.

Homicide may be justifiable—that is, not deserving of any blame—under the following circumstances :—

(1) Where a criminal is executed in accordance with his sentence.

(2) Where an officer of the law whilst performing his duty has of necessity to kill a person who is resisting or preventing him in the execution of his duty.

(3) Where it is committed to prevent a forcible and atrocious crime, such as murder or rape.

Homicide also may be excusable—that is, excused by law but not quite free from blame—as in the following cases :—

(1) Where a person kills another by misadventure or accident, without any intention of harm, whilst doing a lawful act in a proper manner.

(2) Where a person, in defending himself or his wife or family from attack, unavoidably in the course of the struggle kills another.

If homicide cannot be justified or excused it is criminal or felonious. There are four forms of felonious homicide, viz. :—

(1) Murder, which is defined as where a person of sound memory and discretion unlawfully killeth any reasonable

creature in being with malice aforethought either express or implied, the death following within a year and a day.

(2) Manslaughter, which is defined as the unlawful and felonious killing of another without any malice either express or implied.

(3) Infanticide, which is the felony committed by a woman when by any wilful act or omission she causes the death of her newly born child, her mind being then unbalanced. See " Infanticide " and " Child Destruction," Chap. 12.

(4) Suicide, which is self-murder or the killing of one's self.

Murder.—Only persons of sound memory and discretion are liable to conviction for murder ; children under eight, idiots, imbeciles and lunatics are not so liable. A person who is abnormal, suffering from diminished responsibility, shall not be convicted of murder but may be convicted of manslaughter (Homicide Act, 1957, s. 2). The killing must have been unlawful and without justification or excuse. It may be done by direct act or by wicked negligence. The person killed must have been a reasonable creature in being, so to constitute infanticide the child should have been born alive. See also " Abortion," " Child Destruction," and " Infanticide," Chap. 12.

The killing must have been with malice aforethought—that is, some evil intent beforehand to do harm without just cause or excuse.

Malice is express when a person with deliberate design kills another. Such clear intent may be proved by the circumstances of the killing, by previous threats, by lying in wait, etc., etc.

Malice may be implied or presumed from the circumstances attending the homicide, for instance when death occurs from violence done when committing a felony or violence. See " Malice," Chap. 1.

In a prosecution for murder, in addition to proving the homicide, it is necessary to prove that death resulted from a voluntary act on the part of the accused and also malice either express or implied on the part of the accused. The accused is entitled to show by evidence and/or by examination of the evidence against him that the homicide was either unintentional or provoked. The prosecution must prove the prisoner's guilt beyond reasonable doubt (*Woolmington* v. *Director of Public Prosecutions* (1935)).

The deceased must have died of the injury given him by the accused, and within a year and a day after he had received it. If he died after that time the law presumes his death occurred from some other cause.

Circumstantial evidence may be sufficient to establish the guilt of the killer, but it must be very strong to justify conviction in cases where the body of the killed person has not been found. See " Circumstantial Evidence," Chap. 7.

Manslaughter.—The absence of malice will reduce murder to manslaughter. Manslaughter may be voluntary—that is, where a person in a sudden fight kills another—or it may be involuntary—that is, where a person who is doing some non-felonious but unlawful act accidentally kills another, or where a person, by culpably neglecting his duty, accidentally causes the death of another. Also the existence of provocation may reduce murder to manslaughter, but the provocation must have been great and such as would deprive a reasonable person of his self-control. (See *Mancini* v. *Director of Public Prosecutions* (1942)). In such case the sufficiency of the provocation shall be left to the determination of the jury (Homicide Act, 1957, s. 3).

If a person, by his neglect or default, unintentionally causes the death of another, he may be convicted of manslaughter. It will be no defence to plead that the person killed contributed to his own death by his negligence.

Neglect or ill-treatment of helpless persons (such as children, sick, aged, or lunatic persons) which results in death, may be murder if premeditated, or manslaughter if there has been gross and culpable negligence.

A person can be convicted of manslaughter arising out of the driving of a motor vehicle (*Andrews* v. *Director of Public Prosecutions*, (1937)).

Manslaughter in connection with the driving of a motor vehicle can be dealt with as reckless or dangerous driving. See " Dangerous Driving," Chap. 24.

Suicide.—Suicide is where a person kills himself and it is therefore the homicide of one of Her Majesty's subjects, and is a felony, but as the perpetrator is beyond the reach of human justice, no criminal consequences follow.

A person of sound mind and of the age of discretion who voluntarily and deliberately kills himself is termed a **felo de se,** or felon of himself.

Formerly a *felo de se* forfeited his property and received an ignominious burial. These post-mortem penalties have been abolished.

The attempt to commit suicide is a misdemeanour at common law, being an attempt to commit a felony, and the offender on recovery may be arrested and with his consent dealt with summarily (M.C. Act, 1952, s. 19 and First Sched.).

Attempted suicide is not an attempt to commit murder within ss. 11-15 of the Offences against the Person Act, 1861 (*R.* v. *Burgess* (1862)).

If two persons mutually agree to commit suicide together (suicide pact) but only one of them does so, the survivor is guilty of manslaughter (Homicide Act, 1957, s. 4). See also the Accessories and Abettors Act, 1861, Chap. 2.

Legal Consequences of Homicide and kindred Offences.—

Homicide Act, 1957:—

S. 5: The following shall be capital murders:

(a) Murder done in the furtherance or course of theft.

(b) Murder by shooting or causing an explosion.

(c) Murder in resisting lawful arrest, or in assisting an escape or rescue from legal custody.

(d) Murder of a police officer or his assistant acting in the execution of his duty.

(e) Murder of a prison officer or his assistant acting in the execution of his duty.

On conviction of capital murder the penalty may be death (See also Sched. I of this Act).

S. 6: A person convicted of 2 or more murders on different occasions in Great Britain is liable to the death penalty.

S. 7: Death penalty for murder is enforceable only under ss. 5 and 6 of this Act.

S. 9: Where a court is precluded from passing sentence of death for murder, the sentence shall be one of imprisonment for life.

Offences against the Person Act, 1861 :—

S. 1: Murder is a felony. (Persons under eighteen when they commit the crime shall not be sentenced to death or life imprisonment but shall be sentenced to be detained during Her Majesty's pleasure (C. and Y.P. Act, 1933, s. 53, as amended by s. 9, Homicide Act, 1957).

Imprisonment for life instead of sentence of death on conviction of murder shall be pronounced in the case of an expectant mother (Sentence of Death (Expectant Mothers) Act, 1931).

S. 5: Manslaughter is a felony punishable by imprisonment for life, or by fine. Infanticide is punishable as manslaughter (Infanticide Act, 1938). Child destruction (Chap. 12) is punishable by imprisonment for life.

S. 7: To kill another by misfortune or in defending oneself or in any manner without felony is not punishable.

S. 9: Murder or manslaughter by a British subject abroad may be dealt with in the county or place in this country where he is in custody.

S. 4: Conspiracy to murder any person anywhere, or inciting or proposing to murder any person anywhere, is misdemeanour punishable by imprisonment for ten years.

S. 11: Administering or causing to be administered to any person any poison or other destructive thing or wounding or causing grievous bodily harm to any person, with intent to commit murder, is felony.

S. 14: Attempting to administer or cause to be administered any poison or other destructive thing, or shooting at any person, or attempting to discharge any loaded arms at any person, or, attempting to drown, suffocate or strangle any person, with intent to commit murder, is felony.

S. 12: Destroying or damaging by explosives any building with intent to commit murder is felony. (Having or making explosives with intent to commit any of these felonies is a misdemeanour (s. 64).)

S. 13: Setting fire to, casting away or destroying any ship or vessel with intent to commit murder is felony.

S. 15: Any attempt to commit murder, by any means other than those specified, is felony.

S. 16: Sending, uttering, etc., a letter or writing threatening to murder any person is felony. See " Threats and Menaces," Chap. 8.

S. 67 gives the heavy penalties to which accessories to any of these felonies are liable.

All these serious offences must be tried at Assizes.

Persons under 17 cannot be dealt with by a summary court for homicide, they must be remanded for trial by a Higher Court (M.C. Act, 1952, ss. 20, 21).

A Chief Officer of Police, by the Prosecution of Offences Regulations, 1946 (see Appendix III), is bound to give information with respect to every offence punishable by death to the Director of Public Prosecutions, therefore every case of murder must be reported to the Director, and also every offence of attempted murder and manslaughter.

Search warrant, 1861 Act.—S. 64 of the Offences against the Person Act, 1861, makes it a misdemeanour knowingly to have in possession or make any gunpowder, explosive substance or any dangerous or noxious thing or any machine, engine, instrument or thing, with intent by means thereof to commit, or for the purpose of enabling any other person to commit, any of the felonies in this Act mentioned, and s. 65 empowers a Justice, on reasonable cause on oath, to issue a warrant to search any house or place where the same is suspected to be for such purpose as hereinbefore mentioned.

(101)

Chapter X

OFFENCES AGAINST FEMALES

Contents

Sexual Offences.—In a case in which a man is charged with a sexual offence against a female the words of Sir Matthew Hale relative to rape should be remembered : " It is an accusation easy to be made and hard to be proved, but harder to be defended by the party accused though innocent." The first consideration is the credibility of the female's story. The question of consent and corroboration available must then be considered.

The following circumstances will support her evidence : good reputation, reporting the occurrence without delay, marks of violence on her person, signs of struggle at the scene, and any other evidence corroborating her statement.

The following will weaken her testimony : bad reputation, concealment of the occurrence for any unreasonable length of time, making no outcry in a place where she might have been heard, and no corroboration of her story.

In general, the evidence of one witness in sexual cases should be corroborated in some material particular by other evidence implicating the accused, otherwise it will be the evidence of the female alone against that of the man. The fact that she made a complaint is admissible in evidence. See " Hearsay Evidence," Chap. 7.

In a case of alleged rape the injured female should without delay, if she consents, be examined by a doctor. If she is under sixteen her parents' consent should be obtained. This examination cannot be made without her consent, but her refusal to undergo such an examination will naturally discredit her story.

The Sexual Offences Act, 1956 purports to consolidate the statute law relating to sexual crimes, abduction, procuration and prostitution of females and kindred offences.

It contains 56 sections and 4 Schedules and came into force on 1st January, 1957.

This Act has repealed the Criminal Law Amendment Acts, 1885, 1912, 1922, 1928, 1951, the Vagrancy Act, 1898, the Punishment of Incest Act, 1908, the Attempted Rape Act, 1948 and parts of other Acts (4th Sched.).

Felonies and attempts at felonies under the Act are indictable but not triable at Quarter Sessions and they are punishable by imprisonment (2nd Sched., Part 1).

The mode of trial and penalties for " offences " under this Act, are dealt with in Part II of the 2nd Sched., which directs that many of these " offences " in the Act are indictable (but several of them are not triable at Quarter Sessions), that some are indictable subject to the sanction of the Attorney General or prosecution by the Director of Public Prosecutions, that some are merely indictable, that some are indictable or triable summarily, and that some are triable summarily subject to the right of the accused under M.C. Act, 1952, s. 25, to claim trial on indictment.

" Sexual intercourse " whether natural or unnatural shall be deemed complete upon proof of penetration only (s. 44). In the Act " man " without the addition of " boy " or vice versa does not prevent any provision of the Act applying to any person to whom it would have applied if both words were used, and similarly with the words " woman " and " girl " (s. 46).

Under s. 40 a constable may arrest a person without a warrant if he has reasonable cause to suspect him of having committed or of attempting to commit an offence under s. 22 (procuring a woman to be a prostitute) or s. 23 (procuring a girl under 21 to have unlawful sexual intercourse).

Under s. 41 anyone may arrest without a warrant a person found committing an offence under s. 30 (man living on prostitution), s. 31 (woman controlling a prostitute) or s. 32 (man soliciting in public place for immoral purposes).

S. 42 allows a justice, on sworn information that there is reasonable cause to suspect that a house or part of it is used by a woman for prostitution and that a man residing or frequenting the house is living wholly or in part on her earnings, to issue a warrant authorising a constable to enter and search the house and to arrest the man.

The C. and Y.P. Act, 1933, s. 40, allows the issue of a warrant to search for and remove a child or young person. In addition s. 43 of this Sexual Offences Act, 1956, empowers a justice to issue a warrant to search for and remove a woman detained for immoral purposes and so detained against her will or if she is under 16 or is a defective (see s. 45) or is under 18 and is so detained against the will of her parent or guardian.

S. 39 directs that the wife or husband of the accused shall be competent to give evidence on a charge of any offence under this 1956 Act, for the defence or the prosecution (except in so far it is excluded in the case of s. 12 (buggery), s. 15 (indecent assault on a man) and s. 16 (assault with intent to commit buggery)). Provided that:

(a) the wife or husband shall not be compellable to give evidence or to disclose in evidence any communication made to him or her during the marriage by the accused, and

(b) the failure of the wife or husband of the accused to give evidence shall not be commented on by the prosecution.

This section 39 shall not affect s. 1 of the Criminal Evidence Act, 1898 or any case where the wife or the husband of the accused may at common law be called as a witness without the consent of the accused.

Rape and Similar Offences.—Sexual Offences Act, 1956, s. 1. It is a felony for a man to rape a woman and it will be rape where a man induces a married woman to have sexual intercourse with him by impersonating her husband.

Rape is a felony at common law being the unlawful carnal knowledge of a female by force or fraud against her will. By ss. 2, 3, 4 it is an offence to procure a woman to have unlawful sexual intercourse in any part of the world

(a) by threats or intimidation (s. 2)

(b) by false pretensions or false representations (s. 3)

(c) by applying or administering to or causing to be taken by, a woman any drug, matter or thing with intent to stupefy or overpower her so as thereby to enable any man to do so (s. 4).

There cannot be a conviction of any of these offences on the evidence on one witness only unless the witness is corroborated in some material particular by evidence implicating the accused.

Carnal knowledge means penetration to any degree, and to constitute rape there must be proof of penetration. It is no excuse if the woman consented through fear or fraud or after the fact, or that she was a prostitute. The consent of the woman is a good defence, but such consent must have been freely given and not induced by fraud, threats, etc. If the woman is of weak intellect and incapable of giving a true consent the accused may be convicted of rape.

A boy under the age of fourteen cannot be convicted of rape as it is presumed that he is physically incapable of the act. Generally speaking a husband cannot be convicted of rape upon his wife (but a charge of assault may be made), but he can be so convicted if husband and wife have been legally separated (*R. v. Clarke* (1949)). A husband, a boy under fourteen, and a woman may be liable as principals in the second degree as present aiding and abetting in the felony of rape. A boy under fourteen can be convicted of indecent assault.

Sexual Offences Act, 1956, s. 5.—It is a felony for a man to have unlawful sexual intercourse with a girl under 13.

S. 6. It is an offence for a man to have unlawful sexual intercourse with a girl not under 13 but under 16.

However if the girl is under 16 the man will not be guilty of this offence if:

(a) the girl is his " wife " (an invalid marriage as she is under age) or

(b) the man is under 24, has not been previously charged with a like offence and has reasonable cause for his belief that the girl is 16 or over.

Section 7. It is an offence for a man to have unlawful sexual intercourse with a woman whom he knows to be an idiot or imbecile.

Section 8. It is an offence for a man to have unlawful sexual intercourse with a woman who is under care or treatment in an institution, etc., or out on licence or under guardianship under the Mental Deficiency Act, 1913. But he will not be guilty of this offence if he does not know and has no reason to suspect her to be a defective.

Section 9. It is an offence for a person to procure a woman who is a defective to have unlawful sexual intercourse in any part of the world. But he will not be guilty of this offence if he does not know and has no reason to suspect her to be a defective.

By s. 45 of this Act " Defective " means a person having mental defectiveness (i.e. arrested or incomplete development of mind existing before the age of 18 due to inherent causes or disease or injury)

(a) of a degree requiring care, supervision and control or in the case of a child rendering him incapable of receiving education at school: or

(b) coupled with strongly vicious or criminal propensities requiring care, control etc. for the protection of others.

Carnal knowledge, or the attempt at such, of any female person of unsound mind by any person in charge of her is a misdemeanour, and her consent or alleged consent will not be a defence (Lunacy Act, 1890, s. 324).

Any offence of rape and carnal knowledge of mental defectives or of girls under 13 must be reported to the Director of Public Prosecutions (see Appendix III).

Indecent Assault.—Sexual Offences Act, 1956, s. 14. It is an offence for a person to make an indecent assault on a woman. A girl under 16 cannot in law give any consent to such an assault. (See also s. 28 (later) for indecent assault on a girl under 16.) However where marriage is invalid (the wife being under 16) the husband will not be guilty of this offence if he has reasonable cause to believe her to be his wife.

A woman who is a defective cannot in law consent to such an assault but the person who so assaults her will be guilty of this offence only if he knew or had reason to suspect her to be a defective.

A constable has power to arrest without warrant for indecent assaults on young persons (C. and Y.P. Act, 1933, s. 13).

Indecent assault on any person (male or female) under 16 may be dealt with summarily if the court is satisfied and the accused consents (M.C. Act, 1952, s. 19 and 1st Sched.). Certain indecent assaults should be reported to the Director of Public Prosecutions (see Appendix III).

Incest.—Sexual Offences Act, 1956, s. 10. It is an offence for a man to have sexual intercourse with a woman whom he knows to be his grand-daughter, daughter, sister or mother.

" Sister " in this section includes half-sister and the relation above in this section applies although not traced through lawful wedlock.

Section 11. It is an offence for a woman aged 16 or over to permit a man whom she knows to be her grandfather, father, brother or son to have sexual intercourse with her by her consent. " Brother " in this section includes half-brother and the relationship above in this section applies although not traced through lawful wedlock.

Under s. 38 of the Act, on a man being convicted of incest or attempted incest against a girl under 21 the court may, by order, divest him of all authority over her, etc.

Procuration.—Procuration is the obtaining of females for immoral purposes. The practice is often referred to as the white slave traffic, particularly in connection with the procuring of girls to go abroad for immoral purposes.

There is considerable risk in females accepting employment abroad unless there is sufficient evidence as to the *bona fide* character of the engagement. The real object of the employer or agent may be concealed under the pretext of engaging the victim for some theatrical or other employment.

Any case of suspicion should be reported to the Commissioner of Metropolitan Police, who is the central authority for this country under the International Agreement of 1904, arrived at to try to put an end to this white slave traffic. Also, both at home and abroad, friendless or unprotected girls are liable to fall into the hands of unscrupulous persons.

Sexual Offences Act, 1956, s. 22. It is an offence for a person to procure:

(*a*) a woman to become in any part of the world a common prostitute: or

(*b*) a woman to leave the United Kingdom intending her to become an inmate of or frequent a brothel elsewhere: or

(*c*) a woman to leave her usual place of abode in the United Kingdom, intending her to become an inmate of or frequent a brothel in any part of the world for the purposes of prostitution.

Conviction of any of the above offences cannot take place on the evidence of one witness only unless the witness is corroborated in some material particular by evidence implicating the accused.

Section 23. It is an offence for a person to procure a girl under 21 to have unlawful sexual intercourse in any part of the world with a third person.

In such an offence, to ensure conviction, the evidence of only one witness must be corroborated materially by evidence implicating the accused.

Section 24. It is an offence for a person to detain a woman against her will on any premises with the intention that she shall have unlawful sexual intercourse with men or a particular man or to detain a woman against her will in a brothel. This section states that withholding her clothes or any of her property or threatening legal proceedings if she takes away clothes provided for her by him or on his directions shall be deemed to be such detention.

Also the woman shall not be liable to any legal proceedings for taking or having any clothes she needed to enable her to leave such premises or brothel.

Sections 25, 26 and 27 declare that where a person who is the owner or occupier of any premises or who has or acts or assists in the management or control of any premises, induces or knowingly suffers a female (see below) to resort or be on those premises for the purpose of having unlawful sexual connection with men or a particular man, such person commits crime as follows:—

(a) it is felony if the female is a girl under 13 (s. 25)

(b) it is an offence if the female is a girl not under 13 but is under 16 (s. 26).

(c) it is an offence if the female is a defective (see s. 45) but if such person did not know and had no reason to suspect her to be a defective he will not be guilty of this offence (s. 27)

Children and Young Persons Act, 1933, s. 61. A child or young person (under seventeen) who has no parent or guardian or an unfit or neglectful parent or guardian and is falling in to bad associations or is exposed to moral danger, or is beyond control (or who is illtreated or neglected etc.; C. and Y.P. Act, 1952, s. 1) or who has been subjected to a personal offence (as mentioned in the First Schedule to the Act) or is a member of a household where same has occurred, (or is a female member of a household where a member has committed or attempted to commit incest; Sexual Offences Act, 1956, Third Sched.) may be dealt with as needing care or protection. See " Care or Protection " Chap. 12.

Abduction of Females.—Sexual Offences Act, 1956, s. 17. It is felony for a person to take away or detain a woman against her will with the intention that she shall marry or have unlawful sexual intercourse with that or any other person if she is so taken away or detained either by force or for the sake of her property or expectations of property (being any interest in property the property of a person to whom she is a next of kin).

Section 18. It is felony for a person to take or detain a girl under 21 out of the possession of her parent or guardian (who is any person having the lawful care or charge of her) against his will, if she has property (or any interest in property) or expectations of property (being a next of kin) and is so taken or detained by fraud and with the intention that she shall marry or have unlawful sexual intercourse with that or any other person.

Section 19. It is an offence for a person to take an unmarried girl under 18 out of the possession of her parent or guardian (person who has lawful care or charge of her) against his will, if she is so taken with the intention that she shall have unlawful sexual intercourse with men or a particular man. However belief on reasonable cause that the girl is 18 or over will avoid this offence.

C. and Y.P. Act, 1933, s. 40 provides for a warrant to search for and remove such a girl in cases of necessity.

Sexual Offences Act, 1956, s. 20. It is an offence for a person acting without lawful authority to take an unmarried girl under 16 out of the possession of her parent or guardian (lawful) against his will.

Section 21. It is an offence for a person to take a woman who is a defective out of the possession of her parent or guardian (lawful) against her will if she is taken with the intention that she shall have unlawful sexual intercourse with men or with a particular man.

However a person is not guilty of this offence if he does not know and has no reason to suspect her to be a defective.

Prostitution.—Sexual Offences Act, 1956, s. 28. It is an offence for a person to cause or encourage the prostitution of, or the commission of unlawful sexual intercourse with, or of an indecent assault on, a girl under 16 for whom he is responsible.

This section states that a person shall be deemed to have caused or encouraged this offence if he knowingly allowed her to consort with or to enter or continue in the employment of any prostitute or person of known immoral character.

Under the section the parent or legal guardian and any person who has actual possession or control or custody or charge or care of such girl are so responsible for her as regards this section. " Parent " and " legal guardian " are explained in this section.

Section 29. It is an offence for a person to cause or encourage the prostitution in any part of the world of a woman who is a defective. Unless he does not know and has no reason to suspect her to be a defective.

Section 30. It is an offence for a man knowingly to live wholly or in part on the earnings of prostitution.

Under this section, a man, unless he proves the contrary, will be presumed to commit this offence, if he lives with or is habitually in the company of a prostitute, or exercises control, direction or influence over a prostitute's movements in a way which shows he is aiding, abetting or compelling her prostitution with others.

Section 31. It is an offence for a woman for purposes of gain to exercise control, direction or influence over a prostitute's movements in a way which shows she is aiding, abetting or compelling her prostitution.

Section 32. It is an offence for a man persistently to solicit or importune in a public place for immoral purposes.

Section 36. It is an offence for the tenant or occupier of any premises knowingly to permit the whole or part of the premises to be used for the purposes of habitual prostitution.

NOTE.—Offences under ss. 30, 31, 32 may be dealt with summarily or on indictment. Offences under s. 36 may be dealt with summarily (see 2nd Sched.).

A common prostitute is a female who for reward offers her body commonly for sexual connection or for acts of lewdness. Lewd conduct by a *virgo intacta* without sexual intercourse may amount to prostitution *(R. v. De Munch* (1918)).

Vagrancy Act, 1824, s. 3. Every common prostitute wandering in the public streets or public highway or in **any** place of public resort and behaving in a riotous or indecent manner may be arrested by any person when found so offending and summarily punished as an idle and disorderly person. See " Vagrancy Acts," Chap. 27.

Town Police Clauses Act, 1847, s. 28. Any common prostitute or night walker loitering and importuning passengers for the purpose of prostitution in any street in any urban district (where the Act is in force) to the obstruction or annoyance of the residents or passengers, may be arrested by any constable who sees the offence committed and summarily punished. (This offence is known as " soliciting.")

Public Health Acts Amendment Act, 1907, s. 81, states that the above offences are also punishable when committed in any place of public resort or recreation ground under the control of the local authority or in any unfenced ground adjoining any street, in any urban district, where the section is in force by Order.

Harbouring Prostitutes.—Town Police Clauses Act, 1847, s. 35. It is an offence for any person keeping any house, shop, room, or other place of public resort in any urban district (where the Act is in force) for the sale or consumption of refreshments of any kind, knowingly to suffer common prostitutes or reputed thieves to assemble and continue there.

Refreshment Houses Act, 1860, s. 32. It is an offence for a person licensed to keep a refreshment house under the Act knowingly to suffer prostitutes, etc., to assemble or continue on his premises.

Licensing Act, 1953, s. 139. The holder of a Justices' licence (and the holder of an occasional licence (s. 148)) shall not knowingly permit his premises to be the habitual resort or place of meeting of reputed prostitutes. He may only allow such to remain in his premises to obtain reasonable refreshment for such time as is necessary for the purpose.

Brothels.—A common brothel is a house or room used by persons of opposite sexes for the purpose of prostitution.

Keeping a brothel is a misdemeanour at common law, being a common nuisance as endangering the public peace and corrupting both sexes.

The Disorderly Houses Acts, 1751 and 1818, declare that the person managing a bawdy house, gaming house or brothel or other disorderly house (which is a nuisance at common law) will be deemed the keeper thereof, though not the real owner or keeper, and allows the issue of a warrant to arrest such person.

A disorderly house means premises kept open to persons and so carried on as to contravene law and good order.

Sexual Offences Act, 1956, s. 33. It is an offence for a person to keep a brothel or to manage or act or assist in the management of a brothel.

Section 34. It is an offence for the lessee or landlord of any premises to let the whole or part of the premises with the knowledge that it is to be used, in whole or in part, as a brothel, or, where the whole or part of the premises is used as a brothel, to be wilfully a party to that use continuing.

Section 35. It is an offence for the tenant or occupier or person in charge of any premises to permit the whole or part of the premises to be used as a brothel The rest of this section and the First Schedule to the Act deal with the rights and duties of the landlord or lessor of such premises.

Offences under the above three sections maybe dealt with summarily as directed in the 2nd Schedule to the Act.

Licensing Act, 1953, s. 140. The holder of a Justices' licence (or of an occasional licence (s. 148)) shall not permit his premises to be a brothel. On conviction for this offence, whether under this section or otherwise, his licence shall be forfeited, and by s. 30 of this Act he is disqualified for holding a Justices' licence.

A licensee was held guilty of this offence although no evidence of a previous case of like kind on the premises was given, and although he was absent from the premises at the time (*R.* v. *Holland, Lincolnshire Justices* (1882)).

Prevention of Crimes Act, 1871, s. 11. Every person who occupies or keeps a brothel and knowingly lodges or harbours thieves or reputed thieves or permits them to assemble thereon or allows the deposit of stolen goods therein commits a summary offence.

Children and Young Persons Act, 1933, s. 3. It is a misdemeanour punishable on indictment or on summary conviction for any person having the custody, charge or care of any child or young person aged four or upwards and under sixteen to allow such child or young person to reside in or frequent a brothel.

Arrest and Search Warrant.—As will be seen later under " Arrest, Search Warrant and Procedure " in Chap. 12, the Children and Young Persons Act, 1933, ss. 13, 40, gives constables certain powers of arrest without warrant and allows justices to issue search warrants in cases where children or young persons are subjected to any of the offences mentioned in the 1st Schedule to the Act, which now includes many offences under the Sexual Offences Act, 1956.

Also ss. 40, 41 of this 1956 Act gives further powers of arrest without warrant for certain offences (see above).

Chapter XI

INDECENCY

Contents

Indecent Conduct.—Offences against decency may be committed by language and behaviour, by the giving of some display or exhibition, by exposure of the person, or by making public any indecent matter. For indecent assault see " Assault," Chap. 8.

Indecent Language.—" Indecent " may be defined as unbecoming, not decent, contrary to propriety, or offensive to modesty.

" Obscene," which is an adjective of similar but somewhat stronger meaning, conveys the idea of something disgusting, filthy, repulsive, or offensive to chastity or delicacy.

" Profane " indicates something unclean, polluted, disrespectful, irreverent, impious, or blasphemous.

The Profane Oaths Act, 1745, directs that a person who shall profanely curse or swear may be prosecuted within 8 days and fined.

Town Police Clauses Act, 1847, s. 28. It is a summary offence for any person to use any profane or obscene language or to sing any profane or obscene song or ballad in any street in any urban district (including any place to which the public have a right of access, also any place of public resort and any unfenced ground adjoining any street in any urban district) where this section is in force by Order (Public Health Acts Amendment Act, 1907, s. 81), to the annoyance of the residents or passengers, and the offender may be arrested without warrant.

Byelaws. In many districts it is an offence, by byelaw, to make use of any indecent language, gesture or conduct.

For indecent behaviour of prostitutes, see " Prostitution," Chap. 10.

Indecent Exhibitions.—Any indecent performance or exhibition is a common nuisance and is indictable as a misdemeanour at common law.

Vagrancy Act, 1824, s. 4. Any person wilfully exposing to view in any street, highway or public place any indecent exhibition may be arrested without warrant and convicted as a rogue and vagabond (s. 6).

Town Police Clauses Act, 1847, s. 28. It is a summary offence to exhibit to public view any profane, indecent or obscene representation in any street in any urban district (where the Act is in force), to the annoyance of residents or passengers, and the offender may be arrested without warrant.

Byelaws. In many districts byelaws and regulations deal with indecent shows and entertainments.

Indecent Exposure.—It is a public nuisance and therefore indictable as a misdemeanour at common law publicly to expose the naked person.

Such an exposure will be public at common law if made in a place where it is seen by other persons.

Vagrancy Act, 1824, s. 4. It is a summary offence for any person wilfully, openly, lewdly and obscenely to expose his person with intent to insult any female, and the offender may be arrested without warrant and convicted as a rogue and a vagabond.

If possible a female who has been so insulted should be called as a witness, but if such female cannot be traced or is not available to give evidence, accused may be convicted of this offence on other evidence proving that he systematically exposed himself with an apparent intent to insult females.

Town Police Clauses Act, 1847, s. 28. It is a summary offence wilfully and indecently to expose the person in any street in any urban district (where the Act is in force), to the annoyance of residents or passengers, and the offender may be arrested without warrant.

For indecent assault on a female, see " Indecent Assault " Chap. 10, and for indecent assault on a male and gross indecency between males, see " Statutory Assaults," Chap. 8, and " Unnatural Crimes " (later).

A public bath or bathing place will be a public and open place as regards offences against decency (Public Health Act, 1936, s. 224).

Indecent Publications and Advertisements.—Any publication, sale, exhibition to public view, or circulation through the post, of anything of an indecent or obscene nature is an offence.

Vagrancy Acts, 1824 (s. 4) and 1838 (s. 2). Every person wilfully exposing to view in any street, highway or public place, or in the window or other part of any shop or building situate in any street, highway or public place, any obscene print, picture, or other indecent exhibitions, may be arrested without warrant and convicted as a rogue and a vagabond.

Town Police Clauses Act, 1847, s. 28. It is an offence for any person publicly to offer for sale or distribution or to exhibit to public view any profane, indecent or obscene book, paper, print, drawing, painting or representation, in any street in any urban district (where the Act is in force) (for extent of " street " see " Indecent Language "), to the annoyance of the residents or passengers, and the offender may be arrested without warrant.

Indecent Advertisements Act, 1889. It is a summary offence to do any of the following acts in connection with any picture or printed or written matter of an indecent or obscene nature :—

(1) To affix to or inscribe same on any building, wall, hoarding, gate, fence, post, tree or other thing whatsoever, so as to be visible to any person in any street, public highway or footpath.

(2) To affix or inscribe same on any public urinal.

(3) To deliver, attempt to deliver or exhibit same to any inhabitant or person in any street, highway or footpath.

(4) To throw down same into the area of any house.

(5) To exhibit same to public view in the window of any house or shop.

It is also an offence to give or deliver to any other person any such indecent pictures or writings with intent that same should be so affixed, inscribed, delivered or exhibited.

Any advertisement relating to syphilis, nervous debility or other infirmity arising from or relating to sexual intercourse will be deemed indecent matter within the meaning of this Act, if it is attached to anything so as to be visible to any person in any public highway or footpath or put up in any public urinal or delivered or attempted to be delivered to any person in any public highway or footpath, except where such an advertisement is published by any local or public authority.

Any constable may arrest without warrant any person whom he finds committing any offence against this Act.

Venereal Disease Act, 1917. It is a misdemeanour (which may be dealt with summarily) for any person to advertise in any manner any treatment for venereal disease.

However, this prohibition does not apply to advertisements, recommendations, etc., published by any local or public authority.

Obscene Publications Act, 1857. A Stipendiary Magistrate or two Justices, on complaint on oath that complainant has reason to believe and does believe that any obscene books, papers, pictures or other representations are kept in any house, room or other place for the purpose of sale or distribution or exhibition for gain, and that one or more such articles have been sold, distributed, exhibited, lent or otherwise published as aforesaid at or in connection with such place, and such Stipendiary or Justices being satisfied that such belief is well founded and that any of such articles are of such a character and description that their publication would be a misdemeanour, may grant a warrant to any police officer to enter such place in the daytime, using such force as may be necessary, and to search for and seize all such articles found therein and bring same before the Justices. Thereupon the Stipendiary or Justices shall issue summons to the occupier of such house or place to appear within seven days before Petty Sessions to show cause why such articles should not be destroyed.

A magistrates' court if satisfied as to their obscenity shall order their destruction (s. 1). "Obscenity" means that which has a tendency to deprave and corrupt.

The publishing of obscene matter is a misdemeanour at common law and this 1857 Act gives power to seize and destroy obscene matter before it is made public (see *Cox* v. *Stinton* (1951)).

A publication could be " obscene " if part of it was obscene (*Paget Publications, Ltd.* v. *Watson* (1952)).

The misdemeanour (being indictable as a public nuisance) of publishing, exhibiting or selling any indecent or obscene book, writing, picture or model or any other indecent or obscene article or thing whatsoever, whether similar to the things before mentioned or not, may be dealt with summarily, if the Court thinks it expedient so to do and if the accused consents (M.C. Act. 1952, s. 19 and First Sched.).

Customs Consolidation Act, 1876, s. 42. The importation into this country of any indecent or obscene prints, paintings, photographs, books, etc., or any indecent or obscene articles, is prohibited and such articles are forfeited.

Judicial Proceedings (Regulation of Reports) Act, 1926. It is a summary offence to print or publish in relation to any judicial proceedings any indecent matter or details the publication of which would be calculated to injure public morals, or any particulars of divorce or marriage judicial proceedings, other than the names, etc., of the parties and witnesses, a concise statement of the charges and defences, the law points raised, and the summing up, finding and judgment of the Court. Prosecution under the Act requires the sanction of the Attorney-General.

This prohibition does not apply to printing for the use of Courts or to books of law reports or to publications intended for circulation among the legal and medical professions.

Children and Young Persons Act, 1933. In proceedings arising out of any offence or conduct contrary to decency or morality the Court may direct that press reports shall not identify any child or young person concerned (s. 39). The press shall not, in their reports, identify any child or young person concerned in any proceedings in a Juvenile Court unless the Court or the Secretary of State so permit (s. 49). See " Treatment of Youthful Offenders," Chap. 12.

Post Office Act, 1953, s. 11. It is a misdemeanour to enclose any indecent or obscene print, painting, photograph, book or card or any indecent or obscene article in any postal packet, or to have on any postal packet or on the cover thereof any words, marks or designs of an indecent, obscene or grossly offensive character. An offender may be dealt with summarily or on indictment. See Prosecution of Offences Regulations, 1946, (Appendix III) for cases of indecent or obscene matter which are to be reported to the Director of Public Prosecutions.

Unnatural Crimes.—Sexual Offences Act, 1956, s. 12. It is felony for a person to commit buggery with another person or with an animal.

See s. 39 (in Chap. X) as regards the evidence, and this also affects ss. 15 and 16 which follow here.

This s. 39 does not apply in the case of this section except on a charge of the offence with a person under 17. And a person shall be presumed to be under 17 unless the contrary is proved if it is so stated in the charge of indictment and the person appears to the court to have been so at the time of the offence.

Section 13. It is an offence for a man to commit an act of gross indecency with another man, whether in public or private, or to be a party to the commission by a man of an act of gross indecency with another man, or to procure the commission by a man of an act of gross indecency with another man.

Section 16. It is an offence for a person to assault another person with intent to commit buggery.

However s. 39 of this Act (see above) as to the evidence of the husband or wife of the accused does not apply as regards this section except on a charge of an assault (apparently this assault) on a person under 17 (who by this section shall be presumed to be under 17, unless the contrary is proved (see under s. 12 above)).

Section 15. It is an offence to make an indecent assault on a man.

A boy under 16 cannot in law give any consent which prevents an act being such an assault.

A defective cannot in law consent to such an act but a person is only to be treated as guilty of an indecent assault on a defective by reason of that incapacity to consent if such person knew or had reason to suspect him to be a defective.

However s. 39 of this Act (evidence of wife or husband) as noted in Chap. 10, does not apply as regards this section except on a charge of indecent assault on a boy under 17 (or apparently under 17 unless the contrary is proved).

This offence could be dealt with summarily (see 2nd Sched.).

Section 32. It is an offence for a man persistently to solicit or importune in a public place for immoral purposes.

This can be prosecuted on indictment or summarily (see 2nd Sched.).

Chapter XII

CHILDREN AND PERSONS UNDER 21

Contents

Abortion.—Abortion may be defined as the unlawful taking or administering of poison or other noxious thing or the unlawful use of any means whatsoever with intent to procure miscarriage.

Offences against the Person Act, 1861, deals with this crime and with the three classes of persons who may be involved.

(1) The woman. It is felony for any woman being with child and with intent to procure her own miscarriage, unlawfully to take any poison or other noxious thing or use any instrument or other means whatsoever (s. 58).

(2) The person administering, etc. It is felony for any person, with intent to procure the miscarriage of any woman whether she be or be not with child, unlawfully to administer to her or cause to be taken by her any poison or other noxious thing or use any instrument or other means whatsoever (s. 58).

(3) The person supplying the means. It is a misdemeanour for any person unlawfully to supply or procure any poison or other noxious thing or any instrument or thing whatsoever, knowing that the same is intended to be unlawfully used or employed with intent to procure the miscarriage of any woman whether she be or be not with child (s. 59).

Publishing any advertisement of any article in terms calculated to lead to its use for abortion is a summary offence under ss. 9 and 10 of the Pharmacy and Medicines Act, 1941, and the consent of the Attorney-General is required for a prosecution.

Any offence of abortion must be reported to the Director of Public Prosecutions (see Appendix III).

Child Destruction.—This felony is committed where a person, with intent to destroy the life of a child capable of being born alive, by any wilful act causes the child to die before it has an existence independent of its mother. Provided that a person shall not be found guilty of this felony unless it is proved that such act was not done to preserve the life of the mother. Evidence of pregnancy for twenty-eight weeks or more shall be *prima facie* proof that the child was capable of being born alive.

If tried for murder, manslaughter, infanticide or abortion, the accused may be convicted of child destruction. If tried for child destruction there may be a conviction for abortion or concealment of birth (Infant Life (Preservation) Act, 1929). ·

Infanticide.—Under the Infanticide Act, 1938, where a woman by any wilful act or omission causes the death of her child under the age of 12 months, but at the time of the act or omission the balance of her mind was disturbed by reason of her not having fully recovered from the effect of giving birth to the child or the effect of lactation, she shall be guilty of the felony of infanticide which is punishable as manslaughter.

If a woman is tried for the murder of her child under the age of 12 months the jury may return a verdict of murder or of infanticide.

On the indictment for the murder of a child the jury may return a verdict of manslaughter or of guilty but insane or of concealment of birth (which verdict may be given on an indictment for infanticide).

Under s. 1 of the Children and Young Persons Act, 1933, a person of or over 16 indicted for infanticide or manslaughter of a person under 16 may be found guilty of cruelty under the Act.

Concealment of Birth is a misdemeanour and is committed by every person who, when a child has been born (alive or dead), endeavours to conceal the birth by any secret disposition of the dead body of the child. Any person tried for the murder of any such child may be convicted of endeavouring to conceal the birth thereof (Offences against the Person Act, 1861, s. 60).

As evidence is required to prove that a child has been born, the mother should be examined as soon as possible by a doctor, but only if she consents, for if she does not consent such an examination would amount to an assault upon her. The dead body of the child should be found and identified. However, where the body was cremated and thus got rid of, the mother, indicted for murder, was convicted of concealment of birth (*R.* v. *Kersey* (1908))., The body should be examined by a doctor to ascertain whether the child was born alive, and, if so, by what means it died. Denial of the birth of the child is not sufficient, as there must have been some act of secret disposal of the body. Any " secret disposition " is sufficient, and every person who uses any such endeavours to conceal the birth is liable, and where another person may be liable it is immaterial whether there be any evidence against the mother or not. As the offence is a misdemeanour, an arrest should not be made without a warrant.

Abandoning Child.—It is a misdemeanour unlawfully to abandon or expose any child under the age of two years whereby its life is endangered or its health is or is likely to be permanently injured (Offences against the Person Act, 1861, s. 27).

Children and Young Persons.—The main statutes dealing with children and young persons and persons under 21 are the Children and Young Persons Act, 1932, the Children and Young Persons Act, 1933, the Children and Young Persons Act, 1956, the Children and Young Persons Act, 1938, the Education Acts, 1944 and 1946, the Criminal Justice, Act, 1948, the Children Act, 1948, the Children and Young Persons (Amendment) Act, 1952, and the Children Act, 1958 (operative on April 1, 1959).

Children and Young Persons Act, 1933, is the principal Act.

Part I arranges for the prevention of cruelty and gives the various offences and the power of arrest without warrant for the offences given in the 1st Schedule to the Act.

Part II deals with employment, entertainments, dangerous performances, and employment abroad.

Part III gives the procedure as regards proceedings in connection with children and young persons, juvenile courts and juvenile offenders and those in need of care or protection.

Part IV deals with remand homes, approved schools and fit persons with amendments by the 1956 Act.

Part V gives control over voluntary homes.

Part VI contains various supplementary provisions.

In criminal law, a " child " means a person under the age of fourteen years (1933 Act, s. 107). A " young person " means a person who has attained the age of fourteen years and is under the age of seventeen years (1933 Act, s. 107 and 1932 Act, s. 70; see also s. 20 M.C. Act, 1952). An " adult " is a person who is of the age of seventeen years or upwards (M.C. Act, 1952, s. 19).

" Place of Safety " means any remand home or police station or any home provided by a local authority (C. Act, 1948, 3rd

Sched.), or any hospital, surgery or any other suitable place the occupier of which is willing temporarily to receive an infant, child or young person (1933 Act, s. 107).

" Street " includes any highway and any public bridge, road, lane, footway, square, court, alley or passage, whether a thoroughfare or not (1933 Act, s. 107).

" Public Place " includes any public park, garden, sea beach or railway station and any ground to which the public for the time being have or are permitted to have access whether on payment or otherwise (1933 Act, s. 107).

" Guardian " includes any person who, in the opinion of the Court, has for the time being the charge of or control over the child or young person (1933 Act, s. 107 and M.C. Act, 1952, s. 126).

Where the age of any person at any time is material for the purposes of the Act, his age at the material time shall be deemed to be that which appears to the Court, after considering any available evidence, to have been his age at that time (M.C. Act, 1952, s. 126).

Where any powers or duties are conferred by Part II of the 1933 Act on local authorities, the " local authority " shall be the local education authority (1933 Act, s. 96, as amended by the Education Act, 1944, 8th Sched, and C. Act, 1948, 3rd Sched.).

An education authority may institute proceedings for any offence under these Acts (1933 Act, s. 98, and C. Act, 1948, 3rd Sched.).

The procedure in Courts with respect to juveniles is regulated by the Summary Jurisdiction (Children and Young Persons) Rules, 1933, 1938, 1950, 1952 and 1953.

If a juvenile is charged with an offence and is not defended and he makes assertions, the Juvenile Court may question him to clear up such assertions. If a Juvenile Court finds a juvenile guilty of an offence or decides that he needs care or protection, information regarding him shall be obtained and any written report from a probation officer, local authority or doctor may be received without being read aloud provided that the substance of the report is told to the juvenile and his parent or guardian (if present) and that further evidence may be given, and the Court may require the parent or guardian of the juvenile to withdraw from the Court.

When a Court places a juvenile under the supervision of a probation officer or other person it shall give the juvenile a written notice explaining the effect of the order of the Court.

The term " juvenile " is herein used to indicate a person under 17 and so includes " children " and " young persons."

Child Protection.—The Children Act, 1958, makes fresh provision for the protection of children living away from their parents. Part I (ss. 1–17) deals with the supervision of " foster " children by local authorities, and supersedes ss. 206–220 of the Public Health Act, 1936, and ss. 35–37 of the Children Act, 1948.

It is the duty of local authorities to ensure the well-being of " foster " children (s. 1). A " foster " child is one below the upper limit of compulsory school age whose care and maintenance are undertaken for reward for more than one month by a person who is not a relative or guardian of his, but not one whose well-being is already the responsibility of some competent authority (s. 2).

Persons maintaining " foster " children must notify the local authority and provide particulars such as name, age, place of birth etc. (s. 3). The local authority has power to inspect premises, impose conditions or prohibit the keeping of " foster " children (s. 4). Any person aggrieved by any requirement imposed under section 4 may appeal to a juvenile court (s. 5). Certain disqualifications for keeping " foster " children are detailed in section 6. A juvenile court may order the removal of a child from unsuitable surroundings (s. 7).

Under s. 40 of C. & Y.P. Act, 1933, a warrant authorising the search for a child may be issued on suspicion that unnecessary suffering is being caused to a child. Any refusal to allow the visiting of a " foster " child gives reasonable ground for such a suspicion (1958 Act, s. 8).

Failure to make any of the notifications required or making a false or misleading notice; refusing to allow the visiting of any " foster " child by a duly authorised officer; failure to comply with any requirements imposed by a local authority; maintaining a " foster " child in contravention of s. 6 or refusing to comply with an order for the removal of any " foster " child; or obstructing any person in the execution of such an order, shall be summary offences punishable by imprisonment up to 6 months or a fine up to £100 or both (s. 14).

Under the Nurseries and Child Minders Regulation Act, 1948, any person who for reward receives in his home more than two children under 5 from more than one household, to be looked after for the day or a substantial part of the day or for longer period not exceeding 6 days, commits a summary offence unless registered with the local health authority (ss. 1 and 4). The occupier of any premises (other than premises wholly or mainly used as a private dwelling) where children (under compulsory school age 15) are received to be looked after for the day or a substantial part of a day or for any longer period not exceeding 6 days, commits a summary offence unless the premises are registered with the local health authority (ss. 1 and 4). The local health authority may register fit persons and fit premises and impose requirements (s. 2). It will issue certificates of registration (s. 3) and may cancel same for cause (s. 5). It will authorise inspection of premises and children, and if admission is refused a justice may issue a warrant authorising entry (s. 7). The local health authority may prosecute offences under the Act (s. 11). The Act does not apply to hospitals, schools and approved nursery schools and institutions (s. 8).

The Children Act, 1948, makes further provisions for the welfare of certain juveniles up to the age of 18. It will be the duty of the local authority (the council of a county or county borough, s. 38) to take into their care a child under 17 who has no parents or guardian or who is abandoned or lost or whose parents or guardian are prevented from properly maintaining him and who requires their intervention. If it does so it should be responsible until he is 18. However, the care of such child may later be taken over by a parent or guardian or relative or friend (s. 1). If it takes over care of such a child, the local authority may, by resolution, assume parental rights (until he is 18, s. 4), if his parents are dead and he has no guardian or if his parents or guardian have abandoned him or are incapable or unfit and consent or if a juvenile court so order if no consent is given (s. 2).

It will be a summary offence to induce, assist, etc., such a child to run away or to harbour such a runaway (s. 3). The local authority shall be a " fit person " to whom a court may commit a child or young person (s. 5). The parent of a child under 16 in the care of the local authority shall keep the authority informed of his address ; if he does not he commits a summary offence (s. 10). The local authority may board out a child in their care or maintain him in a home (provided by the authority under s. 15) or place him in a voluntary home (see later) or send him if over compulsory school age to a hostel (provided under s. 19) or maintain him in premises under their control (s. 13). A local authority may provide accommodation for the temporary reception of children (s. 15). Such accommodation may be made available for children under 12 in custody instead of their being sent to a remand home, and such a place will be known as a " special reception centre." Such children may be committed there by the court or sent there by the police (C. and Y.P. Amendment Act, 1952, s. 3). The local authority may procure or assist the emigration of any child in their care, with the consent of the Secretary of State (s. 17). Sections 23–26 deal with contributions payable to the local authority in respect to children in their care. Every local authority shall establish a children's committee to carry out their functions under these 1933, 1936 and 1948 Acts, and also regarding the adoption of children, unless exempted by the Secretary of State (ss. 39, 40). A local authority shall appoint a children's officer and provide an adequate staff (s. 41). A local authority shall make provision, in homes provided by them under s. 15, for children removed to a " place of safety " (s. 51). The Adminstration of Children's Homes Regs., 1951, deal with these homes. S. 103 of the C. and Y.P. Act, 1933, authorised the Secretary of State to appoint inspectors for the purposes of the Children Acts. These inspectors are authorised to enter all places referred to in these

Acts, on production of their written authority and any obstruction of these inspectors will be a summary offence (s. 54).

" Child " in the Children Act, 1948, means generally a person under 18, " guardian " means a person so appointed by deed or will or by a court, " parent " of an illegitimate child means his mother and a person who has adopted a child is his " parent " under the Act (s. 59).

Cruelty to Children and Young Persons.—Part I of the Children and Young Persons Act, 1933, deals with cruelty to juveniles and with certain other similar offences.

The offences under Part I are as follows :—

(1) *Cruelty.*—That is, any person who has attained the age of sixteen years who has the custody, charge or care of *any person under sixteen*, wilfully assaulting, ill-treating, neglecting, abandoning or exposing such juvenile or causing or procuring same to be done, in a manner likely to cause him unnecessary suffering or injury to health.

It is a misdemeanour punishable on indictment or summarily by fine and (or) imprisonment not exceeding six months.

Failure to provide adequate food, clothing, medical aid or lodging for such juvenile or failure to take steps to get same provided under the National Assistance Act, 1948, will be deemed to be " neglect " likely to cause injury to health under this section, on the part of the person legally liable to maintain such juvenile.

If the death of an infant under three was caused by suffocation (not due to disease or foreign body in the throat) while in bed with a person of sixteen or over, who had gone to bed under the influence of drink, that person will be deemed to have neglected the infant in a manner likely to cause injury to health (s. 1).

If actual suffering or injury or its likelihood is prevented by the action of another person or if the juvenile dies, the responsible person may be convicted under this section.

If the person responsible is indicted for infanticide or manslaughter, the jury may find him guilty of an offence under this section.

If it is proved that the person convicted was in any way interested in any money accruable or payable on the death of the juvenile and knew it, the punishment may be heavier.

Nothing in this section shall affect the right of any parent, teacher or other person in lawful control or charge to administer punishment to a child or young person (s. 1).

Assaults on children and young persons may also be dealt with as assaults. See Chap. 8, " Statutory Assaults."

(2) *Brothels.*—Any person having the custody, charge or care of a person of the age of four and under sixteen, allowing such

juvenile to reside in or frequent a brothel. Misdemeanour, and is also punishable summarily by fine and (or) imprisonment up to six months (s. 3). See Chap. 10, " Persons in a Brothel."

(3) *Begging.*—Any person causing or procuring or when having the custody, charge or care of such juvenile, allowing a person under sixteen to be in any street, premises or place for the purpose of begging or getting alms in any manner. Summary offence (s. 4).

If a person singing etc. in a public place has with him a child lent or hired to him, the child shall be deemed to be there for the getting of alms (s. 4).

(4) *Intoxicants.*—It is a summary offence for any person to give or cause to be given to any child under five any intoxicating liquor, except on doctor's orders or in case of sickness or other urgent cause (s. 5).

(5) *Tobacco or cigarette papers.*—Sale to persons under sixteen is a summary offence (s. 7). See " Smoking by Juveniles " later.

(6) *Pawnbrokers.*—Must not take pledges from persons under fourteen (s. 8). See Chap. 31, " Pawnbrokers."

(7) *Old Metal.*—Dealers must not purchase old metal from persons under sixteen (s. 9). See Chap. 31, " Dealers in Old Metals."

(8) *Vagrants and Children.*—It is a summary offence for a person habitually to wander from place to place and take with him any child of five or more or any young person still liable to compulsory schooling, unless he can prove that the child or young person is not, by so " wandering " prevented from receiving efficient full-time education. Any constable, on reasonable grounds of suspicion, may arrest without warrant such person and take the child or young person to a place of safety (s. 10, and Education Act, 1944, 8th Sched.).

(9) *Unprotected Fire.*—Where any person of sixteen or over who has the custody, charge or care of any child under twelve, allows such child to be in any room containing an open fire grate or any heating appliance liable to cause injury by contact not sufficiently protected to guard against the risk, without taking reasonable precautions against the risk of the child being burnt or scalded and by reason thereof the child is killed or suffers serious injury. Summary offence (s. 11 and s. 8 of the C. and Y.P. (Amendment) Act, 1952).

See also the Heating Appliances (Fireguards) Act, 1952.

(10) *Entertainments.*—Failing to provide for the safety of children at entertainments is a summary offence (s. 12). See Chap. 37, " Ingress and Egress."

As regards juveniles and licensed premises see Licensing Act, 1953, ss. 126 to 129, Chap. 38.

(11) Under s. 56 of the Offences against the Person Act, 1861, it is felony to unlawfully, by force or fraud, lead or take away or decoy or entice away or detain any child under 14, with intent to deprive the parent or lawful custodian of the possession of such child, or with intent to steal any article on such child, or with any such intent to receive or harbour any such child knowing it has been so abducted, except where the abductor has claimed a right to the possession of such child or is the mother or has claimed to be the father of such illegitimate child.

Custody, charge or care of a child or young person :—
The parent or legal guardian or person legally liable to maintain him is presumed to have the custody of him, and desertion by the father does not in itself end his custody.

A person to whose charge he is committed by any person who has the custody of him, is presumed to have charge of him.

A person having actual possession or control of him is presumed to have care of him (s. 17).

Arrest, Search Warrant and Procedure.—Any constable may arrest without warrant :—

(1) Any person who within his view commits any of the offences in the First Schedule to the Act, if he does not know and cannot ascertain his name and residence.

(2) Any person who has committed or whom he has reason to believe to have committed, any of the offences in the First Schedule to the Act, if he has reasonable ground for believing such person will abscond or if he does not know and cannot ascertain his name and address (s. 13).

First Schedule to Act of 1933 as amended by the Sexual Offences Act, 1956.—This schedule mentions the following offences where committed against children or young persons—

Murder, manslaughter, infanticide.

Offences against the Person Act, 1861 : s. 27 (abandoning or exposing a child under two); s. 56 (kidnapping child under fourteen); s. 5 (manslaughter); s. 42 (assault); s. 43 (aggravated assault on boy under fourteen or female).

Children and Young Persons Act, 1933, s. 1 (cruelty to juvenile under sixteen); s. 3 (allowing juvenile of four and under sixteen to be in a brothel) ; s. 4 (causing or allowing juvenile under sixteen to be used for begging) ; s. 11 and s. 8, 1952 Act (exposing child under twelve to risk of burning) ; s. 23 (causing or allowing juvenile under sixteen to take part in public dangerous performance) and

Sexual Offences Act, 1956, offences under ss. 2 to 7, 10 to 16, 19, 20, 22 to 26, and 28, and any attempt to commit offences under ss. 2, 5, 6, 7, 10, 11, 12, 22, 23. Section 99 (2) of the C. and Y.P. Act, 1933, shall apply where necessary.

Any other offence involving bodily injury.

After such an arrest without warrant the prisoner shall be released on bail at the police station, unless his release would tend to defeat the ends of justice or cause danger to the juvenile concerned (s. 13). See Chap. 5, " Bail by Police."

A constable or any person authorised by a Justice may take to a place of safety any juvenile in respect of whom any of the First Schedule offences has been or is believed to have been committed or who is about to be brought to Court as needing care or protection (s. 67).

Search Warrant.—A Justice may issue a warrant authorising any constable named therein to enter, if need be by force, any place specified in the warrant, and either to search for and remove to a place of safety any child or young person if it is found that he has been or is being assaulted, ill-treated or neglected or the subject of any First Schedule offence, or to remove a juvenile to a place of safety. The juvenile need not be named and the warrant may direct the arrest of any person accused. The person laying the information may accompany the constable unless the Justice otherwise directs and the Justice may direct the attendance of a doctor (s. 40).

Procedure.—The same information or summons may charge any of the above First Schedule offences in respect to two or more juveniles. The same information or summons may also charge a person as having the care, custody or charge, and charge him with the offences of assault, neglect, abandonment or exposure together or separately. The dates of the acts making up a continuous offence need not be specified. For summary conviction the offence should have been committed, wholly or partly, within six months before the information was laid. Evidence of previous acts making up the offence may be taken (s. 14).

The wife or husband of the accused is a competent witness for the prosecution or the defence without the consent of the accused but is not compellable to give evidence (s. 15).

The unsworn evidence of a child of tender years in offence cases may be received if the Court is satisfied that the child has sufficient intelligence and understands the duty of speaking the truth, but such evidence must be corroborated (s. 38).

In the case of any First Schedule offence, the presence of the juvenile at the hearing of the case may be dispensed with if the Court does not consider it essential (s. 41).

In a First Schedule offence case, if the attendance of the injured juvenile would involve serious danger to his life or health, and a doctor gives evidence to that effect, a Justice may take the juvenile's deposition and send it to the Court (s. 42). Such a deposition is admissible in evidence, on medical evidence of the juvenile's condition, provided that notice of the intention to take it had been served on the accused and that he or his lawyer had (or might have had if he had chosen to be present) an opportunity of cross-examining the juvenile on his deposition (s. 43).

Smoking by Juveniles.—S. 7 of the Children and Young Persons Act, 1933, deals with person under the age of sixteen years smoking tobacco (which includes cigarettes).

It is a summary offence to sell to anyone apparently under the age of sixteen years, any tobacco or cigarette papers, whether for his own use or not.

However, sale of tobacco other than cigarettes shall not be an offence if seller had no reason to believe that the tobacco was for the use of the juvenile buyer.

It is the duty of a constable and of a park-keeper in uniform to seize tobacco or cigarette papers in the possession of any person apparently under the age of sixteen whom he finds smoking in any street or public place (including any ground to which the public have access, whether on payment or otherwise, s. 107).

It is not an offence to sell to, and there is no power of seizure in the case of :—

(1) Boy messengers in uniform in the course of their employment ;

(2) Persons employed by tobacconists for the purpose of their business.

On proof that any automatic machine for the sale of tobacco kept on any premises is being extensively used by persons apparently under sixteen, a Magistrates' Court may order the owner of the machine or the occupier of the place where the machine is kept to take specified precautions to prevent the practice or if necessary to remove the machine.

Care or Protection of Juveniles.—Children and Young Person Acts, 1933, 1952, s. 61. A child (under 14) or young person (under 17) needs care or protection when he—

(1) has no parent or guardian or a parent or guardian unfit or neglectful and is falling into bad associations or is exposed to moral danger (which will include being destitute, wandering without abode and means, begging) or is beyond control (or is ill-treated or neglected in a manner likely to cause him unnecessary suffering or injury to health, s. 1, 1952 Act) ; or

(2) has been subject to an offence mentioned in the First Schedule to the Act or is a member of a household where any such offence (including incest or attempted incest; Sexual Offences Act, 1956, 3rd Sched.) has been committed and in such case requires care or protection; or

(3) is a person liable to compulsory education prevented from receiving education by being taken wandering. (See " Vagrants and Children," s. 10 above.)

S. 62. Any local authority, constable, or person or society duly authorised by the Secretary of State (the N.S.P.C.C. will be so authorised), who has reasonable grounds for believing that a person under seventeen needs care or protection (as above described), may bring him before a Juvenile Court. (It will be the duty of the local authority to investigate information received of any such case, s. 2, 1952 Act). (He may be brought on summons or on warrant, but if not on either notice shall be served by the applicant on his parent or guardian, S.J. (Children and Young Persons) Rules, 1933, 1938, 1950, 1952, and 1953.) Also any Court which has convicted a person for an offence mentioned in the 1st Schedule or under s. 10 for wandering and thereby preventing education, may also deal with the juvenile or direct him to be brought before a Juvenile Court and the local authority shall do so (s. 63).

The Court may send a juvenile needing care or protection to an approved school (see later) or commit him to the care of a fit person or bind over the parent or guardian to exercise proper care and guardianship or (and) place him under the supervision of a probation officer or some other named person for up to three years (s. 62) and may add a requirement as to his residence or mental treatment provided that in the case of a young person he consents to it (C.J. Act. 1948, s. 74).

S. 64, as amended by 1952 Act. If the parent or guardian proves he is unable to control a person under seventeen and consents to the order, a Juvenile Court may send the juvenile to an approved school or place him under the supervision (with similar requirement as to residence or mental treatment, C.J. Act, 1948, s. 74) of a probation officer or other named person for up to three years or commit him to the care of a fit person, (s. 1, 1938 Act). S. 65 has been amended to allow a local authority to bring a refractory child or young person before the Juvenile Court.

S. 66. Where a juvenile has been ordered to be under supervision, if he is under 17 and it is considered necessary, he may be brought before a juvenile court and may be sent to an approved school or committed to the care of a fit person.

If a court considers that a young person brought before them under any of the preceding conditions (ss. 62-66, 1933 Act) needs inquiry into his physical or mental condition, it may send him to a suitable remand centre if one is available (C.J. Act, 1948, s. 75).

S. 67. A constable or any person authorised by any Court or Justice may take to a place of safety (where he may be detained until he can be brought before a Juvenile Court) any person under seventeen in respect of whom an offence under the First Schedule to the Act, has been or is believed to have been committed or who is about to be brought before a Juvenile Court as needing care or protection or refractory. The Court has power to make an interim order (remand) for his detention in a place of safety or for his committal to the care of a fit person, for periods each not exceeding twenty-eight days, until the Court is in a position to decide what to do with the juvenile. See also s. 6 of 1938 Act and s. 3 and Sched., 1952 Act, as to further interim orders.

If the court proposes to make such an interim order but the person is too unruly or depraved for a remand home, the court may send him to a suitable available remand centre, and if while in a remand home on interim order, he proves too unruly or depraved a court may send him to a suitable available remand centre (C.J. Act, 1948, s. 75).

Education.—The Education Act, 1944, has made several alterations in the Children and Young Persons Act, 1933. Compulsory school age is now between 5 years and 15 years (s. 35). The parent or guardian or person having the actual custody is bound to cause such person to receive efficient full-time education (s. 36). For non-attendance at school the local Education Authority may serve a school attendance order (s. 37). The parent will be guilty of an offence if his " child " does not attend school regularly (s. 39). School attendance may be enforced by fine and/or imprisonment and the Court may direct that the " child " be brought before a Juvenile Court which may deal with him under s. 62 of the C. and Y. P. Act, 1933, as needing care or protection (s. 40). "Child" here means a person not over compulsory school age (s. 114).

Employment of Juveniles.—Children and Young Persons Act, 1933, Part II (ss. 18-30) deals with the employment of children and young persons. S. 18 imposes restrictions on the employment of children, and s. 30 directs that any person assisting in any trade or occupation carried on for profit shall be deemed to be employed although he receives no reward for his labour.

For the purposes of byelaws made by the local authority under Part II of this 1933 Act the expression " child " shall have the same meaning as it has for the purposes of the said Part II (Education Act, 1944, s. 120 (5)). Also for the purposes of any enactment relating to the employment of children and young persons any person not over compulsory school age shall be deemed to be a child within the meaning of that enactment (Education Act, 1944, s. 58).

However, a chorister taking part in religious services or practices, whether paid or not, shall not be deemed to be employed (s. 30) and a child of twelve or over broadcasting for the B.B.C. and persons in approved schools are exempted (s. 29).

The general restrictions are as follows :—

(1) No child shall be employed until his age is two years less than the age at which compulsory schooling ceases (viz. thirteen years). However, byelaws may allow the parent or guardian to

employ a child in light agricultural or horticultural work (s. 18).

(2) No child shall be employed before the close of his day's school hours. However, byelaws may allow a child to be employed for one hour before his day's school hour (s. 18).

(3) No child shall be employed before 6 A.M. or after 8 P.M. nor for more than two hours on any of his school days. However, this restriction does not apply to a child of twelve or over, duly licensed to take part in an entertainment (see later) (s. 18).

(4) No child shall be employed on any Sunday for more than two hours (s. 18).

(5) No child shall be employed to lift, carry, or move anything so heavy as to be likely to cause injury to him (s. 18).

A local authority (the Education Authority, s. 96) may make byelaws restricting still further the employment of children (s. 18, and Education Act, 1944, 8th Sched.).

A local authority after approval by Parliament may make byelaws dealing with the employment of persons under eighteen other than children (s. 19). The Young Persons (Employment) Act, 1938, regulates the hours of employment of persons under 18 in certain occupations. See also Shops Act, 1950.

Street Trading.—No person under sixteen shall engage or be employed in street trading, but byelaws may allow persons of fourteen up to sixteen to be so employed by their parents. A local authority may make byelaws regulating or prohibiting street trading by persons under eighteen (s. 20). A person under eighteen who engages in street trading in contravention of above, is liable to fine on summary conviction (s. 21).

" Street trading " includes hawking of newspapers, matches, flowers and other articles, playing, singing or performing for profit, shoe-blacking and other like occupations carried on in streets or public places (s. 30).

If a person is employed in contravention of any of the above restrictions, his employer (unless he proves he used all due diligence to observe the law) and any person (other than the employee) to whose act or default the contravention is attributable, are liable to fine on summary conviction (s. 21). For the right of entry to make enquiries see " Powers of Entry (Employment) " later.

Entertainments by Children.—Children and Young Persons Act, 1933, Part II, s. 22. A child (under fourteen) shall not, unless duly licensed, take part in any entertainment in connection with which any charge, whether for admission or not, is made to any of the audience.

However a licence shall not be necessary (apart from any restrictions on employment) if the child has not taken part in any such entertainments on more than six occasions during the preceding six months and if the net proceeds do not go to the private profit of the promoters.

Provided, however, that this exception does not apply on liquor licensed premises unless either the premises are also licensed for stage plays or music, singing or dancing, or two Justices have in writing specially authorised the child to take part.

Causing or procuring or being the parent or guardian allowing a child to take part in an entertainment in contravention of above, is a summary offence.

The local authority (the Education Authority, s. 96) may grant a licence for a child of twelve or upwards, who is residing in their area, to take part in specified entertainments on week days, provided the child is fit to take part and will be properly treated. See the Employment of Children in Entertainments Rules, 1933, 1945 and 1946.

The licensee shall give seven days' notice to the local authority of any area in which the entertainment is to take place and that authority has power to vary, extend or revoke the licence, subject to an appeal to the Board of Education.

For right of entry to make enquiries, see " Powers of Entry (Employment) " later.

Dangerous Performances by Juveniles.—Children and Young Persons Act, 1933, Part II.

(1) No person under sixteen shall take part in any public performance in which his life or limbs are endangered. Causing or procuring or being the parent or guardian allowing him to do so is a summary offence which may be prosecuted only by or with the authority of the Chief Officer of Police (s. 23) ;

(2) No person under twelve shall be trained to take part in performances of a dangerous nature (including acrobatic and contortionist work, s. 30) ; and

(3) No person under sixteen shall be trained to take part in such performances except on licence (s. 24).

Causing or procuring or being the parent or guardian allowing any such training except on licence is a summary offence punishable by fine (s. 24).

A petty sessional court may grant a licence for a person of twelve and under sixteen years to be so trained. The applicant for the licence shall give seven days' notice to the Chief Officer of Police of the district where the juvenile is to be trained, and he may oppose the grant. The licence shall specify the place or places where such person is to be trained and conditions for his protection may be included. It may be revoked by the Court on cause shown by any person (s. 24).

For the right of entry to make enquiries, see " Powers of Entry (Employment) " later.

Powers of Entry (Employment).—Children and Young Persons Act, 1933, s. 28. On reasonable cause to believe that the provisions of Part II as to employment, entertainments and dangerous performances or of any byelaw made thereunder, are being contravened with respect to any person, the local authority or any constable may obtain from a Justice a written order giving power to enter at any reasonable time within forty-eight hours of the making of the order, any place in or in connection with which such person is or is believed to be employed, trained, etc., and to make enquiries therein with respect to such person. If a licence is in existence in respect to entertainments or dangerous performances, any authorised officer of the local authority or any constable may enter the place specified and make enquiries therein as to the person to whom the licence relates. It is a summary offence to obstruct such constable or officer or to refuse to answer or answer falsely any enquiry thus authorised.

Employment Abroad. Restrictions.—The Children and Young Persons Act, Part II, s. 25, directs that no person shall cause or procure or, having the custody charge or care of him, allow to go abroad for the purpose of singing, playing, performing or being exhibited, for profit :—

(1) Any person under fourteen.
(2) Any person who is fourteen years of age or upwards and under eighteen, unless a licence has been granted for the purpose. (" Abroad " means outside Great Britain and Ireland, s. 30).

These restrictions do not apply to a person only temporarily resident in Great Britain and Ireland (s. 25).

Seven days after giving notice to the Chief Officer of Police for the district in which the juvenile resides, application for a licence may be made to the Chief Magistrate or Magistrate at Bow Street, London, or to a stipendiary magistrate duly authorised under the section. Conditions may be attached and any such licence may be revoked, varied or extended (s. 25).

Contravention of the above is a summary offence, and if a person procured any such juvenile to go abroad by false pretence or false representation he is liable on indictment to two years' imprisonment (s. 26).

A constable or any person authorised by a Justice may take to a place of safety any juvenile under seventeen who there is reason to believe is about to go abroad in contravention of the above restrictions (s. 26).

Treatment of Youthful Offenders.—The Children and Young Persons Act, 1933, and the Criminal Justice Act, 1948, make special provision for the treatment of youthful offenders who are children or young persons (under 17) or are under 21.

After arrest with or without warrant if a youthful offender

under 17 cannot be brought forthwith before a Magistrates' Court, he shall be released by the police on bail with or without sureties unless the charge is homicide or other grave crime, or unless it is necessary in the interests of the juvenile to remove him from association with criminals or prostitutes or unless it is considered that his release would defeat the ends of justice (1933 Act, s. 32) and if detained and under 12 he may be sent to a special reception centre instead of to a remand home (1952 Act, Sched.). See " Bail by Police," Chap. 5.

If such prisoner is not so released after arrest and is not sent to a special reception centre he shall be detained in a remand home (until he can be brought before a Court), unless the police certify in writing for the information of the Court that it is impracticable to do so, or that he is so unruly that he cannot be safely so detained or that by reason of his health or condition it is inadvisable so to detain him (1933 Act, s. 32).

Where a court (or justice) remands or commits for trial or sentence a person under 21 charged with or convicted of an offence and not released on bail if under 12, he may be sent to a special reception centre (1952 Act, Sched.), if not he should be sent to a remand home if under 14, to a remand home if not less than 14 but under 17 unless too unruly or depraved, and to a remand centre (if available) if not less than 17 or if 14 or more and too unruly or depraved for a remand home (C.J. Act, 1948, s. 27 (1)).

Where a person (16-21) is committed or remanded by a magistrates' court with a view to Borstal training, he should be sent to a suitable available remand centre and if not, to prison, but if he is under 17 he may be sent to a remand home unless he is too unruly or depraved (M.C. Act, 1952, s. 28). Where an offender liable to imprisonment and not less than 14 but under 17 is remanded in custody for inquiry into his physical or mental condition, the court may send him to a suitable remand centre (if available) instead of to a remand home (M.C. Act, 1952, s. 26).

Any court (or justice) may order the transfer of a person from a remand home to another remand home, or in the case of a person not less than 14 who is too unruly or depraved for a remand home, to a suitable remand centre and if one is not available, to a prison (C.J. Act, 1948, s. 27 (5)).

If not less than 14, a person in custody charged with an offence may have his finger prints taken by order of a magistrates' court (M.C. Act, 1952, s. 40). See " Finger Prints," Chap. 5.

When a juvenile has been arrested or taken to a place of safety, the police or person who took him there shall warn the parent or guardian to attend the Court. If a juvenile is brought for any reason before a Court, the parent or guardian if available should be required to attend the Court unless the Court thinks it would be unreasonable (1933 Act, s. 34). His attendance may be enforced by summons or warrant (S. J. (Children and Young Persons) Rules, 1933, 1938, 1950, 1952 and 1953).

When a child or young person is to be brought before a justice or justices charged with an offence or needing care or protection notification of the date and reason for bringing such juvenile, shall be given forthwith to :—

(1) A probation officer for the petty sessional division, and

(2) The local authority for the district in which the juvenile is resident (or of the place of the offence, etc., if residence is not known).

The local authority except in cases of a trivial nature or unless it is arranged that a probation officer will do so, shall provide the Court with information as to the home, school, health and character of the juvenile.

This notification shall be given by the police where the juvenile is charged with an offence, and in any other case (i.e. care or protection) by the person bringing the juvenile before the Court (1933 Act, s. 35 and 1952 Act, Sched.).

While detained in a police station or being conveyed to or from a Court or while waiting before or after attendance at Court, a juvenile shall be prevented from associating with an adult (not being a relative) charged with any offence other than the offence with which the juvenile is jointly charged. If a girl she shall be under the care of a woman (1933 Act, s. 31).

In the case of any proceedings arising out of any offence or conduct contrary to decency or morality, the Court may direct that no newspaper report shall give the picture, name, address or school or any particulars calculated to identify any child or young person concerned in the proceedings, either as accused, prosecutor or witness. Breach of any such direction of the Court is punishable summarily by fine (1933 Act, s. 39).

Unless the Court or the Secretary of State by order permit, no newspaper report of any proceedings in a Juvenile Court shall give the picture, name, address, school or any particulars calculated to identify any child or young person concerned in the proceedings as accused, prosecutor or witness. Any contravention is punishable summarily by fine (1933 Act, s. 49).

Charges against children and young persons (and also applications for orders or licences relating to them) shall be heard by Juvenile Courts. However, this does not apply to a joint charge against a person under seventeen and a person of seventeen or over, nor does it apply when a person under seventeen is charged and another person of seventeen or upwards is charged with aiding, abetting, causing, procuring, allowing or permitting that offence, and a Magistrates' Court may continue dealing with a case even though it transpires in the course of the proceedings that the person concerned is a person under seventeen (1933 Act, s. 46).

A Juvenile Court may deal with a charge or an application relating to a person believed to be a child or young person although it is discovered that the person is not a juvenile (1933 Act, s. 48 (1)).

Any Justice or Justices may entertain an application for bail or remand and hear the evidence, no matter what the age of the defendant is (1933 Act, s. 46 (2)).

If a juvenile is remanded by a Juvenile Court for information to be obtained concerning him, the remand may be for periods not exceeding 21 days and another Juvenile Court may subsequently deal with him (1933 Act, s. 48 (3)).

Any Court by or before which a child or young person is found guilty of an offence other than homicide, may remit the case to a Juvenile Court to deal with the offender (1933 Act, s. 56).

The Summary Jurisdiction (Children and Young Person) Rules, 1933, 1938, 1950, 1952 and 1953, deal with the procedure in Court respecting juvenile offenders and juveniles in need of care or protestion. See Stone's Justices' Manual.

Punishment of Youthful Offenders.—It shall be conclusively presumed that no child under eight can be guilty of any offence (C. and Y.P. Act, s. 50). A person of the age of eight and under fourteen is criminally responsible for his offences (except a boy for rape or carnal knowledge) if it is proved that he had sufficient discretion and capacity to know what he was doing was wrong.

Such a child (8 up to 14) shall be dealt with by a Juvenile Court for any offence other than homicide, but a Court may commit him for trial for an indictable offence if a person of fourteen or over is charged jointly with him (M.C. Act, 1952, s. 21).

He may not be fined more than 40s. (M.C. Act, 1952, s. 32). He cannot be sentenced to death (1933 Act, s. 53), or imprisonment but he may be committed for up to a month to a remand home (1933 Act, s. 54). See later as to sending to an approved school.

A person of fourteen and upwards is liable for his offences.

A young person (14-17) may be dealt with summarily, with his consent, at any time, for any indictable offence except homicide. Any fine shall not exceed £10 (M.C. Act, 1952, s. 20). A magistrates' court shall not impose imprisonment on him (M.C. Act, 1952, s. 107), but if he is 15 or over, imprisonment may be ordered by Assizes or Quarter Sessions (C.J. Act, 1948, s. 17 (1)). Instead of imprisonment he may be committed to a remand home for up to one month (C. and Y.P. Act, 1933, s. 54) or he may be sent to a suitable detention centre if one is available (C.J. Act, 1948, s. 18).

If a child or young person is convicted on indictment of attempt to murder, manslaughter or wounding with intent to do grievous bodily harm, the court may sentence him to be detained for a specified period and in such case he will be detained as directed by the Secretary of State (C. and Y.P. Act, 1933, s. 53).

If a child or young person is charged with any offence for which fine, damages or costs may be imposed, the court may impose same and may in any case and shall if the offender is a child order that it should be paid by the parent or guardian, unless the parent or guardian cannot be found or has not conduced to the commission of the offence and if a child or young person is charged with any offence, the court may order his parent or guardian to give security for his good behaviour (1933 Act, s. 55). See also C.J. Act, 1948. s. 11.

A child or young person found guilty of an offence punishable with imprisonment in the case of an adult, may be sent by a court to an approved school or committed to the care of a fit person (1933 Act, s. 57).

The words " conviction " and " sentence " shall not be used in relation to children and young persons dealt with summarily and are to be replaced by " found guilty " and " order " (1933 Act, s. 59). No conviction or finding of guilty of a child or young person shall be regarded as a conviction of felony for the purpose of any disqualification attaching to felony (1933 Act, s. 51).

No court (or justice) shall impose imprisonment on a person under 21, unless the court is of opinion that no other method of dealing with him is appropriate (C.J. Act, 1948, s. 17 (2)). A magistrates' court shall not pass a sentence of imprisonment on a first offender of or over 21 unless the court is of opinion that no other method of dealing with him is appropriate (First Offenders Act, 1958, s. 1).

Where a magistrates' court has power (or would have but for this Act) to impose imprisonment on a person under 21 but not less than 12 or to deal with him for breach of a probation order, the court may order him to attend at an available attendance centre (C.J. Act, 1948, s. 19). See later.

A court (or justice) instead of imposing imprisonment on a person under 21 but not less than 14, may order him to be detained in a detention centre (C.J. Act, 1948, s. 18). See later.

A person under 21 but not less than 16 who is convicted of an offence punishable with imprisonment may be sentenced to Borstal (C.J Act 1948, s. 20). See " Borstal Institution," Chap. 28.

A person not less than 17 who is convicted under the provisions of the Act of an indictable offence by a magistrates' court may be committed in custody to Quarter Sessions for heavier sentence (M.C .Act, 1952, s. 29).

Appeal.—There is a right of appeal to Quarter Sessions under the C. and Y.P. Act, 1933, in connection with youthful offenders against an order committing to the care of a fit person, sending to an approved school, placing under supervision of a probation officer or other person, requiring recognisance to exercise proper care, requiring a contribution, altering payment of an affiliation order, requiring an automatic tobacco machine to be removed, etc. (s.102), requiring parent to pay the fine, etc. (s. 55), decision of Juvenile Court to which a case had been remitted (s. 56), directing local authority to pay contribution to approved school (s. 90) and variation of trust money (s. 91).

Remand Homes.—A county and a county borough council shall provide for its area remand homes where children and young persons may be kept in custody (C. and Y.P. Act, 1933, s. 77). Any juvenile who escapes or is taken away without lawful authority from a remand home (or from a person to whom he has been boarded out by the local authority, or from a person to whose care he has been committed, s. 85), may be arrested without warrant and brought back (see C. and Y.P. Act, 1956). It is a summary offence to assist or induce any such escape or to take away without lawful authority or to harbour or conceal or prevent from returning to a remand home or special reception centre any such juvenile (1933 Act, s. 78 and Schedule to 1952 Act and 1956 Act, s. 3). See the Remand Homes Rules, 1939.

Where a court (or justice) remands or commits for trial or sentence, in custody, a person under 14 he shall be committed to a remand home or special reception centre if under 12. If he is under 17 he shall be committed to a remand home unless too unruly or depraved (C.J. Act, 1948, s. 27). From a date to be specified no premises shall be used as a remand home unless approved by the Secretary of State who may make rules for the management of such homes (C.J. Act, 1948, s. 49) and cause them to be inspected (1948 Act, 9th Sched.).

Remand Centres.—These places of detention have been directed by the Criminal Justice Act, 1948. A remand centre is a place for the detention of persons not less than 14, but under 21, who are remanded or committed in custody for trial or sentence. They should have facilities for the observation of a prisoner's physical or mental condition (Prison Act, 1952, s. 43). If a person not less than 14 but under 17 is committed or remanded but is too unruly or depraved for a remand home, he should be sent to an available remand centre (C.J. Act, 1948, s. 27 (1)). A person of 16 to 21 committed in custody to Quarter Sessions with a view to Borstal training should go to a suitable available remand centre (M.C. Act, 1952, s. 28). A person not less than 14 but under 17, who is liable to imprisonment and is remanded in custody for inquiry into his physical or mental condition may be committed to a suitable available remand centre (M.C. Act, 1952, s. 26).

A court dealing with a case of a refractory young person (14-17), or one in need of care or protection, or supervision may, on interim order under s. 67 of the C. and Y.P. Act, 1933, commit the young person to an available remand centre for inquiry into his physical or mental condition. Also a young person too unruly or depraved for a remand home may be sent or removed, on such an interim order, to a suitable available remand centre (C.J. Act, 1948, s. 75). These centres will be set up gradually for particular areas.

Detention Centres.—These places of detention are to be established under the Criminal Justice Act, 1948. A detention centre is a place in which persons not less than 14 but under 21 may be detained for short periods under suitable discipline (Prison Act, 1952, s. 43). Where a court (or justice) has or would have had, but for this Act, power to impose imprisonment on a person under 21 but not less than 14, the court considering every other method (except imprisonment) is not appropriate, may order him to be detained in an available detention centre for 3 months, or less or up to 6 months in special circumstances. However a person cannot be sent to a detention centre if previously he was sentenced to imprisonment or Borstal training or had previously been, since the age of 17, in a detention centre (C.J. Act, 1948, s. 18). A child or young person found guilty of an offence and liable to imprisonment if he were an adult, can be committed for a month to a remand home (1933 Act, s. 54) but should be sent to a detention centre if 14 or over and if a suitable one is available (C.J. Act, 1948, s. 18). These centres will be available gradually to be regulated by the Detention Centre Rules, 1952.

Attendance Centres.—The establishment of these has been directed by the Criminal Justice Act, 1948. An attendance centre is a place at which offenders not less than 12 but under 21, may be ordered to attend at specified times to be given under supervision appropriate occupation and instruction. The Secretary of State may make arrangements for such places with any local or police authority (C.J. Act, 1948, s. 48). If a magistrates' court has or would have had but for this Act, power to impose imprisonment on a person not less than 12 but under 21, or to deal with such a person for breach of a probation order, the court may order him to attend at an available attendance centre for a number of hours not exceeding 12. Such an order may not be made in the case of certain previous offenders mentioned in the section. If the person fails to attend or contravenes the rules, he may be brought on summons or warrant before a magistrates' court and be dealt with for the original offence (C.J. Act, 1948, s. 19). The Attendance Centre Rules, 1958 deal with discipline, rules, records, etc. (C.J. Act, 1948, s. 52).

Approved Schools.—The Children Act, 1908, provided for Industrial Schools for those likely to grow up in the ways of crime and Reformatory Schools for youthful offenders. These provisions were repealed and replaced by those of the Children and Young Persons Act, 1933, as follows.

An approved school is a school approved by the Secretary of State (s. 107) for the education and training of persons sent there in pursuance of this 1933 Act, and which is carried on in accordance with the provisions of the Fourth Schedule to the Act (ss. 79, 80 and 81). See the Approved School Rules, 1933 and 1949.

Certain approved schools have been classified as suitable for persons of specified class or description and persons of such class or description should first be sent to the appropriate classifying school (C. and Y.P. (Amendment) Act, 1952, s. 6) where the allocation of the person sent there will be made to the school most suited to his needs.

Children and young persons may be ordered to approved schools under the following sections of the Act :—

(1) S. 62, as needing care or protection.

(2) S. 64 and s. 5, C. and Y.P. (Amendment) Act, 1952, as uncontrollable by parent or guardian.

(3) Non-compliance with a school attendance order (Education Act, 1944, s 40).

(4) S. 66, if under supervision, on the application of his probation officer.

(5) S. 57, when guilty of an offence punishable in the case of an adult with imprisonment.

(6) S. 84 (8), on application of the local authority to whose care they had been committed.

(7) S. 58, by order of the Secretary of State, in the cases specified in the section (certain juvenile offenders).

A Court shall not order a child under ten to an approved school unless for good reason it is satisfied he cannot be suitably dealt with otherwise (s. 44).

Regard must be had to the religious persuasion of the child or young person (s. 68).

The Court shall order the juvenile to be sent to the available approved school deemed most suitable to the case (s. 70 and s. 6 C. and Y.P. (Amendment) Act, 1952, re classifying schools) and pending the carrying into effect of the order, may remand him in custody or to the care of a fit person for periods not exceeding twenty-eight days (s. 69). The order shall state whether the local authority, the probation officer or the police authority is to be responsible for conveying the juvenile to his school (ss. 70, 72).

If a child or young person has been ordered to an approved school and cannot be found, and if a Magistrates' Court is satisfied on information that some person can produce him, the Court may issue a summons to such person to produce the child or young person in Court. If he fails to do so without reasonable excuse, he may be summarily convicted and fined. Also any person harbouring or concealing such child or young person is liable on summary conviction to imprisonment and (or) fine (s. 72).

A child may be detained in an approved school for three years from date of the order or until the expiration of 4 months after he ceases to be of compulsory school age (C.J. Act, 1948, s. 71). A young person under sixteen will be kept there for three years, and if he has attained the age of sixteen at date of the order he will be kept there until he is 19½ (1933 Act, s. 71, and C.J. Act, 1948, s. 72). If considered necessary and if the Secretary of State approves, a juvenile who has not been detained in Borstal or convicted of a grave crime (see s. 53) may be kept in an approved school for a further six months, provided that he is not to be detained after he attains the age of 19½ (1933 Act, s. 73, and C.J. Act, 1948, s. 72).

After discharge from an approved school the managers of the school have certain powers of supervision, and of recalling the person if he is under 19½ (1933 Act, s. 74, and C.J. Act, 1948, s. 72).

It is a summary offence for any person subject to a contribution order not to notify any change of address to the person entitled to receive the contributions (s. 87). See also ss. 86 to 91, and Part III of the Children Act, 1948, as regards contributions.

The Fourth Schedule to the 1933 Act provides for the administration of approved schools. A juvenile who escapes or is absent without leave from an approved school may be arrested without warrant and brought back to the school, and, with the authority of the Secretary of State may be brought at any time before a magistrates' court (1933 Act, s. 82, 1956 Act and C.J. Act, 1948, 9th Sched.). If a juvenile is guilty of serious misconduct in his approved school, the manager, with the authority of the Secretary of State, may bring him before a magistrates' court (1933 Act, 4th Sched.). In such cases the magistrates' court may make a new approved school order lasting if he was 16 or over until he is 19½, or extend his detention in the school by up to 6 months or if 16, sentence him possibly to Borstal training (C.J. Act, 1948, s. 72).

It is a summary offence to assist or induce a juvenile to escape or stay away, or to harbour or conceal such juvenile or to prevent him from returning to his school. If there is reasonable ground to believe that some person could produce the absentee, such person may be summoned to produce him and if he fails to do so without reasonable excuse, he may be summarily convicted and fined (s. 82).

Care of a Fit Person.—The Children and Young Persons Act, 1933, authorises a Court to make an order committing a child or young person to the care of any fit person, whether a relative or not, who is willing to undertake the care of him, and if considered advisable, to also make an order placing the juvenile under the supervision of a probation officer.

A local authority shall be a " fit person " for the purpose of such an order (s. 76).

This course may be directed in the following cases :—

(1) Where a Juvenile Court finds that a person under seventeen is in need of " care or protection " (s. 62).

(2) Where a Juvenile Court finds that a child (under 14) has not complied with a school attendance order (Education Act, 1944, s. 40).

(3) Where any Court finds a person under seventeen guilty of an offence punishable in the case of an adult with imprisonment (C. and Y.P. Act, 1933, s. 57).

(4) Where a person under seventeen was placed under supervision and his probation officer recommends it as desirable (s. 66)

(5) Pending decision as to what is to be done regarding a child or young person needing care or protection, etc., for periods each not exceeding twenty-eight days (s. 67).

(6) Pending the child or young person's departure to an approved school, for periods each not exceeding twenty-eight days (s. 69).

(7) In refractory cases (C. and Y.P. Act, 1938).

Such an order will normally remain in force until the juvenile is eighteen. His religious persuasion shall be considered and the fit person shall have the same rights and powers and the liabilities as to maintenance as if he were the parent, and the juvenile shall continue in his care (s. 75). If he runs away or is taken away without lawful authority he may be arrested without warrant and brought back to the person having the care of him, and if not received by such person may be brought before a Juvenile Court, and it is an offence to assist, etc., his escape (1933 Act, s. 85, Children Act, 1948, 3rd Sched. and Children and Young Persons Act, 1956, s. 1).

The Secretary of State may discharge a juvenile from such " care " and he may authorise his emigration (s. 84). A Juvenile Court, on the application of any person, may vary or revoke the order (s. 84, and s. 2, 1938 Act).

A contribution order may be made directing payments to the fit person (1933 Act, ss. 86-91, and Children Act, 1948, Part III). See " Approved Schools."

Voluntary Homes and Voluntary Organizations.—Children and Young Persons Act, 1933, Part V (ss. 92-94) and Children Act, 1948, Part IV (ss. 27-34). Voluntary homes are homes or other institutions for the boarding, care and maintenance of poor children (up to 18), supported wholly or partly by voluntary contribution or endowments, not being schools (1933 Act, s. 92, and 1948 Act, ss. 27, 28).

Such homes must be registered with the Secretary of State, who has power to cancel the registration of unsatisfactory homes and to require the local authority to remove and take care of the children. It will be a summary offence to carry on an unregistered " home " (1948 Act, s. 29).

The person in charge of such a home shall send particulars, as prescribed, to the Secretary of State every year and failure to do so will be a summary offence (1933 Act, s. 93).

Such a home is subject to government inspection and any obstruction of the inspector will be a summary offence and a search warrant may be obtained (1933 Act, s. 94)

The Secretary of State may, by regulations, control the conduct of such homes and any arrangements by voluntary organisations for the emigration of children or for the boarding out of children. Contravention will be a summary offence (1948 Act, s. 33).

If a child over compulsory school age was either in the care of the local authority or of a voluntary organization but is so no longer, the local authority, if necessary, shall advise and befriend him up to 18 or leave the voluntary organization to do so. If he goes to another area, the local authority of that area shall be informed (1948 Act, s. 34).

A voluntary organization means a body which carries on activities otherwise than for profit, but does not include any public or local authority (1948 Act, s. 59).

Harmful Publications:—The C. and Y.P. (Harmful Publications) Act, 1955 makes it a summary offence to print, publish, sell or let on hire or have for the purpose of sale or letting on hire any book, magazine, etc. consisting wholly or mainly of stories told in pictures portraying the commission of crimes or acts of violence or cruelty or repulsive or horrible incidents in such a way as would tend to corrupt a child or young person (under 17) into whose hands it might fall or be likely to fall. Prosecution can be only by or with the consent of the Attorney General. A search warrant under the Act may be obtained. Importation of such works, their printing plates and films is prohibited.

Ages fixed by Law.

Under 1. Death of such infant caused by mother may be infanticide. F. (Infanticide Act, 1938.)

Under 2. Abandoning or exposing such child so as to endanger life or health. M. (Offences against Person Act, 1861, s. 27.)

Under 3. Suffocation of such child in bed caused by drunkenness of person over 16. O. (C. & Y.P. Act, 1933, s 1.)

Under 5. Intoxicants must not be given to such child unless for a good reason. O. (C. & Y.P. Act, 1933, s. 5.) Minding for reward such children from more than one household needs registration. (Nurseries and Child Minders Act, 1948, ss. 1, 4.)

Over 5. Education compulsory (Education Act, 1944, s. 35.)

Over 5 to 15. Person habitually wandering from place to place with such child and unable to prove that child gets efficient education. O. (C. & Y.P. Act, 1933, s. 10; Education Act, 1944, 8th Sched.)

Under 7. Drunk in charge of such child in public place or licensed premises. O. (Licensing Act, 1902, s. 2.)

Under 8. Not criminally responsible for his acts (C. & Y.P. Act, 1933, s. 50).

Under 10. Approved school :—normally ought not to be sent there unless Court considers child cannot be suitably dealt with otherwise (C. & Y.P. Act, 1933, s. 44).

Under 12.   Such child must not be trained in dangerous performances (C. & Y.P. Act, 1933, s. 24).

Exposing child under 12 to risk of burning or scalding in a room (C. & Y.P. Acts, 1933, s. 11 and 1952, s. 8).

Child under 12 may be sent to a special reception centre (C. & Y.P. (Amendment) Act, 1952 s. 3).

Over 12.   May be licensed to take part on week days in public entertainments (by the Local Authority) (s. 22), or to be trained in performances of a dangerous nature (by a Court). (C. & Y.P. Act, 1933, s. 24.)

Under 13.   Defilement of girl under thirteen. Sexual Offences Act, 1956, s. 5.

Occupier, etc., of premises inducing or suffering her to be there for that purpose. Sexual Offences Act, 1956, s. 25.

Gunpowder must not be sold to such child. **O.** (Explosives Act, 1875, s. 31.)

Prohibited from riding on or driving vehicles, machinery or implements used in agriculture. (Agriculture (Safety, Health and Welfare Provisions) Act, 1956).

Under 14.   Such person is a " child " (C. & Y.P. Act, 1933, s. 107) and if over 8 is in law responsible for offences (except rape). If proved to have sufficient capacity to know what he or she is doing, should be dealt with by a Juvenile Court (1933 Act, s. 46) except for homicide (Magistrates Courts Act, 1952, s. 21), and may not be fined more than 40s. (M.C. Act, 1952, s. 32). He may be sent to a remand home (C. & Y.P. Act, 1933, s. 54) or to an approved school (s. 57).

If remanded or committed in custody he should be sent to a remand home (Criminal Justice Act, 1948, s. 27 (1)).

" Child " of tender years who does not understand the nature of an oath may give unsworn evidence in offence cases if of sufficient intelligence and understands the duty of speaking the truth. (C. & Y.P. Act, 1933, s. 38.)

Court :—must not be in a Court unless as defendant or witness or a child in arms (1933 Act, s. 36).

Employment abroad for singing, etc., for profit prohibited. (C. & Y.P. Act, 1933, ss. 25, 26.)

Entertainments :—taking part in is prohibited where charge is made for admission, unless child is twelve or over and duly licensed by the Education Authority. **O.** However, may occasionally do so where no private profit goes to promoters, provided that this will not apply in liquor licensed premises unless place is licensed for entertainments or two Justices approve. (C. & Y.P. Act, 1933, s. 22.)

Firearm or ammunition (except 20 in. shotgun or airgun, etc.)—must not have nor may they be lent or given (or sold) to him. **O.** (Firearms Act, 1937, s. 19.)

Kidnapping or knowingly harbouring such child when stolen. **F.** (Offences Against Person Act, 1861, s. 56).

Licensed premises :—must not be in the bar during permitted hours unless resident or merely passing through or in railway refreshment rooms. (Licensing Act, 1953, s.126.)

Licensed premises :—Must not be sent there for or supplied with intoxicants except in properly closed vessels. (Licensing Act, 1953, s. 128.)

Pawnbroker must not take pawn from such child. **O.** (C. & Y.P. Act, 1933, s. 8.)

Rags dealer :—must not give child any article whatsoever. (Public Health Act, 1936, s. 154.)

Rape :—such a boy cannot be convicted of rape or carnal knowledge, but may be for indecent assault.

Over **14.** Is a " young person " up to 17 (C. & Y.P. Act, 1933, s. 107) and is responsible criminally for acts. He should consent to any requirements in a probation order (C.J. Act, 1948, s. 3 (5)). If in custody for an offence a summary court may order his finger prints to be taken by the police (Magistrates' Courts Act, 1952, s. 40).

Under **15.** Education is compulsory. A person under 15 who does not comply with a school attendance order may be sent to an approved school or to care of fit person or be placed under supervision, and the parent or guardian is punishable. Employment of such person is limited under s. 18 of C. & Y.P. Act, 1933 and any byelaws made thereunder. (Education Act, 1944, ss. 35, 40, 44, 58, and 8th Sched.)

Any person who for reward, receives a " foster child " of compulsory school age must notify the local authority, also any change of residence or its death or removal (Children Act, 1958).

The law protects such children under compulsory school age who are maintained for reward apart from their parents (Children Act, 1948, s. 5).

Quarter Sessions, Assizes or Magistrates' Courts shall

not impose imprisonment on him (Crim. Justice Act, 1948, s. 17 (1)).

Over 15. A child of 15 in the care of the local authority may be placed in a local authority hostel until he is 21 (Children Act, 1948, s. 13).

Under 16. Abduction of such girl. (Sexual Offences Act, 1956, s. 20.)

Alien:—need not register until aged sixteen. (Aliens Order, 1953, Arts. 14, 19.)

Begging :—causing or procuring or allowing such person to be in any place for alms. **O.** (C. & Y.P. Act, 1933, s. 4.)

Brothel :—if aged four and under 16 must not be allowed by person having charge to reside in or frequent a brothel. **M.** (C. & Y.P. Act, 1933, s. 3.)

Tobacco or cigarette papers must not be sold to such person unless to a boy messenger in uniform or an employee in the trade, for others. (C. & Y.P. Act, 1933, s. 7.)

Cruelty :—to such person by person over 16. **M.** (C. & Y.P. Act, 1933, s. 1.)

Dangerous performances :—causing, procuring or allowing such person to take part in same in public (C. & Y.P. Act, 1933, s. 23), or the training for same except when over 12 and on licence. **O.** (s. 24.)

Defilement of girl of thirteen and under sixteen. (Sexual Offences Act, 1956, s. 6.)

Occupier, etc., of premises inducing or knowingly suffering her to be there for that purpose. (Sexual Offences Act, 1956, s. 26.)

Indecent assault on person under 16:—consent no defence. (Sexual Offences Act, 1956, ss. 14, 15.)

Marriage of person under sixteen is void. (Marriage Act, 1949, s. 2.)

Motor vehicle :—Such person must not drive a motor vehicle on a road and must not take out a driving licence. (Road Traffic Act, 1930, s. 9.)

Old metal must not be purchased by dealers from such person. **O.** (C. & Y.P. Act, 1933, s. 9.)

Seduction, prostitution, unlawful carnal knowledge or indecent assault on such girl must not be caused or encouraged by person having charge of her. (Sexual Offences Act, 1956, s. 28.)

Smoking by such person in public place entails seizure of the tobacco and cigarette papers. (C. & Y.P. Act, 1933, s. 7.)

Street betting with such person is a serious offence **O.** or **M.** (Street Betting Act, 1906.)

Street trading by such person is prohibited, except when allowed by byelaw for young person employed by parent. (C. & Y.P. Act, 1933, s. 20.)

Parent of such child who is in the care of the local authority shall keep the authority informed of his address. **O.** (Children Act, 1948, s. 10.)

Over 16.   Borstal institution :—may be sent there if over 16 and under 21. (Crim. Justice Act, 1948, s. 20.)

Incest :—female of sixteen or over who consents to incest against herself. (Sexual Offences Act, 1956, s. 11.)

Indictment of such person for manslaughter of person under sixteen or infanticide may result in conviction for cruelty. (C. & Y.P. Act, 1933, s. 1.)

Motor cycle or invalid carriage only may be driven on a road by such person who is under 17. (Road Traffic Act, 1930, s. 9.)

Licensed premises :—Such person (16-18) may have beer, porter, perry or cider with a meal not in the bar. Licensing Act, 1953, s. 129.)

Under 17.   If over 14 such person is a " young person " (C. & Y.P. Act, 1933, s. 107), and is responsible in law for his or her offences. Must be dealt with by a Juvenile Court except when jointly charged with a person of 17 or over, or where another, over 17, is charged with aiding, etc., the offence (s. 46), or for homicide. Can be dealt with summarily by consent for any indictable offence except homicide. Any fine must not exceed £10 (Magistrates' Courts Act 1952, s. 20).

Approved school :—may be sent there. But if under 10 only for very good reason (C. & Y.P. Act, 1933, ss. 44, 57.)

Bail :—at a police station must be released on bail unless good reason to the contrary. (C. & Y.P. Act, 1933, s. 32.)

Care of fit person:—may be committed to. (C. & Y.P. Act, 1933, ss. 57, 69, 84, 85.)

Care or protection :—when such is required Court may deal with him. (C. & Y.P. Act, 1933, ss. 61-63.)

Employment abroad :—may be taken to a place of safety if about to go abroad for singing, etc., for profit, without the necessary licence. (C. & Y.P. Act, 1933, s. 26.)

Firearm or ammunition :—must not purchase or hire and same must not be sold or hired to such person. **O.** (Firearms Act, 1937, s. 19.)

Pedlar's certificate must not be issued to such person.
(Pedlars Acts, 1871 and 1881.),

Prisoners :—must not be allowed to associate with
adult prisoners except relatives or persons jointly
charged. A girl must be under care of a woman.
(C. & Y.P. Act, 1933, s. 31.)

Such person, if refractory and uncontrollable, may
be sent to an approved school or put on probation
or committed to the care of a fit person. (C. & Y.P.
Act, 1933, s. 64, and 1938 Act, s. 1.)

A summary court shall not impose imprisonment on
him (Magistrates' Courts Act, 1952, s. 107).

Instead of committal to a remand home, a court (or
justice) may send a young person (14-17) to an
available detention centre. (Criminal Justice Act,
1948, s. 18 (4)).

If a magistrates' court or justice remand or commit a
young person (14-17) in custody he should be
sent to a remand home unless too unruly or
depraved (Criminal Justice Act, 1948, s. 27 (1)).

Where a young person (14-17) is remanded in custody
by a court or justice for inquiry into his physical
or mental condition he may be sent to an available
remand centre (Magistrates' Courts Act, 1952, s. 26).

If the young person is before a court for care or
protection and inquiry into his physical or mental
condition is desirable, the court can send him,
on an interim order, to an available remand centre
(Criminal Justice Act, 1948, s. 75).

If the young person is remanded or committed in
custody to Quarter Sessions for Borstal training he
should go to a remand home unless too unruly or
depraved (Magistrates' Courts Act, 1952, s. 28).

The local authority shall provide for such a juvenile
who is abandoned, lost, etc., and keep him in
its care until he is 18 (Children Act, 1948, s. 1).

Must not be in sole charge of an aircraft in motion
(Air Navigation Order, Art. 9, B).

Over 17.   Such person is an " adult."

Motor car (and motor cycle and invalid carriage)
may be driven on a road by a duly licensed person
of seventeen. (Road Traffic Act, 1930, s. 9.)

A magistrates' court which convicts him of an
indictable offence may commit him, in custody, to
Quarter Sessions for heavier sentence (Magistrates'
Courts Act, 1952, s. 29).

Under 18.   Abduction of such unmarried girl with unlawful and
carnal intent. (Sexual Offences Act, 1956, s. 19.)

Betting with such person on any " track," and his employment for betting work on any track, is prohibited. **O.** (Betting and Lotteries Act, 1934, s. 15.)

Employment of such persons over fifteen and under eighteen may be regulated by byelaws. **O.** (C. & Y.P. Act, 1933, ss. 19, 20, Education Act, 1944, 8th Sched.)

Employment abroad to sing, etc., for profit is prohibited unless over fourteen and with licence. (C. & Y.P. Act, 1933, s. 25.)

Licensed premises :—intoxicants must not be supplied for consumption by him on the premises except beer, porter, cider or perry with a meal to a person of 16-18. **O.** (Licensing Act, 1953, s. 129.)

Public Service vehicle :—must not be licensed as a conductor. (Road Traffic Act, 1930, s. 77.)

The protection provisions of the Children Act, 1948- may continue to apply until such a lost, abandoned child is 18 (s.1) and the local authority may assume parental rights (s. 2).

Such a person remains a " child " as far as the Children Act, 1948, is concerned (s. 59), and within Part I of the Children Act, 1958 (s. 17).

Over 18. Care of a fit person shall cease when juvenile is eighteen. (C. & Y.P. Act, 1933, s. 75.)

Over 19½. Approved school :—detention should cease at nineteen and a half. (C. & Y.P. Act, 1933, ss. 58, 73, and Crim. Justice Act, 1948, s. 72.)

Under 21. Abduction of such girl on account of her fortune with intent to marry or carnally know her. (Sexual Offences Act, 1956, s. 18.)

Betting circulars must not be sent to such person. **M.** (Betting and Loans (Infants) Act, 1892, s. 1.)

Borstal Institution may be ordered if over sixteen and under twenty-one. (Crim. Justice Act, 1948, s. 20.)

When committed or remanded in custody by a magistrates' court for Borstal training he should be sent to an available remand centre, and if not, to prison, but if under 17 he may be sent to a remand home unless too unruly or depraved (Magistrates' Courts Act, 1952, s. 28).

Loans circulars must not be sent to such person. **M.** (Betting and Loans (Infants) Act, 1892, s. 2.)

Motors :—locomotives, tractors and heavy motor cars must not be driven on a road by such person except tractors used primarily for work on land in connection with agriculture (Road Traffic Act, 1930,

s. 9, and Emergency Laws (Misc. Provisions) Act, 1953, Sched. 1.)

Procuration of such a girl for unlawful carnal connection. (Sexual Offences Act, 1956, s. 23.)

Public service vehicle :—must not be licensed as a driver. (Road Traffic Act, 1930 s. 77.)

No court or justice shall impose imprisonment on him unless no other method of dealing with him is appropriate (Crim. Justice Act, 1948, s. 17 (2)).

If 12 and up to 21 he can be ordered to attend at an attendance centre instead of imprisonment or for breach of a probation order (Crim. Justice Act, 1948, s. 19).

If remanded or committed in custody and 17 or over or if over 14 and too unruly or depraved he should be sent to an available remand centre (Crim. Justice Act, 1948, s. 27).

Marriage on the authority of a certificate from a superintendent registrar, of a person under 21 who is not a widow or widower requires consent of parent or guardian or Court, as perscribed by s. 3, Marriage Act, 1949.

Of or over 21 If a first offender, a magistrates' court cannot impose imprisonment on him unless no other method is appropriate (First Offenders Act, 1958, s. 1).

Over 21.   If a persistent offender he can be sentenced to corrective training (Crim. Justice Act, 1948, s. 21 (1)).

Under 24.   In the case of a man under 24 his reasonable belief that the girl was sixteen or over, will be a defence on the first occasion on which he is charged with the defilement of a girl of thirteen and under sixteen. (Sexual Offences Act, 1956, s. 6.)

30 *or over.*   If a " persistent offender " he can be sentenced to preventive detention (Crim. Justice Act, 1948, s. 21 (2)).

NOTE.—The above ages refer to males and females unless otherwise indicated. A person attains a given age at the first moment of the day preceding his birthday, see note, 95 J.P. 172.

PART III.—OFFENCES IN CONNECTION WITH PROPERTY

Chapter XIII

BREAKING IN

Contents

Breaking into Premises.—Any breaking into premises with felonious intent is a serious felony punishable with imprisonment.

At Common Law the breaking and entering of the dwelling-house of another or of a church in the night-time with intent to commit a felony therein, was known as burglary and was punishable by death, but any breaking in by day was only a misdemeanour.

Night and day breakings in are now provided against by the Larceny Act, 1916, and may be classified as burglary, housebreaking and sacrilege.

Burglary.—The felony of burglary is committed by any person who :—

(1) In the night breaks and enters the dwelling-house of another with intent to commit a felony therein, or

(2) In the night breaks out of the dwelling-house of another, having entered the said dwelling-house with intent to commit a felony therein or having committed any felony in the said dwelling-house (s. 25).

Four points must be considered and proved, viz. :—

(1) *The time.* It must be night-time—that is, the interval between 9 P.M. and 6 A.M. (s. 46). The breaking must have taken place during night-time. If breaking precedes entering both must have taken place at night though not necessarily on the same night. When entry precedes breaking the entry need not have taken place at night.

(2) *The place.* It must be a dwelling-house in which people habitually sleep or any building accessory to the dwelling-house, occupied along with it and communicating with it either directly or by means of a covered and enclosed passage (s. 46 (2)). " Dwelling-house " means some permanent structure in which some person or persons habitually sleep as member or members of the household that occupies and dwells in it. A dwelling-house remains a " dwelling-house " even though the residents are absent, provided such absence is temporary and there is an intention of returning. If a dwelling-house is divided into several distinct sets of chambers or rooms each is a " dwelling-house."

(3) *The manner.* There must be a breaking and an entering. The breaking may be either :—

(*a*) Actual, as occurs when the burglar disturbs any of the means provided for keeping people out. There need not be an actual breaking of anything ; it will be sufficient to turn a key or lift a latch or raise a closed window. It is not " burglary " to enter by an open door or window, but after such a non-burglarious entry it would be burglary to subsequently break an inner door. Entry by use of a false key would amount to a " breaking."

(*b*) Constructive, which occurs when admission is obtained by getting some inmate of the house, by force or by fraud, to open. For example, entrance on threats of violence, or by knocking at the door and securing entry on pretence of having legitimate business inside.

There must be some entering of the dwelling-house, and the least insertion of some part of the body is sufficient. If there is no bodily entry but an instrument is used to break the premises, it is not burglary unless the instrument was inserted to effect the contemplated felony, i.e. to hook out goods or to shoot a person.

If there is a breaking but no proof of entry, the offender may be convicted of the attempt to commit burglary.

Burglary is also committed when a person " breaks out " in the night-time, after a previous entry with intent to commit felony or after committing a felony therein.

(4) *The intent.* There must be an intent to commit some felony, whether executed or not. For example to steal, to kill, to commit rape. This felonious intention must exist at the time of breaking and entering, and evidence should be given of the facts from which the intent may be presumed. If the intent is to commit a misdemeanour it is not burglary.

Night Offences akin to Burglary.—The Larceny Act, 1916 also deals with some night offences which are akin to burglary but which do not amount to burglary. These crimes are :—

Entering any dwelling-house in the night-time with intent to commit a felony. In such a case there is no breaking. The offence is felony (s. 27 (1)).

Being found by night armed with any dangerous or offensive weapon or instrument with intent to break or enter into any building and to commit any felony therein. M. (S. 28 (1)).

Being found by night having in possession without lawful excuse (the proof whereof lies on the accused) any key, picklock, crow, jack, bit or other housebreaking implement. M. (S. 28 (2)). Almost anything may be such an instrument.

Being found by night with face blackened or disguised with intent to commit any felony. M. (S. 28 (3)).

Being found by night in any building with intent to commit any felony therein. M. (S. 28 (4)).

Any person to whom any property is offered to be sold, pawned or delivered, if he has reasonable cause to suspect that any offence has been committed against this Act with respect to such property, shall, if it is in his power, arrest the person offering the same and take him and such property before a justice (s. 41).

Any person may arrest without warrant any person found committing any of the above offences, and a constable may arrest without warrant any person he finds lying or loitering in any highway, yard or other place during the night whom he has good cause to suspect of having committed or being about to commit any felony against the Act (s. 41). " Night " in the Larceny Act, 1916, means the interval between 9 P.M. and 6 A.M. on the following day (s. 46). See " Loiterers and Suspected Persons," Chap. 28.

Housebreaking.—Only a misdemeanour at common law, housebreaking is now a felony by the Larceny Act, 1916, and it consists of :—

(1) The breaking and entering of any dwelling-house or any building within the curtilage thereof and occupied therewith, or any schoolhouse, shop, warehouse, counting-house, office, store, garage, pavilion, factory, workshop or Government, municipal or public building, and committing any felony therein (s. 26 (1)), or

(2) The breaking out of the same, having committed any felony therein (s. 26 (2)), or

(3) The breaking and entering of the same or of any place of Divine worship, or any building within the curtilage, with intent to commit any felony therein (s. 27 (2)), or

(4) Entering any dwelling-house in the night with intent to commit any felony therein (s. 27 (1)).

Housebreaking differs from burglary in that it extends to a wider range of buildings, including shops, offices and stores, whereas burglary is confined to dwelling-houses. Also burglary must occur during the night-time (9 P.M. to 6 A.M.), while housebreaking, except for the one case of entering (without breaking) a dwelling-house in the night with felonious intent (s. 27 (1)), may take place at any time.

Premises were broken into and property stolen. Very shortly afterwards a person was found in possession of the stolen property which is good evidence of the house-breaking. It is not " receiving " as a man cannot receive from himself (*R*. v. *Loughlin* (1951)).

Any person may arrest without warrant any person found housebreaking (s. 41).

The curtilage is a court or enclosed space attached to a dwelling-house.

Sacrilege.—Larceny Act, 1916, s. 24. The felony of sacrilege is committed by :—

(1) Breaking and entering any place of Divine worship and committing any felony therein, or

(2) Breaking out of any place of Divine worship, having committed any felony therein.

This felony may be committed at any time and in respect to any place of Divine worship. The breaking and entering of a place of Divine worship with felonious intent is housebreaking (s. 27 (2)). See above.

Any person has power to arrest without warrant any person found committing this felony of sacrilege (s. 41).

As regards persons found in premises for any unlawful purpose, found in possession of housebreaking implements, or found armed with intent to commit felony (Vagrancy Act, 1824), see " Loiterers and Suspected Persons," Chap. 28.

Any expression of " time " in any Act of Parliament unless otherwise stated means Greenwich mean time (Statutes (Definition of Time) Act, 1880), but where there is any reference to a point of time in any enactment, regulation, rule, document, etc., the time referred to shall, during summer time, be deemed to be the time as fixed for general purposes by these Acts (Summer Time Act, 1922, and later Acts).

Chapter XIV

LARCENY

Contents

Larceny in General.—Stealing or depriving a person of his property was from the earliest times regarded as a serious offence. It was called larceny, and was a felony at common law. It has been defined as the felonious taking and carrying away of the personal goods of another with the intention of depriving the rightful owner of same.

The crime at common law was only possible in connection with personal goods of some value. There had to be a taking and moving of the goods, because change of possession was the root of the idea of theft.

Various statutes made the stealing of many specific articles larceny, thus supplementing the Common Law, and section 1 of the Larceny Act, 1916, has given a statutory definition of stealing.

Forms of Stealing.—The stealing of another's property may be committed either by violence or without violence. Breaking into premises is usually followed by stealing, but the various forms of this crime have already been treated as distinct offences. See " Breaking into Premises," Chap. 13.

The main forms of crime in connection with the stealing or depriving a person dishonestly of his property are as follows :—

(1) Larceny. See " Larceny by Statute," which deals with simple larceny, stealing from the person, larceny in a dwelling-house, larceny by a servant or by a bailee, larceny by mistake or by finding, and other larcenies by statute.

(2) Stealing from the person with violence. See " Robbery."

(3) Larceny by means of fraud. See " Larceny by Trick."

(4) Obtaining goods by false pretences. See " False Pretences."

(5) Embezzlement or the stealing of property on the way to its owner. See " Embezzlement."

(6) Frauds by agents, trustees, etc. See " Conversion."

(7) Offences in relation to bankruptcy. See " Bankruptcy Offences."

(8) False personation for wrongdoing. See " Personation."

(9) Receiving property knowing it to have been stolen. See " Receiving Stolen Property."

" Blackmailing," or the obtaining or endeavouring to obtain money, etc., from another by threats, is dealt with under " Threats and Menaces," Chap. 8.

Property and Possession.—These terms are used in distinguishing the various forms of stealing and need explanation.

When a person owns a thing he is said to have the property in it—that is, his right to have it and enjoy it as against everyone else, his right of ownership. See " Property in General," Chap. 18.

When a person has control over a thing he is said to have possession of it, and his possession may be actual and physical or constructive. Constructive possession is a legal possession though not actually physical ; for example, a person keeps a thing in his house or in some place over which he exercises control, or he leaves it in the control of his servant, as in the case of his driver, while out with his car. When a man becomes owner of a thing he acquires the property in it, and when it comes under his control he gets possession of it. He may part with possession but still retain his property in a thing, e.g. by lending it or entrusting it to a bailee.

If the owner loses possession by stealing (either furtively or by means of a trick), but has not given up his property in the article, it is larceny, a felony.

If the owner does not get possession of a thing in which he has the property and it is stolen by certain persons when it is on the way into his possession, it is embezzlement, a felony.

If the owner hands over the possession of and the property in an article, induced to do so by false representation, it is false pretences, a misdemeanour.

If the owner gives credit on the strength of some fraud and is thereby at a loss, it is obtaining credit by fraud, which is a statutory misdemeanour.

The expression " property " as fully defined in s. 46 of the Larceny Act, 1916, includes any real or personal property, money, debts and legacies, documents giving title to property and any property into or for which the same has been converted or exchanged and anything acquired by such conversion or exchange.

Larceny by Statute.—The Larceny Act, 1916, defines stealing as follows :—

S. 1.   For the purposes of this Act :—

(1) A person steals who, without the consent of the owner, fraudulently and without a claim of right made in good faith,

takes and carries away anything capable of being stolen, with intent at the time of such taking permanently to deprive the owner thereof.

Provided that a person may be guilty of stealing any such thing notwithstanding that he has lawful possession thereof, if, being a bailee or part owner thereof, he fraudulently converts the same to his own use or to the use of any person other than the owner.

(2) (i) The expression " takes " includes obtaining the possession :—

(a) by any trick ;

(b) by intimidation ;

(c) under a mistake on the part of the owner, with knowledge on the part of the taker that possession has been so obtained ;

(d) by finding, where at the time of the finding the finder believes that the owner can be discovered by taking reasonable steps.

(ii) The expression " carries away " includes any removal of anything from the place which it occupies, but in the case of a thing attached, only if it has been completely detached.

(iii) The expression " owner " includes any part owner or person having possession or control of or a special property in anything capable of being stolen.

(3) Everything which has value, and is the property of any person, and if adhering to the realty then after severance therefrom, shall be capable of being stolen.

Provided that (a) save as expressly provided in the Act with respect to fixtures, growing things and ore from mines, anything attached to or forming part of the realty shall not be capable of being stolen by the person who severs the same from the realty, unless after severance he has abandoned possession thereof ; and (b) the carcase of a creature wild by nature and not reduced into possession while living, shall not be capable of being stolen by the person who has killed such creature, unless after killing it he has abandoned possession of the carcase.

Notes on this definition.—A bailee is a person entrusted with property for some purpose, usually to re-deliver to the owner or to deliver to somebody else, e.g. a tailor given a coat to repair or a messenger given a parcel to deliver. A bailee can commit larceny of the goods entrusted to him or fraudulent conversion (see " Conversion "), or may unlawfully pawn them. (See " Pawnbrokers," Chap. 31.)

The stealing must be without the consent of the owner. His consent must be a true consent, not consent induced by deceit, as in the case of larceny by trick. See " Larceny by Trick."

As a general rule a person cannot steal his own property, but he may steal his own property from his bailee or from a person who has some special property in it.

If the taker has acted under a *bona fide* claim of right it will not be larceny.

An example of larceny by mistake would be where a man receives too much money in change and, knowing that a mistake has been made, keeps the excess money.

As regards finding, when a person finds an article he should take reasonable steps to discover the owner, such as reporting the matter to the police or to the occupier of the premises on which he finds the article. If an article has been lost or mislaid under circumstances that would enable the owner to find it, e.g. leaving a bag in a hired vehicle, any appropriation of it by another person would be larceny.

To constitute larceny of things attached to the realty (such as growing grass) or of carcases of wild creatures, such things or carcases must have been first detached or killed and then abandoned, and the taker must have then come (or returned) and taken them away. When anything attached to the land (such as grass) has been severed from the land it is still the property of the owner of the land and is capable of being stolen.

If ownership of an article has been abandoned and nobody has any claim to it a taker cannot be found guilty of larceny unless there is evidence of felonious intent.

Acts of Parliament (see later) provide for the larceny of very many specified articles, some of which were not the subject of larceny at Common Law.

If the taking has been in the nature of a borrowing, the taker intending at the time not to deprive the owner permanently of the thing, it is not larceny. However the taking wrongfully of another person's property but without intention to steal it (a bicycle in this case) followed later by action showing intention to deprive the owner permanently of his property amounts to larceny (*R*. v. *Riley* (1853) and *Ruse* v. *Reed* (1949)). See later for " Taking of a motor vehicle." Larceny may be committed even though the taking was not for the benefit of the thief or even for anyone's benefit, so long as there was an intent to deprive the owner permanently.

Simple larceny is stealing for which no special punishment is provided by any statute, and is a felony punishable with imprisonment not exceeding five years (Larceny Act, 1916, s. 2). This s.2 does not create an offence, it merely arranges the penalty. Larceny is a felony at Common Law. Directions as to other penalties are given in s. 37 of the Act as amended by C.J. Act, 1948, 10th Sched.

Compound larceny is stealing accompanied by circumstances of an aggravated nature and for which special punishment is provided by Act of Parliament, varying in severity in different cases. Thus by the sections of the Larceny Acts, larceny aggravated from the nature of the person, place or thing concerned is liable to punishment varying from imprisonment for life down to fine.

A trial for larceny may take place where the offence was committed or where the accused was arrested or is in custody or where he has the stolen property in his possession. (M.C. Act, 1952, ss. 2, 3; C.J. Act, 1925, s. 11 and Larceny Act, 1916, s. 39.)

Statutory Larcenies (Larceny Acts, 1861 and 1916).

(1) *Larceny from the person.*

Stealing any property from the person of another. F. Fourteen years. (1916 Act, s. 14.)

For stealing from the person with violence. See " Robbery."

(2) *Larceny by particular persons.*

Clerk or servant stealing any property belonging to or in the possession or power of his employer. F. Fourteen years. (1916 Act, s. 17 (1).)

Person employed in the public service of the Crown or in the police stealing any property of the Crown or in his possession by virtue of his employment. F. Fourteen years. (1916 Act, s. 17 (2).)

Officer of the Post Office stealing or embezzling a postal packet in course of transmission by post. F. Imprisonment for life or seven years. (1916 Act, s. 18.) See " Post Office," Chap. 26.

Officer of the Bank of England or Ireland stealing any money, security, etc., belonging to or entrusted to such bank. F. Imprisonment for life. (1916 Act, s. 19.)

Tenant or lodger stealing any chattel or fixture let to him with any house or lodging. F. (1916 Act, s. 16.) See " Landlord and Tenant," Chap. 29.

For kindred offences see " Embezzlement " and " Conversion."

(3) *Larceny in particular places.*

Houses. Stealing in a dwelling-house any property (*a*) either to the value of £5 or more (triable summarily with accused's consent M.C. Act, 1952, ss. 19, 20 and 1st Sched.) or (*b*) by putting any person therein in bodily fear by menaces or threats. F. Fourteen years. (1916 Act, s. 13.)

Ships, docks or wrecks. Stealing any goods in vessels in ports, canals, or rivers, or from docks, or from wrecks or vessels in distress. F. Fourteen years. (1916 Act, s. 15.)

Workshops, etc. Stealing any textile goods in process of manufacture, to the value of 10s., in any building, field or place. F. Fourteen years. (1916 Act, s. 9.)

Mines. Stealing the ore of any metal or any coal from a mine. F. (1916 Act, s. 11.) Miners removing or concealing any ore with intent to defraud the owner, etc. F. (1861 Act, s. 39.)

(4) *Larceny of particular things.*

Animals. Stealing any horse, cattle or sheep. F. Fourteen years. (1916 Act, s. 3.)

Killing any animal with intent to steal the carcase, skin or any part of the animal killed is felony if the stealing of the animal would have amounted to felony. (1916 Act, s. 4.)

It is an offence to steal deer (see " Larceny of Animals," Chap. 35), hares and rabbits (see " Poaching Offences," Chap. 19), dogs (see " Dogs," Chap. 35), domestic animals (see " Larceny of Animals," Chap. 35), domestic birds (see " Birds," Chap. 35), fish (see " Fishery Laws," Chap. 19).

Documents. Stealing any document of title to lands, or any document of any Court or other legal document, or any original document relating to the business of any public office. F. (1916 Act, s. 7.)

Fraudulently destroying, etc., any valuable security or any document of title to lands. F. (1861 Act, ss. 27 and 28.) Fraudulently removing or unlawfully and maliciously injuring or destroying any original document belonging to any Court. F. (1861 Act, s. 30.)

Electricity. Maliciously or fraudulently abstracting, diverting or using any electricity. F. (1916 Act, s. 10.)

Fences. Stealing any part of any fence, stile, or gate, or not satisfactorily accounting for the possession of any part of any fence, stile, or gate, value at least 1s. Summary offence. (1861 Act, ss. 34 and 35.)

Fixtures. Stealing the glass or woodwork of a building, any metal or utensil or fixture fixed in or to any building, anything metal fixed in land or as a fence or in any street, square, public place or burial ground. F. (1916 Act, s. 8 (1).)

Fruits, vegetables, etc. Stealing, destroying or damaging with intent to steal any plant, root, fruit or vegetable production growing in any garden, orchard, pleasure ground, hothouse, etc. Summary offence (1861 Act, s. 36) ; and after a previous summary conviction for same. F. (1916 Act, s. 8 (3).) Stealing any cultivated root or plant used for the food of man or beast or for medicine, distilling, dyeing, or any manufacture, and growing in any land, open or enclosed, not being a garden, orchard, pleasure or nursery ground. Summary offence. (1861 Act, s. 37.)

Postal packets (mails). Stealing a mail bag, or any postal packet in course of transmission by post, or any property out of such postal packet, or stopping a mail with intent to rob the mail. F. Imprisonment for life. (1916 Act, s. 12.) See " Post Office," Chap. 26.

Trees and shrubs. Stealing the whole or any part of any tree or shrub wheresoever growing (value 1s. at least) or being in possession of same and not satisfactorily accounting for same. Summary offence (1861 Act, ss. 33 and 35) ; but after two previous summary convictions for same. F. (1916 Act, s. 8 (2).)

Stealing the whole or any part of any tree or shrub growing in any park, gardens or grounds (value exceeding £1), or growing anywhere (value exceeding £5). F. (1916 Act, s. 8 (2).)

Water and gas—if stored in pipes or reservoirs for sale or use—may be the subject of larceny at common law, and as same have value and are the property of a person (1916 Act, s. 1 (3) and s. 2) it would appear that larceny by statute is possible. See Water Act, 1945, Sched. III, s. 66, and Gas Act, 1948, Sched. III (29) for fraudulent acts.

Wills. Stealing any will or other testamentary disposition. F. Imprisonment for life. (1916 Act, s. 6.) Fraudulently destroying, obliterating or concealing any will or codicil during the life of the testator or after his death. F. (1861 Act, s. 29.)

Power of Arrest without Warrant.—In addition to the common law power of arrest without warrant for felony, the Larceny Acts (ss. 103 and 104 of 1861 Act and s. 41 of 1916 Act) give wide power of arrest without warrant to constables and to private persons as follows :—

(1) Any person may arrest without warrant any person found committing any offence under the Larceny Acts (except angling in the daytime, 1861 Act, s. 103, and threatening to publish with intent to extort, 1916 Act, s. 31). (1861 Act, s. 103 and 1916 Act, s. 41.)

(2) Any person, to whom property is offered to be sold, pawned or delivered, if he has reasonable cause to suspect that an offence under the Larceny Acts has been committed with respect to such property, should, if in his power, arrest the person offering the same. (1861 Act, s. 103 and 1916 Act, s. 41.)

(3) Any constable may arrest without warrant any person he finds lying or loitering in any highway, yard or other place during the night (9 P.M. to 6 A.M.) and whom he has good cause to suspect of having committed or being about to commit any felony against the Larceny Acts, and take him as soon as reasonably may be before a Justice to be dealt with according to law. (1861 Act, s. 104 and 1916 Act, s. 41). If no other specific charge application to have him bound over may be made.

For power to search for stolen property, see " Search Warrant,'' Chap. 5. Also a search warrant can be granted by a Justice (s. 42).

Summary Punishment.—By s. 19 of the Magistrates' Courts Act, 1952, the Justices may, if they consider it expedient and if the accused consents, deal summarily with the following larceny offences given in the First Sched. to the Act.

1916 Act. Sections 2 (simple larceny), 4 (killing animals with intent to steal), 5 (dog-stealing), 8 (stealing fixtures, trees, etc.), 9 (stealing goods in course of manufacture), 10 (stealing electricity), 12 (stealing postal packets), 13 (a) (stealing to value of £5 in dwelling-house), 14 (larceny from the person), 15 (1 and (2) (larceny from ships and docks), 16 (larceny by tenants or lodgers), 17 (1) and (2) (larceny and embezzlement by clerks or servants), 18 (larceny by postal official), 20 (conversion of property value not exceeding £20), 32 (1) (false pretences), 33 (1) and (2) (receiving property stolen in the United Kingdom), 35 (aiding and abetting in any of the previously mentioned offences).

1861 Act. Section 27 (fraudulently destroying any valuable security).

Robbery.—Robbery is the felonious taking of property from another against his will, accompanied by violence or putting in fear. It is in effect larceny aggravated by violence or terror.

Larceny Act, 1916, s. 23, declares the following to be felonies :—

(1) To assault any person with intent to rob. Penalty, five years.

(2) To rob any person. Penalty, fourteen years.

(3) Being armed with any offensive weapon or instrument, to rob or assault with intent to rob any person.

(4) Being together with one other person or more, to rob or assault with intent to rob any person.

(5) To rob any person and at the time or immediately before or immediately after, to use any personal violence to any person.

The last three offences are regarded as so serious that those guilty may be sent to imprisonment for life (see also Larceny Act, 1916, s. 37, as amended by C.J. Act, 1948, 10th Sched.) These last three offences are termed " robbery with violence " to indicate that some weapon or more than one person, or some actual physical violence, was involved in the act of robbery.

The term " highway robbery " refers merely to a robbery which takes place on a highway ; robbery may take place in a house or field as well as on a highway.

As the gist of the offence is the force and terror accompanying the larceny of the property, therefore it should be shown that the injured party was actually in fear, or that the circumstances were such that the Court may presume some fear of danger, or that violence was actually used.

The Prevention of Crime Act, 1953, is intended to prevent ill disposed persons from committing acts of violence leading to robbery.

It makes it an offence, punishable summarily or on indictment, for any person to have with him in any public place any offensive weapon without lawful authority or reasonable excuse, the proof thereof to lie on him.

In this connection " public place " means any highway and any premises or place to which the public have access, and " offensive weapon " means any article made or adapted for use for causing injury to the person or intended by its carrier for such use by him. A constable may arrest without warrant any person whom he has reasonable cause to believe to be committing this offence if he is not satisfied as to that person's identity or place of residence, or has reasonable cause to believe that arrest is necessary in order to prevent the commission by him of any other offence in which an offensive weapon might be used.

A firearm or imitation firearm though it is not loaded or is incapable of discharging any missile is deemed to be an offensive weapon or instrument for the purpose of robbery. (Firearms Act, 1937, s. 23.)

Larceny by Trick.—As this felony closely resembles false pretences, it is now specially considered. In an ordinary case of larceny the thief deprives the owner of his possession of the article and of the benefits of his ownership, against the owner's consent and without his knowledge. However, in some cases the owner hands over possession of an article to the thief, being induced to do so by some trick or fraud, but without any intention of parting with his property in the article. This is commonly termed larceny by trick.

In larceny by trick the thief obtains possession of the article by means of some trick or fraudulent expedient. The owner is deceived, and as a result parts with possession, therefore the thief is regarded as having stolen and " taken " the article, although the owner has willingly handed it over (Larceny Act, 1916, s. 1).

The owner's consent is not true consent, as it was obtained by fraud, and the owner does not intend to part with his property in the article. Larceny by trick is a felony, and, therefore, there is power to arrest without warrant. False pretences is a misdemeanour, therefore to arrest a warrant is necessary, except in the cases where the offender is caught committing the offence, as then the Larceny Act, 1916, s. 41, gives power to arrest without warrant.

Under s. 44 of the Larceny Act, 1916, a person indicted for stealing may, on evidence that he took the article in such manner as would amount to false pretences be found guilty by the jury of false pretences, and a person indicted for false pretences may be convicted of false pretences although the evidence showed that he stole the property in question.

Examples of this Felony.—" *Ringing the changes.*" For example, putting down a sixpence and six pennies and asking for a shilling in return ; getting the shilling and leaving it with the money already on the counter ; asking for and receiving a florin in exchange for the lot. Here the thief gets two shillings for one shilling and so steals a shilling by trick.

" *Welshing.*" For example, a person at a race meeting, just before a race, makes a bet with a bookmaker. The horse backed wins, but the bookmaker departs with the money and is not to be found or refuses to pay up when the person tries to collect his winnings (which include the amount he staked and which he did not intend to part with unless the horse lost).

" *Ring-dropping.*" The accused displays a ring which he says he has just found or which he pretends to pick up or which he suggests has been illicitly acquired. He offers to leave this apparently valuable ring with an onlooker on condition the latter will deposit cash or some valuable as security. If this is done the accused departs with the money or valuable and later the ring is found to be almost valueless.

" *Confidence trick.*" Where following a quickly developed acquaintance the accused, by a plausible tale and apparent proof of his own honesty, induces the victim in his turn to deposit cash or valuables in accused's possession as a proof of honesty, and then accused disappears with the property. This trick has many forms. Other examples of larceny by trick are :—

Obtaining articles from an automatic machine by putting in metal discs, not money.

Servant sent to a house with goods ordered and with instructions not to leave them without getting payment, but being induced by some trick to part with the goods without payment.

Obtaining goods from a messenger by falsely pretending to be the person to whom the goods were to be delivered.

Asking for change of £1, obtaining the change, and departing with both the £1 and the change.

In all such cases it is larceny, because the victim did not intend or was not authorised to part with the property in the money or articles the possession of which he has handed over to the thief who has taken them fraudulently and without a claim of right (s. 1). The charge against the thief is larceny.

False Pretences.—This term is applied to the offence of obtaining property fraudulently by means of a false representation that some facts exist or existed. It is a misdemeanour by statute. The attempt is a misdemeanour at Common Law.

Larceny Act, 1916, s. 32 (1). Every person who by any false pretence, with intent to defraud,

(*a*) obtains from any other person any chattel, money or valuable security, or

(*b*) causes or procures any money to be paid or any chattel or valuable security to be delivered to himself or to any other person, for the use or benefit or on account of himself or any other person,

shall be guilty of a misdemeanour. Penalty, five years.

The following points, as indicated in above description of the offence, are material in a case of false pretences, viz. :—

(1) The making of a false pretence. The pretence must have been false, but mere exaggeration or trade puffing will not be sufficient. It may be made in writing, and if so the circumstances may amount to forgery, for which the punishment is more severe. It may be in words or by the conduct and acts of the accused. It should be a pretence of an existing

CHAPTER XIV.—LARCENY 163

fact or of some fact that has existed. A promise that a certain state of things shall exist in the future or that something will be done in the future is not sufficient. A promise is not a pretence, so a promise as to the future will not in itself make the offence. (See *R.* v. *Dent* (1955).) However, a promise to do something together with a false representation that the promiser has the power to do that thing, may be false pretences ; for example, a married man posing as unmarried promises that he will marry a girl and thus gets money from her. Also there are some decided cases which suggest that a promise to do a thing in the future may amount to a false pretence that the maker has a present intention and power to do so. (See *R.* v. *Naylor* (1865), *R.* v. *Bancroft* (1909), and *R.* v. *Carpenter* (1912).) The nature of the false pretence should be set out in the information or summons.

(2) The obtaining of the property by means of the false pretence. If the property was not obtained or if the injured party was not taken in by the false pretence but, however, parted with his property, the accused may be convicted of the misdemeanour of attempting to obtain it by false pretences. The property obtained should have been some definite thing, as it is not " false pretences " to obtain some advantage, such as a ride in a train. The change of ownership of the article must have been caused by the false pretence, viz. the defrauded person, believing the false pretence to be true, parted with his money or goods.

(3) The intent to defraud. It will not be necessary to prove an intent to defraud any particular person ; it is sufficient to prove that the accused did the act with a general intent to defraud (see Larceny Act, 1916, s. 40 (1)). The intent will usually be shown by the circumstances.

Evidence of similar acts or conduct on the part of the accused is admissible to prove the intent to defraud, as showing a systematic course of dishonest conduct on his part.

Any person may arrest without warrant any person he finds committing this offence (Larceny Act, 1916, s. 41). A case of false pretences may be dealt with summarily under M.C. Act, 1952, s. 19 and 1st Sched., if the accused consents.

Other similar Offences.—Obtaining credit by fraud. Debtors Act, 1869, s. 13. It is a misdemeanour if in incurring any debt or liability (liability for money or money's worth) any person obtains credit under false pretences or by means of any other fraud. A person who orders and obtains a meal in a restaurant without having the means to pay for it, or who orders goods without either the means or the intention of paying for them, will be guilty of this offence, which may be punished summarily if accused consents to trial (M.C. Act,1952, s. 19, 1st Sched.).

Evidence of credit obtained from other persons previously is admissible as showing system and negativing accident or mistake (*R.* v. *Wyatt* (1903)).

Companies Act, 1948, ss. 328-334. Where a company has gone into liquidation, any of its officers who have obtained credit by fraud or committed other frauds in connection with the company are guilty of misdemeanour and may be prosecuted summarily. The officers are similarly liable if proper accounts were not kept, and directors may be held personally responsible for any fraudulent trading.

Cheating, or the fraudulent obtaining of another's property by some deceitful practice which affects or may affect the general public, is a misdemeanour at common law. For example, selling by false weights or selling inferior articles under some false mark or description.

Larceny Act, 1916, s. 32 (2). It is misdemeanour for a person, by any false pretence, with intent to defraud or injure any other person, to fraudulently cause or induce any other person,

(a) to make, destroy, etc., any valuable security or,

(b) to attach any name or seal to any paper in order that same may be afterwards made into or used as a valuable security.

National Insurance Act, 1946, s. 52. It is a summary offence to make any false representation or statement to obtain benefit, etc., under the Act.

Proceedings may be taken within 12 months from the commission of the offence or within 3 months after the offence comes to light. See also National Insurance Act, 1946, s. 52, and National Insurance (Industrial Injuries) Act, 1946, s. 67, for somewhat similar provisions.

Police Pensions Act, 1948, s. 7.   Any fraudulent attempt to obtain any pension or benefit under the Act is punishable either on indictment or summarily.

For cheating at play, see Chap. 36. For misrepresentations by moneylenders, see Chap. 31. For vagrancy frauds and national assistance frauds, see Chap. 27.

Embezzlement.—Embezzlement is the felony committed when a servant or clerk converts to his own use anything received by him for his employer before it has passed into the possession of his employer.

To embezzle originally meant to make away with secretly, and embezzlement had to be made a special offence because the servant or clerk is in lawful possession of money, etc., which he receives on behalf of his master, and the misappropriation of such money is not larceny.

This crime is defined by s. 17 of the Larceny Act, 1916, thus :—

Every person who being a clerk or servant or person employed in the capacity of a clerk or servant, fraudulently embezzles the whole or any part of any chattel, money or valuable security delivered to or received or taken into possession by him for or in the name or on the account of his master or employer shall be guilty of felony.

Under the Larceny Act, 1916, the following may be liable to prosecution for embezzlement : Clerks or servants, employees in the public service of the Crown or in the police, officers of a local marine board (s. 17), postal servants *re* postal packets (ss. 18 and 33, and Post Office Act, 1953, s. 57), officers of the Bank of England or Ireland (s. 19), and a co-partner or one of two or more persons owning an interest in any property (s. 40 (4)).

Also several statutes deal directly with embezzlement by specified classes of persons. For example: customs officers (Customs and Excise Act, 1952), and employees of councils of counties or county boroughs (Local Government Act, 1933, s. 120)

Essentials of the Crime of Embezzlement.

(1) The offender must have been employed as described in the various Acts referred to above or be a co-partner or a clerk or servant. A clerk or servant within the meaning of the Act is a person whom the master not only employs but also directs as to when and how the work should be carried on. If the accused is merely an agent employed to do certain work but not bound as to when and how it is to be done, he may not be convicted of embezzlement, though he may be convicted of conversion. A clerk or servant is generally paid a salary, while an agent is usually paid by commission.

(2) The accused must have received the money or goods from some third person, for or on account of his employer, in the course of his employment as clerk, servant, etc. If he appropriates money, etc., which he has received from his employer directly or indirectly, it is larceny ; and if he receives money, etc., for his employer and places it in the possession of his employer (i.e. in the till, in the shop, etc.) and then takes it out and appropriates it, it is also larceny, but it is not embezzlement. However, if indicted for embezzlement a man may be found guilty of stealing, and if indicted for stealing he may be found guilty of embezzlement (Larceny Act, 1916, s. 44 (2)).

(3) The accused must have fraudulently embezzled some specific sum of money or some property. A general deficiency in accounts is not sufficient, nor is mere neglect to account for moneys received sufficient proof of embezzlement. However, a dishonest clerk or servant who is not liable for embezzlement may be made amenable for false accounting. See Chap. 17.

The offences of embezzlement, fraudulent conversion, false accounting and larceny are closely connected, so the facts of an alleged offence of embezzlement should be carefully considered,

A case of embezzlement, stealing, or unlawful disposing of materials, etc., by any hired person to whom they may have been entrusted to prepare or work up, may be dealt with summarily under the Frauds by Workmen Act, 1777. A servant who, contrary to orders, takes his master's corn or other food to give the same to his master's animals, does not commit felony, but may be dealt with summarily under the Misappropriation by Servants Act, 1863.

Conversion.—Conversion is the offence committed by a person who is entrusted with property not his own and who deals wrongfully with it. The essence of the offence is fraud. It may be committed by agents, factors, trustees, directors and municipal officials, and it is a misdemeanour under ss. 20, 21 and 22 of the Larceny Act, 1916.

Conversion may be committed by the following :—

(1) An agent who fraudulently converts to the benefit of himself, or of any person not authorised to benefit, any property or part thereof or proceeds thereof :—

(a) Over which he has been entrusted with power of attorney, viz. legal power to dispose of such property (s. 20 (1) (i)) ;

(b) Entrusted to him for safe custody or to deal with in any particular manner (s. 20 (1) (iv) (a)) ;

(c) Received by him for or on account of another person (s. 20 (1) (iv) (b)).

(2) A factor or agent entrusted with possession of goods or of any document of title to goods for the purpose of sale or otherwise, who, without the authority of his principal, for the benefit of himself or any other person other than his principal and in violation of good faith :—

(a) Gives such goods or documents as a pledge or security for money, etc., borrowed or received by him ; or

(b) Accepts any advance of money, etc., on agreement to deposit, transfer or deliver such goods or documents (s. 22).

Thus it is a misdemeanour for a factor to obtain advances on the security of goods entrusted to his care unless he has the authority of his principal. However, the section declares that a factor is not liable to prosecution under the section where any such pledging is done for an amount which does not exceed the amount which is justly due and owing to him from his principal (s. 22).

(3) A trustee, being so created by deed, will or written instrument, or who is an executor, administrator, etc., as defined in section 46, who, with intent to defraud, converts the property concerned in the trust to the benefit of himself or some other person or purpose outside the purpose of the trust. A prosecution under this section must have the sanction of the Attorney-General, and also the sanction of the Court or Judge before whom any civil proceedings come (s. 21).

(4) A director, member or officer of any body corporate or public company who fraudulently takes for the benefit of

himself or any purpose other than the purposes of the company, any of the property of the company (s. 20 (1) (ii)).

(5) Any person authorised to receive moneys dealt with in the Municipal Corporations Acts, who appropriates (or applies) the same otherwise than as directed by law (s. 20 (1) (iii)).

A Municipal Corporation can raise money, etc., as laid down in these Acts, and this section makes it a misdemeanour for any person to apply corporate money otherwise than as directed by the Acts. Offences under s. 20 where the money or property does not exceed £20 may be dealt with summarily with the consent of the accused (M.C. Act, 1952, s. 19 and 1st Sched.).

If a person has had to make admissions or disclosures in the course of any compulsory process of law *re* bankruptcy he is protected by s. 43 (2) and (3) of this Act if he is prosecuted for any of the above offences.

Proof of general deficiency is not sufficient, and fraudulent conversion of specific property should be proved (*R.* v. *Sheaf* (1925)). Any offence of fraudulent conversion by a public official, solicitor or trustee must be reported to the Director of Public Prosecutions (see Appendix III).

Bankruptcy Offences.—The Bankruptcy Act, 1914, creates many offences against the criminal law, and the following are some of the misdemeanours that may be committed by bankrupts :—

(1) Fraudulently removing property to the value of £10 or upwards (s. 154) ;

(2) Concealing, destroying, falsifying, etc., books and documents (s. 154) ;

(3) Obtaining property on credit by any false representation or other fraud and not paying for same (s. 154) ;

(4) Obtaining credit to the extent of £10 or upwards from any person without informing him that he is an undischarged bankrupt (s. 155) ;

(5) An undischarged bankrupt engaging in business under another name and not disclosing to all persons with whom he does business the name under which he was adjudicated bankrupt (s. 155) ;

(6) Concealing, disposing or removing property with intent to defraud creditors (s. 156). See also Debtors Act, 1869, which deals with persons defrauding their creditors by transferring or removing their property.

One bankruptcy offence is a felony, namely : quitting England and taking with him, or attempting or making preparation to quit England and take with him, any part of his property to the amount of twenty pounds or upwards which ought by law to be divided amongst his creditors (s. 159).

It is a misdemeanour for a creditor wilfully and with intent to defraud to make a false claim in a bankruptcy (s. 160).

Certain of these offences can only be prosecuted on order of the Court and by s. 164 summary proceedings shall not be taken after one year after first discovery of the offence nor after three years from the date of the offence. See Stone, title " Bankrupt and Fraudulent Debtors."

Personation.—Personation is the passing oneself off as another. False personation is a cheat punishable on indictment at common law, but apparently only if the cheat is of such a nature as affects or is likely to affect the public at large. Personation not covered by statute may amount to conspiracy to produce a public mischief by false pretences.

The wearing of or masquerading in the clothing of the opposite sex is not in itself an offence. The attendant circumstances, however, may justify prosecution for some specific offence, e.g. under s. 4, Vagrancy Act, 1824. See Chap. 27.

False Personation Act, 1874. It is felony to falsely and deceitfully personate any person with intent fraudulently to obtain any land, chattel, money, valuable security or property.

Forgery Acts, 1861 and 1870, and Companies Act, 1948, **s. 84.** It is felony to falsely and deceitfully personate the owner of stocks, shares, etc., and thereby take or attempt to take the owner's interest therein or money therefrom.

Personating a woman's husband, and thereby having connection with her is rape. See Chap. 10.

Personation of a voter at an election is a felony. See Chap. 21.

Falsely pretending to act under the authority of a County Court is a felony (County Courts Act, 1934, s. 177).

Personating bail, viz. without lawful authority or excuse (the proof of which is on the party accused) acknowledging in the name of any other person any recognizance or bail before any Court, is a felony (Forgery Act, 1861, s. 34).

False personation of anyone in order to receive money payable out of Navy Funds is a misdemeanour, and may also be dealt with summarily (Admiralty Powers Act, 1865).

False personation for any purpose prejudicial to the safety or interests of the State is a misdemeanour. See " Official Secrets Acts," Chap. 20.

Personation of a customs and excise officer for any unlawful purpose is punishable summarily or on indictment and the offender may be detained (s. 7) by a constable, etc. (s. 274) (Customs and Excise Act, 1952).

County Police Act, 1839, s. 15. It is a summary offence for any person who is not a constable appointed under the Act to put on the dress or take the name, designation or character of a constable, for the purpose of doing or procuring to be done any

act which he could not do or get done of his own authority, or
for any other unlawful purpose.

See also s. 12, Town Police Clauses Act, 1847, if it applies in the
police district by local Act.

Special Constables Orders, 1923, 1948. It is a summary
offence to put on the dress or accoutrements or take the name,
designation or character of a special constable for any unlawful
purpose or without proper authority. See " Uniforms," Chap. 30.

Receiving Stolen Property.—Receiving stolen property,
knowing it to have been stolen, was a misdemeanour at Common
Law. However, s. 33 of the Larceny Act, 1916, now provides that
it is either felony or misdemeanour according to the nature of the
offence by which the owner was deprived of his property.

Larceny Act, 1916, s. 33. Every person who receives any
property, knowing the same to have been stolen or obtained in
any way whatsoever under circumstances which amount to
felony or misdemeanour, shall be guilty of an offence of the like
degree (felony or misdemeanour). This section also provides that
any person who receives any mail bag, postal packet, money or
property (the taking of which being a felony), knowing same to
have been feloniously taken, shall be guilty of felony, and that
receivers or possessors of goods stolen outside the United Kingdom are similarly guilty of either felony or misdemeanour,
according to the nature of the principal offence.

A "receiver" may be tried and convicted whether the " thief "
has or has not been detected. Any number of the " receivers "
may be charged and tried together (s. 40 (3)), and one (or more)
may be convicted (s. 44 (5)). A " receiver " may be tried in the
place where he " receives " property stolen elsewhere (ss. 33, 39).

To justify a prosecution there should be evidence :—

(1) That the property was stolen or obtained under circumstances amounting to felony or misdemeanour, viz. the principal
offence.

(2) That the property was in the possession or control of the
accused. He " receives " as soon as he obtains control over it
but he cannot " receive " from himself (*R*. v. *Loughlin* (1951)).

(3)That the accused knew at the time he received the
property that it had been stolen or criminally obtained. The
fact of having stolen property in possession may not be sufficient
proof of guilty knowledge. However, the possession of property
recently stolen raises the presumption that the possessor had
stolen or received it with guilty knowledge, and he should
explain his possession of it to the satisfaction of the jury.
Guilty knowledge may be proved by circumstantial evidence ;
for example, accused concealed the property or denied its
possession, accused bought it for much less than its value, or
sold it cheaply or " on the quiet."

Guilty knowledge may be inferred if accused gives no explanation to account for possession or if the jury do not believe any explanation offered. (*R.* v. *Aves* (1950)).

The circumstances in which accused received or got possession of goods may of themselves prove that they were stolen and that he knew they were stolen.

In a prosecution for receiving or having in possession stolen property, special evidence of guilty knowledge may be given. See " Extent of Evidence," Chap. 7.

For " Restitution of Stolen Property," see Chap. 18.

Where the stealing or taking of any property is punishable summarily under the Larceny Act, 1861, the person who knowingly receives such property may be dealt with summarily (Larceny Act, 1861, s. 97).

Knowingly buying or receiving stolen or embezzled materials from persons employed in various manufactures (iron, cotton, etc.) is punishable summarily (Frauds by Workmen Acts, 1748, 1777).

On the conviction of a pawnbroker for receiving stolen property the Court may forfeit his licence. See Chap. 31.

The keeper or occupier of a lodging-house, or place where intoxicants are sold, or place of public entertainment or resort, who knowingly lodges or harbours thieves or reputed thieves, or allows them to meet or assemble therein, or allows the deposit of goods therein (having reasonable cause for believing them stolen) commits a summary offence, and his licence (if any) may be forfeited on a first offence, and shall be forfeited on a second conviction (he being then disqualified for any such licence for two years). If two convictions occur within three years in respect of the same premises, the Court shall disqualify such premises for any such licence for a year (Prevention of Crimes Act, 1871, s. 10).

See also Chap. 10 for a similar offence by brothel-keepers.

Taking, etc., of a Motor Vehicle.—It is an offence to take and drive away any motor vehicle without having either the owner's consent or other lawful authority.

Any unlawful moving of the vehicle constitutes " taking away " (*Shimmall* v. *Fisher and Others* (1951)).

The offence can be committed anywhere; " road " is not mentioned in the section.

If the vehicle is not moved but it is clear that a person is in it without authority or cause and obviously about to drive it away it would be an attempt to commit the offence and therefore also a common law misdemeanour and in any case it would be an offence under s. 29 of the Act. (See later).

A constable may arrest without warrant any person reasonably suspected by him of having committed or of attempting to commit this offence.

The offender is liable, on summary conviction, to imprisonment

up to 3 months or fine up to £50, or, on conviction on indictment, to imprisonment up to 12 months or fine up to £100 or both.

However, the accused is not liable to conviction if the Magistrates'
Court or jury are satisfied that he acted in the reasonable belief
either that he had lawful authority or that the owner, in the
circumstances of the case, would have given his consent if he had
been asked therefor.

If a person is indicted for stealing a motor vehicle the jury
may find him guilty of an offence under this section (Road Traffic
Act, 1930, s. 28).

It is a summary offence for any person, without lawful authority
or reasonable cause—

(1) To take or retain hold of or get on to a motor vehicle or
trailer while in motion on a road for the purpose of being drawn
or carried (stealing a ride and a dangerous practice) ; or

(2) To get on to or tamper with the brake or other part of
the mechanism of a motor vehicle while it is on a road or local
authority parking place (this may be action preparatory to
stealing or likely to cause damage) (R.T. Act, 1930, s. 29).

Under s. 19 and First Sched. M.C. Act, 1952, an attempt to
commit any indictable offence which may be dealt with summarily
may be dealt with summarily, so an attempt to take and drive
away a motor vehicle without authority, being indictable, can be
dealt with summarily if the accused consents to summary trial.

See *R.* v. *Fussell* (1951).

Chapter XV

MALICIOUS DAMAGE

Contents

Malicious Damage to Property.—The burning of a house was the only form of malicious injury that was a crime at common law. See " Arson." All other forms of malicious damage were formerly regarded as trespasses with civil remedy only, but now the Malicious Damage Act, 1861, deals with many forms of malicious injury to property of every description.

It is provided by section 58 that the malice need not be against the owner of the property damaged ; the " evil intent beforehand to do harm " being sufficient to constitute the offence.

Malicious Damage Act, 1861. It is a crime to unlawfully and maliciously kill, maim or wound animals or to destroy, pull down or damage property as follows :—

Animals.—Any cattle (such as oxen, horses, sheep, etc.). Felony. (S. 40.) Any dog, bird, beast or other animal not being cattle but being either the subject of larceny at common law (see "Larceny of Animals, Chap. 35 ") or being ordinarily kept in a state of confinement or for any domestic purpose. Summary offence. (S. 41.)

Bridges, viaducts or aqueducts. Felony. (S. 33.)

Buildings, machinery, steam-engines or mine erections. by persons riotously and tumultuously assembled to the disturbance of the peace. Felony if demolished. Misdemeanour if damaged. (Ss. 11 and 12.)

Canals, rivers, dams, sluices, quays, etc. F. (Ss. 30, 31.)

Fences, walls, gates or stiles. Summary offence. (S. 25.)

Fishponds, mill ponds, reservoirs or pools. Misdemeanour (S. 32.) See also " Fishery Laws," Chap. 19.

Hop-binds growing on poles in any plantation of hops. Felony. (S. 19.)

Houses or fixtures attached, if done by tenants. Misdemeanour. (S. 13.) See " Landlord and Tenant," Chap. 29.

Machinery, used for agriculture or in any manufacture, Felony (Ss. 14 and 15.)

Mines, by letting in water, damaging machinery, etc. Felony. (Ss. 28 and 29.)

Ships, otherwise than by fire or explosives. Felony. (S. 46.)

Trees, shrubs or underwood :—

(a) Wheresoever growing, if damage amounts to one shilling at least. Summary offence. (S. 22.)

(b) Growing in any park, garden, orchard, etc., if damage exceeds one pound. Felony. (S. 20.)

(c) Growing elsewhere than in a garden or ground adjoining or belonging to a dwelling-house, if damage exceeds five pounds value. Felony. (S. 21.) (Both these felonies may be dealt with summarily if accused consents (M.C. Act, 1952, s. 19 and 1st Sched.).

Roots, plants, fruit or vegetables, growing in any garden, orchard, nursery ground or greenhouse. Summary offence, (S. 23.)

(As regards damage to allotment gardens, see the Allotments Act, 1922. The Town Gardens Protection Act, 1863, empowers the police to arrest persons found damaging public grounds in towns.)

Roots or plants, cultivated and used for food, medicine, distilling, dyeing or for any manufacture, and growing in any land open or enclosed which is not a garden or orchard. Summary offence. (S. 24.)

Works of art, such as books, pictures, statues, etc., kept in museums, churches, public buildings, etc., and public statues or monuments. Misdemeanour. (S. 39.)

Property in general.—It is a misdemeanour to unlawfully and maliciously commit any damage, injury or spoil to or upon any real or personal property whatsoever either of a public or private nature, for which no punishment is provided by this Act (s. 51).

If accused consents he may be dealt with summarily (M.C. Act, 1952, s. 19 and 1st Sched.).

Malicious damage by burning. See " Arson," below.

Malicious injury by means of explosives. See Chap. 33.

For threats to cause damage, see " Threats and Menaces," Chap. 8. Also see " Railways " and " Telegraphs," Chap. 26.

There is no provision in the Act for awarding compensation on conviction of an indictable offence under the 1861 Act.

Power of Arrest.—Any person found committing any offence under the Act may be arrested without warrant by any constable, or the owner of the property, or his servant or any person authorised by him (s. 61).

Any constable may arrest without warrant any person he finds lying or loitering in any highway, yard or other place during the night and whom he has good cause to suspect of having committed or being about to commit any felony against the Act (s. 57).

See also " Loiterers and Suspected Persons," Chap. 28.

The following section may cover most cases of malicious damage. Criminal Justice Administration Act, 1914, s. 14. If any person wilfully or maliciously commits any damage to any real or personal property whatsoever, either of a public or private nature, and the amount of the damage does not exceed £20, he may be dealt with summarily, and punished, and ordered to pay compensation (or he may be sent for trial on indictment if the damage exceeds £5).

If damage is committed by a person acting under a *bona fide* and reasonable supposition of right, or if the damage is merely nominal and not producing any actual harm, the Criminal Law as to malicious damage will not apply.

For compensation for damage see " Restitution of Stolen Property," Chap. 18.

Sabotage is a word applied to indicate malicious damage to machinery or apparatus used in trade and industry. It comes from the French word " sabot," meaning wooden shoe or socket for a railway rail and the damaging of railway apparatus or machinery by a workman's boot was therefore called " sabotage."

This term is used to indicate malicious damage done to his employer's machinery or property by an ill-disposed employee and it is felony (see ss. 14, 15, 1861 Act). The word has recently come into political use as describing interference with government plans.

Arson.—Arson is the unlawful and malicious setting fire to buildings and property, including crops, vegetable produce, coal mines, and ships, and is a felony by common law and by statute.

At Common Law arson was confined to the malicious and wilful burning of the house of another, including every outhouse appertaining to the dwelling.

To constitute the felony of arson it must be proved that the act of burning was both wilful and malicious, but the malice need not necessarily be against the owner of the property burned. The person in possession of the burned property can be guilty of arson, as his intent may be to injure or defraud some other person (Malicious Damage Act, 1861, ss. 58 and 59).

Any burning of some part of the property is sufficient. Burning by mere negligence or accident will not amount to the felony.

The Malicious Damage Act, 1861, greatly expanded the scope of the offence and makes it felony to unlawfully and maliciously set fire to any :—

(1) Church or other place of Divine worship (s. 1).

(2) Dwelling-house when any person was therein (s. 2).

(3) House, warehouse, shop, shed, etc., or any building used in farming, trade or manufacture, whether in possession of the offender or of any other person, with intent thereby to injure or defraud any person (s. 3).

(4) Station, warehouse or other building belonging to any railway, port, docks or harbour or to any canal or other navigation (s. 4).

(5) Public building (s. 5).

(6) Building other than such above mentioned (s. 6).

(7) Matter or thing being in, against, or under any building under such circumstances that if the building was thereby set fire to, the offence would amount to felony (s. 7). Any attempt to set fire to any building or thing in, against or under it, etc., is also a felony (s. 8).

(8) Crops of hay, corn, grass, grain or pulse or of any cultivated vegetable produce whether standing or cut down or any part of any wood or plantation of trees, or any heath, gorse, furze or fern (s. 16). (This felony may be tried summarily if the accused consents (M.C. Act, 1952, s. 19 and 1st Sched.).

(9) Stack of corn, grain, hay, straw, etc., or of any cultivated vegetable produce, or of furze, gorse, heath, fern, turf, peat, coals, charcoal, wood or bark (s. 17). Any attempt to set fire to any of the things mentioned in sections 16 and 17 is also a felony (s. 18).

(10) Mine of coal or other mineral fuel (s. 26). Any attempt to set fire to a coal mine is also a felony (s. 27).

(11) Ship or vessel whether complete or unfinished, or to cast away or destroy same (s. 42).

(12) Ship or vessel, or to cast away or destroy same, with intent thereby to prejudice the owner of same or of any goods on board the same, or the insurer of same (s. 43).

Any attempt to commit the felonies mentioned in sections 42 and 43 is also a felony (s. 44).

The arson or destruction of any of H.M. ships, arsenals, magazines, dockyards, stores, etc., is felony punishable by death (Dockyards, etc., Protection Act, 1772, s. 1), and every such case must be reported to the Director of Public Prosecutions (see Appendix III).

For powers of arrest, see " Malicious Damage," above.

Chapter XVI

COINAGE

Contents

COUNTERFEITING the Sovereign's money was regarded as a most heinous crime, and in 1351 the Statute of Treasons made it high treason. It is a felony under the Coinage Offences Act, 1936, which repealed the Coinage Offences Act, 1861, and the Counterfeit Medal Act, 1883. The provisions of the Coinage Offences Act, 1936, relating to silver coin now extend to the cupro-nickel coinage established by the Coinage Act, 1946 (see s. 5 (1)), and will extend to coin of any other metal or mixture of metals specified in a proclamation under the Coinage Act, 1946, s. 3 (c).

" Current coin " means any coin which has been coined in any of Her Majesty's mints, or is lawfully current, by proclamation or otherwise, in any part of Her Majesty's Dominions or is lawfully current in any foreign country (1936 Act, s. 17).

" Counterfeit coin " means coin which is not current coin but is falsely made resembling any current coin, and includes any current coin which has been gilt, silvered or altered in any manner so as to resemble any current coin of a higher denomination (s. 17).

" Uttering coin " means the passing off or putting into circulation of coin.

" Uttering " includes " tendering " and " passing off." If a coin is offered in payment but refused by the person to whom it was tendered it is an " uttering." The offence is charged as " tendering, uttering or putting off."

" Impairing coin " means the clipping, diminishing or lightening of current gold or silver coin with intent to pass it off when so diminished as current coin.

Current gold or silver coin suspected to have been diminished otherwise than by reasonable wearing may be bent, cut, broken or defaced by any person to whom it is tendered, the loss to fall on the person tendering if it proves to be impaired or counterfeit (s. 14).

The offences may be grouped in four classes :—

(1) *Making or altering.*

Falsely making or counterfeiting any coin resembling any current coin. F. (S. 1.)

Casing over or colouring any coin resembling any current gold or silver coin, or gilding, silvering, colouring, altering, filing or preparing in any way any coin or piece of metal with intent to make it resemble or pass for current gold or silver coin. F. (S. 2.)

Impairing, diminishing or lightening any current gold or silver coin with intent that it might then pass as current coin. F. (S. 3.)

Defacing any current coin by stamping thereon any names or words. M. Coin so defaced is not legal tender (s. 4).

Without lawful authority or excuse, knowingly making, mending, buying, selling or having in possession any coining tools or instruments. F. (S. 9.)

Without lawful authority or excuse, knowingly conveying coining tools, coins, or metal out of any of Her Majesty's mints. F. (S. 10.)

Without lawful authority or excuse, making, selling or having in possession for sale, any medal, cast, coin, or other like thing made wholly or partially of metal and either resembling current gold or silver coin or having a device resembling a device on such current coin or being so made that it can, by colouring, etc., be made to resemble such current coin. M. (S. 8.) There is no power of arrest without warrant for this offence (s. 11).

It is a summary offence to melt down, break up or use otherwise than as currency, any gold or silver coin current in the United Kingdom or in any British Possession or foreign country, except under licence from the Treasury (Gold and Silver (Export Control) Act, 1920, s. 2).

(2) *Dealing in counterfeit coin.*

Without lawful authority or excuse, buying, selling or trafficking in any counterfeit coin (complete or incomplete) at a lower rate or value than the same purports to be. F. (S. 6.)

Without lawful authority or excuse, knowingly importing into this country any counterfeit gold or silver coin. F. (S. 7.)

Without lawful authority or excuse, knowingly exporting counterfeit coin. M. (S. 7.)

Selling any coin, medal, etc., resembling current gold or silver coin. M. (S. 8.) (See above under " Making or altering.")

(3) *Uttering.*

Knowingly uttering any false or counterfeit current coin. M. (S. 5.)

Knowingly uttering any counterfeit current gold or silver coin and having in possession at the time any other such coin, or on the same day or within ten days knowingly uttering any other such coin. M. 2nd offence. F. (S. 5.)

Uttering counterfeit current gold or silver coin of the realm, or knowingly having three or more such coins in possession, having been previously convicted of a similar offence or of any felony under the Act. F. (S. 5.)

With intent to defraud, uttering as current gold or silver coin, any coin, medal, etc., resembling current coin but being of less value. M. (S. 5.)

Uttering any current coin of the realm defaced by having words, etc., stamped on it. Summary offence, but the consent of the Attorney-General is required for a prosecution. (S. 4, and see under " Making " above.)

The uttering is complete even if the counterfeit is not complete (s. 5).

(4) *Possession.*

Knowingly having in possession three or more counterfeit current gold or silver coins with intent to utter same. M. 2nd offence. F. (S. 5.)

Knowingly having in possession three or more counterfeit current copper coins with intent to utter same. M. (S. 5.)

Unlawfully and knowingly having in possession any clippings, filings, dust, etc., obtained by impairing or diminishing any current gold or silver coin. F. (S. 3.) As regards possession of coinage tools, see " Making," above.

Having in possession for sale any coin, medal, etc., resembling current gold or silver coin. M. (S. 8.) (See under " Making," above.)

Arrest, Seizure and Evidence.—Any person may arrest anyone found committing any offence against the Act, except the offence under s. 8, regarding medals, etc. (s. 11).

Counterfeit coin, coining instruments, or any filings, dust, etc., produced by sweating gold or silver coin, found in any place or in possession of anyone without lawful excuse, may be seized by any person and brought before a Justice. On reasonable cause of suspicion a Justice may issue a warrant to search premises by day or by night, and seize counterfeit coin, instruments, etc. (s. 11).

Persons found uttering counterfeit coins may be arrested without warrant. All the counterfeit coins should be secured and marked so that they may be afterwards identified.

Counterfeiting may be proved by circumstantial evidence, such as finding coining instruments and pieces of finished or partly finished counterfeit coin on defendant's premises. The offence is complete even though the counterfeiting may not have been quite finished (s. 1).

Any credible witness may prove coin counterfeit (s. 13).

Where " lawful authority or excuse " is put forward as a defence, such must be proved by the accused (ss. 6-10).

" Possession " under the Act includes not only the personal possession or custody of the article, but also the knowingly having it in the possession of any other person or in some building or place (s. 17).

Intent may be proved by evidence sufficient to allow the jury to infer it ; for example, accused attempted to pass the coin, or had similar coins in his possession. Guilty knowledge may be proved by evidence that accused had previously uttered counterfeit coin or had other counterfeit coins in his possession at the time.

All the misdemeanours under the Coinage Act, 1936, may be dealt with summarily if the Justices consider it expedient and if the accused consents (M.C. Act, 1952, s. 19 and 1st Sched.).

Any offence against the Coinage Offences Act, 1936, and the Gold and Silver (Export Control) Act, 1920, s. 2, must be reported to the Director of Public Prosecutions (see Appendix III).

Counterfeit Currency (Convention) Act, 1935.—This Act declares that currency notes issued by the Government of any country outside the United Kingdom and legal tender in that country, are deemed to be bank-notes within the Forgery Act, 1913, and this Act (s. 1).

Section 2 of the Revenue Act, 1889, which prohibits the importation of imitation coin, shall apply also to imitation foreign coin (s. 3). See also the Customs and Excise Act, 1952.

Attempts to commit offences in connection with counterfeit currency are extraditable (s. 4).

Chapter XVII

FORGERY

Contents

Forgery.—Forgery is the making of a false document (or writing) in order that it may be used as genuine or the counterfeiting of certain specified seals and dies, and forgery with intent to defraud or deceive is punishable. This definition is given in s. 1 of the Forgery Act, 1913, which consolidated and amended the law relating to forgery, and which makes the forgery of many documents felony and the forgery of all other documents misdemeanour, when committed with the intent to defraud or deceive, as the case may be.

At Common Law forgery was the fraudulent making or alteration of a writing to the prejudice of another man's right and was a misdemeanour.

A document is false within the meaning of the Act :—

(1) If the whole or any material part thereof purports to be made by or on behalf of a person who did not make it or authorise its making, or

(2) If, though properly authorised, the time or place of making or the identifying mark is falsely stated therein, or

(3) If any unauthorised material alteration has been made in it, or

(4) If it purports to be made by or for a fictitious or deceased person, or

(5) If it has been made with the intention that it should pass as having been made by some person other than the maker or authoriser (s. 1).

Under s. 35, C.J. Act, 1925, a document false in any way and made to be used as genuine is a forged document.

The uttering of a forged document, etc., is felony where the forgery is felony, and misdemeanour where the forgery is a misdemeanour, and is committed when a person, knowing the same to be forged and with intent to defraud or deceive, uses, offers, publishes, delivers, disposes of, tenders or exposes for payment, sale or exchange, exchanges, tenders in evidence or puts it off in any way (s. 6).

In a prosecution for forgery the intent should be shown. The intent to defraud applies particularly to documents of a private nature, such as deeds, wills, etc., and the intent to deceive mainly concerns documents of an official nature, such as birth certificates, court records, etc. To deceive is to induce a person to believe a thing is true which is false, and to defraud is to induce by deceit a person to act to his injury. It is not necessary to prove intent to defraud or deceive any particular person (s. 17). Such intent generally is sufficient.

Under section 16 of the Forgery Act, 1913, a search warrant can issue, on reasonable cause to believe that any person has in his custody or possession, without lawful authority or excuse, any banknote, or implement or materials for the forgery of a banknote, or any forged document, seal or die or any implements, etc., used or intended to be used for the forgery of any document. This warrant authorises search and seizure.

While the principal statute is the Forgery Act, 1913, other statutes created forgery offences ; for instance, the Forgery Act, 1861, the Stamp Duties Management Act, 1891, the Post Office Act, 1953, and the Customs and Excise Act, 1952. The main offences under these Acts will now be given, followed by the offences relating to paper money.

Principal Forgery Felonies.

(1) Forgery, with intent to defraud, of many specified valuable documents, such as wills, probates, bank-notes, deeds, bonds, valuable securities, insurance policies, etc., etc. (1913 Act, s. 2). Some of these offences if value does not exceed £20 and accused consents may be dealt with summarily. (M.C. Act, 1952, s. 19 and 1st Sched.)

(2) Forgery, with intent to defraud or deceive, of certain documents, mostly of an official nature, such as records of births, baptisms, marriages, deaths or burials, marriage licences, documents of any Court of Justice, etc., etc. (1913 Act, s. 3).

Any offence against these two sections (2 and 3) must be reported to the Director of Public Prosecutions (see Appendix III).

(3) Forgery with intent to defraud or deceive, of certain seals and dies, such as the Great Seal, a seal of any Court of Justice, a die required by law for marking gold or silver, etc., etc. (1913 Act, s. 5).

(4) Uttering, knowingly and with intent, any forged document, seal or die, the forging of which is felony (1913 Act, s. 6).

(5) With intent to defraud, demanding, receiving or obtaining or endeavouring to obtain any money or other property on forged instruments (1913 Act, s. 7). May be dealt with summarily if the value does not exceed £20 and accused consents (M.C. Act, 1952, s. 19 and 1st Sched.).

(6) Without lawful authority or excuse, having in possession any forged stamp, die or label, as specified (1913 Act, s. 8).

(7) Altering a money order with intent to defraud, or knowingly offering or uttering any such altered money order (Post Office Act, 1953, s. 23).

(8) An officer of any Court knowingly uttering any false copy or certificate of any record, or any person knowingly delivering any false process or order of Court to any person or professing to act under any such false process (Forgery Act, 1861, s. 28).

(9) Acknowledging any recognizance or other instrument before any Court or authorised person, in the name of any other person, without lawful authority or excuse (Forgery Act, 1861, s. 34).

(10) Destroying, injuring, falsifying, etc., any official records of births, baptisms, marriages, deaths or burials (Forgery Act, 1861, ss. 36 and 37).

(11) Unlawfully dealing with the hall-marks on gold or silver wares (Gold and Silver Wares Act, 1844).

(12) Fraudulently printing, altering, obliterating, mutilating, or " faking " in any way, any stamp (impressed or adhesive indicating any duty or fee, s. 27), or selling or using any fraudulently made stamp or knowingly and without lawful excuse having a fraudulently made stamp in possession (Stamp Duties Management Act, 1891, s. 13). Felonies under this section may be dealt with summarily with the accused's consent (M.C. Act, 1952, s. 19 and 1st Sched.).

See also " Post Office," Chap. 26.

Principal Forgery Misdemeanours.

(1) Forgery, with intent to defraud, of any document which it is not felony by statute to forge (1913 Act, s. 4).

(2) Forgery, with intent to defraud or deceive, of any public document the forgery of which is not felony by statute (1913 Act, s. 4).

(3) Uttering, knowingly and with intent, any forged document, seal or die, the forgery of which is misdemeanour (1913 Act, s. 6).

(4) Forgery of any trade mark. See " Trade Marks," Chap. 32.

(5) Forgery of any passport or the knowingly making of a false statement for the purpose of procuring a passport (Criminal Justice Act, 1925, s. 36). This offence may be punished summarily with consent of accused (M.C. Act, 1952, s. 19 and 1st Sched.). See " Aliens," Chap. 29.

(6) Making false statements, etc., to procure naval pay, pension or allowance (Admiralty Powers Act, 1865, s. 6).

(7) Forgery or deceitful use of any licence or certificate of insurance or security (Road Traffic Act, 1930, s. 112). See " False Motor Vehicle Licences, Certificates, etc." Chap. 24.

Forgery of a motor index mark or licence or registration book is a summary offence (Vehicles (Excise) Act, 1949, s. 21).

Forgery of or using a false certificate issued under the National Service Act is a summary offence. (N.S. Act, 1948, s. 30).

Offences as regards Paper Money.

(1) Forgery, with intent to defraud, of any bank-note (defined in s. 18 of the Act) or valuable security (such as a currency note). F. (1913 Act, s. 2.)

(2) Uttering, knowingly and with intent, any forged bank-note or valuable security. F. (1913 Act, s. 6.)

(3) Without lawful authority or excuse, knowingly purchasing, receiving or having in possession any forged bank-note. F. (1913 Act, s. 8.)

(4) Without lawful authority or excuse, making, using or knowingly having in possession, any paper intended to resemble and pass as special paper used for bank-notes, Treasury bills or London County bills or as revenue paper, or the instruments for making or dealing with such paper. F. (1913 Act, s. 9.)

(5) Without lawful authority or excuse, engraving or making on any material any words or devices resembling those on bank-notes or stock or dividend certificates, or having such engraved material in possession, or having in possession any paper upon which such words or devices have been printed. F. (1913 Act, s. 9.)

(6) Making, using or uttering for any purpose whatsoever any document purporting to be, or in any way resembling, or so nearly resembling as to be calculated to deceive, any currency or bank-note. Summary offence. Such documents and their plates, etc., may be ordered to be destroyed. Any person whose name appears on such a document is *prima facie* liable and he must give the name and address of the printer to the police (Criminal Justice Act, 1925, s. 38).

(7) The Currency and Bank-Notes Acts, 1914 and 1928, allow the Bank of England to issue bank-notes for one pound and for ten shillings, and such bank-notes shall be current and legal tender in Great Britain and Northern Ireland (1928 Act, s. 1). Currency or Treasury notes are to be deemed bank-notes (s. 4).

If any person prints, stamps or impresses on any bank-note, any words, letters or figures, he will commit a summary offence, punishable by fine not exceeding one pound (s. 12).

Under the Counterfeit Currency (Convention) Act, 1935, currency notes of other countries which are legal tender are deemed to be bank-notes within the Forgery Act, 1913 (s. 1), and any forged bank-note or plant for forging same which is seized shall be delivered to the Secretary of State by order of the Court or Justice (s. 2). Attempts to forge same are extraditable (s. 4).

False Accounting.—False accounting is a misdemeanour by statute, and is committed when a person responsible for correct entries in accounts makes false accounts with intent to defraud. This offence is akin to embezzlement and to forgery.

Falsification by Clerks.—It is a misdemeanour for any clerk, officer or servant, wilfully and with intent to defraud :—

(1) To destroy, alter, mutilate or falsify any book, paper, writing, valuable security or account which belongs to, or is in possession of, or has been received by him for or on behalf of his employer, or

(2) To make or concur in making any false entry or to omit, alter or concur in omitting or altering any material particular from or in any such book, document or account (Falsification of Accounts Act, 1875, s. 1).

These misdemeanours may be dealt with summarily if accused consents (M.C. Act, s. 19 and 1st Sched.).

Falsification by Company Officials.—It is a misdemeanour for any director or official of any body corporate or public company :—

(1) To receive or possess himself of any of the property of the company otherwise than in payment of a just debt or demand and with intent to defraud to omit to have a true and full entry thereof made in the books of the company (Larceny Act, 1861, s. 82).

(2) With intent to defraud, to destroy, alter, mutilate, falsify, etc., any of the books, accounts or valuable securities belonging to the company (Larceny Act, 1861, s. 83).

(3) To make or publish any written statement or account which he knows to be false in any material particular, with intent to deceive or defraud any member or creditor of the company, or with intent to induce any person to become a shareholder or partner therein or to entrust any property to such company or to enter into any security for the benefit thereof (Larceny Act, 1861, s. 84).

Musical Copyright Acts.—These Acts of 1902 and 1906 forbid the sale of pirated copies of any musical work and give certain powers to the police.

" Pirated copies " means any copies of any musical work reproduced without the consent of the owner of the copyright in such work (1906 Act, s. 3).

It is a summary offence to reproduce, sell, expose or have in possession for sale any pirated copies of any musical work, or to have in possession any plates for printing or reproducing pirated copies of any musical work (1906 Act, s. 1).

If any person hawks or offers for sale in the street any pirated copies of music, such copies may be seized by any constable on the request in writing of the apparent owner of the copyright or of his agent and at the risk of such owner. Any music so seized must be brought before a Court (1902 Act, s. 2).

If the owner has given a general written authority to the Chief Officer of Police requesting the arrest, at the owner's risk, of all persons found offering for sale pirated copies or committing offences under this section, in respect to the musical works specified in such written authority, a constable may arrest without warrant any person found in a street or public place selling, offering or having for sale any pirated copies of such musical works (1906 Act, s. 1).

A Magistrates' Court, if satisfied by sworn information that there is reasonable ground for suspecting that an offence against the Act is being committed on any premises, may grant a search warrant authorising entry, search and seizure between the hours of 6 A.M. and 9 P.M. (1906 Act, s. 2).

Factories Act, 1937.—The forgery of certificates, the making or using of false entries or false declarations required under the Act, or false personation in connection with the Act is an offence (s. 135) punishable summarily (s. 140).

Chapter XVIII

PROPERTY

Contents

Property in General.—The word "property " has several meanings, but in police circles it is used to signify money, things or goods which come into the possession of the police, such as stolen property, lost property, prisoners' property, etc.

In legal textbooks the word " property " is also used to indicate the exclusive right of possessing, enjoying and disposing of a thing ; in other words, to mean the title or right of ownership that an owner possesses with respect to a thing which is his property.

What the expression " property " in the Larceny Act, 1916, includes is given fully in s. 46 of the Act. See " Property and Possession," Chap. 14.

The owner, therefore, is said to have property in a thing which he owns. Thus the word " property " may in one sense mean an article, thing, house, or estate, and it may be used in another sense to indicate the owner's rights over that article, thing, house, or estate.

The great majority of crimes are committed in respect of property, especially as regards its possession.

For stealing and other unlawful procuring of property see " Larceny " (and its allied offences), " Breaking in," " Dealers in Old Metals," " Pawnbrokers," " Wrecks," " Public Stores," and " Army and Navy Property."

For injury to property see " Malicious Damage " and " Arson."

For possession of stolen property see " Receiving Stolen Property " and " Warrants."

For restoration of property see " Restitution of Stolen Property " and " Police (Property) Act."

For property lost and found see " Treasure Trove " and " Larceny by Statute."

Advertising rewards for the return of lost or stolen property is dealt with under the heading " Compounding Offences," Chap. 2.

Treasure Trove.—Treasure trove (or treasure found) is where any gold or silver, in coin, plate or bullion, is found hidden in a house or in the earth or other private place.

If the owner is unknown the treasure belongs to the Crown. The finding should be reported to the coroner, who may hold an inquest to determine whether articles of gold or silver so found are treasure trove or not. See " Courts of Justice," Chap. 4.

Concealing the discovery of any treasure trove is an offence, being a misdemeanour at common law, and the offence may be committed by a person who receives the treasure trove knowing it is treasure trove from the finder who was ignorant of its nature.

Police (Property) Act.—The Police (Property) Act, 1897, deals with the disposal of property which has come into police possession in connection with criminal matters.

On application either by the police or by a claimant of such property or where the owner cannot be ascertained a Magistrates' Court may make an order disposing, as it thinks right, of any property which has come into the possession of the police:—

(1) In connection with any criminal charge, or

(2) Under s. 103 of the Larceny Act, 1861 (seizure of stolen property on apprehension of the thief or alleged offender, or on search warrant), or

(3) Under s. 34 of the Pawnbrokers Act, 1872 (where pawn-brokers take possession of articles believed stolen, etc.), or

(4) Under s. 66 of the Metropolitan Police Act, 1839 (seizure of suspected stolen property), or s. 48 of the City of London Police Act, 1839.

Within 6 months after such an order a person may take legal proceedings for recovery of the property against the possessor under the order (s. 1).

Regulations of February 14, 1898, made under this Act by the Secretary of State, provide that all property which has so come into the possession of the police, where the owner has not been ascertained and no order of a Court has been made with respect thereto, shall be kept by the police for one year and then sold. If such property is a perishable article or if its custody involves unreasonable expense or inconvenience, the same shall be sold as soon as conveniently may be.

The proceeds of such sales are to be paid to the Police Property Fund, from which payment may be made for any expenses incurred in the conveyance, custody and sale of such property, for reasonable compensation to persons by whom property has been delivered to the police, and for any other purposes authorised by the Secretary of State. Contributions therefrom may be made for the benefit of discharged prisoners.

Where any property has been taken from a person charged before a magistrates' court with any offence, the police shall report same to the court and the court considering that it or part of it may be returned to the accused consistently with the interests of justice and the safe custody of the accused, may direct that it or part of it shall be returned to the accused or to such other person as he may require (M.C. Act, 1952, s. 39).

Restitution of Stolen Property.—When property is stolen, the thief deprives the owner of all the benefits of his ownership, but he does not deprive the owner of his ownership. The article itself is gone, but the owner still retains his property in the article —that is, his legal right of ownership over the article.

If the owner prosecutes to conviction a person for the felony or misdemeanour of stealing, taking, obtaining, extorting, embezzling, converting, disposing of or knowingly receiving his property, Assizes or Quarter Sessions can order its restoration subject to exceptions given in the section (Larceny Act, 1916, s. 45). A like power of ordering such restoration is given to a Magistrates' Court which convicts the offender summarily for any of the above offences which are not summary offences (M.C. Act, 1952, s. 33).

Where any court has ordered restitution as above and such property had been sold to an innocent purchaser, the court may order payment, not exceeding the proceeds of such sale, to such purchaser out of any moneys taken from the offender on his arrest. (Larceny Act, 1916, s. 45 ; M.C. Act, 1952, s. 33.)

A Magistrates' Court has also power to make an order under the Police (Property) Act, 1897, restoring to the owner any stolen property which has come into the possession of the police under the circumstances given in the Act. This covers cases in which a thief has been acquitted, or a person has been charged on summons or warrant but not arrested, or in which all the stolen property has not been included in the charge, or in which stolen property has been recovered as mentioned in the Act.

Under s. 30 of the Pawnbrokers Act, 1872, where a person is convicted summarily of unlawfully pawning goods or of stealing or fraudulently obtaining goods and pawning them, or where in the course of any proceedings it appears to a Magistrates' Court that goods have been unlawfully pawned, the Court may order the goods to be restored to the owner, either without payment or on payment or part payment of the loan to the pawnbroker according to what the Court considers just and fitting. However, this section will not apply if the goods were pledged for more than ten pounds.

The general rule as regards any sale or transfer of property is that the purchaser or receiver, even if he acts *bona fide* and pays the fair value, acquires no better right to the ownership of the property than what the seller or giver had. Thus the true owner of an article which has been stolen or lost has the right to take civil action to recover it or its value.

There are two exceptions to this rule.

(1) Sale in market overt (or open). When stolen goods are

sold in open fair or market for value to a *bona fide* customer, the ownership of the goods becomes vested in the purchaser. This exception to the rule is necessary to facilitate trade. However, if the owner prosecutes the thief or guilty receiver and he is convicted, the property is to be restored to the owner (Larceny Act, 1916, s. 45), the conviction cancelling the effect of the sale in market overt.

(2) Money or negotiable securities. The ownership of money or negotiable securities (such as bills of exchange and promissory notes), transferred as currency for value and to an innocent recipient, passes to that recipient, and there can be no restoration of the original article. See Larceny Act, 1916, s. 45 (2) (*a*).

This is necessary to secure free circulation of money in the general interests of the community. However, a recipient of stolen money or securities should prove that he received same in good faith and for value.

Where goods have been obtained by fraud or other wrongful means (such as false pretences) not amounting to stealing, a Court has to be most careful about making an order of restitution for fear that there might have been a sale of the goods to a *bona fide* purchaser.

See Sale of Goods Act, 1893, s. 24, and Larceny Act, 1916, s. 45.

Larceny Act, 1916, s. 46, defines " property " as including any property into which the original property has been converted or changed and anything acquired by such conversion or exchange therefore an owner of stolen money may recover from the thief any article which the thief has purchased with the stolen money. See Stone, under title " Restitution ".

A Court which convicts a person of felony may, if it thinks fit, on application of any person aggrieved, award any sum not exceeding £100 by way of satisfaction or compensation for any loss of property suffered by the applicant through the said felony. (Forfeiture Act, 1870, s. 4, and M.C. Act, 1952, s. 34.)

A Court, on making a probation order or an order for absolute or conditional discharge may (apart from costs) order the offender to pay damages for injury or compensation for loss, in summary cases up to £100 or greater sum if allowable under any other enactment (C.J. Act, 1948, s. 11 (2)).

Public Stores.—The Public Stores Act, 1875, applies to all stores under the care or control of any public department or office or of any person in the service of Her Majesty, and such stores are known as Her Majesty's Stores.

Certain marks (such as the broad arrow, a crown, Her Majesty's arms, coloured threads in the materials, etc., as described in the Act) are appropriated for distinguishing public stores. It is a misdemeanour to apply these marks to any stores without lawful authority, and it is felony to obliterate such marks with intent to conceal Her Majesty's property in any such stores (ss.4 and. 5)

Any person charged with having in possession any of Her Majesty's stores reasonably suspected of being stolen or unlawfully obtained, and who does not account satisfactorily to the Court how he came by the same, will be deemed guilty of a misdemeanour and may be punished summarily (s. 7).

If such stores are found in the possession of :—

(1) A person in Her Majesty's service, or
(2) A person in the service of a public department, or
(3) A dealer in old metals or marine stores, or
(4) A pawnbroker,

and he is taken or summoned before a Magistrates' Court, and the Court is satisfied such stores are or were Her Majesty's property, if such person does not satisfy the Court that he came lawfully by such stores, he will be liable to conviction and fine up to £5 (s. 9).

For the purposes of this Act stores shall be deemed to be in the possession of any person if he knowingly has them in the possession of any other person or in any premises, field or place, open or enclosed, whether occupied by himself or not, and whether for the use or benefit of himself or of another (s. 10).

A constable, if authorised in writing by a department, may stop, search and detain any vehicle or person reasonably suspected of conveying any such stores stolen or unlawfully obtained (s. 6). See also " Property of H.M. Forces," Chap. 30.

Wrecks.—The Minister of Transport and Civil Aviation has the general superintendence of all matters relating to shipwrecks, and may appoint any person to be a receiver of wreck and look after wrecked property in accordance with the Merchant Shipping Act, 1894.

In addition to the shipwrecked vessel, " wreck " will include goods cast into the sea while the ship is in danger and which sink (jetsam), goods which float on the surface (flotsam) and goods at the bottom of the sea and tied to a buoy (lagan).

A receiver of wreck has power to requisition all necessary assistance for the preservation of shipwrecked persons, vessels, cargo, etc. He must be notified by the finder of all wreck found, and all wreck found which is not taken by the owner must be delivered to him. It is an offence to take wreck or to keep possession of wreck, or to refuse to deliver wreck to the receiver, who may take such wreck by force if necessary. The receiver may obtain a search warrant to search for and seize concealed wreck. The receiver has full power to protect wreck ; he may arrest persons plundering or interfering with same, and may use force to suppress any interference or obstruction.

The Merchant Shipping Act, 1894, also makes it an offence to interfere with lighthouses or their lights, lightships, buoys or beacons, or to exhibit any light or fire in such a manner as to be mistaken for a light from a lighthouse, after notice to screen or extinguish such light.

The Malicious Damage Act, 1861, ss. 47 to 49, makes it felony to exhibit false lights or signals with intent to bring any vessel into danger or to do anything tending to the loss or destruction of any vessel, or to remove or conceal buoys and other sea marks or to destroy wrecks or any articles belonging thereto.

The Offences against the Person Act, 1861, s. 17, makes it felony to prevent or impede any person in his endeavour to save life at a shipwreck, and section 37 makes it a misdemeanour to assault any person, lawfully authorised, who is carrying out his duty in connection with a wreck.

Larceny Act, 1861, ss. 65 and 66, directs that any person in whose possession wreck is found, or who is offering for sale wreck or goods reasonably suspected to have been unlawfully taken from a wreck, may be summoned to show cause, and if he cannot satisfy the Justice that he came lawfully by such goods he may be imprisoned and the goods returned to their owner. Any person to whom such goods are offered for sale, any customs or excise officer, or any peace officer, may seize such goods and inform a Justice so that proceedings may be taken.

Larceny Act, 1916, s. 15, renders it felony for any person to steal any part of a vessel in distress or wrecked, or articles of any kind belonging to such vessel.

Hire Purchase Act, 1938.—This Act, as amended by the Hire Purchase Act, 1954, defines a " hire purchase agreement " as one for the bailment of goods under which the bailee may buy the goods or under which the property in the goods will or may pass to the bailee, and a " credit-sale agreement " as one for the sale of goods under which the purchase price is payable by five or more instalments (s. 21).

The Act applies to all such agreements under which the purchase price does not exceed £1,000 in the case of livestock (horses, cattle, sheep, goats, pigs or poultry, (s. 21) and £300 in any other case (s. 1, as amended in 1954).

Certain requirements are prescribed as necessary before any such agreements are entered into, so that the cash price may be quite definite (ss. 2 and 3) and the seller is bound to supply documents and information on request (s. 6).

In the case of a hire purchase agreement, the hirer is given the right to determine by payment the agreement before the final payment falls due (s. 4). Certain provisions in any agreement shall be void including any condition allowing the owner to enter on premises to take possession of goods let under a hire purchase agreement (s. 5), and the hirer is bound to give information as to the whereabouts of the goods on penalty of fine (s. 7).

If one third of the hire purchase price has been paid or tendered, the owner shall not enforce any right to recover possession of the goods otherwise than by an action (s. 11).

This restriction on recovery applies to hire purchase agreements (to which the Act applies) made before or after the commencement of the Act (s. 20) and in such case if after the commencement of the Act the hirer refuses to give up possession of the goods to the owner the hirer shall not, by reason only of the refusal, be liable to the owner for conversion of the goods (s. 17).

The Act does not apply to hire purchase or credit-sale agreements made before January 1, 1939, (or in the case of the 1954 amendments, 30th August, 1954) except as above-mentioned and some other points as given in s. 20.

Chapter XIX

POACHING

Contents

Poaching Offences.—Poaching is the offence committed by a person who pursues, kills, or takes certain game birds and animals on land where he has no right to go. It amounts to trespass on land accompanied by taking or attempting to take certain property.

Poaching Prevention Act, 1862 : Under this Act " game " includes hares, rabbits, woodcocks, snipe, also pheasants, partridges, grouse, black or moor game and their eggs.

Any constable, in any highway, street or public place, may search any person whom he may have good cause to suspect of coming from any land where he shall have been unlawfully in pursuit of game and having in his possession any game unlawfully obtained or any gun, part of a gun or nets or engines used for the killing or taking of game.

Such constable may also stop and search any conveyance in or upon which he shall have good cause to suspect that any such game or article or thing is being carried by any such person.

Should any such game, article or thing be found, he may seize and detain same. He has no power under this Act to arrest, or to seize dogs or ferrets.

If a constable makes such a seizure he should summon the person, and the Court, if satisfied that the accused had obtained such game by unlawfully going on any land or had used such article or thing for unlawfully killing or taking game or had been accessory thereto, may fine him £5 and forfeit such game, gun, etc., ordering the same to be sold or destroyed. (S.2)

Night Poaching Acts, 1828 and 1844 : Under these Acts " game " includes hares, pheasants, partridges, grouse, heath or moor game, black game and bustards.

Unlawfully taking or destroying any game or rabbits by night in any land (open or enclosed) or public road, highway or path, is a summary offence.

By night unlawfully entering or being on any land, whether open or enclosed, with any gun, net, engine or other instrument for the purpose of taking or destroying game is a summary offence.

Offenders, as above described, who assault or offer violence with any offensive weapon to owners or occupiers of land, their gamekeepers, servants or their assistants, commit misdemeanour.

Three or more persons together unlawfully by night entering or being on any land, open or enclosed, to take or destroy game or rabbits, any of such persons being armed with any offensive weapon, commit misdemeanour.

Under these Acts the " night " commences at the expiration of the first hour after sunset and ends at the beginning of the first hour before sunrise.

Owners, occupiers, gamekeepers and their assistants may arrest any such offenders caught in the act or in pursuit, and deliver them to any peace officer.

Game Act, 1831 : Under this Act " game " includes hares, pheasants, partridges, grouse, heath or moor game, black game and bustards.

The following are summary offences :—

Trespassing in search or pursuit of game or of woodcocks, snipe, quails, landrails or rabbits, on any land—

(1) In the day-time (s. 30) ;

(2) And not giving real name and address, or wilfully continuing or returning upon the land when required to quit and give name and address by the owner or occupier or other authorised person, who in such latter case may arrest the offender and bring him before a Justice (s. 31) ;

(3) In the day-time in company with four or more persons, any of such persons having a gun and any of such persons using violence or threat to prevent any other person approaching them for the purpose of requiring them to quit or to tell their names (s. 32).

The daytime in this Act commences at the beginning of the last hour before sunrise and ends at the expiration of the first hour after sunset (s. 34).

Any prosecution should be commenced within three months of the offence (s. 41).

The Act does not apply to persons hunting or coursing with hounds or greyhounds (s. 35).

Larceny Act, 1861, s. 17 : To unlawfully kill or take any hare or rabbit in any warren or ground lawfully used for the breeding or keeping of hares or rabbits, whether enclosed or not :—

(1) during the night-time (as defined above under Night Poaching Acts) is a misdemeanour ;

(2) during the day-time (as defined above) is a summary offence.

But this section does not affect any person taking rabbits in the daytime on the tide banks in Lincolnshire.

It is also a summary offence at any time to set or use any snare or engine in any such warren for hares or rabbits (s. 17).

Game Laws.—Several statutes, such as the Game Act, 1831, the Game Licences Act, 1860, the Ground Game Act, 1880, and the Ground Game (Amendment) Act, 1906, deal with matters affecting game birds and animals.

The unlawful pursuit and taking of game is dealt with under " Poaching Offences."

Generally speaking, a breach of the Game Laws is an excise offence, and proceedings are taken by the Inland Revenue.

Game is defined as including hares, pheasants, partridges, grouse, heath or moor game, black game and bustards (Game Act, 1831, s. 2).

A person must not take, kill or pursue or use any dog, gun or other instrument for the purpose of taking, killing or pursuing any game or woodcock, snipe, quail or landrail, or coney or deer, without a game certificate (s. 23 of the Game Act, 1831, as amended by the Game Licences Act, 1860, which in s. 5 gives the cases where the possession of a game certificate is not necessary).

However the Ministry of Agriculture, Fisheries and Food may require in writing, any person to kill, take or destroy on specified land rabbits, hares, deer, foxes, etc. Non compliance will be a summary offence (Agriculture Act, 1947, ss. 98, 100 and Pests Act, 1954, s. 2).

A person who holds a game certificate does not require a gun licence, but the possession of a gun licence under the Gun Licence Act, 1870, is no defence to a prosecution for acting without a game certificate.

Before a person may deal in game he must be licensed by the District or Borough Council, and he must also obtain an excise licence from the Post Office. See " Game Dealers," Chap. 31.

Under the Game Act, 1931, s. 3 it is unlawful to take or kill game on Sunday or Christmas Day, and also during the close seasons, which are :—

Pheasants, between February 1 and October 1.
Partridges, between February 1 and September 1.
Grouse, between December 10 and August 12.
Black game, between December 10 and August 20.
Bustards, between March 1 and September 1.
Quail, between February 14 and July 1.

Other birds are in general now protected throughout the year. See " Birds," Chap. 35.

Hares.—It is illegal to sell or expose native hares for sale during the months of March, April, May, June and July. (Hares Preservation Act, 1892.)

Fishery Laws.—The law provides for the preservation or conservation of fish in the rivers and waters of the country and for the protection of the rights of owners of fisheries.

The Minister of Agriculture, Fisheries and Food has power to constitute Fishery Boards in charge of fishery districts, who may appoint water bailiffs and make byelaws fixing the close seasons for fish and for many other purposes.

Salmon and Fresh-water Fisheries Act, 1923.

S. 61 : Fishery Boards grant licences to fish for salmon or trout.

S. 63 : It is an offence to fish for or take salmon or trout otherwise than by means of an instrument which the fisherman is duly licensed to use for that purpose.

S. 64 : Any constable, water bailiff, member of a Fishery Board, or person producing his licence under this Act may require any person found fishing for salmon or trout to produce his licence and give his name and address. Failure to comply is an offence.

The following acts in connection with salmon, trout or fresh-water fish are summary offences under this statute :—

S. 1 : To use any light, or otter, spear, stroke haul, or like instrument for taking fish, or to have same in possession under circumstances showing the intent to use same for that purpose, or to throw missiles into water for that purpose.

S. 2 : To use fish roe for the purpose of fishing, or to buy, sell or have salmon or trout roe for that purpose.

S. 3 : To knowingly take any such fish which is unclean or immature, or to have in possession any such unclean or immature fish.

S. 4 : To wilfully disturb any spawn or spawning fish.

S. 8 : To cause or knowingly permit any poisonous substances or trade effluents to flow or be put into any waters containing fish. See also Rivers (Prevention of Pollution) Act, 1951.

S. 9 : To use dynamite or other explosive substance or to put any noxious material into any waters or to destroy any dam or sluice, with intent thereby to take or destroy fish.

(See also s. 32 of the Malicious Damage Act, 1861, Chap. 15.)

Ss. 6 and 7 : To use nets in a certain manner or to use nets with meshes smaller than the dimensions prescribed.

Ss. 11 and 28 : To use fixed nets or other fixed engines unless duly authorised.

Ss. 26, 27, 29 and 31 : To fish for or take or obstruct any salmon or trout during the close seasons, or during the weekly close time (usually 6 A.M. Saturday to 6 A.M. Monday) except with rod and line.

Ss. 30 and 32 : To buy, sell or have in possession for sale any salmon between Aug. 31 and Feb. 1, or any trout between Aug. 31 and March 1, except salmon or trout (Amendment Act, 1929) caught abroad, or preserved abroad, or preserved within this country between Feb. 1 (or March 1, as regards trout) and Aug. 31.

S. 35 : To fish for eels by rod and line or fish for or take any fresh-water fish in any river or lake or water communicating with any river, during the annual close season for fresh-water fish (usually between March 14 and June 16). Fresh-water fish include any fish living in fresh water exclusive of salmon and trout, eels and migratory fish.

This Act of 1923 contains many other provisions for the protection of fish. It gives power of entry, search, and seizure of fish and instruments, to duly appointed water bailiffs, who are deemed to be constables for the enforcement of the Act, and persons resisting or obstructing them are guilty of an offence against the Act (s. 67).

Any person who during the night is found illegally taking fish or at or near waters with intent illegally to take fish, or having in his possession any prohibited instrument, may be arrested without warrant by any water bailiff and his assistants and delivered to the police (s. 71).

Larceny Act, 1861, s. 24. It is a misdemeanour to unlawfully and wilfully take or destroy any fish in any water in any land adjoining or belonging to the dwelling-house of any person who owns such water or has a right of fishery therein, but persons merely angling in such waters during the day-time commit only a summary offence (for which there is no power of arrest without warrant).

It is a summary offence to unlawfully and wilfully take or destroy or attempt to take or destroy any fish in any other waters which shall be private property or in which there is a private right of fishery, but if the offence is committed by angling in the day-time the maximum fine is smaller, and the offender is not liable to arrest under the Act (s. 24). Under s. 25 the owner or his servants may seize the tackle of such fishers, but the angler in the day-time whose tackle has been seized is thereby exempted from any other penalty.

Sea-Fishing Industry Act, 1933, s. 4 (as substituted by s. 38 of the Sea Fish Industry Act, 1938). No person shall in Great Britain sell, expose or offer for sale, or have in possession for sale, any sea fish of a size smaller than that prescribed by Order. The market authority (in their market), any officer of police and certain fishery officials, in order to enforce the section, may, at all reasonable times, board any fishing boat or enter any premises used for any business for the treatment, storage or sale of sea-fish, search for and examine any sea-fish and seize any sea-fish kept in contravention of the section.

" Sea fish " means fish (fresh or cured) of any kind found in the sea and includes lobsters, mussels, crabs, shrimps, prawns, oysters, cockles, and any other shell fish, but does not include salmon or migratory trout (s. 9).

Immature Sea-Fish Order, 1948, gives the following minimum

sizes (inches long)—hake (13), haddock (9½), plaice (9), dabs (9), soles (9), whiting (9½), lemon soles (9), witches (9), megrims (9).

Sea Fish Industry Act, 1938. This Act deals with the white fish industry and defines " white fish " as fish of any kind found in the sea other than herring, salmon and migratory trout and includes shell fish (s. 62). See also the White Fish and Herring Industries Acts, 1948, 1953, and the Sea Fish Industry Act, 1951.

Trespass.—The word " trespass " is used to describe the act of entering or being upon land or premises without any right to be thereon.

Civil action in the County Court may be taken against a trespasser, but the mere fact of a person trespassing does not make him liable under the criminal law.

A trespasser who refuses to leave on request may by his conduct tend to provoke a breach of the peace and thereby become liable to arrest and prosecution. See Chap. 22.

If a trespasser causes any damage to any real or personal property whatsoever either of a public or private nature by his trespassing he may be prosecuted summarily for committing wilful or malicious damage which in the opinion of the Court does not exceed the value of £20, and may be imprisoned or fined and the Court may award reasonable compensation to the person aggrieved. However, the section will not apply if the " trespasser " acted under a fair and reasonable supposition that he had a right to do the act complained of (C.J.A. Act, 1914, s. 14), but to sustain a conviction there must be proof of some actual damage. See Stone, under title " Property."

The Justices should be satisfied that there was real damage and a wilful act for the purpose of committing damage.

Trespassing in pursuit of game is dealt with under " Poaching." For trespass on railway premises, see " Railways," Chap. 26.

A trespasser on premises may be removed, but he should first be requested to depart, and no more force than is necessary to remove him should be used. A person is entitled to protect himself and property against trespassers, but he will be liable criminally if he uses unnecessary violence.

Persons found in any premises or enclosed area for any unlawful purpose may be arrested and dealt with under s. 4, Vagrancy Act, 1824. See " Loiterers, etc.," Chap. 28.

Under s. 31 of the Offences against the Person Act, 1861, it is a misdemeanour to set any spring-gun, man-trap or other engine calculated to destroy human life or inflict grievous bodily harm upon a trespasser or other person coming into contact therewith, or for the occupier to knowingly permit any such engine to remain so set, provided that this section does not make it illegal to set traps to destroy vermin or to set spring guns or other engines from sunset to sunrise in a dwelling-house for the protection thereof.

As regards commons and waste lands, the public have rights of access for air and exercise subject to any regulations affecting such land.

It is a summary offence (40s. fine) without lawful authority to draw or drive upon such land any carriage, cart, caravan or other vehicle or to camp or light any fire thereon or to fail to observe any conditions lawfully prescribed (Law of Property Act, 1925, s. 193).

See also s. 14, Road Traffic Act, 1930, as to the summary offence of driving a motor vehicle on land not part of a road (" Regulation of Traffic," Chap. 24).

PART IV.—OFFENCES AFFECTING THE COMMUNITY IN GENERAL

Chapter XX

OFFENCES AGAINST THE STATE AND RELIGION

Contents

Treason.—Treason means treachery. It is a betraying or breach of faith and in law denotes the grave crime of treachery towards the Sovereign as head of the State or any betraying of the State itself. Blackstone terms it the highest civil crime which any man can possibly commit.

The Treason Acts declare certain offences to be treason : for example, compassing the death of the Sovereign, levying war against the Sovereign, adhering to the Sovereign's enemies.

Treason is a most serious crime, being directed against the security of the State, and is punishable on conviction by death. All persons concerned in any treason are regarded as principals.

Any knowledge and concealment of treason, even without any assent to it, is termed misprision of treason, and is a misdemeanour at common law. The procedure in treason cases is to be the same as in murder cases (Treason Act, 1945).

A person charged with treason shall not be admitted to bail except by order of a judge of the High Court or the Secretary of State (M.C. Act, 1952, s. 8).

Many acts directed against the safety or interests of the State are also punishable under the Official Secrets Acts. See " Official Secrets Acts."

Treason Felony Act, 1848 : Under this statute the following acts of treason may be prosecuted and dealt with as felonies (imprisonment for life).

(1) Compassing to deprive or depose the Sovereign from the style, honour and name of the Crown of the United Kingdom or of any other of his Dominions.

(2) Levying war against the Sovereign within the United Kingdom in order by force or constraint to compel him to change his measures or counsels, or to intimidate or overawe Parliament.

(3) Stirring up any foreigner with force to invade the United Kingdom or any other part of the Sovereign's dominions.

See also " Incitement to Disaffection," Chap. 30.

Every case of treason must be reported to the Director of Public Prosecutions (see Appendix III).

Sedition.—Sedition is a general term covering attempts to excite discontent or disaffection, disorder or tumult, or to subvert the Government, constitution or laws of the country.

Sedition, being against the safety of the State, is a misdemeanour at common law.

Sedition consists of acts, writings or conduct which do not amount to treason, but which must be punished in the interests of the State, for if unchecked, sedition leads to disorder, and possibly to revolution.

It is a crime against society nearly allied to that of treason.

The offence of sedition is usually committed by writing or speaking words which may pervert the minds of the people and cause general disaffection or public disorder.

It will be for a jury to decide whether such writings or words are seditious.

A writing of a seditious nature is known as a seditious libel (see " Libel," Chap. 23), and the writer cannot plead the truth of his libel as an excuse for his publishing it.

A speaker at a meeting who has used seditious words may be indicted for his seditious speech, and the circumstances of the meeting itself may render the meeting an unlawful assembly.

Seditious conduct may be dealt with as conduct likely to lead to a breach of the peace, and those concerned may be bound over by the Court. See " Breach of the Peace and Sureties," Chap. 22.

An alien may be punished on indictment or summarily for any attempt to cause sedition or disaffection or to promote industrial unrest (Aliens Restriction (Amendment) Act, 1919, s. 3).

See Stone, under title " Sedition."

Any offence of sedition and seditious libel must be reported to the Director of Public Prosecutions (see Appendix III).

Drilling.—Under the Unlawful Drilling Act, 1819, all meetings of persons for the purpose of training or drilling to the use of arms or for practising military movements without lawful authority are prohibited. Every person present at such meeting for the purpose of drilling and training others or who trains or drills others or assists therein, and every person present for the purpose of being drilled or trained or who is drilled or trained thereat is guilty of a misdemeanour.

Any such unlawful meeting may be dispersed by any Justice or by any constable and his assistants, and those present may be arrested and detained.

Under the Firearms Act, 1920, s. 16, a Secretary of State or any officer deputed by him for the purpose has power to authorise meetings and assemblies for the purpose of training or drilling as above mentioned. See also " Public Order Act 1936," Chap. 22.

Official Secrets Acts. The Official Secrets Act, 1911 amended and supplemented by the Official Secrets Acts, 1920 and 1939, deals with spying and other practices prejudicial to the safety or interests of the State.

In the interests of the State certain premises and localities are declared to be " prohibited places," and the Acts aim at preventing spying on such places.

A " prohibited place " includes any work of defence, camp, ship, aircraft, telegraph station, munition factory, etc., etc., belonging to or occupied by the Crown ; any place where munitions of war or documents relating thereto are made or kept on behalf of the Crown ; and any railway, road, canal, work of public character or place declared to be a prohibited place by order of the Secretary of State (1911 Act, s. 3).

Felony. For any purpose prejudicial to the safety or interests of the State, to approach, inspect or enter any prohibited place, or to make any sketch, model or note likely to be of any use to an enemy, (including a potential enemy *R.* v. *Parrott* (1913)), or to obtain, record, or communicate to any other person any secret official code or password or any document or information which might be useful to an enemy. The prosecution may give evidence of the accused's character (1911 Act, s 1).

Misdemeanours. For any person in possession of information of a secret official nature, or relating to a prohibited place, or obtained in contravention of the Act, or entrusted in confidence to him by a person holding office under Her Majesty, or procured by virtue of his office under Her Majesty, to communicate same to any unauthorised person, or to use same in any manner prejudicial to the safety or interests of the State, or to unauthorisedly retain same, or to unreasonably endanger the safety of same (1911 Act, s. 2).

A constable is a person who holds office under Her Majesty (*Lewis* v. *Cattle* (1938)). He is a public servant and an officer of the Crown (*Fisher* v. *Oldham Corporation* (1930)).

To communicate any information relating to munitions of war to any foreign power, or in any other manner prejudicial to the safety or interests of the State (1911 Act, s. 2, and 1920 Act).

To knowingly receive any document, information, etc., communicated to him in contravention of the Act (1911 Act, s. 2).

To knowingly harbour any person about to commit or who has committed an offence under the Act, or to wilfully omit or refuse to disclose to a superintendent of police any information he may have regarding such person (1911 Act, s. 7, and 1920 Act).

For the purpose of gaining admission to a prohibited place or for any other purpose prejudicial to the safety or interests of the

State, **to use, without lawful authority, any official uniform,** or to make any false declaration or application, or to forge any pass or other official document, or to personate any official, or to use or have without authority any genuine or counterfeit official die, seal or stamp (1920 Act, s. 1).

Without lawful authority, to retain for any purpose prejudicial to the safety or interests of the State, any official document, or to fail to comply with any direction respecting same (1920 Act, s. 1).

Without lawful authority, to communicate to any other person any official information issued for one's own use alone, or to have in possession official information issued for the use of some person other than himself (1920 Act, s. 1).

On obtaining possession of any official document by finding or otherwise, to neglect or fail to restore it to the person for whose use it was issued, or to a police constable (1920 Act, s. 1).

To interfere in any way with a police officer or any member of Her Majesty's Forces engaged on guard or other duty in relation to any prohibited place (1920 Act, s. 3).

To fail to give on demand to a chief officer of police duly so authorised by a Secretary of State or so acting in a case of great emergency, any information in one's power relating to an offence or suspected offence under s. 1 of the 1911 Act, or to fail to attend at such reasonable time and place as may be specified to furnish such information (Official Secrets Act, 1939).

Any attempt, aid, incitement, etc., to an offence under the Acts will be as punishable as the offence concerned (1920 Act, s. 7).

Summary Offences. A Secretary of State, by warrant, may require any person who owns or controls any cable or wireless telegraphic apparatus to produce any or all telegrams received or sent by him. Failure to do so is punishable summarily (1920 Act, s. 4).

Every person who carries on the business of receiving for reward, letters, telegrams or other postal packets for delivery or forwarding to the persons for whom they are intended (known as an " **accommodation address** "), must be registered with the Chief Officer of Police of the district, and must keep a book in which he must record :—

(1) The name and address of every person for whom any postal packet is received or who has requested that postal packets received may be sent to him ;

(2) Any instructions as to the sending of postal packets ;

(3) The place of sending, the date of posting (as per post-mark) and the date of receipt of every postal packet received, also the name of sender if given thereon, and the registration particulars if it is registered ;

(4) The date of delivery and name and address of the person to whom any postal packet is delivered ;

(5) If a postal packet is forwarded, the date and name and address of person to whom it is forwarded.

He must not deliver a letter to any person until that person has signed a receipt for same in this book, nor must he give the letter to any other person or send it on to any other address, unless he has received written instructions to that effect signed by the addressee.

This book and all postal packets and instructions regarding same must be kept at all reasonable times open to inspection by any police constable. Any contravention of the above rules or false information given or false entry made is an offence and is punishable summarily (1920 Act, s. 5).

Power of Arrest. Any person found committing, or reasonably suspected of having committed or having attempted to commit or being about to commit an offence under the Act, may be arrested without warrant (1911 Act, s. 6).

Power of Search. On reasonable grounds a Justice may grant a search warrant authorising any constable named therein to enter at any time any premises or place named, and to search same and every person found therein, and to seize any document or thing found in connection with which there is reasonable ground for suspecting that an offence under the Act has been or is about to be committed.

In a case of great emergency necessitating immediate action in the interests of the State, a superintendent of police can, by a written order, give any constable the like authority as may be given by a Justice's search warrant (1911 Act, s. 9). See Chap. 5.

Prosecution. Any person charged with any offence under these Acts may be arrested, or a warrant for his arrest may be issued and executed, and such person may be remanded in custody or on bail, but no further proceedings or prosecution may be taken without the consent of the Attorney-General (1911 Act, s. 8).

Any offence under these Acts must be reported to the Director of Public Prosecutions (see Appendix III).

During trial the court may be cleared. See " Open Court," Chap. 4.

Piracy is robbery on the sea, and is the taking of a ship or any of its contents on the high seas from the control of those lawfully entitled, and taking it away without any authority. It is a felony at common law and under the Piracy Acts, and if accompanied by violence it is punishable with death and therefore every such case must be reported to the Director of Public Prosecutions (see Appendix III).

Foreign Enlistment Act, 1870. This statute is intended to prevent British subjects from assisting any foreign State at war with a friendly State. It is a misdemeanour for any British subject, without licence, to enlist in the service of, or to recruit for, or to leave this country with intent to enlist in the service of, or to convey illegally enlisted persons to, any foreign State at war with another State at peace with this country. It is also a misdemeanour to build, equip or despatch a vessel knowing same is to be employed in the service of such a State, or to prepare, without licence, any military or naval expedition against any friendly State.

Blasphemy is the use of language (spoken or written) having a tendency to vilify the Christian religion or the Bible. The offence lies in the attacking of Christianity in an indecent manner, with intent to bring religion into contempt, corrupt public morals and shock or insult believers. It is a misdemeanour at common law. See Stone, under title " Blasphemy."

Disturbing Public Worship.—Any wilful and malicious or contemptuous disturbance of persons assembled for religious worship, or any interference with the person officiating or any of those there assembled is punishable by fine at Quarter Sessions (Places of Religious Worship Act, 1812, s. 12, and Religious Disabilities Act, 1846).

Riotous, violent or indecent behaviour (known as " brawling ") in any place of religious worship at any time or in any churchyard or burial ground is a summary offence, and the offender may be arrested by a constable or churchwarden (Ecclesiastical Courts Jurisdiction Act, 1860, ss. 2 and 3). See also " Clergymen," Chap. 29, and Stone, under title " Church."

Bigamy. Bigamy is the crime committed by a person who being legally married goes through a lawful form of marriage with another person during the life of the former husband or wife.

This second " marriage " is void, and the crime lies in the profanation of the solemn ceremony of marriage, such profanation being regarded as an outrage on public decency. Bigamy is a felony by statute and is punishable at Assizes with seven years imprisonment.

Offences against the Person Act, 1861, s. 57 : Whosoever being married shall marry any other person during the life of the former husband or wife, whether the second marriage shall have taken place in England or Ireland or elsewhere, shall be guilty of felony.

This section does not apply (and no offence is committed) in the case of a second marriage contracted :—

(1) Outside England and Ireland by a person who is not a subject of Her Majesty's, or

(2) By a person divorced (decree having been made absolute) from his or her wife or husband, or

(3) By a person whose former marriage has been declared void by a Court of competent jurisdiction, or

(4) By a person whose husband or wife has been continuously absent for seven years then last past and was not known by such person to be living within that time.

Having regard to the above description of the felony, it will be necessary that the prosecution should prove the following in a case of bigamy :—

(1) The first marriage and that it was a valid marriage. This is usually proved by a certified copy from the marriage register. An admission of the marriage by the accused is not sufficient. It must be proved that the marriage was a valid or binding marriage, and if after this has been proved, the accused asserts that it was not valid (if it is invalid the second marriage is not bigamous) the onus of proof that it is invalid rests on him.

(2) The identity of the parties, viz. that they are the persons mentioned in the marriage certificates produced. The best proof will be the evidence of persons present at the marriages.

(3) The second marriage ceremony.

This can usually be proved by a certified copy of the marriage register. It must be proved that this second ceremony was a lawful ceremony of marriage. It is immaterial whether the ceremony took place in England or abroad so long as it is legal according to the law of the place where celebrated. It is no defence to show that this second marriage was invalid or void by law.

(4) That the first husband or wife was alive when the second marriage took place.

This can be proved by the production of the first husband or wife, or by evidence that he or she was alive at the time.

(5) If the first husband or wife had been absent for seven years then past, the prosecution should prove that the accused knew he or she was alive at the time. If this cannot be proved the accused may be acquitted under section 57 as above.

However, *bona fide* belief on reasonable grounds that the wife (or husband) is dead even within 7 years is a good defence (*R.* v. *Tolson* (1889)).

The second " husband " or " wife " can give evidence, as he or she is not legally the husband or wife of the accused. The real husband or wife of the accused may be called as a witness for the prosecution or for the defence and without the consent of the accused, but he or she cannot be compelled to give evidence. (Criminal Justice Administration Act, 1914, s. 28 (3)).

Chapter XXI

PUBLIC JUSTICE OFFENCES

Contents

Contempt of Court.—A contempt of court is any disobedience to its rules or any disregard of its dignity as a Court of law. It is an interference with the course of justice and is a misdemeanour at common law.

The offence may be committed by disorderly behaviour in a Court, disobedience of the order of a Court, manufacture of false evidence to mislead a Court, intimidation of the parties or witnesses, publication of comments or information likely to prejudice the hearing of a case, etc.

Criminal Justice Act, 1925, s. 41. It is a summary offence to take any photograph in any Court of Justice or to make any sketch in any Court for publication of a judge, recorder, registrar, justice or coroner, a juror, a witness, or a party to any proceedings before the Court, or to publish any such photograph or sketch. This protection covers the persons named while in or entering or leaving a Court-room or the premises in which a Court is held.

For press reports as to Juvenile Courts, etc., see " Treatment of Youthful Offenders," Chap. 12.

Justices have no power to commit persons summarily for contempt, but higher Courts may deal summarily with such cases. Proceedings may be taken by indictment triable at Assizes or by criminal information in the Queen's Bench Division.

A Magistrates' Court may order a person to find sureties for his good behaviour if his conduct in Court is disrespectful or unmannerly, obstructive or insulting, or likely to lead to a breach of the peace. If such person fails to give the required surety he may be committed to prison in default of giving surety.

Usually Justices will direct such an offender to be removed from the Court.

Escape.—It is a misdemeanour at common law for a prisoner, whether innocent or guilty, to escape without the use of force from lawful custody on a criminal charge.

If a prisoner escapes by force the offence is felony if he was in custody on a charge of treason or felony, and it is misdemeanour if he had been in custody on a minor charge.

If a prisoner makes a voluntary escape by consent or connivance of his custodian, the custodian will be deemed guilty of the same kind of offence for which the prisoner was in custody.

Any constable or other person who has a prisoner lawfully in his custody and who negligently suffers him to go at large commits a misdemeanour at common law.

Every person is bound to hold a lawful prisoner and to deliver him up to the proper authority. If a prisoner escapes and is not briskly pursued and taken again before he has been lost sight of, the escape will be considered a " negligent " escape.

To aid a prisoner in custody for treason or felony to make his escape from prison or from the officer conveying him under warrant to prison is a felony (Prison Escape Act, 1742). For " Rescue," see below.

Criminal Justice Act, 1948, s. 66, states that any person required or authorised by or under the Act to be taken to any place or to be kept in custody, shall, while being so taken or kept, be deemed to be in legal custody, and s. 65 authorises arrest without warrant of certain persons unlawfully at large. See Chap. III.

Prison Breach is escape by force from a lawful imprisonment by means of some actual breaking of the prison or place of custody, and is felony or misdemeanour according to the offence for which the person was in prison. Under s. 39 of the Prison Act, 1952, it is a felony for any person to aid a prisoner in escaping or attempting to escape from any prison. An unsuccessful attempt to break out of prison or any conspiracy to effect prison breach is a misdemeanour at common law.

Rescue.—Rescue is the forcible liberation of a prisoner from lawful custody.

The offence is treason, felony or misdemeanour, according to the offence of the person rescued, but if the person rescued is not convicted of his original offence, the rescue is a misdemeanour.

For attempted rescue and assaulting the police, see " Assault," Chap. 8, and as regards the prisoner, see " Escape."

The forcible rescue of goods which have been lawfully seized under legal process is a misdemeanour at common law.

Under the County Courts Act, 1934, the rescue or attempted rescue of goods seized under process of a County Court is a summary offence and a Court bailiff may arrest the offender and bring him before the Judge (s. 124) and an assault on an officer of the Court acting in the execution of his duty is also a summary offence and a Court bailiff may arrest the offender and bring him before the Judge (s. 31).

Pound Breach, or the forcible rescue of cattle by breach of the pound in which they had been lawfully placed, is a misdemeanour at common law.

To release or attempt to rescue or release any cattle impounded under the Highway Act before the same shall have been legally discharged, or to damage the pound, is a summary offence (Highway Act, 1835, s. 75; Town Police Clauses Act, 1847, s. 26).

Under the Pound Breach Act, 1843, it is a summary offence to release or attempt to release any cattle or other beasts lawfully seized for the purpose of being impounded or on the way to or from the pound, or to in any way damage the pound. See " Impounding Animals," Chap. 24.

Perjury.—Perjury is a misdemeanour at common law and also by statute. It was made an offence because the taking of a wilful false oath in a Court of law is an abuse of public justice. The law relating to perjury and kindred offences was consolidated by the Perjury Act, 1911, as follows.

(1) *Perjury.*—Perjury is the crime committed by a person lawfully sworn as a witness or interpreter in a judicial proceeding who wilfully makes a statement material in that proceeding which he knows to be false or does not believe to be true (1911 Act, s. 1).

" Lawfully sworn " includes affirmation and declaration as well as any oath administered without objection by the person sworn (1911 Act, s. 15).

" Judicial proceeding " includes a proceeding before any Court, tribunal or person having by law power to hear, receive and examine evidence on oath.

" Material statement " is one such as might affect the decision of the Court, tribunal or person, and the Judge at the trial will decide whether the statement is or is not material (1911 Act, s. 1).

It must be clear that the perjury was deliberate and wilful, not merely carelessness or mistake.

(2) *False Statements on Oath not in Judicial Proceedings.*—If a person is authorised or required by law to make any statement on oath for any purpose and is lawfully sworn otherwise than in a judicial proceeding, and he wilfully makes a statement which is material for that purpose and which he knows to be false or does not believe to be true. M.

If a person wilfully uses any false affidavit for the purposes of the Bills of Sale Act, 1878. M. (1911 Act, s. 2.)

(3) *False Statements.*—It is a misdemeanour to wilfully and falsely make statements :—

(*a*) As to marriage, such as false oaths, declarations, notices, certificates, particulars required, representations, etc. (1911 Act, s. 3).

Such offences may be dealt with summarily within twelve months (Criminal Justice Act, 1925, s. 28).

(*b*) As to births or deaths, such as false particulars, certificates, declarations, etc. (1911 Act, s. 4), and such offences may be dealt with summarily and within twelve months (Criminal Justice Act, 1925, s. 28).

(*c*) To obtain registration on, or a certificate of registration from, any register kept by law of persons qualified by law to practise any vocation or calling (1911 Act, s. 6).

(For example, medical, dental, pharmaceutical, etc., registers.)

(4) *False Declarations not on Oath.*—It is a misdemeanour to knowingly and wilfully make otherwise than on oath a statement false in a material particular in :—

(*a*) A statutory declaration, or

(*b*) Any account, certificate, report or other document authorised or required by any Act of Parliament, or

(*c*) Any oral declaration or answer required under any Act of Parliament (1911 Act, s. 5). False statements in statutory declarations may be punished summarily on consent of accused to trial (M.C. Act, 1952, s. 19 and 1st Sched.).

(5) *Subornation of Perjury.*—This is the common law misdemeanour of procuring another to commit perjury. It is a misdemeanour to aid, abet, counsel, procure, incite or attempt to procure another person to commit an offence against the Act (1911 Act, s. 7).

Corroboration is necessary to ensure a conviction for any offence against this Act, as the evidence of one witness alone as to the falsity of the statement will not be regarded as sufficient (1911 Act, s. 13). One witness together with proof of other material and relevant facts substantially confirming his testimony will meet the requirements as without corroboration it would be merely one oath against another. See " Corroboration," Chap. 7.

A Judge or person presiding over a Court, or a Justice sitting in special sessions, or a Sheriff dealing with a writ of inquiry or trial, if of opinion that a witness in the proceedings before him has been guilty of perjury, may order the prosecution of that witness for such perjury, and may commit him for trial (1911 Acts, ss. 9 and 10).

False statements in company documents.—It is a misdemeanour for any person to knowingly and wilfully make a statement, false in any material particular, in any balance sheet, report or other document required for the purposes of several sections of the Act, as specified in the 15th Schedule, and the offence may be dealt with summarily (Companies Act, 1948, s. 438).

False statements in declarations, certificates or writings made to be used as evidence of the service of any document or the hand-writing or seal of any person is punishable summarily by imprisonment up to 6 months or fine up to £100 or both (M.C. Act, 1952, s. 82).

Bribery is the offering to or the receiving by any person of any undue reward in order to incline him to do or to reward him for doing a thing contrary to the rules of honesty and integrity.

At Common Law the bribery of any person who has a duty to do anything in which the public are interested, particularly the administration of justice, is a misdemeanour, and statute law also makes certain forms of bribery misdemeanour.

In the offence of bribery the giver and the receiver are equally guilty, and an unsuccessful attempt to bribe is also an offence.

Public Bodies Corrupt Practices Act, 1889, s. 1, makes it a misdemeanour for any person to corruptly solicit, receive or agree to receive for himself or for any other person, or to promise, give or offer to any person, any gift, loan, reward or advantage whatever, as an inducement to or reward for or otherwise on account of, any member, officer or servant of a public body (such as a county, city or town council, board, etc.) doing or forbearing to do anything in respect of any matter or transaction whatsoever, actual or proposed, in which said public body is concerned. Thus any bribery and corruption in connection with the members and servants of public bodies is a misdemeanour by statute, but by section 4 no prosecution under the Act may be instituted without the consent of the Attorney-General.

Prevention of Corruption Act, 1906 : This statute deals with the corruption of and by any agent or person employed by or acting for another, and makes the following offences mis-demeanours triable on indictment or summarily :—

(1) For any agent to corruptly accept, obtain or agree to accept, or to attempt to obtain from any person for himself or for any other person, any gift or consideration, as an inducement or reward for doing or not doing any act in relation to his principal's affairs or business, or for showing or not showing favour or disfavour to any person in relation to his principal's affairs or business ;

(2) For any person to corruptly offer, give or agree to give any gift or consideration to any agent for like reason ;

(3) For any person to knowingly give to any agent, or for any agent to knowingly use with intent to deceive his principal, any receipt, account or document which is false or incorrect in any material particular and which to his knowledge is intended to mislead the principal.

A person serving under the Crown or under any corporation, borough, county or district council is an agent under this Act. So also is a police constable.

The consent of the Attorney-General is necessary before a prosecution may be instituted, the information must be on oath and Quarter Sessions cannot deal with the case.

Prevention of Corruption Act, 1916, declares that when money or other consideration is paid, given to or received by a person in the employment of the Crown or of a public body, by or from a person holding or seeking to obtain a contract from the Crown or public body, such money or consideration shall be deemed to have been given or received corruptly unless the contrary is proved.

This statute extends the expression " public body " (1889 Act, s. 1) to include local and public authorities of all descriptions, and states that a person serving under any such body is an agent within the meaning of the Prevention of Corruption Act, 1906.

Any offence of bribery and corruption of or by a public official must be reported to the Director of Public Prosecutions (see Appendix III).

As regards bribery and other corrupt practices at elections, see " Election Offences," below.

Licensing Act, 1953, s. 142, it is a summary offence for any holder of a Justice's licence to bribe or attempt to bribe any constable. See " Conduct of Licensed Premises," Chap. 38. Bribery of an officer of customs and excise is a serious offence and the offender may be detained (Customs and Excise Act, 1952, s. 9).

Extortion.—It is a misdemeanour at common law for any public officer to extort or unlawfully take, by virtue of his official position, any money or thing of value that is not due to him or more than is due, or before it is due.

Misconduct by Public Officers.—Generally speaking, any misconduct by an officer of justice, either by wrong-doing or by culpable neglect, is a common law misdemeanour.

For stealing or embezzlement by a public officer, see Chap 14.

County Police Act, 1839, s. 12, Metropolitan Police Act, 1839, s. 14, and Municipal Corporations Act, 1882, s. 194, declare that any county, metropolitan or county borough constable who is guilty of any neglect of duty is liable on summary conviction to fine or imprisonment.

The Crown Proceedings Act 1947 gives the right to sue the Crown (authorised departments or the Attorney General, s.17) by civil proceedings in accordance with the provisions of the Act.

Election Offences.—The Representation of the People Act, 1949, deals with parliamentary and local government elections. The franchise is the right to vote and in polling (voting) votes are given by secret ballot.

Personation is the voting as some other person living or dead or fictitious and application for or the marking of a ballot paper shall be deemed to be voting. It is a corrupt practice (s. 47). It is a felony and aiding, abetting, counselling or procuring it is also a felony. Two witnesses are necessary to prove it (s. 146).

Other Voting Offences are dealt with in ss. 48, 49 and are illegal practices and any tampering with, destruction, stealing of, etc., of ballot papers or nomination papers are offences (s. 52). Breaches of the secrecy of voting will be summary offences (s. 53).

Bribery.—That is directly or indirectly using any consideration of value to induce a voter to vote or refrain from voting is a corrupt practice (s. 99).

Treating is the providing or accepting any meat, drink, entertainment or provision for corruptly influencing any person to vote or refrain from voting and is a corrupt practice (s. 100).

Undue Influence is the using or threatening to use any force, restraint or threats against any person to make him vote or refrain from voting or impeding or preventing the free exercise of the franchise. It is a corrupt practice (s. 101). A corrupt practice is punishable on indictment or summarily (s. 146). An illegal practice is punishable summarily (s. 147). It will be the duty of the Director of Public Prosecutions to inquire into any allegations of corrupt or illegal practices and to institute such prosecutions as he may consider necessary (s. 159).

It will be an illegal practice for any person to act or incite others to act in a disorderly manner for the purpose of preventing the transaction of the business at a political meeting held between the dates of the issue of and the return to a writ for a parliamentary election in the constituency or at a meeting in the electoral area for a local government election held on or within three weeks before the day of election.

If any constable reasonably suspects any person of committing this offence, he may, if so requested by the chairman of the meeting, require that person to give him his name and address. If such person refuses or fails to do so or gives a false name and address, he will be liable on summary conviction to fine up to 40s. If he refuses his name and address or if the constable reasonably suspects him of giving a false name and address, the constable may without warrant arrest him (s. 84). No member of a police force shall in any manner try to persuade any person to give or not to give his vote in any constituency or electoral area wholly or partly within the police area. Penalty on summary conviction, fine up to £100.

If such illegal canvassing is committed by a member of a county police force in reference to the election of a borough councillor, he shall forfeit £10, half to the person who sues for it within 6 months and half to the Treasurer of the county (s. 87).

Second Schedule to the Act.—A constable shall not be admitted to vote in person elsewhere than at his own political station, except on production and surrender of a certificate as to his employment signed by the prescribed officer of police or by the returning officer (Para. 33).

If a person misconducts himself in a polling station or fails to obey the presiding officer he may be removed by order of the presiding officer by a constable and such person, if charged with the commission of an offence in the polling station, may be dealt with as a person arrested by a constable, without a warrant, for an offence (Para. 34).

If a person applies in a polling station for a ballot paper and the candidate or his election or polling ·agent declares to the presiding officer that he has reasonable cause to believe that such person has committed personation and undertakes to substantiate the charge in a court of law, the presiding officer may order a constable to arrest him and he shall be dealt with as a person arrested without warrant for an offence (Para. 37). The Act was followed by the Representation of the People Regs. 1950, 1954.

Public Mischief.—All offences of a public nature, that is, all such acts or attempts as tend to the prejudice of the community, are indictable.

Committing an act tending towards public mischief is a misdemeanour at common law. A person who falsely represented to the police that she had been robbed and who gave a description of the alleged robber was convicted of this offence and bound over (*R.* v. *Manley* (1932)). However a public mischief charge will be strengthened if conspiracy is also present.

Justices have a general power to bind over to be of good behaviour for any act of misbehaviour. See " Surety for Good Behaviour," Chap. 22.

Obstructing Public Justice.—Any conspiracy to obstruct prevent, pervert or defeat the course of public justice or falsely to accuse of any crime is a misdemeanour.

It is not necessary that proceedings should have already commenced at the time when the conspiracy to conceal or to prevent proceedings takes place. Public justice requires that every crime should be suitably dealt with (*R.* v. *Sharpe and Stringer,* (1938)).

See also " Accessories," " Compounding Offences," " Compounding a Felony," Chap. 2, and " Conspiracy," Chap. 23.

NOTE.—Any offence of public mischief or of conspiracy to pervert or defeat the course of justice must be reported to the Director of Public Prosecutions (see Appendix III).

Chapter XXII

PUBLIC ORDER

Contents

Breach of the Peace and Sureties.—The "Queen's Peace" or shortly " the peace " is the normal state of society, and any interruption of that peace and good order which ought to prevail in a civilised country is a breach of the peace. Breaches of the peace may be serious, affecting large numbers of people, such as riots ; they may involve comparatively few persons, such as affrays ; and they may consist of acts of violence confined to two or more persons, such as assaults.

For offensive conduct in a public place or at a public meeting which is likely to cause a breach of the peace, a constable can arrest without warrant. See " Public Order Act, 1936," later.

The Justices are empowered to take measures to prevent any apprehended or likely breach of the peace, and may, on evidence produced before them, order a person to enter into a recognizance and find sureties either to keep the peace or to be of good behaviour.

The process is termed " binding over " to keep the peace or to be of good behaviour. Upon complaint by any person a Magistrates' Court may hear the complainant and defendant and their witnesses and may make an order adjudging the defendant to enter into a recognizance, with or without sureties, to keep the peace or to be of good behaviour towards the complainant. If he fails to comply with the order the Court may commit him to custody for up to six months or until he sooner complies with the order (M.C. Act, 1952, s. 91).

For breach of such an order, forfeiture of the recognizances may be ordered. See " Recognizance," Chap. 5.

Where a magistrates' court has committed a person to custody in default of finding sureties ordered on complaint of another person, the committed person or his representative by complaint against that other person, may apply to the Court which, on fresh evidence, may reduce the amount of any surety or dispense with them or otherwise deal with the case as it thinks just. (M.C. Act, 1952, s. 94 and Rules r. 66.)

Before binding over a person, the Court should hear evidence from both sides. Even if no application that a person be bound over is made, the Court may, if it thinks fit, bind over that person.

Binding over is a precautionary measure, to be adopted when there is reasonable ground to anticipate some present or future danger. It is not a conviction or a punishment. It should not be ordered for some act that is past and is not likely to be repeated, but it may be added to a punishment for a definite offence, as, in a case of assault, allowed by C.J. Act, 1925, s. 39.

Surety of the Peace.—Persons engaged in committing a breach of the peace may be arrested by a constable and ordered by the Justices to give surety of the peace. If a person has just cause to fear that another will do him or his family some bodily harm or damage his property, he may demand the surety of the peace against him.

Threats of violence or threats to injure or procure others to injure the complainant will jnstify binding over to keep the peace.

An applicant should satisfy the Court that he is actually under fear and that he has cause to be so.

If the parties are before the Court on another charge, the Court, if satisfied that there is a fear of future danger, may exercise their power of binding over.

Surety for Good Behaviour.—This surety is more comprehensive than the surety of the peace, as it includes the surety of the peace, and a person who is bound over to be of good behaviour is also bound to the peace.

All disturbers of the peace may be bound over to be of good behaviour, and it need not be proved or even suggested that any person is put in fear. The statute 34 Edward III, c. 1, 1360-1, authorises Justices to take security of their good behaviour from " all them that be not of good fame." When a person is bound over to keep the peace or be of good behaviour he can appeal to Quarter Sessions. (Magistrates Courts (Appeals from Binding over Orders) Act, 1956).

Generally speaking, the Court can bind over to be of good behaviour for any act of misbehaviour, but Justices may not exercise this power for rash, unmannerly or quarrelsome words, unless they tend to a breach of the peace or to scandalise the Government.

This power to bind over to be of good behaviour is limited only by the discretion of the Court. It is not confined to breach of the peace. It is preventive justice to prevent a person doing something against the law. (See *R*. v. *Sandbach, ex parte Williams* (1935)).

Affray.—An affray is a public offence to the terror of the Queen's subjects such as the fighting of two or more persons in some public place to the terror of the people. It is a misdemeanour at common law.

If the fighting occurs in some private place it is an assault and not an affray. An affray differs from a riot in that an affray is not premeditated and in that it requires three or more persons to constitute a riot, whereas two persons can make an affray.

If two persons fight in a street or public place, but not to the terror of the people, it is not an affray, but such conduct may be dealt with as an assault or breach of the peace.

A constable should quell an affray which happens in his presence. He may arrest the offenders without warrant and bring them before a Justice, who may commit them for trial for the misdemeanour or bind them over to keep the peace. See Chap. 3.

Unlawful Assembly.—An assembly of persons is unlawful at Common Law when it is composed of three or more persons who have met together to carry into effect some illegal purpose or who have met in such numbers or under such circumstances as to endanger the public peace or cause alarm and apprehension to Her Majesty's subjects. An unlawful assembly, therefore, would be any gathering of three or more persons for any unlawful purpose or with intent to carry out any common purpose in such a manner as is likely to endanger the peace, as shown by the large numbers assembled or by the circumstances of the assembly.

Any meeting of numbers of people with such circumstances of terror as cannot but endanger the peace and cause alarm among the Queen's subjects is an unlawful assembly.

All persons who join an unlawful assembly and all who give support to it are liable to prosecution for misdemeanour at common law. It does not matter whether the object of the meeting be lawful or unlawful, for, if the circumstances accompanying it (e.g. great numbers, etc.) are, in the opinion of firm and rational men, likely to endanger the peace, the meeting will be an unlawful assembly.

It is the duty of the police to disperse and put an end to an unlawful assembly, arresting the ringleaders and persons who offer resistance either on the spot if it is possible and advisable, or subsequently by warrant. As an alternative, proceedings may subsequently be taken against individuals by summons for any assaults, obstruction, etc., that may have taken place. An unchecked unlawful assembly may end in a riot.

Riot.—A riot is a tumultuous disturbance of the peace by three persons or more, assembling together of their own authority, with an intent mutually to assist one another against anyone who shall oppose them in the execution of some enterprise of a private nature, and afterwards actually executing the same in a violent and turbulent manner, to the terror of the people, whether the act intended were of itself lawful or unlawful (Archbold).

The assembly becomes a riot when those assembled begin to

execute their enterprise by a breach of the peace to the terror of the public.

If a number of people meet together and suddenly quarrel and fight amongst themselves it is an affray (see " Affray "), not a riot ; but if they divide into parties and the parties fight together, each party with a common purpose, it is a riot.

Riot is a misdemeanour at common law, and all persons encouraging, promoting or taking part are liable.

A rout is where three or more assemble with a common purpose to do an unlawful act and make some advances towards doing it. A rout is the step just previous to a riot. Rout is a misdemeanour at common law.

It is the duty of the police to suppress a riot, using force if necessary, and they have authority to call on all other subjects of the Queen to assist them in so doing. It is the duty of every citizen to assist in suppressing a riot.

It is a misdemeanour at common law for a person to refuse to assist a constable in the execution of his duty when duly called on to do so and the person is capable of so doing and has no lawful excuse for refusing.

Any two Justices may order all licensed premises to remain closed during any time they may appoint, in or near the place where any riot or tumult happens or is expected to happen (Licensing Act, 1953, s. 158).

When twelve or more persons are riotously and unlawfully assembled to the disturbance of the public peace, and when they are required, by proclamation read by a Magistrate, Sheriff, Sub-Sheriff or Mayor, to disperse, then if such persons (twelve or more) riotously continue together for the space of one hour they will be guilty of felony and may be arrested by any Justice, Sheriff, Mayor, or Peace Officer or other person commanded by them (Riot Act, 1714, s. 3).

The proclamation to disperse should be in these words :—" Our Sovereign Lady the Queen chargeth and commandeth all persons, being assembled, immediately to disperse themselves and peaceably to depart to their habitations or to their lawful business, upon the pains contained in the Act made in the first year of King George, for preventing tumults and riotous assemblies. God Save the Queen." The person reading this proclamation must command silence and must read the whole proclamation. All members of the tumultuous assembly who then remain together after the hour expires may be arrested, proceeded against as felons within the following twelve months (Riot Act, 1714, s. 1).

The reading of this proclamation is termed " reading the Riot Act." Its effect is to make the parties felons, but if the assembly is riotous the parties are guilty of riot at common law and may be dispersed at once, if possible, without reading the Riot Act.

It is felony to oppose or hinder the reading of the Riot Act so that it is not read, and persons who, knowing of such prevention, remain together to the number of twelve or more for more than an hour thereafter are also guilty of felony. (Riot Act, 1714, s. 5).

Riot damage.—If persons riotously and tumultuously assembled to the disturbance of the peace demolish or destroy any house, building, or mine works they are guilty of felony, and if they injure or damage any such building they are guilty of misdemeanour (Malicious Damage Act, 1861, ss. 11 and 12).

Under the Riot (Damages) Act, 1886, a person whose house or premises has been damaged or the property therein injured, stolen or destroyed by rioters may claim compensation from the Police Authority in accordance with the Secretary of State's Regulations dated 1 Oct, 1921, which also apply in the case of rioters plundering a wreck.

Forcible Entry and Detainer.—Forcible entry is the taking possession of lands or buildings by force and without the authority of the law. It is a misdemeanour by statute and at Common Law.

The offence lies in the use of violence, such as threats, force, large numbers of people, etc., and the fact that the offender had a right to enter the premises will not justify such use of violence.

Proceedings are by indictment, and charges of assault, etc., may also be made, if the circumstances justify same.

An entry without force may be a trespass. See Chap. 19.

Forcible detainer is the continuing to hold possession by force of lands or buildings which have been entered wrongfully.

This is a similar misdemeanour and will be committed by a person who, without any right to the property, forcibly keeps possession.

However, a trespasser may be removed from premises by the rightful owner provided that no more force is used than is necessary for his removal and that his goods are removed with proper care.

Labour Disputes.—Any combination of workmen for the purpose of securing a rise in wages or an alteration in their conditions of employment was at one time illegal. In 1825 the laws against such combinations were repealed, and in 1871 trade unions were made lawful.

In 1875 section 3 of the Conspiracy and Protection of Property Act exempted trade unions from liability to the law as regards conspiracy (see " Conspiracy ") by enacting that an agreement or combination by two or more persons to do or procure to be done any act in contemplation or furtherance of a trade dispute should not be indictable as a conspiracy, if such act, when committed by one person, would not be punishable as a crime.

However, this section does not exempt from punishment any person guilty of a conspiracy for which a punishment is directed by any Act of Parliament, and it does not affect the law relating to riot, unlawful assembly, breach of the peace, or sedition, or any offence against the State or the Sovereign.

In 1906 the Trade Disputes Act further declared that an act done in pursuance of an agreement or combination by two or more persons should, if done in contemplation or furtherance of a trade dispute, not be actionable unless it would be actionable if done singly.

The Trade Disputes and Trade Unions Act, 1927, declared that certain strikes and lock-outs were illegal, and that any act done in contemplation or furtherance of an illegal strike should not be deemed to be done in contemplation or furtherance of a trade dispute. However, this 1927 Act was repealed by the Trades Disputes and Trade Unions Act, 1946.

Intimidation.—Conspiracy and Protection of Property Act, 1875, s. 7. Every person commits a summary offence, but may claim trial by jury on indictment who, with a view to compel any other person to abstain from doing or to do any act which such other person has a legal right to do or abstain from doing, wrongfully and without legal authority :

(1) uses violence to or intimidates such other person or his wife or children or injures his property, or

(2) persistently follows such other person about from place to place, or

(3) hides any tools, clothing or other property owned or used by such other person, or deprives him of or hinders him in the use thereof, or

(4) follows such other person with two or more other persons in a disorderly manner in or through any street or road, or

(5) watches or besets the house or place where such other person resides or works or carries on business or happens to be, or the approach to such house or place.

However, the Trade Disputes Act, 1906, s. 2, made it lawful for one or more persons, in contemplation or furtherance of a trade dispute, to attend at or near a house or place where a person resides or works or carries on business or happens to be, merely for the purpose of peacefully obtaining or communicating information, or of peacefully persuading any person to work or abstain from working. This is known as " peaceful picketing."

Breaking Contract of Service.—Conspiracy and Protection of Property Act, 1875, ss. 4 and 5 : It is a summary offence for any person employed in the supply of gas or water to wilfully and maliciously break his contract of service knowing that the consequences will be to deprive the inhabitants of their supply of gas or water, and for any person to wilfully and maliciously break a contract of service or hiring knowing that the probable consequences will be to endanger life or property.

See Stone, under title " Labour Laws."

Public Order Act, 1936.—This Act deals with political uniforms, private quasi-military associations, processions, offensive conduct and public meetings.

Under the Act, " meeting " means a meeting held for the purpose of discussion of matters of public interest or for the expression of views thereon. " Public meeting " includes any meeting in a public place and any meeting which the public or any section thereof are permitted to attend, whether on payment or otherwise.

" Public procession " means a procession in a public place.

" Public place " means any highway, public park or garden, any sea beach, and any public bridge, road, lane footway, square, court, alley or passage whether a thoroughfare or not ; and includes any open space to which, for the time being, the public have or are permitted to have access, whether on payment or otherwise (s. 9).

Excepting the offences under sections 2 and 6, an offence under the Act is punishable summarily by imprisonment not exceeding three months or (and) £50 fine (s. 7).

Political uniforms. S. 1.—It will be a summary offence for any person to wear uniform signifying his association with any political organisation or with the promotion of any political object, in any public place or at any public meeting, unless such wearing has been permitted on special occasion by the Chief Officer of Police, by order made with the consent of the Secretary of State (s. 1). A constable may arrest without warrant any person reasonably suspected to be committing this offence (s. 7). A Court may remand in custody for eight days only or on bail, but no further proceedings shall be taken without the consent of the Attorney-General (s. 1).

Quasi-military organisations. S. 2.—It will be an offence (punishable summarily or on indictment : s. 7) for any person to take part in the control or management or in the organising or training of any association of persons whose members or adherents are :

(1) organised or trained or equipped for the purpose of enabling them to be employed in usurping the functions of the police or armed forces of the Crown, or

(2) organised and trained or organised and equipped either for the purpose of enabling them to be employed for the use or display of physical force in promoting any political object or in such manner as to arouse reasonable apprehension that they are organised and either trained or equipped for that purpose.

A prosecution shall not be instituted without the consent of the Attorney-General.

The High Court, on application by the Attorney-General, has power to deal with the property of any such association. A Judge of the High Court may grant a search warrant to enter any place or premises within one month and search the place or premises and persons therein (women to be searched by a woman) and seize anything found which is reasonably suspected to be evidence of this offence.

Proof of things done or words written, spoken or published, by any person taking part in the control or management or in organising, etc., shall be admissible as evidence of the purposes for which or the manner in which members, etc., of the association were organised or trained or equipped.

This section 2 shall not prohibit the employment, arrangements for or instruction in their duties of a reasonable number of persons as stewards to assist in preserving order at any public meeting held upon private premises (s. 2), that is premises to which the public have access (on payment or otherwise) only by permission of the owner, occupier or lessee of the premises (s. 9). Nor does it prohibit their being furnished with badges or other distinguishing signs (s. 2).

Processions. S. 3.—If the Chief Officer of Police, having regard to the time or place and the circumstances and to the route taken or proposed to be taken by any public procession, has reasonable ground for apprehending that the procession may occasion serious public disorder, he may give directions imposing upon the organisers or the processionists such conditions as may appear to him necessary for preserving public order, including prescribing the route and prohibiting entry of any public place specified.

Provided no conditions restricting display of flags, banners or emblems shall be imposed except such as are reasonably necessary to prevent risk of a breach of the peace.

If he considers that under existing circumstances in a borough or urban district the above powers will not be sufficient to prevent serious public disorder arising from the holding of public processions in any part of the area, the Chief Officer of Police shall apply to the Council of the Borough or District for an order prohibiting for a specified period (not exceeding three months) all public processions or any specified class of public procession, and the Council, with the consent of the Secretary of State, may make such an order. The Commissioners of the City of London and of the Metropolis have the same power, as above given to Councils, in their police areas.

Any person who knowingly fails to comply with any directions or conditions so prescribed under the section, or who organises or assists in organising any public procession held or intended to be held in contravention of such an order or incites any person to take part in same, will commit a summary offence.

Arranging the route etc. of an unlawful procession amounts to organizing it (*Flockhart* v. *Robertson* (1950)).

Offensive Weapons. S. 4.—It will be a summary offence for any person while present at any public meeting or on the occasion of any public procession, to have with him any offensive weapon, otherwise than in pursuance of lawful authority. A person shall not be deemed to be acting in pursuance of lawful authority unless he is acting in his capacity as a servant of the Crown or of either House of Parliament or of any local authority or as a member of a recognised corps (viz. rifle club, miniature rifle club or cadet corps duly approved : s. 9) or as a member of a fire brigade or as a constable. A constable may without warrant arrest any person reasonably suspected to be committing this offence (s. 7). See also under " Robbery," Chap. 14.

Offensive Conduct. S. 5.—It will be a summary offence for any person in any public place or at any public meeting to use threatening, abusive or insulting words or behaviour with intent to provoke a breach of the peace or whereby a breach of the peace is likely to be occasioned. A constable may without warrant arrest any person reasonably suspected to be committing this offence (s. 7).

Public Meetings.—Public Meeting Act, 1908, s. 1, makes it a summary offence for any person at a lawful public meeting to act in a disorderly manner for the purpose of preventing the transaction of the business for which the meeting was called together. Inciting another to commit the offence will be a like offence. See also " Offensive Conduct " above, and " Election Offences," Chap. 21.

The following has been added to this Act by s. 6 of the Public Order Act. If a constable reasonably suspects any person of committing the above offence he may if requested to do so by the chairman of the meeting require that person to give his name and address. If such person refuses or fails to do so or gives a false name and address, he will commit a summary offence. (40s. fine.) If such person refuses or fails to give his name and address or if the constable reasonably suspects him of giving a false name and address, the constable may without warrant arrest him.

Meetings.—There is no right to hold meetings in any public place, as such places are for people to pass along. Every unauthorised obstruction of the highway is illegal as being either an offence by some statute or byelaw or indictable as a common nuisance. Streets are for passage, and passage is superior to everything else, and nothing short of absolute necessity will justify a person in obstructing a highway. An obstruction is committed even if only part of the highway is obstructed. However, meetings may be permissible in certain public places in accordance with local custom, but usually not as of right.

When a meeting is held in a private place, those present, whether there by payment, by ticket, or free, are there by permission of the persons responsible for the meeting, and if requested to leave they should leave the premises. (See below as regards the police.)

A person who does not leave on such request becomes a trespasser and may be put out by reasonably necessary force. If such a trespasser uses violence to those removing him he commits a breach of the peace. The chairman of such a meeting has authority to regulate the proceedings. He may call on a disorderly person to keep quiet or else leave the meeting, and if such request is disobeyed he may direct the removal of such person. The stewards or agents of the promoters of the meeting may then use reasonably necessary force to eject the disturber, and if he resists and uses violence he will be liable for having committed a breach of the peace. See " Arrest," Chap. 3.

It has been held that the police are entitled to enter and remain on private premises (in this case it was a meeting in a hired hall and the public were invited to attend without charge for admission) when there are reasonable grounds for believing that an offence or a breach of the peace is likely to be committed thereon. A constable in the execution of his duty has a right to enter and remain on private premises when he has reasonable ground for believing that an offence is imminent or is likely to be committed (*Thomas* v. *Sawkins* (1935)).

As regards meetings in streets it has been held that as it is the duty of the police to prevent an apprehended breach of the peace and accordingly to prohibit and prevent a meeting which would likely result in a disturbance if held, a person attempting to hold the meeting and refusing to desist was rightly convicted of obstructing a police inspector in the execution of his duty (*Duncan* v. *Jones* (1935)).

Prevention of Violence (Temporary Provisions) Act, 1939. —This Act was to prevent the commission of acts of violence designed to influence public opinion or government policy with respect to Irish affairs. It was to remain in force for two years but was continued yearly by the annual Expiring Laws Continuance Acts. However it was not continued by Expiring Laws Continuance Act, 1954.

The 1939 Act gave power to arrest without warrant and authorised search warrants and authority, in case of emergency, to search any premises or place.

Emergency Powers :—The Emergency Powers Act, 1920, empowers the Sovereign to issue proclamations of emergency. This can be done if it appears that action has been taken or immediately threatened by persons and is of such a nature and on so extensive a scale as to be calculated, by interfering with the supply and distribution of food, water, fuel or light or with the means of locomotion, to deprive the community of the essentials of life.

No such proclamation shall be in force for more than one month without prejudice to the issue of another proclamation at or before the end of that period.

Regulations may be made for securing the essentials of life and should be laid before Parliament for approval of their continuance.

The Emergency Powers (Defence) Acts, 1939-45, authorised the making of Defence Regulations. Certain of the Defence Regulations have been continued. Notes on these continued emergency regulations are given in Appendix IV at the end of this book.

Chapter XXIII

CONSPIRACY AND DEFAMATION

Contents

Conspiracy.—Conspiracy is the crime committed when two or more persons combine together to execute some act for the purpose of injuring some other person or the public. It is a misdemeanour at common law.

The essence of the crime is the agreement of two or more persons to do some unlawful act or to do some lawful act by unlawful means, and it is not necessary that any act should have been done in pursuance of the agreement. It is an offence of confederacy or combination. Unless a third person is charged with them, husband and wife cannot be jointly charged with the crime as the law regards them to be one. All the accused need not be brought to trial together ; one person may be prosecuted for conspiracy with others known or unknown. Everything said, written or done by any one of the conspirators in furtherance of their common purpose will be evidence against the other conspirators.

There may be a conspiracy to defraud any person or persons, to injure an individual by some wrongful act or by blackmailing him, to commit some offence or some public mischief, etc.

It may be possible to deal with an act of fraud which does not come within the definition of false pretences as a conspiracy.

For conspiracy to murder, see Chap. 9.

See also " Labour Disputes " and " Intimidation," Chap. 22, and " Obstructing Public Justice," Chap. 21.

Libel.—The offence termed libel consists in making public in some way a defamatory document concerning some person, class of persons, or system so as to tend to bring him, them, or it into hatred, contempt or ridicule. Libel is a misdemeanour when it is likely to cause a breach of the peace by exciting feelings of revenge, stirring up hatred against persons, or tending to disturb the peace and good order of the country.

The mere writing of a libel is not an offence, but the offence is committed when the libel is published, viz. communicated to some other person or persons by means of writing, printing, pictures, etc.

In criminal proceedings, communication of the libel to the injured person is sufficient, as it may provoke him to a breach of the peace, and the truth of the libel will not be a good defence unless accused can prove that the publication of it was for the public benefit.

Criminal proceedings for libel are as a rule not undertaken unless some public interest is concerned, something affecting the State and the general administration and interest of the country.

Any offence of libel *re* persons occupying judicial or public offices must be reported to the Director of Public Prosecutions (see Appendix III).

Libel Act, 1843, ss. 4 and 5. It is a misdemeanour to maliciously publish any defamatory libel, and the punishment is greater should it be charged and proved that it was published, knowing it to be false.

Larceny Act, 1916, s. 31 : It is a misdemeanour to publish or threaten to publish any libel upon any other person, living or dead, or to threaten to publish or propose to abstain from publishing or to offer to prevent the publishing of any matter or thing touching any other person, living or dead, with intent to extort. See " Threats and Menaces," Chap. 8.

If the intention of publication is to excite disaffection against the Sovereign, the Government, the administration of justice, or to incite to crime, disaffection, etc., the libel becomes a seditious libel. See " Sedition," Chap. 20.

If the writing blasphemes God or turns the Christian religion into contempt or ridicule, etc., the person responsible may be indicted for blasphemous libel.

A libel may be dealt with as an obscene libel, if the matter therein is obscene and likely to deprave and corrupt those into whose hands it might fall. See Appendix III.

As regards the privilege extended to fair and accurate newspaper reports of proceedings in Courts or at public meetings and meetings of public bodies, and to departmental and police publications, see the Law of Libel Amendment Act, 1888.

The Newspaper Libel and Registration Act, 1881, deals with summary court proceedings in respect of libels published in newspapers.

Slander is the utterance in words of defamatory matter, viz· matter which directly or indirectly tends to expose any person, persons or system to hatred, contempt or ridicule. It is thus a kind of verbal libel and redress may be obtained by civil action for damages.

Slander may be indictable if the words are seditious, blasphemous or obscene, or tend to provoke a breach of the peace.

The law as to libel, slander and other malicious falsehoods has been amended by the Defamation Act. 1952.

PART V.—TRAFFIC LAW

Chapter XXIV

TRAFFIC

Contents

Road Traffic Acts. General Note.—*The Road Traffic Acts*, 1930, 1931, 1933, 1934, 1936, 1937, 1956 and the Transport Acts, 1947 and 1953 provide for the regulation of motor vehicles and road traffic in general; they created and regulate the new class of " public service vehicles "; and they empower the Minister of Transport to make regulations as to the construction, use and equipment of motor vehicles, and as to many other matters in connection with traffic.

These Acts repealed the Locomotives Acts and the Motor Car Act ; they have superseded the Stage Carriage Act and the Town Police Clauses Acts so far as they relate to public service vehicles ; and they revoked certain sections of several other statutes. " Motor vehicles " means " mechanically propelled vehicles intended or adapted for use on roads," and trailers mean " vehicles drawn by motor vehicles," (1930 Act, s. 1, 1933 Act, s. 36) but the application of the Acts is limited in some respects with regard to tramcars, trolley vehicles and " Crown " vehicles as will be noted later. See also s. 36 of the 1933 Act.

In addition to repealing certain statute law, s. 122 of the 1930 Act repealed so much of the provisions of any local Act as confers or imposes on any person any power, right or obligation, which by any of the repealed enactments or by the Act (except Part V.) is conferred or imposed on any person.

This provision therefore affects local byelaws relating to traffic.

The maximum penalty for an offence under the Acts for which no special penalty is provided is £20 fine, and for a second or subsequent conviction £50 fine or three months imprisonment (1930 Act, s. 113).

The 1931 Act is a short amending Act. The 1930 Act is the principal Act and Parts I., II., III. and IV. of the 1930 and 1934 Acts are to be construed together as one. These Parts are as follows :—

Part I. Regulation of Motor Vehicles. Ss. 1-34 of 1930 and ss. 1-9 of 1934.

This Part deals with classification ; licensing of drivers ; speed limits and driving offences ; accidents ; weights and weighing of motor vehicles ; taking of or meddling with motor vehicles ; and miscellaneous matters. Part I. does not apply to tramcars and only the sections relating to the licensing of drivers, dangerous and careless driving, drunkenness and inquiry into accidents apply to trolley vehicles. It applies to Crown vehicles subject to certain exemptions in favour of vehicles used by the armed forces of the Crown, for which see " Motor Vehicles of H.M. Forces," Chap. 30.

Part II. Insurance against Third Party Risks. Ss. 35-44 of 1930 and ss. 10-17 of 1934.

This Part compels the insurance of the use of motor vehicles in respect of third party risks and the production by drivers of certificates of insurance or of other evidence of adequate insurance. It does not apply to Crown vehicles, tramcars, trolley vehicles, and invalid carriages.

Part III. Highway Law. Ss. 45-60 of 1930 and ss. 18-23 of 1934.

This Part provides for a highway code ; the restriction of road traffic ; traffic direction ; prevention of danger from vehicles, ropes, etc. ; and miscellaneous matters. This Part applies to all vehicles, and it applies to Crown vehicles, with the exception of s. 54 of the 1930 Act, which provides for the recovery of expenses due to extraordinary traffic on a road.

Part IV. Regulation of Public Service Vehicles. Ss. 62-98 and 100 of 1930 and ss. 26-30 of 1934.

This Part deals with public service vehicles; traffic areas and Traffic Commissioners; public service vehicle licences; road service licences; drivers' and conductors' licences; and the regulation of drivers, conductors and passengers. It includes a direction as to the persons who are entitled to take proceedings for offences under Part IV. (a chief officer of police, etc., s. 95, 1930 Act) and the special provisions as to London.

Part V of the 1930 Act deals with the running of public service vehicles by Local Authorities.

Part VI of the 1930 Act and Part V. of the 1934 Act deal

with legal proceedings and penalties, the interpretation of expressions used and the repeal of existing law.

" Crown Vehicles " mean vehicles in the public service of the Crown. Parts I. and III. (less s. 54 and subject to certain exceptions) apply, and the person " responsible " for an offence in connection with a Crown vehicle, other than the driver of the vehicle will be the person named for the purpose by the department concerned unless the Court is satisfied that the driver only was responsible (s. 121 (2), 1930 Act).

Road and Rail Traffic Act, 1933.—This Act provides for the licensing of goods vehicles on roads (ss. 1-26, 34-36), for which see " Goods Vehicles," Chap. 25.

It made several amendments in the R.T. Act, 1930, and has been supplemented by the Transport Act, 1947, which created the British Transport Commission which has taken over the railways and certain transport undertakings. Traffic Commissioners and the Licensing Authorities grant licences. (R.T. Act, 1956, Sched. 8 (40).

Road Traffic (Driving Licences) Acts, 1936 and 1947, allow the exemption from driving licence of a steersman on a vehicle limited to 5 m.p.h. speed. They also allow the issue of provisional (learners') licences, and limited licences in connection with the driving of heavy goods vehicles.

Road Traffic Act, 1937, allows extended currency periods for carriers' goods licences.

Road Traffic Act, 1956. This Act has 55 sections and 9 schedules of which many sections and much of the schedules have been brought into force by the Road Traffic Act, 1956 (Commencement Orders 1956, 1957 and 1958).

The Act contains general provisions relating to road traffic (ss. 1-18), provisions regarding parking places (ss. 19-25), directions as to enforcement (ss. 26-32), traffic regulations (ss. 33-38), changes in the classification etc., of public service vehicles (ss. 39-40) and miscellaneous provisions (ss. 41-55).

Of the 9 schedules the 1st deals with tests of vehicles, the 3rd concerns parking places, the 4th gives the offences for which disqualification or endorsement may be ordered, the 6th affects the classification of vehicles, the 7th deals with offences in respect of motor cyclists helmets, the 8th has 41 lots of amendments to the Road Lighting and Traffic Acts and the 9th repeals some previous law regarding Road traffic.

These Motor Vehicles Acts have been supplemented by the Motor Vehicles (Construction and Use) Regulations, 1955-1957, and the Motor Vehicles (Construction and Use) (Tracklaying Vehicles) Regulations 1955 and 1957, which will be referred to subsequently as the Construction and Use Regs., and the Tracklaying Vehicles Regs. (see Appendix II).

Highways, Streets and Roads.—" Highway " means a strip of land over which every member of the public may lawfully pass The public have only the right to pass along the highway. A *cul-de-sac* or way closed at one end so that there is no thoroughfare may be a highway.

Highways are common to the public, and " highway," in the full sense, is a public road over which all the subjects of the realm have a right to pass and repass (Stephen's Commentaries).

" Street " for the purposes of the Public Health Act, 1875 (see s. 4), includes any highway, road, lane, footway, square, court, alley, or passage, whether a thoroughfare or not ; and the term is usually applied to a road with houses in a town or urban district ; it has a similar meaning in the Public Health Act, 1936.

A highway or street includes any footways or footpaths at the sides, and offences in relation to " highways " or " streets " may be committed on the footway as well as in the carriage-way. However, there are several distinct offences confined to footways and they will be indicated separately.

The Road Transport Lighting Act, 1957, states that a " road," for the purposes of the Act, means any highway and any other road to which the public has access (s. 17).

This includes the private forecourt of a hotel to which the public have access habitually without let or hindrance (*Bugge* v. *Taylor* (1941)). But see also *Thomas* v. *Dando* (1951) where the forecourt was not habitually used by the public. A road generally includes its footpath (or pavement) which would include its grass verge.

" Road," means any highway and any other road to which the public has access, and includes bridges over which a road passes (1930 Act, s. 121, and 1956 Act, s. 54). (The ' road ' includes the footway as well as the carriage way (*Bryant* v. *Marx*) (1932).)

Public highways and streets are maintained by the Local Authorities. The police deal with highway and street offences which affect the public and report to Local Authorities any interference with the highways and streets.

Generally speaking, any wrongful act or omission upon or near a highway which interferes with the public right to freely, safely and conveniently pass along the highway may be held to be a nuisance at common law, and therefore indictable and punishable.

A person who has sustained damage by reason of a nuisance may sue for damages and (or) an injunction to end the nuisance.

Obstruction.—Members of the public have a right to pass along any public highway, and any interference with that right amounts to obstruction. Only absolute necessity will justify any obstruction of the highway.

Any unauthorised obstruction of the highway is a nuisance and indictable as a misdemeanour at common law. Several statutes provide penalties for various forms of obstruction, but if any particular form of obstruction is not expressly penalised by statute, the offender may be indicted for the nuisance. For example, a shopkeeper whose display in his windows collected large crowds, thereby obstructing the highway, has been convicted on indictment for nuisance.

Obstruction may be caused by :—

(1) Persons—who in any way wilfully obstruct the free passage of any highway or footway.

(2) Things—which by their presence on the highway or footway interfere with the public right to pass along. The persons responsible are liable.

(3) Vehicles—for which the driver or person in charge is liable. The law cases as to obstruction were reviewed in *Gill* v. *Carson* (1917), and the test is the unreasonable use of the highway. In *Solomon* v. *Durbridge* (1956) it was held that a motor car could become an unnecessary obstruction of the highway if it was left at a particular place for too long.

The several obstruction offences are given in subsequent sections, under " Highways Act," " Other Highway Nuisances and Dangers," " Town Police Clauses Act," " Other Street Nuisances and Dangers," " Regulation of Traffic," also see " Obstruction," Appendix 2.

In addition to the statutes dealing with obstruction on the highways generally throughout the country, and with obstruction in the streets of cities, towns or urban districts, many localities have local byelaws and regulations dealing with particular forms of obstruction, such as jostling on the footpaths.

The statute law under which road obstruction is usually dealt with is :—

(1) Highway Act, 1835, ss. 72 and 78, obstruction in any way of the free passage of the highway.

(2) Town Police Clauses Act, 1847, s. 28 (where it applies). Wilful obstruction of the street by vehicle or animal, to the obstruction, annoyance or danger of the residents or passengers.

(3) Construction and Use Regs., reg. 89 and Tracklaying Vehicles Regs., reg. 67. Unnecessary obstruction of the road by a motor vehicle or its trailer. See " Obstruction ," Appendix 2.

Highway Act, 1835, s. 72 : The following acts are summary offences :—

Tethering any horse, ass, sheep, mule, swine or cattle on any highway so as to suffer or permit the tethered animal to be thereon.

Causing any injury or damage to be done to the highway or its hedges, posts, rails, walls or fences.

Wilfully destroying or injuring the surface of any highway.

Wilfully or wantonly pulling up, cutting down, removing or damaging the posts, blocks or stones fixed by the surveyor.

Digging or cutting down the banks which are the securities and defence of the highway.

Breaking, damaging or throwing down the stones, bricks or wood fixed upon the parapets of bridges or otherwise injuring or defacing same.

Pulling down, destroying, obliterating or defacing any mile-stone or post, graduated or direction post or stone, erected upon any highway.

Playing at football or any other game on any part of the highway to the annoyance of any passenger or passengers.

Any hawker, gipsy or other person travelling, pitching any tent, booth, stall or stand, or encamping upon any part of any highway.

Making or assisting to make any fire, or wantonly firing off any gun or pistol, or setting fire to or wantonly letting off or throwing any squib or other firework whatsoever, within 50 feet of the centre of the carriage-way, or baiting any bull upon or near any highway, or laying any timber, stone, rubbish or other matter or thing whatsoever upon the highway, to the injury of such highway or to the injury, interruption or personal danger of any person travelling thereon.

Suffering any filth, dirt, lime, or other offensive matter or thing whatsoever to run or flow into or upon any highway from any lands or premises adjacent thereto.

Wilfully obstructing, in any way, the free passage of any highway.

Penalty, 40s. fine and cost of damage occasioned.

The following offences under s. 72 are confined to footways :—

Wilfully riding upon any footpath or causeway by the side of any road, made or set apart for the use or accommodation of foot passengers. " Footpath " means a way over which the public have a right of way on foot only (1956 Act, s. 54).

Wilfully leading or driving any horse, ass, sheep, mule, swine, cattle or carriage of any description (including bicycles and other similar machines (Local Government Act, 1888, s. 85)) or any truck or sledge upon any such footpath or causeway.

Wilfully obstructing the passage of any footway. (A shop-keeper may be liable for obstruction because of a queue out-side his shop if he is not carrying on his business in the ordinary way, *Fabbri* v. *Morris* (1947).)

Under s. 78 it is a summary offence for any person, by negligence or misbehaviour to prevent, hinder or interrupt the free passage of any person, wagon cart or other carriage, or horses, mules or other beasts of burden on any highway.

The Highway Act, 1835, specifies several offences relating to or on highways. Under s. 78 any driver offending against the Act may be arrested by any person who sees the offence com-mitted and brought before a Justice. Section 79 empowers any person witnessing an offence against the Act to arrest the offender if his name be unknown, and bring him before a Justice. This Act is in force throughout the whole country.

Also see later under " Regulation of Traffic," " Dangerous, etc., Driving " and "Carts and Wagons," Chap. 25.

Other Highway Nuisances and Dangers.—In addition to the foregoing offences the following acts are dealt with by Statutes applying to the whole country.

Barbed Wire Act, 1893 : Barbed wire on a fence adjoining the highway and likely to be injurious to persons or animals on the highway is dangerous and the local Council may serve notice on the owner requiring him to abate the nuisance. If he does not obey a Magistrates' Court may order him to do so.

Construction and Use Regs., 1955, Reg. 89 (and Tracklaying Vehicles Regs., Reg. 67). No person in charge of a motor vehicle or trailer shall cause or permit it to stand on a road so as to cause any unnecessary obstruction thereof.

Road Traffic Act, 1930, s. 50 : Leaving a vehicle or trailer at rest on a road in a dangerous position is an offence. See " Regulation of Traffic."

S. 51 : It is an offence to place or cause to be placed any rope, wire or other apparatus across a highway or any part thereof in such a manner as to be likely to cause danger to persons using the highway, unless all necessary means had been taken to give adequate warning of the danger.

S. 52 : Machines and machinery are now allowable, unscreened, next or on the highway when used for purposes connected with agriculture, forestry, building or road work. Highway Act, 1835, s. 70, compelled screens, etc., when steam engines were within 25 yards of the highway.

S. 56 : The highway authority have power to require the removal of (and to remove) any unauthorised structure (including any machine, pump, post or other obstructing object) set up on the highway.

S. 33 declares that the Act does not authorise any person to use on any road any vehicle so constructed or used as to cause a public or private nuisance. See also " Dangerous Vehicle," Appendix II.

Town Police Clauses Act, 1847, s. 28 (where it applies), declares that the following acts are offences when they are committed in any street (which includes any road, square, court, alley and thoroughfare, or public passage (s. 3), and means a place to which the public have a right of access, including the footpaths), in a town or urban district to the obstruction, annoyance or danger of the residents or passengers :—

Exposing for show, hire or sale (except in a market or fair) any horse or other animal.

Exhibiting in a caravan or otherwise any show or public entertainment.

Shoeing, bleeding or farrying any horse or animal (except in case of accident).

Cleaning, exercising, training, breaking or turning loose any horse or animal.

Making or repairing any part of any carriage (except necessary repairs after accidents).

Slaughtering or dressing any cattle or any part thereof (except in cases of accident).

Placing any line, cord or pole across any street or hanging or placing any clothes thereon.

Wantonly discharging any firearm or throwing or discharging any stone or other missile.

Making any bonfire or throwing or setting fire to any firework.

Wilfully and wantonly disturbing any inhabitant by pulling or ringing any door bell or knocking at any door.

Wilfully or unlawfully extinguishing the light of any lamp.

Flying any kite or making or using any slide upon ice or snow.

Cleaning or preparing any cask or tub, or cutting, etc., any timber or stone, or slaking, sifting or screening lime.

Throwing or laying down any stones, coal, timber or other material (except building materials so enclosed as to prevent mischief to passengers).

Beating or shaking any carpet, rug or mat (except door-mats before 8 A.M.).

Fixing or placing any flower-pot, box or other heavy article in any upper window without sufficiently guarding same against being blown down.

Throwing from any roof or any part of a building any slate, brick, rubbish or other thing (except snow so as not to fall on passengers).

Ordering or permitting any person in his service to stand on the sill of a window so as to carry out any operation on the outside (unless such window is in the basement storey).

Leaving open any vault or cellar or underground entrance without a sufficient fence or handrail, or leaving the covering of same defective.

Insufficiently fencing any area, pit or sewer left open, or leaving same without a sufficient light after sunset.

Throwing or laying any dirt, litter or ashes or any rubbish on any street.

Causing any offensive matter to run from any premises into any street.

Keeping swine (or pigsty) in or near any street so as to be a common nuisance.

(It is not an offence to lay sand or other materials in time of frost to prevent accidents, or to lay litter, etc., to prevent the freezing of pipes or to prevent noise in case of sickness, but same must be removed when the occasion for them ceases.)

The following offences are confined to footways :—

Wilfully causing any obstruction in any public footpath by means of any cart, carriage, sledge, truck, barrow, animal or other means (viz. of the same kind).

Leading or driving any horse or other animal or drawing or driving any cart, carriage, sledge, truck, or barrow upon any footway of any street.

Fastening any horse or other animal so that it stands across or upon any footway.

Placing or leaving any furniture, goods, wares or merchandise or any cask, tub, basket, pail, or bucket, or placing or using any standing place, stool, bench, stall, or show-board on the footway.

Placing any blind, shade, covering, awning or other projection over or along any such footway unless 8 feet in height at least in every part from the ground.

Placing, hanging up or otherwise exposing to sale any goods, wares, merchandise, matter or thing whatsoever, so that the same project into or over any footway or beyond the line of any house, shop or building at which the same are so exposed, so as to obstruct or incommode the passage of any person over or along such footway.

Rolling or carrying any cask, tub, hoop, or wheel, or any ladder, plank, pole, timber, or log of wood upon any footway, except for the purpose of loading or unloading any cart or carriage or for the purpose of crossing the footway.

All these acts in contravention of s. 28 are offences in urban districts when committed to the obstruction, annoyance or danger of the residents or passengers.

The penalty is 40s. fine or fourteen days imprisonment.

It is the duty of the Highway Authority to provide footpaths and margins by the side of roads wherever they deem it necessary or desirable for the safety of foot passengers or live stock (R.T. Act, 1930, s. 58).

This section 28 of the Town Police Clauses Act, 1847, creates a number of offences in connection with streets and allows a constable to arrest any person whom he sees committing any of these offences (and as there is power of arrest without warrant a warrant may be issued, C.J.A. Act, 1914, s. 27). The police can prosecute (lay the information) for offences under this s. 28 because they have the power of arrest for them. For other offences under this 1847 Act and the Public Health Acts proceedings may taken by an aggrieved person, by a local authority or with the consent of the Attorney General (*Sheffield Corporation* v. *Kitson* (1929)). This section applies only in towns and urban districts (s. 171, Public Health Act, 1875), and in those rural districts to which it has been extended by Special Order under s. 276 of the Public Health Act, 1875, and s. 13, Public Health Act, 1936.

Other Street Nuisances and Dangers.—The following offences are usually reported to the surveyor of the local council :—

The Towns Improvement Clauses Act, 1847, contains several regulations affecting streets, which apply in urban districts (s. 160, Public Health Act, 1875) and deal with, amongst other matters, damage to street names or house numbers (s. 64), projections in front of buildings which interfere with free passage (s. 69), doors or gates opening outwards on streets (s. 71), adequate coverings for openings in footpaths (s. 73),water shoots on houses (s. 74), dangerous buildings (ss. 75-78), interference with road repair work (s. 79), precautions to be taken (by way of hoardings, fencing and lighting) during repair work to buildings (ss. 80-82), and repairing of dangerous places (s. 83).

The Public Health Acts also contain rules applying to the streets of urban districts, with respect to the following matters :—

1875 Act : Wilful damage to streets (s. 149).

1907 Act : Depositing building materials, rubbish or other thing in the street and having same or any excavation in the street insufficiently fenced or lighted (s. 29), repairing or enclosing dangerous places (s. 30), fencing land adjoining streets (s. 31), secure erection of hoardings (s. 32), routes for leading or driving animals (s. 80).

1925 Act: Lopping of trees, etc., overhanging highways, etc., (s. 23 as added to by R.T. Act, 1956, Sched. 8 (5)), fixing rails, beams, cables, wires, etc., over, along or across a street (s. 25).

1936 Act : Dangerous buildings (s. 58), interference with dustbins and refuse tips (s. 76), public sanitary conveniences (ss. 87-89), exposure in public of persons or articles liable to convey infectious disease (ss. 148-165).

Impounding Animals.—Cattle and animals of the like kind constitute a nuisance and a danger to the public when straying on the highway, and when so found may be taken by any person to the pound or place set apart for that purpose. Cattle may be on the highway only for the purpose of passing and repassing.

Highway Act, 1864, s. 25, provides that any horse, mule, ass, cattle, sheep, goat or swine found straying on or lying about any highway may be removed by any person to the fields or stables of the owner or to the common pound. The owner of same is liable to a summary fine of 5s. per animal (total penalty not to exceed 30s.) together with the expense of so removing the animals and the pound fees.

Town Police Clauses Act, 1847, ss. 24 and 25, declares that any cattle, including horses, asses, mules, sheep, goats and swine, found at large in any street in any urban district without any person having the charge thereof, may be impounded by any constable or resident, and detained there until a penalty not exceeding 40s. is paid, together with the expenses of impounding and feeding such cattle. If same be not paid within three days, the cattle may be sold, after seven days notice to the owner if known or seven days after advertisement in a local newspaper.

Protection of Animals Act, 1911, s. 7, enacts that any person who impounds any animal is bound to supply it with sufficient food and water, and that if an animal is left in a pound without sufficient food or water for six successive hours or longer, any person may enter the pound and supply same. The cost of food and water supplied to an impounded animal may be recovered summarily from the owner. See " Cruelty to Animals," Chap. 35.

It is an offence to release animals which are being taken to pound or which have been impounded. See " Pound Breach," Chap. 21.

Highway Code.—Road Traffic Act, 1930, s. 45, directs the Minister of Transport to prepare a " highway code " comprising directions for the guidance of persons using roads, and allows him to revise it from time to time. Such code and any revision thereof must be approved by Parliament.

This code is printed and available to the public (see 1956 Act, Sched. 8 (18)).

Failure by a person to observe any provision of this code shall not of itself render him liable to criminal proceedings, but such a failure may in any civil or criminal proceedings be relied upon as tending to establish or to negative any liability which is in question in such proceedings (s. 45).

The code contains advice and directions to all users of the highway, to drivers of motor vehicles, to motor cyclists, to drivers of horse-drawn vehicles, to persons in charge of animals, to pedal cyclists, and to pedestrians. It gives the various traffic signs and signals and the Law's demands upon road users together with some hints on driving and cycling.

Regulation of Traffic.—The police in the pursuance of their duty to maintain order have a general power to regulate traffic so that every person may freely and safely pass and repass on the highway.

Every constable in uniform engaged for the time being in the regulation of traffic has power to regulate traffic (1930 Act, s. 49 and 1956 Act, s. 14). Several statutes prescribe rules which must be obeyed by the drivers of vehicles. Breaches of these rules are summary offences, as will be seen by the following extracts from the Acts in question.

Many localities have local byelaws for the regulation of traffic.

Proceedings are taken by the police when breaches of these laws and byelaws are detected.

Highway Act, 1835, s. 77 : No person is to act as driver of more than two carts or wagons or other such carriages on a highway, but one person may act as driver of two such carriages provided same are not drawn by more than one horse each and the horse of the hindmost is attached by a rein not exceeding 4 feet in length to the back of the foremost. Penalty, 20*s*. fine.

S. 78 : The following acts are offences punishable by £5 fine (or £10 if the driver be the owner) or imprisonment in default.

Driver of any wagon, cart or other carriage of any kind riding upon same or upon any horse drawing same, on the highway, and not having another person on foot or on horseback to guide the same. (Carts and carriages driven with reins and conducted by some person holding the reins of all the horses drawing the same are excepted.)

Driver of any carriage whatsoever on the highway quitting the same and going on the other side of the highway fence, or being negligently or wilfully at such distance from such carriage or in such a situation that he cannot have the direction and govern-ment of the horses or cattle drawing the same.

Driver of any carriage whatsoever leaving any cart or carriage on the highway so as to obstruct the passage thereof.

Driver ot any wagon, cart or other carriage whatsoever or of any horses, mules or other beasts of burden, meeting any other carriage or beasts of burden, and not keeping his carriage or beasts on the left or near side of the road.

Any person in any manner wilfully preventing any other person from passing him or any wagon, cart or other carriage or beasts of burden under his care upon such highway, or by negligence or misbehaviour preventing, hindering or interrupting the free passage of any person, carriage or beast of burden on any highway, or not keeping his carriage or beast of burden on the left or near side of the road for the purpose of allowing such passage.

Town Police Clauses Act, 1847, s. 28 : The following acts are offences when committed in any street in any urban district to the obstruction, annoyance or danger of the inhabitants or passengers :—

Having the care of any wagon, cart or carriage and riding on the shafts, or without having reins and holding the same riding on such carriage or on any animal drawing the same, or being at such a distance as not to have due control over every animal drawing the same.

Meeting another carriage and not keeping his carriage to the left or near side. Passing another carriage and not keeping his carriage on the right or off side (except in cases of actual necessity or some sufficient reason for deviation).

Wilfully preventing, by obstructing the street, any person or carriage from passing him or any carriage under his care.

Driving at one time more than two carts or wagons, or if driving two, not having the halter of the horse in the last cart or wagon securely fastened to the back of the first, or having such halter of a greater length from such fastening to the horse's head than 4 feet.

Causing any public carriage, sledge, truck or barrow, with or without horses, or any beast of burden, to stand longer than is necessary for loading or unloading goods, or for taking up or setting down passengers (except vehicles and beasts of burden standing for hire in any place appointed for that purpose by the Local Authority).

By means of any cart, carriage, sledge, truck or barrow or any animal, wilfully interrupting any public crossing, or wilfully causing any obstruction in any public footpath or other thoroughfare.

Causing any tree, timber, or iron beam to be drawn on any carriage without having sufficient means of safely guiding the same.

Penalty, 40s. fine or fourteen days imprisonment.

Under ss. 21 and 22 of this Act the Local Authority, to prevent obstruction, may make orders for the route of vehicles, horses and persons.

Road and Rail Traffic Act, 1933, s. 30 : The bridge authority, by proper notice in proper position at each end of a bridge over which a road passes, may prohibit the use of the bridge by motor vehicles weighing laden more than a specified weight, not less than five tons, either absolutely or when travelling at more than a specified speed. It will be an offence to contravene such notice, unless the bridge authority has given a permit to do so. Persons aggrieved by such prohibition or restriction may apply to the Minister of Transport who may modify or cancel same. This section will operate by Order (1956 Act, 8th Sched. (32)).

Road Traffic Act, 1930, s. 54 : If extraordinary expense in the repair of a road is due to excessive weight or other extraordinary traffic, the cost of such damage is recoverable from the person responsible for such traffic (except in the case of Crown vehicles, s. 121 (2)).

Ss. 46 and 59, R.T. Act, 1930; s. 29, R and R.T. Act, 1933 and s. 33 of the Road Traffic Act, 1956 authorise the Minister of Transport and Civil Aviation to make orders regulating traffic on roads. The procedure to be followed in making these orders is governed by the Traffic Regulation Orders (Procedure) (England and Wales) Regs, 1957.

S. 47 : A highway authortiy, to obviate danger to the public or serious damage to the highway, may by notice restrict or prohibit temporarily the use of a road by vehicles.

It may also, on occasion of works being executed or proposed to be executed (Public Utilities Street Works Act, 1950) on a road, prohibit or restrict traffic by Order. Notices of such a notice or Order must be posted on the road, giving the alternative routes for traffic. Such notices or Orders shall not apply to tramcars or trolley vehicles. See 1956 Act, s. 34, which has amended this s. 47 with regard to traffic regulation during road repairs, etc. S. 45 of the 1956 Act increases the powers of local authorities to construct, maintain, etc., works in the carriageway.

S. 48: Traffic signs may be erected on or near roads by the highway authority in conformity with the directions of the Minister of Transport, and they should be of the prescribed size, colour and type, except where the Minister authorises a sign of another character. " Traffic sign " means any object or device (whether fixed or portable) for conveying warnings, information, requirements, restrictions, or prohibitions of any description prescribed or authorised by s. 48 (2) of the Act of 1930 to traffic on roads or any specified description of traffic, and any line or mark on a road for conveying such warnings, (R.T. Act, 1956, s. 35). No other traffic signs are permissible, except those re bridges, and those placed by any tramway, trolley vehicle, light railway, dock or harbour undertaking. The 1956 Act, ss. 35, 37, 38, extend the law re traffic signs, special traffic signs and temporary traffic signs.

The highway Authority may give written notice to the owner or occupier of land to remove any unauthorised traffic sign and has power to remove it.

Traffic Signs Regs. and General Directions 1957, give the traffic signs which may be placed on or near roads and directions as to their use. Many of these signs are merely of a warning or informative character, and disregard of them, while not punishable as a specific offence under s. 49 of the Road Traffic Act, 1930, may increase any liability for careless or dangerous driving.

Not stopping at a stop line in obedience to a light signal or a police signal (Reg. 21) will be an offence under s. 49.

Disobedience of signals used in connection with road works (Reg. 29) may also be an offence.

As regards light signals, " green " indicates that a vehicle may proceed with due regard to the safety of other users of the road and subject to the directions of any police officer regulating traffic; " red " and " red with amber " prohibit movement beyond the stop line until green shows. " Amber " shown alone also prohibits movement beyond the stop line except in a case where the vehicle is so close to the stop line that it cannot safely be stopped before passing the line (Reg. 27).

The traffic signs, " Halt at major road ahead," " Slow major road ahead," " Keep left dual carriageway," " Turn left dual carriageway," " Keep left," " Stop for weight check," " Stop " (which may be used only where one-way traffic working is necessary owing to a temporary closure to vehicular traffic of a width of the carriageway) and the " Red light signal " (whether fixed or portable) are authorised and it is an offence to disobey them (Reg. 5).

For the traffic sign " Stop, children crossing " see School Crossing Patrols Act, 1953, *post*.

R.T. Act, 1930, s. 49, as amended by 3rd Sched. R.T. Act 1934. It is an offence for any person driving or propelling any vehicle,

(*a*) to neglect or refuse to stop the vehicle or to make it proceed in or keep to a particular line of traffic, when directed to do so by a police constable, for the time being engaged in the regulation of traffic on a road, in the execution of his duty,

(*b*) to fail to conform to the indication given by any traffic sign, lawfully placed on or near any road and being lawfully authorised. The offender must be duly warned, as per s. 21, 1930 Act, of likely prosecution (1956 Act, s. 30).

A traffic signal on or near a road as a traffic sign shall be deemed to be of the prescribed size, colour and type or of another author-ised character and to be lawfully there unless the contrary is proved (R.T. Act, 1934, s. 36 and Emergency Laws (Transi-tional Provisions) Act, 1946, 2nd Sched.). Therefore the onus is placed on a defendant to prove the signal is not legal if he so alleges.

S. 20 (3) : Any person driving a motor vehicle on a road shall stop the vehicle on being so required by a police constable in uniform. Failure to do so is punishable by fine.

S. 50 : It is an offence for any person in charge of a vehicle to cause or permit the vehicle, or any trailer drawn thereby, to remain at rest on any road in such a position or in such condition or in such circumstances as to be likely to cause danger to other persons using the road. An offender must be warned, as per s. 21, 1930 Act, of likely prosecution (1956 Act, s. 30).

S. 14 : The driving of a motor vehicle, without lawful authority, on to or upon any common land, moor land or other land (not being part of a road), or on any road being a bridleway or footpath, is an offence except when done for the purpose of saving life, extinguishing fire or other like emergency, or on land within 15 yards of a road for the purpose only of parking the vehicle on that land. However, this section does not affect the rights of the public on commons or waste lands or any byelaws as to land, or the law of trespass, and it does not confer any right to park a vehicle on any land. (See " Trespass," Chap. 19.)

For rules as to control of vehicle, use of horn, obstruction, quitting vehicle, reversing, view of traffic, etc., see " Construction and Use of Motor Vehicles," Chap. 25 and Appendix 2.

R.T. Act, 1956, s. 14. A person on foot who proceeds across or along the carriageway in contravention of a direction to stop given by a constable in uniform regulating traffic in the road will commit a summary offence liable to fine. Such an offender shall give his name and address, on request, to a constable. Failure to do so will be a summary offence liable to fine.

A Traffic Safety Code for road works was issued in May 1957 giving guidance as to the lighting etc. of road obstructions and for temporary traffic control (M.T.C.A. Memo No. 736).

Removal of Vehicles (England and Wales) Regulations, 1957.—Where a vehicle has broken down or is permitted to remain at rest on a road so as to be likely to cause danger to or obstruction to other persons using the road or is allowed to rest on a road in contravention of any relevant law (see Schedule to Regulations) a constable may require the owner or person in charge to remove it as directed. Failure to comply will be a summary offence. A constable may arrange for the removal of a vehicle in the foregoing circumstances and he may also do so if it seems to have been abandoned.

" Obstruction " as above will occur if the vehicle is too near a road junction or too far from the edge of the carriageway or so near another vehicle, that the constable considers that the passage of other vehicles is unduly restricted.

Parking.—Under the Public Health Act, 1925, s. 68, a Local Authority may by order authorise the use, as a free parking place, of any part of a street not within the London Traffic Area, provided such use does not unreasonably prevent access to any premises adjoining the street or does not cause a nuisance etc.

In London " parking places " are designated under powers contained in the London Traffic Act, 1924, s. 10.

By s. 9(1) of the Road Traffic Act, 1956, " parking places " on highways may be designated in London and the local authority may make charges for vehicles left on such parking places. In certain streets the provisions of this section have been implemented and " parking meters " installed for the collection of charges. This power may be ordered to extend to places outside London.

See also " Obstruction " above.

Pedestrian Crossings.—R.T. Act, 1934, s. 18 allows the establishment of road crossings for pedestrians and the making of regulations respecting their use. This section has been amended giving increased power to the Minister regarding such crossings and increasing the penalty for contravention (1956 Act, s. 46).

The Pedestrian Crossings Regs., 1954, revoked previous similar regulations and apply everywhere. They have been amended by the Pedestrian Crossings (England and Wales) (Amendment) Regs., 1958.

Reg. 3: Every crossing for foot passengers on a road shall be indicated as prescribed in the First Schedule. Part 1 of this Schedule directs two lines of studs across the carriage way. Part 2 directs that every crossing where there are no light signals or police control shall be further marked by black and white stripes between the lines of studs (viz., " Zebra Crossings "). At or near each end of such a crossing there shall be a yellow globe with flashing or constant light on a black and white banded post. The approach for vehicular traffic to an uncontrolled crossing (zebra crossing) shall be indicated by 2 lines of studs (each stud about one foot apart) situated between 42 feet and 48 feet from crossings on roads subject to a speed limit of 30 m.p.h. or less, and between 70 feet and 80 feet on roads where no such speed limit in in force.

Reg. 5: A vehicle must not stop in a crossing unless prevented from proceeding by circumstances beyond the driver's control or has to stop to avoid accident.

Reg. 8: No foot passenger shall remain in a crossing longer than is necessary for passing across with reasonable despatch.

An " uncontrolled crossing " means one to which Part 2 of the Schedule applies (no light signals) or where traffic is not being controlled by a police officer in uniform (Reg. 2).

Reg. 4: Every foot passenger in an uncontrolled crossing has precedence over any vehicle and its driver shall afford such precedence. If a street refuge or central reservation interrupts such crossing each side of the crossing will be a separate crossing.

Reg. 6: A vehicle (not a solo bicycle) shall not stop in the carriage way between the double line of studs in the road before the crossing is reached and the uncontrolled crossing with its light on black and white post except, as allowed by Reg. 7, it is unable to proceed or has to stop to avoid accident or for fire brigade, ambulance or police purposes, or defence purposes, or building operations or for road works purposes.

Contraventions of Regs. 4, 5, 6, or 8 are punishable summarily by fine. (See s. 46, 1956 Act.)

A street refuge in a pedestrian crossing is not part of the crossing and a pedestrian when leaving such a refuge must not do so negligently (*Wilkinson* v. *Chetham-Strode* (1940)).

School Crossing Patrols Act, 1953.—This Act allows county and county borough Councils to appoint persons as school crossing patrols to patrol at places where children are crossing or seek to cross roads on their way to or from school, between 8 a.m. and 5-30 p.m. Any such patrol must be trained and wear uniform. When such a patrol exhibits the prescribed sign " Stop Children Crossing " the driver of a vehicle must stop and allow the children to cross the road. If the driver does not stop he commits a summary offence liable to fine of £20. There is also liability to disqualification or endorsement on subsequent convictions R.T. Act, 1956, 4th Sched. See also Traffic Signs (School Crossing Patrols) Regs., 1953.

Dangerous, etc., Driving.—Several statutes deal with the driving of vehicles on the highway, prescribing punishment for certain acts which cause or may cause injury to person or property.

Highway Act, 1835, s. 78 : The driver of any carriage what-soever on any part of any highway, by negligence or wilful misbehaviour, causing any hurt or damage to any person, horse, cattle or goods conveyed in any carriage passing or being upon such highway.

(Bicycles, tricycles and other similar machines are carriages within the meaning of the Highway Acts (Local Government Act, 1888, s. 85)).

Any person riding any horse or beast or driving any sort of carriage, riding or driving the same furiously so as to endanger the life or limb of any passenger. Penalty £5 fine, or £10 if driver is also the owner. Any person witnessing these offences may arrest without warrant.

Town Police Clauses Act, 1847, s. 28 : Any person in any street (in any urban district) to the obstruction, annoyance or danger of the residents or passengers, riding or driving furiously any horse or carriage, or driving furiously any cattle. Penalty 40s. fine or fourteen days imprisonment. Any constable witnessing the offence may arrest without warrant and convey the offender before a justice. A bicycle is a carriage *(Taylor* v. *Goodwin* (1879)).

Offences against the Person Act, 1861, s. 35 : Any person, having the charge of any carriage or vehicle, by wanton or furious driving or racing or other wilful misconduct or by wilful neglect, doing or causing to be done any bodily harm to any person. Misdemeanour.

Public Health Act, 1925, s. 74 (2) : Any person riding or driving so as to endanger the life or limb of any person or to the common danger of the passengers in any street, not being a street within the Metropolitan Police District (wherein the Metropolitan Police Act, 1839, gives similar powers), may be arrested without warrant by any constable who witnesses the occurrence, and may be fined.

This provision is restricted to urban districts but may be applied, by Order, to rural districts. See s. 27 Crim. Justice Adm. Act, 1914, as to proceedings where there was no arrest.

Road Traffic Act, 1930, s. 11 : Any person driving a motor vehicle on a road recklessly or at a speed or in a manner which is dangerous to the public having regard to all the circumstances of the case, including the nature, condition and use of the road and the amount of traffic which is actually at the time, or which might reasonably be expected to be, on the road, commits an offence.

1956 Act, Sched. 8 (12). Penalty on summary conviction fine not exceeding £100 and maybe in addition imprisonment not exceeding on first conviction 4 months and on second or subsequent conviction 6 months. Also the period of disqualification imposed under s. 11, 1930 Act is given in s. 26 of the 1956 Act.

On conviction on indictment imprisonment not exceeding two years and (or) a fine (R.T. Act, 1934, s.4).

A conviction shall be endorsed on his licence, and he may be disqualified from having a licence. On second or subsequent conviction his disqualification shall be ordered unless the Court having regard to the lapse of time (3 years or more) since the last previous conviction or for any other special reason, orders otherwise. But the Court has power to disqualify on a first conviction (for " special reason," see " Penalties," later). A person, present in the vehicle at the time and convicted of aiding, abetting, etc., the offence, may also be punished (s. 11 and s. 26, 1956 Act).

When by such reckless driving (see s. 11 above) a person causes the death of another person he is liable to up to 5 years imprisonment on conviction on indictment (not triable at Quarter Sessions). However the jury may convict him of the offence under s. 11 whether or not notice of prosecution under s. 21, 1930 Act was given. Any inquest should be adjourned (R.T. Act, 1956, s. 8).

On trial on indictment for manslaughter in connection with the driving of a motor vehicle, the jury may find the accused guilty of reckless or dangerous driving whether or not the requisite notice under s. 21 of the R.T. Act, 1930 (see below), was served on him (R.T. Act, 1934, s. 34).

In a case of driving at a speed dangerous to the public, it is not necessary to prove actual danger ; potential danger must be considered (*Kingman* v. *Seagar* (1937), and *Bracegirdle* v. *Oxley* (1946)).

S. 12 : Any person driving a motor vehicle on a road without due care and attention or without reasonable consideration for other persons using the road commits an offence (" careless driving "). There are two separate offences in this section and it is a question of fact for the justices.

Inexperience of a learner is no excuse. There is only one standard of careful driving (*McCrone* v. *Riding* (1938)). A driver who allows himself to be overtaken by sleep while driving is at least guilty of the offence of driving without due care and attention (*Kay* v. *Butterworth* (1945)).

If a Magistrates' Court considers a charge of reckless or dangerous driving (s. 11) is not proved, then during the hearing or immediately thereafter, the Court may direct or allow a charge of careless driving (s. 12) to be preferred forthwith and may proceed with the charge provided the accused is given an opportunity of answering it or may adjourn the hearing if it considers that the accused is prejudiced in his defence to the new charge. If notice under s. 21 of the R.T. Act, 1930, was given or was not required for the first charge (s. 11) no further notice is necessary in respect to the new charge under s. 12 (R.T. Act, 1934, s. 35).

A conviction for careless driving shall be endorsed on the licence unless the Court for special reason direct otherwise (R.T. Act, 1934, s. 5), and the offender shall be liable to fine up to £40, on second or subsequent conviction up to £80 fine or to imprisonment up to 3 months or both (R.T. Act, 1956, Sched. 8 (12)) but is not liable to disqualification on a first conviction (R.T. Act, 1930, s. 12). For special reason see " Penalties," later.

If a Court convicts for reckless or dangerous driving or for careless driving or for driving under the influence of drink or a drug (1956 Act, s. 26 and Sched. 8 (35)), the Court in addition to any other penalty may order accused to be disqualified until he has passed a driving test, for which he may get a provisional driving licence (R.T. Act, 1934, s. 6 (3) and (4)).

R.T. Act, 1930, s. 20 (2) : A constable may arrest without warrant any driver who within his view commits any of these reckless or dangerous or careless driving offences under ss. 11 and 12, unless the driver either gives his name and address or produces his licence for examination.

S. 20 (1) : If it is alleged that a driver has committed any of these driving offences under ss. 11 and 12 and he refuses, on being so required by any person having reasonable ground for so requiring, to give his name or address, or gives a false name or address, he will commit an offence.

S. 21 : If a person is prosecuted for the above offences of reckless or dangerous or careless driving (but see s. 35 (2), R.T. Act, 1934) or for exceeding the prescribed limit of speed (see " Speed Limits "), he will escape conviction unless either:—

(a) he was warned at the time of the offence that his prosecution for one or other of these offences would be considered, or

(b) a summons for the offence was served on him within fourteen days of the commission of the offence, or

(c) within the said fourteen days, notice of the intended prosecution was served on or sent by registered post to him or the person registered as owner of the vehicle at the time of the offence.

However, failure to comply with this requirement will not be a bar to conviction if the Court is satisfied that neither the name and address of the accused nor the name and address of the owner could with reasonable diligence have been ascertained in time to serve the summons or send the notice within the fourteen days, or that the accused by his own conduct contributed to the failure.

S. 13 : To promote or take part in a race or trial of speed between motor vehicles on a public highway is an offence punishable by up to three months imprisonment or £50 fine or both.

A person convicted of this offence shall be disqualified for at least twelve months from having a licence unless the Court, for special reasons, orders otherwise. For special reason see " Penalties," later.

No person shall promote or take part in a trial of any description between motor vehicles on a footpath or bridleway (right of way on foot and on or with a horse, s. 54) unless the trial has been authorised by the local authority (County Council) with the consent of the owner or occupier of the land (R.T.Act, 1956, s. 12).

S. 15 : It is an offence, punishable on indictment or summarily, to drive or attempt to drive a motor vehicle on a road or other public place, when under the influence of drink or a drug to such an extent as to be incapable of having proper control of the vehicle. (See" Drunkenness," Chap. 38.). Medical evidence is not necessary.

S. 16 : It is not lawful for more than one person in addition to the driver to be carried on any two-wheeled motor cycle, or for such one person to be carried otherwise than sitting astride the cycle on a proper seat securely fixed to the cycle behind the driver's seat (" pillion "). On contravention of this section the driver is liable to a fine.

S. 29 : Taking hold of or getting on to a motor vehicle or trailer while in motion on a road, for the purpose of being drawn or carried, otherwise than with lawful authority or reasonable cause is an offence. Also getting on to a motor vehicle or tampering with the brake or other part of its mechanism while it is on a road or local authority parking place, otherwise than with lawful authority or reasonable cause is an offence under the Act.

S. 33 : Driving over Menai Bridge except in accordance with any regulations is an offence. The 1931 Regulations, as amended, were revoked and none are at present in force.

It is not lawful for more than one person to be carried on a road on a pedal bicycle unless it is constructed or adapted for the carriage of more than one person. " Person carried " includes the rider. If this section is contravened each person carried is liable to a fine. (R.T. Act, 1934, s. 20.)

R.T. Act, 1930, s. 19 : To protect the public from the danger arising from drivers suffering from excessive fatigue, the hours of driving duty of drivers of public service vehicles, heavy and light locomotives, motor tractors, and motor vehicles constructed to carry goods, are limited by this section to :—

(*a*) Any continuous period of $5\frac{1}{2}$ hours ; or

(*b*) Continuous periods totalling eleven hours in any period of twenty-four hours commencing 2 A.M.

Any two or more periods of time shall be reckoned as continuous unless separated by at least half an hour in which the driver can get rest and refreshment. Driving time shall include time spent on other work in connection with the vehicle or its load.

A driver should have at least 10 consecutive hours for rest in any period of 24 hours calculated from the commencement of any period of driving, but 9 consecutive hours for rest in the 24 will be sufficient if he has at least 12 consecutive hours for rest in the next following period of 24 hours. (See later for variation.)

By s. 31, R. & R.T. Act, 1933, time during which a driver is bound to obey directions or remain on or near the vehicle or at a place where he cannot rest away from the vehicle shall not be deemed " rest time."

Also by s. 7, R.T. Act, 1934, times for rest and refreshment allowed to drivers of stage carriages during their hours of duty may be taken into consideration as regards their hours of duty.

However, these rules do not apply to ambulances, fire machines (s. 19) and vehicles under control of the armed forces of the Crown (see s. 121), nor to vehicles used for agriculture or forestry elsewhere than on a road, and the prescribed hours may be varied by the Minister of Transport (s. 19).

Any person driving, or causing or permitting any person employed by him or subject to his orders to drive in contravention of this section, commits an offence, but will escape conviction if he proves to the Court that the contravention was due to unavoidable delay in the journey arising out of circumstances which he could not reasonably have foreseen (s. 19).

Variation of Provisions of s. 19. *Order*, 1937, has altered the above hours in connection with public service vehicles as follows:

One period of driving duty (with intervals) may continue for $8\frac{1}{2}$ hours in the 24. If $8\frac{1}{2}$ hours is worked in two periods one period may last $6\frac{1}{2}$ hours (with intervals) if the driver gets 12 consecutive hours rest in the 24.

Eight consecutive hours rest on one day of the week may be substituted for drivers of express and contract carriages if there is a 4-hour rest at a destination, and also for a stage carriage driver if he gets 12 consecutive hours rest on the following day.

Variation of Provisions of s. 19. *Order*, 1934, has altered the prescribed hours, in connection with heavy and light locomotives. motor tractors and goods vehicles authorised under A and B licences (see " Goods Vehicles," Chap. 25), as follows:—

(*a*) If only one period of 8 hours is worked in the 24 hours, 8 hours may be substituted for the $5\frac{1}{2}$ hours continuous period if the driver is allowed intervals for rest and refreshment of not less than 40 minutes in the aggregate.

(*b*) If the driver is employed by the week and receives one complete day's rest of 24 hours in each week, the limit of 11 hours aggregate driving time in a 24-hours period may be extended to 12 hours provided that some part of the time is occupied in waiting or other work.

This 12 hours is usually allowed in respect to such vehicles authorised under " C " licences on 2 days in each of the last three weeks of December.

Lights on Vehicles.—The use of lights on vehicles at night is regulated by the Road Transport Lighting Act, 1957, as amended by the Road Transport Lighting (Amendment) Act, 1958. References are to the Act of 1957 unless otherwise stated.

These Acts regulate the lighting of vehicles (including vehicle machines and implements) used " during the hours of darkness " on any public highway and any other road to which the public has access but do not apply to tramcars or vehicles used on railway lines (s. 16). Provisions as to the position, etc., of the lamps and reflectors to be carried are contained in the Road Vehicles Lighting Regulations, 1954, and R.V.L. (Amendment) Regs., 1955, the Road Vehicles Lighting (Standing Vehicles) (Exemption) (General) Regs., 1956, and the Road Vehicles Lighting (Amendment) Regs., 1958.

Hours of Darkness.—Night is referred to in the Acts as the "hours of darkness" which, by s. 17 of the 1957 Act means the time between half an hour after sunset and half an hour before sunrise, throughout the whole year. See also M.Vs. (C. and U.) Regs., 1955 and 1957 (Reg. 90 and T.68).

Lights and Reflectors to be carried on Vehicles.—During the hours of darkness every lamp shall be kept properly trimmed, lighted, and in a clean and efficient condition (s. 1) and shall be attached to the vehicle in the prescribed manner. Also any person who causes or permits a vehicle to be on any road during the hours of darkness must provide the necessary lamps (s. 1).

A vehicle shall not show a red light to the front, and it shall not show any light to the rear other than a red light, apart from any lamps used for illuminating the inside of the vehicle or any number plate, taximeter, or signalling device, or any route or destination boards of any public service vehicle (s. 2), but lamps may show white light to the rear for the purpose of reversing (s. 2) and bicycles and tricycles may carry amber coloured reflectors on the pedals (1958 Act, s. 1).

(1) *Lights on Road Vehicles Generally.*—The lights to be carried on all vehicles (except those dealt with individually below) are as follows:

(a) Two lamps showing white light to the front (1957 Act, s. 1). These are known as " obligatory front lamps " (Regs., 1954, r. 3).

(b) Two lamps showing red light to the rear (s. 1). These are known as " obligatory rear lamps " (1954 Regs., r. 3).

(c) Two red reflectors (s. 1).

(2) *Pedal cycles and tricycles.*—Only one front white light and one rear red light are necessary for a solo bicycle or a tricycle not propelled by mechanical power, which also must have a red rear reflector (s. 6).

No lamp need be carried by a solo bicycle or a tricycle not propelled by mechanical power when wheeled by a person on foot as near as possible to the left or near edge of the carriage-way (s. 6).

Lights need be not shown when a bicycle or a tricycle not propelled by mechanical power is stationary owing to traffic exigencies or traffic signals or directions if it is as near as possible to the near side of the carriage-way (s. 6).

A bicycle propelled by mechanical power but not having a side-car must have one front white lamp and one red rear lamp and one red rear reflector (s. 6). If such a bicycle has a sidecar attached it should have two such front and rear lamps and two red rear reflectors.

(3) *Invalid Carriages.*—That is mechanically propelled vehicles whose weight unladen does not exceed 5 cwt. and which are specially made for and used by disabled persons (s. 17). Such a vehicle need show only one white light to the front (s. 6). It must carry two red rear lights and two red rear reflectors (s. 1).

(4) *Motor Cycles.*—If no sidecar is attached, only one white light to the front and one red light to the rear are necessary also one red rear reflector (s. 6). No lights are necessary whilst such a solo bicycle is being wheeled by a person on foot as near as possible to the left or near edge of the carriage way (s. 6).

A motor cycle combination shall have two front white lights (which need not be at the same height from the ground (R.V.L. Regs., 1954, r. 6) and two red rear lights also two red reflectors (s. 1). Whilst being wheeled on the road such combinations shall show all the obligatory lights.

(5) *Animal-drawn vehicles (horse carts, etc.).*—Two front white lights two red rear lights and two red rear reflectors are necessary (s. 1). By s. 4 of the Act, it is however provided that a vehicle need not carry separate lamps for different purposes if it carries a lamp satisfying all requirements for those purposes in itself. This would seem to allow horse carts, etc., to continue to use lamps showing white light to the front and red light to the rear.

(6) *Animal-drawn vehicles used for agricultural purposes.*—These vehicles when engaged for the time being in carrying agricultural produce of an inflammable nature in the course of the internal operations of the farm need not carry lamps (s. 7).

An agricultural implement being so drawn, or any animal-drawn vehicle used for the time being by a person engaged in agriculture for the conveyance of his agricultural produce or articles required by him for use in agriculture, must show one white light to the front attached to the right or off-side of the vehicle (s. 7). Two red rear reflectors are necessary (s. 1). If the vehicle or implement carries a projecting or overhanging load it will be subject to the provisions as to such (see below) with the substitution of references to red reflectors instead of to the tail light. The term " agriculture " covers the use of land as meadow or pasture or orchard or as a market garden or allotment, but it does not include woodland (s. 17).

(7) *Vehicles drawn or propelled by hand (such as hand-carts, wheelbarrows, perambulators, etc.).*—*Under the R.V. Lighting Regs., 1954.—*

(a) If such vehicle and any load is not more than 2½ feet wide, 6 feet long and 4½ feet high, it need not carry any lamps provided it is kept as near as possible to the edge of the carriageway during the hours of darkness.

(b) If such vehicle and any load exceeds any or all of the preceding measurements but is not more than 4 feet wide, it need show only one obligatory front light and a red rear lamp or a red rear reflector.

(c) If such vehicle and any load exceeds 4 feet in width it must carry two lamps showing white light to the front. It must also have a red rear reflector or a red rear lamp (Reg. 26).

(d) If the vehicle carries a load extending more than 3½ feet behind its tail light, a red rear lamp must also be carried so that no part of the load projects more than 3½ feet beyond it. Any red rear reflector on such a vehicle must be fixed on the offside within at least 16 inches from the side.

(8) *Towed Vehicles.*—When a vehicle is drawing or towing one or more other vehicles, the drawing vehicle must show its obligatory front lights and the last or hindmost vehicle must show its two obligatory red rear lights and two red reflectors (s. 9). No other lights need be displayed, except:

(1) If the distance between any two of the vehicles exceeds 5 feet, both vehicles must be fully lighted;

(2) If any part of any vehicle being towed or if its load projects or overhangs on either side more than 12 inches beyond the centre of the white light lamp carried on the same side by the drawing vehicle or by any preceding vehicle which is also being drawn by the same vehicle, such broader vehicle must display on the projecting side a front white light so placed that no part of the vehicle or its load projects outward more than 12 inches beyond the centre of such lamp (s. 9).

(3) If any towed or towing vehicle otherwise exempt from carrying lights projects laterally beyond the other vehicles by more than 12 inches then it will have to carry a white front light and a red rear light to indicate the projection. As to the position of the rear red light see under " Projecting or Overhanging Loads " below.

Also under s. 1 of the R.T. Act, 1930, and s. 36 of the R. & R.T. Act, 1933, any towed vehicle being a " vehicle drawn by a motor vehicle " may be regarded as a trailer at the time (see *Wallace* v. *Major* (1946), and Reg. 3 of the R.V.L. Regs., 1954) and the number of such drawn vehicles is limited under s. 18 of the R.T. Act, 1930. See " Trailers " in Appendix II.

(9) *Projecting or Overhanging Loads.*—If a load on a vehicle projects to the rear more than 3½ feet behind its tail lamp or any red reflector, a separate red rear lamp must be carried so that no part of the load projects to the rear more than 3½ feet behind that

rear lamp. Such a " projecting " lamp may be in addition to or in substitution for any lamp showing red to the rear or any reflector s. 8). In relation to: (a) a vehicle carrying a fire escape; and (b) a mechanically propelled vehicle being a land tractor or an agricultural tractor on which is mounted an agricultural implement, instead of 3½ feet the distance shall be 6 feet (Road Vehicles Lighting (Projecting Loads) Regs., 1958, Reg. 4).

If a load overhangs laterally by more than 12 inches measured— (a) from the outermost part of the vehicle on the same side as that on which the load overhangs; or (b) if the vehicle is drawing one or more vehicles, from the outermost part of the rearmost vehicle on the same side as that on which the load overhangs, the vehicle shall carry a rear lamp in the ' relevant position " to indicate the overhang (Reg. 5 (1)).

" Relevant position " means a position on any side on which the load overhangs laterally, which is as near as practicable to the outer edge of the load and which is such that no part of the load projects outwards more than 12 inches beyond a vertical line through the nearest part of the illuminated area of the rear lamp (Reg. 5 (2)).

This regulation applies to a towed vehicle which need not carry red rear lights by virtue of s. 9 of R.T.L. Act, 1957, but it does not apply to any vehicle carrying loose agricultural produce not baled or crated (Reg. 5 (3 & 4)).

Rear lamps marking projecting loads must at night be kept properly trimmed, lighted and in a clean and efficient condition (Reg. 6).

N.B.—Grasscutters (motor mowers) which are mechanically propelled but usable only under control of pedestrians are to be treated as not being motor vehicles and as vehicles propelled by hand. (1957 Act, s.10).

Multi-purpose lamps.—Nothing in these Lighting Acts shall require a vehicle to carry separate lamps for different purposes if it carries a lamp satisfying all the requirements which would be applicable to separate lamps carried by it for these purposes (s. 4).

Any multi-purpose lamp (showing white light to the front and red light to the rear) on a sidecar, tractor, hand or horse drawn vehicle should be at least 16 inches from the side of the vehicle (Reg. 8, 1951).

Reversing White Lights.—A vehicle may carry one or two reversing lights showing a white light to the rear only for the purposes of reversing (1957 Act, s. 2).

Any such light shall be electric (not exceeding 24 watts) non-dazzling and switched on either automatically by use of the reverse gear or by a switch operated by the driver. In vehicles manufactured after 1st July, 1954, this switch must serve no other

purpose and there must be a device to show that the light is on.
Only when the vehicle is reversing shall the reversing white light
be shown (Regs. 19 to 22).

Rear Lamps.—Such lamp must show red light to the rear
(1957 Act, s. 1). The area of such lamp shall be 2 inch diameter or
equivalent area if not circular when on vehicles except in the case
of motor cycles, sidecars, bicycles, tricycles, agricultural implements, trailer pumps, hand-propelled and horse-drawn vehicles
when the diameter may be 1½ inch or equivalent area if not
round. In the case of motor cycles and sidecars the electric bulbs
must not be less than 6 watts. When two rear lamps are carried
they must look alike and be so wired that if one goes out the other
remains alight (Reg. 18, 1954) and this Reg. shall not apply to
existing public service vehicles (Reg. 16).

Every obligatory rear lamp shall be marked with the specifica
tion number B.S. 2516, and " Grade I " or " Grade II " (except
in the case of a cycle the cylinder capacity of which does not
exceed 250 cubic centimetres when it may have a lamp of " Grade
Cycles ") and it must be marked with the name or means of identification of the manufacturer. (This paragraph will apply to an
obligatory rear lamp fitted with an electric bulb and carried on a
mechanically propelled vehicle first registered after 1st April,
1959 or carried on any vehicle supplied by its manufacturer after
that date (R.V.L.(A.) Regs., 1958)).

Obligatory red rear lamps should be fixed on a vehicle in
accordance with the First Schedule to the 1954 Regs. On a
vehicle (a) constructed or adapted to carry goods or burden, and
(b) carrying a load projecting to the rear in such manner that the
rear lights would not be visible from a reasonable distance, the
lamps shall be attached to the load in the prescribed positions
(R.V.L.(A.) Regs., 1958).

Red Reflectors.—The 1957 Act, s. 1 directs that every vehicle
on any road during the hours of darkness must carry two unobscured and efficient red reflectors. Reflector in this section means
one facing to the rear (s. 1). A person who causes or permits a
vehicle to be on a road must provide same. Bicycles, tricycles
and solo motor cycles need have only one. Every red reflector
carried on a vehicle shall:

(1) Be of the required standard of efficiency as regards red
reflecting power and shall not reflect any letter, number or
other mark.

(2) Have an exposed reflecting surface giving a circle of 1¼
inches diameter (later on a 1½ inch diameter and, if not round,
an equivalent area, will be ordered).

(3) Be clean and unobscured and plainly visible from the rear.

(4) Be fixed in a vertical position and facing squarely to the
rear, on the centre line or offside of the vehicle, not less than 15
inches above the ground, and so that no part of the vehicle

projects to the rear of the reflector more than 30 inches, or 20 inches in the case of bicycles (Regs. 23, 24 and 2nd Sched.).

A group of small reflectors close together will count as an obligatory reflector (see Reg. 25). Every reflector shall be marked with specification number B.S. 2515, " Grade I " or " Grade II " and the name or means of identification of the manufacturer.

The foregoing paragraph will apply to reflectors carried on a mechanically propelled vehicle first registered after 1st April, 1959, or carried on any vehicle supplied by its manufacturer after that date; and carried on any vehicle after 1st October 1967.

It is an offence to sell or offer for sale any red reflector not complying with the prescribed conditions (1957 Act, s. 12).

On a vehicle (a) constructed or adapted to carry goods or burden, and (b) carrying a load projecting to the rear in such manner that the reflectors would be obscured the reflectors shall be attached to the load in the prescribed positions (R.V.L. (A.) Regs., 1958).

Lighting of Rear Identification or Registration Mark.— Whenever during the hours of darkness a mechanically propelled vehicle not being a works truck is upon a public road, a lamp shall be kept burning thereon so contrived as to illuminate by means of reflection, transparency or otherwise, and render easily distinguishable every letter and figure of the registration mark on the back of the vehicle or on the back of the rearmost vehicle attached to the vehicle (Reg. and Lic. Regs., 1955, Regs. 25, 26).

NOTE:—The identification mark is now called registration mark. See " Identification Mark ", Chap. XXV.

On every mechanically propelled vehicle registered for the first time on or after 1st October, 1938, not being a works truck, this illuminated rear registration mark must be easily distinguishable in the absence of fog by an observer behind the vehicle who is more than 10 feet distant and not more than 60 feet directly behind (50 feet behind in the case of a motor bicycle, an invalid carriage, or pedestrian controlled vehicle), provided that this does not apply where the police authorise vehicles without lights on adequately lighted parking places or hackney carriage stands (Reg. and Lic. Regs., 1955, Reg. 26).

If the rear registration mark is so constructed and used that it is illuminated by transparency or translucency, the letters and figures must, when so illuminated during the hours of darkness, appear either red or white (Reg. and Lic. Regs., 1955, Reg. 21 and 3rd Sched.).

Front Lamps.—Under the Road Vehicles Lighting Regulations, 1954:

(a) An obligatory front lamp shall be so fixed that its centre is not higher than 5 feet from the ground. This does not apply to public service vehicles. (On horse-drawn vehicles it may not exceed 5 feet 9 inches from the ground (Reg. 5).

Every electric light (over 7 watts) or acetylene lamp showing light to the front must be fixed not more than 3 feet 6 inches from the ground and except in the case of a lamp used only in fog or falling snow, not less than 2 feet from the ground. Provided that this will not apply to a vehicle registered before 1st January, 1952, a vehicle for combative purposes or a vehicle supplied to the Forces before 1st January, 1956 (Regs. 9, 10).

(b) An obligatory front lamp shall be fixed so that no part of the vehicle or its equipment (except mirror and indicator Reg. 3) extends more than 12 inches beyond the centre of the lamp on the side that the lamp is placed. This does not apply to motor or pedal bicycles or to tower wagons (Reg. 5).

(c) On horse-drawn vehicles, such a front lamp shall not be behind the axle if only one axle, and it shall not be more than 18 inches behind the front axle in the case of a vehicle having more than one axle (Reg. 5).

(d) If there is only one obligatory front lamp, it shall be fixed on the off-side of the vehicle except in the case of a solo motor or pedal bicycle (Reg. 7).

(e) If two obligatory front lamps are carried, they shall be fixed on opposite sides of the vehicle, and, except in the case of a bicycle with sidecar, they shall be fixed at the same height from the ground (Reg. 6).

Anti-Dazzle.—Unless allowed by regulation, no light from a vehicle other than a dipping headlight, shall be moved by swivelling, deflecting or otherwise while the vehicle is in motion (s. 3)—except in the case of a bicycle or tricycle, amber coloured reflectors attached to or incorporated in or forming part of the pedals are permissible (R.T.L. (A.) Act, 1958). Under the Road Vehicles Lighting Regulations, 1954, no front lamp (electric or acetylene) shall be used on any vehicle other than a pedal bicycle or tricycle unless it is so made, fitted and kept, that the beam of light from it:

(1) is permanently deflected downwards so that it cannot dazzle a person standing more than 25 feet distant, whose eye level is not less than 3 feet 6 inch high; or

(2) can be deflected downwards or both downwards and to the left so that it cannot dazzle such a person, or

(3) can be extinguished by a device which leaves a non-dazzling beam of light (as under (1)), or

(4) can be extinguished by a device which at same time either deflects the light from another lamp downwards or both downwards and to the left so that it cannot dazzle (see (1) above), or brings into or leaves in operation a non-dazzling light from lamps other than the obligatory front lamps (Reg. 10). Provided that a lamp will not comply with (1) unless its centre is not less than 2 feet from the ground unless it is used only in fog or falling snow (Reg. 10).

The above does not apply to any direction indicator or lamp

with an electric bulb or bulbs not exceeding 7 watts in power and having frosted glass or other light-diffusing material (Reg. 10).

It applies to electric light lamps and acetylene light lamps on vehicles (Reg. 10).

The light from not more than two front lamps (other than the obligatory front lamps) may be deflected to either side by the movements of the front wheels provided such lamps are not more than 3 feet 6 inches from the ground (Reg. 11).

Every electric light bulb in a front lamp in a motor vehicle shall have the wattage indelibly marked on the glass or on the metal cap (Reg. 12).

No bulb or bulbs over 7 watts power in a front lamp shall be kept lighted while the vehicle is stationary in a road. However, this shall not apply during an enforced stoppage of the vehicle; to a public service vehicle stopping to set down or pick up passengers; to interior lighting of vehicles; to break-down vehicles or tower-wagons in use at their special work; to direction indicators; to searchlights or special lamps used for naval, military, air force, police or fire brigade purposes or to searchlights or special lamps on vehicles used for repairs to sewers, gas, electricity or water mains whilst repairs are being made (Reg. (13).

Parking Lights.—This subject has been dealt with by Road Vehicles Lighting (Standing Vehicles) (Exemption) (General) Regs., 1956, for the whole country except London, which was dealt with by similar (Exemption) Regs., 1955. The Regs. apply to passenger vehicles, goods vehicles, invalid carriages and motor cycles and pedal cycles with or without sidecars but do not apply to vehicles needing special lamps (see s. 8, 1957 Act) or with trailers. (Reg. 3).

" Passenger Vehicle " here means motor vehicle (not cycle or invalid carriage) made solely for passengers and their effects and adapted to carry not more than 7 persons and the driver.

" Goods Vehicle " here means motor vehicle of unladen weight not exceeding 2 tons, made or adapted for carriage of any burden (Reg. 2).

Parking without lights is allowable as above on a road (" road " includes part of a road (Reg. 2)) having a speed limit provided that (a) the vehicle is close to left of the road and if it is one-way close to left or right of the road as the case may be. (b) the vehicle is not more than 25 yards from a street lamp. (c) the vehicle is not within 15 yards of a road junction. (d) the road is so specified in written consent by the Chief of Police and the prescribed traffic sign is on or near the lamppost (Reg. 4, 5). Reg. 28 of the 1954 Regs. is revoked (Reg. 1) but a vehicle permitted to park on a parking place or hackney carriage stand need not show lights if the Chief of Police has given written consent (Reg. 6). Such a vehicle (as above) may park on a road having a speed limit without the lights then required by law provided it : —

(a) Stands with left side close to edge of road.

(b) is not more than 100 yards from a street lamp.

(c) is not within 15 yards of a road junction.

(d) shows a white light to front and a red light to rear (Reg. 7).

These lights are termed " parking lights ". They must be on the off side of the vehicle not less than 15 inches or more than 6 feet from the ground and clearly visible (Regs. 8, 9). These Regs. deal only with lights and do not affect the law regarding obstruction (Reg. 10).

The 1957 Act empowers the Minister to make regulations regarding the lighting of vehicles parked on a road or in a parking place or moving on a road and as regards traffic signs in connection therewith.

Extent of Acts and Regulations.—The 1957 Act applies to vehicles and persons in the public service of the Crown and the service or the department concerned should be asked to name the person responsible for any alleged offence. It applies to vehicles of every description and machines and implements of any kind drawn or propelled along roads (s. 17). It does not apply to railroad vehicles or to tramcars (s. 16).

The Minister is given wide powers to make regulations exempting vehicles from the provisions of the Act, and may vary the requirements (see ss. 10 & 11).

Penalties.—Any person who causes or permits any vehicle to be on the road in contravention of this Act or of regulations made thereunder, or who otherwise fails to comply with these provisions, commits a summary offence and is liable to a fine of £5, and to a fine of £20 for a second or subsequent offence (s. 12). No power of arrest without warrant is given by the Act. The person driving or being in charge of a vehicle has a good defence if he proves that the offence arose through the negligence or default of some other person whose duty it was to provide the vehicle with lamps or reflectors (s. 12). It shall be the duty of the person who causes or permits a vehicle to be on any road during the hours of darkness to provide the vehicle with the prescribed lamps and reflectors (s. 1).

A person is liable to the penalty which is the law at the time when his offence is dealt with in Court. (*D.P.P.* v. *Lamb* (1941)).

Road Vehicles Lighting (*Special Exemption and Amendment*) *Regs.* 1954, deal with vehicles used for Naval, Military, or Air Force purposes, and vehicles of the visiting forces.

Vehicles used on manoeuvres, and vehicles used in training, on special occasions when notice within 48 hours is given to the police, are exempt from all the requirements as to lighting, Searchlights may be used on such vehicles.

Where from six to twelve such vehicles are proceeding in convoy on tactical or driving exercises after notice to the police, white lights on front vehicle, faint underneath white lights on the middle vehicles and red rear light on last vehicle are allowable.

Vehicles constructed or adapted for combative purposes should have red rear lamps and red reflectors not more than 5 feet from the ground.

Vehicles of a visiting force should comply with the rules regarding vehicles from abroad, which follow.

Vehicles from Abroad.—The 1954 Lighting Regulations as to lamps and reflectors (Parts II to VI) shall not apply to any motor vehicle brought temporarily into Great Britain by a person resident abroad, provided such vehicle complies with Paras. (b) to (e) of Part V of the Annex to the Convention on Road Traffic, Geneva, 19th Sept., 1949 (Reg. 4, 1954).

Such vehicles should have two front white lights and a red rear light; motor cycles one front and one rear. They need not have red reflectors (Reg. 29, 1954).

Definitions, Lighting Act 1957.—" Hours of darkness " means the time between half an hour after sunset and half an hour before sunrise.

" Public passenger vehicle " means a vehicle (other than a tramcar) carrying passengers for hire or reward on a road.

" Vehicle " means a vehicle of any description and includes a machine or implement drawn or propelled along roads whether by animal or mechanical power.

" Road " means any highway and any other road to which the public has access (s. 17).

Classification of Motor Vehicles.—Road Traffic Act, 1930, s. 1, refers to " motor vehicles " as including all mechanically propelled vehicles intended or adapted for use on roads, and s. 2 (as amended by 1956 Act Sched. 8 (9)) divides them (exclusive of tramcars and trolley vehicles) into seven classes; unladen weight being the main consideration. These seven classes are as follows:—

(1) Heavy locomotives : viz. not constructed to carry any load and of weight unladen exceeding 11½ tons.

(2) Light locomotives : viz. not constructed to carry any load, and of weight unladen exceeding 7¼ tons, but not exceeding 11½ tons.

(3) Motor tractors : viz. not constructed to carry any load and of weight unladen not exceeding 7¼ tons.

Above three classes include the heavy drawing vehicles which do not themselves carry any load. However, fuel, water, tools and equipment for their propulsion, also apparatus such as a crane, dynamo, etc., as a permanent fixture will not be a " load."

(4) Heavy motor cars : viz. constructed to carry a load or passengers, of weight unladen exceeding $2\frac{1}{2}$ tons, and not defined as " motor cars."

If the vehicle is so constructed that a trailer may be partly superimposed on it so that a substantial part of the weight of the trailer rests on the vehicle it shall be deemed to be a vehicle constructed to carry a load. The vehicle plus trailer is an " articulated " vehicle.

(5) Motor cars : viz. constructed to carry a load or passengers not defined as motor cycles or invalid carriages and of weight unladen not exceeding—

(a) 3 tons, if constructed solely for carriage of passengers and their effects, and adapted to carry not more than seven passengers and a driver, and having prescribed tyres, or

(b) $2\frac{1}{2}$ tons, in any other case.

" Motor car " also includes a gas-propelled goods vehicle of maximum weight unladen not exceeding $3\frac{1}{2}$ tons, and a goods vehicle not gas propelled if maximum weight does not exceed 3 tons. See 1956 Act Sched. 8 (9).

(6) Motor cycles : viz. of weight unladen not exceeding 8 cwt., with less than four wheels, and not defined as " invalid carriages."

A tricar therefore *may* be a " motor cycle."

Any side-car attached, in compliance with the prescribed conditions, is part of the vehicle and is not a trailer.

Motor scooters and bicycles and tricycles with attachment for propulsion by mechanical power are " motor vehicles " and as such should be registered and licenced. Grasscutters are not to be treated as motor vehicles.

(7) Invalid carriages : viz. of weight unladen not exceeding 5 cwt. and specially made (not merely adapted) for use of and used solely by persons suffering from some physical defect or disability (s. 2).

Vehicles drawn by motor vehicles are, in s. 1, 1930 Act, referred to as " trailers." (See also s. 36, R. & R.T. Act, 1933).

S. 3 : It will be an offence for any person to use or cause or permit to be used on a road, any motor vehicle or trailer which does not comply with the regulations as to construction, weight and equipment, applicable to the class of vehicle to which it belongs. However, any regulations under the Act, which vary the rules as to construction or weight, must exempt therefrom for at least five years, any vehicles registered before the expiration of one year from the making of the regulations, and the Minister of Transport and Civil Aviation has power to authorise the use on roads of special types of motor vehicles, for which see Sched. 8 (16) of the 1956 Act.

The Regulations as to construction and use, and as to special types of motor vehicles are given in Chapter 25.

R.T. Act, 1934, s. 8 : The sale, supply or offer to sell or supply a motor vehicle or trailer for delivery in such a condition that its use on a road in such condition would be unlawful as not complying with the regulations as to construction, weight and equipment (including brakes, steering gear or tyres or lighting equipment subject to the defence that it would not be used during hours of darkness until properly lighted; see s. 7, 1956 Act), shall be an offence.

It is also an offence to alter a motor vehicle or trailer so as to render its condition such that its use on a road would be unlawful.

However, a person shall not be convicted of an offence under this section in respect to sale, supply, offer or alteration if he proves it was done for export from Great Britain or with reasonable cause to believe that the vehicle would not be used on a road in Great Britain or would not be so used until put into lawful condition (s. 8, 1934 Act).

Driving Licence.—Road Traffic Act, 1930, s. 4 (1) : It is an offence for a person to drive a motor vehicle on a road unless he holds a driving licence (covering the driving of a vehicle on that class or description : R.T. (Driving Licences) Act, 1936). It is also an offence to employ a person to do so unless he (the driver) holds a driving licence.

" Driver," where a separate person acts as steersman of a motor vehicle, includes that person as well as any other person engaged in the driving of the vehicle (s. 121, R.T. Act, 1930).

A person who steers a motor vehicle down a slope without the engine running is a " driver " (*Saycell* v. *Bool* (1948)).

A person steering a towed broken down motor vehicle is not a " driver " (*Wallace* v. *Major* (1946)).

(A person without licence may act as steersman of a vehicle limited to 5 m.p.h. speed or of a heavy goods vehicle if under the orders of a licensed driver (R.T. (Driving Licences) Act, 1936).

Any person driving a motor vehicle on a road shall, on being so required by a police constable, produce his licence for examination so as to enable the constable to ascertain the name and address of the holder of the licence, the date of issue and the authority by which it was issued, and if he fails to do so he is liable to fine.

However, if within five days after any such request, such driver produces the licence in person at such police station as may be specified by him at the time its production was required, he shall not be convicted of this offence (s. 4, (5) 1930 Act).

Under s. 31, 1956 Act, a constable may require a person whose licence is revoked, to produce it and then he may seize it and deliver it to the licensing authority. A constable, on reasonable belief that a licence under Part I of the 1930 Act (driving) was obtained by a false statement may require the holder to produce it (he may seize it and summon such holder; s. 112, 1930 Act).

In both these cases 5 days is allowed for production at a specified police station.

A person believed to be the driver of a motor vehicle when an accident has occurred owing to its presence on a road or who is believed to have committed an offence in relation to the use of a motor vehicle on a road or who has accompanied the holder of a provisional licence to drive on such occasions, may be required to give his name and address and that of the owner of the vehicle (s. 31).

A constable has power to seize any licence produced, if he has reasonable cause to believe it forged, deceitfully used, etc. (s. 112). See " False Motor Vehicle Licences, Certificates etc."

S. 9 : Prescribes minimum ages at which persons may drive motor vehicles on roads, viz. :

(1) Sixteen for persons driving motor cycles and invalid carriages.   This may be varied by regulations under s. 10, 1956 Act.

(2) Seventeen for persons driving motor cars.

(3) Twenty-one for persons driving heavy motor vehicles.

A person under 16 shall not drive a motor vehicle on a road.

A person under seventeen shall not drive a motor vehicle other than a motor cycle or an invalid carriage on a road.

A person under twenty-one shall not drive a heavy or light locomotive, a motor tractor or a heavy motor car on a road. This restriction on persons under twenty-one driving such " heavy " vehicles on roads does not apply to a tractor used primarily for work on land in connection with agriculture (Emergency Laws (Misc. Provisions) Act, 1953), nor does it apply (see s. 121) to such heavy vehicles used for Naval, Military or Air Force purposes.

" Agricultural tractor " means a motor tractor used primarily for work on land in connection with agriculture (M.Vs. (Driving Licences) (Amendment) Regs. 1950).

Any person driving or causing or permitting driving in contravention of this s. 9 will be guilty of an offence.

S.4 : A driving licence is granted by the Council of the county or county borough in which the applicant resides. It may specify that the holder is restricted to driving a particular group, class or classes of motor vehicles (see 2nd Sched., Driving Licences Regs., 1950). The 1956 Act, s. 48, deals with the fees and duration of driving licences.

This section came into operation on the 1st September 1957 and provides that a driving licence shall remain in force for 3 years from the date of issue, and the fee shall be 15 shillings.

By the Motor Vehicles (Driving Licences) (Grouping of Applications) Regs. 1957, applications for driving licences were divided into groups to ensure an even spread of work in the issue of three-year driving licences. If an applicant's surname begins with any letter from O to Z, renewal before 1 September 1959 will be for

for one year, fee 5s., but on and after that date for three years, fee 15s.

Under s. 6 of the R.T. Act, 1934, a driving licence shall not be granted (as from 1 June, 1935) unless the applicant passes the test of competence to drive (see ss. 16, 17, R.T. Act, 1956). Provisional driving licences issued on or after 1 March 1958 are for six months, fee 10s. (1956 Act s. 18 (2) and Motor Vehicles (Driving Licences) (Amendment) Regs. 1958). He may apply to a Magistrates' Court to determine whether his driving test was properly conducted and another test may be ordered (R.T. Act, 1934, s.6).

A person is disqualified from obtaining a driving licence :

(a) if he holds another driving licence which is in force, whether suspended or not ;

(b) if he is disqualified by age or a conviction or order of a Court (but in the latter case he may get a provisional licence so as to learn to drive—R.T. Act, 1934, s. 6 (4)).

S. 5 : An applicant must make a declaration in the prescribed form as to his physical fitness, and if from his declaration (or on inquiry; 1956 Act, Sched. 8 (10)) it appears he is suffering from any disease or physical disability as is specified or is likely to cause driving by him to be a source of danger to the public, the licence shall be refused.

However, a licence to drive an invalid carriage may be granted if the applicant is considered fit to drive such carriage, and, except in the case of the prescribed disabilities (see later), an applicant may claim a test as to his fitness to drive so as to justify the grant of a licence which may be limited to the driving of vehicles of a particular construction or design.

A provisional licence for six months (with conditions, see later) may be granted to permit a person to learn to drive so as to pass this test or any compulsory test. Failure to comply with the conditions is an offence.

A Council may revoke a driving licence if satisfied the holder is suffering from such disease or disability as is likely to render his driving a source of danger to the public, but such licence holder, except in cases of the prescribed disabilities, (for which see later) may claim a driving test.

A person who is refused a driving licence or whose licence is revoked for physical unfitness may appeal to a Magistrates' Court of the petty sessional division in which he resides.

S. 32 : The holder of a driving licence (in force) granted in Northern Ireland may drive in Great Britain, under the terms of his licence, provided the Minister of Transport has certified as satisfactory the driving licence system ot Northern Ireland. The Minister so certified on December 1, 1930. Such a driver is bound to produce his licence for examination as directed above, and if he is disqualified by a conviction or order of a Court he must give his licence to the Court for transmission to the Minister of Transport, to whom also a Court shall send particulars of any conviction of any such driver which it considers ought to be endorsed on his licence.

The driver of a foreign-owned motor vehicle which is temporarily in this country should have a special driving licence (see " Foreign-owned Motor Vehicles," Chap 25) or an ordinary driving licence.

Motor Vehicles (Driving Licences) Regs., 1950.—An applicant for a licence to drive a motor vehicle shall supply particulars on the prescribed application form, and pay the fee (Reg. 4).

If he suffers from epilepsy ; certified mental defect or disorder ; sudden attacks of disabling giddiness or fainting ; inability to read at 25 yards in good daylight (with glasses, if worn) the identification marks of a motor car, he cannot get a driving licence and is not entitled to claim a driving test (Reg. 5)

The prescribed test of competence to drive includes knowledge of the Highway Code ; competence to properly drive a vehicle of the same class as that on which tested ; ability to read a motor car number plate at 25 yards ; ability to manipulate the engine, to stop, reverse, turn, signal and obey signals (Reg. 6 and 3rd Sch.).

Examiners appointed by the Minister of Transport will conduct the tests for members of the general public, and Crown Departments, Police, Fire Brigades and certain employers may test their employees (Regs. 7, 8 and 9).

Any person requiring a test may apply to the clerk of the Licensing Authority (Reg. 10).

A person who passes the test will be given a certificate to that effect, which he must deliver up to the Licensing Authority before his driving licence can be issued (Reg. 11).

If a person fails he must wait a month before another test can be given (Reg. 12). An applicant must provide a motor vehicle for the test (Reg. 13), and pay the fee (Reg. 14). See M.V. (Driving Licences) (Amendment) Regs., 1956 and 1957.

Non-resident holders of foreign driving licences and permits need not be so tested (Reg. 15). (1957 Regs.)

Provisional licences (to learn) are granted subject to the condition that until the holder has passed a test he shall, except in case of a vehicle (other than a motor car or an electrically propelled goods vehicle exceeding 16 cwts.) which is not constructed or adapted to carry more than one person, be supervised in his vehicle by a person who holds a full licence to drive the same class of vehicle and who has passed a test or has held a driving licence for 2 years and the vehicle shall display the prescribed letter " L " (in red on white ground) on front and rear of the vehicle. Also the learner driver of a solo motor cycle with seat made for carriage of passenger must not carry on his motor cycle any person who is not qualified to drive a motor cycle (Reg. 16) but this requirement does not apply to a pedal cycle of the tandem type to which additional means of propulsion by mechanical means are attached (Amendment Regs., 1950).

A person granted a driving licence shall forthwith sign it in ink, and if he fails to do so or if on production of licence to any person entitled to demand its production it does not bear his usual signature in ink he shall be guilty of an offence (Reg. 17).

The Licensing Authority shall keep a record of driving licences (and endorsements) and shall supply to the police without fee, on application, a copy of the particulars of any licence granted by them (Regs. 19, 20).

For other driving licences see " Public Service Vehicles " and " Heavy Goods Vehicles," Chap. 25.

Speed Limits for Motor Vehicles.—It shall not be lawful for any person to drive a motor vehicle on a road at a speed exceeding a speed limit imposed by or under any enactment, and on summary conviction an offender is liable to fine. (s. 10, R.T. Act, 1930, and s. 2, R.T. Act, 1934).

A first or second conviction for exceeding a speed limit shall not render the offender liable to disqualification for holding a licence (s. 2, R.T. Act, 1934). A conviction for exceeding a speed limit shall be endorsed on the offender's driving licence unless for any special reason the Court thinks fit to order otherwise (s. 5, R.T. Act, 1934). For special reasons, see " Penalties," later.

A person prosecuted for exceeding a speed limit shall not be liable to be convicted solely on the evidence of one witness to the effect that in his opinion the person prosecuted was driving at a speed exceeding that limit (s. 2, R.T. Act, 1934). Corroborative evidence of a speedometer or stop watch may be accepted by the Court (*Penny* v. *Nicholas* (1950)). See later "Exemptions, etc." See s. 21, 1930 Act as to warning of prosecution.

A speed limit may be either

(1) The speed specified by law as the maximum speed at which the particular class or description of motor vehicle may be driven on a road (s. 10, R.T. Act, 1930).

These speed limits are given in Appendix I.

(2) The general speed limit of 30 miles per hour in " built-up areas " as imposed under s. 1 of the R.T. Act, 1934.

General Speed Limit in Built-Up Areas.—By s. 1 of the R.T. Act, 1934, a general speed limit of 30 m.p.h. in built-up areas for all motor vehicles was imposed originally to continue to 31 Dec., 1939, and this has been made permanent by s. 4 (1) 1956 Act, but the remainder of this s. 4 and Sched. 8 (34) deal with other speed limits. Some roads in London have a general speed limit of 40 m.p.h.

It is therefore not lawful for any person (except for police, fire brigade and ambulance purposes, s. 3) to drive a motor vehicle on a road in a built-up area at a speed exceeding any speed limit prescribed for such road.

A road in a built-up area means :—

(a) A road in which there is a system of street lighting by lamps placed not more than 200 yards apart, unless a Direction has been given that it is *not* to be deemed a road in a built-up area, and

(b) a road of which a Direction has been given that it is to be deemed to be a road in a built-up area (irrespective of its lighting system), (and such a road is to be indicated by traffic signs).

Any such Direction may be given by an order of the local authority with the consent of the Minister of Transport and Civil Aviation, and the Minister may also direct that a particular road is not to be deemed to be a road in a built-up area.

Any contravention of a speed limit is an offence under s. 10 of the R.T. Act, 1930, as amended by s. 2 of the R.T. Act, 1934.

It is punishable by fine. The offender's driving licence shall be endorsed unless the Court, for special reason, orders otherwise (s. 5, 1934 Act).

The prescribed traffic signs shall be erected as so to give adequate guidance to drivers as to where this speed limit begins and ceases (s. 1). These signs are prescribed by the Traffic Signs (30 m.p.h. Speed Limit) Regs., 1957. The figures 30 in black on a white circle surrounded by a red ring will indicate that this speed limit is in force, and a transverse black bar in a white circle will indicate that this speed limit is not in force on the road.

These signs will be fitted with reflectors or will be illuminated, and they are to be erected in accordance with the Traffic Signs (30 m.p.h. Speed Limit) (England and Wales) Directions 1957.

The Traffic Signs (30 m.p.h. Speed Limit) (England and Wales) Directions 1958 amend the Directions of 1957 by stating that the 1957 Directions are not to apply in certain cases where a speed limit of 40 m.p.h. is in force on roads in London.

Exemptions from Speed Limit.—Any vehicle used for police, ambulance or fire brigade purposes is exempt from any speed limits if their observance would be likely to hinder the use of the vehicle for the purpose for which it is being used (s. 3, 1934 Act).

The speed limits may be varied in relation to motor vehicles of the armed forces of the Crown or used for salvage purposes (s. 121, R.T. Act, 1930, and Third Schedule, R.T. Act, 1934).

No speed limit is imposed on motor vehicles for combative purposes, training, conveyance of personnel, use with guns, mobile cranes for aircraft, tracklayers for combat or guns, fire tenders and ambulances, owned by the Admiralty the War

Department or the Air Ministry and used for naval, military or air force purposes or vehicles so used while being driven by persons for the time being subject to the orders of any member of the armed forces of the Crown, or on motor vehicles used for salvage purposes pursuant to Part IX of the Merchant Shipping Act, 1894 (Motor Vehicles (Variation of Speed Limit) Regs., 1947).

These exemptions also apply to vehicles in the service of a visiting force (M.V. (Variation of Speed Limit) Regs., 1954).

The speed limits prescribed shall not apply in the case of vehicles while being used in the conduct of experiments or trials under s. 6, Roads Improvement Act, 1925 (Variation of Speed Limit Regs., 1956).

The evidence of a single witness that he had timed a motor vehicle over a measured distance by a stop-watch and thereby ascertained its rate of speed is evidence of fact and is not merely opinion, and a Court is entitled to convict on such evidence (*Plancq* v. *Marks* (1906)). Corroboration by the evidence of another witness is not necessary (*Russell* v. *Beesley* (1937)).

Road Traffic Act, 1930, s. 10, prescribes fine and (or) three months imprisonment for:—

(1) Any person aiding, abetting, counselling or procuring any person employed by him to drive or subject to his orders in driving to exceed a speed limit, or

(2) Any person inciting to commit this offence.

These penalties are not affected by the M.C. Act, 1952, 5th Schedule.

If an employer issues a time table or gives directions under which it is not practicable to complete a journey without exceeding any speed limit, same may be produced as *prima facie* evidence that he procured or incited his employees to commit this offence.

S. 21: Notice of prosecution is necessary. See " Dangerous Driving ".

Accidents.—*Road Traffic Act*, 1930, s. 22: If in any case, owing to the presence of a motor vehicle an accident occurs whereby personal injury is caused to any person other than the driver of that motor vehicle or damage is caused to any vehicle other than that motor vehicle or a trailer drawn thereby or to any animal other than an animal in or on that motor vehicle or a trailer drawn thereby (1956 Act, Sched. 8 (15)), on a road, the driver of such vehicle shall stop and, if required so to do by any person having reasonable grounds for so requiring, give his name and address, and also the name and address of the owner and the identification marks of the vehicle.

If for any reason he does not so give his name and address to any such person, such driver shall report the accident at a police station or to a police constable as soon as reasonably practicable and in any case within twenty-four hours of the accident. Failure to comply with this section is an offence. " Animal " here means any horse, cattle, ass, mule, sheep, pig, goat or dog.

This liability to report extends to every case where the driver has not in fact given his name and address, for example, no one asked for it or no one was present at the time (*Peek* v. *Towle* (1945)).

Refusal, on reasonable requirement, to give name and address is an offence not excused by subsequent report to the police (*Dawson* v. *Winter* (1932)).

If the driver gives his name and address (or drivers exchange names and addresses) as required, there is no duty to report to the police (*Adair* v. *Fleming* 1932) and *Green* v. *Dunn* (1953)).

A driver did not know he had collided with a stationary car and did not report. He was convicted but the K.B.D. quashed the conviction (*Harding* v. *Price* (1948)).

This s. 22 imposes a duty, so failure to report where the driver was unaware of the act was not an offence.

S. 40 (2) : If an accident involving *personal injury* to another person occurs owing to the presence of a motor vehicle (except invalid carriages, tramcars, trolley vehicles, and Crown vehicles) on a road, and if the driver does not at the time produce his certificate of insurance or security (see " Insurance Certificates ") to a police constable or to some person who, having reasonable grounds for so doing, has required its production, such driver shall, as soon as possible and within twenty-four hours, report the accident at a police station or to a police constable and produce his " certificate." Failure to do so is an offence. However, he shall not be convicted of an offence under this subsection by reason only of failure to produce his certificate, if within five days after the accident he produces the certificate in person at a police station specified by him at the time the accident was reported.

Therefore after any such " personal injury " accident, the driver, in addition to stopping and giving his name and address, etc., or reporting to the police as directed under s. 22 above, must produce his certificate of insurance either to some person at the scene or to the police within twenty-four hours (subject to the five days of grace allowed for production at a specified station).

S. 23 : If an accident arises out of the presence of a motor vehicle (tramcars excepted) on a road, the Minister may direct inquiry into the cause and any person authorised by him has power to inspect any vehicle concerned and to enter premises for the purpose. It will be an offence to obstruct him. The Minister may also direct a public inquiry to be held. Any report by or to the Minister as a result of an inquiry under this section shall not be used in evidence by or on behalf of any person by or against whom legal proceedings are instituted in consequence of the accident.

Insurance Certificates.—Part II. of the R.T. Act, 1930, as supplemented by Part II. of the R.T. Act, 1934, compels provision to be made in respect of third-party risks arising out of the use of motor vehicles, but by s. 35 (5) it does not extend to invalid carriages or tramcars or trolley vehicles, and it has not been applied to vehicles in the public service of the Crown, for which see s. 121 (2).

Insurance is compulsory in respect of any liability which may be incurred in respect of the death or bodily injury (or emergency treatment, s. 16, 1934 Act), to any person caused by or arising out of the use of the motor vehicle on a road, provided, however, that such insurance need not cover liability for death or injury in course of employment to a person employed by the insured person ; liability for death or injury to persons carried on the vehicle (except where persons are carried for hire or reward or in pursuance of a contract of employment) ; or any contractual liability (ss. 36 and 37 of 1930 Act). But this proviso does not exclude the liability for emergency treatment (s. 16 (4) of 1934 Act).

R.T. Act, 1930, s. 35 : It shall not be lawful for any person to use or to cause or permit any other person to use a motor vehicle on a road unless there is in force in relation to the user of the vehicle by that person or that other person such a policy of insuance or covering note, or such a security in respect of third-party risks as complies with the Act. A person convicted of this offence is liable to three months' imprisonment or £50 fine or both. (Note that it is " use," not " drive.")

Under s. 6 R.T. Act 1930, he may be disqualified, and under Schedule. 4, R.T. Act 1956, he may be disqualified or his licence endorsed. S. 29, 1956 Act, mentions a good defence to this charge and withdraws the power of the court to limit the disqualification to the driving of a motor vehicle of the same class or description.

Exceptional hardship is not a special reason and belief that he was properly insured is not a special reason unless based on reasonable grounds (*Knowler* v. *Rennison* (1947)). See also special reasons under " Penalties ".

However, vehicles owned and used by a police authority, a local authority, or a person who deposits £15,000, as laid down in the section, are exempt from the provisions of this section. Also vehicles driven for police purposes by or under direction of the police, or driven for salvage purposes under the Merchant Shipping Act, 1894 (R.T. Act, 1934, Third Schedule).

S. 36 : This section gives the requirements in respect of a policy of insurance and provides that the person taking out the policy should have a " certificate of insurance " in the prescribed form. Policy of insurance includes covering note.

If any payment is made by an insurer in respect to death or bodily injury arising out of the use of a motor vehicle and the person has received treatment at a hospital not carried on for profit, the insurer shall pay the reasonable hospital expenses up to £50 per in-patient and £5 per out-patient (R. & R.T. Act, 1933, s. 33).

S. 37 : This section gives the requirements in respect of a " security," which is an undertaking to make good, up to at least £5,000 (£25,000 in the case of public service vehicles) any liability (third-party risks) required by the Act to be covered by a policy of insurance. The person so " secured " must obtain a " certificate of security " in the prescribed form.

R.T. Act, 1934, s. 10 : Subject to the conditions prescribed in this section it shall be the duty of an insurer to pay any sum payable on judgment given against the person insured, in respect of third-party risks.

S. 11 : The bankruptcy, etc., of an insured person shall not affect certain claims by third parties.

S. 12 : Certain restrictions on the scope of a policy covering third-party risks limiting the age or mental or physical condition of drivers, the condition of the vehicle, the number of persons carried, the goods carried, etc., etc., shall be of no effect as regards the liabilities for third-party injuries which must be covered under s. 36 of the 1930 Act. The insurer in such case remains liable but he may recover from the insured person any amount he has paid.

S. 13 : It will be the duty of a person against whom a claim is made in respect of any liability for death or bodily injury arising out of the use of a motor vehicle on a road, to give particulars of his insurance to the person making the claim. To fail to do so or to give false information is an offence.

S. 14 : The holder of a certificate of insurance shall, within seven days, surrender it to the insurer if the policy is cancelled by consent or by virtue of any provision in the policy. If the certificate is lost or destroyed he shall make a statutory declaration to that effect.

S. 15 : These provisions of the Act apply also to securities in respect to third-party risks.

S. 16 : If bodily or fatal injury to a person is caused by or arises out of the use of a motor vehicle on a road and emergency medical or surgical treatment or examination is immediately required and effected by a doctor or hospital, the person who was using the vehicle at the time is responsible for payment for same at the rate of 12s. 6d. per person so treated and mileage in excess of two miles at 6d. per mile.

S. 17 : A claim for payment for such emergency treatment

may be made orally at the time or in writing (personal delivery or registered letter) within seven days, to the person who was using the vehicle, and the amount will be recoverable as a simple contract debt. The police shall, on request, furnish such claimant with any information available as to the vehicle and its driver.

R.T. Act, 1930, s. 39 : Provision may be made by regulations to require a person to produce evidence either of proper " insurance " or of exemption before he can get a Road Fund licence for his motor vehicle. (See later for the regulations.)

S. 40 (1) : Any person driving a motor vehicle (except invalid carriages, tramcars, trolley vehicles and Crown vehicles) (including the persons mentioned in s. 31, 1956 Act, as given above) on a road shall, on being so required by a police constable, give his name and address and the name and address of the owner of the vehicle *and* produce his certificate (that is, the certificate of insurance or the certificate of security or evidence that the vehicle was not being driven in contravention of this Part of the Act). Failure to do so is an offence. However, if he personally produces the " certificate " within the five days following at a police station specified by him at the time of such demand, he shall not be convicted of the offence by reason only of failure to produce his certificate.

S. 40 (2) : If an accident involving personal injury to another person has occurred owing to the presence of a motor vehicle on a road, the driver, in addition to other requirements, must produce his certificate either at the scene to the police or some other person who has reason for asking for it or to the police within twenty-four hours, but cannot be convicted of failing to produce it if he has personally produced it at a police station specified by him at the time the accident was reported and within five days after the occurrence of the accident.

S. 40 (3) : The owner of a motor vehicle is bound to give such information as he may be required by or on behalf of a chief officer of police to give for the purpose of determining whether the use of the vehicle was or was not properly insured on any occasion when the driver was bound, under this section, to produce his certificate. Failure to do so is an offence. See also s. 113 (3) under " Penalties, etc."

S. 112 (4) : If a constable has reasonable cause to believe any certificate so produced to him is forged, false, etc., he may seize it. See " False Motor Vehicle Licences, Certificates, etc." later.

The Motor Vehicles (Third Party Risks) Regs., 1941, 1949, and 1951, as amended by M.Vs. (Third Party Risks Deposits) Rules, 1952, deal with these certificates and prescribe the particulars which must be inscribed thereon. The driver of a motor vehicle may have, according to the nature of the " insurance " :—

(1) A certificate of insurance (Form A or Form B). This will be signed by the insuring person or company and will give the name of the policy holder, the effective date of commencement and date of expiry, the persons or classes of persons entitled to drive, the limitations as to use, and either the identification mark of the vehicle or the description of vehicle insured (Reg. 5).

A covering note may precede issue of certificate of insurance.

(2) A certificate of security (Form D). This will be signed by the authorised person, and will give the name of the holder of security, the effective date of commencement and date of expiry, and the conditions to which security is subject (Reg. 5).

(3) A certificate of deposit (Form E). This will give the identification mark of the vehicle, will certify the owner has deposited the £15,000, and will be signed by the owner of the vehicle (Reg. 8).

(4) A certificate of ownership by a local or police authority (Form F). This will give the identification mark of the vehicle and will be signed by someone on behalf of the authority (Reg 8).

(5) An International Motor Insurance Card. See " Foreign-Owned Motor Vehicles," Chap. 25.

If the holder of a policy or security is entitled to drive any motor vehicle other than that specified in it, he may have a further certificate of insurance or security (Reg. 7).

A person applying for a Road Fund licence must produce any necessary certificate of insurance or security (or evidence that the vehicle is properly insured or is exempt from insurance). But this does not apply to persons who let motor vehicles on hire as regards any such vehicle intended to be used solely for such purpose and driven by the hirer or persons under his control (Reg. 11).

Insuring companies, local authorities and persons depositing £15,000, must keep a record of the certificates they issue and of the vehicles concerned, and are bound to furnish particulars to the police on request (Reg. 12).

Any contravention of or failure to comply with these regulations renders the offender liable to a fine of five pounds (Reg. 38).

NOTE.—The Motor Insurers' Bureau may pay compensation to a person injured by a non-insured vehicle. Any insurance office will supply information on this matter.

X **False Motor Vehicle Licences, Certificates, etc.**—*R.T. Act*, 1960, s. 112. It is a misdemeanour, which may be punished summarily by imprisonment up to four months, or by fine up to £100, or both, to commit any of the following acts, with intent to deceive, in respect of any licence or " certificate " of insurance or security (or prescribed evidence thereof) under the Act :—

(1) Forging or altering.

(2) Using or lending to or allowing to be used by any other person.

(3) Making or having any document so closely resembling same as to be calculated to deceive.

The following acts in connection with such licences and certificates are punishable summarily (s. 113 (1)) by imprisonment up to six months, or by fine, or both :—

(1) Knowingly making any false statement for the purpose of obtaining the grant of a licence to oneself or any other person.

(2) Making any false statement or withholding any material information so as to obtain the issue of a certificate of insurance or security.

(3) Issuing any certificate of insurance or security which is to his knowledge false in any material particular.

If any such licence or certificate or document in lieu thereof is produced to a constable by the driver of a motor vehicle and he has reasonable cause to believe that any of the above offences has been committed in relation to it, he may seize the document. See s. 31, 1956 Act, given above.

Such driver, unless the document has been returned to him or unless he is prosecuted for this offence, shall be summoned to account for his possession of the document.

R. and R.T. Act, 1933, s. 34 : It is a misdemeanour punishable similarly, to commit similar offences with respect to licences, appointments, documents, plates or marks necessary for goods vehicles under the Act, or to alter an entry made in the current records as to hours and journeys which must be kept under s. 16.

False statements made knowingly to obtain (or prevent, Third Sched., 1934 Act) the grant or variation of a licence under the Act are also punishable under the section.

A constable, examiner, or certifying officer has similar power to seize suspected documents and plates and to prosecute. (See also " Goods Vehicles," Chap. 25.)

R.T. Act, 1934, s. 33 (1) : Proceedings for any of the above offences may be brought within six months from date of commission or within a period which exceeds neither three months from date of knowledge of the offence nor one year from date of its commission, whichever period is the longer.

Penalties.—Road Traffic Act, 1930.—S. 113 (2) : Any offence under the Act (or the 1934 Act) unless another penalty is specially provided, is punishable summarily by fine not exceeding £20, and in case of a second or subsequent conviction by fine not exceeding £50, or imprisonment not exceeding three months.

S. 111: Contravention of or failing to comply with any regulation made under the Act, if not otherwise punishable, shall be liable to summary fine not exceeding £20.

S. 121 : In the Act the term " owner " in relation to a vehicle which is the subject of a hiring or hire purchase agreement means the person in possession of the vehicle under that agreement. " Driver " includes any separate person acting as steersman of a motor vehicle as well as any other person engaged in the driving of the vehicle.

S. 113 (3) directs that where the driver of a vehicle is alleged to be guilty of an offence under the Act :—

(a) the owner of the vehicle shall give such information as he may be required by or on behalf of a chief officer of police to give as to the identity of the driver. Failure to do so is an offence, unless the owner satisfies the Court that he did not know and could not with reasonable diligence have ascertained who the driver was ;

(b) any other person, if so required, shall give any information which it is in his power to give and which may lead to the identification of the driver. Failure to do so is an offence. 1956 Act, s. 32, extends these powers to obtain information as to the identity of the driver to:

(1) offences under this Act relating to parking places

(2) offences against regulations made under s. 10, London Traffic Act, 1924

(3) offences against any other enactment relating to the use of vehicles on roads (N.B. This is a wide extension).

Where on summary trial for any of these offences, the identity of the driver is required and the accused has been asked for it and has written stating that he was the driver, the court may accept the statement (M.C. Act, 1957, s. 2).

S. 41 (2), Criminal Justice Act, 1948, providing for proof of admissions in certain traffic offences as to the identity of driver or owner of a vehicle shall apply to any offence to which s. 113 (3) applies.

In the case of any offence under the 1956 Act relating to parking places, this power (under s. 113 (3), 1930 Act) to require information shall be exercisable by the police, or, in writing, by the local authority for the parking place.

S. 40 (3) directs that the owner of a motor vehicle must give information to the police as to its insurance, when the driver was bound to produce his certificate of insurance (see above).

Some of the offences created by the 1930 Act are punishable by imprisonment exceeding three months and, therefore, the persons charged have the right to claim trial by jury and should be so informed by the court.

These offences are reckless or dangerous driving (s. 11), driving under the influence of drink or drugs (s. 15), making, using, etc., false licences and insurance " certificates," and making false statements to obtain the grant of same(s. 112, and s. 34, R. & R.T.

Act, 1933), and driving or procuring a licence whilst disqualified (s. 7 (4)).

Some offences are punishable summarily by imprisonment up to 3 months, including racing or speed trials on a road (s. 13), unlawfully taking a motor vehicle (s. 28), using an uninsured vehicle (s. 35), procuring a licence but concealing any endorsement which ought to be disclosed (s. 8), a second offence of procuring or inciting the exceeding of a speed limit (s. 10), and a second conviction of any " offence " (see s. 113 (2)) under the Act.

S. 6 : A Court which convicts a person for any criminal offence in connection with the driving of a motor vehicle (not being an offence under Part IV re Public Service Vehicles) has certain powers as regards disqualifying him for holding or obtaining a driving licence for such period as the Court thinks fit, and as regards endorsing particulars of the conviction and of any disqualification on his driving licence.

This s. 6 directed that any court which convicts a person of any criminal offence in connection with the driving of a motor vehicle (not being an offence under Part IV, Public service vehicles) may (except when otherwise expressly provided) order disqualification for such a period as the court thinks fit and may (or shall in case of disqualification) order endorsement on his licence.

This section also allows an appeal against disqualification but Sched. 8 (11), 1956 Act, altered this to the effect that a Court, if it thinks fit, may suspend the disqualification pending an appeal against the conviction or order.

1956 Act, s. 26 (2), states that a reference to " any criminal offence " (as above) shall now be a reference to the following offences specified in the 4th Sched. to the Act (which therefore are the offences for which disqualification or endorsement may be ordered) :

(1) Any offence against s. 4 (1), 1930 Act or s. 31, 1934 Act (driving or employing a person to drive without a licence) or under s. 5 (3), 1930 Act (failure to comply with the conditions of a provisional licence).

(2) Any offence under s. 7 (4), 1930 Act (applying for or obtaining a licence or driving, while disqualified).

(3) Any offence against s. 9, 1930 Act (restriction of driving by young persons).

(4) Any offence committed in respect of a motor vehicle against any statutory restriction of speed on a road, including any offence under s. 13, 1930 Act (prohibition of motor racing and speed trials on highways).

(5) Manslaughter by the driver of a motor vehicle, any offence under s. 35, Offences Against the Person Act, 1861 (causing bodily harm) committed by the person having charge of a motor vehicle, or any offence under s. 8, 1956 Act (causing death by recklessly or dangerously driving) or any offence under

ss. 11 or 12, 1930 Act (reckless, dangerous, careless or inconsiderate driving) committed in respect of a motor vehicle.

(6) Any offence under s. 9, 1956 Act (person in charge of a motor vehicle on a road or other public place when under the influence of drink or drug so as to be incapable of having proper control), or any offence under s. 15, 1930 Act (driving or attempting to drive when under the influence of drink or a drug) committed in respect of a motor vehicle.

(7) Any offence under s. 16, 1930 Act (unlawful pillion riding) committed by the driver of a motor vehicle.

(8) Any offence under s. 28, 1930 Act (taking away motor vehicle without owner's consent or other authority).

(9) Any offence under s. 2 (1), 1956 Act (using or permitting or causing on a road a motor vehicle which has no test certificate if one was obligatory; not yet in force).

(10) An offence under any statutory provision committed in respect of a motor vehicle, being an offence:—

(a) of failure to conform to the indication given by a traffic sign or to comply with a direction given by a police constable, or

(b) of failure to comply with a requirement to proceed or not to proceed in a specified direction or along a specified part of the carriageway

(c) of using a vehicle on a road, or causing or permitting a vehicle to be so used, so as, by the condition of the vehicle or its parts or accessories, the number of passengers carried by it, or the weight, distribution, packing or adjustment of its load, to cause, or to be likely to cause, danger, and in particular (but without prejudice to the generality of this paragraph) of contravening any requirement as to brakes, steering gear or tyres or any other requirement prescribed under s. 1 (1), 1956 Act (tests of the condition of vehicles; not yet in force).

And any offence in respect of a motor vehicle under s. 50, 1930 Act (leaving a vehicle in a dangerous position on a road), s. 18 (8), 1934 Act (pedestrian crossings), s. 1 (5), Street Playground Act, 1938, or s. 2 (2), School Crossing Patrols Act, 1953.

(11) Any offence under s. 35, 1930 Act (compulsory third-party insurance).

(12) Any offence in respect of a motor vehicle under the Road Transport Lighting Act, 1957.

Disqualification from the Date of Conviction :—

(1) Must take place unless the Court for special reasons orders otherwise, in the following cases:

promoting or taking part in racing or speed trials on a road (s. 13, 1930 Act) ;

being incapable of proper control through drink or a drug (s. 15).

(2) Must be ordered, unless the Court having regard to the lapse of time (3 years or more, 1956, Sched. 8 (12)) since the last previous conviction or for other special reason orders otherwise, on a second or subsequent conviction for reckless or dangerous driving and may be ordered on a first conviction (s. 11, 1930 Act).

(3) Cannot be ordered for any offence under Part IV. (public service vehicles).

(4) May be ordered on any conviction of a " criminal offence " in connection with the driving of a motor vehicle (see above).

(5) A person convicted of dangerous or careless driving (or driving under the influence of drink or a drug; Sched. 8 (35), 1956 Act) whether or not ordered to be disqualified for a period, may be disqualified until he has passed the prescribed test of competence to drive (R.T. Act, 1934, s. 6 (3) and 1956 Act, s. 26 (4)).

A " special reason " is one which is special to the facts which constitute the offence. A circumstance peculiar to the offender is not a special reason (*R.* v. *Crossan* (1939), *Whittal* v. *Kirby* (1946), *Knowler* v. *Rennison* (1947), *Jowett-Shooter* v. *Franklin* (1949) *Lines* v. *Hersom* (1951) and *Thomas George Wickins* (1958)).

There may be an appeal against an order of disqualification (1930 Act, s. 6) and the Court may, pending the appeal, suspend the operation of the order (1956 Act, s. 28 and Sched. 8 11)). Where the Court has a discretion for special reasons, it would appear that an appeal against the sentence would not be barred by s. 83, M.C. Act, 1952, which excludes appeal against a sentence passed where the summary court has no discretion as to the making of the order. S. 26, 1956 Act deals with fines and disqualifications.

Particulars of a disqualification shall be sent by the Court to the council of the area where the person resides and to the council which granted his driving licence (s. 8 (6), 1930 Act).

A licence shall be suspended (be of no effect) during the period of disqualification (s. 7 (2)).

The Court shall forward the licence to the council which granted it and the council shall keep it until disqualification ceases and the owner asks for it in writing (s. 8 (6)).

If a person whilst disqualified applies for or obtains a licence, or drives a motor vehicle (or motor vehicle which he is forbidden to drive) on a road, he commits an offence and any such licence shall be of no effect. Penalty, up to six months imprisonment, or up to £50 fine if the Court find special circumstances in the case, or both (s. 7 (4)).

A person so disqualified may apply to the Court to remove the disqualification. The justice to whom the complaint is made shall

issue a summons to the superintendent of police of the county or
the chief constable of the borough, in which the Court had made
the order, or to a constable designated for the purpose by the
superintendent or chief constable, requiring him to appear before
the magistrates' court of his area, to show cause why an order
should not be made on the complaint. If such an order is made the
court shall notify the council which has been notified of the disqualification (M.C. Rules, 1952, r. 78). The Court on considering
the circumstances of the case may order the disqualification to be
removed and endorse his licence accordingly or may refuse the
application, but if refused the person must wait 3 months before
again applying (s. 7 (3), 1930 Act). The periods for applications
for removal of disqualifications are given in s. 27, 1956 Act.

A person under the prescribed age (see "Driving Licence" above)
is thereby disqualified for holding or obtaining any driving licence
which his age prohibits him from having (s. 9, 1930 Act).

Endorsement:—

(1) Must be ordered—for any offence of reckless or dangerous
driving (s. 11), or in any case where a person is disqualified by
virtue of a conviction or by an order of the Court (s. 6).

(2) Must be ordered unless the Court for special reason orders
otherwise, on conviction for exceeding a speed limit or for
careless driving (R.T. Act, 1934, s. 5). For " special reason "
see *Whittall* v. *Kirby* (1946), above.

(3) Cannot be ordered—for any offence under Part IV.,
1930 Act (Public Service Vehicles) (s. 6).

(4) May be ordered—on conviction of an offence specified in
the 4th Schedule to the 1956 Act (see *ante*).

An order for endorsement operates as an order that any licence
held at the time or subsequently obtained shall be so endorsed
until the holder becomes entitled to have a licence free from
endorsement (s. 8 (1), 1930 Act).

A person is so entitled when no such order has been made
against him during a continuous period of three years or upwards,
and in reckoning this continuous period of three years any period
during which he was disqualified must be excluded. However,
an endorsement of a speed conviction will count against him
for only one clear year (s. 5, R.T. Act, 1934). The Court shall
send notice of any endorsement it has ordered to the Council of the
area in which the offender resides and to the Council which granted
his licence (s. 8 (6), 1930 Act).

On the issue of a new licence any endorsements on the previous
licence shall be copied on to the new licence unless the holder is
entitled to have a licence free from endorsements (s. 8 (3)).

If an order for endorsement is made, the offender :—

(1) If he holds a licence, shall, if so required by the Court,
produce his licence for endorsement within five days or such
longer time as the Court may fix.

(2) If he does not hold a licence but subsequently obtains one, shall within five days after obtaining it produce it to the Court for endorsement.

Failure to do so is a summary offence, and the licence becomes suspended from the expiration of such time until it is so produced (s. 8 (2)).

However, in cases of prosecution for exceeding a speed limit, reckless or dangerous driving, careless driving and driving under the influence of drink or drugs, the defendant shall have his driving licence in Court or send it to the Clerk of the Court to reach him not later than the day before the hearing.

If convicted the Court may require production of the licence, and if it is not then produced to the Court, the holder shall be guilty of an offence and the licence becomes suspended until it is produced to the Court (s. 33 (3) and (4), R.T. Act, 1934).

If any person whose licence has been ordered to be endorsed and who is not entitled to have a clear licence, applies for or obtains a licence without giving particulars of the order, he commits an offence (liable summarily to three months imprisonment or £50 fine, or on indictment to six months imprisonment or fine), and any licence so obtained shall be of no effect (s. 8 (4)).

Particulars of a conviction endorsed on a driving licence may be produced as *prima facie* evidence of the conviction (s. 33 (2), R.T. Act, 1934).

Where an order for endorsement is compulsory (the Court having no discretion) after conviction it is not a " sentence " against which there may be an appeal, but the offender, if he did not plead guilty may appeal against his conviction (M.C. Act, 1952, s. 83).

Police Powers—Road Traffic Act, 1930.—When a motor vehicle is on a road, this Act gives a constable certain powers regarding it, its driver, its owner, and the person in charge of it. These powers may be summarised as follows :—

(1) Stop the vehicle—a constable in uniform can so require at any time (s. 20 (3)). See " Regulation of Traffic."

(2) Traffic signals—the driver of any vehicle must obey a constable regulating traffic (s. 49). See " Regulation of Traffic."

(3) Name and address of driver and of owner—must be given by driver on request (s. 40 (1)). See " Insurance Certificates " and " Accidents ".

(4) Driving licence—driver, on request, must produce it for examination, either then or within five days at a specified police station (s. 4 (5)). See " Driving Licence."

(5) Insurance " certificate "—driver, on request, must produce it either then or within five days at a specified police station (s. 40 (1)). See " Insurance Certificates."

If personal injury has happened and if it is not produced at the scene, the driver within twenty-four hours must report the accident at a police station or to a constable, and also produce his " certificate," either then or within five days at a specified police station (s. 40 (2)). See " Accidents."

(6) False documents, seizure—on reasonable cause to believe a licence, " certificate," plate, etc., is forged, false, altered, or used with intent to deceive it may be seized (s. 112, and s. 34, R. & R.T. Act, 1933). See " False Motor Vehicle Licences and Certificates."

(7) Arrest without warrant—when person driving or in charge is incapable of having proper control through drink or drug (s. 15). See " Drunkenness," Chap. 38.

When driving recklessly, dangerously, or carelessly, unless driver gives name and address or produces licence (s. 20 (2)). See " Dangerous, etc., Driving."

When suspected of attempting to take or having taken the vehicle without lawful authority (s. 28). See " Taking, etc., of a Motor Vehicle," Chap. 14.

(8) Information—owner must give information as to the identity of driver alleged to be guilty of any offence under the Act, also any other person must give any information in his power to give which may lead to such identification (s. 113 (3)). See " Penalties, etc., R.T. Act," and " Evidence by Certificate," Chap. 7.

Owner must give information as to driver, insurance, etc., of vehicle on any occasion on which driver was bound to produce his insurance " certificate " (s. 40 (3)). See " Insurance Certificates."

Police shall supply information to enable recovery of payment for emergency treatment (s. 17, R.T. Act, 1934).

(9) Weighing—when a constable, authorised on behalf of the highway authority by his Police Authority or Chief Officer produces his authority he can require the person in charge of a motor vehicle to allow it to be weighed (R.T. Act. 1930, s. 27). See " Weight," Appendix II.

Chapter XXV

ROAD VEHICLES

Contents

Vehicles.—The word " vehicle " may be used as a comprehensive term to include every conveyance the movement of which upon the highway goes to make up the expression " traffic," or more particularly " vehicular traffic." In this sense the Oxford English Dictionary defines " vehicle " as meaning any means of carriage, conveyance, or transport ; a means of conveyance provided with wheels or runners and used for the carriage of persons or goods. Passenger vehicle means a vehicle constructed solely for the carriage of passengers and their effects (M.V. (C. & U.) and Tracklaying Regs. 1957).

The Highway Act, 1835, and the Town Police Clauses Act, 1847, dealt with highways and streets and used the word " carriage " to include the vehicles of the period, such as carriages, wagons, carts and other animal-drawn vehicles, sledges, trucks, and barrows.

The Local Government Act, 1888, s. 85, declares that bicycles, tricycles, and other similar machines are " carriages " within the meaning of the Highway Acts.

The Road Traffic Act, 1930, s. 31, enacts that any motor vehicle or trailer shall be deemed to be a carriage within the meaning of any Act and of any rule, regulation or byelaw made under any Act, and if used as a carriage of any particular class, shall, for the purpose of any enactment relating to carriages of that class, be deemed to be a carriage of that class.

Thus, generally speaking, all road vehicles are " carriages," and owners and drivers have to comply with the law dealing with carriages, as well as to obey the particular rules affecting the class of vehicle they own or drive.

Road vehicles, irrespective of the power by which they are drawn or propelled, are either :

(1) Private vehicles, that is to say, vehicles which are not licensed by any authority to convey members of the public or goods for hire or reward, or

(2) Public vehicles, meaning vehicles which, under licence of the proper authority, carry on the roads passengers or goods for payment. Such vehicles are of various types, but all should have been passed by some authority as suitable for the purpose of carrying persons or goods on the highway for hire.

Public vehicles consist of :

(1) Tramcars and trolley vehicles. These vehicles, are allowed on the roads under statutory authority. For the purposes of the Road Traffic Act, 1930, and the Road Transport Lighting Act, 1957, " tramcar " includes any carriage used on any road by virtue of an Order made under the Light Railways Act, 1896, and " trolley vehicle " means a mechanically propelled vehicle adapted for use upon roads without rails and moved by power transmitted thereto from some external source. See also R.T. Act, 1956, s. 54.

The provisions of Part I. (Regulation of Motor Vehicles) of the 1930 Act do not apply to tramcars, and the provisions as to the licensing of drivers to drive on the road (ss. 4-8), dangerous and careless driving (ss. 11 and 12), drunkenness of drivers (s. 15), and inquiries into accidents (s. 23) apply to trolley vehicles (s. 1).

However, the drivers of tramcars and trolley vehicles must obey traffic directions (s. 49) and must not leave their vehicles at rest in dangerous positions (s. 50).

(2) Hackney carriages and stage coaches. These are vehicles which are licensed by the Local Authority for standing or plying for hire in the streets of its district. They are dealt with later under " Hackney Carriages and Stage Coaches."

(3) Public service vehicles. These are certain classes of motor vehicles which are licensed for the carrying of passengers for hire or reward. They are regulated by Parts IV. of the R.T. Act, 1930, and R.T. Act, 1934, and particulars are given later under " Public Service Vehicles."

(4) Licensed goods vehicles, see later.

Special regulations apply to the nature and (or) use of a vehicle and are given under the following headings:—

Carts and Wagons.
Pedal Cycles.
Hackney Carriages and Stage Coaches.
Public Service Vehicles.
Goods Vehicles.
Mechanically Propelled Vehicles.

Carts and Wagons.—Horse-drawn carts, wagons and other vehicles of the like kind are carriages within the various statutes dealing with vehicles and traffic. Such vehicles must bear the names and addresses of their owners.

Highway Act, 1835 : Under section 76, the owner's name and address must be painted on some conspicuous part of the off side of every wagon, cart or other such carriage except motor vehicles and trailers (see Road Traffic Act, 1930, Sch. 5), or on the off-side shaft thereof,in large legible letters(white upon black or black upon white not less than 1 inch in height) whilst same is used on any highway. If the owner uses or allows such a carriage to be used on the highway without the name and address, or suffers same to become illegible, or has a false name or address thereon, he maybe fined.

Under section 78, the driver of any wagon, cart or other such carriage, not having the owner's name painted and remaining legible thereon, who refuses to give the true name of the owner, may be arrested by any person who sees the offence committed and maybe fined.

Pedal Cycles.—Bicycles, tricycles and other similar machines are carriages within the Highways Acts (Local Government Act, 1888, s. 85).

Pedal cycles must display front white and rear red lights and reflectors during the hours of darkness. See " Lights on Vehicles ," Chap. 24.

Only one person may travel on a pedal cycle unless it is prepared for the carriage of more than one person. See " Dangerous Driving," Chap. 24.

It is an offence for a pedal cyclist to hold on to a motor vehicle for the purpose of being drawn, unless with lawful authority, or reasonable excuse. See " Dangerous Driving," also " Taking, etc., of a Motor Vehicle," Chap. 14. R.T. Act, 1930, s. 59, allows the making of regulations as to the fitting of appliances on pedal cycles and tricycles for giving warning of their approach on roads.

R.T. Act, 1934, s. 21, allows the making of regulations as to brakes on pedal cycles and tricycles.

Brakes on Pedal Cycles Regs., 1954, apply to pedal bicycles and pedal tricycles.

Every cycle having any wheel with outside diameter exceeding 18 inches shall:

(1) if it is " freewheeled " have two independent braking systems, one acting on the front wheel or wheels and the other acting on a rear wheel.

(2) if it is " fixedwheeled " have a braking system acting on the front wheel or wheels.

If it is a tricycle not constructed or adapted for the carriage of goods it will be sufficient to have two independent braking systems acting on the front wheel if it has two rear wheels or on the rear wheel if it has two front wheels.

Every other cycle shall have at least one braking system (Reg. 4). All braking systems shall be efficient and kept in proper working order and should not act directly on tyres (Reg. 5). No person shall ride or cause or permit a cycle to be ridden on a road unless it complies with these Regulations (Reg. 3). Above Regulations do not apply to a cycle with pedals acting directly upon any wheel or to a cycle brought temporarily into the country by a person resident abroad (Reg. 6). A police officer in uniform may test and inspect the brakes of any cycle on a road. He may do so on premises where the cycle is, within 48 hours of any accident in which the cycle was involved, if the owner of the premises consents (Reg. 8).

N.B. " owner " in this Regulation may include the occupier.

R.T. Act, 1956, s. 11 applies to persons riding pedal bicycles and pedal tricycles the following sections of the 1930 Act:—

S. 11 (1) (reckless and dangerous driving).

S. 12 (1) (careless driving).

S. 15 (1) and (4) (driving under the influence of drink or a drug) but not the attempting to so drive.

S. 20 (powers to stop drivers and get their names and addresses and to arrest them in certain cases) except the asking for production of licences.

S. 21 (giving warning of intended prosecution) in cases under s. 11 and 12 above but not to registered owners.

And s. 35, 1934 Act (which enables charge of careless driving to be substituted for reckless or dangerous driving).

However these offences, in such case, will not be indictable and any fines imposed will be smaller.

R.T. Act, 1956, s. 13. When this section is in force, it will be an offence (up to £10 fine) for any person to promote or take part in a race or trial of speed on a public highway between pedal cycles or pedal tricycles, unless it is authorised and conducted by or under regulations to be made by the Minister and in such event the police can issue traffic directions.

Hackney Carriages and Stage Coaches.—A hackney carriage, for traffic purposes, is a vehicle which stands or plies for hire in the streets, the driver putting the whole carriage at the disposal of the hirer, and the vehicle, if a motor vehicle, being adapted to carry less than eight passengers.

These hackney carriages, when they stand or ply for hire in an urban district or a rural district to which the Town Police Clauses Act, 1847, applies, require to be licensed by the Local Authority (s. 37), and if mechanically propelled they are usually called taxi-cabs or taxis.

A stage coach or stage carriage is a vehicle which proceeds from stage to stage and which stands or plies for hire for passengers at separate fares in the streets.

A tramcar is a stage carriage for the purposes of the Stage Carriages Act, 1832 (*Chapman* v. *Kirke* (1948)).

Such stage coaches when they stand or ply for hire in the districts mentioned below should be licensed for the purpose by the Local Authority, and they are usually horse-drawn wagonettes or chars-a-banc.

Above vehicles are regulated by the Town Police Clauses Acts, 1847 and 1889, which are in force in towns and urban districts and in those rural districts which have procured the necessary Order from the Home Office. The provisions of these Acts as to hackney carriages and stage coaches are incorporated with the Public Health Act, 1875 (see ss. 171, 276).

Town Police Clauses Act, 1847, s. 38, declares that every wheeled carriage, whatever may be its form or construction, used in standing or plying for hire in any street within the district shall be deemed to be a hackney carriage, but that the term shall not include any stage coach standing or plying for passengers to be carried for hire at separate fares. (However, certain offences are common to hackney carriages and stage coaches. See later.)

Town Police Clauses Act, 1889, s. 3, defines the term " omnibus " as including every char-a-banc, wagonette, stage coach and other carriage plying or standing for hire for passengers at separate fares within the district (tramcars and omnibuses used for certain specified purposes being excepted).

However, the Road Traffic Act, 1956, has restricted the extent of these definitions, as under s. 39 any motor vehicle which either carries passengers at separate fares or which is adapted to carry eight or more passengers is now a " public service vehicle," and as such it must be licensed by the Licensing Authority and not by the Local Authority (see " Public Service Vehicles "). Accordingly a motor vehicle to be a " hackney carriage " must be a vehicle adapted to carry less than eight passengers, and the term " stage coach " is used as applying to animal-drawn vehicles carrying passengers at separate fares.

Moreover, the Road Traffic Act, 1930 (5th Schedule), has repealed all the provisions of the Town Police Clauses Acts so far as they relate to public service vehicles, with the result that the rules of the Town Police Clauses Acts, 1847 and 1889, apply only to hackney carriages (as now defined) and to horse-drawn and other non-mechanically propelled " omnibuses " which are here termed stage coaches.

Under these Town Police Clauses Acts (where they apply) it is necessary that the proprietors, the drivers and conductors, and the hackney carriages and stage coaches shall be licensed by the local council. The local council at its discretion may license such vehicles and persons, and the proprietors, drivers and conductors must comply with the provisions of the Acts and of any byelaws made by the council for the regulation of such vehicles.

Such local byelaws usually prescribe rules for the conduct of the drivers and conductors, for the safety and comfort of the vehicles, for the standing places allotted for the vehicles, and for the fares which may be charged. They also provide that property left in the vehicles by passengers should be brought to an office so that same may be regained by the owners and the authorised rewards recovered for the finders.

The Town Police Clauses Act, 1847, creates certain offences as regards hackney carriages, and the Town Police Clauses Act, 1889, directs that certain of the sections of the 1847 Act shall apply to " omnibuses," a term which covers stage coaches as defined above.

Therefore hackney carriage and stage coach offences under the Town Police Clauses Act, 1847, include the following :—

S. 45 : Plying for hire with an unlicensed vehicle.

S. 47 : Driver plying for hire without licence.

Ss. 51, 52 : Number of persons to be carried must be displayed outside ; no more need be carried, and that number must be carried if required.

S. 54 : Demanding more than the previously agreed fare.

S. 58 : Taking more than the authorised fare.

S. 61 : Driver being intoxicated while driving, or driver injuring or endangering any person or property by furious driving or any other wilful misconduct. (See also Stage Carriage Act, 1832, s. 48.)

S. 62 : Leaving vehicle unattended in street.

S. 64 : Obstruction of the street or of any other carriage, or of the hiring of any other hackney carriage (or stage coach).

S. 66 : Hirer refusing to pay the authorised fare.

S. 67 : Any user wilfully injuring the carriage.

The offences under the Town Police Clauses Act, 1847, which are peculiar to hackney carriages include :—

S. 53 : Refusing, without reasonable excuse, to take a hirer or would-be hirer to any place within the district.

S. 55 : Agreement to pay more than the legal fare is not binding, and any excess paid may be recovered and the driver punished.

S. 57 : If driven to a place there to wait, the driver is entitled to his fare and a deposit for waiting, but if he then goes away or refuses to account for the deposit he commits an offence.

S. 59 : No person may be carried without the express consent of the hirer.

Public Health Act, 1936, ss. 159, 160. The person in charge of a public conveyance must have it disinfected after it has conveyed any person suffering from a notifiable disease.

Such person must not enter or be conveyed in a public conveyance carrying passengers at separate fares and need not be taken in any other public conveyance until the cost of disinfection is paid.

The Stage Carriages Act, 1832, and the Railway Passenger Duty Act, 1842 (as modified by the Road Traffic Act, 1930, 5th Sched.), provides that a stage coach and a tramcar shall not carry a greater number of passengers than it is constructed to carry. The number to be carried shall be painted outside (at back) and inside, and fit and proper seats (16 inches space) shall be provided.

Vehicles (Excise) Act, 1949, s. 27, defines hackney carriage as a mechanically propelled vehicle standing or plying for hire.

As no place is mentioned this definition covers a carriage standing or plying for hire in any yard, premises or other private place, as well as in any street. This definition is an excise definition for revenue purposes only. If such an excise " hackney carriage " is mechanically propelled and a less rate of duty has been paid on it because it is used for hire work, then, in addition to its registration marks it must carry a hackney carriage plate, as set out in the 4th Sched., showing its seating capacity. (Road Vehicles (Reg. and Lic.) Regs. 31, 32). The fact that a vehicle has this excise " hackney carriage " licence and plate does not render it a hackney carriage competent to stand or ply for hire in a street in a district to which the Town Police Clauses Act, 1847, applies. Standing or plying for hire in a street of such district is allowable only when the vehicle is specially licensed for the purpose by the local Council, and such a locally licensed vehicle should carry a plate, bearing its licence number, and its driver should carry a numbered badge, both provided by the Council. In such case the additional " hackney carriage " plate is not necessary.

Public Service Vehicles.—R.T. Act, 1930, Part IV. R.T. Act, 1934, Part IV., and R.T. Act, 1956 ss. 39–40) deal with certain motor vehicles used in the service of the public in carrying passengers for hire, and such vehicles are termed public service vehicles.

1956 Act, s. 39, defines " public service vehicle " to mean a motor vehicle used for carrying passengers for hire or reward which either (a) is carrying passengers at separate fares or (b) is not carrying passengers at separate fares but is adapted to carry eight or more passengers, and which is not a tramcar or a trolley vehicle.

However by s. 40 and 6th Sched. a vehicle adapted to carry less than 8 passengers and carrying passengers at separate fares for race meetings, public gatherings, etc. (Part I) for certain journeys with 4 passengers or less (Part II) for overseas visitors (Part III) and under certain conditions (Part IV, all Parts of the 6th Sched.) shall not be treated as a public service vehicle. Also a public service vehicle carrying passengers at separate fares shall be treated as a " contract carriage " when used for overseas visitors (Part III) or under certain conditions (Part IV of 6th Sched.). See also the provisions of the rest of s. 40 and the supplementary provisions of Part V of the 6th Sched. (s. 40).

A vehicle carrying for hire or reward agricultural workers to or from work during the six months from June 1st, shall be deemed not a public service vehicle (Emergency Laws (Misc. Provisions) Act, 1953).

1956 Act, s. 39 divides public service vehicles into three classes:—

(1) *Stage Carriages.*—Viz. public service vehicles carrying passengers for hire or reward at separate fares and not being express carriages as hereinafter defined (s. 39).

For example, an omnibus service.

A " stage carriage " must have a public service vehicle licence and must be worked under a road service licence.

(2) *Express Carriages.*—Viz. public service vehicles carrying passengers for hire or reward at separate fares none of which is less than 1s. or any greater sum prescribed by regulations.

However, a composite fare for more than one journey shall not be taken as representing the aggregate of fares of any less amount and no account shall be taken of any fare which is charged in the case of passengers of particular descriptions if a fare of 1s. or more is charged for the like service in the case of all passengers not falling within any of those descriptions (1956 Act, s. 39).

For example, a motor coach service.

If a " separate fare " motor vehicle does not comply with these conditions it will be regarded as a stage carriage.

An " express carriage " must have a public service vehicle licence, and must be operated under a road service licence.

(3) *Contract Carriages.*—Viz. public service vehicles not carrying passengers at separate fares. (1956 Act, s. 39).

However, a public service vehicle carrying passengers at separate fares will be treated as a " contract carriage " in the circumstances (as noted above) under Parts III or IV, 6th Sched. (1956 Act, s. 40).

A " contract carriage " must have a public service vehicle licence. The holder of the licence must keep a record and the driver carry a work ticket (Contract Carriage Records Regs. 1951).

R.T. Act, 1930, ss. 62-66; *R. and R.T. Act*, 1933, s. 27; and *R.T. Act*, 1956, Sched. 8 (40): England, Wales and Scotland are divided into twelve traffic areas. Each traffic area has a Licensing Authority which issues licences. It also has Traffic Commissioners. These traffic areas (and their headquarters) are as follows:—Northern

(Newcastle-on-Tyne), Yorkshire (Leeds), North Western (Manchester), West Midland (Birmingham), East Midland (Nottingham), Eastern (Cambridge), South Wales (Cardiff), Western (Bristol), South Eastern (London), Metropolitan (London), Northern Scotland (Aberdeen), and Southern Scotland (Edinburgh).

The old Acts (e.g. Town Police Clauses Act, 1847) regulating passenger-carrying vehicles were, by the 5th Schedule to the 1930 Act, repealed so far as they related to public service vehicles.

The following Public Service Vehicles Regulations deal with the matters indicated by their descriptive titles and prescribe fine for contraventions:—

(1) *Licences and Certificates* Regs., 1952, 1957.

(2) *Conditions of Fitness* Regs., 1958, 1959.

(3) *Equipment and Use* Regs., 1958.

(4) *Drivers' and Conductors' Licences* Regs., 1934.

(5) *Conduct of Drivers, Conductors and Passengers* Regs., 1936 and 1946. See ss. 84 and 85, 1930 Act.

(6) *Lost Property* Regs., 1934, 1958.

(7) *International Circulation* Regs., 1957. See " Foreign-owned Motor Vehicles " later.

Under the Records of Licences Regs., 1933, the Licensing Authority are to keep duplicates of the licences granted by them which are as follows :—

(1) *Public Service Vehicle Licence.*—This licence may be in three forms, viz. :

(*a*) Stage carriage licence. Such a licence will also entitle the holder to use the vehicle as a contract carriage, or, subject to any conditions on his road service licence, as an express carriage.

(*b*) Express carriage licence. Under this licence the holder may use the vehicle as a contract carriage. He may also use the vehicle on a service of stage carriages if he has the consent in writing of the Licensing Authority of the area in which it is to be so used.

(*c*) Contract carriage licence.

R.T. Act 1930.—It is an offence for any person to cause or permit a motor vehicle to be used on any road as a stage carriage, express carriage, or contract carriage unless he holds the appropriate public service vehicle licence for the vehicle (s. 67).

Applications for these licences shall be made to the Licensing Authority of the traffic area within or from which the vehicle is intended to be ordinarily operated (s. 78).

A public service vehicle licence will last one year from the date on which it takes effect, unless previously revoked, and if suspended it will be of no effect during the time of suspension (s. 80). Such a licence is valid in every other traffic area (s. 73).

Licences and Certificates Regs., 1952.—The fee for the licence is £4 (Reg. 17). The licence shall be carried in a container on left side of vehicle or on the windscreen adjacent to the excise licence, so as to be clearly legible (Reg. 19). If the vehicle is let on hire and used as a stage or express carriage, there shall be a notice on the front or on near side of vehicle bearing the words " On hire to " and the name of the holder of the road service licence under which it is used (Reg. 20).

R.T. Act 1930.—A public service vehicle licence may be refused or suspended or revoked, if the Licensing Authority considers, from the conduct of the person or the manner in which the vehicle is being used, that he is not a fit person to hold the licence (s. 67).

A public service vehicle licence for a motor vehicle adapted to carry eight or more passengers shall not be granted unless a " certificate of fitness " has been issued and is in force in respect to the vehicle (s. 68). See also Sched. 8 (22 and 23), R.T. Act, 1956.

Certifying officers appointed by the Minister of Transport examine vehicles and issue certificates of fitness (s. 69).

A certificate of fitness shall continue in force for from five years to one year (as specified in the certificate), unless previously revoked or cancelled.

The fee for the certificate is £5 (Reg. 24). Change of ownership does not render the certificate invalid (Reg. 26).

The Minister of Transport and a certifying officer have power to revoke a certificate of fitness. If the certificate is revoked or if the vehicle ceases to be a vehicle in respect of which such a certificate is in force, its licence ceases to be of effect (s. 68).

Public service vehicle examiners appointed by the Minister will inspect public service vehicles. Any certifying officer or examiner, on production, if so required, of his authority, may enter and inspect any public service vehicle, and for that purpose may require a public service vehicle to be stopped or may enter premises. Obstructing him or failing to so stop a vehicle is an offence (s. 69).

The holder of a public service vehicle licence must report to the Licensing Authority :—

(*a*) of the area where it occurs, any failure of or damage to the vehicle calculated to affect the safety of the public ;

(*b*) of the area in which licence was issued, any alteration of the vehicle (s. 70).

Failure to do so is an offence (s. 70).

If a certifying officer or examiner finds that a public service vehicle is or is likely to become unfit for service unless its defects are remedied, he may suspend the licence, and shall so notify the licensee and the Licensing Authority which granted the licence. Suspension lasts until removed (s. 71).

Conditions of Fitness Regs.—A certificate of fitness shall not be issued unless the vehicle complies with the conditions prescribed in these Regulations. The conditions deal with the stability, suspension, turning circle, clearance, life guards, guard rails, side overhang, brakes, steering, hub projection, fuel tanks, carburettors, exhaust pipes, locking of nuts, electrical equipment, body, steps, platforms, stairs, entrances, exits, doors, gangways, seats, windows, markings, ventilation, driver's accommodation, windscreens and wipers, passengers' communication with driver, wireless apparatus, luggage racks, general construction etc.

Equipment and Use Regs.—As regards the use of a public service vehicle: whilst passengers are carried every entrance, exit and gangway shall be kept clear of obstruction but neither standing passengers nor the drawing of a gas-producing trailer shall be deemed obstruction (Reg. 6). No person shall be on the right of the driver, who must not be obstructed in any way (Reg. 7).

The body, etc., shall be kept clean and in good condition (Reg. 8). The internal lamps shall be alight during the hours of darkness when passengers are carried (Reg. 9). Steering arms shall be kept free from rust (Reg. 10).

Petrol tanks shall not be opened or filled while the engine is running (Reg. 11). A conductor is necessary on a stage carriage with a seating capacity for more than 20 passengers; but is not necessary on a single decked vehicle with a seating capacity for not more than 26 if no adult fare is less than 6*d.*, nor on any single decked vehicle if the traffic commissioner has certified that one is not necessary (Reg. 12). No highly inflammable or dangerous substance shall be carried unless safely packed (Reg. 13). Name and address of licence holder shall be displayed on the near side of the vehicle (Reg. 14). Every public service vehicle shall carry suitable and efficient fire extinguishing apparatus which must be maintained in good working order (Reg. 15).

Every vehicle used as an express or contract carriage shall carry a suitable receptacle, easily accessible and properly marked, containing the prescribed first aid dressings which must be maintained in good condition. It must also carry a lifting jack (Reg. 16).

The Public Service Vehicles and Trolley Vehicles (Carrying Capacity) Regs., 1954, direct that the seating capacity of such vehicles shall be clearly marked either inside and visible from outside or on the rear or near side of the vehicle (Reg. 8).

The number of seated passengers shall not exceed the fixed carrying capacity (but if only children up to 15 and their attendants up to 6 persons are carried three children will count as two passengers except in certain 12-seater vehicles where only up to 9 children may be so counted) and no standing passengers may be carried, except where it is allowed by the following Regulations (Reg. 3).

During peak traffic or to avoid hardship a stage carriage or trolley vehicle may carry standing passengers on the lower deck of a double decker or on a single decker, up to one third of the seating capacity on the deck, or eight, whichever number is the less (Reg. 4).

The Licensing Authority may authorise an express or contract carriage to carry some standing passengers (Regs. 5 and 6).

No standing passengers shall be carried on a half decked vehicle or on the upper deck of a double decker or if there is any vacant seat or unless a conductor is carried, or on a public service vehicle with a seating capacity not exceeding 12 in respect of which the first certificate of fitness was issued on or after 11 April, 1958.

However the Licensing Authority may certify that a conductor is not required on the particular service on which a single decker is used (Reg. 7 as amended by 1958 Regs.).

(2) *Road Service Licence.*—R.T. Act 1930. This is a licence to a person allowing him to provide a specified road service. A vehicle shall not be used as a stage carriage or an express carriage except under such a licence. Conditions may be attached. (Such conditions may be varied and there maybe an appeal to the Minister of Transport and Civil Aviation, 1956 Act, s. 47). A road service licence will be necessary in respect of any route (s. 72).

It is an offence for any person to use or cause or permit to be used a vehicle in contravention of this section, or for the holder of a road service licence to wilfully or negligently fail to comply with any condition attached to his licence (s. 72 (10)).

Applications for this licence shall be made to the Traffic Commissioners within whose area the proposed route or any part thereof is situate (s. 78). It is not valid in any other traffic area unless backed (or endorsed) by the Commissioners of that other area, which may also attach conditions as respects its own area (s. 73).

However, licences for " corridor " areas (where passengers are merely carried through another traffic area) need not be so backed (R.T. Act, 1934, s. 28).

The licence may be for one or more periods or occasions, or the date of its expiry may be prescribed. It is usually three years (Duration Regs., 1937 and 1938).

When the Commissioners grant a road service licence it shall send particulars of it to every chief officer of police and every local authority in whose district or area any such service is to be provided (s. 72 (9)). The Commissioners may revoke or suspend a road service licence for non-compliance with its conditions, and if so shall notify the police and local authorities of the places concerned (s. 74). Licence holders must supply particulars of arrangements with other persons re passenger transport facilities (s. 76).

Licences and Certificates Regs.—An application for a road service licence or backing (to allow running in another traffic area) shall be accompanied by a notice giving the prescribed particulars of the service (Reg. 39). This notice will be published in the " Notices and Proceedings " periodically issued by the Commissioners of the area, which also contains the dates and places of their Public sittings to hear applications and their decisions (Reg. 41). Objections to applications shall be in writing, giving the grounds (Reg. 43). The Commissioners may vary conditions already imposed, on giving notice to persons affected (Reg. 46). The dates prescribed for the expiry of licences and backings (s. 80 of Act) are the last days of February, June and November (Reg. 45).

If the licensee ceases to operate the service he shall notify the Commissioners forthwith and return the licence (Reg. 48).

The fee for the licence is £1 for each year or part of a year. If not for more than three days the fee is 2s. per day (Reg. 44). A special occasional service may be licensed fee 5s. (Reg. 47).

(3) *Drivers' and Conductors' Licences.*—R.T. Act 1930. A person shall not drive or act as conductor of a public service vehicle on a road unless he is duly licensed by the Traffic Commissioners. A person shall not employ any unlicensed person to drive or act as conductor of a public service vehicle on a road (s. 77).

A person is disqualified for such a driver's licence until he is 21, and for such a conductor's licence until he is 18.

A driver's licence may be limited to such types of vehicles as may be specified in the licence.

A licence as driver or conductor may be suspended or revoked by the Authority who granted it if the holder is considered unfit to hold it by reason of his conduct or physical disability.

Any contravention of this section will be an offence (s. 77).

Application for licence shall be made to the Authority of the area in which the applicant resides (s. 78). It may last three years from the date on which it takes effect, unless previously revoked, and if suspended shall be of no effect during the time of suspension (s. 80). It will be valid in every traffic area (s. 73).

Drivers' and Conductors' Licences Regs.—An applicant shall supply the prescribed information, which includes a certificate of character and a medical certificate (Reg. 5). The fee is 1s. per year (Reg. 7). He shall immediately sign his licence with his ordinary signature (Reg. 8), but shall write nothing else on it (Reg. 9). A licensee shall notify any change of address within 7 days (Reg. 10). He shall produce his licence, or give the address at which it will be available for the next 5 days, on request of any constable, certifying officer, public service vehicle or goods vehicle examiner or person duly authorised by the Licensing Authority (Reg. 11).

He shall be issued a badge (the property of the Minister) bearing a distinguishing letter and number and shall wear it in a conspicuous position when acting as driver or conductor (Reg. 14). If his licence is suspended or revoked he shall return the licence and badge (Regs. 13, 15). He shall report any loss, defacement, etc., of his licence or badge (Regs. 12, 17). He shall keep the badge in his possession and shall not cause or permit it to be worn by any other person (Reg. 19).

Lost Property Regs.—Any person who finds property accidentally left in a public service vehicle shall immediately hand it to the conductor (or driver if no conductor) (Reg. 4). The conductor shall search his vehicle for left property before or at the end of any journey. Within 24 hours he shall hand any such property to the operator of the service, or if he is going off duty, to his relief conductor, who has the like responsibility. However, if claimed by a person who satisfies the conductor that he is the owner, it shall be returned to such person forthwith without fee or reward and the conductor shall report the facts to the operator (Reg. 5).

Particulars of any found property shall reach the operator within 2 days and he shall keep a record of same, available at all reasonable times for inspection by the police and Licensing Authority (Reg. 6). The operator is responsible for safe custody of such property (see also s. 30, R.T. Act, 1934), and if the name and address of the owner is readily ascertainable he should be notified by the operator (Reg. 7).

Unclaimed property, after 3 months, vests in the operator, who may give it to the conductor or sell it (Reg. 8). If such property is returned to the owner he shall pay the operator a fee of 1/-, and if the value exceeds 2s., an additional sum (one-twelfth of the value and not exceeding £4) as a reward to be paid to the conductor (Reg. 9) into whose possession the property first came (Reg. 11).

The operator, after 48 hours, may destroy or sell perishable unclaimed property, and may at any time dispose of objectionable property (Reg. 10). The operator has the right to open bags, packages, etc., so as to trace the identity of owners or to ascertain the contents (Reg. 13). If property is claimed the operator may require the claimant to open the package, etc., and submit the contents for examination (Reg. 14). Contravention of or failure to comply with the regulations is a summary offence, fine not exceeding £5 (Reg. 15).

The regulations as to the conduct of drivers and conductors are given below.

General Provisions re *Public Service Vehicles.*—R.T. Act, 1930, s. 81: Gives a right of appeal within a month to the Minister of

Transport in connection with the refusal, granting, etc., of public service vehicle licences, road service licences and certificates of fitness.

R.T. Act, 1956, 8th Sched. (25) deals with appeals and any regulations thereon.

The holder of a road service licence or backing or certificate is bound to produce it for examination at his principal place of business on request of any police officer, certifying officer, public service vehicle examiner or person authorised by the Commissioners (Licences and Certificates Regs., Reg. 9).

S. 82 : Allows an appeal to Summary Courts in connection with the refusal, revocation, suspension, etc., of drivers' and conductors' licences.

S. 83 : Authorises the police and local authority to inspect, without payment, the record of all licences which shall be kept by the Licensing Authority (Records of Licences Regs., 1933), and to take copies or extracts therefrom. Certified copies of entries made in this record are admissible in evidence.

S. 84 : Empowers the making of regulations as to the conduct of passengers in public service vehicles ; penalty on contravention, fine not exceeding £5.

S. 85 : Regulations as to the conduct of drivers and conductors may be made and the penalty for any breach to be fine up to £5.

Conduct of Drivers, Conductors and Passengers Regs.—A driver or conductor of a public service vehicle when acting as such, shall be civil, ensure the safety of passengers, correctly give the route, fare and destination, give his name and name and address of employer, and particulars of his licence to any constable or person having reasonable cause to ask for it, help any person having authority to examine the vehicles and shall not smoke in the vehicle on the journey or when passengers are on board (Reg. 4).

A driver when driving shall not talk with the conductor or other persons unless for safety reasons (Reg. 5). A conductor shall enforce the regulations relating to the conduct of passengers, see that the route, fare and destination notices are properly displayed, and shall not talk to the driver, except to stop the vehicle (Reg. 6).

A driver of a stage or express carriage shall, when he stops, stop the vehicle close to the left of the road and must not stop there unreasonably long (Reg. 7). A conductor of a stage or express carriage shall not delay unreasonably in signalling to the driver to start (Reg. 8).

Public Service Vehicles :—A passenger or intending passenger shall not be disorderly, enter or alight save by the doors provided, impede passengers wilfully and unreasonably, enter or remain when told not to do so because the vehicle is full or not allowed to pick up there, travel on the upper deck unless occupying a seat, travel in any part which is not for passengers, wilfully interfere with the vehicle or with any person, distract the driver's attention save to stop the vehicle, signal the vehicle to start, damage or soil the vehicle, distribute in the vehicle any printed, etc., matter or advertising articles, wilfully interfere with any notice on the vehicle, use any noisy instrument in the vehicle or make excessive noise, throw money, bottles, litter, etc., out of the vehicle, throw out any article, flag, streamer, etc., overhanging the road, or obstruct any person in the course of his duty (Reg. 9).

Stage and Express Carriages :—A passenger or intending passenger shall not smoke where smoking is prohibited or sell any article in the vehicle (Reg. 9). If his condition or clothing is offensive he shall not enter or remain in the vehicle after an authorised person has requested him to leave and tendered his fare if previously paid.

He shall not have loaded firearms or any dangerous or offensive article, and requires the consent of an authorised person to have any bulky or cumbersome article. He shall not bring in any animal without the consent of an authorised person, or retain it after request to remove it (Reg. 10). He shall not use a defaced or altered ticket or an expired period or season ticket with intent to avoid payment of a fare or a non-transferable ticket issued to another person.

On request (unless he holds a ticket) he shall declare his journey, pay his fare and take his ticket, and shall show it when required or pay the fare. Leaving without paying and with intent to avoid payment will be an offence. At the end of his journey if required he shall surrender his ticket, and if requested, leave the vehicle. A season ticket holder shall, if required, give up his ticket at the expiry of the period (Reg. 11). An employee of the licensee is an " authorised person " (Reg. 2).

General Powers :—Any passenger reasonably suspected of contravening these regulations shall give his name and address to the driver or conductor or to a constable, on demand. Any passenger contravening these regulations may be removed from the vehicle by the driver or conductor, or on request of the driver or conductor by any constable (Reg. 12).

R.T. Act, 1930. s. 85 : A licensed driver or conductor who contravenes any regulations under the Act as to his conduct may be fined £5, and the Court may endorse the conviction on his licence (under this Part of the Act), which must be produced within a reasonable time for endorsement on penalty of committing an offence.

S. 90 : A local authority outside the London Traffic Area with the Minister's sanction may make orders as to the use of highways by public service vehicles (see s. 29, R.T. Act, 1934).

S. 95 : Except in the case of a breach of the regulations as to the conduct of passengers in public service vehicles (made under s. 84) proceedings for an offence under this Part IV of the Act shall not in England and Wales be instituted except :—

(a) by or on behalf of the Director of Public Prosecutions, or

(b) by a person authorised in that behalf by the Licensing Authority, a chief officer of police, or the Council of a county, county borough, or county district. But proceedings for an offence, by or on behalf of the Minister may be taken for an offence under s. 75 (accounts, records and returns); 1956 Act, Sched. 8 (26).

S. 98 : This section, as amended and supplemented by the London Passenger Transport Act, 1933 (see s. 51 and 11th Sch.), makes special provision for the Metropolitan Traffic Area which comprises London and adjoining counties and towns.

In this area a Traffic Commissioner (Sched. 8 (4), R.T. Act, 1956) will licence all public service vehicles, tramcars and trolley vehicles.

Drivers and conductors of public service vehicles, tramcars and trolley vehicles will be licensed by the Commissioner of Metropolitan Police (Metropolitan Traffic Area (Drivers' and Conductors' Licences) Orders, 1934, 1943).

Lost property found in omnibuses, tramcars and trolley vehicles, which hitherto had been dealt with by the police at the Lost Property Office, Lambeth Road, has, since 1 Oct, 1933, been dealt with by the London Passenger Transport Board (now the London Transport Executive by virtue of the Transport Act, 1947). This Board was established to provide and control all local passenger transport in the prescribed London Passenger Transport Area, and it took over and operated the Underground and Metropolitan railways, the tram and trolley vehicle systems, and road services of stage and express carriages (also contract carriages) within the area (London Passenger Transport Act, 1933). Hackney carriages (taxis) and horse-drawn " stage carriages," and their drivers (and conductors) remain under the control of the Commissioner of Metropolitan Police.

Ss. 101-110 constitute Part V of the 1930 Act, and deal with the running of public service vehicles by local authorities.

A local authority which operates a tramway, light railway, trolley vehicle or omnibus undertaking, may, as part of that undertaking, run public service vehicles on any road within their district, and with the consent of the Authority for the area in which any other road is situate they may run on that road (s. 101).

However, by s. 108, nothing in Part V shall be in derogation of the provisions of Part IV of the Act, and s. 72 (8) renders road service licences necessary. Also the Act does not authorise a local authority to run a public service vehicle as a contract carriage or on certain roads and premises (s. 101). See P.S.V. (Travel Concessions) Act, 1955, allowing local authorities to allow free travel or reduced fares.

Goods Vehicles.—By the Road and Rail Traffic Act, 1933, and the Transport Act, 1947, motor vehicles and trailers constructed or adapted for the carriage of goods and used on roads in any traffic area (see s. 27, R. and R. Traffic Act, 1933), for the carriage of goods were, with some important exceptions, brought under the control of the Traffic Commissioners for that area (1956 Act, Sched. 8 (40)).

The British Transport Commission established under the Transport Act, 1947, was authorised to take over vehicles used under A and B licences for long distances (40 miles or more) for hire or reward, subject to some exceptions (See the British Transport Commision Acts, 1947, 1949 and 1950); but by the Transport Act, 1953, s. 1, the Commission should dispose of them as quickly as practicable. Vehicles (Excise) Act, 1949, gives the duties payable on such vehicles and defines " goods vehicles " as mechanically propelled vehicles constructed or adapted for use and used for the conveyance of goods or burden whether in the course of trade or otherwise (s. 27).

However Finance Act, 1952, s. 7 states that a vehicle of unladen weight exceeding 12 cwt. made for conveyance of goods but not used for such conveyance for hire or reward or trade or business is not a " goods vehicle " under the 1949 Act. S. 5 gives certain exemptions from excise duty payable under the 1949 Act.

Licensing and regulation of goods vehicles.—R. and R. Traffic Act, 1933. " Goods vehicle " means a motor vehicle constructed or adapted for use for the carriage of goods or a trailer so constructed or adapted (s. 1 (2)). See also Tracklaying Regs. 1957.

" Motor Vehicle " means a mechanically propelled vehicle intended or adapted for use on roads (s. 36).

" Carriage of goods " includes the haulage of goods (s. 36), therefore the Act applies to locomotives and tractors. " Goods " includes goods or burden of any description (s. 36).

" Trailer " means a vehicle drawn by a motor vehicle (s. 36).

It is an offence for any person, except under licence under the Act, to use a goods vehicle on a road for the carriage of goods:—

(*a*) for hire or reward, or

(*b*) for or in connection with any trade or business carried on by him (s. 1 (1)).

However by s. 1 (5) the following acts shall not be deemed to be a carrying of the goods for hire or reward:—

(1) delivery or collection of goods sold, used or hired in the course of his trade or business ;

(2) delivery or collection of goods for process or treatment in the course of his trade or business ;

(3) carriage by a person engaged in agriculture of goods in connection with the business of agriculture carried on by

another person in the locality in a vehicle licensed under the Act (C. Licence) for carriage of goods in connection with his agricultural business ;

(4) carriage of goods in a vehicle used under trade licence.

(5) carriage of goods in a vehicle used by a manufacturer agent or dealer for demonstration purposes (s. 1 (5)).

The following vehicles are exempted from licence (s. 1 (7)) :—

(1) vehicles (and their trailers) used under reduced rates of taxation exclusively for agricultural or other ancillary purposes;

(2) trailers drawn by vehicles constructed solely to carry not more than seven persons (exclusive of driver) and their effects and not used for the carriage of goods for hire or reward ;

(3) tramcars and trolley vehicles ;

(4) public service vehicles duly licensed as such

(5) hackney carriages, when used as such.

(6) vehicles used for the purposes of funerals ;

(7) vehicles used for a local authority in road cleansing, watering, disposal of refuse, or for weights and measures or sale of food and drugs purposes :

(8) vehicles used for police, fire brigade or ambulance purposes ;

(9) vehicles towing disabled vehicles or removing goods from disabled vehicles ;

(10) vehicles used for miners' rescue purposes ;

(11) vehicles of any class or description specified in regulations, used for any purpose or for any purpose so specified (R.T. Act, 1956, Sched. 8 (29)).

Road and Rail Traffic Act (Exemption) Regs., 1957, exempt from the necessity of having carriers licences (under s. 1 of the 1933 Act) the use of the following vehicles:—

(a) Hired for Armed or visiting Forces purposes;

(b) Used for Civil Defence purposes;

(c) Without permanent bodies and on test, etc.;

(d) Used between neighbouring premises;

(e) Trailers used for road works;

(f) Road rollers with road works trailers or water carts;

(g) Tower wagons and their trailers;

(h) Used for lifeboat purposes;

(i) Used by highway authorities for weighing vehicles under s. 27, R.T. Act, 1930;

(j) Used under limited trade licences;

(k) Motor cars, dual purpose vehicles or motor cycles used by commercial travellers soliciting orders, etc., but not used for goods other than samples;

(l) Pedestrian controlled vehicles;

(m) Motor cars, dual purpose vehicles or motor cycles carrying the drivers' tools, etc., for their business;

(n) Used by doctors, nurses, dentists or veterinary surgeons for carriage of their instruments, etc.;

(o) Passenger vehicles (not more than 7 seats) with trailer if no goods are carried for hire or reward;

(p) Tractors, ploughing machines and other agricultural engines used for agricultural and similar purposes.

(q) Farmers' dual purpose vehicles.

(r) Vehicle with plant.

(s) Vehicle distributing grit, salt etc., on roads.

The performance by a local or public authority of its functions shall be deemed to be the carrying on of a business (s. 1 (6)).

The person by whom the vehicle is being used is the driver if the vehicle belongs to him or is hired or loaned to him, and in any other case it will be the person whose agent or servant the driver is (s. 1 (3)).

There are three kinds of carrier licence (R. and R. Traffic Act, 1933, s. 2), viz. :—

(1) *The " A " or Public Carrier's Licence.*—This will entitle the holder to use the vehicles as authorised in the licence, for the carriage of goods for hire or reward or in connection with his own business as a carrier of goods. The period of currency for this licence will normally be 5 years.

However the licensee may be allowed to use designated vehicles, on contract for not less than a year with a " non-carrying " person, for carriage of goods for that person's business (1933 Act, s. 7)

Special conditions cannot be attached to this licence.

(2) *The " B " or Limited Carrier's Licence.*—This will entitle the holder to use the vehicles as authorised in the licence, as he thinks fit from time to time, either for the carriage of goods for or in connection with his trade or business, or for the carriage of goods for hire or reward subject to any special conditions prescribed in his licence, which may be varied by written authority of a Commissioner (Road Vehicles and Drivers Order, 1952).

This licence will usually be for a period of two years.

Special conditions may be attached to this licence limiting the use of the vehicles for carriage of goods for hire or reward to certain goods, certain districts, etc. (s. 8 (3)).

" Authorised vehicle " in relation to a licence under this 1933 Act means a vehicle authorised to be used thereunder whether or not it is used for a purpose requiring such licence and whether it is hired or on loan to him (R.T. Act, 1956, s. 43 (5)).

(3) *The " C " or Private Carrier's Licence.*—This will entitle the holder to use the vehicles as authorised in the licence, for the carriage of goods in connection with his trade or business,

subject to the condition that none of these vehicles shall be used for the carriage of goods for hire or reward.

However see above, where under s. 1 (5) delivery or collection of goods in the course of his trade or business, etc., shall not be deemed to be a carrying of goods for hire or reward.

The currency period for this licence will normally be 5 years. Special conditions cannot be attached to this licence.

(4) *A " short term " licence* of any of the above 3 classes of licence may be granted so as to allow goods vehicles to be used temporarily. On applications for licences short term licences may be granted for 12 months (" A " licence), 6 months (" B " licence) or 3 months (s. 3).

The Goods Vehicles (Licences and Prohibitions) Regs., 1952, 1953 and 1957, regulate the procedure for applications for licences: the publication of a periodical statement called " Applications and Decisions " (Reg. 9); the identification of authorised vehicles (Reg. 12, see later); the fees for licences (Reg. 19); the production of licences (Reg. 18, see later); the transfer of an authorised vehicle (Reg. 21); appeals to the Transport Tribunal (Reg. 23) and the currency period of carriers' licence (Reg. 26). The penalty for any contravention is £5 fine (Reg. 2).

The Chairman of the Licensing Authority of the area will grant these licences (s. 4). He will have discretion to grant or refuse or vary " A " and " B " licences, but he must grant " C " licences unless the applicants' licences have been suspended or revoked (ss. 6, 7).

Applications shall be made on the prescribed forms. Notices of applications for " A " and " B " licences will be published in " Applications and Decisions " and persons already providing transport facilities may submit objections (s. 11).

See also R.T. Act, 1956, s. 43 (2) respecting objections.

1933 Act. A licence will authorise the use of specified motor vehicles, or of a maximum number of motor vehicles and trailers (s. 2 (6)). No vehicle may be specified at the same time in more than one licence (s. 2 (8)). A person may hold two or more licences of the same or different classes (s. 2 (9)). A licence is personal to the licensee.

The holder of a licence shall produce it for examination when required to do so by any constable or examiner or person authorised by the licensing authority and may elect whether to produce it at his base, head office or principal place of business (Reg. 18).

Licences shall be subject to the following conditions (ss. 8, 9).

(1) The authorised vehicles shall be maintained in a fit and serviceable condition.

(2) The law as to speed, weight and loading shall be complied with.

(3) The law as to the hours of duty and rest of drivers shall be observed.

(4) The provisions as to keeping of records shall be complied with.

It will also be a condition of all " A " and " B " licences that the law as to fair wages and conditions of employment shall be complied with. As stated above, special conditions may be attached to " B " licences. Failure to comply with a condition shall be an offence (s. 9).

The licensing authority may revoke or suspend licences for breach of conditions of the licence (s. 13). There is a right of appeal to the Transport Tribunal (1933 Act, s. 15, and 1947 Act, s. 73).

See 1956 R.T. Act, ss. 43, 44, regarding the conditions of carrier's licences and the suspension or revocation of " A " and " B " licences.

Examiners of goods vehicles.—" Examiners " shall be appointed to see that goods vehicles are maintained in a fit and serviceable condition and to secure the observance of the provisions of the Road Traffic Act, 1930, and of the R. & R.T. Act, 1933.

An examiner may enter and inspect any goods vehicle and for that purpose may detain the vehicle, and he may at any time which is reasonable, enter any premises on which he has reason to believe that a goods vehicle is kept. It will be an offence to obstruct him in the performance of his duty.

For good reason he may prohibit (by written notice) the use of a goods vehicle on a road for the carriage of goods, and any disobedience of such a prohibition will be an offence (s. 17).

He has the same power in the case of goods vehicles as a constable under the R.T. Act, 1930, to require the production of documents (driving licences, s. 4, and insurance certificates, s. 40) and the giving of information (ss. 40, 113) by persons driving motor vehicles (R. T. Act, 1930). He also has power to require a vehicle to be weighed, under s. 27 of the R.T. Act, 1930 (s. 18). A certifying officer shall have the same powers and duties as an " examiner " (s. 19).

Keeping of records.—Current records shall be kept by holders of licences and these current records shall show :—

(a) as respects every driver and attendant the times at which he commenced and ceased work and particulars of intervals of rest ;

(b) as respects every journey of a vehicle on which goods are carried under the licence, particulars of the journey and of the greatest weight of goods carried and the description and destination of the goods carried.

The forms and keeping of these records are prescribed by the

Goods Vehicles (Keeping of Records) Regs., 1935, which direct
that drivers shall carry these records and make entries therein.
Partial exemption is allowed in the case of vehicles used in the
business of agriculture or of a travelling showman, and dispensa-
tions may be granted in particular cases.

Each record shall be preserved for three months, or longer if the
Chief Officer of Police or the licensing authority so direct, and it
shall be produced for inspection when so required by any person
authorised by them (s. 16 as amended by 2nd Sched. Emergency
Laws (Transitional Provisions) Act, 1946).

Regulations under this s. 16 may contain exemptions and
requirements (R.T. Act, 1956, Sched. 8 (30)).

A police constable and an examiner may at any time require
the person in charge of any goods vehicle to produce and permit
him to inspect and copy any document which must be carried on
the vehicle under the Act or Regulations, and may detain the
vehicle for such time as is required for the purpose. Failure to
obey will be an offence (s. 18).

Identification of authorised vehicles.—The vehicles authorised to be used under a carrier's (goods) licence will be specified
either particularly or the maximum number in the licence, and
Reg. 12 of the Licence and Prohibitions Regs., 1952, directs
that:—

A holder of a licence shall be issued an identity certificate in
respect of each vehicle authorised to be used under his licence.
During the time a vehicle is operated under the licence, a
valid identity certificate shall be affixed to the vehicle in a
water-proof container on the left or near side of the vehicle, or
on left side of windscreen or to any general trade plate at front
or rear.

The certificate for a trailer can be on the trailer or on the
drawing vehicle.

Identity certificates bear the date of expiry, and for " A "
licences the letter A in red, and " B " licences the letter B in
blue.

Offences and Penalties.—*Goods Vehicles.*—It is a misdemeanour punishable on indictment (2 years) or summarily (4
months and (or) £100 fine) to forge, alter, or allow to be used
by another, any licence, or any document, plate or mark by
which an authorised vehicle is to be identified, or to have anything
so closely resembling a licence, document, plate or mark as to be
calculated to deceive, or to alter an entry made in a record
under s. 16 of the Act. It is also an offence knowingly to make
any false statement for the purpose of obtaining the grant or
variation of a licence.

On reasonable belief that an offence, as above, has been committed in relation to any document or plate carried on a motor

vehicle or by its driver, a constable or examiner may seize the document or plate, and take proceedings (s. 34).

An offence under the Act is punishable summarily by fine.

Contravention of any regulation made under the Act may be made punishable summarily by fine not exceeding £20 (s. 35).

Heavy Goods Vehicles.—A " heavy goods vehicle " is a vehicle which is constructed or adapted for hauling or carrying goods or burden of any description and which is a heavy or light locomotive, a motor tractor, a heavy motor car or a motor car so constructed that it may take a partly superimposed trailer and bear a substantial part of its weight (R.T. Act, 1934, s. 31).

A person shall not drive a heavy goods vehicle on a road unless he is licensed for the purpose under this s. 31 or is licensed to drive single deck public service vehicles and it would be an offence to employ a person not so licensed to drive a heavy goods vehicle on a road (s. 31), but this has been suspended until further Order by s. 8, Emergency Laws (Miscellaneous Provisions) Act, 1953. A steersman is exempt from licence (Road Traffic (Driving Licences) Act, 1936).

However, the requirement does not apply to the driving of vehicles used exclusively for agricultural purposes and on which the reduced excise duty of £2 has been paid.

These licences would be grantable by the Traffic Commissioners of the area. Tests may be imposed, provisional licences for 3 months may be issued (1936 Act, and see also Sched. 8 (38), R.T. Act, 1956), and a licence may be for 3 years, unless it is sooner suspended or revoked for misconduct as a driver or for physical disability. An aggrieved person may appeal to the local Magistrates' Court (s. 31).

This licence is in addition to the necessary motor driving licence. The grant of these licences under s. 31 is regulated by the Heavy Goods Vehicles (Drivers' Licences) Regs., 1936, 1938, under which the holder shall forthwith sign his licence, and on request of any police constable or person duly authorised he shall produce it for examination or state the address at which it will be available during the next five days, on penalty of fine, but these Regs. are suspended as the holder of a Driving Licence (Group A) may drive any heavy goods vehicle (Road Vehicles and Drivers Order, 1952).

Mechanically Propelled Vehicles.—In the interests of the public and of the State every mechanically propelled vehicle used on the roads comes under legal regulation in many ways. As indicated in Chapter 24 such vehicles are classified and speed limits are prescribed ; driving licences are necessary and the use of such vehicles must be insured against third party risks. From the steam-driven heavy locomotive to the motor scooter, all have to contribute (unless specially exempted) to the revenue.

The Vehicles (Excise) Act, 1949, imposes excise duties and provides for their collection. In addition, the Act directs that they should be registered and licensed, and that they should carry excise licences and identification (registration) marks.

This Act repealed the relevant parts of various Finance Acts (1940 to 1948) and of the Roads Act, 1920, but orders and regulations made under such Acts in force at the commencement of the Act, continue in force as if made under the Act (s. 30).

The Road Vehicles (Registration and Licensing) Regulations, 1955, repealed all similar previous regulations.

For the purposes of these Regulations

" Bicycle " means a mechanically propelled bicycle (including a motor scooter, a bicycle with attachment for propelling it mechanically and a motor bicycle used for drawing a trailer or sidecar) not exceeding eight cwt. unladen.

" Invalid carriage " means a mechanically propelled vehicle (including a cycle with attachment for propelling it mechanically) not exceeding 5 cwt. unladen, and adapted and used for an invalid or invalids.

" Owner " as regards a vehicle means the person by whom the vehicle is kept and used.

" Pedestrian controlled vehicle " means a mechanically propelled vehicle with 3 or more wheels, not exceeding 8 cwt. unladen and neither made nor adapted for use nor used for the carriage of a driver or passenger.

" Tricycle " means a mechanically propelled tricycle (including a motor scooter and a tricycle with attachment for mechanical propulsion) not exceeding 8 cwts. unladen and not being a pedestrian controlled vehicle.

" Works truck " means a mechanically propelled vehicle designed for use in private premises and used on a road only in passing from one part of any such premises to another or to other private premises in the immediate neighbourhood (Reg. 1).

The Road Traffic Act, 1930, provides for their construction and use, and empowers the Minister of Transport and Civil Aviation to make regulations for the purpose.

The law on these matters is summarised as follows:—

1. Registration of Vehicles.—By s. 1 of the Vehicles (Excise) Act, 1949, mechanically propelled vehicles used on public roads must pay excise duties and persons keeping them take out appropriate licences.

Such duties are to be levied by the County and County Borough Councils (s. 8 and R.T.A., 1930, s. 77). See Road Vehicles (Excise Duties and Licences) Orders, 1953 and 1957.

Every person applying for such licence must make a declaration and furnish the prescribed particulars to the Council (s. 9).

On the first issue of such a licence, the Council concerned must register the vehicle and assign it a registration mark (s. 16) which must be fixed on the vehicle or on any other vehicle drawn by it or on both in the prescribed manner (s. 17) and which will attach to the vehicle until it is broken up, destroyed or sent permanently out of Great Britain (R. and L. Regs., 1955, Reg. 14).

The owner of a vehicle who requires a licence shall apply on the prescribed declaration form either to the Council in whose area the vehicle will be ordinarily kept, or where the owner has not previously obtained or had transferred to him a licence for the vehicle, to the Council in whose area the vehicle is. In any case the Council of the area in which the vehicle is to be ordinarily kept will get all the records and the motor vehicle will be registered in its Register (Regs. 2 and 3).

Such owner (except the owner of a tramcar) will receive a registration book containing particulars as to the vehicle. This book must not be altered, defaced, etc., and must be produced at any reasonable time for inspection by a police officer or local taxation officer (Reg. 6).

If the character or use of a vehicle is altered so as to necessitate a higher rate of duty, the owner must make out a new declaration and send it with registration book and licence to the Council concerned (Reg. 8).

If any other alteration is made in a vehicle affecting the particulars given in the last declaration made regarding the vehicle, the owner must notify same in writing to the Council concerned, sending also the registration book (Reg. 7).

On the sale or change of ownership of vehicle, the then owner must give the registration book to the new owner, and also notify in writing the change of ownership to the Council which has last registered the vehicle. The new owner, if he does not intend to use the vehicle on the roads, must notify in writing the Council concerned of the change of ownership, but if he intends to use the vehicle on the roads he must insert his name and address in the registration book and give it to the Council concerned and if he has not been given the current licence he must take out a licence. Where the vehicle is to be used under a trade licence and trade plates this notification is not necessary for three months, unless in the meantime the vehicle has been transferred to a new owner. The Council will return the book to him direct, or, if the vehicle is to be kept in the area of another Council, through that other Council, which will register the vehicle in its register (Reg. 9 as amended by 1957 and 1958 Regs.).

On a change of address the owner must enter his new address in the registration book and send the book to the Council concerned (Reg. 10).

When a vehicle is broken up, destroyed, or sent permanently out of Great Britain the owner must notify the Council concerned and send it the registration book (Reg. 11).

If a registration book is lost, destroyed, mutilated, defaced or illegible, the owner must apply to the Council concerned for a duplicate. Where a duplicate has been issued to replace a lost book, and the book is found later on, the owner must take all reasonable steps to regain it and return it to the Council (Reg. 12). Every Council must keep a " Register " (Reg. 19) and an extract from it certified as true by the official in charge is admissible in evidence (Evidence Act, 1851, s. 14).

A Council on application shall supply full particulars concerning any vehicle registered with it, to the police, to any other licensing authority, or in connection with parking place functions, to any other local authority or to the Customs and Excise—free, and shall supply to any person showing reasonable cause the name and address of the owner and the particulars of the last licence—1s. fee (Reg. 27 as amended by 1958 Regs.).

Where a mechanically propelled vehicle is exempt from licence duty, any licence issued is marked " Nil," but in the case of such vehicle used exclusively on private roads, the owner must make the usual declaration, and he will get a registration book but not a licence (Reg. 33).

It is a summary offence to supply false or misleading particulars in any declaration for a licence or in any notification to a Council regarding any change in registration (1949 Act, ss. 9, 16). It is also a summary offence to forge, fraudulently alter or use, or fraudulently lend or allow to be used by any other person any identification mark or licence or registration book under the Act (1949 Act, s. 21).

2. Licensing of Vehicles.—Vehicles (Excise) Act 1949. All mechanically propelled vehicles used on a public road, (that is a road repairable at the public expense, s. 27) except those vehicles specially exempted, must pay excise duties. These duties are to be paid upon licences to be taken out by the persons keeping same (s. 1). These licences are either general trade licences, limited trade licences or ordinary road fund licences (see later). The particulars to be furnished on application for such licences are given in the Road Vehicles (Excise) (Prescribed Particulars) Regs., 1957.

It is an excise offence for any person to use on a public road any such vehicle for which a licence is not in force (s. 15).

Where it is alleged that an unlicensed vehicle has been used on a public road, the owner shall give any information required by police or Council as to the driver and any person using the vehicle, and any other person if so required shall give any information he can give as to the identity of the driver or user. Failure to comply with above will be a summary offence (s. 15).

The licence is issued for the vehicle specified in the application and does not entitle the licensee to use any other vehicle (s. 9).

R. and L. Regs., 1955. If the character or use of a vehicle is

altered so as to render a higher rate of duty payable, the owner
must make a fresh declaration and will receive an amended
licence (Reg. 8).

If any alteration is made in a vehicle which affects the registration particulars, the owner shall notify the Council and send his
registration book for amendment. If it affects the licence, the
licence should be sent to the Council for an amended licence
(Reg. 7).

When a licence has been taken out for a vehicle, and the
vehicle is used in an altered condition or in a manner or for a
purpose which renders it chargeable for a higher rate of duty the
person so using such vehicle is liable to an excise penalty (s. 13).
However, the duty at a higher rate is not chargeable unless the
vehicle as used satisfies all the conditions which would bring it
into the class or description liable to the higher rate of duty (s. 13).

On sale or change of ownership, the former owner may deliver
the licence, which is transferable with the vehicle. If this is not
done the new owner must take out a licence for the vehicle
(Reg. 9 as amended by R.V.L. Regs., 1957 and 1958).

Upon or not more than fourteen days before the expiration of
a licence, application may be made either to the Council or to
an authorised post office within the area, on the prescribed
form, for a renewal of the licence, and the certificate of insurance
shall be produced. However, renewal cannot be made at a
post office (i) after 14 days from the date of expiry; (ii) unless the
old licence is delivered up to the post office; (iii) to a person who
lets such vehicles on hire if the vehicle in question is to be used
solely for hiring out to be driven by the hirer or his agents (Reg.
17 as amended by R.V. (R. & L.) (A.) Regs., 1957). However,
licences for tractors and goods vehicles are issued by County
Councils (1953 Amendment Regs.).

The following mechanically propelled vehicles are exempt
from excise duty by s. 7, Vehicles (Excise) Act, 1949:—

> Fire engines ; vehicles kept by a local authority while being
> used for the purposes of their fire brigade service; ambulances;
> road rollers ; vehicles used on tram lines not being tram cars
> used for passengers; vehicles used solely for haulage of lifeboats
> and their gear; vehicles not exceeding 5 cwt. used for invalids;
> road construction vehicles used solely for such machinery on
> public roads ; vehicles used for clearing snow from public
> roads by snow ploughs ; vehicles brought into Great Britain
> for the time being licensed under s. 13, Finance Act, 1920, or
> s. 9, Roads Act, 1920, in their application to Northern Ireland
> and " foreign " vehicles whose owners are making only a
> temporary stay (M.V. (International Circulation) Act, 1952,
> s. 30).

Application must be made and a registration book and licence marked " Nil '' is issued to be carried in the prescribed manner (R. & L. Regs., 1955, Reg. 33).

In the case of vehicles belonging to the Crown (except those used or appropriated for use for naval, military or air force purposes) declaration must be made, the vehicle is registered and given a registration mark. Registration books are not issued nor are licences. Every such vehicle shall carry a Certificate of Crown ownership. In the case of vehicles used exclusively on roads not repairable at the public expense and vehicles to be used on public roads solely in passing from land occupied by the owners to other land also occupied by the owners and for distances not exceeding a total of six miles in any week if so authorised by the Minister (s. 7 of 1949 Act), a declaration must be made and a registration book issued but no licence (Reg. 33).

A licence may be taken out for one calendar year or for one, two or three quarterly periods, but no licence lasts longer than December 31 of the year. The quarters of the year normally end on March 24, June 30, Sept. 30 and Dec. 31 (Road Vehicles (Part Year Licensing) Order, 1957).

Authorised trade goods vehicles exceeding 11 tons weight unladen may have short term road fund licences.

The holder of a licence can surrender it and claim a refund of duty (s. 12). Duty paid may also be refunded on proof of non-user of the vehicle on public roads (R. & L. Regs., 1955, Reg. 28).

The council may require proof that the vehicle accords with the declaration made (Reg. 15) and may require proof of the unladen weight of a vehicle (Reg. 16).

3. Trade Licences.—These are special licences issued at lower rates to motor traders, viz. manufacturers, repairers, or dealers in mechanically propelled vehicles (Vehicles (Excise) Act, 1949, s. 10). A person who has a business wholly or mainly of collecting and delivering motor vehicles and not including any other activities except as manufacturer, repairer or dealer in motor vehicles shall be deemed to be a dealer in mechanically propelled vehicles (Finance Act, 1952, s. 7). With such licences, special plates are supplied and when same are carried no other registration mark or licence is necessary. (R. & L. Regs., 1955, Part II, Regs., 29, 30).

Trade licences are of two kinds—the General Trade Licence and the Limited Trade Licence.

The following rules apply to both kinds of trade licences.

A trade licence contains :—

(1) Name and address of the person so licensed.
(2) Number of identification plate allotted.
(3) Date of expiry of licence.
(4) Amount of duty paid.
(5) Date stamp of office of issue.
(6) Serial number of licence.

This trade licence must be carried in a holder attached to the supplied plate fixed in front of the vehicle, so as to be clearly visible at all times by daylight from the front of the vehicle when in use on a public road under that trade licence.

A trade licence must not be used by any person other than the person to whom it was issued, who must not allow or suffer it to be used by any other person. But no offence under this article is committed if the licensee or a person in his employment and acting under authority is present and in charge of the vehicle or if it is a one-person machine being used by a prospective purchaser for test or trial. A trade licence must not be used on a vehicle other than a mechanically propelled vehicle which is in the possession of the licensee in the course of his business as maker, dealer, etc., or is a mechanically propelled vehicle which is for the time being laid up by its owner, and it must never be used on a vehicle which is being used for the conveyance of passengers for profit or reward.

A trade licence may be taken out by a motor trader in pursuance of s. 10 of the Act in respect of—

(a) all vehicles used by him or

(b) all vehicles used by him of the classes liable to duty under s. 2 of the Act (mechanically propelled vehicles not exceeding 8 cwt. unladen such as bicycles, tricycles, etc.) (R. & L. Regs., 1955, Regs., 29, 30).

It should be noted that the lending or hiring out of trade plates is illegal. One or more trade licences of either or both kinds may be taken out, but only one vehicle may be on the road at any time under one licence.

If the holder of a trade licence or licences uses on a public road under trade licences at any one time a greater number of vehicles than authorised by his licence or licences, he will commit a summary offence with excise penalty (1949 Act, s. 15).

One trade plate for front and one for rear of a vehicle are issued with each trade licence. They are the property of the Council and should be returned on expiry of the licence. The holder of a trade licence should notify the Council of any change of address. If trade plates are used (and they must be fixed in the manner prescribed for registration marks) on a vehicle no other registration mark need be carried (Regs., 29, 30).

The special plates are lent by the Council and are either red or white (as described later). At present they are rectangular or square in form, and each plate bears a crown and " G.R. " or " E.R. " in a circle in the top right-hand corner. The letters on them must be those of the index mark allotted to the Council which issues the licence. The numbering will consist of four figures, the series running from 0001 to 0999. The square plate has the number at the top and the letters below, and may be used only on cycles or invalid carriages. The rectangular plate has the figures first, then the letters, all in line, and may be used on any vehicle.

Trade licences are of two kinds :—

(1) General Trade Licence.—It is subject to the rules given above. This licence shall not be used on a vehicle on a public road except for the purposes given in Reg. 29 of the 1955 Regs.—viz.—

(1) moving a laid up motor vehicle to another place of storage;

(2) on a motor vehicle, with or without trailer, for any purpose connected with the business of maker, repairer or dealer in motor vehicles of the holder;

(3) on a motor vehicle drawing a trailer in connection with any business as a maker, repairer or dealer in trailers, carried on by the licensee in conjunction with his business as maker, repairer or dealer in motor vehicles;

(4) with or without a trailer whilst the motor vehicle is *bona fide* being used for any of the said purposes for any other additional purpose of the holder of the licence.

General trade licence plates are signal red in colour, and all letters and figures thereon and a half-inch border all round the plate are white in colour.

There are two forms of general trade licence, viz. :—

(*a*) That for all vehicles used by the licensee.

It costs £25. It is rectangular in shape and is carried in a rectangular holder fixed above the top of the rectangular front plate on cars, or in centre of square front plate on cycles. It is marked " G.T.P."

(*b*) That for all cycles under 8 cwt., tricycles and invalid carriages.

It costs £5. It is trapezoidal in shape and is carried in a trapezoidal-shaped holder in the centre of the square front plate. It is marked " G.T.P. for cycles and invalid carriages."

(2) Limited Trade Licence.—This licence is granted subject to the rules which apply to both kinds of trade licences. The holder may use it on a public road on a motor vehicle with or without a trailer for one or more of the following ten purposes:—

(1) Test or trial during or after construction or repair.

(2) Proceeding to or from a public weighbridge or any place for registration or inspection by a Council.

(3) Test or trial for a prospective purchaser.

(4) Delivery to a purchaser.

(5) Delivery to another maker, dealer or repairer. or *vice versa*.

(6) Proceeding to or from a workshop for work thereon.

(7) Towing or carrying a vehicle broken down on a road or towing a trolley vehicle.

(8) Proceeding to or from a railway station. aerodrome or wharf for shipment, etc.

(9) Proceeding to or from a storage place or saleroom.

(10) Taking a laid-up vehicle from one storage place to another.

Nothing in the above provisions shall authorise the use of a vehicle or its trailer under a Limited Trade Licence if the duplicate entries (see later) are not properly completed and carried on the vehicle or for any of the following purposes :—

(a) To carry any person other than the driver (or 2 drivers if a steam vehicle) or an authorised inspector or one person in a broken down vehicle which is being towed or not more than 2 other persons each of whom is either the holder of the licence or his employee necessarily present, or a prospective purchaser or his nominee, who is in either case carried on the vehicle itself and not on any trailer drawn thereby.

(b) To carry any goods or load in the course of trade or for delivery or removal, but a load of ballast (sand, scrap, etc.) may be carried for the purpose of testing the vehicle, but a partly superimposed trailer will not be a " load " nor will a vehicle broken down on a road be a " load" and " goods " will not include goods not carried for hire or reward in new vehicles in course of delivery to a purchaser or for export (R. & L. Regs., 1955, Reg. 30).

" Trailer " in this Regulation 30 does not include a mechanically propelled vehicle unless it is one which is authorised to be carried by the mechanically propelled vehicle by which it is drawn and no other trailer is drawn by that vehicle.

The holder of a limited trade licence is liable for any contravention (even if it is contrary to his orders) by his servants of the Regs. or of the conditions under which this licence is taken out (*Griffiths* v. *Studebakers* (1923)).

The holder of a limited trade licence will be supplied by the Council with a book in which particulars of the use of the licence on each occasion must be entered in duplicate before the licence is so used. One copy of the entry must be carried in the vehicle during the whole of the journey (as stated above) and one copy must remain in the book. This book, as also the duplicate entries, must be produced at all reasonable times for inspection by any police or local taxation officer. It is an offence to deface, mutilate, alter, falsify, or obliterate any entry in the book or in the copy carried on the vehicle, or to make any false or misleading entry therein (Reg. 30).

Limited trade licence plates are pure white in colour, and all the letters and figures thereon and a half-inch border all round are signal red in colour.

There are two forms of limited trade licences, viz. :—

(a) That for all vehicles used by the licensee.

It costs £5. It is triangular in shape and is carried in a triangular holder fixed above the top of the rectangular front plate on cars, or in the centre of the square front plate on cycles. It is marked " L.T.P."

(b) That for all cycles (under 8 cwt.), tricycles and invalid carriages.

It costs £1. It is diamond-shaped and is carried in a diamond-shaped holder in the centre of the square front plate. It is marked " L.T.P. for cycles and invalid carriages.'

4. Excise Motor Licence.—This licence (formerly called the Road Fund Licence) under the Act shall in the prescribed manner be fixed to and exhibited on the vehicle in respect to which it is issued (Vehicles (Excise) Act, 1949, s. 9 and R. & L. Regs., 1955, Reg. 4).

The licence has entered upon it :—

(1) The registration mark of the vehicle.

(2) Horse-power and seating capacity or weight unladen (or the letters " MAX.").

(3) Class and make of the vehicle.

(4) Amount of duty paid (or the word " Nil ").

(5) Name of licensing authority and date of issue (Reg. 13). It will also show the date on which it expires.

In the case of all mechanically propelled vehicles (except tramcars) it must be attached to and carried on the vehicle at all times when the vehicle is in use on a public road (Reg. 4).

Position of Licence :—

(1) Bicycles, motor scooters, bicycles with trailers, tricycles and invalid carriages—on near side in front of driving seat.

(2) Bicycles with side-car—on near side of handle-bar or on near side of combination in front of driving seat.

(3) Pedestrian controlled vehicles—on near side of vehicle.

(4) All other vehicles (except when on or near windscreen)— on near side, facing to near side of road, between two parallel lines as prescribed and not less than 2½ feet or more than 6½ feet from the ground.

It must be clearly visible at all times by daylight to a person standing at the near side of the vehicle.

It must be carried in a metal weather-proof holder (circular or rectangular with cross-bars) with cover of transparent white glass. However, if the front glass wind-screen extends to the near side, the licence may be carried facing forwards at the near lower corner of wind-screen, either in a holder within 2 inches of the screen before or behind it, or in a weather-proof container upon the screen, so as to be clearly visible from in front at all times by daylight (Reg. 4, and 2nd Schedule).

No person shall alter, deface, mutilate or add anything to any such licence, or exhibit on a vehicle any licence which has been altered, defaced, mutilated, or added to, or upon which the particulars have become illegible or the colour altered by fading or otherwise, or exhibit any colourable imitation of a licence (Reg. 5).

If a licence is lost, destroyed, mutilated, defaced, illegible, or altered, the owner must procure a duplicate from the Council. If a lost licence is found after a duplicate has been issued the owner must take all reasonable steps to regain it and return it to the Council (R. & L. Regs., 1955, Reg. 12).

Where from any cause a licence becomes void otherwise than by effluxion of time, it shall at once be delivered up to the Council where the vehicle was last registered (Reg. 18). A licence for the next period issued in advance may at once be exhibited on the vehicle (Reg. 4). Using an unlicensed vehicle is an excise offence (1949 Act, s. 15). For fraudulent use of road fund licence see " Registration of vehicles " above.

5. Identification or Registration Mark.—Under the Vehicles (Excise) Act, 1949, the mark indicating the Council with which a mechanically propelled vehicle is first registered (the index mark consisting of one or more letters) and the registered number of the vehicle (one or more figures) must be fixed on the vehicle in the prescribed manner (s. 17). If this mark is not so fixed, or if, being so fixed, it is in any way obscured or rendered or allowed to become not easily distinguishable, the driver is liable to summary fine (s. 19). However, a driver charged with obscuring, etc., such mark is not liable to conviction if he proves he has taken all reasonable steps to prevent it being obscured. Also, a driver is not liable to the penalty if he proves he had no reasonable opportunity of registering the vehicle and was driving it on a public road for the purpose of registering it (s. 19).

A registration mark is assigned to a vehicle and not to its owner, and it attaches to that vehicle until the same is broken up, destroyed or sent permanently out of Great Britain (R. & L. Regs., 1955, Reg. 14), or until it is transferred to another vehicle by special arrangement with the licensing authority.

It is an offence to forge or fraudulently alter or use or fraudulently lend or allow to be used by any other person any mark for identifying a vehicle (1949 Act, s. 21).

Shape and Position.—The registration mark consists of the index mark and the registration number, and it must be shown on a flat rectangular plate or on a flat unbroken rectangular surface forming part of the vehicle (R. & L. Regs., 1955, Reg. 21).

The registration mark shall be exhibited on the front and back of the vehicle in a vertical position so that the letters and figures thereon shall be easily distinguishable, except in the case of a works truck when the mark shall be vertical on both sides or on the back of the vehicle.

An invalid carriage, a pedestrian controlled vehicle and a bicycle may have the front registration mark on a flat plate with duplicate faces (see 3rd Sched.) fixed on the vehicle in a vertical position or may have it on both sides of the vehicle on flat surface of the front mud-guard (Reg. 22).

However, the rules as regards vehicles registered for the first time on or after Oct. 1, 1938 not being works trucks are as follows:

(a) The registration mark shall be exhibited on the front and rear of the vehicle.

(b) The front registration mark on a bicycle, pedestrian controlled vehicle or invalid carriage must be vertical on both sides of a plate on the vehicle, so as to be easily distinguishable from both sides of the vehicle. The rear mark should be easily distinguishable in normal daylight by an observer more than 10 ft. and not more than 60 ft. distant.

(c) In all other cases the front and rear marks shall be exhibited so as to be easily distinguishable in normal daylight by an observer more than 10 ft. and not more than 75 ft. distant from directly in front or rear (R. & L. Regs., 1955, Reg. 26).

During the hours of darkness the rear identification mark (except that of a works truck) must be illuminated (Regs., 25, 26). See " Lights on Vehicles," Chap. 24.

No other figures or letters and no design or ornamentation shall be placed near the registration mark in such a manner as to be liable to render it more difficult to read or distinguish the identification mark of the vehicle when in motion (R. & L. Regs., 1955, Regs. 22 and 26).

When one or more vehicles are attached, either in front or behind the vehicle, the registration mark (or a duplicate) must be exhibited on the front of the foremost and on the rear of the rearmost vehicle. However in the case of vehicles drawn by a " restricted vehicle " (an agricultural vehicle, 1949 Act, s. 4 (2), or a vehicle passing for short distances from land to land owned by same owner, 1949 Act, s. 7 (4)), the rearmost vehicle can carry the registration mark of any other restricted vehicle owned by the same owner (R. &. L Regs., 1955, Reg. 23).

The letters allocated are given in the Road Vehicles (Index Marks) Regs., 1951, 1955 and 1959.

Form and Description.—The registration mark should be a flat plate or on a flat part of the vehicle (Reg. 21). It may be in either of the shapes prescribed by diagram, viz. the index letters may be either above or below or to the left or right of the registration figures. Each letter or figure shall be 3½ in. high, ⅝ in. broad, and take up (except the figure 1) 2½ in. width.

There shall be ½ in. space between each adjoining letter or figure and also from each letter or figure to the edge of the top or bottom of the black surface, and there shall be a margin of 1 in. between the sides of the black surface and the nearest letter or figure.

If the letters are above or below the figures, the distance must be ¾ in. and if the letters are on the left or right of the figures, there shall be a space of 1½ in. between.

In the case of invalid carriages, pedestrian controlled vehicles and bicycles, as regards the front registration mark, the above dimensions may be halved, but as regards the rear registration mark the dimensions are about two-thirds the size of those on cars and must not be less than the following. All letters and figures shall be 2½ in. high, ⅜ in. broad, and take up (except the figure 1) 1¾ in. width. There shall be ½ in. space between each adjoining letter or figure and ½ in. margin from any letter or figure to the edge of the top, bottom and sides of the black surface. If the letters are above or below the figures the distance should be ½ in., and if the letters are on the left or right side the figures there should be a space of 1 in. between.

The registration mark may be so constructed that it can be illuminated by transparency or translucency (viz. light can shine through). If so, the letters and figures of the front mark, when illuminated, shall appear white, and those of the rear mark shall appear white or red. See " Lights on Vehicles," Chap. 24. At all other times the letters and figures must appear white (or silver or light grey) against a black background.

If the registration mark is not so constructed, the letters and figures must be indelibly inscribed or so attached as not to be readily detachable, in white (or silver or light grey), upon a black surface. A flat plate of cast or pressed metal having raised letters and figures may be used (R. & L. Regs., 1955, Reg. 21 and 3rd Sched.).

The registration mark supplied with a general trade licence is on a red plate, the letters and figures being white. That attached to a limited trade licence is on a white plate, the letters and figures being red. Such " trade " vehicles need not carry the ordinary registration marks (Reg. 29). See "Trade Licences."

A mechanically propelled hackney carriage (used for carrying passengers for hire), must, in addition to the registration mark, carry a distinctive sign indicating that it is a hackney carriage and the number of persons it seats (1949 Act, s. 18).

This applies when the rate of duty paid is less than the rate of duty payable had the vehicle been licensed as a private vehicle.

It does not apply to a tramcar, or to a vehicle licensed by a Local Authority to ply for hire, which carries an outside mark, as prescribed by the Local Authority, indicating that it is a hackney vehicle licensed for public hire. See " Hackney Carriages."

If the hackney vehicle is temporarily adapted for and used solely for the conveyance of goods in the course of trade, the distinctive sign need not be displayed while the vehicle is being so used (Reg. 31).

This distinctive hackney carriage sign consists of a semi-circular black mark, having a white, silver or light grey border and the words " Hackney Carriage . . . Seats " in white non-detachable letters. It must bear a number indicating the seating capacity of the vehicle. This mark may be on a plate or on the flat surface of the vehicle. It must be placed on the back of the vehicle: it must be vertical and must be clearly visible at all times (R. & L. Regs., 1955, Reg. 31 and 4th Schedule).

6. Foreign-Owned Motor Vehicles.—The Motor Vehicles (International Circulation) Order 1957, made under M.V. (I.C.) Act of 1952, came into operation on the 7 August 1957 and contains provisions affecting motor vehicles and drivers from abroad. Persons resident outside the United Kingdom who hold a Convention Driving Permit or a Domestic Driving Permit may for one year drive in Great Britain motor vehicles of the class they are authorized by their permits to drive without holding driving licences issued under the R.T. Act 1930. Such persons may for one year drive public service or heavy goods vehicles brought temporarily into Great Britain which they are authorized by their permits to drive without holding public service or heavy goods vehicle driving licences, and, if over 18, may drive heavy motor vehicles temporarily brought into Great Britain, even though they may be under 21 (Art. 2).

Under the Motor Vehicles (International Circulation) Regulations 1957, Registration Authorities (R.A.C., A.A., R.S.A.C. or London County Council) may grant an international circulation permit for certain motor vehicles brought temporarily into Great Britain by persons resident outside the United Kingdom who comply with certain requirements (Reg. 1). This permit may last 90 days (Reg. 2). It must be carried in a holder on the vehicle in the same manner as an excise licence (Reg. 3).

On the expiry of the permit or if such vehicle is destroyed, transferred to another or is removed from this country, the permit shall be surrendered to a Registration Authority (Reg. 4).

A registration authority may allow the vehicle to retain the identification mark of its own country, otherwise the identification mark will be QA, QB, etc., and a registered number. A registration mark need not be exhibited at the front of the vehicle if that is not required by the law under which, or the authority by whom, the registration mark was issued. A nationality sign shall be exhibited on the back of the vehicle, except vehicles registered by the British Authorities in Germany or the United States authorities in Germany or France (Reg. 5).

Where a registration authority assigns to the owner an identification mark of the Q series under Reg. 5, he will also be given a registration card. This card must be surrendered with the international circulation permit if the latter is surrendered under Reg. 4. The registration card must be produced for inspection at any reasonable time on request by a police or local taxation officer. It must not be altered, defaced etc., and if it is lost, destroyed, mutilated, defaced, or becomes illegible the owner must apply for a duplicate (Reg. 6).

Excise licences may be granted for vehicles brought temporarily into Great Britain by persons who have not a principal place of business or usual place of abode in Great Britain (Reg. 7).

Contraventions of these Regulations are punishable summarily.

The use of a foreign-owned motor vehicle in this country must be duly insured in respect of third party risks in this country. The owner should have an " International Motor Insurance Card " which is to be regarded as an insurance policy covering third party risks (M.V. (International Motor Insurance Card) Regs., 1957). See " Insurance Certificates," Chap. 24.

As regards motor vehicles brought from Northern Ireland, Isle of Man, Jersey or Guernsey, they should have certificates of insurance or security complying with their own law and covering the driving of the vehicles in Great Britain. (Motor Vehicles (Third Party Risks) Regs., 1941, 1949 and Rules, 1952 and Reg. 12 of the International Motor Insurance Card Regs., 1957, contains a special provision for motor vehicles from Northern Ireland.)

A central register of foreign-owned vehicles and their specially licensed drivers is kept by the London County Council to whom the issue and surrender of such permits, licences and certificates must be reported by the Clubs and Association concerned. All convictions of such drivers must be reported to the London County Council.

The distinctive mark carried to indicate the nationality of a vehicle consists of letters in white on a black oval plate carried on the back of the vehicle. For example, A indicates Austria, GB Great Britain, and C.H. Switzerland (Confédération Helvétique).

These vehicles are exempt from the Lighting Regulations if they have two front white lights and a red rear light and comply with the Geneva Convention, 1949. See " Lights on Vehicles " Chap. 24.

They are also exempt from many of the Construction Regulations. See Appendix II.

The Public Service Vehicles (International Circulation) Regs. 1948, deal with single-decked public service vehicles brought into Great Britain (with passengers therefor) for not more than 90 days.

7. Construction and Use of Motor Vehicles and Trailers. —For the purpose of regulations dealing with their construction and use motor vehicles and their trailers have been divided into two classes—viz. wheeled vehicles and tracklaying vehicles.

The Motor Vehicles (Construction and Use) Regulations, 1955, deal mainly with wheeled vehicles.

" Wheeled " means that the whole weight of the vehicle is transmitted to the road surface by means of wheels.

" Tracklaying " means that the vehicle is so designed and constructed that its weight is transmitted to the road surface either by means of continuous tracks or by a combination of wheels and continuous tracks in such circumstances that the weight transmitted to the road surface by the tracks is not less than half the weight of the vehicle (Reg. 3 and T. 3).

Reg. 5 directs that every motor cycle and invalid carriage shall be so constructed that it is a wheeled vehicle, and that every motor vehicle and trailer shall be so constructed that it is either a wheeled vehicle or a track laying vehicle.

The Motor Vehicles (Construction and Use) (Tracklaying Vehicles) Regulations, 1955, apply to tracklaying vehicles only (T. Reg. 4).

Both Regulations contain the provision that every motor vehicle first registered before the expiration of one year from the making of any of these regulations by which the requirements as regards the construction or weight of any class or description of vehicles are varied, shall be exempt from the requirements of that regulation for a period of 5 years from the making thereof, provided it complies with any prior regulations affecting it (Reg. 4 and T. Reg. 4).

If any person uses or causes or permits the use on a road of a motor vehicle or trailer in contravention of

(1) The rules as to construction, weight and equipment of wheeled or tracklaying motor vehicles or trailers, as prescribed by the Motor Vehicles (Construction and Use) Regulations, in Part II (Regs. 5 to 58) and Part IV (Reg. 106) of the Regulations and in Part II (Regs. 5 to 39) and Part IV (Reg. 79) of the Regulations (Tracklaying), 1955, he commits an offence under s. 3, Road Traffic Act, 1930. Penalty, fine not exceeding £20, and heavier fines for second or subsequent offences (s. 113, R.T. Act, 1930).

(2) The rules governing the use of motor vehicles and trailers, as prescribed by Part III (Regs. 59 to 105) of the Regulations he commits an offence punishable by fine not exceeding £20 (Reg. 104).

(3) The rules governing the use of tracklaying motor vehicles and trailers, as prescribed by Part III (Regs. 40 to 78) of the Regulations (Tracklaying), 1955, he commits an offence punishable by fine not exceeding £20 (T. Reg. 77).

Details of the subjects of the above-mentioned regulations have been arranged alphabetically and are given in Appendix II.

Chapter XXVI
COMMUNICATIONS
Contents

Post Office.—The Post Office Act, 1953, deals with many offences in connection with the postal service, and these offences are usually prosecuted under the direction of the Postmaster-General.

The postal service is a State monopoly, and it is unlawful for any unauthorised person to carry on a letter service (ss. 3, 4).

Interference with the Postal Service.—It is a felony for any person to steal any mailbag, or to stop a mail with intent to rob or search, or to steal any postal packet (or anything out of it) in course of transmission by post (s. 52). See also " Statutory Larcenies " Chap. 14.

It is a felony to unlawfully take away or open a mail bag or unlawfully take a postal packet in course of transmission by post out of a mail bag, in transmission in any vehicle, ship or aircraft on behalf of the Post Office (s. 53). Knowingly receiving anything whose taking is felony under the Act is also felony (s. 54).

It is a misdemeanour for any person to fraudulently or wilfully detain or refuse to deliver up any postal packet or mailbag which is in course of transmission by post and ought to have been delivered to any other person, or which has been found by him or any other person (s. 55).

The wilful and malicious (with intent to injure any other person) opening or interfering with the due delivery of any postal packet which ought to have been delivered to that other person, is a misdemeanour when committed by a person not in the employment of the Post Office and who is not the parent or guardian of the person to whom the letter is addressed (s. 56).

Placing in or against any post office letter-box or telephone kiosk any dangerous, noxious or deleterious substance, or committing any injury or nuisance to same may be punished summarily or on indictment (s. 60).

Without authority affixing any notice or other thing, or painting or disfiguring any Post Office property, is a summary offence (s.61).

Any wilful obstruction or molestation of a postal official in the execution of his duty, or of the course of business in a post office, is a summary offence and the offender can be removed by any constable on demand (s. 65).

Any imitations without due authority of post office stamps, envelopes, forms and marks, also fictitious stamps are prohibited, and are summary offences (ss. 62, 63).

Without authority displaying marks on any house, box or place implying that same is an official post office, letter-box, telephone box, etc., is a summary offence (s. 64).

The forgery or larceny of money orders (or postal orders) is a felony (s. 23). See " Forgery," Chap. 17.

Prohibited Postal Packets.—Sending any postal packet containing any dangerous, noxious or deleterious substance or anything likely to injure other postal packets or any officer of the Post Office, or any indecent or obscene picture book, writing or article, or having on the outside any marks of an indecent, obscene or grossly offensive character, is a misdemeanour punishable summarily or on indictment (s. 11).

Offences by Postal Officials.—Embezzling, secreting or destroying any postal packet in course of transmission by post is a felony (s. 57).

Opening contrary to his duty any postal packet in course of transmission by post or wilfully delaying or detaining same is a misdemeanour, but the Secretary of State by warrant may direct the opening, delaying or detention of postal packets (s. 58).

Any carelessness, negligence or misconduct when in charge of a mailbag or postal packet in course of transmission by post is punishable summarily (s. 59).

Proceedings may be taken against the Crown in respect of loss or damage to a registered inland postal packet due to wrongful act, neglect or default by an agent of the Crown in dealing with the packet (Crown Proceedings Act, 1947, s. 9).

Definition.—" Postal packet " means a letter, post card, newspaper and every packet or article transmissible by post and includes a telegram (s. 87).

" In transmission by post " covers the period from the time of its being delivered to the post office to the time of its being delivered to the person to whom it is addressed (s. 87).

For " Accommodation Addresses " see " Official Secrets Acts," Chap. 20. Also see " Evidence by Certificate," Chap. 7.

It is a summary offence to use the words " Royal Mail " or " Royal Air Mail " on any premises, vehicle, etc., without authority (s. 64).

It is a summary offence to telephone any message which is grossly offensive or indecent, or menacing, or false or persistently unreasonable for the purpose of causing annoyance, etc. (s.66).

Telegraphs.—Several Telegraph Acts have dealt with the telegraph service since 1863. The Postmaster-General is now responsible for the public telegraph and telephone services, and a telegram is a " postal packet " under the Post Office Act.

Telegrams must be promptly and accurately transmitted, their contents must not be improperly disclosed, and there must be no misuse of the service.

These statutes make it an offence for :—

(1) Any person in the employment of a telegraph company—

to wilfully or negligently omit or delay to transmit or deliver any message (1863 Act, s. 45), or

to improperly divulge to any person the purport of any telegram (1863 Act, s. 45, and Post Office Protection Act, 1884, s. 11).

(2) Any person connected with the Post Office to disclose, contrary to his duty, the contents of any message entrusted to the Postmaster-General for transmission (1868 Act, s. 20). This offence may be dealt with summarily by consent (M.C. Act, 1952, s. 19 and 1st Sched.).

(3) Any person to forge or wilfully and without due authority alter a telegram, or to utter a telegram knowing same to be forged, or to transmit by telegraph as a telegram or utter as a telegram any message which he knows to be not a telegram, is a misdemeanour (punishable summarily or on indictment) whether he had or had not an intent to defraud (Post Office Protection Act, 1884, s. 11).

In such cases it is necessary to prove that the false telegram was sent with intent to deceive the person to whom it was sent. See also " Forgery," Chap. 17.

Any unlawful and malicious injury to or interference with any part of the telegraph system or any attempt to carry out any such injury or interference may be dealt with as a summary offence (Malicious Damage Act, 1861. ss. 37 and 38). See Chap. 15.

Wireless.—Wireless telegraphy means any system of communication by telegraph without the aid of any wire connecting the points from and at which the messages or other communications are sent and received.

Under the Wireless Telegraphy Act, 1949, it is an offence for any person to establish any wireless telegraphy station or install or use any apparatus for wireless telegraphy without a licence granted by the Postmaster-General (s. 1). A wireless receiving licence costs £1 and lasts one year. A wireless and television receiving licence costs £4 and lasts one year. Any person using an apparatus for interfering with any wireless telegraphy (s. 13) or uses wireless for sending false messages or for listening in without authority to other messages (s. 5) will commit an offence. The offence may be dealt with summarily, and in addition to punishment the apparatus may be forfeited (s. 14).

Proceedings shall not be taken except with the consent of the Postmaster-General.

A Justice on sworn information may issue a search warrant authorising entry and inspection of any premises, vehicle, vessel or aircraft specified and test of apparatus (s. 15). A blind person on certificate from the local county or county borough council may get a licence free (s. 2).

See Wireless Telegraphy Act, 1949 (Commencement) Order, 1954, which put ss. 1 to 8 into operation.

Railways.—Several Railway Regulation Acts provide for the protection of railway property against malicious injury and for the proper carrying out of railway traffic.

Any wilful obstruction of a railway servant in the execution of his duty or wilful trespass on railway premises is punishable summarily, and offenders may be arrested by railway officials or railway special constables (1840 and 1842 Acts). Any malicious act with intent to obstruct, upset or damage any engine, carriage or truck using a railway is a felony, and any unlawful act or wilful neglect which obstructs such engine, etc., is a misdemeanour (Malicious Damage Act, 1861, ss. 35 and 36).

Any malicious act with intent to endanger the safety of any person travelling on a railway is a felony, and any unlawful act or wilful neglect which endangers the safety of any person so travelling is a misdemeanour (Offences against the Person Act, 1861, ss. 32, 33 and 34).

Offences under the Railways Acts are as a rule dealt with by the railway police and officials of the railways concerned.

Intoxicating liquor may be sold for consumption on railway passenger vehicles without a licence from the Justices, provided that an excise licence under s. 154, Customs and Excise Act, 1952, has been taken out (Licensing Act, 1953, s. 164).

The railways were nationalised by the Transport Act, 1947, and the powers of the old companies were given to the British Transport Commission which by the Transport Act, 1953, s. 16, has to prepare a scheme for their reorganization.

As well as the general law dealt with above there is also the following special railway Act—The British Transport Commission Act, 1949.

In addition to other matters this Act allows stone throwing, etc., and trespass to be dealt with summarily (40s. fine) without the necessity of proving deliberate malice, as follows :—

(1) Unlawfully throwing or causing to fall or strike at, against, into or upon any engine, tender, motor, carriage or truck, or any works or apparatus on any railway, any wood, stone or other matter or thing likely to cause damage or injury to persons or property (s. 56).

(2) Trespassing upon any of the railway lines or upon any railway embankment or cutting or upon any other lands of the Commission in dangerous proximity to any such lines of railway or other works or to any electrical apparatus used for or in connection with the railway. But no person shall be subject to a penalty unless notices warning persons not to trespass have been placed and renewed as necessary (s. 55).

Merchant Shipping Acts.—The Merchant Shipping Act, 1894, amended by later Acts, deals with the ships and men of our merchant service.

These Acts regulate the conditions of service of the mercantile marine, dealing also with desertion and disciplinary offences.

If a sailor deserts or is absent without leave the captain, mate, owner, etc., may take him and convey him on board. If required the police are to assist, but if the sailor so requires he must first be brought before a court or magistrate (1894 Act, s. 222).

If a sailor of a fishing-boat deserts or is absent without leave the captain or owner may take him (the police, if required, assisting) before some officer who has power to issue a warrant for his arrest. An officer of the Ministry of Transport and Civil Aviation, on the information of the captain, owner or agent of a fishing-boat, may issue a warrant to arrest a sailor charged with desertion or other ship offence. This warrant lasts ninety-six hours and must be executed by the police, who will bring the sailor before the officer, who, if necessary, will send him before a Magistrates' Court (1894 Act, ss. 380 and 381).

Persons in passenger steamers who are guilty of misconduct in connection with the payment of their fares or their behaviour on board may be detained by the captain and his assistants and conveyed before a Justice to be dealt with summarily (1894 Act, s. 287). See " Drunkenness," Chap. 38.

Passenger vessels may have an excise retailer's licence for sale of intoxicants (Customs and Excise Act, 1952, s. 153).

Air Navigation.—The Civil Aviation Act, 1949, deals with this subject. If an aircraft is so flown as to be the cause of unnecessary danger to any person or property, the pilot and the owner or hirer may be convicted summarily (s. 11). Any offence under the Act or Regulations thereunder and any offence committed on a British aircraft shall be deemed to have been committed in any place where the offender may for the time being be (ss. 60, 62).

Special constables may be appointed by 2 Justices for duty as constables on premises controlled by the Minister of Transport and Civil Aviation (s. 37).

Trespassing on the land of a licensed aerodrome, if warning notices had been posted, is a summary offence (s. 38). A person shall not fly or cause or permit any other person to fly an aircraft unless there is in force a policy of insurance or a security against third party risks in relation to such flying. This will not apply if the owner is a local authority or a police authority or if the aircraft is being used for police purposes or if the presented amount has been deposited with the High Court (s. 43). The hirer of an aircraft for more than 14 days will be regarded as the owner (s. 49). This insurance is on the same lines as motor insurance and there must be certificates of insurance or security (s. 44).

S. 8 of the Act confers power to make Orders in Council regulating air navigation and for carrying out the Chicago Convention of 7 Dec., 1944, regarding international civil aviation.

Public Health (Aircraft) Regs., 1952, prescribe measures to prevent the spread of infectious diseases by aircraft.

The Air Navigation Order, 1954, as amended 1956, with some amendment orders in 1957 and 1958 has revoked all previous similar Orders and now regulates the use of aircraft. It has 76 Articles and 4 Schedules, regulating the identity, rules of the air, etc., fees and classification of aircraft. " Aircraft " includes all balloons, kites, gliders, airships and flying machines. " Airship " means an aircraft using gas lighter than air as support and having means of propulsion and control. " Flying machine " means an aircraft heavier than air and having means of mechanical propulsion. " Military aircraft " includes naval, military and air force aircraft (Art. 73). In the order the Minister of Transport and Civil Aviation is referred to as " the Minister " (Art. 73).

No aircraft shall fly in the United Kingdom unless it is registered (Art. 1) or allowed to do so by special permission of the Minister (Art. 2). The Minister registers aircraft in the United Kingdom (Art. 3 and 4), and he may cancel registration and it may become void (Arts. 5 to 7).

No aircraft shall fly unless it bears the nationality and registration marks required by the law of the country in which it is registered (Art. 8). Aircraft registered in the United Kingdom shall bear the capital letter " G " and the four capital Roman letters assigned to it by the Minister, painted, etc., on the machine and inscribed on a metal plate, with name and address of owner, affixed inside the machine (Art. 9).

No aircraft shall fly unless there is in force in respect thereof a certificate of airworthiness, except in the case of a balloon not carrying passengers for payment or a kite or an aircraft with special permit from the Minister (Arts. 11 to 16 which also deal with maintenance).

Aircraft registered in the United Kingdom are liable to inspection and modification by order of the Minister (Art. 14).

Various precautionary action as regards equipment, loading, etc., must be taken by the person in command and the pilot of an aircraft registered in the United Kingdom before it flies or attempts to fly (Arts. 17 to 20).

An aircraft shall not fly unless every member of the operating crew (pilots, flight navigators, flight engineers and radio operators (Art. 73)) holds a licence, and every member of such crew must have a licence entitling him to so act. There are some exceptions to this (Art. 21). Articles 22, 23 and 24 relate to these licences and crews.

A Student Pilot's licence may be granted by the Minister to enable the holder to qualify as pilot of a flying machine (Art. 25).

The various logbooks which must be kept in respect of an aircraft registered in the United Kingdom are given in Article 27.

Arts. 28, 29 and 30 detail the documents to be carried in such an aircraft when flying. Art. 32 gives the offences in relation to documents.

The person in command of an aircraft shall, on landing or departure, produce to an authorised person any of the following documents—certificates of registration and airworthiness, licences of operating crew, journey logbook, etc.; if engaged in international navigation a list of any passengers and their places of embarkation and destination and manifest of any goods. However, there is an allowance of 5 days within which to produce documents at a specified police station. The operator of an aircraft registered in the United Kingdom shall on demand by an authorised person, produce within a reasonable time—any certificate of registration or air-worthiness, any log-book, not being a journey logbook, etc. The holder of any licence under the order shall, on demand by an authorised person, produce the licence—however in some cases he may have 5 days within which to produce it at a specified police station. The holder of a personal flying log kept by every member of an operating crew, learner, etc. shall produce it within a reasonable time, on demand by an authorised person. " Authorised person " includes an officer of police and a person authorised in writing by the Minister (Art. 30).

No person shall with intent to deceive, forge, alter, etc., any document necessary under this Order, or use any such forged, etc., document or use one to which he is not entitled or lend any such document to another person or make false representation to procure any such document or alter, etc., any entry in any logbook or make wilfully or negligently any materially incorrect entry in a load sheet (Art. 32).

The Minister has power to restrict the flying of aircraft in any district where large numbers of persons are likely to gather or where a flying contest or exhibition is to take place or which may be used for national defence (Art. 35). Article 27 gives the restrictions on the carriage of dangerous goods.

A captive balloon shall not be flown and an airship shall not be moored anywhere and a kite shall not be flown within 3 miles of an aerodrome or elevated over 200 ft. from the ground, except with the permission of the Minister (Art. 38). No person shall commit any act likely to imperil the safety of an aircraft or of any person on board an aircraft (Art. 39). No person shall enter or be in any aircraft while in a state of intoxication and if an aircraft commences to fly carrying any such person it shall be in default (Art. 40). Smoking may be allowed in some compartments of an aircraft (Art. 41). Articles 42 and 43 deal with notices of safety precautions to be displayed and with the exits in aircraft.

No person under 17 shall have sole control of an aircraft in motion, except in the case of a glider of which no person under 16 may have sole control when in motion (Art. 46).

An aircraft registered abroad shall not take or discharge passengers or goods in the United Kingdom except by previous agreement or permission of the Minister (Art. 49).

The Minister may license an aerodrome on conditions (Art. 50) and aerial light houses must be approved by him (Art. 57) and he may take action to have extinguished or properly screened any light which is near an aerodrome or may be mistaken for an aerodrome light and which is dangerous to air navigation (Art. 58).

The Minister or an authorised person has power to detain or otherwise prevent the flight of an aircraft which would be a contravention of the order or would be a cause of danger to persons or goods in the aircraft or to other persons or property elsewhere, or which is unfit for flight. An " authorised person " for the purposes of this Article means a person authorised in writing by the Minister. (Art. 61).

Customs and Excise Act, 1952 requires aircraft flying to or from abroad to depart from or land at a Customs Airport (for customs clearance). If such an aircraft lands at a place other than a customs airport the commander should notify a customs officer or a constable. He should not allow goods to be unloaded without the officer's consent and no crew or passenger shall depart without the consent of an officer or constable save when necessary for safety (s. 15). Any customs officer or constable may prevent departure of an aircraft for abroad which is leaving from a place not a customs airport or from a customs airport before clearance is given (s. 25). S. 152 of this Act allows passenger aircraft to have an excise retailer's licence for the sale of intoxicants without having a justice's licence (see s. 164, Licensing Act, 1953).

Any person authorised in writing by the Minister and any officer of police has the right of access at all reasonable times by day or night to any aerodrome or place where an aircraft has landed for the purpose of inspecting the aerodrome or aircraft or any document he has power to demand under the Order and for detaining the aircraft under the provisions of the Order (Art. 62). No person shall obstruct or impede any person acting in the exercise of his powers or the performance of his duties under the provisions of the Order (Art. 63).

Art. 67 deals with the penalties for breaches of the Order. The general penalty is fine or imprisonment not exceeding six months or both, on summary conviction.

However certain minor contraventions such as failure to sign licence, failure to carry documents or to produce them on demand, are liable on summary conviction to fine.

Failure to apply for licence or certificate is not punishable under this Article (Art. 69).

The Order applies to all aircraft registered in the United Kingdom wherever they may be and to all other aircraft when within the United Kingdom unless the contrary intention appears in the Order (Art. 68).

With the exception of air force aircraft, no State aircraft (military, customs and police) shall fly over or land in the United Kingdom (except when ordered by signals to land) unless properly authorised (Art. 71).

Schedule II gives the rules of the air and air traffic control.

Low Flying—Rule 15.—(1) Subject to the provisions of paragraphs (2) and (3):—

(*a*) An aircraft other than a helicopter shall not fly over any congested area below (i) such height as would enable the aircraft to alight clear of the area and without danger to persons or property on the surface, in the event of failure of a power unit, or (ii) a height of 1,500 feet above the highest fixed object within 2,000 feet of the aircraft, whichever is the higher.

(*b*) A helicopter shall not fly below such height as would enable it to alight without danger to persons or property on the surface, in the event of failure of a power unit.

(*c*) Except with the written permission of the Minister a helicopter shall not fly (i) over a congested area below a height of 1,500 feet above the highest fixed object within 2,000 feet of the helicopter; (ii) over an area prescribed for the purposes of this paragraph below such height as would enable it to alight clear of the area in the event of failure of a power unit.

(*d*) An aircraft shall not fly over, or within 1,000 yards of, any assembly in the open air of more than 1,000 persons, except with the written permission of the Minister and the written consent of the organisers nor, even with such consent, below such height as would enable it to alight clear of the assembly in the event of failure of a power unit. Provided that where a person is charged with a contravention of this paragraph, it shall be a good defence to prove that the flight of the aircraft over, or within 1,000 yards of, the assembly was made at a reasonable height and for a reason not connected with the assembly or with the event which was the occasion for the assembly.

(*e*) An aircraft shall not fly closer than 500 feet to any person, vessel, vehicle or structure.

(2) (*a*) Paragraphs (1) (*d*) and (*e*) shall not apply to an aircraft in the service of a police authority.

(*b*) Paragraphs (1) (*d*) and (*e*) shall not apply to the flight of an aircraft over or within 1,000 yards of an assembly of persons witnessing an aircraft race or contest or exhibition of flying, if the aircraft is taking part in such race, etc., or is engaged in a flight arranged by or made with the written consent of the organisers.

(c) Paragraph (1) (e) shall not apply to (i) any aircraft while it is engaged in sowing any seed or spraying land or water; (ii) any aircraft while it is landing or taking off in accordance with normal aviation practice.

(3) Nothing in this Rule shall prohibit any aircraft from (a) taking off, landing or practising approaches to landing, or (b) flying for the purpose of checking navigational aids or procedures at a Government or licensed aerodrome, or (c) flying for the purpose of saving life. Providing that in the case of practising approaches to landing, it is confined to the airspace customarily used by aircraft.

Aerobatic flights over towns or populous areas are prohibited (Rule 19).

Air Accidents.—The Civil Aviation (Investigation of Accidents) Regs., 1951, direct that when an accident occurs to a civil aircraft involving death or serious injury to any person, or serious damage to an aircraft, particulars should be notified to the local police and to the Minister of Transport and Civil Aviation by the pilot or owner or operator (Arts. 3 and 4). " Aircraft " includes all balloons (captive or free), gliders, airships and flying machines (Art. 1).

Such an aircraft should not be removed or interfered with for three days unless by authority, except when necessary to save life or to prevent danger or obstruction, etc. (Art. 5).

An Inspector of Accidents will investigate the accident (Arts. 6 to 8), and if necessary, a special Court will be appointed to hold a public inquiry (Arts. 9 and 10).

The Air Navigation (General) Regulations, 1954, as amended in 1956, with some amendments in 1957, contain 232 regulations dealing with certificates, licences and other matters in connection with aircraft. The Air Navigation (Radio) Regulations, 1954, prescribe the rules for radio operators and apparatus in aircraft.

The Air Navigation (Stowaways) Order, 1949 (with some amendments in 1957), deals with persons who hide in aircraft without proper consent.

Smuggling.—Acts of Parliament deal with the importation of goods into the country in three ways :—

(1) The bringing in of some articles is absolutely forbidden ; for example, indecent publications. See Chap. 11.

(2) Certain goods may not be imported unless the prescribed customs duties are paid thereon ; for example, wine, spirits, tobacco, saccharine, various manufactured articles. The duties thus imposed form part of the national revenue, and may protect home industries against foreign competition.

(3) Some articles may not be brought into this country except under official licence or permission ; for example, certain dangerous drugs. See " Dangerous Drugs," Chap. 39.

The importation of any article contrary to the law on the subject is termed " smuggling," and articles so imported illegally are called " contraband goods."

The Customs and Excise Service keep watch at seaports to prevent and detect breaches of the law.

The Customs and Excise Act, 1952 deals with the prevention of smuggling in ss. 68 to 74. Customs officers, coastguard and police may search vehicles and vessels (s. 297). An excise or customs officer may search persons (s. 298) and obtain search warrants for premises (s. 296).

A constable, customs officer, etc., who suspects on reasonable grounds that signalling to smugglers is going on, may enter ships, aircraft, vehicles, houses and places and prevent same which is an offence (s. 71). A person offering goods for sale as smuggled goods is liable to heavy penalty and may be detained (s. 74) by a constable, customs officer, etc. (s. 274) and dealt with by a court (s. 281).

It shall be the duty of every constable and every member of H.M. armed forces or coastguard to assist in the enforcement of the law as set out in the Act (Customs and Excise Act, 1952, s. 5.)

Any contravention or attempted evasion of the laws on the importation of goods is an offence, and the offender may be arrested or summoned.

Tramways.—Under the Tramways Act, 1870, the following acts are punishable summarily by fine—wilful damage (s. 49), wilful injury or obstruction (s. 50), bringing dangerous goods without notice (s. 53), and passenger evading payment of proper fare, and such passenger, if name or address is unknown, may be detained by any tramway servant and all persons called by him to his assistance, until taken before a Justice or otherwise legally discharged (ss. 51, 52).

PART VI.—OTHER STATUTORY OFFENCES AND REGULATIONS

Chapter XXVII

VAGRANCY AND CHARITY

Contents

Vagrancy Acts.—The Vagrancy Act, 1824, was intended to prevent wasters and sturdy beggars from wandering about the country and committing sundry questionable acts by which an easy livelihood might be gained.

Offenders under the Act are arranged in three classes:—

(1) Idle and Disorderly Persons (s. 3).—This term is applied to person committing any of the following offences :—

(1) Begging in any public place (s. 3). See " Begging," later.

(2) Common prostitutes wandering in public places and behaving in an indecent or riotous manner (s. 3). See " Prostitution," Chap. 10.

(3) Pedlars wandering abroad and trading without licence (s. 3). See " Pedlars," Chap. 31.

Above offenders may be committed by one Justice for fourteen days, or by two Justices in Petty Sessions for one month, or may be fined £5.

(2) Rogues and Vagabonds (s. 4).—This term is applied to persons committing any of the following offences :—

(1) Persons convicted a second time of being an idle and disorderly person.

(2) Persons arrested as " idle and disorderly " who violently resist arrest.

(3) Fortune-tellers and suchlike. See " Vagrancy Frauds," later.

(4) Begging by exposing wounds or deformities. See " Vagrancy Frauds."

(5) Collecting alms or charitable contributions under false pretences. See " Vagrancy Frauds."

(6) Sleeping out. See " Vagrancy Frauds."

(7) Exposing to public view obscene or indecent exhibitions. See " Indecent Publications," Chap. 11.

(8) Exposing the person with intent to insult any female. See " Indecent Exposure," Chap. 11.

(9) Having implements with intent to feloniously break into any building.

(10) Being armed with any offensive weapon with intent to commit any felony.

(11) Found in or upon any premises or enclosed yard, garden or area for any unlawful purpose.

(12) Suspected persons or reputed thieves found frequenting or loitering with intent to commit a felony.

For full description of above four offences (9 to 12), see " Loiterers and Suspected Persons," Chap. 28.

(13) Gaming in any public place (added by the Vagrant Act Amendment Act, 1873). See " Gaming " Chap. 36.

Above offenders may be committed by one Justice for fourteen days, or by two Justices in Petty Sessions for three months, or may be fined £25.

(3) Incorrigible Rogue (s. 5).—This term is applied to any person convicted as follows :—

(1) For committing any offence for which he may be dealt with as a rogue and a vagabond (see the fourteen offences above), having been previously convicted as a rogue and a vagabond.

(2) For violently resisting arrest as a rogue and vagabond.

(3) For escaping from a place of confinement before the expiration of the term for which committed or confined under the Vagrancy Act.

Persons convicted by the Justices as incorrigible rogues shall be committed to prison until the next Quarter Sessions, at which the circumstances are to be examined and they may be sentenced to up to twelve months' imprisonment. There is no appeal against such a conviction by Justices, but the prisoner, if given leave, may appeal to the Court of Criminal Appeal against the sentence of Quarter Sessions (Criminal Appeal Act, 1907, s. 20 (2)).

Power of Arrest.—Any person may arrest without warrant anyone found committing an offence against the Act and bring him before a Justice or hand him over to the police (but in the case of fortune tellers only the police can so arrest. See " Vagrancy Frauds," later).

Any constable refusing to take such a prisoner into his custody or any person hindering a constable in the execution of the Act, is liable to fine (s. 6). See Stone, under title " Vagrants."

Note :—Where any statute directs that an offender shall be punished as an idle and disorderly person or as a rogue and vagabond or as an incorrigible rogue, such person shall be punished under the Vagrancy Act (s. 21).

Begging.—As every person really in need of subsistence is entitled to national assistance, the law makes it a summary offence to beg or to try and obtain contributions from the public in any fraudulent manner.

Vagrancy Act, 1824, s. 3 : Every person wandering abroad or placing himself or herself in any public place, street, highway, court, or passage, to beg or gather alms, or causing or procuring or encouraging any child or children so to do, may be punished summarily as an idle and disorderly person.

Children and Young Persons Act, 1933, ss. 4 and 61 : Causing or procuring or allowing any child or young person (under 16) to be in any street, premises or place for the purpose of begging or receiving or inducing alms is a summary offence, and the child or young person may be dealt with as needing care or protection. See Chap. 12.

Pedlars Act, 1871, s. 16 : If a pedlar is convicted of begging, the Court must deprive him of his pedlar's certificate. See Chap. 31.

Vagrancy Frauds.—Persons convicted of the following offences under s. 4 of the Vagrancy Act, 1824, may be punished summarily as rogues and vagabonds.

(1) *Fortune Telling.*—Every person pretending or professing to tell fortunes, or using any subtle craft, means or device by palmistry or otherwise, to deceive or impose on any of Her Majesty's subjects.

(2) *Fraudulent Collections.*—Every person going about as a gatherer or collector of alms, or endeavouring to procure charitable contributions of any nature or kind, under any false or fraudulent pretence.

(3) *Exposing Wounds.*—Every person wandering abroad and endeavouring by the exposure of wounds or deformities to obtain or gather alms.

(4) *Sleeping Out.*—Every person wandering abroad and lodging in any barn or outhouse or in any deserted or un-occupied dwelling or in the open air or under a tent or in any cart or waggon (with or in which he does not travel (1935 Act)) and not giving a good account of himself or herself (1824 Act, s. 4), provided that he declines any reasonably accessible free place of shelter or that he is a person who persistently wanders abroad and sleeps out or that by so sleeping out he causes or appears likely to cause damage, infection with vermin or other offensive consequences to property (Vagrancy Act, 1935). Children and young persons found " sleeping out " may be

dealt with as needing care or protection (Children and Young Persons Act, 1933, s. 61). See Chap. 12.

The police have power to arrest without warrant any persons found committing any of the above offences (s. 6), but in the case of " fortune telling " a constable must not arrest unless he has reason to believe that the offender will abscond or he is not satisfied as to the identity or place of residence of the offender (C.J. Act, 1948, s. 68).

Fraudulent Mediums.—The Fraudulent Mediums Act, 1951, repealed the Witchcraft Act, 1735 and s. 4 of the Vagrancy Act, 1824, so far as it extends to spiritualistic mediums or persons using telepathy; clairvoyance or other similar powers or to persons using fraudulent devices in exercising such powers (s. 2).

However, s. 1 of the Act creates the offence of acting as a spiritualistic medium or using telepathy, clairvoyance or other similar powers with intent to deceive or when so acting using any fraudulent device when it is proved that the person so acted for reward. Proceedings require the consent of the Director of Public Prosecutions and they may be summary (with right to claim trial by jury) or on indictment.

However this section does not apply to anything done solely for the purpose of entertainment.

Charities.—The law places no obstacles in the way of exercising charity, but it has taken some steps to check persons from obtaining undeserved assistance and to regulate the raising of money from the public for charitable purposes.

The Vagrancy Act, 1824, makes begging, obtaining alms by the exposure of wounds and deformities, and fraudulent alms collecting, summary offences, for which see above.

Street Collections.—The Police, Factories, etc. (Miscellaneous Provisions) Act, 1916, s. 5, authorises a police authority to make regulations dealing with the collection of money or the sale of articles (e.g. flags or other tokens) in streets and public places for the benefit of charitable or other purposes. Any such regulations must be confirmed by the Secretary of State and shall not apply to the sale of articles in public places in the ordinary course of trade where no representation is made that any part of the proceeds will be devoted to charity.

Such regulations, when made, usually provide :—

(1) That a permit must be obtained from the police authority for any such street collection or flag day ;

(2) That every collector must have in possession a written authority to collect ;

(3) That collectors must not cause annoyance or obstruction ;

(4) That all money received must at once be placed in a closed receptacle ;

(5) That no person must be rewarded for his services out of the proceeds of the collection, and

(6) That a proper account of the money collected and of the expenses incurred must be submitted to the police authority.

War Charities Act, 1940.—This Act repeals and replaces the War Charities Act, 1916. It makes it a summary offence to make any public appeal for assistance for any war charity, or to attempt to raise money for any such charity by promoting any bazaar, entertainment or similar means, unless the charity is exempted or registered under the Act and the governing body of the charity has in writing approved of such appeal or bazaar, etc. However, this does not apply to a collection at Divine service in a place of public worship, or to any war charity exempted by the Registration Authority from registration under the Act (s. 1).

A " war charity " is defined as any fund, association or undertaking having amongst its principal objects the relief of suffering or distress, caused by, or any other charitable purpose connected with war (*i.e.* any war, War Charities (Definition) Order, 1943).

It does not apply to the Royal Patriotic Fund Corporation nor to any " war charity " administered by a government department (s. 11), but it does to any charity for disabled persons (National Assistance Act, 1948, ss. 29, 41).

Accordingly every " war charity " must make application for registration or exemption to the Registration Authority (the local Council, s. 10), which must keep a Register of War Charities and supply the Charity Commissioners with particulars of same (s. 2). Registered war charities should be properly organised and should keep proper accounts which must be audited and copies sent to the Registration Authority at least once in every twelve months (s. 3).

Under s. 4 the Charity Commissioners may make regulations (see the War Charities Regs., 1940) and failure to comply with them or with the conditions laid down in s. 3 will be a summary offence.

In case of default a war charity may be removed from the register and the Charity Commissioners may take control (s. 5).

The police authority may refuse a licence under the House to House Collections Act, 1939, if the collection is for a " war charity " which is not registered or exempted.

The chief officer of police may grant a certificate for a house to house collection to a " war charity " which is exempted from registration under this Act (s. 7).

It is a summary offence to make false statements or representations under this Act or for any person to falsely represent himself to be an officer or agent of a war charity (s. 8).

An offence under s. 4 can be dealt with summarily with fine

up to £5. Proceedings for any other offence against the Act cannot be taken unless by or with the consent of the Charity Commissioners (Ryder Street, St. James's, London, S.W.1) and the penalty is much greater.

House to House Collections Act, 1939.—This Act directs that no collection for a charitable purpose shall be made unless authorised under the Act (s. 1 (1)). " Collection " means an appeal to the public made by means of visits from house to house (including a place of business) to give, whether for consideration or not, money or other property, and " collector " means a person who makes such an appeal. " Charitable purpose " means any charitable, benevolent or philanthropic purpose whether or not the purpose is charitable within the meaning of any rule of law (s. 11).

If a person promotes such a collection and a collection thereunder is made in any locality, then unless he has a licence in force authorising him so to do, he shall be guilty of an offence (s. 1 (2)), punishable by imprisonment not exceeding 6 months, or fine not exceeding £100 or both (s. 8). A " promoter " of a collection means a person who causes others to act, whether for remuneration or otherwise, as collectors for the collection (s. 11).

If a person acts as collector in any locality for such a collection, then unless there is a licence in force for the collection, he shall be guilty of an offence (s. 1 (3)) punishable by fine up to £5, and on second or subsequent conviction, by imprisonment not exceeding 3 months or fine not exceeding £25 or both (s. 8).

A police constable may require any person whom he believes to be acting as a collector for a charitable purpose to declare to him immediately his name and address and to sign his name. Failure to comply shall be an offence (s. 6) punishable by fine not exceeding £5 (s. 8).

A person may apply in the prescribed manner to the Police Authority of the area for a licence authorising him to promote such a collection in any locality within the police area. A licence may be granted for a definite period not longer than 12 months, but it may be for 18 months if the Police Authority wish to provide for the simultaneous expiration of such licences (s. 2).

A licence may be refused or revoked on any of the following grounds:—

(a) the total amount likely to be applied for charitable purposes is inadequate in proportion to the likely amount of the collection.

(b) remuneration excessive in relation to the amount likely to be applied for charitable purposes is likely to be or has been retained or received out of the proceeds by any person.

(c) the licence would be likely to facilitate begging or causing a child to beg, or that such an offence has been committed in connection with the collection.

(*d*) the applicant or licensee has been convicted of assault, rape, carnal knowledge, indecent assault, abduction, larceny, burglary, housebreaking, blackmail, offence in connection with street collections or any offence involving fraud or dishonesty (see Schedule to the Act) and is therefore not a fit and proper person to hold a licence.

(*e*) The applicant or licensee, in promoting a collection, has failed to exercise due diligence to secure fit and proper collectors or to secure compliance with the Regulations under the Act.

(*f*) The applicant or licensee has refused or neglected to furnish to the Police Authority such information as they may have reasonably required regarding any of the above matters.

If a licence is refused or revoked, the grounds shall be given and there may be an appeal to the Secretary of State (s. 2).

The Police Authority may refuse a licence if the collection is for a war charity which is not registered or exempted under the Act (s. 7, War Charities Act, 1940), and any contravention of a regulation will be an offence (s. 4) punishable by fine not exceeding £5 (s. 8).

If a person, in connection with any appeal made by him to the public representing that it is for a charitable purpose, displays or uses—

(*a*) a prescribed badge or certificate of authority not being such as is held by him for the appeal pursuant to regulations made under the Act, or

(*b*) any badge or device or certificate or other document so nearly resembling a prescribed badge or authority as to be calculated to deceive—he shall be guilty of an offence (s. 5) liable to imprisonment not exceeding 6 months, or fine not exceeding £100, or both (s. 8).

A similar punishment may be imposed on a person guilty of the offence of knowingly or recklessly making a statement false in a material particular, in furnishing any information for the purposes of this Act (s. 8).

Licence from the Police Authority is not necessary in two cases, viz. :—

1. The Secretary of State may, by order, exempt from licence and authorise a collection in the localities described in the Order, by a person (or organisation) who pursues a charitable purpose throughout the whole of England or a substantial part thereof.

Such an Order has the effect of a licence in the localities named (s. 3).

2. A chief officer of police may grant a certificate to a person to collect for a charitable purpose which is local in character and is likely to be completed within a short period of time. A person holding such a certificate may authorise other persons to act as collectors. The holder of such a certificate is exempt

from the requirements of the Act (and Regulations) except sections 5 (unauthorised use of badges, etc.) and 6 (liability to give name, etc., to police) and the penalties for contravention of these two sections (s. 1 (4)).

Any functions conferred on the chief officer of police by the Act or Regulations may be delegated by him to any police officer not below the rank of Inspector (s. 7 (2)).

The chief officer of police may grant a certificate for a house to house collection to a war charity which is exempted from registration under the Act (s. 7, War Charities Act, 1940).

House to House Collections Regulations, 1947.—These Regulations prescribe the form of police certificates, applications for licence or order, collectors' certificates of authority, badges, and accounts to be rendered (7 schedules).

The " chief promoter " of a collection is the person to whom a licence or order is granted, but there may also be promoters taking part in the work.

A " collecting box " means a box or other receptacle for money, securely closed and sealed so that it may not be opened without breaking the seal.

A " receipt book " means a book of detachable receipts consecutively numbered with counterfoils or duplicates correspondingly numbered (Reg. 2).

Every promoter shall exercise all due diligence to secure that collectors are fit and proper persons and that they comply with the Regulations (Reg. 5).

A promoter shall not permit any person to act as a collector unless the person is supplied with—

(a) A certificate of authority, as prescribed

(b) a badge, as prescribed, showing the purpose of the collection, and

(c) if money is to be collected, a collecting box or a receipt book.

The purpose of the collection and a distinguishing number shall be marked on every collecting box or wrapper gummed on it (Reg. 2 (3)) and on every receipt (Reg. 6 (1)).

Every promoter shall secure that no certificate of authority, badge, etc., is issued unless the name and address of the collector with distinguishing number of box or receipt book is entered on a list, and shall secure that same are returned when the collection is finished or when the collector ceases to act as such (Reg. 6 (2)).

Every collector shall—

(a) Sign his name on his certificate of authority and produce it on demand to any police constable or person at a house visited for collecting.

(b) Sign his name on his badge and wear it prominently when collecting, and (*c*) Keep his certificate and badge in his possession and return them to his promoter on demand or when the collection is completed (Reg. 7).

No person under the age of 16 (in London 18) shall act or be authorised to act as a collector of money (Reg. 8).

No collector shall importune any person to the annoyance of such person or remain in or at the door of any house if requested to leave by any occupant thereof (Reg. 9).

When collecting money by a collecting box, a collector shall not receive money save by permitting the giver to place it in the collecting box issued to him. When collecting money by any other means the collector shall enter in the receipt book issued to him, in the presence of the contributor, the name of the contributor with amount given, and give him a signed receipt. All entries shall be in ink or indelible pencil (Reg. 10).

Every collector shall return to a promoter his collecting box or receipt book, with the total amount collected, when the box is full or the receipt book is exhausted or on demand of a promoter or on ceasing to act as collector or when the collection is completed (Reg. 11).

Every returned collecting box shall be examined, and if it contains money shall be opened in the presence of a promoter and another responsible person, contents counted and recorded on a list to be certified by the persons making the examination. Receipt books shall be similarly examined and amounts listed (Reg. 12).

A licence or order may expressly allow collections in which instead of collecting boxes or receipt books, envelopes may be used ; the givers to put their contributions therein and gum down the flaps (Reg. 13).

The chief promoter shall furnish accounts of the collection, as prescribed by Regs. 14, 15 and 16. He shall also ensure that all certificates of authority and badges are destroyed when no longer required for the purpose (Reg. 17).

Any contravention of a regulation will be a summary offence (s. 4) punishable by fine up to £5 (s. 8).

National Assistance.—The previous poor law ceased to have effect (save as provided by the 6th Sched. to the 1948 Act which deals with transitional matters including workhouses, etc.) and was replaced by the National Assistance Act, 1948 (most of which came into force on 5th July, 1948, by order made under s. 68) which provides for assistance to persons in need (s. 1).

It shall be the duty of the National Assistance Board to assist persons who are without sufficient resources to meet their requirements (s. 4). The 2nd Sched. deals with the resources which are to be disregarded. The determination of " need for assistance " shall be by regulations made for the purpose (ss. 5, 6, 15).

A person under 16 shall not apply for " assistance," but may benefit as a dependant of an assisted person (s. 7).

Assistance grants may be in money (s. 8) or may be in kind such as goods or services (s. 12).

Assistance shall not be given for persons in full time remunerative work nor to persons out of work by reason of a trade dispute unless it is allowable under the section (s. 9), but may be given in cases of urgency (s. 11).

Any person aggrieved by a decision of the Board in his case may appeal to the Appeal Tribunal dealt with by the 5th Sched. (s. 14). The Board may provide re-establishment centres for training, etc., persons (s. 16) and reception centres for temporary board and lodging for persons without a settled way of living (" casuals ") and may require local councils to provide and maintain reception centres (s. 17). There is power to deal with persons who persistently resort to reception centres when capable of maintaining themselves (s. 18). Rules and regulations may provide for the management of these centres and contraventions may be dealt with by a summary court (s. 19).

Every local authority (councils of counties or county boroughs, s. 33) has the duty of providing residential accommodation for persons (ordinarily resident in their area or with no settled residence or in urgent need of such accommodation (s. 24)) who by reason of age, infirmity, etc., need care and attention which is not otherwise available to them ; and temporary accommodation for persons (in their area (s. 24)) in urgent need thereof arising out of unforeseen circumstances, and also provide conveyance and health services for such persons (s. 21). Charges shall be made for such accommodation according to ability to pay (s. 22). A local authority may arrange with voluntary organisations to provide such accommodation (s. 26).

A local authority has power (and may be directed) to make welfare arrangements for blind, deaf or dumb, crippled and disabled persons (s. 29) and may employ voluntary organisations for the purpose (s. 30). A local authority may make contributions to any voluntary organisation whose activities include the provision of recreation or meals for old people (s. 31).

Any fund, association, etc., having for a principal object the promotion of the welfare of such disabled persons to whom s. 29 applies shall be deemed to be a war charity under the War Charities Act, 1940, and must be registered by the local authority (s. 41). See " War Charities," above.

Sections 37-40 deal with the registration of homes for disabled or old persons by the local authority and their regulation and inspection. See " Persons Old, Disabled, etc.", Chap. 29.

A man shall be liable to maintain his wife and children and a woman shall be liable to maintain her husband and children (s. 42).

If " assistance " is given the Board or the local authority may apply to a magistrates' court for an order to recover the cost of such maintenance from the person liable to maintain the assisted person or persons (s. 43).

If a person misrepresents or fails to disclose any material fact and thereby the Board or local authority incurs expenditure or fails to recover any sum, it is entitled to recover the amount from such person (s. 45).

Where persons are suffering from grave chronic disease or being aged or infirm are living in insanitary conditions and do not have proper care and attention, on 7 days' notice and on certificate from the medical officer of health, a magistrates' court may order the removal of any such person to a suitable hospital or other place to be detained there as stated in the order. Any disobedience to or obstruction of the execution of such an order is punishable summarily (s. 47).

Where such a person should be removed without delay an Order lasting three weeks may be made without this previous notice (Nat. Assist. (Amendment) Act, 1951, s. 1).

Where a person is admitted to hospital or to accommodation under the Act or removed to hospital under s. 47 and there is danger of loss or damage to any of his movable property, the local council shall take reasonable steps to prevent or mitigate the loss or damage, and may recover the cost from such person (s. 48).

The local authority shall cause to be buried or cremated the body of any person who has died or been found dead in their area when no suitable arrangements have otherwise been made, and may recover the cost from his estate or person liable to maintain him (s. 50).

If a person persistently refuses or neglects to maintain himself or any dependant and assistance or accommodation under the Act has to be afforded, he shall be guilty of an offence punishable on summary conviction (s. 51).

If a person makes any false statement or representation for the purpose of obtaining benefit for himself or for another person or for avoiding any liability under the Act, he shall be guilty of an offence punishable on summary conviction (s. 52).

Any " inspector " under the Act should have a written authority, which he should produce if required, when inspecting and any person who obstructs him shall be liable to fine on summary conviction (s. 55).

The council of a county or county borough may prosecute for any offence under the Act, and any sum due shall be recoverable as a civil debt (s. 56).

War Savings and savings bank deposits of a person may be ascertained under regulations to be made by the Treasury (s. 57).

In this Act " disability " includes mental as well as physical disability. " Requirements " (see s. 4) includes requirements for services for which charges are authorised under the National

Health Service Act, 1951, s. 4. See also National Health Service Act, 1952.

3rd Sched. deals with the committees of local authorities who are to carry out the Act. The 7th Sched. repeals the Poor Law Acts and parts of other Acts.

Common Lodging-Houses.—Public Health Act, 1936. Part IX, ss. 235-248, regulates such premises.

A common lodging-house means a house (other than a national assistance institution) provided for the purpose of accommodating by night poor persons, not being members of the same family, who resort thereto and are allowed to occupy one common room for the purpose of sleeping, or eating, and includes, where part only of a house is so used, the part so used (s. 235).

Letting on weekly tenancies does not prevent premises from coming within this definition (*People's Hostels Ltd.* v. *Turley* (1938)).

No person shall keep a common lodging-house unless he is registered under this Act (s. 236) with the Local Authority, and the deputies of such a keeper shall also be registered (s. 237). Registration may be refused if keepers or deputies are not fit persons ; if premises are not suitable and suitably equipped ; or if such use is likely to cause annoyance or inconvenience to the neighbours (s. 238).

" Registered Common Lodging-House " shall be displayed on the outside of the house ; the keeper or deputy shall be therein from 9 P.M. to 6 A.M. ; lists of lodgers shall be sent to the Local Authority if beggars or vagrants are received ; and free access shall be given at all times to authorised officers (s. 241). Infectious disease shall be notified and a Magistrates' Court may order closing if there is notifiable disease (ss. 242–245).

Contravention of the Act will be a summary offence, fine £5 (s. 246), and registration may be cancelled and the keeper disqualified (s. 247).

It is an offence for the keeper of a lodging-house to knowingly lodge or harbour thieves or reputed thieves (Prevention of Crimes Act, 1871, s. 10). See " Receiving Stolen Property," Chap. 14.

Chapter XXVIII
PREVENTION OF CRIME
Contents

Penalties.—The main preventive of crime is most probably the fear of incurring some penalty. Punishment for crime has been briefly dealt with in Chapter 1, but the Criminal Justice Act, 1948, supplemented by the Prison Act, 1952, has made so many changes in and additions to the methods of punishing offences that it is considered advisable to here set out the relevant provisions of these Acts, as follows:—

C.J. Act, 1948, s. 1: Penal servitude and imprisonment with hard labour are abolished and are to be replaced by imprisonment, and prison divisions are also abolished. The term " convict prison " has disappeared.

S. 2 : The sentence by a court of whipping is abolished.

Ss. 3-6, 8-12, 45-47, 1st, 5th and 8th Schedules relate to the revised probation system, for which see later.

Ss. 7, 8, 12 : Where a court convicts a person of an offence and considers punishment or probation is not appropriate, the court may discharge him absolutely or conditionally. See later.

S. 11 (2) : A court may order a probationer or an absolutely or conditionally discharged offender to pay damages for injury or compensation for loss. See later.

S. 13 : Any court which convicts a person on indictment of felony (not being a felony for which the sentence is fixed by law) has power to fine the offender in lieu of or in addition to dealing with him in any other allowable manner.

Sentence of death shall not be passed on a person convicted of murder which he committed when under the age of 18, but instead he shall be sentenced to be detained during H.M. pleasure (Homicide Act 1957, s. 9).

S. 17: Assizes or Quarter Sessions shall not impose imprisonment on a person under 15. No court (or justice) shall impose imprisonment on a person under 21 unless no other method of dealing with him is appropriate, and if it does so, the court shall state the reason. A magistrates' court shall not impose imprisonment on any person under 17 (M.C. Act, 1952, s. 107). A magistrates' court shall not impose imprisonment on a first offender of or over 21 unless the court is of the opinion that no other method of dealing with him is appropriate (First Offenders Act, 1958, s. 1).

S. 18 : Instead of imposing imprisonment a court (or justice) may order an offender, not less than 14 but under 21, to be detained in a detention centre (if a suitable one is available) for various periods up to 6 months as detailed in the section. See " Detention Centre," Chap. 12.

S. 19 : Instead of imposing imprisonment or punishing for breach of probation order, a magistrates' court may order an offender who is not less than 12 but is under 21, to attend at an attendance centre. See " Attendance Centre," Chap. 12.

S. 20 : An offender not less than 16 but under 21, who is liable to imprisonment, may be sentenced by Assizes or Quarter Sessions to Borstal training. See later.

S. 21 : A person not less than 21 who is convicted on indictment and has previous convictions may be sentenced to corrective training. See later. Such a convicted persistent offender who is not less than 30 may be sentenced to preventive detention. See later.

S. 22: Where a person is convicted on indictment of an offence punishable with imprisonment for 2 years or more and has previous convictions the court, if it sentences him to 12 months imprisonment or more, may order that he shall, for 12 months, be subject to the provisions of s. 29 of the Prisons Act, 1952, as to notifying his address, etc., after discharge. See later.

Where a summary court is satisfied on medical evidence that an offender liable to imprisonment is of unsound mind, the court may make a reception order directing his conveyance to a mental institution (M.C. Act, 1952, s. 30). See "Lunacy," Chap. 39.

Where a summary court convicts a person not less than 17 under the provisions of the Act of an indictable offence and considers he deserves greater punishment than the court can inflict, he can be committed in custody to Quarter Sessions for sentence (M.C. Act, 1952, s. 29).

Prisoners may be released on licence and temporarily discharged on account of ill health (Prison Act, 1952, ss. 25 to 28).

C.J. Act, 1948, s. 69: Where H.M. pardons a person sentenced to death, on condition that he serves a term of imprisonment such person shall be deemed to have been sentenced to such imprisonment.

S. 80 (1) : " Impose imprisonment " means pass a sentence of imprisonment or commit to prison in default of payment of money or for failing to do or abstain from doing anything required to be done or left undone. See also s. 126, M.C. Act, 1952.

" Offence for which the sentence is fixed by law " means an

offence for which the court is required to sentence the offender to death or imprisonment for life or to detention during H.M pleasure

(6) : Where the Act empowers a court, on convicting, to pass a sentence or make an order in lieu of dealing with the offender in any other manner, it does not take away any power of the court to order the offender to pay costs, damages or compensation.

" Fine " includes any pecuniary penalty or pecuniary forfeiture or pecuniary compensation payable under a conviction (M.C. Act, 1952, s. 126).

See also " Punishment for Crime," Chap. 1.

Discharge of Offenders.—The Criminal Justice Act, 1948, has authorised two new methods of dealing with convicted offenders.

S. 7 : Where a court convicts a person of an offence (for which the sentence is not fixed by law) and is of opinion, having regard to the circumstances including the nature of the offence and the character of the offender, that it is inexpedient to inflict punishment and that probation is not appropriate, the court, by order, may discharge him absolutely, or may discharge him conditionally on condition that he commits no offence during a specified period not exceeding 12 months. In the latter case the court shall explain to the offender that if he commits another offence during the period he will be liable to be sentenced for the original offence.

S. 8 : If a person conditionally discharged is convicted and dealt with anywhere in Great Britain for an offence committed during the specified period, a judge or justice, as authorised by this section, may issue summons or warrant to bring him before the court which conditionally discharged him. If that court was a summary court it can deal with him for the original offence. If that court was Assizes or Quarter Sessions and is not being held, the offender shall be committed in custody or on bail, by the summary court of the place where arrested, to the Assizes or Quarter Sessions concerned, to be dealt with for the original offence. Where a person conditionally discharged by a magistrates' court is convicted and dealt with for an offence during the specified period by another magistrates' court, that court, if the first court consents, may also deal with him for the original offence.

S. 11 : A court which conditionally discharges a convicted offender may allow a person to give surety for his good behaviour. If a court discharges an offender absolutely or conditionally it may order him to pay damages for injury or compensation for loss, but a magistrates' court cannot order more than £100 unless more is allowable by any other enactment. This award can be made in addition to an order to pay costs.

S. 12 : An absolute or conditional discharge shall not be deemed to be a conviction (imposing any disqualification or disability) for any purpose other than the purposes of this Act, except where an offender not less than 17 who is conditionally discharged commits another offence and is sentenced for his original offence. However this section will not affect the right of an offender to appeal against his conviction or to plead autrefois convict, nor will it affect the revesting or restoration of any property in consequence of the conviction. A person of or over 21 shall be treated for the purposes of the First Offenders Act, 1958, as a first offender if, but only if, he has not since attaining the age of 17 been convicted of any other offence, except an offence not punishable with imprisonment, and the question whether he has been so convicted shall be determined without regard to s. 12 of the C.J. Act, 1948.

This " discharge " of a convicted offender should not be confused with the discharge of an accused person by examining justices who are not satisfied that there is sufficient evidence to put him on trial for any indictable offence.

Probation of Offenders.—Placing a person on probation used to mean discharging an offender without convicting him or punishing him but binding him over to be under supervision. This system was regulated by the Probation of Offenders Act, 1907, and sections of later Acts, all of which have been repealed by the Criminal Justice Act, 1948, 10th Sched.

This 1948 Act has revised the probation system as follows :—

S. 3 : Where a court convicts a person of an offence (for which the sentence is not fixed by law, see s. 80) the court, having regard to the circumstances including the nature of the offence and the character of the offender, may, instead of sentencing him, make a probation order, that is an order requiring him to be under the supervision of a probation officer for a specified period not less than one year nor more than 3 years. The order may in addition require the offender to comply with such requirements as the court considers necessary for securing his good conduct or for preventing future offences. Such an order may include requirements as to the residence of the offender after the court has considered his home surroundings.

Payment of damages for injury or compensation for loss must not be included in a probation order, but the court, under s. 11 of the Act, may make a separate order dealing with same.

R. v. *Parry* (1950), decided that a fine could not be imposed, in addition to a probation order, as a fine was a sentence.

Before a probation order is made, the court shall explain to the offender the effect of the order (and requirements) and that, if he fails to comply or commits another offence, he will be liable to be sentenced for the original offence. If the offender is not less than 14, the order shall not be made unless he expresses his willingness (consent) to comply with the requirements thereof.

S. 4 : Where a court is satisfied, on medical evidence, that the mental condition of an offender is such as requires and as may be susceptible to treatment but is not such as would justify his being certified as a person of unsound mind or as a mental defective, the court may, if a probation order is made, include a requirement that the offender shall submit to medical treatment as specified in the section. However the offender (or parent or guardian if he is under 17) in such case, if he so desires, is entitled to call rebutting evidence before any such order and requirement is made.

S. 5 and Sched. 1 : A court which makes a probation order may, on the application of the probationer or probation officer, discharge it. A supervising court (which means a magistrates' court or juvenile court for the place named in the order, s. 80) may amend a probation order. It may cancel or add requirements within the limits laid down in the Schedule but cannot reduce the period of probation or extend it beyond the 3 years. If the order is to be amended on the application of the probation officer the court shall summon the probationer to appear and if he is not less than 14, the court cannot amend unless he agrees to comply with the amendment. This is not necessary if the amendment amounts to a reduction of the requirements.

S. 6 : If during the period of probation a probationer fails to comply with any of the requirements of the order, a justice of the supervising court (see above) may issue summons or warrant to bring him before that court.

That court may fine him up to £10 or order him to attend at an attendance centre if he is so liable under the conditions of s. 19 of the Act (see " Attendance Centres," Chap. 12) or, if probation had been ordered by a summary court, may deal with him for the original offence (if so probation would end, s. 5 (4)) or, if the probation order had been made by Assizes or Quarter Sessions, commit him in custody or on bail to appear before that court which may deal with him for the original offence. However a probationer required to submit to mental treatment (under s. 4) who refuses to undergo any surgical or other treatment, shall not be regarded as failing to comply with the requirement if the court considers his refusal was reasonable.

S. 8 : If a probationer has been convicted and dealt with in any part of Great Britain for an offence committed during his period of probation, a judge or justice, authorised under this section, may issue summons or warrant to bring him before the court which made the probation order. If that court was a magistrates' court the summons or warrant should direct his appearance before the supervising court (see above) but if the warrant directs his appearance before Assizes or Quarter Sessions and such court is not being held, he can be brought before a magistrates' court of the place where arrested and that court can commit him in custody or on bail to the Assizes or Quarter Sessions concerned.

If the probation order had been made by Assizes or Quarter Sessions and the subsequent offence had been dealt with by a magistrates' court, that court can commit him in custody or on bail to the Assizes or Quarter Sessions which made the order. If

Assizes or Quarter Sessions convict a person of an offence committed during the period of probation ordered by such a court or by a magistrates' court, the Assize or Quarter Sessions court can deal with him for the original offence. If a magistrates' court convicts a person of an offence committed during a period of probation ordered by another magistrates' court, that court, with the consent of the supervising court of the other place, may deal with him for the original offence.

S. 9 : This section arranges for the operation of probation orders relating to offenders in England who reside or will reside in Scotland.

S. 11 (1) : A court which makes a probation order may allow any person to give security for the good behaviour of the offender. Under s. 55 of the C. and Y.P. Act, 1933, a court may require the parent or guardian of a juvenile to give such security.

(2) : A court on making a probation order, may, in addition to awarding costs, order the offender to pay damages for injury or compensation for loss, in the case of a magistrates' court not exceeding £100 or any greater sum as may be allowed by any other enactment.

S. 12 : A conviction on which a probation order is made shall be deemed not to be a conviction for any purpose other than the purposes of the proceedings in which the order was made and of any subsequent proceedings against the offender under the foregoing provisions of the Act, provided that this shall not apply to the conviction where an offender, not less than 17 when put on probation, is subsequently sentenced for his original offence. Probation after conviction shall not be regarded as a disqualification or disability imposed by law on convicted persons. Probation does not prevent the offender from appealing against his conviction or relying on it in bar of any subsequent proceedings for the same offences nor does it affect the revesting or restoration of any property in consequence of the conviction. This section is disregarded in connection with the First Offenders Act, 1958, see under " Discharge of Offenders ", above.

S. 43 : Where a probation officer makes a report to a court (other than a juvenile court) to assist the court in dealing with an offender, a copy of the report shall be given to the offender or his Counsel or Solicitor. However, if the offender is under 17 and is not represented, a copy need not be given to him, but shall be given to his parent or guardian if present in court.

S. 45 and 5th Sched. make arrangements for probation areas, probation committees, case committees for petty sessional divisions, probation officers and expenses. The 5th Sched. directs that it shall be the duty of probation officers to supervise probationers and other persons placed under their supervision, and to advise, assist and befriend them, to enquire, as directed by the court, into the circumstances or home surroundings of any person so as to assist the court in dealing with his case, to advise, assist and befriend as prescribed, persons who have been released from custody and to perform such duties as may be prescribed or imposed by any enactment. The probation officer under whose supervision a woman or girl is placed shall be a woman. See also the Probation Rules, 1949-1955.

S. 46 : The Secretary of State may approve and make rules for premises for persons required to reside therein by a probation order or a supervision order and such premises shall be known as " approved probation hostels " if the residents are employed outside the premises and in any other case as " approved probation homes."

S. 47 : Any institution which is not an approved probation hostel or home, in which a probationer or supervisee is required to reside otherwise than for mental treatment shall be subject to government inspection and a person appointed by the Secretary of State shall have power to enter and investigate the treatment of residents, and anyone who obstructs him will commit a summary offence.

M.C. Act, 1952, s. 71, allows a court to order a person adjudged to pay a sum by summary conviction, to be placed under the supervision of a named person until the fine is paid. Such a person should befriend and advise the offender so as to induce him to pay and avoid committal to custody and should inform the court as to the offender's circumstances (M.C. Rules, 1952, r. 46).

Borstal Institution.—The Borstal system of detention and training to bring about reformation of youthful offenders, introduced by the Prevention of Crime Act, 1908, and extended by later Acts and Orders, was revised by the Criminal Justice Act, 1948, which repealed the previous law relating to it and which has been supplemented by the Prison Act, 1952.

C.J. Act, 1948, s. 20 (1): When a person not less than 16 but under 21 is convicted on indictment of an offence punishable with inprisonment, and having regard to his character and previous conduct and to the circumstances of the offence, the court considers that it is expedient for his reformation and the prevention of crime that he should undergo a period of training in a Borstal Institution, the court may sentence him to Borstal training. After release the offender shall be subject to supervision and the Secretary of State may alter to imprisonment the latter part of his term of detention (s. 45, Prison Act, 1952).

A magistrates' court which convicts such an offender may, if it considers it appropriate, commit him in custody to Quarter Sessions for sentence to Borstal training (s. 28, M.C. Act, 1952). S. 20 (5): Quarter Sessions may do so or deal with him in any manner in which the magistrates' court might have dealt with him. If Quarter Sessions so sentence him, he may appeal to the Court of Criminal Appeal as if he had been convicted on indictment. (7): Before an offender is committed for such sentence or so sentenced the court concerned must consider a report from the

Prison Authorities on the offender's physical and mental condition and his suitability for such a sentence. If necessary, the offender after conviction may be remanded in custody for a period or periods not exceeding 3 weeks until such report is received and considered. (8): A copy of such report shall be given to the offender or his Counsel or Solicitor.

Prison Act, 1952, s. 43: The Secretary of State may provide Borstal Institutions and the Prison Act shall apply to them and to the persons detained therein, and the regulations as to registration, measurement and photographing of prisoners shall also apply.

Prison Act, 1952, s. 47: The Secretary of State may make rules for the management of Borstal Institutions and the treatment of persons detained therein. See Borstal Rules (No. 2), 1949 and 1952.

S. 46 : A person who is required to be taken to a Borstal Institution may be temporarily detained elsewhere until arrangements can be made for taking him there.

S. 44 : If a person under 21 is serving a sentence of imprisonment, the Secretary of State, after consultation with the judge or chairman of the court which passed the sentence, may authorise his transfer to a Borstal Institution. If a person detained in a Borstal Institution is incorrigible or exercises a bad influence on other inmates the Secretary of State may authorise his transfer to prison for the unexpired period of his detention.

S. 49 : A Borstal trainee who is unlawfully at large may be arrested by a constable without warrant and taken back to the Institution.

S. 45: A person sentenced to Borstal training shall be detained in a Borstal Institution for at least 9 months unless otherwise directed by the Secretary of State and as long as the Prison Commissioners determine but not longer than 3 years. After release such a person, for 4 years from the date of his sentence, shall be under the supervision (with any specified requirements) of a society or person named by the Prison Commissioners, who may at any time modify or cancel the requirements or cancel the supervision. If such a supervisee fails to comply with any of the requirements he may be recalled, by order made by the Prison Commissioners, to a Borstal Institution and is liable to be detained there until the 3 years end or for 6 months after his arrest under the order. If he does not come back voluntarily he will be unlawfully at large and under s. 49 may be arrested by a constable without warrant and taken back to the Borstal Institution.

Persistent Offenders.—A person who is leading persistently a criminal life, committing serious crimes of dishonesty such as burglary and robbery, regularly and habitually, was liable to be treated as a " habitual criminal " and sentenced to preventive detention under the Prevention of Crime Act, 1908.

This Act was repealed by the 10th Sched. of the Criminal Justice Act, 1948, which by s. 21, deals with persistent offenders who have committed several crimes by rendering them liable, if not less than 21, to corrective training, and if not less than 30, to preventive detention. Also a persistent offender, if sentenced to imprisonment may, under s. 26, Prison Act, 1952, be released on licence and placed under supervision.

Corrective Training.—C.J. Act, 1948, s. 21 (1). Where a person not less than 21 is convicted on indictment of an offence punishable with imprisonment for 2 years or more and has been convicted at least twice since he was 17, of offences so punishable on indictment, he may be sentenced to corrective training for at least 2 and not more than 4 years. Such training is to be of a corrective character with a view to his reformation and the prevention of crime, given in prison in the nature of special treatment according to rules made under s. 47 of the Prison Act, 1952. It is imprisonment of a special type. See also ss. 21 (4) and 23, as given below, which also apply to corrective training. This may be followed by supervision if he is released on licence before the expiration of his sentence (s. 26, Prison Act, 1952).

Preventive Detention.—C.J. Act, 1948, s. 21 (2). Where a person not less than 30 is convicted on indictment of an offence punishable with imprisonment for 2 years or more and has been convicted on indictment on at least three previous occasions since the age of 17, of offences so punishable on indictment and was on at least two of these occasions sentenced to Borstal training, imprisonment or corrective training, he may be sentenced to preventive detention for not less than 5 or more than 14 years.

Such detention in prison should be for a substantial time for the protection of the public, with special treatment in accordance with rules made under s. 47 of the Prison Act, 1952, and it may be followed by supervision if released on licence before the expiration of the sentence (s. 26, Prison Act, 1952). Such previous convictions qualifying a criminal for corrective training or preventive detention should have been in Great Britain.

C.J. Act, 1948, s. 21 (4): A report from the Prison Commissioners as to the offender's physical and mental condition and his suitability for a sentence of corrective training or preventive detention shall be considered by the court before passing sentence, and a copy of it shall be given to the offender or his Counsel or Solicitor. Under s. 23 notice of the previous convictions relied on shall be given to the offender and to the court at least 3 days before the trial.

Release on Licence and Supervision.—The provisions of the Prevention of Crime Acts and Penal Servitude Acts relating to convicts on licence and police supervisees have been repealed by the 10th Sched. to the Criminal Justice Act, 1948 and replaced by the following provisions of the C.J. Act, 1948 and the Prison Act, 1952.

C.J. Act, 1948, ss. 3, 4, 9 relate to the supervision by a probation officer which has been dealt with under " Probation of Offenders," above.

Prison Act, 1952, s. 45 deals with supervision after Borstal training for which see " Borstal Institution," above.

S. 26: The Prison Commissioners may release on licence a person sentenced to corrective training or preventive detention after he has served such portion of his sentence as laid down in rules. The Secretary of State may require the release of a person so sentenced at any time.

During his period of release on licence the offender shall comply with the requirements specified in the licence which may include a requirement that he shall be under the supervision of a named person or society. If he fails to comply with any requirement he may, by order, be recalled to prison, and if he does not obey he shall be deemed to be unlawfully at large (and can be arrested by a constable without warrant and taken back to prison, s. 49).

S. 25: A person serving a term of imprisonment may be granted a remission of part of his sentence for his industry and good conduct. If a person under 21 is sentenced to imprisonment, instead of part of his sentence being remitted he may be released on licence.

During his period of release on licence such young offender shall be under the supervision of a named society or person and shall comply with any requirements imposed.

If he fails to comply with any requirement he can be recalled, by order, to prison, and if he does not come he will be unlawfully at large and may be arrested (as above).

S. 27 : The Secretary of State may at any time release on licence with conditions a person serving a term of imprisonment for life. He may cancel or modify the conditions and may at any time by order recall the person to prison. If he does not come he will be unlawfully at large and may be arrested and brought back to prison (see above).

Notifying Address.—Criminal Justice Act, 1948, 10th Sched. repealed the provisions of the Prevention of Crimes Act, 1871 as to released prisoners notifying their addresses to the police and replaced them by s. 22 of the Act which has been amended by s. 29 of the Prison Act, 1952.

C.J. Act, 1948, s. 22: Where a person is convicted on indict-ment of an offence punishable with imprisonment for 2 years or more, and has been convicted on at least 2 previous occasions of offences for which he was sentenced to Borstal training or im-prisonment or has been previously convicted of an offence for which he was sentenced to corrective training, the court, if it sentences him to imprisonment for 12 months or more, *shall*, *unless* having regard to the circumstances including the character of the offender *it otherwise determines*, order that for 12 months from his next discharge from prison he shall be subject to the provisions of s. 29 of the Prison Act, 1952.

If such an order is made the offender on his next discharge from prison and thereafter from time to time as directed shall notify his address to the society appointed by the Prison Commissioners.

If he fails to do this on discharge the society shall, and if he subsequently fails to keep the society so informed, the society may, give notice of the failure to the Commissioner of Metropolitan Police and if possible inform the offender that such notice has been given. A certificate from the Metropolitan Police that such a notice has been received shall be evidence of the fact. From the date on which such notice has been given, the provisions of the First Sched. to the Prison Act, 1952 shall apply, as follows:—

The person shall register his address at a police station appointed by the chief officer of police in the police area in which he is from time to time residing. He shall be deemed to reside at any house or other place of whatever description at which he spends a night.

He shall also report once in each month on such day as directed at the police station at which his address is registered. If he changes his residence he shall register his new address stating his last previous address. This registration and report shall be in person, but the police may allow him to report in writing.

If he fails to comply with any of these requirements (without reasonable excuse) he shall be guilty of a summary offence and liable to 6 months imprisonment or less, and may be arrested without warrant by any constable.

If a failure to register an address it shall be a defence to prove either, that on a journey he remained no longer in the place where he failed to register than was reasonably necessary for the purposes of that journey, or that his absence from his registered address was temporary and he kept the police sufficiently informed of his whereabouts. If a failure to report it shall be a defence to prove that being temporarily absent from his registered address on the day appointed he personally reported at a police station in the police area in which he then was and stated his registered address.

A certificate from a police station certifying that a person failed to register or report or has registered, shall be evidence of the fact in proceedings under this Schedule.

Prison Act, 1952, s. 29: The Secretary of State may by a direction in writing relieve the offender of any requirement of above s. 22 or of the First Schedule, and may impose other requirements and on contravention may cancel the direction.

Special Offenders.—Prevention of Crimes Act, 1871, s. 7, makes it a special offence for any person twice convicted of crime (the second time on indictment) to do certain dishonest or suspicious acts within seven years after his last sentence.

Such an offender may therefore be termed a Special Offender under section 7 of this Act, and he is liable summarily to one year's imprisonment. He has the right to claim trial on indictment.

A special offender is a person who has been convicted on indictment of a crime and a previous conviction of a crime has been proved against him, and who at any time within seven years after the expiration of the sentence passed on him for the last of such crimes :—

(1) Is brought before a Magistrates' Court, charged with getting his livelihood by dishonest means, and the Court is satisfied that there are reasonable grounds for believing such charge is correct, or

(2) Is charged with any offence and on being required by a Magistrates' Court to give his name and address, refuses or gives a false name and address, or

(3) Is found in any place, whether public or private, under such circumstances as to satisfy the Court before whom he is brought that he was about to commit or to aid in the commission of any offence, or was waiting for an opportunity so to do. (If charged with " about to commit " there must be evidence to prove that he was then and there about to commit the offence, *R.* v. *Goodwin* (1944)), or

(4) Is found in or upon any dwelling-house or any building, yard or premises being parcel of and attached to such dwelling-house, or in or upon any shop, warehouse, counting-house, or other place of business or in any garden, orchard, pleasure ground or nursery ground or any building or erection therein, without being able to account to the satisfaction of the Court before whom he is brought for his being found on such premises. (" Found " is not equivalent to " arrested," so actual arrest on the spot is not necessary, *R.* v. *Goodwin* (1944)).

Power to arrest a special offender :—

(1) Any constable, if authorised to do so by his chief officer, may arrest without warrant any such special offender on reasonable grounds for believing he is getting his livelihood by dishonest means.

(2) Any constable may without warrant arrest any such special offender whom he finds in any place, public or private, under circumstances indicating that he was about to commit or to aid in committing any offence, or that he was waiting for an opportunity to commit or aid in committing any offence.

(3) Any constable or the owner or occupier (or his servant or person authorised by him) may without warrant arrest any such special offender found in or upon any dwelling-house, yard, etc., shop or place of business, or garden, pleasure ground,

etc., who does not satisfactorily account for his presence therein (s. 7).

" Crime " in this s. 7 means " crime " as defined in s. 20 of the Prevention of Crimes Act, 1871, as meaning any felony, or the offence of uttering false or counterfeit coin, or of possessing counterfeit gold or silver coin, or obtaining money or goods by false pretences, or conspiracy to defraud, or the misdemeanours in s. 28, Larceny Act, 1916 (which replace those in s. 58, Larceny Act, 1861)—that is, being found by night either in possession of housebreaking implements without lawful excuse, or armed or disguised or in any building with intent to commit any felony.

The expression " offence " is defined in this s. 20 as meaning any act or omission which is not a crime as defined by this Act, and is punishable on indictment or summary conviction.

Loiterers and Suspected Persons.—The police have by law great powers for the arrest and prosecution of persons who by their actions appear likely to commit crime.

Frequenting and Loitering.—Any person may arrest without warrant every suspected person or reputed thief frequenting or loitering about or in any river, canal or navigable stream, dock or basin, or any quay, wharf or warehouse near or adjoining thereto, or any street, highway or avenue leading thereto, or any place of public resort or any place leading thereto, or any street, highway or any place adjacent to a street or highway, with intent to commit felony (Vagrancy Act, 1824, s. 4, amended by Penal Servitude Act, 1891, s. 7).

The prisoner may be convicted of this offence if from the circumstances of the case and from his known character as proved to the Justices, it appears that his intent was to commit a felony. It shall not be necessary to show that the prisoner was guilty of any particular act or acts tending to show his purpose or intent (Prevention of Crimes Act, 1871, s. 15). See also " Extent of Evidence," Chap. 7.

On conviction, prisoner will be treated as a rogue and a vagabond and is liable to three months imprisonment from two Justices (Vagrancy Act, 1824).

A " suspected person " under this section would appear to be a person who has acquired the character of a suspect by reason of his previous conduct.

His previous convictions, etc., need not be known by the police who arrested him (*R.* v. *Clarke* (1950)).

In *Hartley* v. *Ellnor* (1917), it was held that there need not be evidence of a previous conviction or of previous bad character, but that the conduct of the accused on the day in question might be sufficient to render him a suspected person.

In *Ledwith* v. *Roberts* (1937), it was held that there must be some previous act occasioning suspicion prior to the final act indicating the intent to commit felony; in other words, one transaction by itself is not sufficient to justify arrest under the section.

The conduct or character of the person must be such as to show he is a " suspected person."

In *Rawlings* v. *Smith* (1938), it was held that *Ledwith* v. *Roberts* did not overrule *Hartley* v. *Ellnor* and that " frequenting " or " loitering" involves something which is continuous or repeated and does not depend on one single act.

Therefore to justify arrest as a suspected person one single suspicious act is not sufficient, and the prisoner's previous conduct should have been such as would make him a suspected person before his actual behaviour indicating intent to commit felony which occasioned his arrest.

The driver of a motor vehicle may be a " loiterer " and also a " suspected person "—see *Bridge* v. *Campbell* (1947).

A " reputed thief " would appear to be a person who from his associates, conduct, and general mode of living has previously come under notice as a person probably engaged in thieving.

Where prisoner has been previously convicted as a rogue and a vagabond, or where prisoner on arrest as a rogue and a vagabond (as above) violently resists arrest, he shall, on being convicted of the offence for which he was arrested, be deemed an incorrigible rogue, and the Court should commit him to prison until the next Quarter Sessions, and Quarter Sessions can order further imprisonment not exceeding one year (Vagrancy Act, 1824, ss. 5, 10).

Night Loitering.—A constable may arrest without warrant any person he finds lying or loitering in any highway, yard or other place during the night (viz. between 9 P.M. and 6 A.M.) and whom he has good cause to suspect of having committed or being about to commit any felony against the Act, and shall take such person as soon as reasonably may be, before a Justice to be dealt with according to law (Larceny Act, 1916, s. 41, Malicious Damage Act, 1861, s. 57, Offences against the Person Act, 1861, s. 66). In such cases the person can be bound over unless some definite offence can be proved.

The chief felonies under the Acts are larceny or stealing, robbery, sacrilege, burglary, housebreaking, receiving goods feloniously stolen, killing animals with intent to steal, damaging fixtures, trees, etc., with intent to steal and demanding with menaces with intent to steal.

Found on Premises.—Any person may arrest any person found in or upon any dwelling-house, warehouse, coach-house, stable or outhouse, or in any inclosed yard, garden or area for any unlawful purpose. The unlawful purpose must be the commission of some criminal offence. Prisoner will be dealt with as a rogue and a vagabond, and is liable to three months imprisonment (Vagrancy Act, 1824, s. 4).

Any person may arrest without warrant every person who shall be found by night in any building with intent to commit any felony therein. This offence is a misdemeanour (Larceny Act, 1916, s. 28).

The accused need not necessarily be arrested inside the building but there should be evidence that he had been inside it (*R.* v. *Lumsden* (1951)).

Housebreaking Implements.—Any person may arrest any person having in his or her custody or possession any picklock, key, crow, jack, bit or other implement with intent feloniously to break into any dwelling-house, warehouse, coach-house, stable, or outbuilding. Prisoner will be dealt with as a rogue and a vagabond, and is liable to three months imprisonment (Vagrancy Act, 1824, s. 4).

Any person may arrest without warrant every person who shall be found by night having in his possession without lawful excuse (onus of proof rests on such person) any key, picklock, crow, jack, bit or other implement of housebreaking. This offence is a misdemeanour (Larceny Act, 1916, s. 28). (Any implement that may be used for the purpose of housebreaking is such an implement if the jury find it to have been in possession for that purpose. *R.* v. *Oldham* (1852)).

Found Armed, etc., with Intent.—Any person may arrest any person armed with any gun, pistol, hanger, cutlass, bludgeon or other offensive weapon or having upon him or her any instrument with intent to commit any felonious act. Prisoner will be dealt with as a rogue and a vagabond, and is liable to three months imprisonment (Vagrancy Act, 1824, s. 4. See also Firearms Act, 1937, s. 26. See also " Prevention of Crime Act, 1953," Chap. 3, and "Robbery", Chap. 14.).

Any person may arrest without warrant every person who shall be found by night armed with any dangerous weapon or instrument with intent to break into a building (viz. some definite building) and commit any felony therein. This offence is a misdemeanour (Larceny Act, 1916, s. 28).

Any person may arrest without warrant every person who shall be found by night having his face blackened or disguised with intent to commit a felony. This offence is a misdemeanour (Larceny Act, 1916, s. 28). See Chap. 13.

A county borough constable while on duty may arrest any idle and disorderly person whom he finds disturbing the public peace or whom he has just cause to suspect of intention to commit a felony (Municipal Corporations Act, 1882, s. 193 and Police Act, 1946, s. 1).

Found Wandering and Sleeping Out.—Any person may arrest any person found wandering about and lodging in any barn or outhouse, or in any deserted or unoccupied building, or in the open air, etc., as more fully described under " Vagrancy Frauds ".

Chap. 27 and not giving a good account of himself or herself. Prisoner will be treated as rogue and a vagabond and is liable to three months imprisonment (Vagrancy Act, 1824, s. 4. and Vagrancy Act, 1935).

Prisons.—The Prison Act, 1952, has repealed previous Acts relating to prisons and discharged prisoners and contains several provisions formerly in the Criminal Justice Act, 1948, which have been included wherever appropriate in these pages.

S. 8: Every prison officer while acting as such has all the powers, etc. of a constable. See " Arrest," Chap. 3.

S. 13: A person is deemed to be in legal custody while he is confined in or is being taken to or from any prison and while he is working or is otherwise outside the prison in the custody or control of a prison officer.

S. 18: Corporal punishment may be ordered in prisons under Rules and on confirmation by the Secretary of State.

S. 22 deals with the removal of prisoners for judicial or other purposes (see " Habeas Corpus " Chap. 5) as does s. 48 re Scotland, Isle of Man and Channel Islands.

S. 23: For taking a person to or from any prison (or place of detention, s. 43) under competent and proper order, a constable or other officer may act outside the area of his jurisdiction, having all the powers, etc., of his office.

S. 39: Any person who aids any prisoner in escaping or attempting to escape from a prison or who, to help an escape, conveys anything into a prison or to a prisoner or places anything outside a prison for a prisoner, shall be guilty of felony (2 years)— see " Prison Breach," Chap. 21.

S. 40: The unlawful conveyance of spirits or tobacco into a prison or to or for a prisoner, or an officer allowing same, Summary Offence.

S. 41: The unlawful conveyance of any letter or any other thing into or out of a prison or to or for a prisoner. Summary Offence.

S. 43: The following provisions apply to remand centres, detention centres and Borstal institutions:—

S. 6 (board of visitors); s. 13 (legal custody); s. 16 (photographs, etc.); s. 18 (no corporal punishment); s. 19 (justice may visit); s. 22 (removal); s. 23 (constable's power); ss. 31, 32 (allowance to discharged prisoner); s. 39 to 41 (offences re escape, etc.).

The following provisions will not apply—

S. 25 (remission or licence); ss. 26 to 30 (release on licence, address).

S. 49: A constable may arrest without warrant any prisoner unlawfully at large, see " Arrest," Chap. 3.

S. 53: " Prison " does not include a naval, military or air force prison.

S. 55: The following provisions extend to Scotland: ss. 22 (2) and 48 (removal of prisoners) and s. 49 (1) (prisoners unlawfully at large).

2nd Sched. deals with persons in Scotland after discharge from prison, etc., in England.

The Prison Rules, 1949, r. 52 deal with the treatment of prisoners.

———————————

Chapter XXIX

PERSONS

Contents

Aliens.—An alien is a foreigner, a subject or citizen of a foreign country. An alien, while in this country, is subject to its laws just as if he were a British subject.

Under the British Nationality Acts 1948 to 1958 every person who is a citizen of the United Kingdom and Colonies or who is a citizen of Canada, Australia, New Zealand, the Union of South Africa, Newfoundland, India, Pakistan, Federation of Rhodesia and Nyasaland, Ceylon, Ghana, Federation of Malaya and the State of Singapore, may be known either as a British subject or as a Commonwealth citizen, both of which expressions shall have the same meaning (s. 1).

" Alien "as regards the Aliens Order means a person who is not a British subject, a citizen of Eire or a British protected person (from a protectorate, mandated territory) (s. 32).

The Irish Free State, later known as Eire and now called the Republic of Ireland is not part of the United Kingdom but is not a foreign country for the purposes of any law in force in any part of the United Kingdom. An Eire citizen is not a British subject but is not an alien and is treated as a British subject while in the United Kingdom. Northern Ireland remains part of the United Kingdom (Ireland Act, 1949, which also deals with the operation of the British Nationality Act, 1948).

The Aliens Restrictions Acts, 1914 and 1919, deal with the regulation of aliens in the United Kingdom and authorise the issue of Orders in Council thereon. The 1914 Act applied during a state of war or on occasion of imminent national danger or great emergency and its powers were extended for a year in 1919 and were continued yearly by the Expiring Laws Continuance Acts. The onus of proving a person is not an alien rests on that person (1914 Act, s. 1). The term " United Kingdom," unless the context otherwise requires, means Great Britain and Northern Ireland (Royal and Parliamentary Titles Act, 1927). Under the 1919 Act, it is an offence for an alien to attempt to cause dis-affection, or to promote industrial unrest (s. 3). See " Sedition," Chap. 20. An alien must not change his name from the name by which he was known on 4th August, 1914, unless the change is legally authorised (s. 7). An alien, if challenged by any party, shall not sit upon a jury (s. 8), nor shall an alien be appointed to an office in the Civil Service (s. 6). The temporary employment of certain aliens was allowed by orders in 1941 and 1945.

The admission, supervision, etc., of aliens is regulated by the Aliens Orders, 1953 and 1957.

Landings and Embarkation.—An alien shall not land or embark in a ship or aircraft except with leave of an immigration officer, and he should do so at an approved port (Art. 1). This will not apply to the crew of the vessel unless otherwise prohibited or to an alien landing to go on in another aircraft at the port (Art. 2); Also this will not apply to an alien travelling in the " common travel area," (the United Kingdom, Channel Islands, Isle of Man and Republic of Ireland) but will apply to an alien coming from the Republic of Ireland where he landed without leave (Art. 3).

Except with the permission of the Secretary of State leave to land shall not be granted to an alien:

(1) unless he can support himself and dependants and if he comes to employment unless he has a written permit from the Minister of Labour;

(2) if he has been sentenced abroad for an indictable offence;

(3) if he is of unsound mind or mentally defective;

(4) if undesirable for medical reasons (Art. 4).

Leave to land may be granted subject to any specified landing conditions (Arts. 5, 6).

Every person over 16 who lands or embarks shall, if required by an immigration officer, produce in every case a valid passport with photograph or document of identity, and if he is an alien produce a landing or embarkation card (supplied by the ship or aircraft) duly completed. An immigration officer or medical inspector may examine any person seeking to land or embark to ascertain whether he is or not an alien. However this Article does not apply to persons travelling within the "common travel area" (see above) except persons coming from the Republic of Ireland who did not get leave to land there (Art. 7).

If an alien is refused permission to land the ship or aircraft in which he came may be directed to take him away and he may be detained until that is done (Art. 8).

This expulsion power shall apply to any alien landing unlaw-fully, and a member of a crew or a stowaway may be expelled even after two months (Art. 9).

Masters of ships and commanders of aircraft coming into or going out of the " common travel area " shall supply particulars of their passengers and crews (Art. 10).

They shall prevent from landing any persons who have to be examined and may detain them (Art. 11).

Any alien landing or embarking, except within the " common travel area," to or from abroad shall, if required by an immigration officer, declare whether he is carrying any documents and if so shall produce them. An immigration officer or constable may search any such alien and his baggage and detain any documents for examination (Art. 12).

Registration.—There is a central register of aliens. Each police area is a registration district with a local register of aliens. The registration officer is the Chief Constable who can authorise any constable or other person to act for the purposes of the Order (Art. 13). Every alien of or over 16 who is in the United Kingdom must register unless exempted. An alien must attend at his local registration office and produce his passport or other document of identity or explain its absence (Art. 14). An alien who has supplied the particulars before or who is one of the crew of a ship and lands need not register. An alien who has landed need not register until after 3 months after his entry unless required to do so by a landing condition and an alien coming from the Republic of Ireland has to comply with the special provisions of the First Schedule to the Order (Art. 15). Registration certificate costs 5 shillings.

A registered alien who has a residence in the United Kingdom, if he changes his residence, shall report his new residence to the registration officer of the area within 72 hours. When he is absent from his residence for over 2 months he must report his address and any later address and his return to his registration officer. If the alien has no residence and travels about, after 72 hours in any registration district he must report there forthwith, and if he changes address in any district he must report his new address there within 72 hours. If an alien has no address he may have a resident referee to whom he shall report changes of address and who will keep the registration officer informed (Art. 16).

A registered alien shall notify within 72 hours any alteration in the particulars he supplied and shall, if required, give any necessary information to the registration officer including two recent photographs of himself (Art. 17).

Every alien, on demand by an immigration officer or constable, shall produce either his registration certificate or his passport or other document of identity, or else give a satisfactory explanation for not producing. If he does not do so he may be detained for inquiry (Art. 18).

The keeper of any premises furnished or unfurnished where lodging or sleeping accommodation is provided for reward (except premises exempted by the Chief Constable such as schools, hospitals, clubs, etc.), shall keep a register (open to inspection by any constable or authorised person) of all persons over 16 staying there for one night or more. Every such person, on arrival, shall give his name and nationality. If he is an alien, he shall also give particulars of his passport or registration certificate, and on departure give his next destination. The keeper of the premises shall ask for all this and keep a record of same for at least 12 months (Art. 19). Contravention of this Art. 19 by a non-alien or any offence in respect of the register or statement required, is an offence requiring the consent of the Director of Public Prosecutions for a prosecution, (Art 26). See Aliens (Registration in Hotels) Regs. 1946, and the Aliens Order 1957.

Deportation.—The Secretary of State may order the deportation of an alien in the following cases :—

(1) If a Court certifies that the alien has been convicted of (a) any offence for which it has power to impose a sentence of imprisonment in the case of an offender of full age, or (b) any prostitution offence; and the court recommends deportation, or

(2) If he considers deportation would be for the public good.

Also if the Secretary of State approves an alien may be expelled from the Isle of Man and deported (Art. 20). An alien to be deported may be detained until deported. An alien sentenced to imprisonment and recommended for deportation shall be detained until the Secretary of State orders his deportation or his release. A deported alien will be kept on aircraft or ship until it leaves for a specified port where he is to be landed (Art. 21).

General.—An offence against the Order is punishable summarily by fine up to £100 or by up to 6 months imprisonment and the offender may be bound over to comply with the Order. If he fails to enter into recognizances when so bound over he may be sent to prison for up to 6 months (Art. 26).

An offence against the Order includes any contravention or non-compliance with the Order, aiding or abetting an offence against the Order, knowingly harbouring such an offender, making false returns, etc., refusing information, etc., obstructing officer, altering documents under the Order (Art. 25).

A constable or immigration officer may arrest without warrant any person who has committed or is reasonably suspected to have committed an offence against the Order (except an offence against Art. 19 re hotel registers) and any person who may be detained under the Order.

When an alien is thus in custody (which is legal custody) reasonably necessary steps may be taken for photographing, measuring or otherwise identifying him (Art. 28).

The Secretary of State may impose special restrictions on any alien or class of aliens (Art. 22). He may exempt persons from the provisions of the Order (Art. 23).

The Order shall not apply to envoys (and their staffs) or foreign powers accredited to Her Majesty.

A British protected person is not an alien as regards this Order. An alien serving in H.M. Forces or the Forces of India or in the United Kingdom while serving in several allied Forces will not be deemed an alien as regards this Order (Art. 24).

Any police station may be a place of detention for up to 5 days (otherwise prison) under Art. 8 (landing refused), Art. 18 (non production) and Art. 20 (deportation). See Aliens (Places of Detention) Order, 1954.

For the law as to the national status of married women, see the British Nationality Act, 1948.

Husband and Wife.—As regards any defence of coercion or compulsion, see " Excuses for Crime " (Chap. 1) and " Accessories to a Crime " (Chap. 2). As regards conspiracy, see Chap. 23.

As regards the giving of evidence by a wife against her husband, or *vice versa*, see " Accused Persons and their Husbands or Wives," Chap. 7.

At Common Law, as a wife was held to be one person with her husband, the taking by the one of the property of the other was not an offence. However, the Married Women's Property Act, 1882, ss. 12, 16, and the Law Reform, etc., Act, 1935, altered this, and now, as a result of s. 36 of the Larceny Act, 1916 (as amended) :—

(1) A wife has the same remedies and redress for the protection and security of her own separate property as if she were an unmarried woman.

(2) A wife cannot prosecute her husband under the Larceny Act, and *vice versa*, while they are living together.

(3) A wife can prosecute her husband under the Larceny Act, and *vice versa*, if they are living apart and if the act was not done while they were living together, or if the property was taken when leaving or deserting with a view to their ceasing to live together.

Landlord and Tenant.—A landlord of a house may be held responsible if the house is conducted as a brothel. See " Brothels," Chap. 10.

It is a misdemeanour for a tenant of any building to unlawfully and maliciously damage such building or detach any fixture (Malicious Damage Act, 1861, ss. 13 and 59). See Chap. 15

Under the Larceny Act, 1916, it is felony for a tenant or his wife to steal any chattel or fixture let to be used in or with the house (s. 16), or for any person to steal or damage with intent to steal anything fixed in or to any premises, or any tree, shrub, etc., belonging to such premises (s. 8). See " Statutory Larcenies," Chap. 14.

Clergymen.—Ministers of religion are by law specially protected when engaged in carrying out their duties in a place of Divine worship or in a burial ground, as follows :—

Offences against the Person Act, 1861, s. 36 : This section makes it a misdemeanour to obstruct, prevent or endeavour to obstruct or prevent any clergyman or other minister in or from celebrating Divine service or officiating in any place of Divine service or in the performance of the burial service. It is also a misdemeanour to strike or offer any violence to any clergyman or other minister engaged in the discharge of his duties as above.

Ecclesiastical Courts Jurisdiction Act, 1860, s. 2 : It is a summary offence to molest, disturb or by any unlawful means disquiet or misuse any authorised preacher or clergyman celebrating any Divine service or office in any church, chapel or burial ground, and under s. 3 the offender may be arrested by any churchwarden or constable. See " Disturbing Public Worship," Chap. 20.

Lawyers, etc.—It is not lawful for a person who is not a barrister, solicitor or other qualified member of the legal profession to act as such.

It is a summary offence for any unqualified person to wilfully pretend to be a qualified solicitor (Solicitors Act 1957).

Various statutes allow certain authorised persons, who may not be lawyers and usually are not, to conduct Court proceedings before magistrates : for example, national assistance officers, inland revenue officers, factory inspectors, school inspectors, etc.

Various Acts authorise legal proceedings by a local authority for breaches of the Acts. Under s. 277, Local Government Act, 1933, a local authority can authorise any member or officer of the authority to institute and carry on (or defend) summary proceedings. However a police officer is not a servant or agent or officer of a local authority (*Fisher* v. *Oldham Corporation* (1930)).

Doctors.—It is an offence for any person to represent himself to be a registered medical practitioner when in fact he is not one.

A person who is duly qualified to practise any branch of the medical profession may register himself with the Medical Council, and his name will appear on the yearly " Medical Register."

The Medical Act, 1858 as amended by the Medical Act, 1950, makes it a summary offence for any person to wilfully and falsely pretend that he is a physician, doctor, surgeon, apothecary, etc., duly registered under the Act, or that he is recognised in law as a physician, etc.

Dentists.—It is a summary offence for any person to practise or hold himself out as practising dentistry unless he is registered in the Dentists' Register. However, a registered medical practitioner may practise dentistry, and a registered chemist may extract teeth in urgent cases.

A company may carry on the business of dentistry if its business is confined to dentistry and the majority of its directors and all the operating staff are registered dentists.

Hospitals and approved dental schools may also carry on the business of dentistry. See the Dentists Acts, 1956 and 1957.

Veterinary Surgeons.—The Veterinary Surgeons Act, 1881, makes it a summary offence for any person who is not a Member or Fellow of the Royal College of Veterinary Surgeons to state or imply that he is one. See also Veterinary Surgeons Act (1881) Amendment Act, 1920, and Veterinary Surgeons Act, 1948.

A register of the Members and Fellows is kept, and an unregistered person who takes or uses the title of veterinary surgeon commits a summary offence.

Pharmaceutical Chemists.—Under the Pharmacy and Poisons Act, 1933, and the Pharmacy Acts, 1953 and 1954, a person who sells goods by retail as a chemist or who describes himself as a chemist and druggist or druggist or pharmaceutical chemist shall be registered with the Pharmaceutical Society as a pharmacist, on penalty of £20 fine (s. 3). He should also register each year (s, 1), and if he sells poisons he should exhibit his certificate of registration in his premises (s. 8) and have his premises registered (s. 12). The Statutory Committee of the Pharmaceutical Society may remove his name from the register for misconduct (s. 7).

Inspectors are appointed by the Society to enforce this Act (s. 25). See also " Poisons," Chap. 39.

Opticians.—The Opticians Act, 1958 (certain provisions of which came into operation on January 1, 1959) established a General Optical Council to regulate the practice of opticians etc. When ss. 20 to 22 of the Act are brought into operation it will be an offence (subject to certain exceptions) for a person who is not a registered ophthalmic optician to test the sight of another person; restrictions will be placed on the sale and supply of appliances to correct, remedy, or relieve a defect of sight; and penalties will be provided for persons pretending to be registered etc.

Nurses.—The Nurses Act, 1957, authorised a General Nursing Council for England and Wales and this Council keeps a register of nurses for the sick and a roll of assistant nurses. Before any person may be registered as a nurse and use the title " nurse ", he or she must have undergone the prescribed training and have the prescribed experience in the nursing of the sick. The Council may issue certificates of registration and have power to cancel such registration.

Private agencies for the supply of nurses must be licensed by the relevant local authority (Nurses Agencies Act 1957).

It is a summary offence for any person except a registered nurse, an enrolled assistant nurse or a children's nurse to unlawfully assume the name or title of nurse (Nurses Act 1957, s. 27). See also " Nursing Homes ", Chap. 39.

Midwives.—Under the Midwives Act, 1951, a woman may not carry on the occupation of a midwife unless she is duly certified and has her name on the roll of midwives kept by the Central Midwives Board or is exempted by order of the local authority under the Emergency Laws (Misc. Provisions) Act, 1953. It is a summary offence for any woman who is not certified under the Act to use the title of midwife or any description implying that she is a qualified or authorised midwife (s. 8). It is also an offence for any person not certified under the Act to attend a woman in childbirth unless under the supervision of a medical practitioner or unless in a case of sudden or urgent necessity (s. 9).

Local Health Authorities are required to provide domiciliary midwives adequate for the needs of their areas (National Health Service Act, 1946, s. 23), and when this is done it will be a summary offence for an unqualified person to act as a maternity nurse for gain (s. 11).

Master and Servant.—It is a summary offence to falsely personate a master and give a false servant's character, or to give false particulars of service regarding a servant, or for a person when offering himself as a servant to use a false character or give false particulars of his service (Servants' Characters Act, 1792).

Architects.—The Architects (Registration) Act, 1931, established an Architects Registration Council, which keeps a register of architects. The name of a registered person may be struck off the register if he is convicted of a criminal offence or is found guilty of disgraceful conduct as an architect.

Under a similar Act of 1938, a person shall not practise or carry on business as an " architect " unless he is registered, on penalty of fine on summary conviction. This will not apply to the use of the title " naval architect," " landscape architect " or " golf course architect," nor to those in the service of a local authority.

Persons, Old, Disabled, Sick, etc.—Under the National Assistance Act, 1948, it is a summary offence to carry on a home for old or disabled persons unless such home is registered with the local Council which can refuse and cancel such registration. All such homes are liable to official inspection (ss. 37-40).

Persons suffering from grave chronic disease or being aged, etc., who are living in insanitary conditions and do not have proper care and attention, may be removed to suitable premises on medical certificate and order of a magistrates' court (s. 47).

Under the Public Health Act, 1936, the local authority, on order of a Justice, may remove a person suffering from notifiable disease where there is serious risk of the infection spreading, to hospital and detain such person there (ss. 169, 170).

A magistrates' court, on the application of the local authority, may order an infectious person suffering from tuberculosis of the respiratory tract, to be removed to hospital and detained there (s. 172).

Chapter XXX

HER MAJESTY'S FORCES

Contents

Interference with Military.—It is a summary offence for any person wilfully to obstruct or otherwise interfere with any officer, soldier or airman in the execution of his duties. To injure, drug, etc., any soldier so as to enable him to avoid military service is also a summary offence (Army and Air Force Acts, 1955, s. 42). Under the Manœuvres Act, 1958 it is a summary offence wilfully and unlawfully to obstruct or interfere with the execution of duly authorised military manœuvres, or, without due authority, to enter or remain in any camp (such trespasser may be removed by any constable or by order of any commissioned officer).

False Characters.—It is a summary offence for any person joining or offering to join H.M. Naval, Military or Marine Forces, to make use of any forged statements as to his character or employment or of any statement as to his character or employment which to his knowledge is false. It is also a summary offence for any person to make a false written statement as to the character or employment of any man, to be used for the purpose of joining H.M. Forces (Seamen's and Soldiers' False Characters Act, 1906).

False Discharges.—It is a summary offence to forge the certificate of service or discharge of any person who has served in H.M. Forces, or to forge any certificate purporting to be one of service or discharge, or to knowingly make use of any such forged certificate, or to personate the holder of any such certificate (Seamen's and Soldiers' False Characters Act, 1906).

Deserters and Absentees.—The general rule is that on reasonable suspicion a constable may arrest without warrant any deserter or absentee without leave from H.M. regular forces (Navy, Army, Air Force and Marines). See Army and Air Force Acts, 1955, s. 186, and Naval Discipline Act 1957, s. 105.

Such a person may be arrested with or without warrant and should be brought before a Magistrates' Court. The Court may order him to be handed over to an escort or may remand him to prison or police custody to await an escort. His own authorities will subsequently deal with him.

Where the deserter or absentee has surrendered to or has been arrested by the police, a certificate from the officer in charge of the police station concerned giving the facts will be evidence of the matters so stated.

An absentee who has merely overstayed his leave and is willing to rejoin his unit, when an escort is considered unnecessary, may be put on the train for his unit, having been given a railway warrant if necessary.

Any person who denies he is a deserter or absentee or who asks to be taken before a magistrate should be taken before a magistrates' court (Army and Air Force Acts, 1955, s. 186, and the Naval Discipline Act, 1957, s. 105). If he claims that he is not an absentee or deserter and therefore is not subject to military law, the court should take depositions under the M.C. Act and Rules, 1952. If the court decides that he is, he can appeal to the Divisional Court on a case stated and the magistrates' court should admit him to bail pending the decision. If no such appeal the court will commit him to military custody.

See also " Visiting Forces Act," Chap. 2.

Reservists called out for annual training or on permanent service, who without reasonable excuse fail to join the colours, are liable to arrest, also members of the Territorial Army who fail, without reasonable excuse, to report on embodiment ; but the police should not take action in such cases except on instructions from the military authorities.

Men of the Territorial Army who absent themselves from drills or training are not liable to arrest by the police.

It is a summary offence falsely to represent oneself to be a deserter (Army and Air Force Acts, 1955, s. 191, and Naval Discipline Act, 1957, s. 96).

It is a summary offence to procure or attempt to procure a soldier, sailor or airman to desert or absent himself without leave, or knowingly to aid a deserter or absentee without leave (Army and Air Force Acts, 1955, s. 192, and Naval Discipline Act, 1957, s. 97).

Property of Her Majesty's Forces.—Under s. 195, Army and Air Force Acts, 1955 and s. 98 of the Naval Discipline Act, 1957, it is a summary offence to have any illicit dealings with any property of H.M. Forces. See also " Public Stores ", Chap. 18.

Such illicit dealings include any—

(1) Buying, exchanging, taking in pawn, detaining or receiving same from any person on any pretence whatever ;

(2) Soliciting or enticing any person to sell, exchange, pawn or give away same ; and

(3) Assisting or acting for any person in selling, exchanging, pawning or making away with same.

It will be a good defence for accused to prove that he acted in ignorance of the same being such property as described above, or that same was duly sold by the authorities, or that same was the personal property of an ex-member of the Forces.

If such property as above described is found in the possession of any person, he may be brought before a Magistrates' Court, and if the Court has reasonable ground to believe that the property was illegally obtained as above he may be convicted unless he satisfies the Court that he came by the property lawfully.

A Magistrates' Court may issue a warrant to search for such property as in the case of stolen goods.

Any person found committing the above offence may be arrested without warrant, and any person to whom any such army property is offered may, and should, arrest the person offering same for sale, pawn or delivery (Army and Air Force Acts, 1955, s. 195 and Naval Discipline Act, 1957, ss. 98 and 106).

An offence by a serving soldier in connection with government property at his barracks or camp should be dealt with by his commanding officer under military law (*R.* v. *Kirkup* (1950)).

Pensioners.—In general, the making of any false statement or the supplying of any false information in connection with pensions, allowances, etc., is a summary offence.

It is a summary offence for any person to receive, detain or have in possession, as a pledge or security for a debt, any official document or certificate issued in connection with the right of any person to pension, pay, allowances, etc., in connection with service in Her Majesty's Forces. (For a similar provision as regards pensions for civil non-effective services see C.J. Act, 1925, s. 37). It is also a summary offence for any person, without lawful authority or excuse (the proof of which shall lie on such person), to have in his possession any such official document or certificate or any certificate of discharge or any other official document issued in connection with the mobilisation or demobilisation of any of Her Majesty's Forces or its members (Army and Air Force Acts, 1955, s. 196, and Naval Discipline Act, 1957, s. 99).

Uniforms.—Under the Uniforms Act, 1894, it is a summary offence for any person not serving in the Military (or Air) Forces to wear without Her Majesty's permission the uniform of any of these Forces, or any dress having the appearance of or bearing any of the regimental or other distinctive marks of such uniform.

However, this prohibition of the unauthorised use of military uniform is not to prevent any person wearing any uniform in a stage play, music hall, circus, or *bona fide* military representation.

It is also a summary offence for any person not serving in Her Majesty's Naval or Military (or Air) Forces to wear any such uniform or dress resembling same, in such a manner and under such circumstances as to be likely to bring contempt on that uniform. It is a similar offence for any person to employ another to so wear that uniform or dress.

Similar provisions apply to the British Mercantile Marine uniform (British Mercantile Marine Uniform Act, 1919).

Under s. 10 of the Police Act, 1919, it is a summary offence for any person who is not a member of the police force to wear, without the permission of the police authority, any police uniform or dress having the appearance or bearing any of the distinctive marks of that uniform. However, this prohibition is not to prevent any person from wearing any uniform or dress in a stage play, music hall or circus performance.

Using any official uniform without lawful authority for the purpose of gaining admission to a prohibited place or for purposes prejudicial to the safety or interests of the State is a misdemeanour (Official Secrets Act, 1920, s. 1). See " Official Secrets Acts," Chap. 20.

Decorations.—The rule is that any of the Sovereign's decorations or medals may only be worn by persons to whom they have been awarded, or by persons entitled to wear them.

The unauthorised use of any military decoration or medal or medal ribbon or any badge supplied or authorised by the Army or Air Council is prohibited, and it is a summary offence for—

(1) Any unauthorised person to use or wear same or anything as nearly resembling the same as to be calculated to deceive ;

(2) Any person falsely to represent that he is or has been entitled to use or wear same ;

(3) Any person, without lawful authority or excuse, to supply or offer to supply same to a person not authorised to use or wear same.

This section does not prohibit the wearing or supply of ordinary regimental badges or ornaments representing the same (Army and Air Force Acts, 1955, s. 197).

Any illegal dealing in Naval, Military or Air Force decorations and medals, such as buying, taking in pawn, detaining, etc. (as given under "Property of Her Majesty's Forces ") is a summary offence unless same are the personal property of an ex-member of the service or of the legal personal representatives of an officer or soldier who has died.

Billeting.—Power is given by the Army and Air Force Acts, 1955, for the compulsory provision by the police of accommodation for members of Her Majesty's Forces when proceeding on duty from place to place, and this is termed billeting.

Where a billeting requisition has been produced to the chief officer of police for the area specified in the requisition he must, on the demand of the commanding officer or any officer, soldier or airman authorised by him in writing, billet such number of persons or vehicles as may be required by the officer or soldier making the demand, not exceeding the number specified in the requisition. A chief officer of police may delegate these duties to a constable of any class (s. 156).

Billets may be provided in any inn, hotel or other premises providing sleeping accommodation for reward, in any building to which the public habitually have access, or which is wholly or partly maintained out of rates, or in any dwelling, outhouse, warehouse, barn or stables, but not in any other premises (s. 155).

A local authority may make a scheme for provision of billets and where such scheme is in force the chief officer of police must act in accordance with it (s. 157).

The occupiers of premises on which persons or vehicles have been billeted must furnish such accommodation, including meals, as the officer, soldier or airman demanding the billets may require, at the rates prescribed by law (s. 158).

Any person aggrieved by having an undue number of persons billeted upon him, or claiming exemption, may apply to a person or persons appointed on behalf of the local authority by the Minister of Housing and Local Government (s. 159).

Where any damage is caused by the billeting of persons or vehicles the occupier of the premises may recover damages from the Army or Air Council (s. 160).

Any person who refuses to receive and accommodate any person or vehicle billeted on him, or tries to pay off any person billeted on him instead of furnishing the accommodation is liable to summary prosecution (s. 161).

The above provisions apply to civilians employed with the forces (s. 162).

The prices payable for the accommodation provided are prescribed by regulations of the Army or Air Council made with the consent of the Treasury (s. 158).

Requisitioning of Vehicles.—The Army and Air Force Acts, 1955 provide for the compulsory requisitioning of vehicles, aircraft, horses, food, forage and stores for the purposes of Her Majesty's forces.

A requisitioning order may be issued to a commanding officer who may give directions for the provision of all or any of the vehicles, specified in the order. A chief officer of police for any area specified in a requisitioning order must, whenever practicable, arrange for constables to be available for accompanying officers or soldiers requisitioning vehicles (s, 166).

Payment will be made for the use of, and any damage to such vehicles (s. 168).

Any persons failing to furnish any vehicle required by a requisitioning order, or obstructing any officer or other person in the the exercise of his duties as to the requisitioning of vehicles is liable to summary prosecution (s. 171).

The above provisions apply to horses, aircraft, food, forage and stores as they apply to vehicles (s. 172).

Motor Vehicles of H.M. Forces.—Road Traffic Act, 1930, s. 121, provides that Parts I. and III. (less s. 54 *re* extraordinary traffic) of the Act shall apply to persons and vehicles in the public service of the Crown. The person responsible will be the person named in that behalf by the Department concerned. Part II. (insurance) does not apply to such vehicles.

However, s. 121 also provides that the restrictions in the Act :

(1) Preventing persons under 21 from driving heavy motor vehicles (s. 9),

(2) Limiting the number of trailers drawn (s. 18), and

(3) Limiting the drivers' hours of duty (s. 19),

shall not apply in the case of motor vehicles owned by the Admiralty, the War Department, or the Air Ministry, and used for Naval, Military, or Air Force purposes, nor in the case of vehicles so used while driven by persons for the time being subject to the orders of any member of the armed forces of the Crown.

For vehicles of H.M. Armed Forces which are exempt from speed limit see " Exemptions from Speed Limit," Chap. 24 and for exemption of such vehicles from the Construction and Use Regs. see " Special Types of Motor Vehicles," Appendix II.

There are special exemptions as regards the lights to be carried by these vehicles. See " Lights on Vehicles," Chap. 24.

Service in the Forces.—Under the National Service Acts of 1948, 1950, 1955 men between 18 and 26 in the normal case are liable to such service (2 years whole time and up to $3\frac{1}{2}$ years part time, total $5\frac{1}{2}$ years) but certain classes of persons are exempt.

The procedure for calling up is given in the National Service (Miscellaneous) Regs., 1948.

A person so liable must register and should produce his certificate of registration on request to a constable in uniform or at a police station within two days.

He must, on notice, attend for medical examination and if he does not he commits an offence. If ordered by a Court to comply but he does not he may be arrested by a constable without warrant. Employers are bound to reinstate former employees after release from the Forces and retain them for at least 26 weeks. If the employer does not so reinstate he commits an offence and may also be ordered to pay compensation.

The Acts also deal with conscientious objectors and the procedure is given in the above-mentioned regulations.

Incitement to Disaffection Act, 1934.—The offences under this Act are as follows :—

(1) Maliciously and advisedly to endeavour to seduce any member of H.M. Forces from his duty or allegiance to Her Majesty (s. 1).

(2) With intent to commit or to aid, abet, counsel or procure the commission of any offence under s. 1, to have in possession or under control any document of such a nature that the dissemination of copies thereof among members of H.M. Forces would constitute such an offence (s. 2).

No prosecution under the Act shall take place without the consent of the Director of Public Prosecutions, to whom any case must be reported (see Appendix III).

An offender is liable on conviction on indictment to two years imprisonment or £200 fine or both, or on summary conviction to four months' imprisonment or £20 or both, and the Court may order destruction, etc., of documents (s. 3).

If a Judge of the High Court is satisfied by information on oath that there is reasonable ground for suspecting that an offence under the Act has been committed and that evidence of the commission thereof is to be found at any premises or place specified. he may grant a search warrant authorising entry, search and seizure in accordance with the section.

Anything seized may be retained for a month or until conclusion of proceedings commenced within that period, and the Police Property Act, 1897, shall apply to such property (s. 2).

Chapter XXXI

DEALERS

Contents

Dealers in Old Metals and Marine Store Dealers.—The Old Metal Dealers Act, 1861, s. 3, defines a " dealer in old metals " as a person dealing in, buying and selling old metal, scrap metal, broken metal, or partly manufactured metal goods, or defaced or old metal goods, and whether such person deals in such articles only or together with second-hand goods or marine stores. (The same definition is given in s. 13 of the Prevention of Crimes Act, 1871.) The term " old metal " means the articles above mentioned. Merchant Shipping Act, 1894, s. 538, defines a " marine store dealer " as a person dealing in, buying or selling anchors, cables, sails, old junk or old iron or other marine stores of any kind.

In every district in which s. 86 of the Public Health Acts Amendment Act, 1907, has been adopted and advertised by the Local Authority under order of the Secretary of State, every person who carries on business as a " dealer in old metal " or as a " marine store dealer " must register his name and abode and his places of business with the Local Authority, and must keep in a book the description and price of all articles purchased or otherwise acquired by him, and the name, address and occupation of the person from whom same were obtained. Failure to do so is a summary offence.

Any person duly authorised in writing by the Local Authority, on production of such authority, must be allowed free access at all reasonable times to all such places of business to inspect same and the books. Any obstruction of such officer is a summary offence.

Children and Young Persons Act, 1933, s. 9 : It is an offence for a " dealer in old metals " or a " marine store dealer " to purchase any " old metal " from any person apparently under the age of sixteen years, whether such person offers it for sale on his own behalf or on behalf of any other person. Old metal includes the articles mentioned above.

Dealers in Old Metals.—Prevention of Crimes Act, 1871, s. **13** : It is an offence for any dealer in old metals, personally or by any servant or agent, to purchase, receive or bargain for, any of the following metals, whether new or old, in any quantity at one time of less weight than as fixed, viz. lead 112 lbs., and copper, brass, tin, pewter, german silver or spelter 56 lbs., or any composite mainly composed of any such metals.

Old Metal Dealers Act, 1861, s. 4 : A Justice, on sworn information made on reasonable belief that old metal stolen or unlawfully obtained is kept in any place by a dealer in old metals may grant a search warrant to enter such place in the daytime and search for and seize all such old metals there found and bring same before a Justice. Such Justice shall issue a summons requiring such dealer to prove how he came by the said articles.

If any dealer be found in possession of old metal stolen or unlawfully obtained and is taken or summoned before two Justices and it is proved to their satisfaction that at the time he received it he had reasonable cause to believe it was stolen or unlawfully obtained, he is liable to fine, and to imprisonment for a subsequent offence.

S. 5 : When a metal dealer has been so convicted, the Court may order that he be registered by the police for a period not exceeding three years.

S. 6 : Such a compulsorily registered dealer must give notice to the police of any removal of his place of business, and under s. 7 the Justices may authorise police officers to visit his place of business and inspect his books and goods.

S. 8 : Such a registered dealer must keep books recording all old metal purchased and sold, and the names of persons from whom purchased or received. He must not make purchases between 6 P.M. and 9 A.M. He must not part with metals within forty-eight hours. He must not purchase from persons under sixteen, and must not employ persons under sixteen to purchase or receive old metals.

See Stone, under title " Metals."

Marine Store Dealers.—Merchant Shipping Act, 1894, s. 538. Every such dealer as defined above must have his name and the words " Dealer in Marine Stores " painted in letters not less than 6 in. in length on his business premises.

S. 539 : He must keep books and enter therein every article of marine stores with time at which received and name, occupation and address of the person from whom purchased or received.

S. 540 : He or his agent must not purchase marine stores from any person apparently under sixteen.

S. 541 : He must not cut up or unlay any cable or like article exceeding 5 fathoms (30 ft.) in length, without written permit from a Justice.

S. 542 : The maker of any anchor must mark on it his name or initials, with a number and the weight.

Pawnbrokers.—A pawnbroker is a person who carries on the business of taking goods and chattels in pawn, and the term includes any person who keeps a shop for the purchase or sale of goods or chattels and takes in articles and gives thereon money not exceeding £10, on agreement expressed or implied that these articles may afterwards be redeemed or re-purchased on any terms. See ss. 5 and 6 of the Pawnbrokers Act, 1872, which with the Pawnbrokers Act, 1922, is the Act dealing with the pawning or pledging of articles and the licensing of pawnbrokers.

Licence.—A pawnbroker must take out yearly an excise licence from the local County or County Borough Council (Finance Act, 1949, s. 15) for each shop kept by him. This excise licence cannot be issued without the production of a certificate granted by the local Council (see s. 27, Local Government Act, 1894), or stipendiary magistrate, except in the case of pawnbrokers licensed on December 31, 1872, or their successors, who can take out excise licenses without the annual certificate (ss. 37 to 41).

Any person who intends to apply for the first time for this certificate must give notice to the police and to the Council and must post up the necessary public notices (s. 42). Want of good character or the fact that his shop or any adjacent premises owned or occupied by him is frequented by thieves or persons of bad character would be good grounds on which his application might be refused (s. 43). The forgery or the knowingly tendering of a forged certificate for the obtaining of a licence is punishable summarily under the Act (s. 44).

Premises.—A pawnbroker must have his name and the word " Pawnbroker " over the outer door of his shop. He must keep in a conspicuous place in his shop the book of rates containing the information required to be printed on pawn-tickets (s. 13). He must keep and use a pledge book, pawn-tickets and a sale book of pledges, together with declaration forms and receipt forms, all as prescribed by the Act (s. 12), and must produce them when required by a Court (s. 50).

He must not employ any person under the age of sixteen to take pledges in pawn (s. 32).

He must not carry on the business of a pawnbroker on Sunday, Good Friday or Christmas Day (s. 32).

Pledges.—A pawnbroker must give a pawn-ticket for every pledge and if required he must give a receipt at time of redemption. His profit must not exceed that laid down by the Act (see also Pawnbrokers Act, 1922), but if the loan is over 40s. he can make a special contract (ss. 15 and 24).

Every pledge is redeemable within twelve months and seven additional days of grace. After this period an unredeemed pledge which has been pawned for 10s. or under becomes the pawnbroker's absolute property, but a pledge for over 10s. must be sold by public auction (ss. 16, 17, 18 and 19).

If a pledge for over 10s. has been sold, the pawner within three years may inspect the auctioneer's books and recover any surplus from the pawnbroker, who is bound to act *bona fide* in respect to such a sale (ss. 21, 22 and 23).

The holder of a pawn-ticket is presumed to be the person entitled to redeem the article concerned, and the pawnbroker must deliver the pledge to the person producing same on payment of the loan and profit (ss. 25-31).

The pawnbroker is not bound to deliver back a pledge unless the pawn-ticket is delivered to him, but if the ticket is lost, destroyed, stolen or fraudulently taken away, the owner may make a declaration (on a form to be supplied by the pawnbroker) before a Justice and redeem his pledge (ss. 25 and 29).

A pawnbroker must not, under any pretence whatever, purchase, except at public auction, any pledge while in pawn with him, nor must he suffer a pledge to be redeemed from him with a view to his purchasing it, nor must he make any agreement with the pawner for its purchase, sale or redemption within the time of redemption (s. 32).

He must not sell or dispose of any pledge except as authorised by the Act (s. 32).

Prohibitions on Pawning.—A pawnbroker must not take in pawn—

(1) Any article from any person apparently intoxicated (s. 32)

(2) Any article from anyone under fourteen years of age (Children and Young Persons Act, 1933, s. 8).

(3) Any firearm or ammunition to which Part I of the Act applies (Firearms Act, 1937, s. 14).

(4) Any linen, apparel or unfinished goods entrusted to any person to wash, mend, make up, etc. (s. 35).

(5) Any arms, military stores, etc., from a soldier or airman or from any person acting on his behalf (Army and Air Force Act, 1955, s. 195).

(6) Another pawnbroker's ticket, nor can he purchase or exchange same (s. 32).

Pawning Offences by Persons not Pawnbrokers :—

(1) Unlawfully pawning the property of another without the authority of the owner (s. 33). (If done with intention to deprive the owner of his property and the pawner does not intend to redeem it, it is larceny.) See " Larceny," Chap. 14.

(2) Offering in pawn an article and being unable or refusing to give a satisfactory account of the possession thereof (s. 34).

(3) Wilfully giving false information to a pawnbroker as to the ownership of the article offered in pawn, or as to pawner's name and address or as to name and address of the owner of the article (s. 34).

(4) Attempting to redeem a pledge, not being entitled to do so (s. 34).

(5) Assisting or acting for a soldier in pawning any military or air force stores (Army and Air Force Acts, 1955, s. 195.)

Powers of a Pawnbroker.—A pawnbroker may detain and hand over to the police—

(1) Any person committing any of the last four offences (Nos. (2) to (5)) mentioned above.

(2) Any person offering in pawn any article which he reasonably suspects to have been stolen or illegally or clandestinely obtained (s. 34).

(3) Any person who produces to him a pawn-ticket which he reasonably suspects to have been forged or altered (s. 49).

Any person so detained should be delivered into the custody of the police, to be conveyed before a Justice for trial. The Court can compensate such pawnbroker for his expenses, trouble and loss of time (s. 34).

General.—On information sworn by the owner of any article on good cause of suspicion, a Justice can issue a warrant authorising a constable to search, within the hours of business, a pawnbroker's shop, for any article unlawfully pawned. If entry is refused the constable may break in and search, doing no wilful damage (s. 36).

If a pawnbroker is convicted on indictment of any fraud in his business or of receiving stolen goods knowing them to be stolen, the Court before whom he is convicted may forfeit his licence (s. 38).

S. 30 of the Act empowers a Court to order restoration to the owner of goods unlawfully pawned. See " Restitution of Stolen Property," Chap. 18.

All offences against this Act may be dealt with summarily, and the general penalty is a fine not exceeding £10.

Pedlars.—Under the Pedlars Act, 1871, a pedlar is any hawker, pedlar, petty chapman, tinker, caster of metals, mender of chairs or other person who, without any horse or other beast bearing or drawing burden, travels and trades on foot and goes from town to town or to other men's houses, carrying to sell or exposing for sale any goods, wares or merchandise immediately to be delivered or offering for sale his skill in handicraft (s. 3).

It is an offence to act as a pedlar without a certificate (1871 Act, s. 4).

Such a certificate is granted by a chief officer of police when he is satisfied that the applicant—

(1) Has resided in his district during one month previous to his application ;

(2) Is over seventeen years of age ;
(3) Is a person of good character ; and
(4) In good faith intends to carry on the trade of a pedlar.

The certificate remains in force for one year from date of issue, and authorises the person to whom granted to act as a pedlar within any part of the United Kingdom (1871 Act, ss. 5, 6, and Pedlars Act, 1881).

It is a summary offence to make false representations to obtain a certificate or to forge or use any counterfeit certificate (1871 Act, s. 12). It is also an offence to lend, transfer or borrow a pedlar's certificate (1871 Act, ss. 10 and 11).

Any convictions under the Pedlars Acts are to be endorsed on the certificate, and a Court has power, when satisfied a holder is not in good faith carrying on the business of a pedlar or when he is convicted of any offence, to deprive him of his certificate.

If he is convicted of begging the Court must take away his certificate (1871 Act, s. 16).

The following need not have a pedlar's certificate—

(1) Commercial travellers ;
(2) Book agents authorised in writing by the publishers of such books ;
(3) Sellers of vegetables, fish, fruit or victuals ; and
(4) Sellers in legally established public fairs or markets (1871 Act, s. 23).

A pedlar is bound at all times, on demand, to produce and show his certificate to—

(1) Any Justice,
(2) Any constable or officer of police,
(3) Any person to whom he offers his goods for sale,
(4) Any person in whose private grounds or premises he is found.

Refusal or failure to do so is a summary offence (1871 Act, s. 17)·

Any person acting as a pedlar, who has no certificate or who refuses to show his certificate, may be arrested by any person to whom he is bound to produce his licence, and brought before a Justice (1871 Act, s. 18).

Any constable or officer of police is empowered at any time to open and inspect any pack, box, bag, trunk or case in which a pedlar carries his goods. If a pedlar refuses to allow such inspection or prevents or attempts to prevent it, he may be arrested (s. 18) and fined (s. 19, 1871 Act).

Under s. 3 of the Vagrancy Act, 1824, every petty chapman or pedlar wandering abroad and trading without being duly licensed or otherwise authorised by law, may be arrested and dealt with as an idle and disorderly person (see Chap. 27) ; but the holding of a certificate does not help if his conduct brings him within ss. 3, 4, 5, of the Vagrancy Act, 1824 (1871 Act, s. 13).

Hawkers.—A " hawker," under s. 2 of the Hawkers Act, 1888, means any person who travels with a horse or other beast bearing or drawing burden, and goes from place to place or to other men's houses, carrying to sell or exposing for sale any goods, wares or merchandise, or exposing samples or patterns of any goods, wares or merchandise to be afterwards delivered, and includes every person who travels by any means of locomotion to any place in which he does not usually reside or carry on business, and there sells or exposes for sale any goods, wares or merchandise in or at any house, shop, room, booth, stall or other place whatever, hired or used by him for that purpose. A motor vehicle would not appear to be a " stall."

Every such hawker must take out a licence from the County or County Borough Council (Finance Act, 1949, s. 15) and it lasts one year.

This excise licence is granted, otherwise than on renewal, on production of a certificate of good character signed by a clergyman and two householders of the parish in which the applicant resides or by a Justice or superintendent or inspector of police of the district (s. 4). It is a summary offence to forge any certificate for obtaining a hawker's licence or to knowingly make use of any counterfeit certificate or licence (s. 4) or to let to hire or lend such licence (s. 5).

A servant may travel with his master's licence and trade for his master's benefit, but it is an offence for any person to trade with a licence granted to any person other than his master (s. 5).

Every hawker must have his name and the words " Licensed Hawker " upon every box or package and vehicle used for the carriage of his goods, and upon every room or shop in which his goods are sold, and upon every handbill or advertisement which he distributes or publishes. It is an offence for any person not licensed as a hawker to use the words " licensed hawker " or any words importing that he trades as a hawker or is licensed to do so (s. 5).

The following need not take out hawkers' licences :—

(1) Commercial travellers ;

(2) The real worker or maker of goods and his family, selling goods made by them ;

(3) Sellers of fish, fruit, victuals or coal, and

(4) Sellers in any legally established public market or fair (s. 3).

Also the selling of stamps by Post Office officials anywhere, the hawking of bibles, prayer books, etc., and the exchanging of sundries for rags, bones, etc., are treated as exempt from the Hawkers Act.

It is a summary offence for any person to do any act for which a licence under this Act is required—

(1) Without having a proper hawker's licence in force, or

(2) Without, at once on demand by any person, producing a current hawker's licence granted to him or to his master

Any constable may arrest such person and bring him before a Justice, who may deal summarily with him (s. 6).

While the police are empowered to arrest such a person and bring him forthwith before a Justice, to be then and there dealt with, they are not authorised to proceed by summons against a hawker, as the Act is an Excise Act, and the penalties are recoverable only on prosecution by the Council's officers (Finance Act, 1949, s. 15).

Other Hawkers.—Customs and Excise Act, 1952, s. 161 : Hawking spirits or selling same otherwise than in premises licensed for the sale of spirits is an offence and the offender may be arrested.

Customs and Excise Act, 1952, s. 189 : It is an offence for any person to hawk, sell or offer for sale any tobacco or snuff in any place except on his premises licensed for the purpose.

Explosives Act, 1875, s. 30 : It is an offence to hawk, sell or expose for sale gunpowder upon any highway or public place.

The hawking of petroleum must be conducted in accordance with the regulations as to its safe conveyance. See Chap. 33.

As to hawking of pirated copies of music, see Chap. 17.

The conduct and location of street hawkers may be governed by local byelaws and regulations.

It is an offence (Highway Act, 1835, s. 72) for any hawker to pitch any tent, booth, stall or stand on any part of the highway.

Game Dealers.—Before a person may deal in game he must procure—

(1) A local licence from the local Borough or District Council (Local Govt. Act, 1894, ss. 27, 32) and then

(2) An excise licence (which expires on July 1) taken out at the Post Office.

A Council may not grant a game dealer's licence to an innkeeper, a retail beer-seller, a carrier or higgler, an owner, driver or conductor of a public conveyance or mail letter vehicle, or any person in the employ of any of these persons (Game Act, 1831, s. 18, and Game Licences Act, 1860).

Game under the Game Act, 1831, includes hares, pheasants, partridges, grouse, heath or moor game, black cock and bustards, and a game dealer's licence is necessary to deal in such game imported from foreign countries.

A licence is not necessary to deal in snipe, woodcock, quail, landrail, rabbits or deer.

Under the Game Act, 1831, a game dealer's licence is granted for a specified premises, outside of which a board must be fixed indicating that the person named is a licensed dealer, and he must not sell game elsewhere than at such premises (s. 28). He must not buy or sell or knowingly have in possession any bird of game after the expiration of ten days after the end of the open season for such bird. Any other person must not buy or sell such a bird after the same period, or knowingly have same in possession (except for breeding purposes) after the expiration of forty days after the open season (s. 4). See Chap. 19.

Money-lenders.—" Money lender," as defined in the Money lenders Act, 1900, includes every person whose business is that of money-lending, or who holds himself out in any way as carrying on that business, but does not include a pawnbroker, banker, insurance agent, or person whose primary business is not that of lending money, nor does it include certain registered societies and corporations.

The Money-lenders Act, 1927, and the Money-lenders Rules, 1927 made under that Act, regulate the conditions under which a person may carry on the business of a money-lender.

Every money-lender must each year obtain a certificate from the Magistrates' Court of the district in which his business is to be carried on (s. 2).

He must also take out a money-lender's excise licence each year from the local Council or Borough Council (Finance Act, 1949, s. 15). This will not be issued unless he holds a certificate as described above (s. 1).

To obtain a certificate, he must lodge a statement of application, giving the prescribed particulars, with the Clerk to the Justices, and two weeks before the hearing he must send a copy of this statement to the chief constable. He must also, except in the case of a renewal, publish notice of his application in a local newspaper (Money-lenders Rules, 1927).

The Court may refuse to grant a certificate if satisfactory evidence of good character is not produced, or if it is proved that he is not a fit and proper person, or if he is disqualified or has not complied with the rules (s. 2).

A money-lender must take out his excise licence in his true name (s. 1). and his certificate must show his true name and the name under which and the address at which he is authorised to carry on the business of a money-lender (s. 2).

His advertisements and business documents must give his authorised name, and they must not in any way imply that he carries on banking business (s. 4).

A person must not send or cause to be sent to any persons except in response to his written request, any circular or other document advertising the name, address, or telephone number of a money-lender, or containing an invitation to borrow or take any steps as to borrowing money from a money-lender. It is permissible to advertise in the public press or by poster exhibited at an authorised address, provided that the advertisement is restricted to the giving of the money-lender's authorised name and address and stating that he lends money, etc.

A money-lender must not employ an agent or canvasser for his business, and no person must act as such (s. 5). Any contravention of s. 5 is a misdemeanour which may be dealt with summarily.

The Act provides for the form of money-lenders' contracts, prohibits compound interest on loans, directs that written particulars of loans shall be supplied, declares that interest exceeding the rate of 48 per cent. will be presumed excessive, and prohibits the charging of expenses on loans (ss. 6-12).

The time for taking proceedings in respect of money lent by money-lenders is limited to twelve months, with certain exceptions (s. 13).

Special provisions are made as regards pawnbrokers' loans (s. 14).

Offences under the Act may be dealt with summarily, and the Court must endorse convictions on the certificates. The Court may also suspend or forfeit certificates and may disqualify a person from obtaining a certificate (s. 3). Persons whose money-lenders' certificates have been refused or suspended or forfeited, or who have been disqualified from obtaining certificates, have the right of appeal (ss. 2 and 3).

Money-lenders Act, 1900, s. 4 : It is a misdemeanour for a money-lender or his agent, by false statements or misrepresentations, to fraudulently induce or attempt to induce any person to borrow money or to agree to the terms on which money is to be borrowed.

Betting and Loans (Infants) Act, 1892 : It is a misdemeanour for anyone for profit to knowingly send to an infant (under twenty-one years of age) any document inviting him to borrow money (s. 2). It is also a misdemeanour for anyone, except under the authority of a Court, to solicit an infant to make an affidavit or statutory declaration in connection with any loan (s. 4). Both these misdemeanours may be dealt with summarily.

Companies Act, 1948, s. 201 : Every company licensed under the Money-lenders Act, 1927, shall in its business letters, catalogues, circulars and showcards give particulars similar to those required by s. 18 of the Registration of Business Names Act, 1916 (see Chap. 32). The consent of the Board of Trade is necessary for prosecution of this summary offence.

Domestic Servants' Registries.—In every district in which s. 85 of the Public Health Acts Amendment Act, 1907, has been adopted by the Local Authority, every person who carries on for the purpose of private gain the business of keeper of a female domestic servants' registry, must register his name, address and premises where such business is carried on, with the Local Authority.

The Local Authority may make byelaws prescribing the books to be kept and regulating the conduct of such business.

Any person duly authorised in writing by the Local Authority must at all reasonable times be afforded full and free power of entry into such registered premises to inspect such premises and the books required to be kept by byelaw.

It is a summary offence to carry on such business without being registered under this section, to refuse entry as above authorised, to contravene any byelaws made under this section, or to neglect to have a copy of such byelaws hung up in a conspicuous place in the registered premises, and in addition to or in lieu of any pecuniary penalty, the Court may suspend or cancel the registration.

Dealers in Securities.—The business of dealing in securities is regulated by a licensing system which came into operation on 8 August, 1944, under the Prevention of Fraud (Investments) Act, 1939. That Act, as amended, has been repealed and consolidated by an Act of the same name passed in 1958.

By s. 26 of the 1958 Act " Dealing in securities " means making or offering to make with any person or inducing or attempting to induce any person to enter into or offer to enter into (a) any agreement for or with a view to acquiring, disposing of, subscribing for or underwriting securities, or lending or depositing money to or with any industrial and provident society or building society, or (b) any agreement the purpose or pretended purpose of which is to secure a profit to any of the parties from the yield of securities or by reference to fluctuations in the value of securities.

" Securities " means (a) shares or debentures or rights or interests in same ; (b) securities of the Government of any part of H.M. Dominions or the government of any foreign state ; (c) rights in respect of money lent to or deposited with any industrial and provident society or building society, including those under any unit trust scheme (s. 26).

S. 1 : No person shall carry on the business of dealing in securities except he has a *principal's licence*, or act as a servant or agent in such business unless he has a *representative's licence*. Any contravention is punishable summarily or on indictment, but proceedings (except arrest, warrant or demand) require the consent of the Board of Trade or of the Director of Public Prosecutions. (See Appendix III.)

S. 2 : There are many exceptions to this necessity for licences, including members of Stock Exchanges or of associations of dealers in securities (which are recognised by the Board of Trade ; see s. 15) ; the Bank of England ; any statutory or municipal corporation ; any dealer exempted by the Board of Trade (see s. 16) ; any industrial and provident society (see s. 10) ; any building society (see s. 11) ; any manager or trustee under a unit trust scheme authorised by the Board of Trade (see s. 17), and the section also exempts certain actions by persons under certain given circumstances.

These licences are grantable by the Board of Trade, who have power to refuse and revoke them (ss. 3-6), and to make rules for regulating the conduct of business by holders of licences (s. 7). Licence holders have to supply information (s. 8) and the names and addresses of holders of licences have to be published (s. 9).

S. 13 : It is an indictable offence, punishable by penal servitude not exceeding 7 years, for any person to induce or attempt to induce another person to invest money, by any statement, promise or forecast which he knows to be misleading, false or deceptive, or by any dishonest concealment of material facts, or by the reckless making of any statement, promise or forecast which is misleading, false or deceptive.

Any person guilty of conspiracy to commit this offence shall be similarly punishable.

S. 14 : On or after the day appointed by the Board of Trade (8 August, 1944) it has been an offence punishable summarily or on indictment, for any person to distribute, cause to be distributed or have in possession for distribution, any documents which to his knowledge are circulars inviting or inducing persons to invest money in securities. This does not apply to a proper prospectus complying with the Companies Act, 1948, or to circulars sent by licensees or persons exempted from licence by the Act.

Proceedings (apart from arrest or remand) require the consent of the Board of Trade or the Director of Public Prosecutions.

A Justice has power to grant a search warrant for such documents, to which the Police (Property) Act, 1897, applies, subject to orders of a Court.

S. 18 : It is an offence punishable summarily or on indictment to knowingly furnish information, as required under the Act, which is false in a material particular.

S. 19 : Corporations and their officers may be liable for offences against the Act.

S. 20 : Summary proceedings under the Act may be taken in the place where the alleged offender is for the time being.

Under the Prevention of Fraud (Investments) Act Licensing Regulations of 1944 (continued in force under the 1958 Act), applications for principal's and representative's licences must be made to the Board of Trade on the prescribed forms accompanied by the prescribed statutory declarations. Any change in the particulars which are required must be notified to the Board of Trade.

Statutory Rules made in 1939, under s. 7 of the 1939 Act and continued under the Act of 1958, regulate the conduct of business of licensed dealers, that is the holders of principals' licences, who are described as " licensed dealers in securities ".

If a licensed dealer in writing offers securities for sale or invites purchase he must give the information prescribed, and he must issue a contract note giving the prescribed particulars in case of a sale or purchase of securities. However, this will not apply if he is dealing with a person whose business involves the acquisition, disposal or holding of debentures.

He must keep books of account, and a record of every transfer of securities.

He must not deal on terms involving payment by instalments unless the prescribed conditions are fulfilled.

The Prevention of Fraud (Investments) Forms Regulations, 1944, prescribe the undertaking necessary under s. 4 (4) instead of a deposit, and Deposits Regulations, 1944, deal with deposits necessary for principals' licences. Both the regulations continue in force under the 1958 Act.

The Borrowing (Control and Guarantees) Act, 1946, as amended 1949, with the Control of Borrowing Order, 1947, require, subject to certain exemptions, the consent of the Treasury to the borrowing of large sums of money and to the issue of shares and securities. Contraventions of the Order are punishable on summary conviction or on indictment (1946 Act, Para. 1 of Schedule).

The Exchange Control Act, 1947, puts the Treasury in control of gold and foreign currency, of the issue of securities, of the import or export of money or securities, etc., etc., and Part II. of the 5th Schedule provides for penalties on summary conviction or on indictment of offences under the Act.

Owners of gold or foreign currency should sell same to authorised dealers unless the Treasury permits otherwise,

Chapter XXXII

TRADE

Contents

Business Names.—The Registration of Business Names Act, 1916, directs that every person or firm having a place of business in this country and carrying on any business or profession (s. 22) under a business name which does not consist of the true surnames of such person or partners or the corporate name of the corporation, must register under this Act (s. 1).

Registration is effected by sending the prescribed particulars to the Register Office of the Board of Trade, and this should be done within fourteen days after the firm or person commences business. Any change in the particulars of registration should also be reported to the Register Office within fourteen days after such change. The Registrar supplies a Certificate of Registration which must be exhibited in a conspicuous position at the principal place of business. He can refuse registration (Companies Act, 1947, s. 116).

Every person or firm required under this Act to be so registered must mention in business letters, catalogues, circulars, and show-cards, on which the business name appears and which are sent to any person, the present surname (with Christian name or initials), any former Christian name or surname and the nationality if not British, of the person or persons carrying on such business or profession (s. 18).

A registered company, a company incorporated outside Great Britain which has, since November 23, 1916, established a place of business in Great Britain, and a company licensed under the Money-lenders Act, 1927, should give similar particulars on its business letters, etc., which it issues or sends to any person in any part of H.M. Dominions. The consent of the Board of Trade is necessary for prosecution (Companies Act, 1948, s. 201).

It is an offence punishable by fine (summarily, s. 442) for anyone to trade under any title of which " Limited " or any contraction of that word is the last word, unless duly incorporated (as a company) with limited liability (Companies Act, 1948, s. 439). The Companies Act, 1948, gives a number of offences which might be committed by officers of companies and allows proceedings for any offence under the Act to be taken by the Director of Public Prosecutions or by the Board of Trade at any time within 12 months of discovery of the offence and not exceeding 3 years from the commission of the offence.

Printing and Publishing.—It is a summary offence for any person to print any paper or book meant to be published or dispersed, without putting his name and address thereon, or to publish or disperse copies of same. Certain works are excepted, including engravings, address and business cards, price lists, sale catalogues of goods or estates, law proceedings, papers printed by authority of any public board or public office in the discharge of their duties.

An information for this offence must be in the name of the Attorney-General or Solicitor-General (Newspapers, Printers, and Reading Rooms Repeal Act, 1869). See Stone, under title " Printers."

Trade Marks.—A trade mark means a mark to be applied to goods which are the subject of trade, manufacture, or merchandise, and which is duly registered in the Register of Trade Marks. It is the property of its owner, and the Merchandise Marks Acts and Trade Marks Acts protect owners and the public against any fraudulent or improper use of trade marks.

It is an offence to forge any trade mark or to falsely apply to goods any trade mark or to apply any false trade description to goods or to fraudulently sell goods with false trade marks or false descriptions (Merchandise Marks Acts, 1887 and 1953).

Subject to the provisions of s. 6 of the Geneva Conventions Act, 1957, it shall be a summary offence to use for any purpose whatever,—

(1) Without the authority of the Army Council:—

(*a*) the emblem of a red cross with vertical and horizontal arms of the same length, on and surrounded by a white ground, or the designation " Red Cross " or " Geneva Cross ".

(*b*) the emblem of a red crescent moon on, and surrounded by a white ground, or the designation " Red Crescent ".

(*c*) the emblem in red surrounded by a white ground of a lion passing from right to left of the observer, holding a scimitar in its right forepaw, with the upper half of the sun shooting forth rays above the lion's back, or the designation " Red Lion and Sun ".

(2) Without the authority of the Board of Trade:—Any design of a white or silver cross with vertical and horizontal arms of the same length, on and surrounded by a red ground, being the heraldic emblem of the Swiss Confederation, or any other design so nearly resembling it which might be mistaken for it.

In such cases the consent of the Director of Public Prosecutions must be obtained before prosecution.

Medical units of H.M. Forces use the Red Cross. The British Red Cross Society, the St. John Ambulance Association and the St. Andrew's Ambulance Association have been authorised to use the Red Cross emblem for certain voluntary aid purposes.

Hall-Marks.—Hall-marks are the marks on gold and silver wares which indicate that the metal therein is of the requisite standard of purity, also the date and place of testing.

For unlawfully dealing with hall-marks see " Forgery," **Chap.** 17.

Pure or fine gold or silver is rather soft and does not wear well, and an alloy or small quantity of baser metal is added to render it harder and more durable. To check fraud, the law makes it compulsory that gold and silver domestic plate and watch cases and 22 carat gold wedding rings should be assayed (or tested) and hall-marked. Such articles must be sent to an Assay Office, where they are tested to ascertain the proportion of gold or silver therein and duly stamped with the hall-marks.

There are seven Assay Offices, viz. London, Birmingham, Chester, Sheffield, Edinburgh, Glasgow and Dublin.

The hall-marks for gold and silver articles are as follows :—

(1) The **standard mark,** showing the amount of pure metal in the article.

(2) The **hall-mark proper,** which is the local town or city mark, showing where the article was assayed and stamped. The following hall-marks are now in use :—

Leopard's head for London ; anchor for Birmingham ; dagger between three wheat sheaves for Chester ; York rose for Sheffield (gold only) ; crown for Sheffield (silver only) ; castle with three towers for Edinburgh ; tree, fish, bell and bird for Glasgow ; and figure of Hibernia with harp for Dublin.

(3) The **date mark,** which consists of one letter of the alphabet. Each Assay Office has its own set of letters and can tell the date of stamping an article by the letter on it.

(4) The **maker's mark,** which consists of two or more letters, being the initials of the firm, the proprietor or the partners of the firm.

Formerly there was also a " duty mark," the King's head, but the duty on plate and the duty mark were abolished in 1890.

Gold Articles.—Standard or sovereign gold consists of 22 carats (or parts) fine or pure gold and 2 carats alloy, in every 24 carats. The term " carat " is not a real weight for gold ; it is used merely to denote the quality.

In gold plate four standards are now allowed, viz. 22, 18, 14, and 9 carat. These standards are shown by figures on the gold articles, with a crown in the case of 22 and 18 carat gold.

For London, Birmingham and Chester the crown is the standard mark for 22 and 18 carat gold. A piece of 22 or 18 carat gold plate assayed at one of these offices would bear thereon a crown and the figures 22 or 18. The crown is not stamped on articles of lower standards. 14 and .585 in rectangles indicate 14 carat gold. 9 and .375 in rectangles means 9 carat gold. (Gold Wares (Standard of Fineness) Order, 1932.)

Therefore a piece of 18 carat gold plate assayed in Birmingham should bear the following hall-marks :—a crown and the figures 18, both in rectangles, an anchor, a letter of the alphabet, and the maker's initials.

If stamped in London the same marks would be used, with the exception of the hall-mark proper, a leopard's head being used instead of an anchor.

It should be noted that a lion passant (or walking) was the 22 carat gold standard mark up to the year 1844, but in that year it was replaced by the crown and 22. For 18 carat gold the standard mark since 1798 has been the crown and 18.

Silver Articles.—The standard for silver articles is 11 oz. 2 dwts. of pure silver and 18 dwts. of alloy, to the pound troy, which is equivalent to 0.925 pure silver. This is known as sterling silver.

There is also a higher standard which is 0.959 pure silver, viz. 11 oz. 10 dwts. pure silver and only 10 dwts. of alloy. Such silver is known as Britannia silver and bears the figure of Britannia. It, however, is too soft and is seldom met with. This higher standard was compulsory from 1697 to 1720, and silver plate of that time is known as Queen Anne silver.

The standard mark for silver is the lion passant (or walking).

Silver articles should also bear local hall-marks, date marks and makers' marks similar to those on gold articles.

A sterling silver article assayed in Birmingham should therefore bear the following hall-marks :—Lion passant, anchor, date letter and initials of maker.

It is not compulsory to hall-mark gold and silver watch chains.

Weights and Measures.—By law a uniform system of weights and measures must be used for trade purposes throughout the country. See the Weights and Measures Acts, 1878 to 1936.

The Weights and Measures Act, 1878, prescribes this uniform system of what are termed imperial weights and measures.

It is a summary offence to sell by any weight or measure which is not one of the imperial weights or measures (s. 19).

Articles sold by weight must be sold by avoirdupois weight, but gold, diamonds and other precious metals and stones may be sold by troy weight, and drugs may be sold by apothecaries' weight (s. 20).

Every weight and measure used for trade must be verified as correct and must be stamped accordingly (s. 29).

It is a summary offence to use or have in possession for use for trade, any false or unjust or unstamped or unauthorised weight or measure (s. 25). See also Customs and Excise Act, 1952, s. 303.

Any wilful fraud in the use of any weight or measure is a summary offence (s. 26).

Coal must be sold by weight except in case of sale and delivery direct from the colliery with written consent of the purchaser. A weight ticket must be delivered with coal where the quantity delivered by any vehicle exceeds 2 cwt. (1889 Act).

Inspectors are appointed by Local Authorities to enforce these statutes regarding weights and measures. The inspectors keep the local standard weights and measures, verify and stamp weights and measures, and inspect trade premises to examine the weights and measures therein.

The use of a weight or measure of the metric system in trade was made lawful by Weights and Measures (Metric System) Act, 1897.

Food and Drugs.—The law designed to ensure that articles consumed by the people shall be wholesome and shall not be sold to the prejudice of the purchasers has been consolidated by the Food and Drugs Act, 1955, followed by the Food Hygiene Regs., 1955. " Food " includes every article used for food or drink by man other than drugs and water, and includes articles used in the preparation of human food (1955 Act, s. 135).

" Food " includes drink, chewing gum, and other products of the like nature and use, and substances used as ingredients in the preparation of food or drink or of such products but does not include (a) water, live animals or birds (b) fodder feeding stuffs for animals, birds or fish (c) articles or substances used only as drugs (1955 Act, s. 135).

It is a summary offence to mix, with a view to sale, anything with any article of food so as to render it injurious to health, or anything with any drug or medicine (except by way of compounding) so as to injuriously affect its quality or potency or to sell or have for sale any such article (1955 Act, s. 1). It is also an offence, generally speaking, to sell to the prejudice of the purchaser any article of food or any drug, which is not of the nature, substance or quality of the article demanded by the purchaser (1955 Act, s. 2).

These are the main offences regarding the adulteration of food and drugs.

This Act also deals with unsound food, prevention of contamination of food, false warranty, false labels, hygiene in sale of food, etc., etc.

The Act is enforced by Local Authorities who appoint inspectors for the purpose. Public analysts are also employed to deal with samples of food and drugs submitted to them for test to detect whether there has been any adulteration.

Unsound or bad food may be dealt with under s. 9 of the Food and Drugs Act, 1955. See " Food," Chap. 39.

The Sale of Food (Weights and Measures) Act, 1926, declares that in selling any article of food by weight, measure or number a person shall not deliver a less weight, measure or number than is purported to be sold. It is also an offence, when selling or offering for sale any article of food, to make any misrepresentation in any manner calculated to mislead the purchaser as to weight, measure or number. See Stone, under titles " Food and Drugs," and " Weights and Measures."

Shops.—The Shops Act, 1950, repealed previous Acts dealing with shops and consolidates the previous law thereon.

It has been amended by the Shops (Revocation of Winter Closing Hours Provisions) Order, 1952, which revoked all the provisions of the Act which related to special closing hours during winter.

" Shop " includes any premises where any retail trade or business is carried on. " Retail trade or business " includes barbers or hairdressers, sale of refreshments or intoxicants, lending books or periodicals for gain and retail sales by auction but not sale of programmes or catalogues at places of amusement (s. 74). Part I includes ss. 1-16.

S. 1 directs that every shop shall be closed for serving of customers not later than 1 p.m. on one weekday in every week. This day may be fixed by the local authority subject to the directions of the section. This shall not prevent the serving of a customer already in the shop before closing or supply in a case of illness or supply of necessaries for a ship on arrival or departure.

This weekly half holiday does not apply (unless extended to any of them by the local authority) to shops whose only trade or business is the sale of intoxicants, refreshments, aircraft, cycle and motor accessories, newspapers etc., meat and other perishable articles, tobacco etc., medicines, etc., also railway bookstalls and retail trade at exhibitions or shows (First Schedule). S. 2 directs the closing of shops for serving of customers not later than 9 p.m. on the late day and 8 p.m. on any other day of the week (the late day shall be Saturday unless some other day is fixed by the local authority, S. 3). Such general closing shall not prevent serving a customer already in the shop or supply in case of illness.

Also the Second Schedule allows the sale of meals or refreshments for consumption on the premises or in trains, newly cooked food for consumption off the premises, intoxicants, tobacco, etc., on licensed premises during permitted hours ; tobacco, sweets, etc., in theatres, etc., to the audience ; medicines ; sales from railway bookstalls; motor, cycle or aircraft accessories ; stores for H.M. Forces or for ships on arrival or departure ; also business at post offices, all these during closing hours.

S. 4 : A local authority may fix 10 p.m. on the late day or 9.30 p.m. on any other week day for closing hours for sale of tobacco, etc.

S. 6 : For sale of table waters, confectionery or ice cream the late day hour may be 10 p.m. and 9.30 p.m. on any other day of the week.

Local Authorities may make " closing orders " not earlier than 7 p.m. as to the hours of all shops or shops of a specified class (ss. 8–11).

By s. 12 it shall not be lawful to carry on in any place, not being a shop, retail trade or business of any class at a time when it would be unlawful to keep a shop open for retail trade or business of that class. This does not apply to a barber attending a customer at customer's residence, nor to an auction of private effects in a dwelling house, nor to the sale of newspapers.

S. 13 deals with shops in which several trades or businesses are carried on.

S. 14 gives the penalties for offences under the above Part I (ss. 1-16) of the Act.

" Local authority " in the Act means the Common Council of the City of London, the Council of a municipal borough, the District Council of any urban district with a population of 20,000 or more, and elsewhere the County Council (s. 73).

Part II (ss. 17-39) of the Act deals with the conditions of employment in shops, including such subjects as half holidays (ss. 17, 18) ; meal times (ss. 19, 20) ; special arrangements re shop assistants in premises for the sale of refreshments (s. 21) ; Sunday employment (ss. 22, 23) ; hours of employment of young persons 16 to 18 (ss. 24–26) and of persons under 16 (s. 27) ; night employment (s. 31) and health and comfort of shop workers (ss. 37, 38).

Part III deals with modifications in special cases such as the suspension of the weekly half holiday and alteration of closing hours in holiday resorts, the alteration of closing hours and closing orders for exhibitions or shows or on special occasions such as Christmas (ss. 40-43).

S. 44 exempts premises where post office business is transacted from Part I and ss. 17-20 of the Act.

S. 45 exempts lending libraries not for private profit ; clubs or institutions not for gain and fairs or bazaars or sales of work for charitable or non-private profit purposes from Part I and ss. 17-21 and 37 of the Act.

S. 46 exempts libraries for educational or recreation purposes from Parts I and II of the Act on given conditions.

Part IV (ss. 47-67) deals with Sunday trading.

S. 47. Every shop shall be closed for the serving of customers on Sunday save as otherwise provided in the Act, and except when open for serving of customers for the purpose of the transactions given in the Fifth Schedule—viz. for the sale of : intoxicants ; meals or refreshments (except fried fish and chips at a fried fish and chips shop) ; newly cooked provisions ; sweets, confectionery and ice cream ; flowers, fruit and vegetables (not tinned or bottled) ; milk and cream (not tinned) ; medicines, etc., at duly registered premises'; motor, cycle or aircraft accessories ; tobacco and smokers' requisites ; newspapers and magazines ; books and stationery at main railway and omnibus book stalls ; guide books, postcards, etc., at museums, parks and in vessels ; photos for passports ; sports requisites at sports places ; fodder for horses, etc., at any farm, inn, etc. Also for post office business and funeral undertaker's business.

S. 48 : The local authority may make partial exemption orders for limited opening of shops for the sale of bread and flour confectionery, fish, groceries and other provisions (Sixth Schedule) on Sunday.

S. 49 : The local authority has power to order the closing on Sunday of shops open for the purpose of sale of meals or refreshments for consumption off the premises.

S. 51 : The local authority may provide, by order, for the opening of shops selling bathing or fishing requisites, photo requisites, toys, etc., books, etc., food (Seventh Schedule) at holiday resorts on Sunday.

S. 53 : Jewish shops, if duly registered, may be open, on conditions, up to 2 p.m. on Sunday, if they are closed on Saturday.

S. 54 : In London a local authority may, by order, allow the opening on Sunday up to 2 p.m., on conditions, of certain street markets and district shops.

S. 55 : Goods sold retail shall not be delivered from a shop at any time when it would not be lawful to serve the customer in the shop, but this will not apply on a Sunday which is Christmas Day or is followed by Christmas Day on the Monday.

S. 56 : This Sunday trading prohibition shall not prevent the supply of necessaries to a ship or aircraft on arrival or departure ; the supply of goods to a club for the club ; the cooking on Sunday before 1.30 p.m. of food for a customer ; the supply of goods required in the case of illness.

A barber or hairdresser may at any time attend infirm persons or persons resident in a hotel or club, for the purposes of his business. Home handicraft workers may get certificates of exemption from this prohibition which also does not apply to sea-going ships.

S. 58 : This Part IV applies to any place where any retail trade or business is carried on as if that place were a shop, but this does not affect the sale by fishermen of freshly caught fish and the sale of produce at a farm, allotment or similar place.

S. 59 : Sunday trade or business carried on under the provisions of this Act shall not be deemed to be an offence against the Sunday Observance Acts.

S. 60 : Nothing in the above provisions of Part IV as to Sunday trading shall apply to retail dealers in butcher's meat carrying on their business on Sunday, but unless allowed under the following provisions of the Act, it shall not be lawful for any person to carry on the business of a retail dealer in butcher's meat on Sunday and such a shop shall be closed to customers on Sunday (s. 61).

S. 62 : Jewish retail dealers in Kosher meat may open shop on Sunday and serve customers with such meat provided that they are licensed by the local Jewish Committee, close their shops on Saturday, and notify the local authority. (Kosher meat means butcher's meat killed and prepared by the Jewish ritual method (s. 74).)

S. 63 : Butcher's meat must not be delivered except when the shop is lawfully open for customers, but this does not apply when Sunday is Christmas Day or the day before Christmas Day.

S. 65 : Butcher's meat may be sold and delivered at any time for a ship or aircraft on its arrival or departure.

" Butcher's meat " means beef, mutton, veal, lamb or pork (including livers, etc.) whether fresh, chilled, frozen or salted and includes Kosher meat (s. 74).

S. 67 : Contains special provisions respecting barbers and hairdressers in Scotland.

Part V (ss. 68-77) contains general provisions.

S. 71 : It shall be the duty of the local authority to enforce the Act and to take any necessary proceedings through its appointed inspector.

Trading Representations (Disabled Persons) Act 1958.— This Act provides for the registration of persons who sell or solicit orders for their goods by representations that disabled persons are employed in making or packaging the goods or benefit from their sale.

It is an offence punishable by fine up to £100, or up to 3 months' imprisonment, or both, in selling or soliciting orders for goods, for any representation that blind or otherwise disabled persons, (a) are employed in the production, preparation or packing of the goods or (b) benefit (other than as users) from the sale of the goods, to be made during visits from house to house, or by post, unless the person carrying on the business is registered (s. 1).

The Factories Acts, 1937, 1948, deal with the health, safety, welfare and employment of persons in factories and workshops, especially women and young persons, and direct that the dangerous part of any machinery should be securely fenced. A special Government staff of factory inspectors see that the provisions of these Acts are carried out. If any person is killed or dies or suffers bodily injury in consequence of the occupier of a factory having contravened any provision of the Acts or Regulations the occupier will be liable to fine and the whole or part of the fine may be applied for the benefit of the injured person or his family (s. 133). See Stone, under title " Factories and Workshops."

Safety on Farms.—The Threshing Machines Act 1878, directs that to prevent accidents the drum and feeding mouth of a threshing machine worked by any motive power other than manual labour shall be securely fenced. Any constable, on reasonable cause, may enter premises and inspect such a machine.

Under the Chaff Cutting Machines (Accidents) Act 1897, the feeding mouth of such a machine should have a safety fitting and the flywheel and knives should be securely fenced. A constable, acting upon the instructions of a police officer not below the grade of Inspector may at any time enter on any premises on which he has reasonable cause to believe that such a machine, which does not comply with the Act, is being worked, for the purpose of inspecting the machine.

The above Acts will be repealed when Regulations are made under the powers given to the Minister by s. 1 (7) of the Agriculture (Safety, Health and Welfare Provisions) Act, 1956. This Act also gives power to make regulations for securing the safety, health and welfare of persons employed in agriculture. The following Regs. have been made:—

(1) *The Agriculture (First Aid) Regs.*, 1957, which prescribe the descriptions and quantities of first aid requisites and appliances to be provided for the purposes of s. 6 of the Act, which states that a worker employed in agriculture shall not be employed unless there is provided a first aid box or cupboard which contains first aid requisites and appliances.

(2) *The Agriculture (Ladders) Regs.*, 1957, make it illegal for faulty ladders to be used by persons employed in agriculture.

(3) *The Agriculture (Power Take-off) Regs.*, 1957, provide certain standards of guarding both power take-offs and power take-off shafts on agricultural machines.

(4) *The Agriculture (Avoidance of Accidents to Children) Regs.*, 1958. Under s. 7 (3) of the Act a person who causes or permits a child to ride on or drive a vehicle or machine or ride on an implement in contravention of the regulations shall be guilty of an offence, and under s. 14 this is punishable on summary conviction by a fine not exceeding £50.

In these regulations:—

" child " means a child who has not attained the age of 13 years.

" trailer " means any vehicle used as a trailer whether or not designed to be so used, but does not include any such vehicle drawn by an animal. Any reference to a tractor, machine, implement, trailer or other vehicle includes any drawbar, towbar or coupling which may be used for the purpose of towing or propelling.

No child shall ride on any of the following classes of vehicles or machines while they are being used in agricultural operations or are going to or from the site of such operations:—

(a) Tractors, (b) self-propelled agricultural machines, (c) trailers, (d) trailers into which any conveyor mechanism is built, (e) machines mounted in whole or in part on tractors or vehicles, or towed or propelled by tractors or vehicles, (f) binders or mowers drawn by animals (Reg. 3 (1)).

The foregoing paragraph shall not apply as respects sub-paragraph (c) in circumstances where the child rides (i) on the floor of the trailer, or (ii) on any load carried by the trailer, provided that the trailer has four sides each of which is higher than the load (Reg. 3 (2)).

No child shall drive any tractor, or self-propelled vehicle or machine while that tractor, vehicle or machine is being used in agricultural operations or is going to or from the site of such operations (Reg. 4).

No child shall ride on any of the following implements while they are being towed or propelled: (a) agricultural implements mounted in whole or in part on tractors or vehicles, or towed or propelled by tractors or vehicles, (b) animal drawn rollers (Reg. 5).

Chapter XXXIII

EXPLOSIVES

Contents

Explosives Offences.—The manufacture and keeping of gunpowder and other explosives is governed by the Explosives Acts, 1875, 1923, and Emergency Laws (Misc. Provisions) Act, 1953. See also Control of Explosives Orders, 1953 and 1954, under which to obtain possession of gunpowder or safety fuse requires a licence from the chief officer of police, except in some exempted cases.

" Explosive " includes every substance used or made to produce a practical effect by explosion or a pyrotechnic effect ; for example, gunpowder, dynamite, fulminate, fog signals, fireworks, cartridges, etc., etc.

These Acts and the Orders in Council made thereunder deal with the licences, supervision and safety requirements necessary for such dangerous substances. See the official " Guide to the Explosives Acts".

The following statutes deal with offences in connection with explosives.

Explosive Substances Act, 1883.—This statute gives power to deal with persons using, making or having in possession explosives to use for unlawful objects, and creates the following five felonies :—

(1) Unlawfully and maliciously causing by an explosive substance an explosion of a nature likely to endanger life or cause serious injury to property whether such injury is caused or not (s. 2).

(2) Unlawfully and maliciously doing any act with intent to cause, or conspiring to cause, such an explosion in the United Kingdom, whether such explosion takes place or not (s. 3 (*a*)).

(3) Unlawfully and maliciously making or having in possession or under control any explosive substance with intent by means thereof to endanger life or cause serious injury to property in the United Kingdom or enable others by means

thereof to do so, whether an explosion takes place or not (s. 3 (b)).

(4) Making or knowingly having in possession or under control any explosive substance under such circumstances as to give rise to a reasonable suspicion that it is not for a lawful object, unless the contrary is proved (s. 4).

(5) Being accessory to the commission of any crime under this Act by in any manner whatsoever procuring, aiding, abetting or counselling its commission (s. 5).

Any person within or (being a subject of Her Majesty) without H.M. dominions may be liable under this Act.

A person may be arrested for an offence against the Act and brought before a Justice and remanded, but no further proceedings may be taken without the consent of the Attorney-General (s. 7).

On reasonable ground for believing that such a crime has been committed the Attorney-General may order a special inquiry by a Justice, who can examine witnesses on oath although no person is charged with the commission of the crime. Such witnesses must answer all questions put to them, but they are protected against the consequences of incriminating replies.

" Maliciously " under this Act means wilfully and not by accident, and " explosive substance " includes any materials for making any explosive, also any apparatus or part of apparatus used or intended to be used or adapted for causing any explosion.

A search warrant may be obtained in the same manner as a search warrant under the Explosives Act, 1875 (s. 73). See " Search Warrant," Chap. 5.

Offences against the Person Act, 1861 :—

(1) Causing grievous bodily harm, disfiguring, etc., by unlawful and malicious explosion of any explosive substance. F. (S. 28.)

(2) Using explosives, corrosives, etc., in any manner with intent to cause grievous bodily harm, disfigurement, etc., whether bodily injury be effected or not. F. (S. 29.)

(3) Placing explosives near buildings or ships with intent to do bodily injury to any person, whether explosion or bodily injury be effected or not. F. (S. 30.)

(4) Damaging any building by explosive substance with intent to commit murder. F. (S. 12.)

(5) Knowingly having in possession or making any gunpowder, explosive substance, machine, etc., with intent by means thereof to commit any of the felonies in the Act. M. (S. 64.)

A Justice, on reasonable cause on oath, may issue his warrant to search in the day-time any house, carriage, vessel, place, etc., in which it is suspected any explosive substance is made, kept or carried for the purpose of committing any of these felonies (s. 65). See " Search Warrant, 1861 Act," Chap. 9.

Malicious Damage Act, 1861 :—

(1) Attempting to destroy or damage, by explosion of any explosive substance, any dwelling-house, any person being therein, or any building, whereby any person's life shall be endangered. F. (S. 9.)

(2) Putting any explosive substance in or near any building with intent to destroy or damage any building or anything therein, whether or not any explosion takes place or damage be caused. F. (S. 10.)

(3) Putting any explosive substance in or near any ship or vessel with intent to destroy or damage any ship or vessel or any machinery or goods, whether or not any explosion takes place or injury be caused. F. (S. 45.)

(4) Making or knowingly having in possession any explosive substance or any dangerous thing or any machine, instrument, etc., with intent thereby to commit or to enable another to commit any of the felonies in the Act. M. (S. 54.)

A Justice, under s. 55, may grant a similar search warrant in connection with above offences.

Explosives Act, 1875 :—

(1) Gunpowder is not to be made or kept except on licensed (or registered) premises (ss. 4, 5).

(2) Exposure or sale of gunpowder upon any street or public place. Offence, 40s. fine. (S. 30.)

(3) Sale of gunpowder to child under thirteen years of age. Offence, £5 fine. (S. 31.)

(4) Exposure for sale, of gunpowder over 1 lb. in weight, without it being contained in a substantial receptacle and labelled " gunpowder." Offence, 40s. fine. (S. 32.)

(5) Throwing or firing fireworks on a street or public place. Offence, £5 fine. (S. 80.) See also " Highway Act " and " Town Police Clauses Act," Chap. 24.

(6) Subject to various modifications given in the Act, the provisions as to gunpowder are to apply to every other explosive (s. 39).

The Fireworks Act, 1951 allows the destruction of fireworks which may be dangerous when in the possession of the public (s. 1). Fireworks must bear the address of the factory where made and the name of its occupier, except those weighing less than one-eighth of an ounce, sparklers, jumping crackers and throwdowns and any prescribed in regulations (s. 5).

Petroleum.—The Petroleum (Consolidation) Act, 1928, has repealed the previous Petroleum Acts of 1871, 1879, 1926, and 1928, and consolidated the law on the subject. This Act, in the interests of public safety, regulates the safe keeping of petroleum spirit (commonly known as petrol), and offences against it may be dealt with summarily.

The term " petroleum " includes crude petroleum, oil made

from petroleum, or from coal, shale, peat or other bituminous substances, and other products of petroleum. The term " petroleum spirit " means such petroleum as when tested in the manner set forth in the Act gives off an inflammable vapour at a temperature of less than 73 degrees Fahrenheit (s. 23).

Thus " petroleum spirit " will include petrol, naphtha, benzine and such like highly inflammable bituminous liquids, and certain mixtures of petroleum with other substances, such as quick-drying varnishes.

Where any petroleum spirit is kept at any place, or is being sent or conveyed between any two places in Great Britain, or is sold or exposed or offered for sale, there shall be attached to, or where that is impracticable, displayed near, the vessel containing it, a label showing in conspicuous characters the words " Petroleum Spirit " and the words " Highly Inflammable," and the name and address of the owner, sender, or vendor.

However, petroleum spirit need not be so labelled during the seven days after its importation into this country, nor when carried on any motor vehicle, ship, or aircraft, and intended to be used only for the purposes thereof.

Penalty, £5 fine and forfeiture of the petroleum spirit (s. 5).

Petroleum spirit shall not be kept except under a petroleum spirit licence granted by the Local Authority, save only in the following cases :—

(1) Petroleum spirit kept for private use or sale, which is kept in separate glass, earthenware or metal vessels, securely stopped and containing not more than one pint each, the total amount so kept not exceeding 3 gallons.

(2) Petroleum spirit kept for use in motor vehicles, motor boats, aircraft or specified engines, in accordance with any regulations made by the Secretary of State (see later).

The occupier of any premises in which petroleum spirit is kept in contravention of this section is liable to fine. Any holder of a petroleum spirit licence who contravenes any condition of his licence is liable to fine (s. 1).

The Local Authority for the granting of licences is the County, City or District Council or the harbour authority, and they may attach to any licence such conditions as they may consider expedient as to the safe keeping of petroleum spirit. Such licences may be transferred.

The occupier of a licensed premises must keep posted on the premises a notice setting out the conditions of his licence which have to be observed by his employees, viz. those conditions directing the precautions to be observed against the risk of fire or explosion. It is an offence not to have such a notice posted up, or to pull down or damage any such notice, or to contravene any of the conditions set out in such notice (s. 2).

Ships carrying petroleum spirit as cargo, on entering a

harbour must give notice of such cargo to the harbour authority (ss. 7 and 8).

Any of the provisions of this Act may be applied, by Order in Council, to any substance (s. 19). The Act, with slight modifications, is applied by the Petroleum (Mixtures) Order, 1929, to all mixtures (whether liquid, viscous or solid) of petroleum with any other substances, except mixtures which when tested do not give off an inflammable vapour at a temperature below 73 degrees Fahrenheit.

When loss of life or personal injury occurs by explosion or fire in which petroleum spirit is involved and in or about or in connection with any premises licensed under these Acts, the occupier must forthwith send notice of the matter to the Secretary of State, Home Office, London. If such notice is sent, the inspector of factories need not be notified. If a similar accident occurs in connection with any carriage, ship or boat conveying petroleum spirit or on or from which petroleum spirit is being loaded or unloaded, the owner or master of the carriage, ship or boat must send notice to the Secretary of State, except in cases where the petroleum spirit was for use only on that carriage, ship or boat, or in cases where notice has by law to be sent to some other Government department (s. 13).

The Secretary of State may direct an inquiry to be made by a Government inspector into the cause of any such accident, and if death has been caused the coroner's inquest shall be adjourned to allow of the presence of a Government inspector to watch the proceedings. A Government inspector has full power of entry, examination, etc., when engaged in carrying out any duty under this Act (ss. 14 and 15).

A Government inspector under the Explosives Acts has power to enter, inspect and examine premises licensed under this Act and premises in which petroleum spirit is or may be kept in contravention of the Act or Regulations (s. 16).

Any officer authorised in writing by the Local Authority may require any person who deals in petroleum or who keeps petroleum for the purposes of any trade or industry, to show him every place and vessel in which his petroleum is kept and to give him samples of such petroleum on payment. He may also test such samples on giving such person due notice in writing. Any refusal or wilful obstruction is a summary offence (s. 17).

A Magistrates' Court may give a warrant authorising entry and search for petroleum spirit kept, sent, conveyed, or exposed for sale in contravention of the Act (s. 18).

Petroleum Spirit (Motor Vehicles, etc.) Regulations, 1929.—A licence from the Local Authority is necessary before petroleum spirit (petrol, etc.) may be kept for sale, but petrol for use in motor vehicles, motor boats, aircraft, engines used for propelling agricultural implements, stationary engines kept for domestic or agricultural purposes and generating power, heat or light, or engines used for canal or harbour works or in connection with the making or repair of roads, and which is not kept either wholly or partly for sale, may be kept without licence provided these regulations are observed. These regulations are to the following effect :—

(1) Every storage place for keeping petroleum spirit must be ventilated and have an entrance to the open air. Means of extinguishing fire must be kept there. If attached to a dwelling house or a building where persons assemble it must be separated therefrom by a substantial and not readily inflammable floor or partition. If the spirit is kept in not more than 2 vessels of capacity not exceeding 2 gallons each, there may be an opening in such partition (not in a floor) if it is fitted with a self-closing and fire resisting door (Reg. 5).

(2) The spirit must be kept in strong and sound metal vessels, indelibly marked " Petroleum Spirit—Highly Inflammable " (Regs. 2 to 4). Any fire, etc., must not be near it and it must not be exposed near any fire, etc. (Regs. 9 and 10).

It must not be allowed to run into any sewer or sewer drain (Reg. 12 and s. 27, Public Health Act, 1936). It must not be used in a storage place except as fuel for any such engine kept therein. However, one gill may be used for cleaning or repair work, and it may be used as fuel for any properly constructed lighting or heating apparatus therein (Reg. 11).

(3) Not more than 60 gallons may be kept in any one storage place (Reg. 6).

(4) The spirit must not be kept in any vessel holding more than 2 gallons unless :—

(1) the storage place is over 20 feet from any building or highway ;

(2) provision is made to prevent the spirit flowing out of the storage place ; and

(3) notice is given in writing to the Local Authority previously and every January following (Reg. 7).

(5) The spirit shall not be kept in any place within 20 feet of a building or inflammable substance otherwise than in the fuel tank of a motor vehicle, engine or aircraft and in not more than 2 vessels of capacity not exceeding 2 gallons each, unless notice is given each January to the local authority (Reg. 8).

(6) Additional restrictions apply as regards engines used for making or repairing roads, such as notice to Local Authority, 30 gallons limit, vessels must not exceed 2 gallons capacity and must be kept in an iron locker which must be safely situated (Reg. 13).

CHAPTER XXXIII.—EXPLOSIVES 405

Petrol Pumps.—Any instrument used in trade for measuring liquid fuel or lubricating oil for sale in individual quantities not exceeding 20 gallons, other than a simple independent measure to which the Weights and Measures Acts apply, must be stamped and regularly tested.

Any flexible discharge hose should not exceed 12 feet in length (Measuring Instruments (Liquid Fuel and Lubricating Oil) Regs., 1929).

Petroleum Spirit (Conveyance by Road) Regulations, 1957, provide for the safe conveyance of petroleum spirit by road, but do not apply to its conveyance on any vehicle for use in the propulsion of that vehicle. Reg. 19 prohibits the carrying of vessels containing petroleum spirit on tank wagons or tank trailers, but not in composite vehicles.

They also do not apply to the conveyance on a vehicle of petroleum spirit not exceeding 32 gallons in closed containers holding not more than 2 gallons or in closed metal drums holding not more than 10 gallons, or not exceeding 50 gallons in a single closed steel barrel, but this exception does not apply to tank wagons, tank trailers, public service vehicles and vehicles hawking petroleum spirit (Reg. 12).

Any vehicle used for conveying petroleum spirit shall be strongly constructed and in compliance with the directions of the Regulations (Reg. 22 and Schedule).

A trailer carrying petroleum spirit shall not be drawn by—

(1) Any vehicle other than a motor tractor or a petroleum conveying vehicle, and only one such trailer may be drawn.

(2) A motor tractor unless the exhaust system is in front of the prescribed fire-resisting shield and unless any electric lighting is as prescribed.

(3) A vehicle conveying petroleum other than petroleum spirit unless the vehicle complies with the provisions applying to petroleum spirit conveying vehicles and unless the total amount of petroleum and petroleum spirit conveyed does not exceed 2500 gallons (Reg. 8).

Every vehicle conveying petroleum spirit by road shall be constantly attended by at least one person over 18 years of age, except when halted in an approved place. The driver may be regarded as a person whilst in, or in close proximity to, the vehicle (Reg. 7).

Persons engaged in loading, unloading or conveying petroleum spirit shall observe all precautions necessary for preventing fire or explosion (Reg. 2).

A person on or attending a vehicle conveying petroleum spirit shall not smoke nor carry matches or lighters (Reg. 4).

No fire or artificial light capable of igniting inflammable vapour nor explosive substance nor anything capable of causing fire or explosion shall be allowed or carried on any vehicle conveying petroleum spirit (Reg. 5), and an efficient extinguisher shall be carried on every such vehicle (Reg. 6). Care must be taken to prevent the escape of petroleum spirit into any drain or sewer (Reg. 3).

Petroleum spirit shall not be supplied direct from a vehicle carrying it in bulk to any mechanically propelled vehicle (Reg. 9).

The owner of a vehicle used for conveyance of petroleum spirit is responsible for providing a copy of these Regulations for his employees and shall ensure they know and carry out their provisions (Reg. 26).

Tank Wagons and Tank Trailers.—The filling pipe shall be kept securely closed except when filling the tank (Reg. 13) and the dipping pipe shall be kept securely closed except when filling or emptying the tank or testing the petroleum-spirit contained in the tank on premises licensed for the purpose (Reg. 14). When filling or emptying the tank, a competent person not under 18 years of age shall be in constant attendance, the engine of the vehicle shall be stopped until all tanks are closed (if horse drawn, the horses shall be removed and the wheels scotched), a dangerous static charge of electricity shall be prevented, the delivery piping or hose shall be sound, and it must be ascertained that the tank will hold the quantity to be delivered (Reg. 15). For delivery into a storage tank see Reg. 16.

Such a vehicle shall not draw a trailer unless it is a tank trailer, and if its capacity exceeds 1,500 gallons, it shall not draw a trailer (Reg. 18).

If the conveying vehicle is not a tank wagon or tank trailer, the petroleum spirit shall be in a vessel either of metal, or of glass, earthenware or material of such a nature that it will not permit leakage. If of metal it must be in good condition and not exceeding fifty gallons capacity, or ninety gallons if it contains a mixture with a content of not more than seventy-five per cent of petroleum (1958 Regs.). In the case of glass, etc., containers each vessel shall contain not more than one pint of petroleum spirit and shall be packed in sawdust or other suitable material to prevent movement in an outer container of metal, wood or fibre which must be kept securely closed during conveyance, and the outer container must not contain in the aggregate more than 3 gallons of petroleum spirit. No vessel shall be filled or emptied while on the vehicle, and if empty shall be securely closed (Reg. 23).

The load shall be protected from fire by a fire resisting cover and no part of the load shall project beyond the sides or back of the vehicle nor above the level of the top of the fire resisting shield which is necessary between the engine and the load (Reg. 24).

Any vehicle conveying petroleum spirit shall not draw a trailer which is not used or intended to be used exclusively for conveying petroleum spirit (Reg. 25). If a trailer forms part of an articulated vehicle it is deemed to be one vehicle for the purpose of these Regulations (Reg. 28).

Any contravention of these Regulations is a summary offence
punishable by fine not exceeding £20 and forfeiture of the
petroleum spirit (s. 6, Petrolium Consolidation Act, 1928).

Carbide of Calcium.—Under the Petroleum (Carbide of
Calcium) Orders, 1929, 1947, a vessel containing carbide of
calcium (which is a solid giving off acetylene gas when water or
even moisture is added) must bear in conspicuous letters " Carbide
of Calcium," " Dangerous if not kept dry," " The contents of this
package are liable if brought into contact with moisture to give
off a highly inflammable gas," and the name and address of the
owner, vendor or sender (Art. 3.)

The quantity which may be kept without licence is as follows :—

1. Five pounds, if kept in hermetically closed metal vessels,
each containing not more than 1 lb.

2. Twenty-eight pounds, provided the following conditions
are observed :—

(1) Kept in hermetically closed metal vessels ;
(2) Kept in a dry and well-ventilated place ;
(3) Due precautions to keep away unauthorised persons ;
(4) Notice given to Local Authority ;
(5) If a fixed generator is used, instructions as to its care
and use must be posted up close by.

In all other cases a licence from the Local Authority is necessary
before calcium carbide may be kept (Art. 2).

The Petroleum (Consolidation) Act, 1928, applies to carbide
of calcium.

It must not be passed into a public drain or sewer (s. 27, Public
Health Act, 1936).

Acetylene.—Acetylene is a highly inflammable and explosive
gas, and is, when liquid or compressed or mixed with air or
oxygen, deemed to be an explosive under the Explosives Act,
1875, s. 104.

Orders in Council, 1937, 1947, direct that such acetylene should
not be manufactured, imported, kept, conveyed or sold, but do not
interfere with acetylene mixed with air in a burner for burning or
lighting purposes. The Compressed Acetylene Order, 1919,
declares that acetylene contained in a suitable porous substance
and in metal cylinders properly made, tested and labelled will not
be deemed an explosive.

Celluloid and Cinematograph Film.—The Celluloid and
Cinematograph Film Act, 1922, is intended to lessen the risk
incurred by the storing of such an inflammable substance as
celluloid.

The Act applies to the keeping or storing of—

(1) Raw Celluloid in quantities of over 1 cwt. or in smaller
quantities unless kept in a properly closed metal case.

" Celluloid " includes xylonite and other similar substances containing nitrated cellulose or other nitrated products, but does not include explosives under the Explosives Act, 1875, and " raw celluloid " means celluloid which has not been subjected to any process of manufacture, and celluloid scrap or waste.

(2) Cinematograph Film, in quantities over twenty reels or 80 lb. in weight or in smaller quantities unless each reel is kept in a properly closed metal case.

" Cinematograph film " means any film containing celluloid and intended for use in a cinematograph or similar apparatus.

A temporary deposit in premises of cinematograph film for the purposes of examination, repair, etc., is a " keeping," but a temporary deposit of celluloid or cinematograph film in premises during the course of delivery, conveyance, or transport, will not be a " keeping " under the Act (ss. 2 and 9).

The following must not be used for such keeping or storing :—

(1) Premises situated underneath premises used for residential purposes.

(2) Premises so situated that a fire occurring therein might interfere with the means of escape from the building or any adjoining building.

(3) Premises forming part of a building, unless separated from the building by fire-resisting partitions, or so situated and constructed that a fire therein is not likely to spread to the building and the Local Authority has given its sanction (s. 1).

Before any premises may be used for such keeping or storing, the occupier must furnish the Local Authority (County, County Borough, Urban, District or Rural Council) with a written statement of his name, the address of the premises and the nature of the business there carried on (s. 1 (a)), and must pay the prescribed annual fee (s. 4).

Conditions which must be observed in respect to such premises :—

(1) Such means of escape in the case of fire as the Local Authority may reasonably require must be provided and properly maintained.

(2) The safety regulations in the 1st Schedule of the Act must be duly observed. (Such as, no open fire or light, no smoking or matches, fire extinguishers, etc.).

(3) Any regulations made by the Secretary of State must be duly observed (s. 1).

An officer duly authorised by the Local Authority may at all reasonable times enter premises used or reasonably believed to be used for such keeping or storing. He may take samples for analysis, and it is an offence for any person to refuse entry to, or to hinder or obstruct, or to refuse samples (ss. 5, 6 and 7).

Any contravention of the Act is a summary offence. An employee who contravenes any of the safety and other regulations made under the Act will also be guilty of a summary offence (s. 3). The Act does not apply to :—

(1) Premises licensed under the Cinematograph Act, 1909.

(2) Premises to which the Factories Act, 1937 applies except in the cases mentioned in s. 1 (as given above) in which certain premises must not be used for such keeping and storing (s. 2).

The Cinematograph Film Stripping Regulations, 1939, apply to premises in which the stripping (removal of emulsion from) and drying of cinematograph film is done and which are supervised by the Inspectors of Factories.

Carbon Disulphide.—This is a highly inflammable liquid. It must be conveyed in steel or iron containers each holding not more than 50 gallons, or in bottles each holding not more than 5 pints packed separately in wooden cases, each case containing not more than 3 gallons of it, or in mechanically driven tank wagons securely closed and without trailers. All must be marked " Carbon Disulphide—Highly Inflammable." No fire, etc., is allowable on the vehicle and attendants thereon must not smoke. Means of extinguishing fire must be carried. These rules will not apply when less than 14 lb of the liquid is carried on a vehicle and if the weight of the liquid in any single container other than a metal one does not exceed 7 lb. (ss. 6, 19, Petroleum Consolidation Act, 1928 and Carbon Disulphide (Conveyance by Road) Regs. 1958).

Gas Cylinders' Conveyance :—

The Gas Cylinders (Conveyance) Regulations, 1931, 1947, direct that, when conveyed by road, vessels containing any of the following gases in a compressed state—air, argon, carbon monoxide, coal gas, hydrogen, methane, neon, nitrogen and oxygen—shall have been constructed and tested in the manner prescribed by the Regulations.

Such vessels shall also have been tested in the prescribed manner within the preceding two years, and they shall be marked with the date of the last test, the name and address of the firm by whom compressed and the name of the gas contained.

They shall be painted (near the valve) with the identification colour prescribed for each gas (*e.g.* oxygen, black).

They shall be properly secured so as not to project beyond the sides or ends of the vehicle.

The Regulations do not apply to cylinders whose capacity does not exceed 12 lbs. of water.

The Compressed Gas Cylinders (Fuel for Motor Vehicles) Conveyance Regulations, 1940, provide for the conveyance by road of cylinders containing compressed coal gas, carbon monoxide, hydrogen or methane, and which are fitted to motor vehicles solely for the storage of gaseous fuel under pressure for the propulsion of the vehicle.

Such cylinders shall be made of forged steel or brass or bronze, constructed and tested as prescribed in the Regulations. They shall also have been tested within the preceding two years, and shall bear the date of the test. They shall be marked with the words " For gas propulsion only, working pressure —— lbs. per square inch," and with the water capacity in cubic feet.

A table shall be affixed to the vehicle giving the date of last test, the date of manufacture, the water capacity and the manufacturer's mark and number, of each cylinder.

The Gas Cylinders (Conveyance) Regulations (as above) do not apply to such cylinders.

See also " Gas Propelled Vehicles," Appendix II.

Chapter XXXIV

FIREARMS

Contents

Firearms Act, 1937.—This 1937 Act applies to Great Britain. However, certain provisions of the Act (such as " firearm certificate " and " registered " definitions), affect Northern Ireland, which has its own Firearms Act.

" Firearm " means any lethal barrelled weapon of any description from which any shot, bullet or other missile can be discharged and includes any prohibited weapon (see later), any component part of any such lethal or prohibited weapon, and any accessory to such weapon to diminish noise or flash (s. 32). However, the provisions of Part I (ss. 1-16) of the Act (purchase, possession, transfer, manufacture, repair and sale) do *not* apply to a smooth bore gun with barrel not less than 20 inches long, nor to an airgun, air rifle or air pistol not declared by the Secretary of State to be specially dangerous (s. 16). Such shot-guns, airguns, etc., may therefore be purchased, kept and sold without firearm certificates.

A lethal weapon would appear to be one which could kill or injure. (See *Bryson* v.*Gamage Ltd.* (1907)). A dummy revolver (with solid barrel) was held to be part of a firearm. (See *Cafferata* v. *Wilson* (1936)).

" Ammunition " means ammunition for any firearm and includes grenades, bombs and other like missiles whether capable of use with such a firearm or not, and prohibited ammunition (s. 32).

However, Part I of the Act does not apply to cartridges containing 5 or more shot none exceeding 9/25ths of an inch in diameter, to ammunition for an airgun, air-rifle or air-pistol, nor to blank cartridges not exceeding one inch in diameter (s. 16).

Part I of the Act does not relieve any person using or carrying a firearm from the obligation of having a gun licence or a game licence (s. 15).

Part II contains miscellaneous provisio ns as to fire-arms and ammunition, ss. 17—24.

Firearm Certificate.—Part I, s. 1 (1) : No pe rson shall purchase, acquire or have in possession any firearm or ammunition to which Part I applies, unless he holds a firearm certificate authorising same, in force at the time, or is exempted under the Act. Contravention will be a summary offence.

S. 2 : Application for a certificate shall be made in the pre-scribed form to the Chief Officer of Police of the area in which the applicant resides, who shall grant it if satisfied that the applicant has a good reason for having the firearm or ammunition and can be permitted to have same without danger to the public safety or to the peace. A certificate shall not be granted to a person prohibited by the Act from possessing such firearm (see later) or who is of intemperate habits or of unsound mind or for any reason is unfitted to be entrusted with same.

The certificate shall specify the conditions (if any) subject to which it is held, the nature and number of the firearms and the quantity of ammunition to be purchased and to be held at any one time. Breach of a condition will be a summary offence (s. 1).

The certificate, unless revoked or cancelled, lasts for three years and is renewable for a further three years by the Chief Officer of Police for the area in which the holder resides, and so from time to time.

The Chief Officer may by notice in writing vary any condition other than those prescribed by rules, and may require the certifi-cate to be delivered to him for amendment. A certificate may be varied, on application by the holder.

The Chief Officer of Police of the area may revoke a certificate for any of the above reasons and also if the holder fails to return his certificate for variation. If revoked the holder must, on notice, return the certificate within twenty-one days from date of notice or from dismissal of any appeal, on penalty of £20 fine.

There is an appeal to Quarter Sessions if a Chief Officer refuses to grant or vary or renew a certificate or has revoked it.

A person making any statement he knows to be false, for the procuring of the grant, variation or renewal of a firearm certificate will commit a summary offence.

S. 3 : The fee for grant of certificate is five shillings, and for renewal or variation increasing the number of firearms held or on replacement of a certificate is two shillings and sixpence.

No fee is payable by a rifle club, miniature rifle club or approved cadet corps for a certificate for firearms, etc., to be used solely for target practice or drill, or for a certificate with respect to the equipment of a ship, aircraft signalling apparatus, slaughtering instrument and trophy of war not to be used as a firearm (s. 3).

S. 4 : The following persons are exempt from holding a firearm certificate :

(1) A registered firearms dealer (or his servant) in the ordinary course of that business.

(2) An auctioneer, carrier or warehouseman (or his servant) in the ordinary course of that business.

(3) A licensed slaughterman, having a slaughtering instru-ment in house or yard in which employed.

(4) The proprietor of a slaughterhouse or knacker's yard (or his servant) having custody of same at the house or yard.

(5) A person having firearms, etc., on a ship as part of its equipment. He can get police permit to remove same.

(6) A person having signalling apparatus on an aircraft or in an aerodrome as equipment, or removing same to or from an aircraft at an aerodrome. He can get police permit to move same.

(7) A person carrying a firearm, etc., for sporting purposes only, for another person who holds a certificate.

(8) A member of a rifle club or miniature rifle club or approved cadet corps, when engaged as such a member in or in connection with drill or target practice.

(9) A person carrying on a miniature rifle range or shooting gallery with rifles not exceeding ·23 calibre, and any person using them in such premises. *May purchase or acquire without*

(10) A person in a theatrical performance or rehearsal or in *bet* producing a cinematograph film during the performance.

(11) Any person at an athletic meeting for starting races.

(12) A person who holds a permit in the prescribed form from the Chief Officer of Police of his area, in accordance with the terms of the permit.

A person making any statement which he knows to be false, for the purpose of obtaining such police permit will commit a summary offence.

S. 5 : Persons in the service of Her Majesty (including police, s. 28) in their capacity as such need not have a certificate to enable them to have possession of firearms and ammunition, but must have one to purchase and acquire same, unless duly authorised in writing to acquire same for the public service.

A person in the naval, military or air service of Her Majesty, on application on the prescribed form, satisfying the police that he is required to acquire a firearm or ammunition for his own use in his capacity as such, is entitled to a free firearm certificate authorising him to purchase or acquire same.

Firearms Dealers.—S. 7 : No person shall, by way of trade or business, manufacture, sell, transfer, repair, test or prove ; or expose for sale or transfer ; or have in his possession for sale, transfer, repair, test or proof, any firearm or ammunition to which Part I of the Act applies (see above) unless he is registered as a firearms dealer. Provided that an auctioneer may have and sell by auction any such firearm or ammunition, if he has a police permit for the purpose. Contravention of this section or the making of a knowingly false statement to obtain such a permit will be a summary offence.

S. 8 : The Chief Officer of Police shall keep a register of firearms dealers in his area. He shall register on application as prescribed from a person carrying on such business in his area, but shall not register an applicant prohibited by order of a Court, and need not register an applicant if satisfied he has ceased this business or that he cannot be permitted to carry on such business without danger to the public safety or to the peace.

For the latter two reasons he shall remove a dealer's name from the register after giving him reasonable notice.

The fee is five pounds. There is a right of appeal to Quarter Sessions against the refusal or revocation of registration.

Making a knowingly false statement to obtain registration will be a summary offence.

S. 9 : A person so registered shall be granted a certificate of registration, which shall be surrendered on or before 1st June in each year or on notice that registration has been revoked. A renewal may be granted on application and payment of a fee of one pound.

If the dealer does not apply before 1 June he shall be given notice, and if he then does not apply within twenty-one days his name shall be removed from the register.

S. 10 : A registered dealer shall give particulars of every place within the police area at which he carries on or proposes to carry on the business of firearms dealer, and every such place shall be entered in the register. The Chief Officer of Police may refuse to enter any particular place in his register and he may remove a place from his register, if satisfied that such business cannot be carried on there without danger to the public safety or to the peace. A person aggrieved by such action may appeal to Quarter Sessions.

To carry on such business at a place not in the register or to knowingly make any false statement to procure entry of any place in the register will be a summary offence.

Transfer and Repair of Firearms.—S. 11 : No firearm or ammunition to which Part I of the Act applies shall be :—

(1) Sold or transferred, except to a registered firearms dealer or to a person producing a certificate authorising him to acquire it or who shows he is entitled under the Act to acquire it without holding such firearm certificate. This provision shall not prevent a transfer to a person entitled under the Act to have possession without holding a certificate if the transfer is not by sale or hire, or by way of gift or loan. Nor does it prevent delivery by a carrier or warehouseman in the ordinary course of his business.

(2) Sold, let on hire, given or lent by any person (except it is to a registered firearms dealer or to a person entitled to acquire it without holding a firearm certificate) unless such person complies with any instructions contained in the firearm certificate produced, and in the case of a firearm gives notice within

48 hours by registered post to the Chief Officer of Police by whom the certificate was issued.

(3) Repaired, tested or proved for any person (except for a registered firearms dealer as such) unless such person produces a certificate authorising him to have possession of same or shows that he is entitled under the Act to have possession of it without holding a certificate. Contravention of above or producing a false certificate or personating the holder of a certificate or making any false statement in connection therewith will be a summary offence.

S. 12 : Every person who by way of trade or business manufactures, sells, or transfers firearms or ammunition to which Part I of the Act applies, shall provide and keep a register of transactions and make the entries therein prescribed by Schedule 2, within 24 hours after each transaction. Any police officer, duly authorised in writing by the Chief Officer of Police, shall be allowed on demand to enter the premises of such a person and inspect all stock in hand. Such person on request shall produce his register of transactions for inspection by any police officer duly authorised, by an officer of customs and excise, or by an officer of the county council duly authorised in writing.

Above does not apply to any sale by auction under police permit. Failure to comply with above or knowingly making any false entry in the register will be a summary offence.

S. 13 : If a registered firearms dealer is convicted of an offence under this Act, or of a Customs offence as to import or export of firearms or ammunition to which Part I of the Act applies, the Court may order his name to be removed from the register, and that he (and any employee concerned) shall not be registered as a firearms dealer, and that any person who may knowingly employ such convicted person shall not be (or remain) registered as a firearms dealer, and that the stock of the business shall be disposed of. There may be an appeal to Quarter Sessions against any such order.

S. 14 : No pawnbroker shall take in pawn from any person any firearm or ammunition to which Part I of the Act applies. Contravention will be a summary offence.

Police Powers.

S. 6 : Any constable may demand from any person whom he believes to be in possession of a firearm or ammunition to which Part I of the Act applies (s. 16 excepts smooth-bore guns of 20-inch barrel, airguns, air-rifles and air-pistols and their ammunition, also shot and blank cartridges) the production of his firearm certificate. If such person fails to produce same, or to permit the constable to read same, or to show that he is entitled under the Act to have the firearm or ammunition without certificate, the constable may seize and detain the firearm or ammunition and require the person to give his name and address. If such person refuses or fails to give his true name and address, he is liable to £20 fine on summary conviction. The constable may arrest without warrant any person who so refuses his name or address, or whom he suspects of giving a false name or address or of intending to abscond. See later, under " General," for other police powers.

Prohibited Weapons.—Part II, s. 17 : It shall be unlawful to manufacture, sell, transfer, purchase, acquire or have in possession, without the authority in writing of the Admiralty, the Army Council or the Air Council—(1) any firearm from which, on pressure to the trigger, missiles may continue to be discharged, (2) any weapon for the discharge of any noxious liquid, gas or other thing, (3) any ammunition containing or designed or adapted to contain any such noxious thing.

Contravention of above is punishable on indictment or summarily.

The above authorities may grant permits in writing with conditions attached, and if so the Chief Officer of Police shall grant certificates and register firearms dealers.

Prohibitions in respect to Firearms.

S. 18 : A Secretary of State may by order prohibit the removal of any firearms or ammunition unless the removal is authorised by the Chief Officer of Police of the area from which they are to be removed and unless any other conditions of the order are complied with.

However, no such order shall prohibit the holder of a firearm certificate from carrying with him any firearms, etc., authorised by the certificate. Any police officer may search for and seize any firearms, etc., which he has reason to believe are removed in contravention of any such order. Any contravention of such an order will be a summary offence.

S. 19 : No person under 17 shall purchase or hire any firearm or ammunition, and no person shall sell or hire any firearm or ammunition to a person under 17.

No person under 14 shall accept or borrow any firearm or ammunition to which Part I of the Act applies, and no person shall give or lend same to any person under 14.

No person under 14 shall have in possession **any** firearm or ammunition to which Part I of the Act applies, except when he is entitled to do so without holding a firearm certificate (viz. by carrying for another for sporting purposes or as a member of a rifle club, or in a shooting gallery). No person shall give possession of a firearm or ammunition to a person under 14 except in such circumstances.

Any contravention will be a summary offence.

S. 20 : No person shall sell or transfer any firearm or ammunition to, or repair, prove or test any firearm or ammunition for, any other person whom he knows or has reasonable ground for believing to be drunk or of unsound mind.

Any contravention will be a summary offence.

S. 21, as amended by 9th Sched., C.J. Act, 1948, and 3rd and 4th Sched., Prison Act, 1952: A person sentenced to penal servitude or preventive detention or corrective training, or to 3 months or more imprisonment for any crime, shall not, within 5 years from release, have a firearm or ammunition in his possession. Also a prisoner whilst on licence (after release) under ss. 25, 26, 27, 45, Prison Act, 1952, Third Schedule, or under s. 53, C. and Y.P. Act, 1933, or a person bound over or on probation with a requirement not to possess, use or carry a firearm, during the period of same, shall not have a firearm or ammunition in his possession. However, a person so prohibited may apply to Quarter Sessions for removal of the prohibition. (See Sch. 1.) No person shall sell or transfer, or repair, test or prove a firearm or ammunition for any person known or believed to be so prohibited. Any contravention of this section will be a summary offence.

Criminal Use, etc., of Firearms.

S. 22 : Possession of any firearm or ammunition with intent by means thereof to endanger life or cause serious injury to property, or to enable any other person by means thereof to do so, shall be a felony whether any injury was caused or not.

S. 23 : It shall be an indictable offence, punishable by imprisonment, for any person :

(1) To use or attempt to use a firearm or imitation firearm with intent to resist or prevent the lawful arrest or detention of himself or any other person. If a person commits this offence in respect to his own arrest or detention he is liable to the penalty for the offence in addition to any other penalty ordered for that other offence.

(2) To have same in possession when committing, aiding or abetting or attempting to commit, or at the time of his arrest for, many of the offences under the Malicious Damage Act, 1861 (arson, malicious damage, etc.) ; the Offences Against the Person Act, 1861 (serious assaults, rape, abduction, etc.) ; the Vagrancy Act, 1824, s. 4 (suspected person or reputed thief frequenting or loitering with intent to commit felony) ; the Prevention of Crimes Act, 1871, s. 7 (special offender found in any place of business under suspicious circumstances) ; the Larceny Act, 1916 (larceny, burglary, housebreaking, found at night, etc.) ; and the Road Traffic Act, 1930, s. 28 (taking a motor vehicle), as specified in the 3rd Schedule to this Act, and the Sexual Offences Act, 1956, ss. 1, 17, 18, 20. unless he shows that he had it in his possession for a lawful object.

If an adult (17 or upwards) is committed for trial for either of the above offences, he cannot be dealt with summarily for any other indictable offence with which he is also charged (M.C. Act, 1952, Fifth Schedule).

A firearm or imitation firearm, although it is not loaded or is otherwise incapable of discharging any missile, is deemed to be an offensive weapon or instrument for the purpose of robbery or assault to rob or of being found at night armed with intent to break or enter.

In this section " firearm " means any lethal barrelled weapon of any description from which any shot, bullet or other missile can be discharged and includes any prohibited weapon. " Imitation firearm " means anything which has the appearance of being a firearm within this section (exclusive of a prohibited weapon for discharge of noxious liquid, gas, etc.) whether it is capable of discharging any shot or other missile or not.

S. 24 : No person other than a registered firearms dealer shall shorten the barrel of a smooth bore gun to a length less than 20 inches, or convert into a firearm anything which though like a firearm is made so as to be incapable of discharging any missile through the barrel.

Contravention of above may be punished on indictment or summarily. Purchasing, acquiring or having in possession any shortened smooth bore gun or any so converted firearm, without having a firearm certificate authorising same, will be punishable on indictment or summarily.

General, ss. 25—33.

S. 25, as amended by 9th Sched., C.J. Act, 1948 : Where a person is convicted under this Act or is convicted of crime and sentenced to preventive detention, corrective training or imprisonment or is bound over or put on probation with a requirement not to have a firearm the Court may forfeit or dispose of any firearm or ammunition found in his possession and cancel his firearm certificate.

S. 26 : A Justice on sworn information may grant a search warrant authorising any constable named therein to enter at any time any premises or place named, if necessary by force, and search same and every person found therein and seize any firearm or ammunition found, in connection with which he has reasonable ground for suspecting that an offence under this Act has been, is being or is about to be committed. He may also examine any business books, if it is the premises of a registered firearms dealer. He may arrest without warrant any person found in the premises whom he has reason to believe to be guilty of an offence under this Act.

A Magistrates' Court may order the destruction or disposal of any firearm or ammunition seized under this Act.

S. 27 : After the expiration of 6 months after the commission of an offence under this Act, the Director of Public Prosecutions may institute or direct summary proceedings at any time within 4 years after the commission of the offence.

S. 29 : Notices under the Act may be served by registered post.

S. 33 : The Act does not interfere with the operations of the London and Birmingham proof houses, and it does not apply to an antique firearm sold, transferred or possessed as a curiosity or ornament.

The Firearms Rules, 1937, 1952 and 1954, prescribe the forms necessary for applications, certificates, permits and registration.

Gun Licence Act, 1870.—The Gun Licence Act, 1870, is an Excise Act and makes it an offence for any person to use a gun outside a residence unless he has a licence for the purpose.

S. 2 : The term " gun " under this Act includes a firearm of any description and an air-gun or any other kind of gun from which any shot, bullet or other missile can be discharged.

S. 7 : It is an offence for any person to use or carry a gun otherwise than in a dwelling-house or the curtilage thereof without having in force a licence granted under the Act.

This licence costs 10s., is procurable at a Post Office or County or Borough Office, is dated the day on which it is granted, and expires on July 31 following. Curtilage includes the outbuildings, yard and ground belonging to the house, enclosed within the common wall or fence.

If a gun is carried in parts by two or more persons in company, each person shall be deemed to carry the gun (s. 8).

S. 7 declares that no penalty under the Act will be incurred by the following persons :—

(1) Any person in the naval, military or volunteer service of Her Majesty, or in a police force, using or carrying any gun in the performance of his duty, or when engaged in target practice.

(2) Any person having in force a licence or certificate to kill game.

(3) Any person carrying a gun belonging to a person having in force a licence or certificate to kill game or a licence under this Act, and by order of such person, and for the use of such person only, if the person carrying the gun shall on request of any excise officer, constable, owner or occupier of the land upon which such gun is used or carried, give the true name and address of himself and of his employer.

(4) The occupier of any lands using or carrying a gun for the purpose only of scaring birds or of killing vermin on such lands, or any person using or carrying a gun for the purpose only of scaring birds or killing vermin on any lands by order of the occupier thereof who shall have in force a licence to kill game or a licence under this Act.

(5) Any gunsmith or his servant carrying a gun in the ordinary course of the trade of a gunsmith. or using a gun by way of testing it in a place specially set apart for the purpose.

(6) Any person carrying a gun in the ordinary course of his trade or business as a common carrier.

S. 9 : Any constable or Inland Revenue officer may demand from any person using or carrying a gun (not being a person in the naval, military or volunteer service of Her Majesty or in a police force, using or carrying a gun in the performance of his duty) the production of his licence under this Act.

If such person shall not produce such a licence or a licence to kill game and permit the constable or officer to read same, it shall be lawful for such constable or officer to require such person to declare to him immediately his name and residence. If such person shall refuse to declare the same, the constable or officer may arrest and convey him before a Justice. The Justice may convict him for such refusal to declare his name and address and fine him, and if the fine be not paid forthwith to the constable or officer, the Justice shall commit him to prison for a period not exceeding one month or until the penalty be sooner paid.

S. 10 : Any constable or officer of Inland Revenue who sees any person using or carrying a gun, may enter upon any lands or premises (except a dwelling-house or the curtilage thereof) for the purpose of making the demand specified in s. 9.

S. 4 : As this Act is an Excise Act, proceedings (except those under s. 9) may only be taken by the County or Borough Council concerned, as the licence duties were transferred to Local Authorities in 1908.

Where a police officer detects a person carrying a gun without a licence under the Act (such person not being exempted under s. 7) the facts should be reported to the Council concerned.

Gun Barrel Proof Act, 1868.—This private Act declares that small arms (rifles, shotguns, etc.) are not to be sold, kept for sale pawned, etc., unless the barrels have been duly proved, as shown by the authorised proof marks thereon. The London Gun Makers Company and the Birmingham Proof House may take proceedings under the Act. A search warrant may be obtained by the police to assist in its execution.

Chapter XXXV
ANIMALS
Contents

Diseases of Animals.—The Act now dealing with this subject is the Diseases of Animals Act, 1950, which has repealed the 1894 Act and several other similar Acts and consolidated the law on the matter. The Act empowers the Minister of Agriculture, Fisheries and Food to make Orders, and s. 89 continues in effect all previous Orders and Regulations made under the repealed Acts respecting the various diseases to which animals are liable.

" Animals," unless the context otherwise requires, means cattle, sheep and goats and all other ruminating (cud chewing) animals and swine.

This definition has by Order, 1952, been extended to horses, asses, mules and jennets.

" Cattle " means bulls, cows, oxen, heifers and calves.

" Carcase " means the carcase of an animal and includes part of a carcase.

" Poultry " unless the context otherwise requires, means domestic fowls, turkeys, geese, ducks, guinea fowls, pigeons also pheasants and partridges and this definition by Order, 1953, has been extended to parrots.

" Disease " as regards " animals " means cattle plague (rinder pest), pleuro-pneumonia, foot and mouth disease, sheep pox, sheep scab or swine fever and this definition, by Order, 1952, has been extended to glanders and farcy.

" Disease " as regards " poultry " means fowl pest, fowl cholera, fowl pox, etc., and the definition has been extended to psittacosis, by Order, 1953.

" Horse " includes ass and mule (s. 84).

Ss. 3-7 give the Minister power to deal with diseases of horses and animals. He can order eradication areas and attested (free from disease) areas and can authorise inspection of animals and horses. False statements to obtain compensation and obstruction of an authorised inspector will be summary offences.

S. 8 : Every person having in his possession or under his

charge an animal affected with disease shall keep that animal separate from animals not so affected and notify with all practicable speed the fact to the local police who shall pass on the information as directed by the Minister's Order, see Tuberculosis Order, 1938.

S. 10 : Places and Areas may be declared to be infected with disease and under s. 11 Orders may deal with the movement, isolation, destruction, etc., of animals and the disinfection of persons and places. S. 12 allows the putting up at an infected place, notice forbidding persons to enter without permission.

Ss 13–18 : Empowers the slaughter of animals in cases of cattle plague, pleuro-pneumonia, foot and mouth disease and swine fever, and of animals and horses in cases of other diseases prescribed by Order ; the disposal of the carcases and compensation to the owners.

Ss. 20-23 allow the Minister to make orders regulating the movement and carriage of animals.

Ss. 24-35 deal with the import of animals, also the First and Second Schedules to the Act.

Ss. 36-41 prescribe the conditions for the export of animals and horses (see later).

Ss. 42, 43 allow the Minister to make Orders for periodical sheepdipping or some other remedy for sheep scab, and the examination of sheep.

S. 44 : The Minister may make Orders as to dogs—such as muzzling, collars, stray dogs and the seizure and disposal of unmuzzled and stray dogs and dogs not kept under control.

Ss. 45-51 relate to poultry, the eradication of their diseases, their slaughter in case of disease, their import, their protection in transit and the power of an inspector to enter premises where poultry are kept. See also Live Poultry (Restrictions) Order, 1957, and Live Poultry (Movement Records) Orders, 1954 and 1956 and the Disinfection Order, 1956.

S. 59 : " Local Authority " means the Council of any borough having a population of not less than 10,000 ; the Council of a Metropolitan borough ; the County Council (for the rest of a County) ; any " body " appointed by the Minister as such for a port, and a local authority shall enforce the Act.

S. 71 : The police shall execute and enforce this Act and every Order of the Minister. When a person is seen or found committing or is reasonably suspected of being engaged in committing an offence against this Act, a constable without warrant may stop and detain him and if his name and address are not known to the constable and the person fails to give them to the satisfaction of the constable, the constable may, without warrant, apprehend him. The constable may whether stopping or apprehending or not, stop, detain and examine any animal, vehicle, boat or thing to which the suspected offence relates and require same to be forthwith taken back to the place whence unlawfully removed

and execute and enforce that requisition. If any person obstructs
or impedes or assists in so doing a constable or other officer in the
execution of this Act or Order under it, he may be arrested without
warrant.

A person arrested under this section shall be taken with all
practicable speed before a Justice and shall not be detained
without a warrant longer than is necessary for the purpose.
The law as to release of persons on recognizances by police shall
apply in such cases.

The foregoing provisions of this section respecting a constable
extend and apply to any person called by the constable to his
assistance.

A constable shall forthwith report in writing to his Superior
Officer of every case in which he stops any person, animal, vehicle,
boat or thing under this section and of his proceedings consequent
thereon.

S. 73 : An inspector appointed by the Ministry or by the local
authority has all the powers which a constable has under this
Act. He can enter land, premises, vehicles, etc., on reasonable
grounds of suspicion.

Ss. 78–81 : Offences under this Act, or Orders or local regulations are punishable summarily with fine and the more serious
offences, such as doing prohibited acts without licence or using
false licences or digging up buried carcases, etc., may be punished
summarily by imprisonment.

Cruelty to Animals.—Protection of Animals Act, 1911, s. 1 :
This section declares that it is an offence of cruelty punishable
summarily by imprisonment or fine or both, for :—

(1) Any person to do any of the following acts or to cause
or procure or being the owner, to permit same to be done :—

(*a*) Cruelly beat, kick, ill-treat, over-ride, over-drive, over
load, torture, infuriate or terrify any animal ;

(*b*) Cause any unnecessary suffering to any animal either
by doing or omitting to do some act ;

(*c*) Convey or carry any animal in such a manner of
position as to cause that animal any unnecessary suffering
(Diseases of Animals, Act, 1950, s. 22, provides for the supply
of food and water for animals carried by railway companies,
and s. 50 of the Act deals with the conveyance of live
poultry).

(*d*) Subject any animal to any operation which is performed
without due care and humanity. See later.

(2) Any person to cause, procure or assist at the fighting or
baiting of any animal (" animal " includes fowl, s. 15) or to use or
permit any premises to be used for such purpose. Cockfighting
Act, 1952 makes it a summary offence to have possession of
appliances for use in the fighting of domestic fowl for the purpose
of using or permitting its use for such purpose. (The Town Police

Clauses Act, 1847, where it applies, makes it a summary offence by s. 28 for any person in any street to the obstruction, danger or annoyance of residents or passengers to set on or urge any dog or other animal to attack, worry or put in fear any person or animal, and by s. 36, for any person to conduct any place for the fighting, baiting or worrying of any animals).

(3) Any person, wilfully or without reasonable excuse, to administer or cause or procure or being the owner to permit the administration of any poisonous or injurious drug or substance to any animal (see also s. 8 later).

An owner will be deemed to have permitted cruelty if he has failed to exercise reasonable care and supervision in respect to the protection of the animal therefrom.

However, this section will not apply :—

(1) To the destruction of an animal as food for mankind unless it was accompanied by unnecessary suffering, or

(2) To the coursing or hunting of any captive animal, unless it is set free in an injured, mutilated or exhausted condition, or unless (Amendment Act, 1921) it is hunted in an enclosed space from which it has no reasonable chance of escape.

(3) To vivisection carried out under licence.

S. 15 : " Animal " means any domestic or captive animal. " Domestic animal " includes any animal or fowl of whatsoever kind or species which is tame or which has been or is being sufficiently tamed to serve some purpose for the use of man.

" Captive animal " includes any animal (not being a domestic animal), of whatsoever kind or species, including bird, fish and reptile, which is in captivity or confinement or which is maimed, pinioned or subjected to any contrivance to prevent its escape.

Ss. 2 and 3 : On conviction of the owner for cruelty to an animal, the Court may direct that the animal be destroyed, if satisfied it would be cruel to keep it alive, or may deprive the owner of the ownership and make an order as to the disposal of the animal. The court may disqualify him from having custody of any animal or animals (Amendment Act, 1954).

S. 4 : If any person by cruelty to an animal causes any damage to the animal or to any person or property, the Court may order compensation up to £10 to be paid to the person aggrieved.

S. 7 : The person impounding or causing to be impounded any animal in any pound must supply it with food and water on penalty of summary fine. See " Impounding Animals," Chap. 24.

S. 8 : It is a summary offence, punishable by fine, to sell or dispose of any grain or seed which has been rendered poisonous except for *bona fide* use in agriculture, or to lay down or cause to be laid down on any land or building any poison or poisonous matter. It will be a defence to prove that such poison was laid down for the destruction of rats or mice or other small vermin, and that reasonable precautions were taken to prevent injury thereby to dogs, cats, fowls, other domestic animals or wild birds (Protection of Animals Amendment Act, 1927, s. 1).

S. 10 : When a person sets or causes to be set any spring trap likely to catch a hare or rabbit, it is a summary offence punishable by fine, if he does not inspect or cause to be inspected such trap at reasonable intervals and at least once a day.

Rabbit clearance areas may be ordered. Spring traps for animals must, after 31st July, 1958 (or otherwise by Order), be of the approved type. Spring traps for hares or rabbits must not be used elsewhere than in rabbit holes, unless permitted by licence. The knowingly spreading of myxomatosis is illegal (Pests Act, 1954). See also Prevention of Damage by Pests (Threshing and Dismantling of Ricks) Regs. 1950 as to the fencing of ricks before they are dismantled.

S. 12 : A police constable may arrest without warrant any person whom he has reason to believe is guilty of an offence under the Act which is punishable by imprisonment (see s. 1), whether on his own view thereof or on complaint of any other person who shall give his name and address.

When a constable, under this Act, arrests a person in charge of a vehicle or animal, he is empowered to take charge of such vehicle or animal and deposit it in some place of safe custody.

S. 13 : Where proceedings under this Act are taken against the driver or conductor of a vehicle, his employer may be summoned to produce such driver or conductor at the hearing. The owner of the animal may be summoned to produce the animal for the inspection of the Court.

The Transit of Animals Orders 1927, 1930, 1931, 1939, 1947, and the Animals (Sea-Transport) Orders 1930, 1952, provide for the conveyance of animals without unnecessary suffering between home ports and between home and foreign ports.

Operations on Animals.—Cruelty to Animals Act, 1876, makes it an offence to perform on any living animal any experiment calculated to give pain, except on licence and subject to the restrictions prescribed in the Act. Any public exhibition of experiments on living animals calculated to give them pain is illegal. The Act enables a search warrant to be granted to a constable on sworn information that such experiments are being unlawfully carried out. The carrying out of such experiments is termed " vivisection," meaning the cutting up when alive This Act does not apply to invertebrate animals.

Protection of Animals (Anaesthetics) Act, 1954, repealed the Animals (Anaesthetics) Act, 1919, and declares that any operation on the sensitive tissues or bone structures of an animal (not a bird, fish or reptile) without an anaesthetic to prevent pain shall be deemed an operation performed without due care and humanity under s. 1, Protection of Animals Act, 1911.

However this Act does not apply to injections, etc., by hollow needle or operations as specified in the First Schedule such as first aid in an emergency, quick or minor operations, tail docking or castration before certain ages.

Injured Animals.—Protection of Animals Act, 1911, s. 11 : If a police constable finds any animal (meaning any horse, mule, ass, bull, sheep, goat or pig) so diseased or so severely injured or in such a physical condition that in his opinion it cannot be removed without cruelty, he shall, if the owner is absent or refuses to consent to the destruction of the animal, summon a veterinary surgeon residing within a reasonable distance. If such veterinary surgeon certifies that the animal is mortally injured or so severely injured or so diseased or in such physical condition that it is cruel to keep it alive, it will be lawful for the constable, without the consent of the owner, to have the animal slaughtered with as little suffering as practicable and to have the carcase removed from the highway if it is thereon.

If the veterinary surgeon certifies that the animal can without cruelty be removed, the person in charge of the animal should have it removed, and if he fails to do so the constable may cause it to be so removed.

Any expenses incurred by the constable under this section may be recovered from the owner summarily as a civil debt.

If the owner by his cruelty is responsible for the condition of an injured animal, a Court has power to order the destruction of the animal. See " Cruelty to Animals."

Where injury to an animal is the result of cruelty, see " Cruelty to Animals " and where the injury has been malicious and affects the owner, see " Malicious Damage," Chap. 15.

Performing Animals.—Performing Animals (Regulation) Act, 1925, ss. 1 and 5 : No person shall exhibit any performing animal at any entertainment to which the public are admitted whether on payment or otherwise, or train any animal for the purpose of any such exhibition, unless he is registered with the County or Borough Council of the place where he resides.

S. 7 : This Act does not apply to training or exhibition for *bona fide* military, police, agricultural, or sporting purposes.

S. 3 : Any constable or any person authorised by the Local Authority, may enter at all reasonable times and inspect any premises on which any performing animals are trained, exhibited or kept. He can inspect any animals found therein and require the production of the certificate of registration under the Act. However, he is not entitled to go on or behind the stage during any public performance.

S. 2 : On proof of cruelty, a Court may make an order prohibiting such training or exhibition or imposing conditions.

S. 4 : It is a summary offence for—

(1) Any unregistered person to exhibit or train any performing animal ;

(2) Any registered person to exhibit or train any performing

animal with respect to which or in a manner with respect to which he is not registered ;

(3) Any person to obstruct any constable or authorised officer acting under this Act ;

(4) Any person to conceal any animal to avoid inspection ;

(5) Any registered person without reasonable excuse to fail to produce his certificate ;

(6) Any person to fail to comply with any order of a Court made under this Act ;

(7) Any person to apply for registration when prohibited from being so registered.

When a person is convicted under this Act or under the Protection of Animals Acts, the Court may cancel his registration or disqualify him from registration.

Protection of Animals Act, 1934, prohibits any public performance (" rodeo ") in which unbroken horses or untrained bulls are thrown, untrained bulls are struggled with, or horses or bulls are stimulated by any cruelty to buck. The promoters and operators are liable to £100 fine and (or) 3 months imprisonment, and the onus of proof that an animal was broken or trained rests on them.

Cinematograph Films (Animals) Act, 1937, prohibits the public exhibition of film scenes in connection with the production of which, suffering may have been caused to animals.

Horses.—Horse Breeding Act, 1958: A person who keeps a stallion which has attained the age of 2 years without a license or permit commits a summary offence, unless it was 4 years old befor Jan. 1, 1949 or unless it is a thoroughbred or a pony of a prescribed breed. If a person travels for service a stallion exempted under one of these two categories, or exhibits it on any premises not in his occupation with a view to its use for service or permits same to be done, unless the stallion is licensed by the Ministry of Agriculture, Fisheries and Food he commits a summary offence (s. 1 and the Horse Breeding Rules, 1948).

Under s. 10, the person in charge of the stallion must produce the license or a certified copy thereof, to any person engaging the service of the stallion or to any police officer or other authorised person.

It is a summary offence to forge or fraudulently alter or use or to permit to be fraudulently altered or used any such licence or certified copy thereof (s. 11).

Diseases of Animals Act, 1950. No horse, ass or mule may be shipped from any port in Great Britain to any port outside the United Kingdom unless—

(1) A veterinary surgeon appointed by the Minister for such purpose has certified in writing that it is capable of being conveyed to such port and disembarked without cruelty and is capable of being worked without suffering (s. 37) ; or

(2) A thoroughbred horse accompanied by a written certificate from a steward or the secretary of the Jockey Club, that it is travelling for racing or breeding purposes or has arrived in Great Britain not more than one month previous for racing purposes (s. 40).

Any such certificate shall be given to the Master of the vessel who, on demand, shall produce it to any constable or officer of the Ministry and allow a copy of it to be taken (ss. 37, 40).

If any horse examined under s. 37 is found to be in such a physical condition that it is cruel to keep it alive or to be permanently incapable of being worked without suffering the inspector shall forthwith slaughter it or cause it to be slaughtered (s. 37).

If a horse being exported under a veterinary inspectors' certificate has a limb broken or is otherwise seriously injured while on board the ship so as to be incapable of being disembarked without cruelty the Master shall cause it to be slaughtered with a proper killing instrument which must be carried on the ship (s. 39).

Transit of Horses Order, 1951 provides for the proper conveyance of horses in rail and road vehicles and Horses (Sea-Transport) Orders 1952 and 1958 with their conveyance by sea. The Exported Cattle Protection Order, 1957, as amended requires that any cattle exported from Great Britain to any place outside the United Kingdom, the Channel Islands, the Isle of Man or the Republic of Ireland, whether by sea or air, shall be rested for 10 hours before they are loaded. They must be given adequate food, water and shelter, and an animal may be removed from the ship or aircraft if it is likely to be exposed to unnecessary suffering during transit.

The Exported Ponies Protection Order 1958 provides that no pony shall be shipped by sea or by air from Great Britain to any place outside Europe, unless it has been inspected by a veterinary inspector and certified to be capable of being conveyed without unnecessary suffering. " Pony " means any horse not more than 14 hands in height, except a foal travelling with its dam if the dam is over 14 hands.

Docking and Nicking of Horses Act, 1949, prohibits the docking (removal of any bone from the tail) or nicking (severing of any tendon or muscle in the tail) of horses (including ponies and mules) unless a veterinary surgeon certifies it is necessary for their health.

From Jan 1, 1955, no docked horse shall be imported except on licence or for export as soon as practicable.

Knackers.—The Slaughter of Animals Act, 1958 and the Slaughter of Animals (Prevention of Cruelty) Regs., 1958, apply to knackers and knacker's yards. A knacker is a person whose business is to kill animals the flesh of which is not intended for sale for human consumption, and the premises used for such business is a knacker's yard (Reg. 2). See also s. 10, 1958 Act. Sale of Knacker's yard products for human consumption is an offence (Food and Drugs Act, 1955, s. 12).

A knacker, his " yard " and his slaughtermen must be licensed by the local borough or district council (see Food and Drugs Act, 1955). Animals should be killed with as little suffering as possible (s. 1, 1958 Act), and if in pain must be slaughtered without delay (Reg. 18). No horse shall be worked after it has been delivered to a knacker's yard (Reg. 21). Every animal delivered to a knacker's yard shall be kept on the premises until killed and must be slaughtered within 48 hours from the time of delivery (Reg. 22). A person under 15 should not be in a knacker's yard while slaughtering or cutting up of carcases is taking place (Reg. 23).

The occupier of a knacker's yard must keep accurate records of all animals received. The record must be made in ink or indelible pencil within 24 hours of the slaughter of the animal or of its receipt (Reg. 32). The record shall be produced for inspection at all reasonable times on request by an authorised officer of the local authority or the Minister (Reg. 35).

Contravention of the regulations in punishable summarily but a person shall not be guilty if he proves that by reason of accident or other emergency, the contravention was necessary for preventing physical injury or suffering to any person or animal (Reg. 36).

A constable has the right to enter a knacker's yard by day or when business is carried on, to see if any contravention of the Act has occurred. Any person refusing such entry or obstructing him can be punished summarily (Protection of Animals Act, 1911, s. 5).

Dogs.—The law makes an owner responsible for the licensing and custody of his dogs.

Diseases of Animals Act, 1950, s. 44, allows the Minister of Agriculture, Fisheries and Food to make Orders regarding dogs—dealing with their muzzling and control ; collars with name and address of owner ; stray dogs ; seizure and disposal of stray dogs, unmuzzled dogs and dogs not under control.

Licensing of Dogs.—Dog Licences Act, 1867 : It is an offence for any person to keep a dog above the age of six months without having in force a licence to keep such dog, or to keep a greater number of dogs than he is licensed to keep (s. 8). Dog licences last 12 months from date of issue (Finance Act, 1949, s. 13). They are personal licences and are not transferable. They cost 7s. 6d. each and are procurable at a Post Office or County or Borough Council office.

It is also an offence for a licensed person not to produce and deliver his licence to be examined and read by a constable or excise officer within a reasonable time after request for its production (s. 9).

Every person in whose custody, charge or possession or in whose house or premises any dog shall be found or seen, shall be deemed to be the person keeping the same unless the contrary be proved (s. 8).

Customs and Inland Revenue Act, 1878, provides that dogs used as guides by blind persons are exempt from license (s. 21). also hounds under the age of twelve months belonging to masters of hounds and never entered in or used with any pack of hounds (s.20). A certificate of exemption may be obtained for dogs kept and used solely for tending sheep or cattle on a farm or in the exercise of the occupation of a shepherd, on the owner making the prescribed declaration, and obtaining the consent of the local court (s. 22).

Dangerous Dogs.—Town Police Clauses Act, 1847, s. 28 : It is an offence for any person in any street in any district where the Act applies, to the obstruction, annoyance or danger of the residents or passengers—

(1) To suffer to be at large any unmuzzled ferocious dog ;

(2) To set on or urge any dog or other animal to attack, worry or put in fear any person or animal ;

(3) To suffer his dog to be at large knowing or having reasonable ground for believing it to be in a rabid state or to have been bitten by any rabid dog or animal ; or

(4) To suffer any dog to be at large after public notice has been given by any Justice directing dogs to be confined on account of canine madness.

Dogs Act, 1871, s. 2 : A Magistrates' Court may hear any complaint that a dog is dangerous and not kept under proper control, and, if it appears that the dog is dangerous, may order it to be kept by the owner under proper control or destroyed.

Dogs (Amendment) Act, 1938, as amended by 9th Sched., C.J. Act, 1948 : If an order to destroy is made the owner can appeal to Quarter Sessions. If the owner intends to appeal he must give notice accordingly within 14 days and the dog must be kept under proper control during the 14 days and until any appeal is decided. If the owner gives notice that he does not intend to appeal the order for destruction takes effect. If no notice of appeal or non appeal is given the order to destroy the dog takes effect after 14 days.

Dogs Act, 1906, s. 1 (as amended by the Dogs (Amendment) Act, 1928) : The owner of a dog shall be liable in damages for injury done to any cattle or poultry by that dog. It will not be necessary to prove a previous mischievous propensity in the dog or the owner's knowledge of same or that the injury was due to the owner's neglect. The occupier of any premises where the dog was kept or permitted to live or remain at the time of the injury will be presumed to be the owner unless he proves the contrary. If a dog is proved to have injured cattle or poultry or chased sheep it may be dealt with as a dangerous dog under s. 2 of the Dogs Act, 1871. The word " cattle " includes horses, mules, asses, sheep, goats and swine. The word " poultry " includes domestic fowls, turkeys, geese, ducks, guinea-fowls and pigeons (Diseases of Animals Act, 1950). See also Public Health Acts Amendment Act, 1907, s. 81. See *Goodway* v. *Becher* (1951) where it was held that the owner acted reasonably in respect of his shooting a dog in defence of his poultry.

Dogs and Livestock.—Under the Dogs (Protection of Livestock) Act, 1953, the owner or person in charge of a dog which worries livestock on any agricultural land (which is not excluded by Order) will be guilty of a summary offence liable to fine up to £10, on second conviction with same dog, fine up to £50.

" Worrying " means attacking or chasing in such a way as may reasonably be expected to cause injury or suffering. However, the owner or person authorised by him may use a dog to drive off trespassing livestock but not to attack them (s. 1).

" Agricultural land " means arable, meadow or grazing land, or land used for poultry or pig farming, market gardens, allotments, nursery grounds or orchards.

" Livestock " means cattle, sheep, goats, swine, horses, asses, mules or poultry. " Poultry " means domestic fowls, turkeys, geese or ducks (s. 3).

For an offence under the Act no proceedings shall be brought except: (*a*) by or with consent of the local chief officer of police, or (*b*) by the occupier of the land, or (*c*) by the owner of the livestock in question.

If a dog is found on any land and no person is present who admits he is the owner or in charge of it, and a police officer has reasonable cause to believe that the dog has been worrying livestock on that land which appears to him as " agricultural " he may seize the dog and detain it until the owner has claimed it and paid all expenses. If not claimed within 7 days the dog may be treated as a stray dog under s. 3, Dogs Act, 1906, (s. 2).

Stray Dogs.—Dogs Act, 1906, s. 3 : Where a police officer has reason to believe that any dog found in a highway or place of public resort is a stray dog, he may seize the dog and detain it until the owner has claimed it and paid all expenses incurred. Where the owner is known, the police shall serve on him notice in writing that the dog has been seized and may be sold or destroyed if not claimed within seven clear days after service of the notice. Where any dog so seized has been kept for seven clear days, or, if such notice has been served, for seven days after service of notice, and the owner has not claimed the dog and paid all expenses incurred, the police may cause the dog to be sold or destroyed. Such notice may be served personally or by leaving it at, or by sending it by post to, the owner's address. A register of all dogs seized must be kept by the police and be open for inspection at all reasonable times by the public on payment of 1s. fee. The police must properly feed and maintain all seized dogs.

S. 4 (and Dogs (Amendment) Act, 1928) : Any person who takes possession of a stray dog shall forthwith either return the dog to its owner or take the dog to the police station nearest to the place where the dog was found and give particulars of the finding. If the finder wishes to keep the dog he will be given a certificate in the form prescribed and may take the dog, but is bound to keep it for not less than one month. If he does not want it, it will be treated as a seized stray dog. Failure to comply with above is a summary offence. Penalty, £2.

S. 6 (and Dogs (Amendment) Act, 1928) : It is an offence for any person knowingly and without reasonable excuse, to permit the carcase of any head of cattle (including horses, mules, asses, sheep, goats and swine) belonging to him or under his control, to remain unburied in a field or other place to which dogs can gain access.

Control of Dogs.—The Control of Dogs Orders 1930, 1931 ' direct that every dog while in a highway or in a place of public resort shall wear a collar with name and address of the owner inscribed thereon or on a plate or badge attached thereto.

Provided that this requirement shall not apply to any pack of hounds, or to any dog while being used for sporting purposes or for the capture or destruction of vermin or for driving or tending of cattle or sheep.

Any dog not so complying with the order may be seized and treated as a stray dog, and any person committing or aiding, abetting, counselling or procuring the commission of any breach of the Order is liable to fine, or to imprisonment if a second or subsequent similar offence occurs within 12 months.

An Amendment Order of 1930 declares that where a dog is found in such a place not wearing a collar as prescribed, the owner, the person in charge, and any person allowing the dog to be so there, shall each be guilty of an offence.

A Local Authority may, under this Order, make regulations for requiring that dogs shall be kept under control between sunset and sunrise for the prevention of worrying of cattle (including horses, mules, asses, sheep, goats and swine).

Road Traffic Act, 1956, s. 15: A local authority may by Order made after consultation with the police and confirmation by the Minister, designate a road. Then any person who causes or permits a dog to be on a designated road without the dog being held on a lead will commit a summary offence. This shall not apply to dogs for driving sheep or cattle or sporting dogs under proper control.

Injury or Cruelty to Dogs.—Malicious Damage Act, 1861, s. 41 : It is a summary offence to unlawfully and maliciously kill, maim, or wound any dog.

Protection of Animals Act, 1911, s. 9 : It is an offence to use, cause, procure, or being the owner to permit to be used, any dog for the purpose of drawing or helping to draw any cart or truck on any public highway.

Protection of Animals (Cruelty to Dogs) Act, 1933 : If a person is convicted of cruelty to a dog the Court may disqualify him for keeping a dog and for having a dog licence, for such period as the Court thinks fit. If such person during the period of disqualification keeps a dog or applies for or obtains a dog licence he is liable to £25 fine and three months imprisonment. After six months he may apply to the Court to remove the disqualification. Under the Protection of Animals Act, 1911, ss. 2 and 3, the Court may also direct the dog to be destroyed if necessary and may deprive the owner of the ownership.

For general cruelty, see " Cruelty to Animals."

Stealing Dogs.—The stealing of a dog is not a felony, as a dog is not the subject of larceny at common law. A dog is not a " chattel," so the obtaining of a dog by false pretences is not indictable under s. 32, Larceny Act, 1916 (false pretences).

Larceny Act, 1861, ss. 18 and 19 : It is a summary offence to steal any dog, or for anyone to unlawfully have in his possession or on his premises any stolen dog or the skin of any stolen dog, knowing such dog to have been stolen or such skin to be the skin of a stolen dog.

Larceny Act, 1916, s. 5 : It is a misdemeanour for any person—

(1) To steal any dog, after a previous summary conviction of any such offence ;

(2) To unlawfully have in possession or on his premises any stolen dog or the skin thereof, knowing such dog or skin to have been stolen, after a previous summary conviction of any such offence ;

(3) To corruptly take any money or reward directly or indirectly, under pretence or upon account of aiding any person to recover any stolen dog or any dog in possession of a person not its owner. See " Compounding Offences," Chap. 2.

It is a summary offence to retain possession of a stray dog without obtaining the necessary certificate. See " Stray Dogs."

Rabies.—Under the Rabies Order, 1938, every person who has in his possession or charge an animal (including a dog or cat) affected with or suspected of rabies must at once notify the police and isolate such animal which must be slaughtered. The police must at once report the fact to the inspector of the Local Authority and to the Ministry of Agriculture and Fisheries, London.

The Dogs Act, 1871, the Dogs Act, 1906, and the Diseases of Animals Act, 1950, authorise the making of Orders placing restrictions on dogs.

S. 28 of the Town Police Clauses Act, 1847 (where the Act applies) prescribes a summary penalty for owners who allow rabid dogs to be at large or who do not obey a Justices' public notice to keep dogs confined on account of suspicion of rabies.

Birds.—The Protection of Birds Act, 1954 repeals and replaces all the previous Wild Bird Protection Acts, which ranged from 1880 to 1939.

Under s. 1 it is an offence to wilfully kill, injure or take or attempt to do so any wild bird or its nest while in use or its eggs, or to have in possession or control any wild bird recently killed or taken (unless allowed under the Act), but there are many exceptions to this comprehensive section.

" Wild Bird " means any wild bird but in the Act does not include pheasant, partridge, grouse, or moor game, black or heath game or, in Scotland, ptarmigan, except as regards s. 5 (which prohibits certain methods of killing or taking birds) s. 10 (which gives power to grant licences to kill or take birds) and s. 12 (which deals with enforcement of penalties) (s. 14).

The Act deals with 5 classes of wild birds as follows:—

(1) *First Sched. Part I.* This schedule protects certain birds and their eggs at all times. This list of 49 birds includes corn-crake, eagle, quail, swan and certain hawks.

An offence in respect of them is punishable by a special penalty (s. 1).

(2) *First Sched. Part II.* This protects certain birds during the close season. This list of 10 birds includes greylag goose, whimbrel and six species of wild duck.

An offence in respect of them is punishable by special penalty (s. 1).

(3) *Second Sched.* This allows certain birds to be killed or taken at any time by authorised persons. This list of 20 birds includes crow, gull, jackdaw, magpie, rook, sparrow, starling, wood pigeon, oyster-catchers.

An authorised person may kill or take or attempt to do so any of the birds in this Second Schedule or take or destroy their eggs and nests or take the eggs of wild geese, ducks or swans for hatching (s. 2).

" Authorised person " means the owner or occupier (or any person authorised by him) of land on which the action authorised is taken; any person authorised in writing by the local authority of the area; any person authorised in writing by certain bodies such as water or fishery authorities, but such authority does not give any right of entry upon any land.

" Local authority " means amongst others the council of a county, county borough, urban or rural district.

" Occupier " includes any person having the right of hunting, shooting or fishing (s. 14).

(4) *Third Sched.* This allows certain birds to be killed or taken outside the close season. (Except on Sundays in certain areas. Wild Birds (Sundays) Orders, 1955, 1956 and 1957.) This list of 31 birds includes the greylag goose and 4 other kinds of wild geese, mallard, teal, wigeon and 11 other kinds of wild duck, curlew, plover, snipe, woodcock.

The close season for snipe is 1st Feb. to 11th Aug., for wild duck and wild geese 21st Feb. to 31st Aug., for capercaillie and (except in Scotland) woodcock 1st Feb. to 30th Sept., and in any other case 1st Feb. to 31st Aug. (s. 2).

(5) *Fourth Sched.* This covers birds which may not be sold alive unless close ringed and bred in captivity. The list of 60 birds includes blackbird, bullfinch, goldfinch, greenfinch, lark, robin, sparrow, starling, thrush, yellow hammer.

Restrictions on sale, etc.—Unless authorised by licence under s. 10, it will be an offence to sell, offer for sale or have in possession for sale any live bird of the Fourth Schedule other than a close ringed bird bred in captivity, any dead wild bird of the Third Schedule during the period 28th Feb. to 31st Aug., or any dead wild bird or the skin or plumage of a wild bird of some other species unless it was lawfully imported or lawfully killed, or the egg of a wild bird (if such species has nested in this country) except the eggs of gulls for food or feeding purposes and the eggs of wild duck, wild geese and swans for hatching and the eggs of lapwings before 15th April in any year. A justice on sworn information may grant a warrant to any constable to enter and search premises for evidence of an offence under this section (s. 6).

The Secretary of State and other authorities may grant licences authorising the killing or taking etc. of wild birds for various purposes (s. 10).

Prohibitions of methods of killing or taking birds.—It will be an offence (with special penalty), unless on licence under s. 10, to set in position without reasonable precautions, traps, snares etc. likely to injure wild birds (except those for other purposes); to use nets, birdlime etc. to catch birds; to use a live bird, tethered etc., as a decoy; to use a very large bore etc. gun for killing birds; to use artificial light to attract birds other than those in the Second Schedule; to use aircraft or motor vehicle or boat to pursue and kill or take a wild bird.

However a net or cage trap may be used by an authorised person for taking Second Schedule birds or for taking for ringing or marking and a net duck decoy used before this Act is still allowable (s. 5).

Restrictions on importation.—Unless authorised by licence under s. 10, the importation is prohibited of any common quail, alive or dead, of any dead lapwing or on or after April 15 in any year the eggs of any lapwing, and during period from February 1 to August 31 of any dead Third Schedule bird or wild duck or wild goose.

The Secretary of State may expand such restrictions (s. 7).

Captive birds.—It will be an offence with special penalty to keep or confine any bird in a cage or receptacle in which the bird cannot stretch its wings freely, but this will not apply to domestic poultry or birds in course of conveyance or so kept for exhibition (under 72 hours) or while getting veterinary treatment.

It will be a special penalty offence (s. 8).

Bird sanctuaries.—The Secretary of State, may by order allow the establishment of bird sanctuaries within the area of a local authority, within which interference with wild birds and their nests and eggs is prohibited (s. 3). The local authority may institute proceedings for any offence under the order (s. 12).

Penalties etc.—A constable may without warrant stop and search any person found committing an offence against the Act and any vehicle, boat or animal which that person may then be using, and may arrest that person if he fails to give his name and address to the constable's satisfaction, and seize and detain any wild bird nest or egg or any weapon or other article capable of being used to kill or take wild birds which may be in the person's possession.

A " special penalty " is a fine of up to £25, or imprisonment (up to one month for first offence and up to three months for a second or subsequent offence against the Act) or both.

In any other case the penalty may be up to £5 fine; both on summary conviction. Also the Court shall order forfeiture of the bird etc. and may order the forfeiture of any weapon, bird or article used in the offence.

The council of a county or county borough may institute proceedings (s. 12).

Larceny of Birds.—All valuable domestic birds which serve for food, such as poultry and their eggs, and the flesh of wild birds may be the subject of larceny at common law. The Larceny Act, 1861, made it a summary offence to steal or to kill to steal any bird or other animal ordinarily kept in a state of confinement or for any domestic purpose, not being the subject of larceny at common law (s. 21), or to unlawfully and wilfully kill, wound or take any house dove or pigeon under such conditions as shall not amount to larceny at common law (s. 23). It also makes it an offence to have knowingly in possession such birds or their plumage (s. 22). However, the Larceny Act, 1916, s. 1, declares that anything which is of any value and which is the property of any-one, is capable of being stolen, so that any bird which has come into the possession of anyone is capable of being stolen.

Malicious Damage to Birds.—It is a summary offence to un-lawfully and maliciously kill, maim or wound any bird or other animal being either the subject of larceny at common law or being ordinarily kept in a state of confinement or for any domestic purpose (Malicious Damage Act, 1861, s. 41).

Larceny of Animals.—All domestic animals, such as horses, asses, mules, cattle, all animals and birds which are fit for human food, such as sheep, swine and poultry and their products and the flesh of animals and birds which are by nature wild, may be the subject of larceny at common law and the stealing of them will be felony.

Larceny Act, 1916, s. 3 : It is a felony to steal any horse, cattle, or sheep.

S. 4 : It is a felony (triable summarily with accused's consent (M.C. Act, 1952, s. 19 and 1st Sched.)) to wilfully kill an animal with intent to steal the carcase, skin or any part, provided that the stealing of the animal would have amounted to larceny.

S. 1 (3) : The carcase of a creature wild by nature and not reduced into possession shall not be capable of being stolen by the person who has killed it unless after killing it he has abandoned possession of the carcase.

Larceny Act, 1861, ss. 12 and 13 : The unlawful taking or attempting to take any deer kept in the unenclosed part of a forest or chase is a summary offence, but a subsequent offence or the unlawful taking or attempting to take any deer in any enclosed land where deer are usually kept is a felony.

S. 14 : Being in possession of any part of a deer or of any engine for taking deer, and not satisfactorily accounting for same is a summary offence.

S. 15 : Setting or using engines for taking deer is a summary offence.

Ss. 21 and 22 : The stealing or the killing with intent to steal of any bird, beast or other animal ordinarily kept in confinement or for any domestic purpose and not being the subject of larceny at common law, or the knowingly being in possession of such stolen animal or part of it, is a summary offence.

S. 23 : The unlawful killing, wounding or taking of any house dove or pigeon under such circumstances as shall not amount to larceny at common law is a summary offence.

For the taking of dogs, game and fish, see " Dogs," above, and " Poaching Offences," and " Fishery Laws," Chap. 19.

Destructive Imported Animals Act, 1932.—This Act gives power to prohibit and control the importation or keeping of destructive animals which are not native to the country. The musk rat or musquash damages river banks, crops, etc., and the Musk Rats Order, 1932, prohibited their importation or keeping except under licence.

The Musk Rats Order, 1933, prohibits their importation and licences to keep them have been revoked. It is therefore an offence to import or keep or turn loose these pests and the police may seize them. The public are asked to kill any such rats found at large and to notify the Ministry of Agriculture and Fisheries, London, of their existence in any place.

The Grey Squirrels Order, 1937, similarly prohibits the importation into, or the keeping within, Great Britain, of grey squirrels.

Slaughter of Animals.—The law on this subject includes the Slaughter of Animals Act, 1958 and the Slaughter of Animals (Prevention of Cruelty) Regs. 1958. See also " Knackers " above.

No animal to which the 1958 Act applies (i.e. horses, cattle, sheep, swine and goats) shall be slaughtered in a slaughter-house or knacker's yard unless such animal is instantaneously killed or stunned so as to be insensible to pain until it dies. Such killing or stunning shall be by a mechanically operated instrument. However no person shall be liable for any contravention of above, for killing by the approved Jewish method for food or for killing by the approved Mahommedan method for food (s. 1, 1958 Act).

" Slaughter-house " means any premises or place used for the killing of animals the flesh of which is intended for human consumption (s. 10, 1958 Act.)

Slaughter-houses and knacker's yards require to be licensed by the local authority (borough or district council) and there is a right of appeal to a Magistrates' Court (Food and Drugs Act, 1955, ss. 62 to 66 and Slaughter of Animals (Amendment) Act, 1954).

Such premises must display conspicuously " Licensed Slaughter House " or " Licensed Knacker's Yard " as the case may be (Food and Drugs Act, 1955, s. 69).

No animal shall be slaughtered or stunned in a slaughter-house or knacker's yard by any person except a person (18 years or or over) duly licensed by the local authority. (s 3, 1958 Act.)

No swine over 12 weeks old shall be slaughtered in any place other than a slaughter-house or knacker's yard unless it is instantaneously slaughtered or stunned so as to be insensible to pain, in either case by a mechanically operated instrument. However this will not apply to the slaughter of swine at a laboratory or research station, etc. if done for diagnosis of disease or research for veterinary or medical purposes (1958 Act, s. 2). See also the Slaughter of Pigs (Anæthesia) Regs. 1958.

Medical officers of health and sanitary inspectors, officers of the Minister of Food and duly appointed veterinary surgeons have authority to inspect slaughter-houses and knacker's yards (s. 8, 1958 Act).

Contraventions of the Act are punishable summarily but it would be a good defence to prove that by reason of an accident or other emergency the contravention was necessary for preventing physical injury or suffering to any person or animal (s. 5, 1958 Act).

The Regulations of 1958 deal with lairages (premises in which animals awaiting slaughter are confined), slaughter-houses and knacker's yards. They detail the conditions which must be observed to prevent unnecessary pain and suffering to animals therein.

Special provisions apply to knacker's yards and in respect to horses.

Records must be kept of animals received and slaughtered.

Contraventions of these Regulations, except to prevent suffering and in an emergency, are punishable summarily and licences may be cancelled.

Riding Establishments Act, 1939.—S. 3 : " Riding establishment " means any stables or other premises whatsoever at which horses are kept for the purpose of being let out on hire for riding or of being used in providing for payment instruction in riding. It does not include any such establishment conducted solely for military or police purposes or by the London Zoological Society.

"Horse" includes any mare, gelding, pony, foal, colt, filly or stallion and any ass.

S. 2 : If any person—

(a) lets out any horse on hire for riding at a time when the horse is in such a condition that the riding thereof will be likely to cause suffering to the horse; or

(b) uses any horse for providing, in return for payment, instruction in riding at a time when the horse is in such a condition that its use for that purpose will be likely to cause suffering to the horse ; or

(c) keeps any horse which is used for the purpose of being let out on hire for riding or of providing, in return for payment, instruction in riding, in so neglected a state or in such condition that suffering is, or is likely to be, caused to the horse ; or

(d) wilfully obstructs or delays any duly registered veterinary surgeon in the exercise of his powers of entry or inspection under this Act ; or

(e) with intent to avoid such inspection conceals any horse ; he shall be guilty of an offence under the Act—penalty on summary conviction, fine not exceeding £25, or for any subsequent offence, £50.

No prosecution shall be brought under the Act except by the local authority, which must first receive and consider a report on the matter from a registered veterinary surgeon.

" Local authority " means the common council of the City of London, the London County Council, the council of the county borough, borough or urban district, and as respects any other area the council of the county.

S. 1 : A local authority may authorise in writing any registered veterinary surgeon to inspect any premises which they have reason to believe are used as a riding establishment. This authority will give the right to enter the premises at all reasonable times and inspect such parts thereof, and such horses found thereon as may be considered necessary so as to ascertain whether an offence under the Act has been or is being committed.

Pet Animals.—The Pet Animals Act, 1951 deals with the keeping of a pet shop, that is the carrying on at premises of any nature including a private dwelling (and any stall or barrow in a market) of a business of selling animals (any vertebrate animals) as pets or keeping same with a view to their sale. This includes selling or keeping for sale cats and dogs for domestic purposes and any animal for ornamental purposes. However the keeping or selling pedigree animals bred by a person or the offspring of his pet animals are excluded, and the local authority may exempt the breeder of pedigree animals who also sells animals as pets (s. 7).

No person shall keep a pet shop except on licence granted by the local authority (Council of County Borough or County District or Metropolitan Borough or City of London or Scottish County (s. 7)), which can specify conditions and which expires at the end of the year. If the licence is refused there can be an appeal to the local summary court (s. 1). It will be an offence to sell animals as pets in any part of a street or public place, except at a stall or barrow in a market (s. 2) or to sell an animal as a pet to a person under 12 (s. 3).

The local authority may authorise in writing inspection of licensed pet shops and any wilful obstruction or delay of the " inspector " will be an offence (s. 4). Offences may be prosecuted summarily (s. 5) by the local authority (s. 6).

Chapter XXXVI

BETTING

Contents

Betting.—S. 1 of the Betting Act, 1853, deals with betting and the receipt of any money or valuable thing as or for the consideration for any contract or undertaking to pay or give thereafter any money or valuable thing, on any event or contingency of or relating to any horse-race or other race, fight, game, sport or exercise. According to the Oxford Dictionary betting is the staking of money or other value on the event of a doubtful issue. Finance Act, 1916, s. 18, stated that as regards betting duty " bet means a bet on an event of any kind."

Betting is not in itself illegal, but it becomes illegal when carried on under conditions which are in contravention of the law, as follows :

Betting Houses.—Betting Act, 1853, declares that every house, room or other place which is opened, kept or used for the purpose of betting with persons resorting thereto or of receiving deposits on bets is a common nuisance and is to be deemed a common gaming-house (ss. 1 and 2). (See " Gaming " later, also " Betting on Tracks.") This renders ready money betting in houses, etc., illegal, but does not affect credit betting by post, etc., where no money is deposited.

The owner, occupier or person so using the same, and the owner or occupier who knowingly and wilfully permits the same to be so opened, kept or used by any other person, and any person managing or assisting in conducting same, are liable on summary conviction or indictment to imprisonment for six months or fine (s. 3). A person using a public house for taking bets from persons resorting there was convicted under s. 3 (*Milne* v. *City of London Police Commissioner* (1939) and *R.* v. *Porter* (1949)). If the owner or occupier or manager or any assistant receives a deposit on any bet or gives any acknowledgement on the receipt of such a deposit he is liable on summary conviction to imprisonment for three months or fine (s. 4). If any person on behalf of the owner, occupier or user of a betting-house invites other persons to resort thereto for the purpose of making bets or wagers, he is liable to two months imprisonment or fine (s. 7).

A Justice, on sworn information, may issue a warrant authorising the police to enter any house or place suspected to be kept
or used as a betting-house, if necessary by force, and to arrest,
search and bring before a Justice all such persons found therein
and to seize all documents relating to racing or betting found
therein (s. 11).

Persons frequenting betting-houses or gaming houses for such
unlawful games may be bound over (Unlawful Games Act,
1541).

A person innocently on the premises for lawful business cannot
be so bound over (*Roden* v. *Brett* (1936)).

In proceedings under the Betting Act, as the imprisonment may
be six months, a defendant has the right to claim trial by jury
(M.C. Act, 1952, s. 25).

The conviction of the holder of a justices' licence for opening,
keeping or using his premises in contravention of the Betting Act,
1853 will be deemed to be a conviction of an offence under this
section (Licensing Act, 1953, s. 141).

Advertising Betting.—Betting Act, 1853, s. 7 : It is a summary offence, punishable by fine, for any person to exhibit or
publish or cause to be exhibited or published any placard, writing
or advertisement, indicating that any house or place is opened,
kept or used for making bets or wagers by resorting to said house
or place or by paying a deposit (see s. 1) ; or for the purpose of
exhibiting lists for betting ; or with intent to induce any person
to resort to such house or place for the purpose of betting.

Betting Act, 1874, s. 3 : It is a similar offence to send, exhibit
or publish or cause to be exhibited, sent or published, any letter,
circular, telegram, placard, handbill, card or advertisement—

(1) Indicating that any person on application will give information or advice relating to bets made in a place kept for
persons resorting there or to ready-money betting by deposits
(see Betting Act, 1853, s. 1), or

(2) Indicating that any person will make on behalf of any
other person any such bets, or

(3) With intent to induce any person to apply to any place
or person for advice or information relating to such bets, or

(4) Inviting any person to make or take any share in such
bets.

Betting and Loans (Infants) Act, 1892, s. 1 : It is a misdemeanour, punishable summarily, for any person, for the purpose
of earning any profit, to send or cause to be sent to a person he
knows to be an infant (that is, under twenty-one years of age),
any circular, telegram or other document, inviting the person
receiving it to make any bet or to take any share in any betting
transaction or to apply to any person or place for information
or advice for the purpose of any bets or for information as to any

race, game or other contingency upon which betting is generally carried on. If such document names any person to whom payment may be made or from whom information may be obtained, such person will be deemed to have been the sender unless he proves the contrary.

S. 3 : If such document is sent to any person, under full age, at any University, school or other place of education, the sender will be deemed to have known such person was an infant unless he proves he has reasonable ground for believing such person was of full age.

Street Betting.—Street Betting Act, 1906 : It is a summary offence for any person to frequent or loiter in streets or public places, on behalf either of himself or of any other person, for the purpose of bookmaking or betting or wagering or agreeing to bet or wager or paying or receiving or settling bets. Such person shall in any case be liable to forfeit all books, cards, papers and other articles relating to betting found in his possession. Being in a place long enough to effect the purpose is " frequenting " (*Airton* v. *Scott*, (1909)).

A constable may arrest without warrant any person found committing this offence, and may seize and detain any article liable to be forfeited under the Act.

For a second offence the offender is liable to a fine of £20. For a third and subsequent offence, or where it is proved that the offender had any betting transaction with a person under sixteen years of age, the offender may be sentenced to fine or imprisonment, and may be dealt with on indictment or summarily.

For the purposes of this Act, " street " includes any highway and any public bridge, road, lane, footway, square, court, alley or passage, whether a thoroughfare or not, and " public place " includes any public park, garden or sea beach, and any unenclosed ground to which the public for the time being have unrestricted access, and also includes every enclosed place (not being a public park or garden) to which the public have a restricted right of access whether on payment or otherwise if at or near every public entrance there is conspicuously exhibited by the owners or persons having the control of the place a notice prohibiting betting therein. It was held that a public house was not a " public place " under this Act (*Brannan* v. *Peek*, (1948)).

Nothing in this Act applies to any ground used for the purpose of a racecourse for racing with horses, or adjacent thereto, on the days on which races take place.

Football Betting.—Ready-Money Football Betting Act, 1920 makes it a summary offence for any person in the United Kingdom—

(1) To write, print, publish or knowingly circulate any advertisement, circular or coupon of any ready-money football betting business, or

444 PART VI.—OTHER OFFENCES AND REGULATIONS

(2) To knowingly procure or attempt to procure any of such things to be done, or

(3) To knowingly assist therein.

" Ready-money football betting business " means any business or agency, for the making of ready-money bets or wagers, or for the receipt of any money or valuable thing as the consideration for a bet or wager, in connection with any football game.

Gaming.—Various statutes render gaming illegal when carried on in a common gaming-house, in licensed premises and refreshment houses, and in a public place. However gaming parties not for private gain and in small amounts are allowable under the Small Lotteries and Gaming Act 1956.

Gaming amounts to playing a game for money or money's worth.

Gaming-Houses.—The keeping of a common gaming-house is a nuisance and is indictable at common law.

According to Justice Hawkins, a common gaming-house is a house in which a large number of persons are invited habitually to congregate for the purpose of gaming (*Jenks* v. *Turpin* (1884)).

Under the Gaming Act, 1845, and the Gaming-Houses Act, 1854, the keeping of a gaming-house is made a summary offence.

S. 2 of the 1845 Act declares that any house or place kept or used for playing therein at any unlawful game, and where a bank is kept by one or more of the players exclusively of the others, or the chances of any game played therein are not alike favourable to all the players, including the banker or other persons by whom the game is managed or against whom the others stake, play or bet, shall be deemed a common gaming-house and contrary to law

The owner or keeper and every person having the care or management and every person assisting in the conduct of a common gaming-house may be prosecuted summarily, and liable to fine up to £100 or imprisonment up to six months (1845 Act, s. 4).

The owner, occupier or user of any place who shall open, keep, or use, or knowingly and wilfully permit the same to be opened, kept, or used for the purpose of unlawful gaming, and any person assisting therein or advancing money for gaming therein is liable on summary conviction to fine of £500 and imprisonment for twelve months (1854 Act, s. 4).

It is not necessary to prove that the unlawful gaming under s. 2, 1845 Act, was for the gain of anyone, and members of the committee of a members' club in which " fruit " machines were used were convicted under this section (*Daniels* v. *Pinks* (1930)).

All play in a common gaming-house is unlawful gaming. A lawful game as thus played may therefore become unlawful. The question whether any game is unlawful or not is one for the Court to decide. (See *Jenks* v. *Turpin* (1884)).

An " unlawful game " apparently is a game of chance played or money or money's worth.

On sworn information a Justice may issue a warrant (as set out in the First Schedule to the Act), authorising any constable to enter, using such force as may be necessary, any alleged common gaming-house, and search for all instruments of unlawful gaming and to arrest, search and bring before a Justice all keepers of such place and all persons found haunting, resorting and playing therein (1845 Act, s. 3).

Persons obstructing or delaying the entry of constables authorised by such warrant are liable to fine and six months imprisonment (1854 Act, s. 1).

If a constable, so authorised by warrant, is wilfully obstructed in any way in his entry, or if the place is found fitted with any contrivance for unlawful gaming or for concealing, etc., any instruments of gaming, it will be evidence that the same is a common gaming-house and that the persons found therein were unlawfully playing therein (1854 Act, s. 2).

It will not be necessary to prove that any person found playing was playing for any money, wager or stake (1854 Act, s. 5).

If cards, dice, counters or other instruments of gaming used in playing an unlawful game are found in the place entered under a warrant or order issued under this Act or on the person of any found therein, it shall be evidence until the contrary be proved that the place is used as a common gaming-house and the Court may order their destruction (1845 Act, s. 8) if the owner had been arrested and brought before a Justice in compliance with the warrant (*Coughtrey* v. *Porter* (1950)).

Persons found haunting, resorting and playing in any place entered under warrant issued under the Act, may be arrested and searched and brought before a Justice (1845 Act, s. 3). Such persons may be bound over by the Justice not to frequent gaming-houses. Any such person who refuses his name and address or gives a false name and address, either on arrest or when before the Justices, may be fined and imprisoned for a month (1854 Act, s. 3).

The Justices may require any such person to be sworn and give evidence (1854 Act, s. 5).

Small Lotteries and Gaming Act, 1956: Under s. 4, small gaming parties are exempted from the provisions of the Betting Acts and are not unlawful lotteries provided that:—

(1) they are games of chance or chance and skill combined at entertainments for raising money which is not for private gain, and

(2) not more than one payment (not exceeding 5/–) is made for entrance fee or stake, etc., by each player: not more than one distribution of prizes (total not exceeding £20) is made: whole proceeds less expenses are not applied for private gain: expenses must not exceed reasonable cost of the facilities provided.

The place so used will not be deemed a common gaming house.

If two or more of such entertainments are given by the same persons in the same place on any day, this section applies as if they were one entertainment.

If several such entertainments in series take place on several days the prizes may total up to £100.

The law penalising gaming and unlawful games on licensed premises (Licensing Act, 1953, s. 141) and in refreshment houses (Refreshment Houses Act, 1860, s. 32) applies as regards such entertainments.

Gaming in Licensed Premises and Refreshment Houses —Licensing Act, 1953, s. 141. The holder of a Justices' licence shall not suffer any gaming or unlawful game to be carried on in his premises. Summary offence punishable by fine.

The playing of any game for money or money's worth staked by the players is " gaming " under above section.

Unlawful games include roulet, faro, basset, hazard, every game of dice except backgammon, every game of cards which is not a game of mere skill, and I incline to add (said the Judge) any other game of mere chance (*Jenks* v. *Turpin* (1884)).

Gaming may be carried out by means of an automatic machine.

Refreshment Houses Act, 1860, s. 32, makes it a summary offence for any person licensed under the Act to keep a refreshment house, to knowingly suffer any unlawful games or gaming therein.

Gaming in a Public Place.—Vagrant Act Amendment Act, 1873, s. 3, enacts that every person playing or betting by way of wagering or gaming in any street, road, highway or other open and public place, or in any open place to which the public have or are permitted to have access, at or with any table or instrument of gaming or any coin, card, token or other article used as an instrument or means of such wagering or gaming at any game or pretended game of chance, is to be deemed a rogue and vagabond.

The offence is punishable summarily under the Vagrancy Act, 1824, or fine (40s., second offence £5), under this Act.

Cheating at Play.—Gaming Act, 1845, s. 17, declares that every person who, by any fraud or cheating, in playing with cards, dice, or other game, or in taking part in the stakes or wagers, or betting on the players, or in wagering on the event of any game, sport, pastime, or exercise, wins from any other person any money or valuable thing, shall be deemed guilty of obtaining same by a false pretence with intent to cheat or defraud. See " False Pretences," Chap. 14.

Lotteries and Prize Competitions.—A lottery is a distribution of prizes by lot or chance.

The Betting and Lotteries Act, 1934, has repealed previous

law dealing with lotteries and Part II of the Act directs as follows :—

All lotteries are unlawful (s. 21), but the following shall be deemed not to be unlawful provided the prescribed conditions are observed :—

(1) Small lotteries incidental to certain entertainments (s. 23).
(2) Private lotteries (s. 24).
(3) Lotteries of Art Unions (s. 25).
(4) Small lotteries for charitable, sporting, etc., purposes (Small Lotteries and Gaming Act, 1956).

It shall be an offence for any person in connection with any lottery in Great Britain or elsewhere, to print tickets ; to sell or distribute tickets or to offer or advertise or have them in possession for this purpose ; to print, publish, distribute or have for publication or distribution any advertisement or list of prize winners or descriptive matter relating to the lottery calculated to act as an inducement to persons to participate in the lottery or other lotteries ; to bring or invite to send into Great Britain for sale or distribution any ticket or advertisement ; to send or attempt to send out of Great Britain the proceeds or records of such tickets ; to use or knowingly permit the use of any premises for lottery purposes ; to cause or procure or attempt to procure any person to do any of the above acts.

It shall be an offence for which proceedings can be directed only by the Director of Public Prosecutions, to publish in a newspaper (or other periodical publication) any such matter descriptive of a lottery as is calculated to act as an inducement to persons to participate in a lottery. It shall be a defence in a prosecution to prove that the lottery in question was one declared by this Act not to be unlawful and that defendant reasonably believed that none of the prescribed conditions had been broken (s. 22). See also s. 5, Small Lotteries and Gaming Act, 1956.

Small Lotteries promoted as part of bazaars, sales of work, fetes and other entertainments of a similar character shall be deemed not to be unlawful lotteries, but all the following conditions shall be observed :—

(a) The whole proceeds of the entertainment and lottery, after deducting the expenses of the entertainment (excluding the expenses of the lottery), the printing of the lottery tickets, and not more than ten pounds expended on lottery prizes, shall be devoted to purposes other than private gain.

(b) None of the lottery prizes shall be money prizes.

(c) Tickets shall not be sold or issued and the result shall not be declared, except on the premises and during the progress of the entertainment.

(d) The lottery shall not be the only or the only substantial inducement to persons to attend the entertainment.

If any of these conditions are broken every person concerned in the promotion or conduct of the lottery shall be guilty of an offence unless he proves the offence was committed without his knowledge (s. 23).

Small Lotteries and Gaming Act, 1956: Under s. 1, certain small lotteries will not be unlawful if:—

(1) they are promoted on behalf of a society registered by the local authority, the society being one established and conducted wholly or mainly for one or more of the following purposes (a) charitable (b) athletic games or sports (c) other purposes which are not for private gain or commercial undertakings, and the lotteries are to raise money for such a society.

" Local authority " means the council of the county or county borough, etc. (s. 2). " Society " includes club, organisation or association of persons and any separate branch or section of it (s. 1), and

(2) the prescribed conditions are complied with (non compliance will be an offence). They number 13 and include: no prize to exceed £100 and no ticket to cost more than 1/–; total value of tickets sold not to exceed £750: no public advertising: proceeds less expenses (not to exceed 10%) to go to the Society (s. 1).

Full return of the proceeds, etc., shall be made by the promoters to the local authority (s. 3).

Such lotteries may not be held on licensed premises (*Smith and others* v. *Wyles* (1958)).

Private Lottery means a lottery in Great Britain which is promoted for, and in which the sale of tickets is confined to, either (a) members of one society, club or other association established and conducted for purposes not connected with gaming, wagering or lotteries (each local branch of a society to be reckoned as a separate and distinct " society "), or (b) persons who work on the same premises, or (c) persons who reside on the same premises ; and which is promoted by persons to whom, under the terms of the section, tickets may be sold. In the case of a " society " the lottery must be authorised in writing by the governing body of the society. Such a society under the Act means a small local society and not one extending over a large area (*Keehan* v. *Walters* (1948)).

Such a private lottery shall be deemed not to be an unlawful lottery, but all the following conditions shall be observed :—

(a) The whole proceeds less printing expenses shall be devoted to prizes, or in the case of a society, to prizes or to purposes of the society, or to both.

(b) No notice or advertisement of the lottery shall be given except a notice on the premises and particulars on the tickets.

(c) The price of every ticket shall be the same and shall be stated on the ticket.

(d) Every ticket shall bear the name and address of each

of the promoters, a statement of the persons to whom sale is restricted, and a statement that any prize won shall be given only to the person to whom the winning ticket was sold by the promoters. No prize shall be delivered except in accordance with that statement.

(e) No ticket shall be issued except by way of sale and on receipt of the full price, and no money, etc., so received by a promoter shall be returned.

(f) No tickets shall be sent through the post.

If any of the above conditions are broken, each promoter and each person breaking a condition, shall be guilty of an offence, but it will be a defence for a promoter to prove that the offence was committed without his knowledge (s. 24).

Lotteries of Art Unions, promoted and conducted in accordance with the Art Unions Act, 1846, shall be deemed not to be unlawful lotteries (s. 25).

Prize Competitions are restricted to the extent that it shall be unlawful to conduct in or through any newspaper (or other periodical publication, s. 28), or in connection with any trade or business (except pari-mutuel or pool betting carried on by a bookmaker), or the sale of any article to the public :—

(a) Any competition offering prizes for forecasts of the result either of a future event or of a past event the result of which is not yet ascertained or not yet generally known.

(b) Any other competition success in which does not depend to a substantial degree upon the exercise of skill.

Contravention of above is an offence, without prejudice or liability to prosecution under the other provisions of this part of the Act relating to lotteries (s. 26).

The sale of football pool competition coupons by a newspaper and tobacconist shop was held not unlawful as the sale was not in connection with the trade or business (*I.T.P. London, Ltd. v. Winstanley* (1947)).

General.—Any Justice, on sworn information on reasonable suspicion that any premises are being used for the commission of an offence under this Part II of the Act in connection with a lottery, may grant a search warrant, authorising entry at any time or times within one month, search, seizure and removal of documents, money or valuables found therein and reasonably believed to be there for any purpose infringing this Part II of the Act relating to lotteries (s. 27).

Any offence under this Part II of the Act is punishable either on summary conviction (fine up to £100, second offence, fine up to £200 and (or) up to three months' imprisonment), or on indictment (fine up to £500, second offence, fine up to £750 and (or) one year's imprisonment), and the Court shall order to

be forfeited any money produced to the Court which is the proceeds of tickets or prize money, and shall order to be destroyed
all documents produced which relate to the conduct of the
lottery (s. 30). If a body corporate is convicted every director
or officer shall be deemed guilty unless he proves the offence was
committed without his knowledge (s. 29).

The importation for publication in the United Kingdom of
any advertisement or notice relating to a lottery is prohibited
(Revenue Act, 1898, s. 1). Any such material is forfeited and
may be disposed of by the Customs Authorities.

See " Smuggling," Chap. 26.

Betting on Tracks.—*Racecourse Betting Act*, 1928, established
the Racecourse Betting Control Board (s. 2), which is empowered
to grant and revoke certificates of approval in respect of race-
courses (s. 3). This Board may authorise a totalisator (or pari-
mutuel or other betting machine of a like nature) on an approved
racecourse, which means any ground used for racing with horses,
in respect of which there is a certificate of approval under the
Act, and it shall be lawful for persons (of 18 or over, s. 15 of
1934 Act) to bet thereon by means of a lawful totalisator (s. 1).

Nothing in the Betting Act, 1853, shall apply to any approved
racecourse on days on which horse races but no other races take
place thereon (s. 1).

Betting and Lotteries Act, 1934, *Part I*, amends the law on
this subject.

In this Act " track " means premises on which races of any
description, athletic sports or other sporting events take place.
" Bookmaker " includes any person who carries on as principal
or agent, occasionally or regularly, the business of receiving or
negotiating bets or conducting pari-mutuel or pool betting
operations, or who holds out or permits himself to be held out
in any manner as a person who so acts ; but a person shall not
be deemed a bookmaker by reason only of the fact that he
operates a totalisator, and the operating of a totalisator shall be
deemed not to be bookmaking.

" Totalisator " means the totalisator or pari-mutuel or any
other machine or instrument of betting of a like nature whether
mechanically operated or not.

" Dog race " means a race in which an object propelled by
mechanical means is pursued by dogs (s. 20).

The councils of counties and county boroughs (or their committees) shall be the licensing authorities for their areas, empowered to grant licences under the Act, authorising betting
facilities on tracks (s. 5).

Two months' notice of application for licence shall be given,
to the Chief Officer of Police and certain persons (on giving seven
days' notice) are entitled to object to the grant (s. 6).

The licensing authority have power to refuse a licence for certain prescribed reasons (s. 7).

Special provision is made as regards the grant of first licences for existing tracks and the making of a false declaration to obtain such a first licence will be an offence (s. 8).

First licences for existing tracks will be for 5 years (s. 8), and for other tracks 7 years (s. 9), unless revoked for disorderly conduct, alteration of the track, illegal use of a totalisator, or conviction of managers (s. 16).

S. 1 : Betting by bookmaking or by totalisator shall not take place on any track on more than 104 days in any year nor on Good Friday, Christmas Day or Sunday.

These 104 days will be known as " appointed days," and the same 104 days shall be fixed by the licensing authority, for the whole of their area, for the year beginning July 1 (s. 10).

S. 2 : Bookmaking shall not be carried on on any track unless the occupier holds a licence in force under this Act authorising betting facilities on the track.

However, this prohibition shall not apply to :—

(a) An approved horse racecourse on any day on which it is used only for horse races, or

(b) Any track on which bookmaking has not been carried on on more than seven previous days in that year beginning July 1, provided that seven days postal notice of the intended bookmaking has been given to the chief officer of police by the occupier.

Bookmaking shall not be carried on on any licensed track on any day which is not one of the " appointed days " of the licensing area.

S. 3 : Pari-mutuel (" tote ") or pool betting business shall not be carried on on any track except—

(a) On an approved racecourse, by authority of the Race-course Betting Control Board, or

(b) On a licensed track being a dog racecourse, and then only in accordance with the provisions of this Act. (See ss. 4 and 11.)

Save as permitted above, no person shall use any premises whether on a track or not, or cause or knowingly permit any such premises to be used, as a place where persons resorting thereto may effect pari-mutuel or pool betting transactions.

S. 4: Betting by bookmaking or totalisator shall not take place on any day on a dog racecourse in connection with more than 8 dog races, and is restricted also to one continuous period not exceeding 4 hours. However, the licensing authority shall fix four of the " appointed days," to be the same for the whole of their areas and to be known as the " special appointed days." on any of which there may be sixteen dog races and betting for eight hours in the aggregate.

S. 11 : On any licensed track being a dog racecourse, a totalisator may be set up and on any appointed day, while the public are admitted and no other sporting events are taking place on the track, it may be operated for betting with persons resorting to the track, on dog races run on that track on that day.

While it is being thus lawfully operated bookmakers as such shall not be excluded from the track and space for bookmaking shall be afforded them.

Any such totalisator on a dog racecourse shall comply with the Regulations of the Secretary of State, shall be a mechanically or electrically operated apparatus, and shall be operated in accordance with the provisions of the First Schedule to the Act.

S. 12 : The Betting Act, 1853, shall not apply to anything done on a licensed track by a bookmaker on any day on which bookmaking may lawfully be carried on, but the grant of this facility shall not affect the operation of this 1853 Act in relation to the use by a bookmaker for the purposes of his business—

(a) Of any permanent structure other than a structure used by him in common with members of the public, or

(b) Of any position on the track specially reserved for his use by the occupier of the track.

S. 13 : Limits are prescribed to the charges which may be made to bookmakers and their assistants for admission to tracks to carry on their business.

S. 14 : The occupier of a licensed track or his servant or agent or any person holding an interest in the track shall not directly or indirectly engage in bookmaking on that track.

S. 15 : A bookmaker or totalisator shall not have on any track any betting transaction with a person apparently under or known to be under 18 years of age. A person under 18 shall not be employed on any track for bookmaking or commission agent work or in connection with the operation of a totalisator.

S. 17 : The occupier of a licensed track is not required to permit betting thereon at any time at which no totalisator is being operated on that track.

S. 19 : Any person authorised in writing by the licensing authority and any constable, may at all reasonable times enter upon any track to see whether this Act is being complied with. It will be an offence to obstruct him.

Contravention of the provisions of the Act will be an offence punishable summarily (fine and on subsequent conviction fine and (or) up to 3 months imprisonment at the most) or on indictment (fine and on subsequent conviction fine and (or) imprisonment up to one year at the most).

The occupier of a track may plead in defence to charges under ss. 1, 2, 4 13 and 14 that the contravention occurred without his knowledge. If a body corporate is convicted under the Act, every director or officer is deemed guilty unless he proves the offence was committed without his knowledge (s. 29).

Pool Betting Act, 1954.—Under s. 11 of this Act " pool betting business " means a business involving the receiving or negotiating of " bets made by way of pool betting " (as meant in the Finance Acts, (No. 2) 1947, 1948, 1950, 1952) and the Act does not affect a totalisator on an approved racecourse or licensed dog track.

A promoter of such a business must register with the council of the county or county borough where he carries on that business (s. 1). Such council shall appoint an accountant (s. 2).

He must be supplied with the rules of the competitions and such business shall be the promotion of competitions for prizes for making forecasts as to sporting or other events, the stakes and winnings must be wholly in money, and the business must comply with the requirements of the Act as to rules, publicity, information to the accountant, etc. (ss. 3, 4).

It shall be an offence to carry on such a business unregistered or to obstruct the accountant or to fail to comply correctly with his requirements or to contravene the provisions of the Act. An offence may involve the penalties under ss. 29, 30, Betting and Lotteries Act, 1934, on prosecution by the council concerned (s. 5).

The Ready Money Football Betting Act, 1920, (which makes it an offence to publish or circulate any advertising, etc. of such a business) and s. 1, Betting Act, 1853, so far as it relates to the opening, etc., of houses, etc., for the receipt of money, shall not apply as respects pool betting business carried on by post by a registered pool promoter (s. 10).

Chapter XXXVII

PUBLIC ENTERTAINMENTS

Contents

Theatres.—A theatre or place used for the public performance of stage plays must be licensed and comply with the rules and conditions laid down by the Licensing Authority, but authorised naval and military recreation rooms do not need a licence for the public performance of stage plays.

Theatres Act, 1843, s. 2 : It is unlawful for any person to have or keep any house or other place of public resort for the public performance of stage plays, without authority by letters patent from the Crown, or by licence from the Lord Chamberlain (London and its boroughs), or by licence from the County or Borough Council (which may delegate its licensing powers to the Justices (Local Government Act, 1888)).

An offender is liable on summary conviction to a fine of £20 for each day of use.

S. 23 : " Stage-play " includes every tragedy, comedy, farce, opera, interlude, melodrama, pantomime or other entertainment of the stage or any part thereof, but does not include a theatrical representation in any booth or show allowed in any lawful fair or meeting of the like kind.

Ss. 7 and 9 : A licence may only be granted to the actual and responsible manager of the theatre, and the licensing authority may impose rules and conditions and have power to close the theatre.

Ss. 11 and 16 : Persons performing for hire or permitting same in unlicensed places are liable to a fine of £10 a day on summary conviction. If money or other reward is charged for admission, or if intoxicating liquor is sold in the place, every actor therein is deemed to be acting for hire.

The occupier of a booth or portable theatre is not liable under s. 2, but the performers may be liable under s. 11.

Ss. 12-15 : Every new play and every addition to an old play must be submitted to the Lord Chamberlain seven days at least before it is acted. The Lord Chamberlain has power to disallow such play or part of a play, and may forbid the acting of any play or part of a play.

Acting or causing to be acted any new play or part of a play before it has been so allowed or after it has been disallowed, or acting or causing to be acted any play which has been forbidden is a summary offence punishable by fine, and the theatre licence may by order of the Court become void or be suspended under s. 43 of the Criminal Justice Act, 1925.

Customs and Excise Act, 1952, s. 150, allows the proprietor of a duly licensed theatre to take out an excise licence, subject to the local permitted hours, for the retail sale of beer, spirits and wine, without the necessity of having a Justices' licence. (See Licensing Act, 1953, s. 164). However, the theatre Licensing Authority may in granting a theatre licence impose a condition that no excise licence be applied for. See " Excise Licences and Law ", Chap. 38.

Theatrical Employers Registration Act, 1925.—This Act renders it necessary for every theatrical employer to register with the Council of the county or borough in which he resides, and if he has no fixed place of residence he may register with any such Council (s. 3).

Every such Registration Authority keeps a register, open to the public inspection on payment of a fee, and every registered theatrical employer is supplied with a certificate of registration (ss. 1 and 4).

" *Theatrical Employer* " means any person who by himself or any agent engages or employs at any one time three or more theatrical performers (s. 13). However, this Act does not apply to—

(1) Any person who has in force a theatre licence or a licence for music and dancing, and

(2) Any person who, not for gain or in the way of business, employs or engages theatrical performers for charitable objects or other similar purposes (s. 11).

" *Theatrical Performer* " includes any actor, singer, dancer, acrobat, or performer employed in any place of public entertainment, or to rehearse with a view to so acting, etc., or to take part in anything being photographed or otherwise recorded as a picture suitable or intended for exhibition by means of a cinematograph or other similar apparatus. It also includes all persons employed or engaged as a chorus or crowd, but does not include stage hands and members of an orchestra (s. 13).

Offences by a Theatrical Employer under s. 10 of the Act.—

(1) To abandon the theatrical performers during the course

of their engagement. He will be deemed to have abandoned them if he absents himself without paying all wages and expenses due to them, unless he proves his absence was not with that intent (see s. 5 (2)).

(2) To act as a theatrical employer without being registered.

(3) To supply false, misleading or incorrect particulars to the Registration Authority, or fail to inform that authority of any change of circumstances.

(4) To apply for registration while his registration is suspended or cancelled, but under s. 9 he may apply three years after cancellation.

(5) To fail to produce a certificate (if any) or to produce a false certificate, to any Court dealing with a charge under this Act.

(6) To apply for registration on behalf of a company or firm of which any person whose registration has been suspended or cancelled is a director, manager, partner, etc. (see s. 5 (1)).

(7) After his registration has been cancelled and has not been renewed, to act as agent for any other theatrical employer.

A Magistrates Court may fine and imprison for any of the above offences and may also suspend for a period or cancel the registration (s. 6).

A Magistrates' Court may also cancel or suspend registration when it is satisfied that a theatrical employer has deliberately failed to pay money due to theatrical performers (s. 7).

The Theatrical Employers Registration (Amendment) Act, 1928, allows a registration authority to take proceedings for any offence under the 1925 Act, to apply for the suspension or cancellation of a registration, and to oppose the renewal of any cancelled registration. Where an applicant for registration or a registered person has been convicted of any offence involving dishonesty and has been sentenced to prison, the registration authority may refuse his application or cancel or suspend his registration, but if so such person may appeal to a Magistrates' Court.

Cinematograph Acts.—The 1909 Act, as amended and supplemented by the 1952 Act (which by a Commencement Order, 1955, came into force on 1st Jan., 1956) deals with the licensing and safety of cinemas.

Subject to the exceptions in s. 7 of the 1909 Act and to those provided in the 1952 Act, the Acts and Regulations thereunder apply as respects all cinematograph exhibitions whether given by means involving the use of inflammable or non-inflammable films or by means not involving the use of films (s. 1, 1952 Act).

" Cinematograph exhibition " means an exhibition of moving pictures produced on a screen by means which include the projection of light (s. 9, 1952 Act).

No cinematograph exhibition shall be given unless the Safety

Regulations are complied with, or, save as otherwise provided by the Act, elsewhere than in premises licensed for the purpose under the Act (s. 1, 1909 Act as amended by Sched., 1952 Act).

Licences.—A county or borough council may grant such licences or their transfers. A licence may be for a year or for a shorter period, and may be subject to any conditions or restrictions as may be prescribed. For a licence or transfer seven days written notice to the licensing authority and to the chief officer of police is necessary, but notice for a renewal is not necessary (s. 2, 1909 Act amended by Sched., 1952 Act). Without prejudice to any other powers of delegation to committees, district councils, etc., a council may delegate these licensing powers to Justices sitting in petty sessions (s. 5, 1909 Act).

Note.—Such Justices therefore will not act as a court of summary jurisdiction.

The Lord Chamberlain may license premises for this purpose (s. 6, 1909 Act).

Any Act which restricts or regulates premises for public entertainment or amusement shall not apply to premises or ships used, by authority of a Secretary of State or the Admiralty, for officially controlled entertainments and this includes music, etc., plays and cinematograph exhibitions (Revision of the Army and Air Force Acts (Transitional Provisions) Act, 1955, s. 4 and Sched. 3).

Music and dancing licences are not required for cinematograph exhibitions which include representations of persons dancing, etc., with accompanying music. Music played on the premises in the introduction or in intervals of such an exhibition shall be treated as music accompanying the exhibition if the time taken is less than one quarter of the total time of the exhibition on that day (s. 7, 1952 Act).

Children.—The licensing authority in granting a licence shall impose conditions or restrictions prohibiting the admission of children (persons under 16, 1952 Act, s. 9) to exhibitions designated as unsuitable for children. The authority should also consider what conditions or restrictions might be imposed on the admission of children to other cinematograph exhibitions showing works designated as of some other description (s. 3, 1952 Act).

Subject to the provisions of this Act no premises shall be used, except with the *consent* of the licensing authority for a cinematograph exhibition organised wholly or mainly as an exhibition for children. The authority may impose special conditions or restrictions on the grant of the consent (s. 4, 1952 Act).

The " consent " is a sort of licence; seven days notice is necessary: there are powers of entry: penalties may be incurred, see s. 4, 1952 Act.

At such an exhibition a prescribed number of attendants (aged 16 and over) must be present. At any cinematograph exhibition no child under 5 shall be admitted unless in charge of a person aged 16 or over and no child under 12 shall be admitted after 7 p.m. unless in charge of a person aged 16 or over (Cinematograph (Children) (No. 2) Regs., 1955 which apply to exhibitions other than those in private dwelling houses to which the public are not admitted and exempted exhibitions. See Reg. 1).

Exemptions from licence.—When such an exhibition is proposed on premises used occasionally and exceptionally only and not more than on six days in a year for such purpose a licence will not be necessary if the occupier gives 7 days notice to the licensing authority and to the chief officer of police and complies with the Safety Regulations and any conditions imposed by the licensing authority (s. 7 (2), 1909 Act). However see Safety Regs. 28 (necessity for licence), Regs., 29 to 34. Also Regs. 35 to 42, where inflammable films are used.

Where such an exhibition is proposed in a moveable structure a licence will not be necessary if the owner has a licence for the structure granted by his own licensing authority and he gives two days written notice to the licensing authority and to the chief officer of police and complies with the Safety Regulations and any conditions imposed by the licensing authority (s. 7 (3), 1909 Act).

However if inflammable films are used the Safety Regs. 1 to 34 will apply and also the requirements in Safety Regs. 35 to 42, if no inflammable films are used.

If such an exhibition is given in a private dwelling house to which the public are not admitted whether on payment or otherwise the 1909 Act (requiring licence) shall not apply (s. 7 (3) 1909 Act). However see Safety Reg. 28 (necessity for licence) and Regs. 29 to 34 if inflammable films are used.

" Exempted exhibitions " are those to which the public are not admitted or to which the public are admitted without payment (s. 5, 1952 Act). Several exemptions are allowed by this section 5, including exemption from licence if the films are non-inflammable, but under Safety Reg. 28, a licence will be necessary if inflammable films are used. This s. 5 should be studied in full.

Also an " exempted organisation ", which is one certified as not conducted or established for profit may have an exempted exhibition under the s. 5 of the 1952 Act.

Powers.—A constable or any person appointed by the licensing authority may at all reasonable times enter any premises whether licensed or not, in which he has reason to believe that a cinematograph exhibition is being or is about to be given so as to see that the Acts or Regulations or the conditions of any licence have been complied with.

Any person preventing or obstructing the entry of such constable or person will commit a summary offence, fine up to £50. (s. 4, 1909 Act).

The owner of apparatus using it or allowing it to be used or the owner of premises allowing premises to be used in contravention of the Acts or Regulations or of the conditions or restrictions of any licence granted, will commit a summary offence punishable by fine (s. 3, 1909 Act). Any person aggrieved by the refusal or revocation of a licence or consent or by any terms, conditions or restrictions imposed may appeal to Quarter Sessions (s. 6, 1952 Act).

Regulations.—The Cinematograph (Safety) Regs., 1955 and 1958, contain requirements—in Part I (Regs. 1 to 27), generally in connection with such exhibitions, re seats, exits, attendants, fire, lighting, etc.; in Part II (Regs. 28 to 34), additional where inflammable films are used; in Part III (Regs. 35 to 42), where premises are so used only occasionally; in Part IV (Regs. 43 to 47), in connection with television exhibitions; in Part V (Regs. 48 to 51), miscellaneous.

The Cinematograph Films (Animals) Act, 1937, prohibits the public exhibition of film scenes involving cruelty to animals.

Music, Singing and Dancing.—The general rule is that in cities and towns it is necessary for any person who habitually keeps or uses any house, room, garden or other place, for public dancing, singing, music or other entertainment of the like kind, to have a licence for music and dancing.

The requirements of the law vary according to the locality, as follows :—

(1) London and the surrounding area within twenty miles, including Middlesex and Surrey. Within this area licences are necessary and are issued by the Local Councils concerned.

(2) The rest of England and Wales over twenty miles distant from London and outside Middlesex and Surrey. In cities and boroughs where Part IV of the Public Health Acts Amendment Act, 1890, has been adopted, or in areas where local Acts or Orders on the subject are in force, licences are required. In other parts of the country licences are not necessary. See Paterson's Licensing Acts, Chap. 15.

Public Health Acts Amendment Act, 1890, Part IV, s. 51, requires that any house, room, garden, or other place, whether licensed or not for the sale of intoxicants, shall not be kept or used for public dancing, singing, music or other public entertainment of the like kind, without a licence for the purpose from the Justices. The Justices, sitting in Licensing Sessions, may grant, transfer or renew licences for a year or less period, under such terms and conditions and subject to such restrictions as they may determine.

Applicants for new licences or for transfers must give fourteen days' notice to the clerk of the Justices and to the chief of police. No notice need be given of an application for renewal of a licence.

Justices in Petty Sessions may grant without notice a temporary licence for a period not exceeding fourteen days. A notice showing the purpose for which it is licensed must be kept posted on the door or entrance of every place so licensed, and such premises must not be opened for such purpose except on the days and during the hours stated in the licence.

Any house or place kept or used for any of these purposes without a licence shall be deemed a disorderly house and the occupier is liable to a fine of £5 per day. As regards the right to prosecute see " Public Health Acts," Chap. 39. If a licence holder breaks or disregards any of the terms or conditions on which his licence was granted, he is liable to a fine of £20 and a daily penalty of £5, and his licence may be revoked.

Under the Sunday Observance Act, 1780, any house, room, or other place opened or used for public entertainment or amusement on Sunday, and to which persons are admitted on payment, may be deemed a disorderly house or place. The persons responsible may be liable to summary prosecution under s. 51 of the Public Health Acts Amendment Act, 1890, if the section is in force in the locality. But see " Sunday Entertainments," later.

A licence is not required for public singing, dancing, music, stage plays or cinema exhibitions in authorised naval, military and air force recreation rooms, which may be so used on any day (Revision of Army and Air Force Acts (Transitional Provisions) Act, 1955, s. 4 and Sched. 3). If a public swimming bath is used for public music, dancing, stage plays, cinematograph exhibition or other public entertainment of the like kind, the necessary licence must be obtained (Public Health Act, 1936, s. 226).

Billiards.—A billiard licence under the Gaming Act, 1845, is necessary for every house, room, or place, kept for public billiard playing or where a public billiard table or bagatelle board or instrument of like kind is kept at which persons are admitted to play, except in the case of a fully licensed public house, which under this Act is not required to have a billiard licence.

Gaming Act, 1845, s. 10 : The Justices may grant billiard licences at the usual annual Liquor Licensing Sessions. Notice similar to that given in liquor licensing applications is necessary in the case of a grant or transfer. The licence is for a year, and no notice is required for a renewal.

S. 11 : Any person keeping a public billiard table or bagatelle board or like instrument without being duly licensed so to do and not holding a public house licence for the premises, or any person so licensed for billiards who does not keep the words " licensed for billiards " near the door and on the outside of his premises, is liable to prosecution as the keeper of a common gaming-house.

S. 12 : A licensee is liable to summary punishment for any breach of the conditions of his licence. The conditions include the prevention of drunkenness or other disorderly conduct on the premises.

S. 13 : A licensee or a publican having a public billiard table must not allow any person to play at such table or instrument between 1 A.M. and 8 A.M. or at any time on Sundays, Christmas Day, Good Friday, or any days of public fast or thanksgiving, and during these periods and days the billiard rooms must be kept closed.

S. 14 authorises the police to enter at any time any house, room, or place, where any public billiard table or instrument of the like kind is kept for play, and it is a summary offence to refuse admittance. See " Billiards," Chap. 38.

Public Libraries.—Libraries provided for the use of the public under the Public Libraries Act, 1892, and libraries and reading rooms provided by registered societies must be quietly and properly used by persons.

Under the Libraries Offences Act, 1898, any person, who in any public or authorised library, to the annoyance or disturbance of anyone using the same—

(1) Behaves in a disorderly manner,

(2) Uses violent, abusive or obscene language,

(3) Bets or gambles, or

(4) Remains beyond closing hours, after warning,

is liable to a fine of £2 on summary conviction.

Malicious damage to books and other property in a library is a misdemeanour under s. 39 of the Malicious Damage Act, 1861.

Ingress and Egress.—Under the Public Health Act, 1936, s. 59, certain public and other buildings shall have such means of ingress and egress and passages or gangways as the local authority deem satisfactory, regard being had by them to the purposes for which the building is intended to be, or is, used, and the number of persons likely to resort thereto at any one time.

These buildings include—any theatre and any hall, etc., used as a place of public resort ; any restaurant, shop, store or warehouse to which the public are admitted and in which more than twenty persons are employed ; any club which should be registered under the Licensing Act, 1953 ; any school not exempted ; any church or place of public worship dating before 1890, or exempt before this Act.

(The section does not apply to a private house to which the public are admitted occasionally or exceptionally.)

For reasons of safety a Magistrates' Court may order the closing of any such building. On penalty of fine of £20, the person having control of any such building must secure that the means of ingress and egress and the passages and gangways are kept free and unobstructed while persons are assembled in the building.

Children and Young Persons Act, 1933, s. 12 : Where an entertainment for children or at which the majority of the audience are children, is given in any building not a private dwelling-house, and over one hundred children attend, there must be a sufficient number of adult attendants so as to take sufficient precautions for the safety of the children. A constable may enter any building in which he has reason to believe such an entertainment is being or is about to be held, so as to see that this section is complied with, and an officer so authorised by the authority which licenses entertainments has the like power of entering premises so licensed.

This section applies to the whole country.

Sunday Entertainments Act, 1932.—In any area in which licensed cinemas were regularly opened and used on Sundays within the twelve months ended October 6, 1931, and in any area where the electors vote in favour of it and the Houses of Parliament approve the necessary order, the licensing authority for cinemas may permit licensed cinemas to be opened and used on Sundays, subject to conditions that the employees have not been employed on each of the previous six days either by the employer in any occupation or by any other employer in connection with similar entertainments (subject to exemption in case of emergency or ignorance), and that a prescribed part of the proceeds shall be paid to the licensing authority (who shall pay 5 per cent. of the proceeds to the Cinematograph Fund controlled by the Privy Council (s. 2), and the remainder to charitable objects), and to any other conditions that the authority think fit to impose. Breach of any condition is punishable summarily by £20 fine (s. 1).

This section also applies s. 4 of the Cinematograph Act, 1909 (given previously), and therefore a constable has power of entry.

A licensing authority is empowered to grant licences in respect of musical entertainments (that is, concerts of music with or without singing or recitation, s. 5), on Sundays and to attach special conditions thereto (s. 3).

No person shall be guilty of an offence or subject to any penalty under the Sunday Observance Acts, 1625, 1677 and 1780, by reason of his connection with the holding of any cinema entertainment allowed under this Act ; any musical entertainment licensed under this Act or otherwise authorised ; any museum, picture gallery, zoological or botanical garden or aquarium ; or any lecture or debate (s. 4).

Note on Sunday Observance Acts—The 1625 Act ordered fines on persons attending plays or other unlawful pastimes on Sundays. The 1677 Act prohibited tradesmen, etc., from working at their ordinary callings (except from charity or necessity), or publicly selling goods on Sundays (but see " Shops," Chap. 32). The 1780 Act prescribed penalties for the Sunday opening or using for public entertainment or amusement or for debating, of any house, room or other place to which persons are admitted for payment. Such a house or place is to be deemed a disorderly house. The advertising of same is also an offence. The Act allowed proceedings by common informers for their own profit but such actions have been abolished. See " Common Informers," Chap. 1.

Hypnotism Act, 1952.—Where an authority has power to grant licences for public music, singing and dancing (see previously) it has power to attach to the licence conditions regulating or prohibiting hypnotism on any person at the licensed place (s. 1).

No person shall perform hypnotism on any living person at any public entertainment at any unlicensed place unless authorised by the authority to grant music, etc., licences in the area, or by the Council of the County Borough, Borough, Urban or Rural District in a place where there is no authority having power to grant music etc., licences (s. 2).

It will be a summary offence to hypnotise any person under 21 at any public entertainment (s 3).

" Hypnotism " includes mesmerism and any similar process to produce induced sleep or trance in any person but does not include self induced hypnotism (s. 6).

Any police constable may enter any premises where any entertainment is held on reasonable cause to believe that a breach of the Act is being or may be done (s. 4).

Chapter XXXVIII

LIQUOR LICENSING LAWS

Contents

Licensed Premises and Intoxicating Liquor.—A person must not sell intoxicating liquor without an excise licence from the Commissioners of Customs and Excise. Every excise licence holder has to pay duty on his licence, and the Customs and Excise Act, 1952, renders liable to heavy fine any person who makes, or deals wholesale in, or sells by retail intoxicating liquor without the necessary excise licence. The Licensing Act, 1953, s. 120, directs that, subject to the provisions of the Act, a person must not sell or expose for sale by retail any intoxicating liquor unless he holds a Justices' licence authorising him to hold an excise licence for such sale, and that he must not so sell or expose for sale except at the place authorised by the Justices' licence.

Therefore, the general rule is that before a person may legally sell by retail intoxicating liquor, he should have a Justices' licence allowing him to sell same on certain definite premises, and possession of such licence allows him to take out the necessary retailer's licence from the Excise which will become void if the Justices' licence is forfeited or becomes void or expires (Customs and Excise Act, 1952, s. 150).

It is the duty of the police to enforce the provisions of the Licensing Acts, which provide for the licensing of premises by the Justices, for the regulation of such licensed premises, and for the orderly conduct of persons in connection with licensed premises and intoxicants.

The most important of these Acts are the Licensing Acts of 1872 and 1902, and the Licensing Act, 1953.

The 1953 Act repealed and re-enacted the provisions of several Acts such as the Licensing Acts of 1910, 1921 and 1923 and most of the 1949 Act.

In this chapter " 1953 " indicates the Licensing Act, 1953 and " club " means registered club. Several of the provisions of the 1953 Act apply to both licensed premises and clubs.

" Intoxicating Liquor " means spirits, wine, beer, porter, cider perry and sweets (viz. liquor fermented from fruit and sugar), and any fermented, distilled or spirituous liquor which cannot be legally sold without an excise licence (1953, s. 165, and Customs and Excise Act, 1952, s. 307).

" Licensed premises " under these Acts are regarded as premises in respect of which a Justices' licence has been granted and is in force and the provisions of the Acts with respect to licensed premises apply to any premises or place where intoxicating liquor is sold by retail under a licence (see 1953, s. 165).

The Justices may grant a licence for premises within the area of their jurisdiction authorising the sale thereon by retail of some specified kind or kinds of intoxicating liquor. Such premises will then be " licensed premises " and the responsible person must in addition take out an excise licence, as he cannot sell under the Justices' licence alone which is an authority to enable him to obtain an excise licence.

Justices' Licences.—These licences are as follows:—

(1) Publican's licence or spirits on-licence, authorising sale by retail of spirits, beer, wine, cider and sweets for consumption on or off the premises. This is known also as a " full " licence.

(2) Beerhouse licence or beer on-licence, giving same rights with respect to beer and cider.

(3) Wine on-licence, giving same rights with respect to wine and sweets.

(4) Cider on-licence, giving same rights with respect to cider.

(5) Sweets on-licence, giving same rights with respect to sweets.

(6) Spirits off-licence, authorising the sale by retail of spirits (viz. spirits of any description such as whisky, gin, etc.) for consumption off the premises, but not in open vessels (Customs and Excise Act, 1952, s. 149, as amended by Finance Act, 1956, s. 3).

(7) Beer off-licence, authorising the sale by retail of beer and cider for consumption off the premises.

(8) Wine off-licence, giving a similar right with respect to wine and sweets provided that they are not sold in open vessels.

(9) Cider off-licence, giving a similar right with respect to cider.

(10) Sweets off-licence, giving a similar right with respect to sweets.

" Spirits " means spirits of any description and includes all liquors mixed with spirits and all preparations made with spirits except methylated spirits (Customs and Excise Act, 1952, s. 307).

The expression " sweets " in the Licensing Acts means any liquor made from fruit and sugar, or from fruit or sugar mixed with any other material, and which has been fermented, and includes British wines, made wines, mead and metheglin (Customs and Excise Act, 1952, s. 307).

Any of the above five on-licences (allowing sale for consumption on the premises) may be granted as a seven-day licence, or as a six-day licence (viz. to be kept closed on Sundays) (1953, s. 109) or as an early closing licence (viz. to close at night one hour earlier than the usual closing hour), or as a six-day and early closing licence (1953, s. 110).

Forgery of a Justices' licence or knowingly tendering a forged licence is a serious offence (1953, s. 46).

Excise Licences and Law.—The Customs and Excise Act, 1952, has consolidated with amendments much of the law relating to customs and excise.

S. 5 : It will be the duty of every constable and every member of H.M. armed forces or coastguard to assist in the enforcement of the law relating to any assigned matter (that is every duty which by law has to be performed by the Customs and Excise, s. 307).

Obstruction of or interference with any person acting under the Act is a serious offence and the offender may be detained (s. 10).

The following excise licences relating to intoxicants do not need to have the authority of Justices' licences.

(1) A distiller's excise licence for the manufacture of spirits (s. 93). The unlawful making of spirits incurs a heavy penalty and any person found in the premises or place may be detained (s. 106) by a constable, etc. (s. 274). On reasonable grounds of suspicion that a still, spirits, etc., are unlawfully in any building or place a constable may obtain a Justices' search warrant and remove same (s. 296).

(2) An excise licence for the brewing of beer (ss. 125 to 138).

(3) No person shall make sweets (as defined above) for sale unless he holds an excise licence for that purpose (ss. 139 to 142).

(4) No person shall deal wholesale in spirits, beer, wine or sweets without an excise licence in respect of any such liquor.

Dealing wholesale means the sale at any one time to any one person of quantities not less than :

  (a) Spirits, wine or sweets—2 gallons or one dozen reputed quart bottles;

  (b) beer—4½ gallons or 2 dozen reputed quart bottles (s. 146).

(5) Excise retailer's licence for a naval or military canteen duly authorised (s. 150).

(6) Excise retailer's licence for a properly authorised theatre. (s. 150). See " Theatres ", Chap. 37.

(7) Excise retailer's licence for a passenger aircraft—this covers sale of tobacco (s. 152).

(8) Excise retailer's licence for a passenger vessel—this covers sale of tobacco (s. 153).

(9) Excise retailer's licence for a railway passenger vehicle which supplies food (s. 154).

(10) Excise retailer's off-licence to the holder of an excise wholesale dealer's licence (s. 146), if the premises are exclusively used for the sale of intoxicating liquor and mineral waters and there is no internal communication with any other business premises. It does not authorise a sale by retail except to a person holding an excise licence for sale of intoxicants, or to a mess or registered club or for delivery outside Great Britain or to a person engaged in any business carried on by the retailer (Licensing Act, 1953, s. 164).

An excise licence is not necessary for the sale wholesale or by retail of black beer (includes spruce beer, mum, or Berlin white beer, s. 307) (and the Licensing Act, 1953 does not prohibit such sale (s. 164)); perfumes; flavouring essences not for intoxicants; spirits, wine or sweets so medicated as to be medicines ; any liquor under specified gravity or proof limits and sale by chemists of spirits of wine for medical or scientific purposes (s. 157).

The following excise licences are granted annually to persons who hold Justices' licences under the Licensing Act.

S. 148 : No person shall sell by retail any intoxicating liquor otherwise than under and in accordance with an excise licence.

Selling by retail means the sale at any one time to any one person of quantities not exceeding :

  (a) Spirits, wines or sweets—2 gallons or one dozen reputed quart bottles.

  (b) Beer or Cider—4½ gallons or 2 dozen reputed quart bottles.

468 PART VI.—OTHER OFFENCES AND REGULATIONS

S. 149 : An excise licence for the sale by retail of spirits, beer, cider, wine or sweets may be granted for a premises, authorising the sale of liquor specified, viz. :

(a) Retailer's on-licence—for consumption on or off the premises.

(b) Retailer's off-licence—for consumption off the premises only.

A retailer's on-licence for spirits covers sale of beer, cider, wine and sweets as well as spirits.

A retailer's on or off licence for beer covers sale of cider and perry.

A retailer's on or off licence for wine covers sale of sweets.

A retailer's off-licence does not allow sale of spirits or wine or sweets in open vessels.

The Excise charge or duty on its licence is based on the annual value of the premises so licensed and Finance Act, 1911 s. 4 states that " premises " includes any courts, offices, yards and gardens which are occupied and within the curtilage or in the immediate vicinity of the house or place where the liquor is sold, except those not used for the licensing trade. See also Customs and Excise Act, 1952, Sched. 4, Para. 35.

S. 296 : A customs and excise officer who has a writ of assistance or a Justices' search warrant may enter a place and if necessary break into it, search and remove anything liable to forfeiture under the Act, but entry shall not be made by night (between 11 P.M. and 5 A.M., s. 307) except in the company of a constable.

S. 297 : On reasonable suspicion that any vehicle or vessel is carrying any goods which are chargeable with any duty not paid or which are being unlawfully removed or which are liable to forfeiture under the Acts, a customs and excise officer or constable or member of H.M. armed forces or coastguard may stop and search such vehicle or vessel.

Occasional Licence.—On giving 24 hours notice or more to the chief officer of police the holder of a retailer's on-licence may apply to the local court of petty sessions for two justices' consent to the grant of an occasional licence for a place other than his licensed premises.

The Justices have a discretion but shall not consent to the licence unless they consider it is expedient for the convenience and accommodation of the public. They may consent to the licence for a period and between such hours as may be specified (1953, s. 148). When the applicant obtains the Justices' consent the Excise shall grant him an occasional licence authorising sale by him of any intoxicants to which his retailer's licence extends, at such place other than his licensed premises during the period and hours specified in the Justices' consent subject to the 10 p.m., etc., limits as given later. This occasional licence shall be produced on request to any excise officer or constable at any time during the sale of liquor under it.

The licence shall not authorise sale of intoxicants on Sunday, Christmas Day or Good Friday or any day of public thanksgiving or mourning or before sunrise or after 10 p.m. except in the case of a public dinner or ball (Customs and Excise Act, 1952, s. 151).

The Licensing Act, 1953, s. 148 applies the following sections to occasional licences—ss. 136, 138 to 142, 151 and s. 12, Licensing Act, 1872. Occasional Licences and Young Persons Act, 1956, applies ss. 127, 129, as to persons under 18, to occasional licences.

Hotel.—Under s. 1, Hotel Proprietors Act, 1956, an hotel is an establishment which offers food, drink and if so required sleeping accommodation, without special contract, to any traveller who appears able and willing to pay a reasonable sum for what is provided and who is in a fit state to be received.

Under s. 2, the proprietor of an hotel will not be liable for loss or damage to property brought to the hotel except where at the time of the loss or damage sleeping accommodation had been engaged for the traveller and if occurred during the period for which the traveller was a guest (midnight to midnight). Such liability does not extend to vehicles or property therein or to animals.

Such liability will not exceed £50 for one article or £100 in the aggregate except where it was due to the default, etc., of the proprietor or where it was expressly deposited for safe custody or where such deposit was refused, etc., However the prescribed notice (in Schedule to the Act) limiting the liability of the proprietor should be conspicuously displayed in the hotel.

Such an hotel within the meaning of the Act shall be deemed to be an inn (s. 1).

An inn is a house of entertainment for travellers.

Billiards.—A person who holds a publican's licence (*i.e.* who is fully licensed) may have public billiard tables in his licensed premises without having to take out a billiard licence. He must not allow play thereat between 1 A.M. and 8 A.M. or at any time on Sundays, Christmas Day or Good Friday (Gaming Act, 1845, s. 13). See " Billiards," Chap. 37.

Sale of Tobacco.—A licensee may take out an excise licence for the sale of tobacco (Customs and Excise Act, 1952, ss. 173 to 194). The Shops Act, 1950, prescribes closing hours and closing times for shops, but exemption is allowed for shops whose business is the sale of tobacco and smokers' requisites and which may be open for customers during " closing hours " and on

Sundays. Also tobacco may be sold to the audience in theatres, etc., and in liquor licensed premises during permitted hours. See Shops, Chap. 32.

Billeting.—Licensed premises are liable, under s. 155 of the Army Act, 1955, to have soldiers billeted (or lodged) in them. See " Billeting," Chap. 30.

Music, etc.—In urban districts where Part IV of the Public Health Acts Amendment Act, 1890, is in force, any place used for public music, singing, etc., must be licensed by the Justices. This applies to premises licensed under the Licensing Acts, and public music, etc., must not be given on such premises unless the necessary additional licence has been obtained. See " Music, Singing and Dancing," Chap. 37.

However, the licensee may have a piano to be used by his customers, etc., but if the room or place is used for the regular musical entertainment, etc., of the public, he should procure a licence allowing such use.

The Licensing Justices (a committee of the Justices of the district) deal with the licensing of houses for the sale of intoxicants, but any offence against the Licensing Laws is brought before Justices sitting in an ordinary Magistrates' Court, as the Licensing Justices are not a Summary Court. (*Boulter* v. *Kent, J. J.* (1897)).

The Licensing Act, 1953, deals with the constitution of the licensing, confirming and compensation authorities in respect of liquor licensed premises.

Grant of Licences.—New licences are granted at the General or Adjourned General Annual Licensing Meeting held in February and later and have to be subsequently confirmed by a committee in counties of Quarter Sessions and in boroughs of the Borough Justices. Licences last for twelve months from April 5 unless forfeited for misconduct or unless granted for a term of not more than seven years (1953, ss. 6, 45). A provisional new on-licence may be granted for premises about to be constructed or in course of construction, but when the building is completed a final order must be obtained (1953, s. 10).

An applicant for a new licence must—

(1) Advertise his application in a local newspaper between 2 and 4 weeks of the hearing.

(2) Keep affixed notice of his application to a conspicuous part of the premises and on the door (or conspicuous place near) of the local church or chapel or if none on some public and conspicuous place, on two consecutive Sundays within 28 days of his application.

(3) Give twenty-one days' written notice by registered post to the chief officer of police, the clerk to the Licensing Justices and to the rating authority (if urban) or chairman of the parish council or meeting (if rural).

(4) Deposit a plan of the premises with the Clerk to the Licensing Justices, if an on-licence is sought (1953, Third Sched.).

The applicant must attend the Licensing Meeting and make his application, which may be opposed by any person or persons. Evidence will be given and the Licensing Justices will give their decision, granting it with or without conditions or refusing it.

Under s. 9, 1953 such an opponent may also oppose the confirmation of the licence.

Renewal of Licences.—An annual Justices' licence expires annually, and its holder, if he wishes to remain licensed, should apply for its renewal. Licences may be renewed at a General Annual Licensing Meeting, but the holders need not attend unless required to do so by the Licensing Justices. Notice of intention to oppose the renewal of a licence may be given by any person. Such notice should be in writing and should contain the grounds of opposition. It should be served on the holder of the licence not less than seven days previous to the licensing meeting (1953, s. 11).

Even if no written notice of objection has been served, verbal objection may be made at the General Annual Licensing Meeting and the Justices may adjourn the consideration of the matter to another day (1953, s. 11). Usually opposition to renewal come from the police on the ground of misconduct or from the Licensing Justices on the ground of redundancy (viz. too many licensed premises in the locality). Before renewing an on-licence the Justices may require plans of the premises (s. 11) and may, on renewal, order structural alterations necessary for the proper conduct of the business (1953, s. 12) and there may be appeal to Quarter Sessions against such an order (1953, s. 35).

The renewal of an " old " Justices' off-licence which was held by the applicant on June 25, 1902, and of an " old " Justices' on-licence which existed on August 15, 1904, and of an old beerhouse licence in force on May 1, 1869, cannot be refused except on the grounds specified in the Act, viz. misconduct, etc., of the applicant, or the disorderly, etc., character of the premises (1953, ss. 13, 14).

All evidence with respect to the renewal of a licence must be given on oath (1953, s. 11). Evidence regarding the grant or transfer of a licence may not be on oath if the Justices so decide.

A " term " licence for a period up to 7 years does not need annual renewal, but when it expires a new licence has to be applied for if required (1953, s. 6).

Transfer of Licences.—A transfer means the substitution of one person for another, as holder of the Justices' licence for a certain premises. The Licensing Justices—sitting in Transfer Sessions (viz. from four to eight special meetings for the purpose each year) or in a General or Adjourned Annual Licensing Meeting—may authorise the transfer of a Justices' licence in respect to certain premises to one person in substitution for another person who holds or has held the licence.

Transfers may be granted only in the following cases :—

(1) Death of licence holder.

(2) Incapacity of licence holder owing to sickness or other infirmity.

(3) Bankruptcy of licence holder.

(4) Licence holder giving up his occupation of the premises.

(5) Wilful neglect or omission of occupier of premises (who is about to quit the premises) to apply for a renewal.

(6) Where the licence has been forfeited or its holder disqualified and the owner of the premises has obtained a protection order to carry on the business.

(7) Where the licence is in suspense. (See 1953, ss. 89, 97.).

The new licensee must be a fit and proper person to hold a licence (1953, s. 21).

A person desirous of obtaining the transfer of a licence must, fourteen days prior to the Transfer Sessions, give written notice to the chief officer of police to the holder of the licence, the clerk of the licensing Justices and to the Rating Authority if urban and if rural to the chairman of the parish council or meeting.

This notice should give applicant's name, address and occupation during the six months preceding (1953, Third Sched.).

This notice is usually accompanied by a character paper signed by five ratepayers, and the police should verify these signatures and report to the Justices regarding applicant's character.

On death or bankruptcy of the licensee or appointment of a trustee, his personal representative or trustee may carry on the business until the next transfer sessions (1953, s. 22).

If the transfer of a licence becomes necessary, owing to death, forfeiture, etc., the Justices in Petty Sessions may grant a **protection order** (or temporary transfer) enabling the applicant to carry on business pending the grant of a transfer at the usual Transfer Sessions. Such an order would enable the owner of the premises or his agent to preserve the licence if the licence holder has forfeited his licence. For such an order a week's written notice to the police (or shorter notice or no notice in case of emergency) will be sufficient. This protection order is made by endorsement on the existing licence (1953, s. 23).

Removal of a Licence.—This means the removal of a Justices' licence from the premises in respect of which it was granted, to other premises. Such a removal may be either special or ordinary. A " special removal " may be applied for when licensed premises are to be pulled down or occupied for any public purpose, or are rendered unfit for licensed purposes by fire, tempest or other unavoidable calamity. The procedure resembles a renewal (1953, ss. 24, 26 and Third Sched.).

An **ordinary removal** may be applied for when the licensee wishes to carry on his licensed business in other premises, and the procedure is similar to that to be observed when a person applies for a new licence (1953, s. 25 and Third Sched.).

There may be a provisional grant of an ordinary removal to premises about to be constructed (1953, ss. 10, 27).

Appeal.—Any person aggrieved by the refusal or grant of a renewal, transfer, or special removal of a Justices' licence or by an order for structural alterations on renewal of licence may appeal to Quarters Sessions (1953, s. 35).

If a licensee appeals against forfeiture of his licence on conviction, the convicting court may grant a temporary licence until the appeal ends (1953, s. 156).

Register of Licences.—The Clerk of the Licensing Justices (who is the clerk of petty sessions) keeps a register of all Justices' licences granted in the district. This register contains particulars of each licence, convictions of the holders for licensing offences and other matters relating to the licence. The police may inspect this register without payment (1953, ss. 38 to 44).

Disqualified Persons and Premises.—The following are disqualified from holding a Justices' licence:—

(1) Any Sheriff's officer or officer executing the legal process of any Court.

(2) Any person convicted of forging a Justices' licence or of knowingly using a forged Justices' licence, or of permitting his licensed premises to be used as a brothel (1953, s. 30).

(3) Any person during the period he was ordered to be disqualified on conviction for selling intoxicating liquor without a Justices' licence (1953, s, 120).

(4) Any person disqualified under any other Act—for example, a licensed pilot, a person convicted of harbouring thieves.

Premises may be disqualified for receiving a licence if not enough rooms or if below the prescribed annual value or if disqualified as such (1953, ss. 31 to 34).

Permitted Hours.—The Licensing Act, 1953, provides that intoxicants may be sold or supplied in any licensed premises or club for consumption on or off the premises, during certain hours, which are called the " permitted hours."

During the other hours of the day it is an offence to supply or sell or consume or take away any intoxicant (1953, s. 100). This provision applies to licensed premises and registered clubs but it does not prohibit or restrict

(a) sale or supply to or consumption by, residents in the premises

(b) ordering or dispatching intoxicants for consumption off the premises

(c) supplying to or consumption by private friends of the licensee *bona fide* entertained by him at his own expense (*d*) consumption of intoxicants at a meal within half an hour after the end of permitted hours of afternoon or evening, if supplied during permitted hours and served with the meal

(*e*) sale to a trader for his trade or to a registered club for the club

(*f*) sale or supply to any canteen (government or naval authorised, s. 165) or mess (authorised naval, military or air force, s. 165) (1953, s. 100).

(*g*) sale in international airports (Licensing (Airports) Act, 1956, s. 1).

Permitted hours in licensed premises on weekdays if not fixed by the Licensing Justices are 8 hours viz. from 11.30 a.m. to 3 p.m. and from 5.30 to 10 p.m.

The Licensing Justices may fix the 8 hours beginning not earlier than 11 a.m. and not later than 10 p.m. with a break of two hours in the afternoons.

However, they may allow 8 hours ending not later than 10.30 p.m., for a consecutive period of not less than eight weeks in a year, and they may allow the permitted hours to begin before 11 a.m., but not before 9 a.m. (1953, s. 101).

On Sundays, Christmas day and Good Friday the permitted hours for licensed premises are 5. If not fixed by the Licensing Justices they are from 12.30 to 2.30 p.m. and from 7 to 10 p.m. However they may fix the 5 hours as not more than 2 between 12 noon and 3 p.m. and not more than 3 between 6 and 10 p.m. (1953, s. 102).

There are no permitted hours on any Sunday in licensed premises in Wales and Monmouthshire (1953, s. 111).

The permitted hours in registered clubs are given later under " Clubs ".

Where the Licensing Justices are satisfied that the licensed premises are structurally adapted and *bona fide* used or intended to be used for habitually providing substantial refreshment for persons frequenting the premises, the permitted hours on week days may have an added hour at the end of the evening (supper hour extension) during the time the licensee applies the section to his premises after he has given 14 days' notice to the chief of police and until the 4th April in any year. During the said hour intoxicants are to be supplied only for consumption at a meal; no person shall be allowed to consume intoxicants otherwise and any bar shall be closed. A notice of this extension shall be posted in the premises (1953, s. 104).

The permitted hours in the metropolis (administrative county of London with any area outside that county but within the four mile radius from Charing Cross, s. 165) shall on weekdays be nine ending not later than 11 p.m. nor earlier than 10.30 p.m., beginning not earlier than 11 a.m. with a 2 hours' break in the afternoon (1953, s. 112).

In the metropolis outside the City of London the licensing Justices may grant a " special hours certificate " to an hotel or restaurant which has a music and dancing licence and is structurally adapted and *bona fide* used or intended to be used for music and dancing and substantial refreshment is supplied to which intoxicants are ancillary (1953, s. 113).

In such case the permitted hours will be 12.30 to 3 p.m. and 6.30 p.m. to 2 a.m. next morning provided that they cease at midnight on Saturdays and if the music ceases at midnight, cease when the music and dancing ceases.

This section does not authorise sale, supply or consumption of intoxicants at any bar except during the ordinary permitted hours or at a meal within half an hour after end of the ordinary permitted hours in the evening if supplied during these permitted hours and served with the meal (1953, s. 117). A special hours certificate may be revoked on the application of the Commissioner of Police showing cause (1953, s. 118).

It shall be unlawful outside the permitted hours (fixed by or under ss. 101 or 102 of the Act) to supply or consume intoxicants at any party organised for gain on premises kept or habitually used for such organised parties. However, this shall not apply to parties on licensed premises or at a canteen, mess or registered club as part of its activities or for which occasional licence has been granted and the break in the permitted hours shall not be treated as outside the permitted hours.

The suppliers, permitters, deliverers and consumers of intoxicants in contravention of this section are punishable on summary conviction (1953, s. 149).

A search warrant may be granted by a Justice to a constable to enter at any time or times within one month, to search any such premises (as above) and to seize and remove intoxicants, and after seizure to demand name and address of any person found on the premises. Failure to give name and address or giving false name and address shall be a summary offence (1953, s. 150).

The holder of an off-licence must observe the same hours of sale as the holder of an on-licence. Intoxicants for consumption off the premises may be ordered or despatched at any time provided that it does not amount to a " sale " during prohibited hours.

Intoxicants may be taken away by the purchaser only during permitted hours.

Licensed premises may be open at any time for the sale of food and non-intoxicants.

Under 1953 Act, ss. 109, 110, a licensee may hold a licence with a condition that he has no permitted hours on Sundays (six-day licence) or that his permitted hours cease one hour earlier than usual at night (early closing licence).

Exemption Order.—The holder of a Justices' on-licence or the secretary of a club may obtain from the Justices in Petty Sessions an exemption order authorising him to sell and supply intoxicants during non-permitted hours, as specified in the order.

A general order of exemption may be granted where the Justices are satisfied it will be for the accommodation of numbers of persons attending any public market or following any trade or calling. The order must give the hours of exemption (but the premises must be closed between 1 and 2 a.m.) and the days on which same are allowed (1953, s. 106).

A special order of exemption may similarly be granted for licensed premises or clubs for any special occasion or occasions, usually for a ball, dinner or entertainment (1953, s. 107).

Compulsory Closing.—Any two Justices may order the closing of licensed premises in case of riot or tumult, actual or expected and any person acting by the order of any Justice may use any necessary force to close such premises (1953, s. 158).

The Licensed Premises.—The licensee must keep fixed on the premises conspicuously, as directed by the Justices, his name with the word " licensed " followed by a description of his licence and must not indicate that he is authorised to sell any intoxicant he is not authorised to sell (1953, s. 135).

He must produce his licence or order of exemption on demand, to a Justice, constable or officer of customs and excise (1953, s. 153).

A constable may at any time enter licensed premises or premises having a "special hours certificate" for the purpose of preventing or detecting the commission of any offence against the Act. If any person, himself or by any person in his employ or acting with his consent fails to admit a constable demanding entry under this section he commits a summary offence (1953, s. 151).

There must be no internal communication between any licensed premises and any non-licensed premises used for public resort or as a refreshment house. It will be an offence if any person makes or allows to be made or uses any such communication. If the licence holder be convicted of this offence, his licence is forfeited (1953, s. 133).

Structural alterations affecting the area used for drinking must not be made without the Licensing Justices' consent and a magistrates' court, on proof, may declare the licence forfeited or order that the premises be restored to their original condition (1953, s. 134). When renewing a licence the Justices may direct structural alterations to be carried out (1953, s. 12).

Licensed premises or a room in a building part of which is licensed premises shall not be used for a magistrates' court or for licensing sessions or for a coroner's inquest if any other suitable place is provided (1953, s. 157).

Conduct of Licensed Premises.

(1) A licensee must exclude children under fourteen years from the bars (parts used exclusively or mainly for sale and consumption of intoxicants (1953, s. 165)) of licensed premises during the permitted hours. Children of the licensee, or resident but not employed there or merely passing through a bar to some other part of the premises to which there is no other convenient access, or in railway refreshment rooms, or other premises made to be used *bona fide* for any purpose to which the holding of a Justices' licence is merely ancillary are excepted (1953, s. 126).

(2) A licensee must not knowingly suffer to remain on his premises any constable on duty, unless he is there in the execution of his duty; he must not supply any liquor or refreshment by gift or sale to any constable on duty except by authority of his superior officer, and he must not bribe or attempt to bribe any constable (1953, s. 142).

(3) He must not knowingly allow his premises to be the habitual resort or place of meeting of reputed prostitutes. Such persons may remain only the necessary time for the purpose of obtaining reasonable refreshment (1953, s. 139). See also T.P.C. Act, 1847, s. 35.

(4) He must not permit his premises to be a brothel. If convicted his licence is forfeited (1953, s. 140).

(5) He must not allow gaming or any unlawful game on his premises, (1953, s. 141). See Chap. 36.

(6) He must not knowingly harbour thieves or reputed thieves or suffer them to meet or assemble in his premises or deposit their stolen goods there. If so his licence may be forfeited (Prevention of Crimes Act, 1871, s. 10). See Chap. 14.

(7) He must not allow the payment of wages on his premises to workmen not his own employees (Payment of Wages Act, 1883). See Truck Act, 1831, as to payment of wages.

(8) Without prejudice to any other right to refuse admission or expel he may refuse to admit to, or may expel from his premises, any person who is drunken, violent, quarrelsome or disorderly or whose presence thereon would subject him to a penalty under this Act. Any such person who fails to leave when requested commits an offence and any constable when requested shall help to expel any such person using any necessary force (1953, s. 138). See also " Drunkenness," later.

(9) He must not allow children and young persons to sing, play, perform, etc., in his licensed premises, unless within the rules set out under " Employment of Juveniles," Chap. 12.

(10) He must not permit drunkenness or any violent, quarrelsome or riotous conduct to take place on his premises (1953, s. 136).

(11) He must not employ any person under 18 in the bar of

his licensed premises while the bar is open for sale or consumption of intoxicants even if such person gets no wages for his work (1953, s. 127).

(12) He must not without reasonable excuse have in his possession on the licensed premises any intoxicant that he is not authorised to sell (1953, s. 121).

Sale of Intoxicants.

(1) He must not sell any intoxicating liquor to a drunken person (1953, s. 136).

(2) He must not sell or supply any intoxicants to any person who is on the " black list " as a habitual drunkard (see 1902 Act, s. 6).

(3) An on-licence holder or any servant of his must not knowingly sell or allow to be sold any intoxicants to be consumed on the premises, to any person under the age of eighteen years, and they must not knowingly allow any person under eighteen to consume intoxicants in the bar. A person of or over sixteen years may purchase or obtain beer, porter, perry or cider for consumption at a meal to be consumed in the eating-room part of the premises, but not in the bar (1953, s. 129).

(4) The licensee must not knowingly sell or deliver or allow sale or delivery of intoxicants to any child under fourteen years, except in corked and sealed vessels in quantities not less than one reputed pint for consumption off the premises only or at the residence or working place of the purchaser (1953, s. 128).

(5) He must not sell or supply any liquor or refreshment to any constable on duty, unless by the authority of his superior officer (1953, s. 142).

(6) A person, in pursuance of a sale by him of intoxicants shall not deliver himself or by his servant or agent any such liquor from any van, vehicle, basket, etc., unless before despatch it has been ordered, and particulars are entered in a delivery book or invoice carried by the person delivering, and in a day book kept on his premises. Intoxicants must not be delivered at any address not specified in such document and day book. No other intoxicants, not recorded in such document and day book, may be carried in any vehicle or receptacle used for delivery. Any constable has power to examine any such vehicle or document. These rules do not restrict the supply to a trader for his trade, or to a club for the club purposes (1953, s. 122).

(7) Intoxicants must not be supplied on credit in licensed premises or clubs. No person shall sell or supply intoxicants or consume intoxicants in such premises unless same is paid for before or at the time sold or supplied, but where consumed with a meal they may be paid for at the same time the meal is paid for. However this section does not prohibit or restrict sale or

supply of intoxicants in authorised canteens or messes (1953, s. 132).

(8) No person in licensed premises or clubs shall sell or supply an amount of intoxicants exceeding the measure asked for. Giving excess measure is known as the " long pull " and this is forbidden (1953, s. 131).

(9) Intoxicating liquor, sold by retail, not in cask or bottle and not in less quantity than half a pint, must be sold in imperial standard measures (1953, s. 130).

(10) A person must not sell or expose for sale by retail any intoxicating liquor unless he holds a Justices' licence authorising him to hold an excise licence for the sale of that intoxicating liquor, nor at any place except that place for which he is authorised by the Justices' licence (1953 Act, s. 120).

It is an offence for a person to knowingly sell or deliver or cause to be sold or delivered, any spirits, in order that they may be unlawfully retailed, consumed or brought into home use. It is also an offence for any person to receive, buy or procure any spirits from a person not authorised to sell or deliver them (Customs and Excise Act, 1952, s. 161).

However, a *bona fide* commercial traveller may at any place take orders for the intoxicants which his employer is duly licensed to sell. A person in unlicensed premises may order intoxicants which are *bona fide* purchased outside and brought in for his use, he then paying.

(11) A person shall not hawk, or save as permitted by the Act, sell or expose for sale any spirits otherwise than on premises for which he holds a licence to sell spirits (Customs and Excise Act, 1952, s. 161).

(12) A licensee must not allow drinking in contravention of the terms of his licence. If the holder of a Justices' licence which does not allow the sale of a particular intoxicant for consumption on the premises knows or consents to its being drunk on the road near or adjoining his premises or on premises near or adjoining which belong to him etc., or in the licensed premises, he commits an offence. It is also an offence if an " off-licensee " arranges for intoxicants to be taken to be sold for his profit and consumed in some place belonging to him (1953, s. 124).

Nothing in the Act shall apply to the sale or consumption of intoxicants in canteens (authorised by the Secretary of State or the Admiralty, s. 165) (1953, s. 164).

Offences, not of Drunkenness, by non-licensed Persons.

(1) Selling or exposing for sale intoxicating liquor by retail without a Justices' licence (1953, s. 120).

(2) Making, dealing in or selling intoxicants without an excise licence (Customs and Excise Act, 1952, ss. 93, 125, 139, 146, 148, 149).

(3) Consuming in or taking from licensed premises or clubs any intoxicants except during permitted hours. However, consumption on such premises during non-permitted hours is permissible in the case of a resident, a private friend, and a person at a meal (within half an hour), as laid down in s. 100 of the Licensing Act, 1953 (see " Permitted Hours ").

It is not an offence in itself to be on licensed premises during non-permitted hours.

(4) Consuming in licensed premises or clubs any intoxicants which were supplied for a meal during the one hour extension of permitted hours, except at such meal (1953, s. 104).

(5) Consuming in licensed premises or clubs any intoxicant not paid for before or at the time (viz. supplied on credit) except where consumed at a meal (1953, s. 132).

(6) Being in licensed premises and procuring or attempting to procure intoxicating liquor for consumption by any drunken person, or aiding any drunken person in obtaining or consuming any intoxicating liquor in any licensed premises (1953, s. 137).

(7) Purchasing or attempting to purchase any intoxicating liquor
>   (a) by a person for consumption in a bar on licensed premises by a person under 18, or
>   (b) by a person under 18 to be consumed by him in the licensed premises (1953, s. 129).

(8) Causing, etc., a non-resident child under fourteen to be in the bar of licensed premises during the permitted hours (1953, s. 126).

(9) Sending a child under fourteen to licensed premises, etc., to obtain any intoxicating liquor (except in bottles corked and sealed and not less than one pint in quantity) (1953, s. 128).

(10) Giving intoxicants to a child under five years except on a doctor's order or in case of sickness or other emergency (Children and Young Persons Act, 1933, s. 5).

(11) Paying wages on licensed premises (Payment of Wages Act, 1883).

(12) Failing to quit licensed premises, being a person whose presence thereon would subject the licensee to a penalty under the Licensing Acts (see " Conduct of Licensed Premises " above), upon being requested to quit the premises by the licensee or his servant or any constable (1953, s. 138). See also " Drunkenness," later.

Prosecution.—Breaches of the Act are punishable on summary conviction (1953, s. 160). Any person aggrieved by an order or conviction made by a Magistrates' Court may appeal to Quarter Sessions as allowed in summary cases. For appeal against a decision of the Licensing Justices see " Appeal " on a previous page.

Evidence that any person, not the licensee or his employee, consumed or intended to consume intoxicants in the premises shall be evidence that the liquor was sold on behalf of the licensee to that person.

Evidence that a transaction in the nature of a sale took place shall be evidence of a sale without proof that money passed.

Evidence that consumption of intoxicant was about to take place shall be evidence of consumption without proof of actual consumption (1953, s. 154).

Police Powers of Entry.—A constable may at any time enter licensed premises or premises having a special hours certificate under s. 115, for the purpose of preventing or detecting the commission of any offence against this Act. Any failure to admit him will be an offence (1953, s. 151).

A Justice, on sworn information that there is reasonable ground to believe that any intoxicating liquor is sold by retail or exposed or kept for sale by retail at any place where its sale by retail is not authorised, may grant a search warrant to a constable, authorising him to enter, if need be by force, at any time or times, within a month the place named and search for, seize and remove any intoxicating liquor found which the constable has reasonable grounds for supposing to be there for unlawful sale.

When the constable has seized the liquor and its vessels he may demand the name and address of any person found on the premises. It is an offence to fail to comply or to give a false name or address. If such person fails to answer satisfactorily, he may be arrested.

Persons so found on the premises, unless they prove they were there for lawful purpose, are liable to fine (1953, s. 152).

Drunkenness.—Drunkenness in itself is not an offence against the law. There is no legal definition of drunkenness ; it is a state or condition of a person which is the result of his consumption of an intoxicant and which is shown by the loss of control of his faculties. Drunkenness becomes a summary offence when it occurs in a public place or licensed premises or is accompanied by the particular circumstances laid down in certain statutes.

A habitual drunkard is a person who, while not certifiable as a lunatic, is at times dangerous to himself or to others or incapable of managing himself or his affairs, by reason of habitual intemperate drinking of intoxicants, or the habitual taking, except upon medical advice, of opium or other dangerous drugs.

Habitual drunkards may be dealt with under the Inebriates Acts. See Stone, under title " Drunkenness."

The statutes creating the offences in connection with drunkenness in some cases give the constable the power to arrest the offender without warrant. If arrested the offender should be brought to a police station, where he will either be released in due course on bail to be summoned, or detained for prosecution in Court.

These drunkenness offences are as follows :—

1. Every person found drunk in any highway or other public place whether a building or not, or on any licensed premises (1872 Act, s. 12). Unless such person is incapable of taking care of himself he should not be arrested, as he may only be summoned for this 1872 Act offence. This offence is known as simple drunkenness, and is punishable by fine ; up to 10s. for first offence, and to 40s. for the third or subsequent conviction within twelve months. Every person found drunk on licensed premises when such premises are open to the public is liable under this section. One Justice, sitting alone, may deal with this offence (C.J.A. Act, 1914, s. 38).

A person found drunk in any highway or other public place whether a building or not or on any licensed premises, and apparently incapable of taking care of himself may be arrested (1902 Act, s. 1).

This offence is commonly known as " drunk and incapable," and is punishable under s. 12, 1872 Act, or by other Acts dealing with drunkenness, but the offence is " simple drunkenness."

2. Being guilty, while drunk, of riotous or disorderly behaviour in any highway or other public place whether a building or not. Such person may be arrested and the penalty may be 40s. or one month (1872 Act, s. 12).

3. Drunk while in charge on any highway or other public place of any carriage, horse, cattle (including pigs and sheep), or steam engine. A bicycle is such a carriage (*Corkery* v. *Carpenter* (1950)). Such person may be arrested : penalty up to 40s. or one month (1872 Act, s. 12).

4. Drunk when in possession of any loaded firearms. Such person may be arrested ; penalty up to 40s. or one month (1872 Act, s. 12). This offence may be committed anywhere, and no person need have been endangered.

5. Found drunk in any highway or other public place whether a building or not, or on any licensed premises, while having the charge of a child apparently under the age of seven years. Such person may be arrested ; penalty up to 40s. or one month (1902 Act, s. 2).

" Public place," for the purposes of the above five offences, includes any place to which the public have access, whether on payment or otherwise (1902 Act, s. 8).

6. Being under the influence of drink or a drug to such an extent as to be incapable of having proper control of the vehicle when driving or attempting to drive a motor vehicle on a road or other public place. (S. 15, R.T. Act, 1930 and s. 26, R.T. Act, 1956).

Being in charge of a motor vehicle depends on the facts of the case. See *Jowett-Shooter* v. *Franklin* (1949) and *Jones* v. *English* (1951). If a person leaves a motor vehicle on a road or public place he is still in charge of it unless he puts some other person in charge of it. (*Haines* v. *Roberts* (1953)).

It has been held that any place to which the public in fact have access is a " public place " under this section *R.* v. *Collinson* (1931) and *Elkins* v. *Cartlidge* (1947).

A person committing this offence may be arrested without warrant by a constable. He is not liable to prosecution under s. 12, Licensing Act, 1872. (See No. 3 above.)

He is liable, on summary conviction, to imprisonment up to four months or fine up to £100; on second or subsequent conviction he is liable to six months imprisonment or to both fine and imprisonment. Also he may be disqualified until he has passed a driving test (s. 6, 1934, s. 26 and Sched 8 (35)., 1956)

(However, he has the right to claim trial by jury, as the imprisonment may exceed three months.)

On conviction on indictment the penalty may be imprisonment up to two years or a fine or both. See s. 15, Road Traffic Act, 1930 and s. 26, Road Traffic Act, 1956.

On conviction, disqualification for twelve months for holding or obtaining a driving licence automatically follows unless the Court for special reasons orders otherwise. (S. 15, Road Traffic Act, 1930.) His driving licence must be in Court and must be endorsed. See " Penalties—R.T. Act, 1930," Chap. 24, and the decided cases regarding special reasons.

A person who is in charge of a motor vehicle on a road or other public place but is not driving it, who is unfit to drive being so much under the influence of drink or a drug as to be incapable of having proper control of it, commits an offence and may be arrested by a constable without warrant. He is liable to fine or 4 months imprisonment or on indictment to fine or up to 6 months imprisonment or both, but he is not liable to be charged under s. 12, Licensing Act, 1872.

The person shall be deemed not to have been in charge of the vehicle if he proves that at the time there was no likelihood of his driving the vehicle and that he had not driven the vehicle on a road since he became unfit to drive (Road Traffic Act, 1956, s. 9).

7. Being drunk, violent, quarrelsome or disorderly on licensed premises, and failing to quit on request by the licensee, his servant or any constable. A constable is required, on demand of the licensee or his servants, to help to expel every such person from the premises and may use such force as may be required for the purpose (1953, s. 138).

8. Being drunk, riotous, quarrelsome or disorderly in any licensed refreshment house and refusing or neglecting to quit on request from the manager or his servant or any constable. Constables are required to assist in expelling such offenders (Refreshment Houses Act, 1860, s. 41).

9. Being drunk in any street (of any urban district) and

guilty of riotous or indecent behaviour therein, or being guilty
of any violent or indecent behaviour in any police office or
police station house (in any urban district). Penalty up to 40s.
fine or seven days (Town Police Clauses Act, 1847, s. 29 where
the Act is in force). Where s. 81 of the Public Health Acts
Amendment Act, 1907, is in force by order, " street " includes
any unfenced ground adjoining a street and any place of public
resort or recreation ground under the control of the Local
Authority. The Metropolitan Police Act, 1839, s. 58, provides
a similar penalty for similar conduct in the London Metropolitan Police area.

10. The driver of any hackney carriage (in any urban
district) who is intoxicated while driving is liable to £5 fine or
two months in default (Town Police Clauses Act, 1847, s. 61
where in force).

The London Hackney Carriages Act, 1843, s. 28, deals with
a driver of a hackney carriage or a driver or conductor of a
stage carriage in the Metropolitan Police district who is drunk
during his employment as such.

11. Being drunk on board a passenger steamer and refusing to leave same when requested, or being drunk and
persisting in attempting to enter a passenger steamer after
having been refused admission (Merchant Shipping Act, 1894,
s. 287). See " Merchant Shipping Acts," Chap. 26.

Clubs.—A club may be defined as a voluntary association of
a number of persons who meet together for purposes mainly
social but perhaps including other purposes such as sport, politics,
literature, each member contributing a certain sum, and the
association being conducted under rules. A club is not defined
in law, and the Court in any particular case may have to decide
on the facts whether an association is or is not a club.

Registration of Clubs.—The Licensing Act, 1953 deals with
clubs wherein intoxicating liquor is supplied.

If a club occupies premises habitually used for the purposes of a
club where intoxicating liquor is supplied to members or their
guests, the club must be registered under the Act (s. 143).

Registration does not render the club premises licensed
premises, but it allows members to consume intoxicants there and
to bring their friends there and supply them with intoxicating
liquor if it is in accordance with the rules of the club.

Before such a club is opened, and in every January, its secretary
must register it by sending a return to the Clerk of the Justices
with a fee of 5s. This return must contain certain particulars,
including the rules of the club relating to membership, admission
of guests, subscription, permitted hours, and the hours of opening
and closing. The Clerk to the Licensing Justices keeps a Register
of Clubs, which is open to inspection by the police free and by

others on payment of a fee not exceeding 1s. A register containing the names and addresses of the club members and a record of the latest payments of their subscriptions must be kept in the club premises (s. 143).

Sale of Intoxicants in a Club.—This registration authorises the sale and the consumption of intoxicating liquor on the club premises, provided that—

(1) Sale or supply or consumption takes place during permitted hours. These hours shall be fixed by the rules of the club. On week days they can be 8 hours, not earlier than 11 a.m. and not later than 10 p.m. with a break of at least 2 hours in the afternoon. However the Licensing Justices may allow 8½ hours to end at 10.30 p.m. and may allow the hours to begin before 11 a.m. but not earlier than 9 a.m.

On Sundays, Christmas Day and Good Friday only 5 hours are allowed, not more than 2 between noon and 3 p.m. and not more than 3 between 6 and 10 p.m. (1953, s. 103).

A supper hour extension of one hour may be allowed on the conditions laid down in s. 104, and a general or special order of exemption may be granted under ss. 106 and 107.

The permitted hours in the metropolis are 9, ending not later than 11 p.m. (s. 112) and a club may be granted a special hours certificate (ss. 114, 115).

(2) Sale or consumption of intoxicants to be consumed on the premises unless paid for before or at the time is unlawful except with a meal (s. 132), extra measure (the long pull) is prohibited (s. 131) and sale except by standard measure by retail of half a pint or more except in a cask or bottle is illegal (s. 130).

(3) Such liquor must not be supplied or obtained for consumption off the premises except to a member personally on the premises (s. 128).

Striking Club off the Register.—A Magistrates' Court on complaint in writing of any person against the secretary of a club may strike a registered club off the register, on all or any of the following grounds:—

(1) That the club has ceased to exist or that the number of members is less than twenty-five.

(2) That it is not conducted in good faith as a club or that it is kept or habitually used for any unlawful purpose.

(3) That there is frequent drunkenness on the club premises.

(4) That illegal sales of intoxicating liquor have taken place on the club premises (for example, sales to non-members).

(5) That persons who are not members are habitually admitted to the club merely for the purpose of obtaining intoxicating liquor.

(6) That the club occupies premises which must not be used for registered club premises, viz. premises, once licensed premises, whose licence has been forfeited or not renewed during the preceding twelve months, or premises which a Court has ordered not to be used for the purposes of a club.

(7) That persons are habitually admitted as members without an interval of at least forty-eight hours between their nomination and admission.

(8) That the supply of intoxicants is not under the control of the members or of a committee appointed by the members.

If complaint is made and the Court grants a summons it shall be served on the secretary and on such other person as the Court may direct. In addition to striking the club off the register the Court may order that the premises are not to be used for the purposes of a registered club for a specified period. A person aggrieved by such an order may appeal to Quarter Sessions (s. 144).

Search Warrant for Club.—A Justice may grant a search warrant if he is satisfied by information on oath that any registered club is so managed or carried on as to constitute a ground for striking it off the register or that any intoxicating liquor is sold, supplied, or kept for sale or supply, on the premises of any unregistered club.

Such search warrant authorises a constable to enter the club, if needs be by force at any time or times within a month and search the premises and seize any documents relating to the business of the club (s. 145). The police have no legal right to enter and inspect clubs. This section enables them to procure a search warrant authorising entry, inspection, etc. See also the search warrant under s. 152 under " Police Powers of Entry " above.

A club in Oxford of past or present members of the University is specially dealt with in s. 147 of this 1953 Act.

Intoxicants in Unregistered Clubs.—If intoxicating liquor is kept for supply or sale in any unregistered club every officer and member of the club is liable to fine unless he satisfies the Court that it was so kept without his knowledge or consent. If intoxicating liquor is supplied or sold to any member or guest in any unregistered club, the person supplying or selling and every person authorising the supply of sale of the liquor are liable to fine or imprisonment or to both (1953, s. 123).

Note.—In this 1953 Act " chief officer " replaces " superintendent ", but a notice to the latter may be accepted.

Seamen's Canteens.—The Licensing (Seamen's Canteens) Act, 1954 allows the Licensing Justices to grant licences to these canteens (24 now in this country) which authorise the grant of excise on-licences. Food and non-intoxicants must be provided when intoxicants are on sale. The local permitted hours must be observed and the premises must be conducted as directed by the Licensing Act, 1953.

Refreshment Houses.—A refreshment house is any house, room, shop, or building kept for the purpose of sale and consumption therein by the public of any victual or refreshment except beer, cider, wine and spirits. For example, coffee houses and fish and chip shops. If a refreshment house is kept open for public refreshment, resort and entertainment at any time between ten at night and five of the following morning, its keeper or manager must take out an excise refreshment house licence (Refreshment Houses Act, 1860, s. 6). The licence is issued by the county or county borough council (Finance Act, 1949, s. 15).

No Justices' licence is necessary, but if a refreshment house keeper wishes to sell wine or other intoxicating liquor he must obtain the necessary Justices' licence under the Licensing Acts.

It is not necessary to take out an excise refreshment house licence if the premises are closed between 10 P.M. and 5 A.M., or if they are duly licensed for the sale of beer, spirits, etc., or if refreshments are not consumed on the premises between 10 P.M. and 5 A.M.

Conduct of Refreshment Houses.—A person licensed to keep a refreshment house must not :—

(1) Sell or suffer to be sold in the premises any intoxicating liquor (unless he is duly authorised under the Licensing Acts to sell same) ;

(2) Knowingly suffer any unlawful games or gaming therein ;

(3) Knowingly suffer prostitutes, thieves, or drunken and disorderly persons to assemble at or continue in or upon his premises ; or

(4) Do, suffer, or permit any act in contravention of his licence (1860 Act, s. 32). A prosecution under the Act should be taken within 3 months (s. 30).

Any person who is drunk, riotous, quarrelsome, or disorderly in a licensed refreshment house and refuses or neglects to quit such premises on request of the keeper or his servant or any constable, commits an offence, and all constables are required to assist in expelling such a person (1860 Act, s. 41).

It is an offence for the keeper of any refreshment house, whether licensed or not, to knowingly harbour reputed thieves or allow the deposit of stolen goods therein (Prevention of Crimes Act, 1871, s. 10). See " Receiving Stolen Property," Chap. 14.

Closing Hours.—A non-licensed refreshment house must not be kept open for the consumption of refreshments thereon between 10 P.M. and 5 A.M. (1860 Act, s. 6).

Apparently a licensed refreshment house may be kept open at any time.

Police Powers.—A constable, when and so often as he thinks proper, may enter any premises licensed as a refreshment house. If the keeper or his employee refuses to admit a constable demanding admittance, the licensee is liable to fine if proceedings are instituted within seven days. On a second offence the licence may be forfeited and the holder disqualified for two years (1860 Act, s. 18). Increased penalties and disqualification for breaches of this Act are allowed by s. 26 of the Licensing Act, 1949.

Licensing, Carlisle District.—The powers of the Secretary of State for the management of the intoxicating liquor trade in the Carlisle district (as defined in the 9th Sched.) are given in ss. 76 to 80 of the Licensing Act, 1953.

He may sell intoxicants for consumption on or off premises and is assisted by a local advisory committee (s. 76) and he has the monopoly of the liquor trade except where licensed premises or registered clubs existed when state management came into operation and continue to exist (s. 77)

Licensing New Towns.—The Licensing Act, 1953, ss. 68 to 75 deals with liquor licensing matters in new towns on the following lines.

A new town shall have a committee to arrange for licensed premises (s. 68) and which shall make proposals as to the establishment and distribution of such premises and submit them to the Minister of Housing and Local Government for his confirmation (s. 70). The Licensing Justices will deal with the grant of new licences and removals (s. 71).

Methylated Spirits.—Under the Customs and Excise Act 1952, methylated spirits means spirits mixed in Great Britain or Northern Ireland with some other substance in accordance with Regulations made under the Act (s. 307). No person shall make or deal wholesale in same unless he holds an excise licence as an authorised methylator (s. 116) nor shall a person sell same without an excise licence (s. 117).

No person shall prepare or sell as a beverage or mixed with a beverage any methylated spirits or methylalcohol or their mixtures (s. 121).

The sale of methylated spirits is not affected by the Licensing Act, 1953, see s. 164 of that Act.

Chapter XXXIX
PUBLIC HEALTH
Contents

Public Health Acts.—The Public Health Acts form a code of regulations designed to promote the good health of the community. They create many offences which, strictly speaking, are not within the sphere of police work, but it is advisable that police should have some knowledge of these Acts. Offences against these laws are dealt with by the Local Authorities, and as a rule the duty of the police is confined to reporting such breaches of the Acts as may come under their notice.

Portions of these Acts are consolidated in the Public Health Act, 1936, which came into operation on 1st October, 1937. Only a few of its provisions are applicable to London.

S. 298 of the Public Health Act, 1936, states that proceedings for an offence under the Act, shall not, without the consent of the Attorney General, be taken by anyone other than a party aggrieved or a Council or body whose function it is to enforce the Act or byelaws.

Several Public Health Regulations apply to visiting forces. See Appendix V.

Food.—Any place in which food for human consumption is prepared, stored or kept for sale must be kept clean, etc., so as to prevent the risk of contamination to food in the place. (See Food and Drugs Act, 1955, s. 13 and Food Hygiene Regulations, 1955).

A collector of or dealer in rags, old clothes or similar articles must not sell or deliver from premises used for the business or when collecting same, any article of food or drink to any person or any article whatsoever to anyone under fourteen. (Public Health Act, 1936, s. 154).

An authorised officer of a Local Authority may examine any food intended for human consumption which has been sold or is exposed or offered for sale or is kept for sale, and if it appears unfit for human consumption, may seize it and take it to be dealt with by a Justice. (Food and Drugs Act, 1955 s. 9).

Horseflesh.—The flesh of horses, asses or mules may not be sold, exposed or kept for sale for human food elsewhere than in a place on which a notice is displayed stating that horseflesh is sold there (Food and Drugs Act, 1955, s. 24). See " Knackers," Chap. 35.

Infectious (Notifiable) Diseases.—The exposure in public places, shops, public conveyances, etc., of persons or articles liable to convey any notifiable disease will be an offence. Infected articles, conveyances, premises, etc., must be disinfected.

Relatives, attendants or occupiers and doctors must notify certain infectious diseases to the medical officer of health of the district.

The notifiable diseases include smallpox, diphtheria, cholera, croup, erysipelas, scarlet fever, typhus, typhoid, enteric and relapsing fevers. See Public Health Act, 1936, Part V, and s. 343.

Nuisances.—The Local Authority has power to deal with refuse, scavenging, noxious matter, keeping of animals, etc. (1936 Act, Part II, ss. 72-82). Also nuisances of ponds, rivers, etc., and it is an offence to deposit ashes, stones, dust, etc., in rivers, streams, etc. (s. 259).

If the following are in such a state as to be a nuisance or prejudicial to health, viz. any premises, any animal so kept, any accumulation or deposit, any dust or effluvia from any trade, etc., any factory, workshop or workplace, the Local Authority may serve notice on the person responsible requiring him to abate same, which is termed a statutory nuisance. If the nuisance is not abated the person responsible may be summarily prosecuted, fined and ordered to abate the nuisance (1936 Act, Part III, ss. 91-100).

Porters, etc.—The Local Authority may licence (yearly) luggage porters, light porters, public messengers or commissionaires and has power to revoke such licences (Public Health Acts Amendment Act, 1907, s. 84).

Offensive Trades.—Certain noxious or offensive trades, businesses or manufactures, are not to be established without the consent of the Local Authority. Nuisance caused by the effluvia from the products used in trades may be dealt with summarily on proof that same is a nuisance or prejudicial to health (1936 Act, ss. 92, 107-109).

Sanitary Conveniences used in Common.—It is a summary offence for any person to injure or improperly foul same (1936 Act, s. 52).

Smoky Chimneys.—The Clean Air Act 1956 makes provision for abating the pollution of the air, by prohibiting the issue of dark smoke from chimneys, by requiring that new furnaces shall be as far as practicable smokeless and by requiring that grit and dust from furnaces shall be minimised. The duty of enforcing the provisions of the Act is laid on the Local Authority.

Unfit Dwellings.—When any premises used for human habitation appear to be in a condition prejudicial to health the Local Authority may take action (Public Health Act, 1936, s. 83).

Canal boats used as dwellings shall be registered with a Local Authority (1936 Act, Part X, ss. 249-258).

Tents, vans, sheds, movable dwellings, etc., used for human habitation come under ss. 268, 269 of the 1936 Act.

Medicines.—The Pharmacy and Poisons Act, 1933, the Pharmacy and Medicines Act, 1941, the Penicillin Act, 1947 and the Pharmacy Act, 1953, deal with medicines. Directions are given regarding their sale, description and composition. Sale by unauthorised persons is restricted.

Poisons.—The Pharmacy and Poisons Act, 1933 as amended by the Pharmacy and Medicines Act, 1941 and the Pharmacy Act, 1954, deals with the registration of chemists and pharmacists (see " Pharmaceutical Chemists ," Chap. 29), and together with the Poisons Rules, 1952 as amended by the Poisons (No. 2) Rules, 1952 and Poisons Rules, 1953, 1955, the Poisons (No. 2) Rules, 1955, the Poisons Rules of 1957 and 1958, and the Poisons (No. 2) Rules, 1958 made under the Pharmacy and Poisons Act, 1933, regulate the sale and supply of poisons.

Authorised seller of poisons.—This term is applied to—

(1) A registered pharmacist who sells drugs by retail.

(2) A body corporate (or company) which sells drugs by retail, and

(3) A representative continuing the business of a registered pharmacist who is an authorised seller of poisons, but has died or become of unsound mind or bankrupt.

Provided that in all these cases a registered pharmacist is in personal control and his certificate of registration is exhibited on the premises, and provided also that the premises are registered with the Pharmaceutical Society for the purpose.

Poisons List.—A list of the substances which are to be treated as " poisons " has been prepared by an Advisory Committee (called the Poisons Board) and approved by the Secretary of State.

The list is given in the Poisons List Order, 1958, as amended by the Poisons List (No. 2) Order, 1958.

This poisons list is in two parts, viz. :—

Part I, containing poisons which may be sold only by an authorised seller of poisons ; and

Part II, containing poisons which may be sold by an authorised seller of poisons or by a person whose name is on a list kept by the Local Authority of persons entitled to sell poisons named in Part II of the list, and who is known as a " listed seller of Part II poisons."

Local Authority.—This is the council of a county, county

borough or Metropolitan borough and the Common Council of the City of London.

The local authority shall keep a list of persons entitled to sell the poisons in Part II of the Poisons List, and a person having premises in the area may apply to have his name put in the list as a person authorised to sell such poisons in such premises. He must pay a fee and may be refused if he or his premises are not considered fit. If on the list and if he is convicted of an offence the Court may order his name to be removed from the list. To supervise such persons local inspectors shall be appointed who may enter premises, examine, inquire and take samples, and they may prosecute offenders and conduct the proceedings.

The Pharmaceutical Society also has inspectors with similar powers as regards sellers of poisons.

Sale of Poisons.—It shall not be lawful for a person to sell—

(1) Part I poisons—unless he is an authorised seller of poisons, selling on duly registered premises under supervision of a registered pharmacist.

(2) Part II poisons—unless either he is an authorised seller of poisons selling on duly registered premises or his name is in the " local authority's list," and he sells in the premises so authorised.

(3) Any poison—unless the container of the poison is duly labelled with the name and proportion of the poison, the word " poison " and the name and address of seller.

Poison shall not be sold or offered for sale by means of an automatic machine.

Sale of Part I Poisons.—As stated above only an authorised seller of poisons may sell such poisons, and it shall not be lawful—

(*a*) To sell same to any person unless that person is certified in writing (as prescribed) or is known by the seller, to be a person to whom the poison may properly be sold.

(*b*) To deliver same until the sale is recorded (as prescribed) in a book and the purchaser has signed the entry.

Exemption from the above restrictions is allowed in the case of—

(1) Medicines provided or ordered by a doctor, dentist or veterinary surgeon, or by an authorised seller of poisons, but same must be labelled with name and address of the provider and a record (as prescribed) shall be kept.

(2) Wholesale sales, and sales for export, to doctors, etc., hospitals, etc., public services, etc.

Penalty.—The general penalty prescribed for breach of the Act or of any rules made under the Pharmacy and Poisons Act, 1933 is, on summary conviction, fine not exceeding £50, and £10 a day for a continuing offence, and the fact that an employee in supplying poison acted without the authority of the employer will not be a defence.

Proceedings may be taken within twelve months after the offence.

Dangerous Drugs.—The Dangerous Drugs Act, 1951, repealed previous similar Acts and regulates the manufacture, disposal etc., of certain drugs regarded as dangerous.

The law on this subject is intended to prevent any abuse of such drugs and to put a stop to the traffic in them for the purposes of intoxication and stimulation. The constant taking of these drugs (often described as " dope ") has most harmful effect on the general health and they should not be taken unless on medical advice and for remedial purposes.

Part I of the Act (ss. 1–4) deals with raw opium, coca leaves, Indian hemp and its resins which are not to be imported or exported without licence.

Part II (ss. 5–7) prohibits the import or export of opium prepared for smoking and makes it an offence to make, sell, have in possession, smoke, allow in premises for smoking, etc., any such opium.

Part III (ss. 8–10) provides for regulations to control manufacture, sale, use, etc., of medicinal opium, extract of Indian hemp, morphine, cocaine, etc., etc.

Part V (ss 13–26)—s. 14 : A constable or person authorised by the Secretary of State may enter the premises of a person dealing in above drugs and inspect books and stocks of any such drugs, and a Justice, on sworn information, may issue a search warrant authorising entry of premises, search and seizure of any such drugs and documents relating to same. Any delay or obstruction will be an offence.

S. 15 : Breaches of regulations or licences or false statements or aiding, etc. same will be offences punishable summarily or (with consent of the Attorney General or by the Director of Public Prosecutions (s. 18)) on indictment.

S. 18 : Summary proceedings may be taken within 3 months from the date when a Secretary of State gives a certificate that there is evidence sufficient for a prosecution.

S. 19 : A constable may arrest without warrant a person who has committed or attempted to commit any offence against the Act (or Regulations, s. 15) if he has reasonable grounds for believing that the person will abscond unless arrested or if his name and address are unknown and cannot be ascertained.

Dangerous Drugs Regulations, 1953, 1957.—Previous similar regulations are revoked (Reg. 38).

Part I (Regs. 1–4) applies to the raw opium and other drugs mentioned in Part I of the Act and prohibits the supplying, procuring, advertising and possession of same except by duly authorised or licensed persons.

Doctors, veterinary surgeons, authorised sellers of poisons, hospitals, etc., pharmacists, laboratories in hospitals, colleges, etc., public analysts, sampling officers, pharmacy inspectors are authorised so far as is necessary for their functions to have and supply such drugs.

Every such drug must be kept safely in a locked receptacle except when being used. The supplier of such drugs must keep a register of what he receives and what he supplies.

Part II (Regs. 6—18) applies to medicinal opium, extract of Indian hemp, morphine, heroin, cocaine, pethidine, and many other drugs as given in the Third Schedule (See 1957 Regs.)

The manufacture, supply, procuring, advertising and possession of such drugs is prohibited except by authorised or licensed persons.

Reg. 9 : A person who is supplied with such a drug by a doctor or veterinary surgeon or on prescription from same is deemed to be authorised to have it.

Reg. 10 : Doctors, dentists, veterinary surgeons, hospital etc., pharmacists, sisters in charge of wards etc., laboratories in hospitals, colleges, etc., public analysts, sampling officers and inspectors and head dispensers in hospitals are authorised to have and supply such drugs so far as it is necessary for the exercise of the functions of above.

But a dentist should supply same only in course of treatment in his presence and a sister must act under doctor's orders.

The authorised holder of any such drugs must keep them safely in a locked receptacle except when in use.

Reg. 13 : The master of a ship without a doctor may have the necessary drugs and must keep a record of the use of same.

A farmer or stock owner who holds a certificate from the chief officer of police of his area (see Fourth Schedule) may hold up to 32 ounces of tincture of opium to be kept under lock and key and only used for administration to animals.

A certified midwife on a " midwifes supply order " signed by the local medical officer of health may have medicinal opium, tincture of opium and pethidine, to be kept in a locked receptacle, used only in the exercise of her profession and record kept of its use.

Reg. 14 : Deals with the form of a prescription for a dangerous drug and Reg. 15 instructs the supplier how to deal with such a prescription.

Reg. 16 : Gives the requirements as to packages or bottles of such drugs which should be properly marked.

Reg. 17 : Contains the directions as to the keeping of registers and records by suppliers of such drugs.

Part III (Regs. 20–25) applies to methylmorphine (codeine) ethylmorphine (dionin) and compounds. Their manufacture must be under licence.

The supply of same by a wholesale dealer must be under licence and the package or bottle must be marked with the amount and he must keep a register.

The possession of over one pound avoirdupois of same requires a licence. Reg. 25 states that this Part III does not apply to sale or distribution of same by a person other than a wholesale dealer and an authorised seller of poisons may compound and sell any such drug.

Part IV (Regs. 26–40)—Reg. 28 : Requires that a supplier of drugs mentioned in Parts I and II must not deliver to a person such a drug unless such person is authorised or licensed to be in possession of it or he produces a written statement from the authorised recipient that he, as messenger, is empowered to take it to the authorised recipient.

Reg. 34 : A carrier or his servant may have possession of a dangerous drug in the ordinary course of his business.

Reg. 33 : All registers, records, etc., must be preserved for two years, except national health prescriptions.

Reg. 37 : " Register " means a bound book, not loose leaf or card index.

Lunacy.—Under the Lunacy Act, 1890 as amended by the National Health Service Act, 1946, a duly authorised officer of the local health authority or any constable who with reason believes that a person wandering at large is of unsound mind, may apprehend him and take him before a Justice. A Justice, on the sworn information of any person that a person wandering at large is of unsound mind may, by order, require any constable or such authorised officer to apprehend such person and bring him before a Justice (s. 15). The Justice, on medical evidence, may order the person to be taken by such constable or officer to a named mental institution (s. 16). If the constable or officer who has apprehended such a person considers that he should be placed under care and control before the proceedings before a Justice, he may take him to a hospital allocated for such purposes where he can be kept for up to 3 days (s. 20).

Institutions for the reception, care and detention of persons of unsound mind must be duly licensed for the purpose.

A person suffering from mental illness may be received into a mental hospital as a voluntary patient or as a temporary patient (Mental Treatment Act, 1930).

The provisions of the Lunacy and Mental Treatment Acts, 1890 to 1930, and the Mental Deficiency Acts, 1913 to 1938, were extensively amended by the National Health Service Act, 1946, A general purpose of the amendment is to transfer functions of the Board of Control to the Minister of Health : the order effecting it is the National Health Service Act (Appointed Day) Order, 1947.

Magistrates' Courts Act, 1952, s. 30. Where a Magistrates' Court is satisfied that a person charged with any act or omission punishable summarily with imprisonment, did the act or made the omission and is satisfied on the evidence of two doctors that he is of unsound mind and a proper person to be detained, the Court may order him to be received and detained in an institution for persons of unsound mind, and may direct the officer of the local health authority or any constable to convey him there. This is known as a " reception order."

C.J. Act, 1948, s. 62 : Changed the expression " Criminal lunatic asylum " to " Broadmoor Institution " and the term " criminal lunatic " was replaced by "Broadmoor patient." These institutions are now under the control of the Minister of Health.

Mental Deficiency.—The Mental Deficiency Act, 1927, gives a classification of persons who are regarded as defectives within the meaning of the Act, viz. :—

(1) Idiots, that is persons so defective in mind as to be unable to guard themselves against common physical dangers.

(2) Imbeciles, that is persons who are not idiots but are so defective in mind as to be incapable of managing themselves or their affairs, or in the case of children of being taught to do so.

(3) Feeble-minded persons, that is persons who are so defective in mind as to require care and supervision for their own protection or for the protection of others, or in the case of children when their deficiency is such as to render them incapable of receiving education at school.

(4) Moral defectives, that is persons who are mentally defective coupled with strong vicious or criminal propensities and who require care, supervision and control for the protection of others (s. 1).

Mental deficiency means a condition of arrested or incomplete development of mind existing before the age of 18 years, whether arising from inherent causes or induced by disease or injury (s. 1).

Such a defective may be sent to a State or certified institution for defectives or placed under guardianship (Mental Deficiency Act, 1913, s. 2).

If it appears to the police that any person charged with an offence is a defective, it is their duty to bring before the Court such evidence as to his mental condition as may be available, giving notice of the intention to the person charged and to his parent or guardian and informing the local health authority, (1913 Act, s. 8).

The managers of an institution for defectives, and the officials of such institution authorised in writing, have the powers of constables for the purpose of conveying a person to or from the institution or of apprehending him and bringing him back in the case of his escape or refusal to return (1913 Act, s. 62).

If a patient in an institution or absent from an institution under licence or without a licence escapes, he may be arrested without warrant and brought back to the institution, by any constable or by the managers or by any person authorised by them in writing (1913 Act, s. 42). See Stone, under title " Lunacy and Mental Deficiency."

Nursing Homes.—Public Health Act, 1936, ss. 187-195, provides for the registration and inspection of nursing homes, that is, premises for the nursing of persons suffering from any sickness, injury or infirmity, including maternity homes, but not including approved hospitals or certified institutions for mental defectives and lunatics (s. 199).

It is a summary offence for any person to carry on a nursing home without being duly registered in respect thereof by the local authority (County or Borough Council). Any certificate of registration must be kept affixed in a conspicuous place in the home.

The Local Authority has power to refuse registration to unfit persons or premises and to cancel registration. Its authorised officers have power to inspect premises carried on or reasonably believed to be carried on as nursing homes and it is an offence to obstruct them. See also " Nurses," Chap. 29.

Births, Deaths and Marriages.—Under s. 203, Public Health Act, 1936, every birth should be notified within thirty-six hours to the Medical Officer of Health of the district, by the father (if he is residing in the house at the time) and by the person in attendance on the mother.

Under the Births and Deaths Registration Acts, 1874, 1926 and 1953, the birth of every living or stillborn child (except a foetus under 28 weeks gestation) must be reported to the Registrar of Births, Deaths and Marriages within forty-two days. Every death must be reported to the registrar within five days. The body of a deceased person (or of a still-born child) must not be disposed of until the person effecting the disposal has received a certificate from the registrar who has registered the death or an order from the coroner. The person effecting the disposal of the body must within four days notify the registrar as to the date, place, and means of disposal of the body. A dead body is not to be removed out of England without notice to the coroner. Contraventions of these Acts are summary offences.

The Marriage Act, 1949 and its Amendment Acts 1954 and 1958, deal with marriage questions and repeal much previous law on the subject.

It is felony for any person to solemnise matrimony falsely pretending that he is in holy orders (s. 75).

A marriage between persons either of whom is under the age of sixteen shall be void (s. 2). It may be a defence to a charge of defiling a girl over thirteen and under sixteen or of indecent assault (Sexual Offences Act, 1956, ss. 6 & 14).

Only the bare facts of any judicial proceeding to secure divorce or restitution of conjugal rights may be published. See Chap. 11.

The making of false declarations, statements, etc., in connection with the registration of births and deaths and the celebration of marriage is also a misdemeanour under the Perjury Act (see Chap. 21) and the falsifying, etc., of official records of same is a felony under the Forgery Act (see Chap. 17).

Burials.—Under the Burial Laws Amendment Act, 1880, it is a misdemeanour to interfere in any manner with the decent and orderly conducting of any burial, whether it is being carried out with or without a religious service.

Under the Cemeteries Clauses Act, 1847, it is a summary offence to play games or sports, or discharge firearms (save at a military funeral), or commit any nuisance in a cemetery, or to wilfully and unlawfully disturb persons assembled in a cemetery for the purpose of burying any body therein, or to commit any wilful damage in a cemetery.

The Burial Act, 1857, makes it a summary offence to remove any body or remains of a body from a burial ground without licence.

It is a summary offence to knowingly bury any body in a burial ground which has been closed as such by order (Burial Act, 1855).

The body of a suicide should be interred in a burial ground (see Interments Act, 1882).

It is a misdemeanour at common law to remove without lawful authority a dead body from the grave.

The cremation in proper manner (Cremation Acts, 1902, 1952) of a body is permissible, but if there is reasonable ground for holding an inquest it is a misdemeanour to prevent it by destruction of the body.

Councils of county boroughs and county districts shall cause to be buried or cremated the body of any person who has died or been found dead in their area in any case where no suitable arrangements for the disposal of the body have been or are being made otherwise than by the council (National Assistance Act, 1948, s. 50).

A Justice on medical evidence may order a dead body in a building to be removed by the local authority to a mortuary or buried forthwith (Public Health Act, 1936, s. 162).

Fires.—The Fire Services Acts, 1947, 1951, have repealed the False Alarms of Fire Act, 1895, and the Fire Brigades Act, 1938, and direct as follows :

Every county council and county borough council shall be the fire authority for its area (s. 4) and two or more may combine for fire fighting purposes (ss. 5-12). Every fire authority shall make provision for fire fighting purposes of the prescribed standards of efficiency (s. 1) and shall make arrangements for mutual assistance (s. 2). It will have power to provide and maintain fire alarms and to employ its fire brigade for purposes other than fire fighting purposes (s. 3) and shall ensure the provision of an adequate available supply of water (ss. 13-16).

Any false or fraudulent obtaining or attempting to obtain any payment under the Firemen's Pension Scheme may be dealt with on indictment or summarily (s. 26).

" Fire fighting purposes " means the purposes of the extinction of fire and the protection of life and property in case of fire (s. 38).

Any member of a fire brigade on duty or any constable may enter, and if necessary break into, any premises or place in which a fire has or is reasonably believed to have broken out or any premises or place which it is necessary to enter for the purpose of extinguishing a fire or of protecting from acts done for fire fighting purposes without the consent of the owner or occupier ; and may do all such acts and things as he may deem necessary for extinguishing fire or for protecting from fire any such premises or place or rescuing any person or property therein (s. 30 (1)).

Any wilful obstruction or interference with a member of a fire brigade engaged in operations for fire fighting purposes will be a summary offence ; fine up to twenty-five pounds (s. 30 (2)).

The senior officer present of such fire brigade shall have sole charge and control of all the operations for the extinction of a fire and may require the water supply in an area to be shut off so as to give a greater supply for the extinction of the fire (s. 30 (3), (4)).

The senior police officer or in the absence of any police the senior fire brigade officer present at a fire may close to traffic any street or stop or regulate traffic in any street (including any alley, passage, etc., whether a thoroughfare or not (s. 38)) when he considers it is necessary or desirable to do so for fire fighting purposes (s. 30 (5)).

It is a summary offence to knowingly give or cause to be given a false alarm of fire to any fire brigade or to any member thereof (s. 31).

Any person who uses a fire hydrant unauthorisedly or who damages or obstructs a fire hydrant otherwise than in consequence of its lawful use will commit a summary offence (s. 14 (5)).

In urban districts it is a summary offence to wilfully set or cause to be set on fire any chimney (but the offender, if necessary, may be indicted for felony), and if any chimney accidentally goes on fire the person occupying or using the premises is liable to a fine of 10s. unless he satisfies the Court that such fire was not due to any omission, neglect or carelessness of himself or his servant (Town Police Clauses Act, 1847, ss. 30, 31 where the Act applies).

Making a fire on a highway is a summary offence. (Highway Act, 1835, s. 72.)

Coroners and Inquests.—The office of Coroner is of ancient origin, having been instituted in England in the twelfth century as a Crown office by the Norman Kings.

The Coroner was the King's officer in a county or borough charged to keep a record of all sudden (that is unnatural or against the course of nature) deaths, forfeitures and other occurrences by which money or property might fall to the Crown.

The Coroner with the aid of a jury investigated such matters and his inquiry was called an inquisition, hence the term " inquest."

A Coroner's inquest is a Court of law although no person is accused before him. The Coroner examines witnesses on oath, and while usually following the ordinary rules of evidence, he may admit any evidence he thinks fit, especially hearsay evidence. His duty is to ascertain how the deceased came by his death, and he is not bound to follow the usual procedure of Law Courts.

The duties of Coroners are now regulated by the Coroners Acts, 1887 to 1954, and the Coroners Rules, 1953. The 1954 Act is now in force by 1955 Order.

It is the duty of the Coroner to investigate the death of any person, when informed that such death has been sudden, violent or unnatural. Cases of sudden death under any circumstances of suspicion should be reported to the Coroner.

On reasonable grounds of suspicion a Coroner may institute inquiries into any case of death.

A Coroner may also institute inquiries and hold an inquest regarding the finding of gold or silver hidden in any private place. See " Treasure Trove," Chap. 18.

A Coroner must hold an inquest in the following cases :—

(1) When there is reasonable cause to suspect that a person has died either a violent or an unnatural death, or has died a sudden death of which the cause is unknown, or

(2) When a person has died in prison, or

(3) When a person has died under such circumstances as to require an inquest in accordance with any Act of Parliament, e.g. when a person confined in a mental or inebriate institution dies without satisfactory medical evidence as to the cause of death (1887 Act, s. 3).

He must have reasonable cause to suspect that death may have been due to other causes than common illness before he is entitled to hold an inquest. The question whether an inquest ought to be held is one for the Coroner to decide on the circumstances of each individual case.

The body should be lying within his jurisdiction before the Coroner may hold an inquest. It is a misdemeanour at common law to dispose of a body in order to prevent an inquest being held or to obstruct the Coroner or his jury in their inquiry.

Even if the body has been destroyed or is not recoverable, an inquest may be held if the Secretary of State so directs (1926 Act, s. 18).

A Coroner may allow a body to be moved into the jurisdiction of another Coroner so that an inquest may be held there (1926 Act, s. 16).

A Coroner's inquest may be held anywhere, but it must not be held in premises licensed for the sale of intoxicants if other suitable premises are available (Licensing Act, 1953, s. 157). It should be held within a reasonable time after death.

The Coroner should summon a jury if there is reason to suspect that the death was due to—

(1) Murder, manslaughter or infanticide, or

(2) Any accident, poisoning or disease which must be notified to any Government department or official, e.g. mining, factory, explosives, railway and petroleum accidents, and certain industrial poisonings and diseases, or

(3) An accident arising out of the use of a vehicle in a street or public highway, or

(4) Circumstances prejudicial to the health or safety of the public, e.g. food poisoning cases, epidemics, deaths under anaesthetics, or has

(5) Occurred in prison or under such circumstances as to require an inquest under some Statute other than the Coroners Act, 1887.

Apart from this requirement a Coroner may hold an inquest either with or without a jury as he thinks fit (1926 Act, s. 13).

If the Coroner considers it necessary he may order a post mortem examination of the body by a qualified medical man (1926 Act, ss. 21 to 24, and Coroners Rules, 1953, rr. 2 to 10). If the chief officer of police informs the Coroner that a person may be charged with the murder etc. of the deceased, the Coroner should consult him as to the pathologist who is to make the post mortem examination (r. 3). If the chief officer of police desires to be represented at this examination he may be represented by a member of his force (r. 4).

A Coroner's jury consists of not less than seven or more than eleven persons. Any person exempted from ordinary jury service is exempt from service on a Coroner's jury. The Coroner must view the body but the jury need not do so unless they so desire or unless the Coroner so directs (1926 Act, s. 14).

Under the Coroners Rules, 1953, an inquest should be carried on in a formal manner (r. 13) and should be held in public but the Coroner may exclude the public in the interests of national security (r. 14). It should not be held on a Sunday (r. 15). A properly interested person may be allowed by the Coroner to examine any witness either in person or by counsel or solicitor, but the police cannot examine witnesses except through counsel or solicitor (r. 16). The Coroner may examine a witness first and the witness may be examined lastly by his representative (r. 17). The proceedings shall be directed *solely* to ascertain:—

(1) Who the deceased was,

(2) How, when and where he came by his death,

(3) The persons, if any, to be charged should the jury find that death was caused by murder, manslaughter or infanticide,

(4) The particulars required for the registration of his death (r. 26).

The Coroner shall make notes of the evidence at every inquest other than the ones at which he takes depositions (r. 30).

No person shall be allowed to address the Court as to the facts (r. 31).

The Coroner shall sum up the evidence to the jury and direct them as to the law before they consider their verdict (r. 32).

The jury are sworn. The Coroner may accept the verdict of the majority of the jury provided the minority is not more than two (1926 Act, s. 15). There may be an appeal to the Queen's Bench.

If a juror or witness duly summoned to attend an inquest does not attend he may be fined £5 (1887 Act, s. 19). Such an absent witness may also be arrested and brought there on the Coroner's warrant.

A person shall not be summoned to attend as a juror at inquests held in the same Coroner's area on more than 3 days (adjournments excepted) in any year (r. 35).

Any prisoner concerned should always be given the opportunity of attending an inquest, and giving evidence, which he may do after caution from the Coroner. An order may be obtained from the Secretary of State to bring a prisoner to an inquest (C.J. Act, 1948, s. 60 and Prison Act, 1952, s. 22).

The inquisition or finding of a Coroner's jury (viz. their verdict) is to be in writing signed by the jurors and by the Coroner. If it charges any person with murder, manslaughter or infanticide, the Coroner may commit such person for trial (1926 Act, s. 25).

If the chief officer of police requests the Coroner to adjourn an inquest on the ground that a person may be charged with the murder, manslaughter or causing death by reckless or dangerous driving, s. 8, Road Traffic Act, 1956) or infanticide of the deceased, the Coroner shall adjourn the inquest for 14 days or longer and on police application he may grant a further adjournment (Coroners Rules, 1953, r. 22).

If the Coroner is informed before the jury have given their verdict that some person has been charged before examining justices with the murder, manslaughter or infanticide of the deceased, he shall, in the absence of reason to the contrary, adjourn the inquest until after the conclusion of the criminal proceedings, and then, if he thinks fit, he may resume the inquest as a fresh inquest (1926 Act, s. 20).

If a deceased person had a relevant association (s. 12) with a visiting force a Coroner shall not hold an inquest (or shall adjourn it). If on an inquest the Coroner is satisfied that a person (as per s. 2) is or will be charged with the homicide of the deceased, before a court of a " visiting country " he shall adjourn the inquest. In these cases he cannot take further action unless authorised by the Secretary of State (Visiting Forces Act, 1952, s. 7).

Fumigation.—When premises and articles not in the open air are to be fumigated with hydrogen cyanide or any substance added by Order in Council, notification has to be given to the nearest police station and elaborate precautions have to be taken and observed. See the Hydrogen Cyanide (Fumigation) Act 1937, and the Regulations of 1951 thereunder.

Abatement of Litter.—If any person without proper authority throws down, drops or otherwise deposits in, into or from any place in the open air to which the public are entitled or permitted to have access without payment, and leaves anything whatsoever in such circumstances as to cause, contribute to, or tend to lead to, the defacement by litter of any place in the open air, he shall be guilty of an offence punishable on summary conviction by a fine of £10.

Any covered place, open to the air on at least one side, and available for public use shall be treated as being a place in the open air.

Power to institute proceedings for an offence under this Act is given to many local authorities, without prejudice to the powers of any other person. (Litter Act, 1958, s. 1).

APPENDIX I

SPEED LIMITS FOR MOTOR VEHICLES

(See Chapter XXIV, TRAFFIC)

The general speed limit indicated by traffic signs in certain built-up areas for all motor vehicles is 30 m.p.h. except when it is necessary for vehicles being used for ambulance, fire brigade or police purposes to exceed that speed, and some roads in the London area now have a general speed limit of 40 m.p.h. which may also be extended to other roads (R.T. Act 1956, s.4). See also " Exemptions from Speed Limit," Chap. 24.

Maximum speed limits in miles per hour on public roads are prescribed by the First Schedule to the Road Traffic Act, 1930 as substituted by R.T. Act, 1934 and varied so as to have effect as set out in the Schedule to the Motor Vehicles (Variation of Speed Limit) Regulations 1956, as follows:—

SCHEDULE

LIMITS OF SPEED

Class or description of Vehicle (See also paragraph 13)	*Maximum speed,* *miles per hour*
VEHICLES OTHER THAN TRACK-LAYING VEHICLES	

1. *Passenger vehicles*, that is to say vehicles constructed solely for the carriage of passengers and their effects, and *Dual Purpose Vehicles:*—

(1) vehicles having an unladen weight exceeding three tons, or adapted to carry more than seven passengers exclusive of the driver 30

(2) vehicles drawing trailers:—

    (*a*) in the case of a motor car adapted to carry not more than seven passengers exclusive of the driver, if the trailer is a close-coupled four-wheeled trailer or is two-wheeled 30

    (*b*) in the case of a motor cycle, if the trailer is two-wheeled 30

    (*c*) in any other case 20

(3) invalid carriages 20

(4) vehicles not fitted with pneumatic tyres, and vehicles drawing trailers not fitted with pneumatic tyres . . 20

2. *Goods vehicles*, that is to say, vehicles constructed or adapted for use for the conveyance of goods or burden of any description, but not including dual purpose vehicles:—

Class or description of Vehicle (See also paragraph 13)	*Maximum speed,* *miles per hour*
(1) generally	30
(2) vehicles drawing trailers, not being articulated vehicles .	20
(3) vehicles not fitted with pneumatic tyres, if drawing trailers or exceeding one ton, and vehicles drawing trailers not fitted with pneumatic tyres	20
(4) vehicles not fitted with resilient tyres	5

3. *Motor tractors:*—

(1) generally	20
(2) if drawing two or more trailers	5
(3) if not fitted with resilient tyres	5

4. *Heavy locomotives and light locomotives:*—

(1) generally	12
(2) if drawing more than two trailers	5
(3) if not fitted with resilient tyres	5

TRACK-LAYING VEHICLES

5. *Motor Cars and Heavy Motor Cars.*	20

6. *Motor Tractors:*—

(1) generally	20
(2) if drawing two or more trailers	5

7. *Light Locomotives:*—

(1) generally	12
(2) if drawing more than two trailers	5

8. *Heavy Locomotives*	5

9. Track-laying vehicles which do not satisfy both of the following conditions:—

> (a) that the vehicle is fitted with springs between its frame and the weight-carrying rollers, and
>
> (b) that the vehicle is fitted with resilient material between the rims of the weight-carrying rollers and the road surface,

and vehicles drawing track-laying trailers which do not satisfy both of those conditions 12

10. Track-laying vehicles satisfying neither of the said conditions and vehicles drawing track-laying trailers satisfying neither of those conditions 5

11. Combined track-and-wheel vehicles not fitted with resilient tyres, and vehicles drawing trailers which are combined track-and-wheel vehicles not fitted with resilient tyres . 5

12. Vehicles drawing trailers, where the drawing or any of the drawn vehicles, not being a track-laying vehicle, is not fitted with resilient tyres 5

Interpretation and Application

13. A vehicle falling within two or more descriptions specified in this Schedule shall be treated as falling within that description for which the lowest limit of speed is specified.

14. (1) In this Schedule " dual-purpose vehicle " means a vehicle constructed or adapted for the carriage both of passengers and of goods or burden of any description, being a vehicle of which the unladen weight does not exceed two tons and which either:—

(*a*) satisfies the conditions as to construction specified in the next following sub-paragraph, or

b) is so constructed or adapted that the driving power of the engine is, or by the appropriate use of the controls of the vehicle can be, transmitted to all the wheels of the vehicle.

(2) The conditions as to construction referred to in the last foregoing sub-paragraph are the following:—

(*a*) the vehicle must be permanently fitted with a rigid roof, with or without a sliding panel,

(*b*) the area of the vehicle to the rear of the driver's seat must:—

(*i*) be permanently fitted with at least one row of transverse seats (fixed or folding) for two or more passengers and those seats must be properly sprung or cushioned and provided with upholstered backrests, attached either to the seats or to a side or the floor of the vehicle; and

(*ii*) be lit on each side and at the rear by a window or windows of glass or other transparent material having an area or aggregate area of not less than two square feet on each side and not less than one hundred and twenty square inches at the rear;

(*c*) the distance between the rearmost part of the steering wheel and the backrests of the row of transverse seats satisfying the requirements specified in head (*i*) of this sub-paragraph (or, if there is more than one such row of seats, the distance between the rearmost part of the steering wheel and the backrests of the rearmost such row) must, when the seats are ready for use, be not less than one-third of the distance between the rearmost part of the steering wheel and the rearmost part of the floor of the vehicle.

15. In this Schedule " Close-coupled ", in relation to a trailer, means that the wheels on the same side of the trailer are so fitted that at all times while it is in motion they remain parallel to the longitudinal axis of the trailer, and that the distance between the centres of their respective areas of contact with the road surface does not exceed thirty-three inches.

16. In this Schedule " articulated vehicle " means a vehicle with a trailer so attached to the drawing vehicle that part of the

trailer is superimposed upon the drawing vehicle, and when the trailer is uniformly loaded not less than twenty per cent of the weight of its load is borne by the drawing vehicle.

17. In this Schedule, in relation to a vehicle (including a trailer), " fitted with pneumatic tyres " means that every wheel of the vehicle is fitted with pneumatic tyres, and " fitted with resilient tyres " means that every wheel of the vehicle is fitted either with pneumatic tyres or with other soft or elastic tyres.

18. In this Schedule " track-laying " means so designed and constructed that the weight is transmitted to the road surface by means of continuous tracks or by a combination of wheels and continuous tracks, and " combined track-and-wheel vehicle " means a vehicle so designed and constructed that its weight is transmitted to the road surface by a combination of wheels and continuous tracks.

19. A heavy motor car or motor car drawing a trailer and being used as a public service vehicle or as a goods vehicle shall be treated as not drawing a trailer if the trailer is used solely for the carriage of a container or containers for holding, or plant and materials for producing, for the purpose of the propulsion of the drawing vehicle, any fuel that is wholly gaseous at sixty degrees Fahrenheit under a pressure of thirty inches of mercury.

20. (1) Paragraphs 1 to 4 of this Schedule do not apply to, and paragraphs 5 to 12 apply only to, track-laying vehicles and vehicles drawing track-laying trailers or trailers some of which are track-laying.

(2) Paragraphs 1 to 12 of this Schedule do not apply to vehicles for the time being used in the conduct of experiments or trials under section six of the Roads Improvement Act, 1925.

APPENDIX II

REGULATIONS AS TO THE CONSTRUCTION AND USE OF MOTOR VEHICLES AND TRAILERS

(See Chapter XXV, ROAD VEHICLES)

The Motor Vehicles (Construction and Use) Regulations, 1955, 1956, 1957 and No. 2, 1957, apply, except where the context otherwise requires, to wheeled vehicles only (Reg. 4). Every motor vehicle and trailer must be a wheeled or a tracklaying vehicle except motor cycles and invalid carriages which must be wheeled (Reg. 5). Each of these regulations when referred to herein will be indicated by the letters " Reg." and the number of the regulation.

The Construction and Use (Tracklaying Vehicles) Regulations, 1955, 1957 and No. 2, 1957, apply to tracklaying vehicles only (T. 4). Each such regulation when referred to will be indicated by the letter " T " and the number of the regulation.

Many of the regulations governing wheeled or tracklaying vehicles are identical and have been combined under the following alphabetical headings, the references to both Regulations being given. For example, " (Reg. 64 and T. 44) " means that the same rule applies to both wheeled and tracklaying vehicles.

For the penalties for contraventions of these Regulations, see " Construction and Use " at end of Chap. 25.

Exemptions.—Before dealing alphabetically with the subjects of these regulations it will be well to mention specifically certain exemptions allowed.

Road rollers are not subject to Regs. 8, 9, 16, 19, 30 and 36 (Reg. 4) nor to the tracklaying regulations T. 6, 7, 15, 18, 27 and 31 (T. 4).

Vehicles proceeding to a port for export are not subject to Regs. 6 to 9, 11 to 14, 16, 17, 20 to 62 and 74. Regulations 8, 9, 13, 16, 30, 36, 40, 44, 45, 53, 56, 57, 59 to 63 and 65 to 72, apply only to motor vehicles and trailers used upon highways (Reg. 4).

A motor vehicle registered before the end of one year from the making of any regulation affecting construction or weight is exempt from its requirements for 5 years providing it complies with any previous similar regulations (Reg. 4 and T. 4).

Motor vehicles or trailers brought into Great Britain temporarily by a person resident abroad are not subject to many of the Construction Rules of Part II of the Regulations, and only Regs. 6, 27 to 29, 33, 37, 42, 50, 53 and 54 of Part II will apply, provided that such vehicles comply with the requirements of the

International Convention, 1926 or of the Road Traffic Convention, Geneva, 1949 (Reg. 4).

Also Regs. 6 to 9, 11 to 13, 15 to 20, 23 to 72 and 102, and Track-laying Regs. 5 to 7, 9 to 12, 14 to 19, and 22 to 50, also 73 and 75 shall not apply to any vehicle in the service of a visiting force (Reg. 4 and T. 4).

The subjects of the regulations are dealt with alphabetically as follows :—

Abnormal Indivisible Load.—Means a load which cannot without undue expense or undue risk of damage be divided into two or more loads for conveyance on a road (Reg. 3) and owing to its dimensions or weight can only be carried by motor vehicles or trailers the use of which on roads is lawful only by reason of an Order of the Minister of Transport made under s. 3 (1) (*b*) of the Road Traffic Act, 1930 (s. 125, Transport Act, 1947). See " Special Types " later.

Agricultural Trailer.—Means a trailer the property of a person engaged in agriculture which is not used on a road for the conveyance of goods or burden other than agricultural produce or articles required for the purposes of agriculture (Reg. 3 and T. 3).

It need not have springs (Reg. 9 and T. 7), nor trailer plate (Reg. 64 and T. 44), nor soft, elastic or pneumatic tyres when on a highway (Reg. 56 and T. 37), nor brakes if it is a tracklayer (T. 36). If it is merely an agricultural vehicle not constructed to carry a load, it does not count as a " trailer " for the purpose of additional attendants (s. 17) or as regards the number of trailers permissible to be drawn (s. 18, R.T. Act, 1930).

A trailer made before 15 Jan., 1931, for the conveyance of horses and cattle and used for that purpose or for some other purpose connected with agriculture need not have soft, elastic or pneumatic tyres (Reg. 56). An agricultural trailer constructed before 1 July, 1947 and drawn by a motor tractor need not have a braking system if laden weight does not exceed 4 tons and is the only trailer drawn and speed does not exceed 10 m.p.h. (Reg. 55).

Ambulances.—The restrictions as to drivers' hours of duty do not apply (s. 19, R.T. Act, 1930). They may carry gongs or bells (Reg. 19), and use them if necessary at any time (Reg. 84). The speed limits do not apply if their observance would hinder the use of any vehicle for ambulance purposes (s. 3, 1934 Act).

The overhang limit does not apply to a motor car used as an ambulance by a local authority (Reg. 43).

Articulated Vehicle.—Means a heavy motor car or motor car with trailer so attached to the drawing vehicle that part is super-imposed thereon and when trailer is uniformly loaded not less than 20 per cent. of the weight of the load is borne by the drawing vehicle (Reg. 3 and T. 3). In such a case the vehicle itself is deemed to be constructed to carry a load (s. 2 (4), R.T. Act, 1930).

Attendant additional to driver is not necessary (Reg. 105 and T. 78).

Brakes.—If the trailer is permanently attached, the brakes must be capable of being set so as to prevent 2 wheels from revolving, when the trailer is not being drawn (Reg. 55).

Length.—See " Length " later.

The total laden weight shall not exceed 20 tons if the trailer part has less than four wheels. If it has four or more wheels the limit is 24 tons (Reg. 71).

Trailer plate is not necessary (Reg. 64 and T. 44).

Wings are not necessary for the rear wheels of a heavy motor car forming part of an articulated vehicle used only for carriage of round timber (Reg. 41 and T. 33).

Attendants.—Two persons shall be employed in driving or attending a heavy or light locomotive on a highway, and if it draws a trailer or trailers, one or more persons in addition to the two aforesaid shall be employed for attending to the trailer or trailers at the rate of one such additional person for each trailer in excess of one. This does not apply to a road roller while rolling a road. If a motor vehicle other than a locomotive draws a trailer or trailers on a highway one person in addition to the driver must be carried to attend to the trailer or trailers. As regards " attendants," the term " trailer " does not include a vehicle used solely for carrying water for the motor vehicle or any agricultural vehicle not made to carry a load. Any person causing or permitting a breach of this section commits an offence (R.T. Act, 1930, s. 17)

The above requirements as to attendants do not apply to :—

(1) An articulated vehicle (Reg. 105 and T. 78).

(2) A land locomotive or land tractor drawing a land implement (Reg. 105 and T. 78) or a land tractor drawing an agricultural trailer (Reg. 105 and T. 78).

(3) A motor car or motor cycle drawing a trailer with not more than two wheels or a motor car drawing a 4-wheeled trailer with two close coupled wheels on each side (Reg. 105).

(4) A motor tractor drawing a closed meat van between docks, railway stations and wholesale markets (Reg. 105).

(5) A motor tractor drawing a machine or implement used for maintenance, repair or cleansing of roads (Reg. 105 and T. 78).

(6) A motor tractor drawing a trailer designed and used for street cleansing or the collection or disposal of refuse, etc. (Reg. 105).

(7) A works truck drawing any works trailer, weight unladen of each vehicle not exceeding 30 cwt. (Reg. 105 and T. 78).

(8) A heavy motor vehicle or motor car drawing a " gas " trailer (Reg. 105 and T. 78).

(9) A motor vehicle drawing a trailer not over 1 ton weight unladen or a trailer not over 45 cwts. weight carrying permanent

apparatus, or a living van not over 2 tons unladen with pneumatic tyres, if in each case the brakes of the trailer act on the overrun of the trailer (Reg. 105).

(10) In the case of a road roller (Reg. 105).

(11) A motor vehicle belonging to H.M. Services drawing a trailer with brakes which can be applied by the driver of the motor vehicle (Reg. 105).

(12) A motor vehicle drawing a broken down vehicle unable to steer (Reg. 105).

Brakes.—Every motor vehicle (except motor cycles with or without sidecars, invalid carriages and land locomotives first registered on or before 1 Jan., 1932) shall have a braking system so made that it can be set so as to prevent two at least (if a three-wheeler, then one) of the wheels or the tracks from revolving when the vehicle is not being driven or is left unattended (viz. **parking brakes**) (Reg. 10 and T. 8).

A brake drum shall not be deemed to form part of a braking system (Reg. 3 and T. 3) but is part of the wheel (Reg. 3).

Every motor vehicle with a braking system with vacuum or pressure reservoir shall have a device to warn the driver of any impending failure of the vacuum or pressure system. This will apply to vehicles first registered on or after 1 Oct., 1937 (Reg. 11 and T. 10).

Locomotive.—If registered before 1st June, 1955, must have an efficient braking system, the brakes acting on all wheels other than steering wheels or on the tracks so as to stop the locomotive within a reasonable distance. This does not apply to a steam locomotive capable of being reversed by its engine, if first registered on or before 2 Jan., 1933 (Reg. 31).

If registered on or after 1st June, 1955, it must have an efficient braking system or systems with two means of operation (unless it is a road roller with one means of operation) as specified in Reg. 32.

A tracklaying locomotive should have an efficient braking system (T. 28).

Motor Tractor, Heavy Motor Car and Motor Car.—Subject to some exceptions the general rule is as follows :—

Every such vehicle shall have an efficient braking system or systems, in either case having two means of operation, so made that on failure of any part (other than a fixed member or brake shoe anchor pin) by which transmission is effected, the driver will have brakes for half the wheels or for two tracks on opposite sides sufficient to stop the vehicle within a reasonable distance. The application of one means shall not affect the pedal or hand lever of the other means of operation (Regs. 35, 39 and 44). (The foregoing also applies to motor cycles but not to a works truck if it has one means of operating the brakes; Reg. 47). No braking system shall be rendered ineffective by the non-rotation of the engine and the requirement will apply to all wheeled vehicles first registered on or after 1 April, 1938 (and now applies to track layers by T. 29).

The brakes of one means shall be applicable by direct mechanical action. Where any brake shoe can be applied by more than one means of operation all the wheels or tracks shall be fitted with brakes all operatable by one of the means of operation (Regs. 35, 39 and 44 and T. 29). One means shall apply brakes directly to half the wheels of a wheeled vehicle, not through the vehicle's transmission gear. In steam wheeled vehicles the engine is deemed an efficient system with one means of operation if it is capable of being reversed and cannot be disconnected from the driving wheels except by sustained effort of the driver (Regs. 35, 39 and 44).

One braking system with one means of operation will be sufficient for a road roller or a non-steam land tractor (Reg. 35 and T. 29), or a works truck (Regs. 39, 44 and 47).

An efficient system or systems with two means of operation will be sufficient for a wheeled heavy motor car first registered on or before 15 Aug., 1928 (Reg. 39).

If there is a failure of any transmission part of a system it will be sufficient if a brake is available for one wheel of a three-wheeled motor car, or for two wheels of a motor car first registered before 1 Oct., 1938 (Reg. 44).

Motor Cycle.—See above. It shall have an efficient system or systems in either case having two means of operation. On failure of a transmitting part there must be available for one wheel sufficient brakes to stop the cycle (Reg. 47).

Invalid Carriage.—It shall have an efficient braking system, acting on at least two of the wheels so as to stop the vehicle within a reasonable distance (Reg. 51).

Trailer.—Every trailer exceeding 2 cwt. weight unladen shall have an efficient braking system, the brakes acting on at least two wheels when there are not more than four wheels, and on at least four wheels if there are more than four wheels, and on half the wheels of a trailer made after 1 April, 1938. The brakes shall be such as to be applicable by the driver or by some other person on the vehicle or trailer, provided that it will be sufficient in the case of a trailer drawn by a tracklayer or of a trailer not weighing more than 1 ton unladen or of a trailer not made to carry other than a permanent load and not weighing more than 45 cwts. laden, or in the case of a living van not over 2 tons unladen if the brakes of the trailer automatically operate on the overrun of the trailer. Also in the case of an articulated vehicle and in the case of any other trailer the brakes shall be capable of being set as to prevent two at least of the wheels or the tracks from revolving when the trailer is not being drawn (Reg. 55 and T. 36).

The above does not apply to a land implement, a trailer used by or for local authorities for street cleansing and not carrying a load, a broken-down vehicle being towed, an agricultural trailer constructed before 1 July, 1947, drawn by a motor tractor if its laden weight does not exceed 4 tons, and it is the only trailer drawn and its speed does not exceed 10 m.p.h., and also a trailer carrying gas for propelling a goods vehicle under 2 tons weight unladen or public service vehicle drawing it (Reg. 55).

In trailers made on or after 1 April, 1938, the braking system shall be so constructed that it is not rendered ineffective by the non-rotation of the engine of the drawing vehicle (Reg. 55 and T. 36).

For the application of the brakes of a trailer, see " Trailers."

General.—Every part of a braking system and its means of operation shall be kept in good and efficient working order and be properly adjusted while the vehicle or trailer is used on a road (Reg. 76 and T. 54). Brakes may be tested (Reg. 106 and T. 79). See " Testing and Inspection."

See also " Quitting vehicle."

Broken Down Vehicles.—When such are being towed in consequence of the breakdown, the following regulations do not apply: Reg. 9 and T. 7 (springs); Reg. 53 and T. 34, T. 73 (length); Reg. 54 and T. 35 (width); Reg. 55 and T. 36 (brakes); Reg. 64 and T. 44 (trailer plate). See also " Obstruction " and " Tow rope " in this Appendix, and " Towed Vehicles," under " Lights on Vehicles," Chap. 24.

The towed vehicle, for the time a " trailer," is still a motor vehicle and its steersman is the person in charge though not driving it.

Control.—No person actually driving a motor vehicle shall be in such a position that he cannot have proper control over the same or that he cannot retain a full view of the road and traffic ahead (Reg. 86 and T. 64). See " View."

Crane.—If a crane or other special apparatus is more or less permanently fixed on a motor vehicle it is part of the vehicle and is not a " load " (s. 2 (4), R.T. Act, 1930).

There is no restriction on the size of the wheels of a mobile crane (Reg. 13 and T. 12), which also need not have springs (Reg. 9 and T. 7). A mobile crane may be an " engineering plant." See " Special Types of Motor Vehicles."

Dangerous Vehicle.—A motor vehicle, its trailers, and all parts and accessories shall at all times be in such condition and the number of passengers and the conditions of loading shall be such that no danger is caused or is likely to be caused to any person on the vehicle or trailer or on a road (Reg. 73 and T. 51).

The load shall be so secured as not likely to cause danger to any person on the road by its falling wholly or in part. The vehicle or trailer shall not be used for any purpose for which it is so unsuitable as to cause or be likely to cause danger to any person on the vehicle or trailer or on a road (Reg. 73 and T. 51).

The number of passengers on a public service vehicle must not exceed that prescribed by Regulations (Reg. 73).

For any contravention of above see " Penalty ".

Deck.—This means a floor or platform upon which seats are provided for passengers. "Gangway" means a space provided for access to or exit from passengers' seats but does not include a staircase or any space in front of a transverse seat required only for passengers.

" Single decked vehicle " means a vehicle upon which no part of a deck or gangway is vertically above another deck or gangway.

" Double decked vehicle " means one having two decks, one wholly or partially above the other, each deck having a gangway.

" Half decked vehicle " means one which is not single or double decked (Reg. 3).

Direction Indicator.—This means a device on a motor vehicle to enable the driver to indicate his intention to change direction to the right or left (Reg. 3 and T. 3). Every motor vehicle registered on or after 1 Jan. 1936 which has a direction indicator must comply with the provisions of the Sched. to the Regs. of 1957 as to illumination, position, etc.

Every trailer constructed on or after 1st July, 1955, which has a direction indicator must comply with the Sched. of the 1957 Regs. This Sched., also allows a 6 inch sign giving a steady or flashing light, fixed not more than 6 feet behind the windscreen and an additional indicator may be at the rear. If no electricity it may be a 6 inch white hand (Reg. 25 and T. 22).

Driver's Duties.—The driver of a motor vehicle must not unnecessarily drive backwards (see " Reversing "); must not cause obstruction (see " Obstruction "); must when driving be in position for control (see " Control ") and full view (see " View "); must stop engine and put on brakes when leaving the vehicle (see " Quitting Vehicle ") if driving alone a steam vehicle must stop when attending to the furnace (see " Steam Vehicles ") and should not stand his vehicle on his right side of road facing on-coming traffic during the hours of darkness (Reg. 90 but see " Obstruction " later). (Regs. 86 to 91 and T. 64 to 69).

Dual Purpose Vehicle.—This is a vehicle constructed or adapted for the carriage both of passengers and of goods or burden of any description being a vehicle whose unladen weight does not exceed two tons and which either:

(a) Is so constructed that it has a permanent rigid roof with or without sliding panel: that behind the driver's seat there is at least one transverse row of permanent proper seats with backrests; that it has at least one transparent window on each side and in the rear; and that the distance between the steering wheel and the rearmost backrest must not be less than one third of the distance between the steering wheel and the end of the floor, or

(b) is so constructed or adapted that the driving power of the engine is or can be transferred to all the wheels.

Such a vehicle, as regards speed limits, is regarded as a passenger vehicle see M.V.'s (Var. of Speed Limit) Regs., 1956, and M.V.'s (C. & U.) (A.) Regs., 1957.

Fire Vehicles.—If a turntable fire escape is a heavy motor car (over 2½ tons) and does not have pneumatic tyres, it should have soft or elastic tyres (Reg. 40 and T. 32). The restrictions as to drivers' hours of duty do not apply to motor vehicles used for fire brigade purposes (s. 19) and these wheeled vehicles may use gongs, bells and syrens (Reg. 19) at all times when necessary (Reg. 84). The speed limits do not apply if their observance would hinder the use of any vehicle for fire purposes. See "Exemptions from Speed Limit", Chap. 24. A fire escape ladder does not count for length or wheeled vehicle overhang (Reg. 3 and T. 3).

They need not stop engines, etc., when fire fighting (Reg. 91 and see T. 61).

Furniture Vans.—Wheeled trailers specially designed and used for the conveyance of furniture and other similar household effects, if constructed before 15 Jan., 1931, need not have soft elastic or pneumatic tyres (Reg. 56).

Gas-propelled Vehicles.—" Gas " is any fuel that is wholly gaseous at 60° Fahr. under 30 inches pressure of mercury (Reg. 3). .." Gas equipment " is a container for holding or materials for producing gas. " Gas trailer " is one used solely for gas equipment for propulsion of the drawing vehicle (Reg. 3 and T. 3).

Reg. 27 and T. 24 direct that the provisions of the 3rd Sched. to the Regs. shall be complied with in the case of every motor vehicle or trailer which has a container for storage of gas for propulsion of the vehicle. These requirements shall be in addition to any requirements of Regulations for the conveyance of gas.

Attendants for such trailers are not necessary (Reg. 105 and T. 78).

Glass.—All glass fitted to windscreens and outside front facing windows (except glass on the upper deck of a double-decked vehicle) shall be safety glass (Reg. 17 as amended by 1957 Regs., and T. 16).

Safety glass is glass that if fractured does not fly into fragments capable of causing severe cuts (Reg. 3 and T. 3). All glass or transparency fitted to motor vehicles shall be maintained in such condition that it does not obscure the vision of the driver while driving on a road (Reg. 75 and T. 53). See also " Mirror."

Heavy Motor Car.—Means a motor vehicle constructed itself to carry a load or passengers, the weight of which unladen exceeds $2\frac{1}{2}$ tons and which is not a " motor car " (s. 2, R.T. Act, 1930).

Attendants.—If a trailer is drawn on the highway a person additional to the driver shall be carried to attend it (s. 17). See " Attendants ".

Brakes.—It shall have an efficient braking system or systems, in either case with two independent means of operation (Reg. 39 and T. 29). A reversing steam engine will count as one such system, but not on a public service vehicle (Reg. 39). See " Brakes."

Drivers' hours of duty.—See " Dangerous Driving." Chap. 24.

Markings.—The owner shall cause the unladen weight to be marked on the left or near side. This does not apply to a vehicle not registered under the Roads Act, 1920 or the Vehicles (Excise) Act, 1949 (Reg. 59 and T. 40).

Overhang (approximately) shall not exceed 50 per cent. of the distance between the front and rear axles. This does not apply to heavy motor cars first registered before 15 Aug., 1928, nor to works trucks or street cleansers or refuse vehicles nor to a load tipping vehicle if overhang does not exceed 45 inches. Seven twenty-fourths of the length remains the limit for vehicles first registered before 1 Oct., 1938, and in road heating vehicles no part of the heating plant shall be taken into account (Reg. 38).

Trailer.—Only one may be drawn on the highway (s. 18). See " Trailers."

Tyres.—Every wheel of a heavy motor car must have pneumatic tyres except the following which must have pneumatic, soft or elastic tyres:—heavy motor cars registered on or before 2 Jan., 1933: heavy motor cars over 4 tons weight unladen mainly used on rough ground or unmade roads: street cleansers: refuse collectors: turntable fire escapes: tower wagons: works trucks (Reg. 40, T. 32).

Weight.—The total laden weight on a road shall not exceed for a 4-wheeler 14 tons, for a 6-wheeler 20 tons and for over 6 wheels 24 tons. (See Reg. 68).

The total laden weight on a highway of the vehicle and its trailer shall not exceed 22 tons (Reg. 70 and T. 48), provided that in the case of a wheeled trailer drawn by a wheeled heavy motor car the total laden weight may be 24 tons (Reg. 70). If tracklaying and gas propelled the total weight may be 23 tons (T. 48). See " Weight ".

Width shall not exceed 7 ft. 6 in., or if registered on or before 1 July, 1932, and converted to pneumatic tyres, 8 ft., or if a steam vehicle registered before 1 Jan., 1939, 7 ft. 9 in., or if a public service vehicle or a road sweeper, 8 ft. (Reg. 37 and T. 30).

Wings or mudguards are necessary unless the body gives adequate protection, but this does not apply to the rear wheels when part of an articulated vehicle for conveyance of round timber, nor to an unfinished vehicle going to works for completion (Reg. 41 and T. 33) nor to a works truck (Reg. 41).

Horn, etc.—Every motor vehicle, except a works truck, a pedestrian controlled vehicle, a locomotive and a land tractor (and a road roller, Reg. 4 and T. 2), shall be fitted with an instrument capable of giving audible and sufficient warning of its approach or position, which shall not be a gong, bell or syren (Reg. 19 and T. 18). A gong or bell may be used only on vehicles for ambulance, fire brigade, salvage corps or police purposes or for the Land Incident Company of the R.A.S. Corps, and a syren can be used only for fire brigade, salvage corps or police purposes (Reg. 19).

When a motor vehicle is stationary on a road, no person shall use or permit to be used any such instrument with which it is fitted (Reg. 85 and T. 63).

Such instrument shall not be sounded between 11.30 P.M. and 7 A.M. on a road in which there are street lamps not more than 200 yards apart or in any " built-up area," except where necessary for ambulance, fire brigade, salvage corps or police purposes (Reg. 84 and T. 62).

Indivisible Loads.—No limit is prescribed for the length of a trailer constructed and normally used for the conveyance of indivisible loads of exceptional length (Reg. 53 and T. 34). An indivisible load means one which cannot without undue expense or risk of damage be divided into two or more loads for road conveyance (Reg. 3 and T. 3). See " Special Types of Motor Vehicles."

Inspection: See " Testing and Inspection."

Invalid Carriage.—Means a motor vehicle not exceeding 5 cwt. weight unladen and specially made for and used solely by a person suffering from some physical defect or disability (s. 2, R.T. Act, 1930). It must be a wheeled vehicle (Reg. 5).

It shall not be more than 7 ft. 2 in. wide (Reg. 50), and it shall not draw a trailer (Reg. 98). It need not have parking brakes (Reg. 10), nor speed indicator (Reg. 12). It shall have an efficient braking system acting on two wheels (Reg. 51) and wings or other similar fittings to catch mud or water thrown up by the wheels (Reg. 52).

Part II of the R.T. Act, 1930, *re* insurance does not apply to invalid carriages (s. 35).

Land Implement.—Means any implement or machinery used with a land locomotive or land tractor for agriculture, grass cutting, forestry, land levelling, dredging or similar operations, and includes a living van and a trailer carrying only the necessary gear and equipment of the land locomotive or tractor which draws it (Reg. 3 and T. 3).

An attendant additional to the driver is not necessary when drawn by a land locomotive or land tractor (s. 17, R.T. Act, 1930, Reg. 105 and T. 78). Brakes (Reg. 55 and T. 36), wings (Reg. 58 and T. 39), trailer plate (except living vans) (Reg. 64 and T. 44) and springs or resilient material (Reg. 9 and T. 7) are not required. There are no limits to its length (Reg. 53 and T. 34), the diameter of its wheels (Reg. 13 and T. 12) and to its width (Reg. 54 and T. 35). Its tyres need not be soft (Reg. 56 and T. 37).

Land Locomotive.—Means a locomotive (over $7\frac{1}{4}$ tons) designed and used primarily for work on the land for agriculture, forestry, land levelling, dredging and similar operations, which is on a road only when going to and from its land work and which on a road hauls nothing other than land implements (Reg. 3 and T. 3).

If it draws a land implement the requirement as to attendants does not apply (Reg. 105 and T. 78).

If registered before 1 Jan., 1932, it need not have parking brakes (Reg. 10 and T.8). It need not have springs or resilient material (Reg. 9 and T. 7) nor a mirror (Reg. 16 and T. 15). It need not have soft tyres if its smooth soled steering wheels have 5-in. tyres (Reg. 30 and T. 27) and its driving wheels 12-in. wide tyres, all smooth soled or with diagonal iron bars (Reg. 30).

Land Tractor.—Means a motor tractor (under $7\frac{1}{4}$ tons) designed and used primarily for work on the land in connection with agriculture, grass cutting, forestry, land levelling, dredging and similar operations, which belongs to a person engaged in agriculture or forestry or to a contractor for such operations and is not used on a road for hauling any object other than a land implement to or from where it is being used or an agricultural trailer (Reg. 3 and T. 3).

If it draws a land implement the requirement as to attendants does not apply (Reg. 105 and T. 78).

If it is a tracklayer or road roller (T. 29) or if it is not driven by steam one braking system with one means of operation is sufficient (Reg. 35). Springs or resilient material are not necessary (Reg. 9 and T. 7), nor a mirror (Reg. 16 and T. 15), nor a warning instrument (Reg. 19 and T. 18), nor a speed indicator (Reg. 12 and T. 11) and it need not have soft tyres if the steering wheels have $2\frac{1}{2}$-inch smooth soled tyres and the driving wheels have smooth soled or diagonal crossbar tyres 6 in. wide for over 3 ton land tractors and 3 in. wide for land tractors not exceeding 3 tons weight unladen (Reg. 36 and T. 31).

Lavatory.—If a motor vehicle first registered on or after 15 Jan., 1931, or trailer has a urinal, closet, lavatory basin or sink, it shall empty every closet or urinal pan into a tank on the vehicle, properly ventilated and deodorised and no basin or sink shall drain into this tank (Reg. 23), and nothing from such closet, urinal, basin or sink shall be discharged or allowed to leak on to a road (Reg. 80).

Length.—Overall length is exclusive of starting handle, hood when down, turntable fire escape ladder, telescopic fog lamp, snowplough and 12-in. post office letter box (Reg. 3 and T. 3). The maximum overall lengths allowable for motor vehicles are:—

Any motor vehicle other than an articulated vehicle, 30 feet (Reg. 6 and T. 5); an articulated vehicle, 35 feet; an eight-wheeled articulated vehicle registered before 1 January, 1931, 36 feet, and these length limits do not apply to articulated vehicles for indivisible loads of exceptional length if all wheels have pneumatic tyres or if all wheels do not have pneumatic tyres but speed does not exceed 12 m.p.h. (Reg. 6).

For length of public service vehicles see " Public Service Vehicles ".

A tracklaying motor vehicle, 30 feet (T. 5).

A trailer (used on a highway, Reg. 4) shall not exceed 22 ft. in length, but this does not apply to a trailer constructed and used for indivisible loads of exceptional length, to a land implement, to the trailer part of an articulated vehicle, to a broken-down vehicle being towed in consequence of the break down, to a trailer which is a trolley vehicle in course of construction or delivery, to a road tar mixing plant or a road planing machine provided that total length of such vehicle and trailer shall not exceed 60 ft. (Reg. 53 and T. 34).

Locomotive.—Means a motor vehicle exceeding 7¼ tons weight unladen and not constructed itself to carry a load. It is a drawing vehicle. If over 11½ tons it is termed a " heavy locomotive " and if under 11½ tons it is a " light locomotive " (s. 2, R.T. Act, 1930). The regulations apply equally to both types of locomotive save where otherwise indicated (Reg. 3 and T. 3).

Attendants.—When on a highway two persons shall drive or attend it, with one additional attendant for each trailer drawn (s. 17). See " Attendants."

Brakes.—An efficient braking system is necessary (Reg. 31 and T. 28) except in the case of a reversible steam locomotive registered on or before 2 Jan., 1933 (Reg. 31). One person shall be ready to apply the brakes of any trailer drawn, where such brakes do not automatically act on the overrun of the trailer (Reg. 92 and T. 70). See " Brakes."

Drivers' hours of duty.—See " Dangerous Driving," Chap. 24.

Markings.—The owner shall have the unladen weight marked on the left or near side (Reg. 59 and T. 40).

Trailers.—Three may be drawn on a highway (s. 18) and they need not have wings if drawn by a vehicle restricted to 12 m.p.h. (Reg. 58 and T. 39).

Tyres shall be pneumatic soft or elastic when on the highway, but road rollers (Reg. 4 and T. 4) and land locomotives having smooth soled tyres not less than 5 in. wide on steering wheels and driving wheels having 12 in. wide tyres either smooth soled or with diagonal crossbars are excepted (Reg. 30 and T. 27).

Warning instrument or horn is not necessary on a locomotive (Reg. 19 and T. 18).

Weight.—The unladen weight of a heavy tracklaying locomotive shall not exceed 15½ tons but if soft tyres and resilient material it may be 17½ tons (T. 26) and the laden weight shall not exceed the unladen weight by more than 3 tons (T. 45).

Not more than three quarters of the total weight of a locomotive having not more than 4 wheels and registered before 1st June, 1955, shall be transmitted to the road by any two wheels (Reg. 29).

The laden weight of a locomotive shall not exceed 20½ tons but more is allowable if proper springs, soft tyres and more wheels (Reg. 65). The total weight on a road by any 2 wheels in line transversely shall not exceed 11 tons but this does not apply to a road roller or to a vehicle with not more than 4 wheels registered before 1st June, 1955 (Reg. 65).

The total weight of all its trailers laden or unladen whether wheeled or tracklaying, shall not exceed 40 tons (Reg. 66 and T. 46).

Width shall not exceed 9 ft. (Reg. 28 and T. 25).

Markings.—The owner shall cause the following to be plainly marked on some conspicuous place on the left or near side of—

(1) A locomotive—the unladen weight (Reg. 59 and T. 40).

(2) A motor tractor—the unladen weight (Reg. 59 and T. 40).

(3) A heavy motor car—the unladen weight. This does not apply to a vehicle not registered under the Roads Act, 1920 or the Vehicles (Excise) Act, 1949 (Reg. 59 and T. 40). See "Mechanically propelled Vehicles," Chap. 25.

(4) A wheeled trailer fitted with overrun brakes—the unladen weight or in the case of a trailer with permanent plant or apparatus:—the total weight (Reg. 62).

Mascots.—A motor vehicle first registered on or after 1 Oct., 1937, shall not carry a mascot in any position where it is likely to strike any person with whom the vehicle may collide unless the mascot is not liable to cause injury to such person through any projection thereon (Reg. 103 and T. 76).

Meat Vans.—When a motor tractor draws a closed wheeled trailer specially constructed and used for the conveyance of meat between docks and railway stations and wholesale markets it need not have an additional attendant (Reg. 105).

Mirror.—Every motor vehicle (when used on a highway, Reg.

4), shall have a reflecting mirror, so made and fitted, either internally or externally, as to assist the driver if he so desires to become aware of traffic to the rear. Similarly passenger vehicles adapted for more than 7 passengers, goods vehicles and dual purpose vehicles must have at least 2 such mirrors, both external or one internal and one external, so made and fitted as to assist the driver, if he so desires to become aware of traffic to the rear and on both sides rearwards (1957 Regs.). None of the foregoing provisions apply to a motor vehicle drawing a trailer if a person is on the trailer and has an uninterrupted view to the rear and efficient means of communicating to the driver the effect of signals given by drivers in the rear, nor does it apply to land locomotives and land tractors, nor to works trucks if a clear view to the rear nor to pedestrian-controlled vehicle nor to a two-wheeled motor cycle with or without a sidecar attached (Reg. 16 and T. 15), nor to road rollers (Reg. 4 and T. 4).

Motor Car.—Means a motor vehicle constructed itself to carry a load or passengers, which is not a " motor cycle " or " invalid carriage," and the unladen weight of which does not exceed $2\frac{1}{2}$ tons, or 3 tons if made solely to carry not more than seven passengers (s. 2, R.T. Act, 1930). " Motor car " also includes a motor vehicle constructed or adapted for the conveyance of goods or burden of any description:—

(a) which carries a container for gas fuel for the propulsion of the vehicle whose weight does not exceed $3\frac{1}{2}$ tons

(b) which does not carry such container, etc., the weight of the vehicle not exceeding 3 tons (R.T. Act, 1956, Sched. 8 (9)).

Attendants.—If it is wheeled and draws a trailer with not more than two wheels on the highway a person additional to the driver need not be carried to attend it (Reg. 105).

Brakes.—It shall have one or more efficient braking systems, in either case with two means of operation when on a highway (see Reg. 44 and T. 29). See " Brakes."

Drivers' hours of duty (goods).—See " Dangerous Driving," Chap. 24.

Overhang.—It shall not exceed 50 per cent. of the wheelbase provided that the limit will be 7/24ths of the length if the car was registered before 1 Oct., 1938, or if its length does not exceed 20 ft. The regulation does not apply to a car first registered on or before 2 Jan., 1933, not to street cleansing vehicles, refuse vehicles, ambulances and works trucks (Reg. 43).

Trailer.—One may be drawn on the highway (s. 18). See " Trailers."

Tyres.—When on a highway every motor car of unladen weight exceeding 1 ton shall have pneumatic tyres. Motor cars first registered on or before 2 Jan., 1933, works trucks, street cleansers and refuse vehicles if the unladen weight exceeds one ton should have pneumatic, soft or elastic tyres (Reg. 45 and T. 32).

Weights.—The maximum weights allowable in the case of a motor car on the road are 9 tons on 2 transverse wheels, 14 tons on 4 wheels, 20 tons on 6 wheels and 24 tons if more than 6 wheels (Reg. 68).

See T. 48 as regards a tracklaying motor vehicle which is allowed a maximum weight of 22 tons, but if gas propelled 23 tons is allowable.

Wings or mudguards are necessary unless the car body affords adequate protection, but this does not apply to the rear wheels of the motor vehicle part of an articulated vehicle for carriage of round timber nor to an unfinished vehicle going to works for completion nor to a works truck (Reg. 46 and T. 33).

Width shall not exceed 7 ft. 6 in., nor 8 ft. in the case of a public service vehicle or its chassis or a road sweeper (Reg. 42 and T. 30).

Motor Cycle.—Means a motor vehicle with less than four wheels and not exceeding 8 cwt. weight unladen, which is not an " invalid carriage " (s. 2, R.T. Act, 1930). It must be a wheeled vehicle (Reg. 5). It need not have a reflecting mirror if it is two wheeled with or without sidecar (Reg. 16), or springs (Reg. 9). It shall have wings or mudguards except in the case of a works truck (Reg. 49).

Attendant extra to driver for a trailer is not necessary where the trailer has not more than two wheels or has brakes which can be applied by the driver of a motor cycle which belongs to H.M. Services (Reg. 105).

Brakes shall be on one or more efficient systems, in either case with two means of operation (Reg. 47), and " solo " and " combination " motor cycles need not have parking brakes (Reg. 10).

Sidecar wheel shall not be wholly outside the length extremities of the motor cycle (Reg. 95). See " Sidecar."

Trailer over 5 cwt. weight unladen or over 5 ft. wide shall not be drawn (Reg. 97), and from 1 Jan., 1947, a solo motor cycle without sidecar shall not draw a trailer except when towing a broken-down motor cycle in consequence of the breakdown (Reg. 96).

Tyres shall be pneumatic but works trucks and pedestrian-controlled vehicles may have soft or elastic tyres (Reg. 48).

If any person in addition to the driver is carried astride on a two wheeled motor cycle (whether it has a sidecar or not) suitable supports or rests for the feet of such passenger must be available (Reg. 101). See also s. 16, R.T. Act, 1930, which allows only one such pillion rider.

Under R.T. Act, 1956, s. 42, the Minister has made the Motor Cycles (Protective Helmets) Regs., 1957 and these have been amended by 1958 Regs., prescribing the construction, etc., of protective helmets for persons on or in motor cycles, and Sched. 7 of the 1956 Act deals with offences under this s. 42.

Motor Tractor.—Means a motor vehicle not constructed itself to carry a load and of weight unladen not exceeding 7¼ tons (s. 2, R.T. Act, 1930).

Attendants.—When it draws a trailer on the highway an attendant additional to driver shall be carried (s. 17), except when it draws a road repair or cleansing machine (Reg. 105 and T. 78), or a meat trailer, a street cleanser or a refuse collector or is a motor vehicle drawing an unsteerable broken down vehicle or a trailer with brakes applicable by the driver of the drawing vehicle belonging to H.M. Forces (Reg. 105).

Brakes.—It shall have one or more efficient braking systems, in either case with two means of operation (Reg. 35 and T. 29). The reversible engine of a steam tractor will count as one system and one braking system will be sufficient for a non-steam land tractor or road roller (Reg. 35). See " Brakes."

Drivers' hours of duty.—See " Dangerous Driving," Chap. 24.

Markings.—When on a highway the owner shall have the unladen weight marked on the left side (Reg. 59 and T. 40).

Overhang shall not exceed 6 ft. (Reg. 34).

Springs are necessary on the highway, but it need not have them if the tyres are pneumatic and the unladen weight does not exceed 4 tons, or in the case of a tracklayer if there is resilient material between the rims of the rollers and the road surface to support the weight. Also it does not need springs if it was registered on or before 1 Jan., 1932, or if a land tractor for hauling timber or a mobile crane or a works truck (with resilient material in the case of a tracklayer) or a works trailer (Reg. 9 and T. 7) or a wheeled shunter not exceeding 4 tons weight unladen or a vehicle for working on rough ground or unmade roads if unladen weight does not exceed 4 tons, tyres are pneumatic and speed does not exceed 20 m.p.h. or a pedestrian-controlled vehicle with pneumatic tyres on all wheels (Reg. 9).

Trailer.—It may draw on the highway one laden trailer or two unladen trailers (s. 18).

Tyres, when on the highway, shall be pneumatic, soft or elastic, land tractors with prescribed smooth soled or diagonal crossbar tyres excepted (Reg. 36 and T. 31), also road rollers (Reg. 4 and T. 4).

Weight.—The total weight of the tractor and its trailer whether wheeled or tracklaying on a highway shall not exceed 22 tons but in some cases may be up to 32 tons (Reg. 70 and T. 47). See " Weight."

Width shall not exceed 7 ft. 6 in. (Reg. 33 and T. 30).

Noise.—No motor vehicle shall be used on a road in such manner as to cause any excessive noise which could have been avoided by the exercise of reasonable care on the part of the driver (Reg. 82 and T. 60).

No person shall use or cause or permit to be used on a road any motor vehicle or trailer which causes any excessive noise either directly or indirectly as a result of :—

(a) any defect (including any defect in design or construction), lack of repair, or faulty adjustment in the vehicle or trailer or any part or accessory thereof, or

(b) faulty packing or adjustment of the load.

However, it will be a good defence to proceedings under this Regulation to prove that the noise was due to some temporary or accidental cause and could not have been prevented by due diligence and care on the part of the owner or driver.

Also, if the driver or person in charge who is not the owner is prosecuted under this Regulation, it will be a good defence to prove that the noise arose through a defect in design or construction, or through the negligence or fault of some other person whose duty was to keep the vehicle in proper condition or to properly pack the load, and could not have been prevented by reasonable diligence and care on the part of such driver or person in charge (Reg. 81 and T. 59).

The driver shall, when the vehicle is stationary otherwise than through enforced stoppage due to traffic necessities, stop the action of the machinery of the vehicle, so far as may be necessary for the prevention of noise. However, this does not apply so as to prevent the working of the machinery when it is necessary to do so on account of any derangement of it, or when its working is required for some ancillary purpose nor does it apply to a gas-propelled vehicle (Reg. 83 and T. 61). See also " Silencer " and " Horn, etc."

Obstruction.—No person in charge of a motor vehicle or trailer shall cause or permit the motor vehicle or trailer to stand on a road so as to cause any unnecessary obstruction thereof (Reg. 89 and T. 67). The highway is not a parking place unless specially designated as such. The use of a highway must be reasonable.

During the hours of darkness (see Chapter XXIV) no person shall, except with the permission of a police officer in uniform, cause or permit any motor vehicle to stand on any road otherwise than with the left or near side of the vehicle as close as may be to the edge of the carriageway.

However these Regulations shall not apply to:—

(a) Any motor vehicle used for fire brigade, ambulance, police or defence purposes if compliance would hinder the use of the vehicle for such purpose;

(b) any motor vehicle standing on a part of a road specially set aside for parking or for hackney carriages or for public service vehicles or for taking up or setting down passengers if compliance would conflict with the " law " allowing such standing;

(c) any motor vehicle waiting to set down or pick up passengers under Regulations or directions by the chief officer of police;

(d) any motor vehicle in a " one way " road;

(e) any motor vehicle used in connection with building operations, repair of another vehicle, removal of obstruction, maintenance of any road or laying, etc., of a sewer, pipe, wire, cable, post, etc., for gas, water or electricity, if compliance would hinder such use of the vehicle (Reg. 90 and T. 68).

Overhang.—This is the distance from the rear of the vehicle excluding hood when down, post office box up to 12 inches, turntable fire escape ladder and luggage carrier fitted to a seven-passenger motor car, to the non-steering axle of a 4-wheeler or to about the middle of a line joining the rear and middle axle of a 6-wheeler (see Reg. 3.) It shall not exceed 6 ft. in a motor tractor (Reg. 34) nor 50 per cent. of the wheelbase in a heavy motor car with some exceptions given in the regulation (Reg. 38) and in a motor car with some exceptions, including ambulances, works trucks and refuse and street cleansing vehicles (Reg. 43). For side overhang see " Width ".

Pedestrian Controlled Vehicle.—This is a motor vehicle not exceeding 8 cwt. unladen which is controlled by a pedestrian and not constructed or adapted or used for the carriage of a driver or passenger (Reg. 3). The following requirements do not apply to such vehicles—springs if all wheels have pneumatic tyres (Reg. 9); minimum diameter of wheels (Reg. 13); mirror (Reg. 16); certain requirements as to brakes if the vehicle does not exceed 8 cwt. unladen (Reg. 44); pneumatic tyres if all tyres are soft or elastic (Reg. 48) warning instrument (Reg. 19).

For registration and licensing purposes such a vehicle means a mechanically propelled vehicle with 3 or more wheels which does not exceed 8 cwts. unladen and which is neither constructed nor adapted for use nor used for the carriage of a driver or passenger (Road Vehicles (Reg. and Lic.) Regs. 1955, Reg. 1).

Penalty.—If any person uses or causes or permits to be used on any road a motor vehicle or trailer in contravention of or fails to comply with the Regulations governing the use on roads of motor vehicles and trailers (Regs. 59 to 104) or (T. 40 to 78) in Parts III of both Regulations, he commits an offence liable to fine of £20 (Reg. 104 and T. 77).

Police Vehicles.—The speed limits do not apply if their observance would hinder the use of any vehicle for police purposes. (R.T. Act, 1934, s. 3.) See " Exemptions from Speed Limit", Chap. 24. They can carry gongs, bells and syrens (Reg. 19) and may use them when necessary at all times (Reg. 83).

Public Service Vehicles.—Reg. 68 deals with the laden weight of a heavy motor car and of a motor car, but it does not apply to public service vehicles. Such vehicles, if heavy motor cars or motor cars are limited to 9 tons weight on 2 transverse wheels, and to a total of 14 tons on all the wheels, when fully equipped for service with weights for the full number of seated passengers, 140 lbs. for each person. If registered after 31st Dec., 1954, and more than 8 standing passengers may be carried another 140 lbs. for each such passenger in excess of 8 must be included (Reg. 67).

A public service vehicle or its chassis which is a heavy motor car may be 8 ft. wide (Reg. 37) and those which are motor cars or their chassis may also be 8 ft. wide (Reg. 42). Overall length of a public service vehicle shall not exceed 30 ft. (Reg. 6). Overall height shall not exceed 15 feet (Reg. 7).

A public service vehicle shall not draw a trailer but it may draw another empty public service vehicle in an emergency or a gas trailer for its propulsion (Reg. 100).

Quitting Vehicle.—No person shall cause or permit to be on a road any motor vehicle which is not attended by a person duly licensed to drive it unless the engine is stopped and if it has a brake the brake is set so as to effectually prevent its movement.

The stopping of the engine shall not apply to a fire brigade vehicle fighting fire or to a gas propelled vehicle (Reg. 91 and T. 69).

Railway Vehicles.—Wheeled motor tractors not exceeding 4 tons weight unladen used for railway shunting and used on a road only for passing to and from such work need not have springs (Reg. 9).

Refuse Vehicles.—These are vehicles and trailers designed and used for the collection or disposal of refuse or of contents of gullies or cesspools. An attendant for such a wheeled trailer drawn by a motor tractor need not be carried (Reg. 105). Pneumatic tyres are not necessary on such wheeled trailers (Reg. 57), or on such vehicles, wheeled or tracklaying (Reg. 40 and T. 32), but both such cars shall have pneumatic soft or elastic tyres (Reg. 45 and T. 32).

There is no limit to the size of their wheels (Reg. 13 and T. 12), nor to the overhang of their heavy motor cars (Reg. 38).

Reversing.—Every motor vehicle exceeding in weight unladen 8 cwt. shall be capable of being so worked that it may travel forwards or backwards (Reg. 14 and T. 13).

Except in the case of a road roller or other road plant at work no person shall cause a motor vehicle to travel backwards for a greater distance or time than may be requisite for the safety or reasonable convenience of the occupants of the vehicle or of other traffic on the road (Reg. 87 and T. 65).

Road Cleansing Vehicles.—These are vehicles and trailers designed and used for street cleansing. If a motor tractor draws any machine or implement for this purpose an attendant for the trailer need not be carried (Reg. 105 and T. 78). Pneumatic tyres need not be on the wheels of such wheeled trailers (Reg. 57), or of such heavy motor cars, wheeled or tracklaying (Reg. 40 and T. 32), or of such motor cars over 1 ton weight unladen, wheeled or tracklaying (Reg. 45 and T. 32), but both types of motor cars must have, at least soft or elastic tyres. There is no limit to the size of their wheels (Reg. 13 and T. 12) nor to overhang (Regs. 38 and 43). If such a trailer does not carry any load other than its necessary gear and equipment it need not have a braking system (Reg. 55 and T. 36).

A vehicle constructed or adapted for use and used solely for road sweeping may be up to 8 ft. wide (Reg. 37).

Road Repair Vehicles.—When a motor tractor draws any machine or implement used for the maintenance or repair of roads an additional attendant need not be carried (Reg. 105 and T. 78). A heavy motor car exceeding 4 tons weight unladen mainly used in operations on rough ground or unmade roads need not have pneumatic tyres, but should have soft or elastic tyres (Reg. 40 and T. 32), and if it has pneumatic tyres and does not proceed at more than 20 m.p.h. and does not exceed 4 tons in weight it need not have springs (Reg. 9).

Road plant at work may travel backwards (Reg. 87 and T. 65).

Road Rollers.—These vehicles must be registered and carry identification marks. They must display their road fund licences which are marked " nil " in the " duty" space (Reg. & Lic. Regs., 1955, Reg 38). The requirements as to the variation of wheel load and the distribution of weight (Regs. 8 and 29 and T. 6), springs (Reg. 9 and T. 7), reflecting mirrors (Reg. 16 and T. 15), warning instrument or horn (Reg. 19 and T. 18), and soft or elastic tyres (Regs. 30 and 36, T. 27 and 31), do not apply. (Reg. 4 and T. 4.) One braking system with one means of operation will be sufficient if a wheeled vehicle not propelled by steam (Reg. 35) or a tracklayer (T. 29).

The prohibition against travelling backwards for an unnecessary distance does not apply if engaged on road work (Reg. 87 and T. 65). Attendants are not necessary (Reg. 105 and s. 17, R.T. Act, 1930). Its water cart need not have a trailer plate (Reg. 64), its water trailer need not have pneumatic, soft or elastic tyres (Regs. 56 and 57).

Roads Experiments.—Vehicles used under s. 6, Roads Improvement Act, 1925, for experiments or trials on roads, are not subject to the Regulations, see " Special Types ", nor are they subject to the ordinary speed limits (Variation of Speed Limit Regs., 1956).

Salvage Corps.—Such wheeled vehicles may carry gongs, bells and syrens (Reg. 19) and may use them when necessary at all times (Reg. 84).

Showmen's Trailers.—The overall width of a wheeled trailer in use before 15 Jan., 1931, by a travelling showman in connection with his business may be 8 ft. 9 in. (Reg. 54).

Sidecar.—A sidecar shall be so attached to its motor cycle that the wheel thereof is not wholly outside planes perpendicular to the longitudinal axis of the motor cycle passing through the extreme projecting points in the front and in the rear of the motor cycle (Reg. 95). If so attached, and if it complies with the prescribed conditions (e.g. tyres, wings, wheels, glass), the sidecar is regarded as forming part of the motor cycle, and not as being a trailer (Road Traffic Act, 1930, s. 2 (4) (c)).

If a sidecar does not so comply it is a trailer, and for drawing of trailers by motor cycles, see " Trailers."

Signalling by Sound.—See " Horn, etc."

Silencer.—Every vehicle propelled by an internal combustion engine shall be fitted with a silencer, expansion chamber or other contrivance suitable and sufficient for reducing as far as may be reasonable the noise caused by the escape of the exhaust gases from the engine (Reg. 20 and T. 19).

No person shall use or cause or permit to be used on a road any such vehicle so that the exhaust gases pass into the air without first passing through the silencer, which shall be kept in efficient working order and shall not be altered so that the noise of the exhaust gases is made greater (Reg. 77 and T. 55). Silencers may be tested (Reg. 106 and T. 79). See " Testing " ; " Noise."

Smokes, Ashes, etc.—Every motor vehicle shall be so constructed that no avoidable smoke or visible vapour is emitted therefrom (Reg. 21 and T. 20).

If solid fuel is used, there shall be an efficient appliance to prevent the emission of sparks or grit, and also a tray or shield to prevent ashes and cinders from falling on the road (Reg. 22 and T. 21).

No person shall use, cause or permit to be used on a road any motor vehicle from which any smoke, visible vapour, grit, sparks, ashes, cinders or oily substance is emitted if the emission thereof causes or is likely to cause damage to any property or injury to any person who is actually at the time or who reasonably may be expected on the road or is likely to cause danger to any such person as aforesaid (Regs. 79 and T. 58, as amended by 1957 Regs.).

Speed Indicator.—Every motor vehicle registered on or after 1 Oct., 1937, and every public service vehicle when used as an express carriage except land tractors, invalid carriages, works trucks, motor cycles with engine capacity not exceeding 100 c.c., motor cycles neither made nor used for the carriage of a driver or passenger, vehicles not allowed by law to do more than 12 m.p.h. and vehicles incapable of exceeding 12 m.p.h., shall be fitted with an instrument so constructed and in such a position as at all times readily to indicate to the driver within a margin of error of plus or minus 10 per cent., if and when he is driving at a speed greater than allowed by law for the vehicle or greater than 30 m.p.h. if there is no speed limit for the vehicle. If the drawing of a trailer reduces the vehicle's speed limit the instrument need not indicate such lower speed (Reg. 12 and T. 11).

This instrument (speedometer) shall at all material times be kept in good working [order and free from any obstruction which might prevent its being easily read, seen (or heard). It will be a defence to prove any defect occurred during the journey in question or that at the time steps had already been taken to remedy the defect (Reg. 74 and T. 52).

Springs.—Every motor vehicle and every trailer drawn thereby (when used on a highway, Reg. 4) shall have suitable and sufficient springs between each wheel and the frame of the vehicle (Reg. 9 and T. 7).

In the case of tracklayers there shall be resilient material between the rims of the weight-carrying rollers and the road surface so that the weight of the vehicle other than that borne by any wheels is supported by the resilient material. In addition a heavy motor car and a motor car and every trailer drawn thereby shall have springs between the frame of the vehicle and the weight-carrying rollers (T. 7).

Above does not apply to road rollers (Reg. 4 and T. 4), vehicles first registered on or before 1 Jan., 1932, wheeled motor tractors not exceeding 4 tons unladen weight which have pneumatic tyred unsprung wheels, or which are used for railway shunting operations, land vehicles, agricultural trailers and trailers used solely for the haulage of felled trees, motor cycles, pedestrian controlled vehicles having pneumatic tyres, mobile cranes, broken-down vehicles being towed, works trucks and works trailers, provided that if such works vehicles are tracklayers they must have resilient material as described above and vehicles not exceeding 4 tons weight unladen mainly used on rough ground or unmade roads if all wheels have pneumatic tyres and speed does not exceed 20 m.p.h. (Reg. 9 and T. 7).

Steam Vehicles.—A wheeled steam locomotive with engine capable of being reversed, and first registered on or before 2 Jan., 1933, need not have brakes (Reg. 31). If the engine is capable of being reversed, it will be deemed an efficient braking system for a wheeled steam tractor (Reg. 35) and for a wheeled steam heavy motor car or motor car not used as a public service vehicle

(Regs. 39 and 44). The total weight on the road of a wheeled steam heavy motor car or motor car which is not a public service vehicle may be 14 tons (4-wheeler) and 20 tons (6-wheeler). Also the weight on any two transverse wheels of such a vehicle may be 9 tons (see Reg. 68). No smoke, visible vapour, sparks, grit, ashes, cinders or oily substance shall be emitted on a road (Reg. 79). See " Smoke, Ashes, etc."

The driver of a steam vehicle other than a motor car shall stop the vehicle whenever it is necessary to attend to the furnace except where two persons are carried to drive or attend the vehicle (Reg. 88 and T. 66).

Steering Gear.—All steering gear when vehicle or trailer is on the road shall be maintained in good and efficient working order and properly adjusted (Reg. 76 and T. 54). It may be tested (Reg. 106 and T. 79).

Stoplight.—This is a device fitted to a motor vehicle or to a trailer drawn by a motor vehicle for the purpose of showing the intention of the driver to stop or slow down (Reg. 3 and T. 3).

Every stoplight on a motor vehicle registered on or after 1 Jan., 1936 or on a trailer shall be at the rear of the vehicle on the right or on the centre, but there may be another one on the left—both to operate at the same time. Every such light shall be red or amber, diffused through frosted glass or other adequate means and giving a steady light (Reg. 26, as amended by 1957 Regs., and T. 23).

Straddle Carrier:—means a motor vehicle constructed to straddle and lift its load for transportation (Reg. 3). It is not a works truck (Reg. 3). See " Special Types " later.

Television Sets.—Not to be used in a motor vehicle if the screen is visible to the driver or if it might distract the driver of any other vehicle on the road. (Reg. 103A of 1957).

Testing and Inspection.—Any brakes, silencers or steering gear fitted to a motor vehicle or trailer may be inspected and tested by any constable in uniform or by any certifying officer or examiner under R.T. Acts or appointed by the Commissioner of Police of the Metropolis to examine and inspect public carriages, who produces his authority if required, either on a road or with consent of owner of premises on premises (Reg. 106 and T. 79). (To prevent the constable from carrying out such test on a road would be an obstruction of the constable in the execution of his duty and he has power of arrest.) However, examination on premises shall not be made unless either the owner of the vehicle consents or after due notice (48 hours personally or at his address, or 72 hours by registered post) has been served on him, but this does not apply in case of examination within 48 hours of an accident causing injury or damage in which the vehicle was involved (Regs. 106 and T. 79).

When s. 3, 1956 Act is put in force, an authorised examiner may test a motor vehicle or trailer on a road to see that the legal requirements are complied with. Only a constable may stop it for such test. Such an examiner has to produce his authority if so required. Any constable can be authorised so to act by his chief officer.

The driver may elect to have such test deferred to a time and place as arranged under Sched. 1 of the Act, provided that if there has been an accident a constable may require a test forthwith.

S. 1 of this Act, when in force, will allow the Minister to make regulations for the examination of vehicles and for the issue of " test " certificates, and s. 2, when in force, will deal with " obligatory test " certificates for old vehicles.

Tow Rope.—When a motor vehicle tows another vehicle the distance between the two shall not exceed 15 feet, and the tow rope or chain shall be rendered easily distinguishable by other users of the road (Reg. 94 and T. 72). See " Towage of Vehicles," Chap. 24.

Tower Wagon.—If it is a heavy motor car (over $2\frac{1}{2}$ tons) it need not have pneumatic tyres, but tyres shall at least be soft or elastic (Reg. 40 and T. 32).

" Tower wagon " means a goods vehicle which is used for the purposes of an electricity, gas or electric transport undertaking and for no other purpose, and which has a telescopic attachment for overhead work and which is not used for conveyance of any load except articles used in connection therewith (see Vehicles (Excise) Act, 1949, s. 27, and Finance Act, 1956, s. 5).

Tracklaying Vehicle.—A tracklaying (caterpillar) vehicle is one so made that the weight goes on the road either by means of continuous tracks or by a combination of wheels and continuous tracks so that the weight transmitted to the road by the tracks is not less than half the weight of the vehicle (Reg. 3 and T. 3).

Those parts of the track which come into contact with the road surface shall be flat and have a minimum width of half an inch. The total area of each track actually in contact with the road surface at any one time shall be not less than 36 sq. in. in respect of each ton of the total weight on the road surface by means of the tracks, or in the case of a land locomotive or land tractor first registered before 1 Jan., 1936, in respect of each ton of the unladen weight of the vehicle (T. 9).

All the tracks, while on a road, shall be kept in such condition as to be free from any defect which might in any way cause damage to the surface of the road or danger to persons on the vehicle or using the road, and in good and efficient working order and be properly adjusted (T. 56).

The brakes shall act on the tracks (T. 28 and 29) and on the tracks of a trailer (T. 36). See " Brakes."

Trailers.—The R.T. Act, 1930, s. 1, and R. and R.T. Act, 1933, s. 36, refer to vehicles drawn by motor vehicles as " trailers " which therefore has to be taken as the definition of trailers. The expression " trailer " as used in the R.T. Acts and Regulations would appear normally to mean a vehicle without any propelling power of its own at the time which is drawn by a motor vehicle. In the case of *Garner* v. *Burr* (1950) the Court considered that " trailer " included anything which will run on wheels and is being drawn by a tractor or another motor vehicle. The ordinary trailer has some carrying capacity. " Trailer " is defined in the Army Act, 1881 (s. 190, amended 1932), as a carriage constructed or adapted for being drawn by a mechanically propelled carriage.

Every trailer shall be either a wheeled vehicle or a tracklaying vehicle (Reg. 5).

A gas trailer is a trailer used solely for gas equipment for propelling the drawing vehicle (Reg. 3 and T. 3).

The Scottish High Court, in an excise duty case, held that a hut on wheels drawn by a motor lorry was a trailer under the Road Traffic Act (*Horn* v. *Dobson* (1933)).

Attendants.—If one or more trailers are drawn on a highway the general rule is that additional help to the driver shall be provided. See " Attendants" for the exceptions.

Brakes.—A trailer over 2 cwt. weight unladen should have an efficient braking system (Reg. 55 and T. 36). For description and exceptions, see " Brakes." If a trailer is drawn by a locomotive one of the persons driving or attending shall be in a position readily to operate the brakes of the trailer, unless a person other than the driver is in a position and able to apply its brakes. If a trailer is drawn by any other class of motor vehicle the driver shall be in a position readily to operate the brakes on the trailer unless another person is in a position efficiently to apply the brakes of the trailer. However, above does not apply where the trailer has brakes which act on its overrun (Reg. 92 and T. 70) or where it is a broken down vehicle unable to steer (Reg. 92).

No person in charge of a trailer or its drawing vehicle shall cause or permit such trailer to stand detached from the vehicle unless at least one of its wheels or the tracks are prevented from moving by a brake or chain (Reg. 93 and T. 71).

Length.—The maximum length of a trailer (on a highway, Reg. 4) should not exceed 22 ft. (Reg. 53 and T. 34), but for exceptions, see " Length."

Number.—The number of trailers drawn by a motor vehicle on a highway shall not exceed—

(1) three—in the case of a heavy or light locomotive ;

(2) one if laden, two if unladen—in the case of a motor tractor :

(3) one—in the case of a heavy motor car or motor car but if such a vehicle with unladen trailer superimposed breaks down it may be towed by another motor vehicle (Emergency Laws (Misc. Provisions) Act, 1953, Sched. 1). However a heavy motor car or a motor car may draw two trailer pumps used for fire brigade purposes, neither weighing more than 25 cwt. (Road Vehicles (Fire Brigade Trailer Pumps) Order, 1939).

But in this connection the term " trailer " does not include a vehicle used solely for carrying water for the motor vehicle or any agricultural vehicle not made to carry a load.

Any person causing or permitting a breach of this section commits an offence (R.T. Act, 1930, s. 18).

These restrictions on the number of trailers do not apply to vehicles in the service of the armed forces of the Crown (R.T. Act, 1930, s. 121 (2)).

Obstruction.—No person in charge of a trailer shall cause or permit it to stand on a road so as to cause any unnecessary obstruction (Reg. 89 and T. 67).

Prohibitions on Trailers.—No trailer shall be used for convey-ance of passengers for hire or reward (Reg. 99 and T. 74). An invalid carriage shall not draw a trailer (Reg. 98). A motor cycle shall not draw a trailer exceeding 5 cwt. weight unladen or 5 ft. in width (Reg. 97).

A public service vehicle must not draw a trailer but may draw a gas trailer. An empty public service vehicle may tow another empty public service vehicle in case of emergency (Reg. 100). · No trailer other than a gas trailer may be drawn by a motor vehicle which exceeds 26 ft. in length (T. 73).

A motor cycle with not more than two wheels and without a sidecar shall not draw a trailer, but it may tow a broken-down motor cycle in consequence of the breakdown (Reg. 96).

Speed.—If a trailer is drawn the rate of speed is limited. See Appendix I.

Trailer Plate.—One is necessary (Reg. 64 and T. 44), but for exceptions, see " Trailer Plate."

Tyres.—The tyres on any wheels should be pneumatic, soft or elastic (Reg. 56 and T. 37) (when on a highway, Reg. 4), but for exceptions, see " Tyres."

Weight.—The total laden weight of a tracklaying trailer shall not exceed 13 tons (T. 49).

The total weight transmitted to the road by any two transverse wheels of a wheeled trailer shall not exceed 9 tons. The total laden weight of a trailer with less than 6 wheels and not forming part of an articulated vehicle shall not exceed 14 tons (Reg. 69).

The unladen weight of a wheeled trailer with overrun brakes and the total weight of a trailer made to carry plant or other special appliance or apparatus which is a permanent or essentially permanent fixture shall be plainly marked on its left side (Reg. 62).

The maximum total weight of all the trailers, laden or unladen, wheeled or tracklaying, drawn by a locomotive (on a highway, Reg. 4) shall not exceed 40 tons (Reg. 66 and T. 46).

The total laden weight of a wheeled or tracklaying trailer together with that of any motor tractor, heavy motor car or motor car drawing it shall not exceed 22 tons (Reg. 70 and T. 47), or 23 tons if gas-propelled tracklayer (T. 47). However, it may be 24 tons in the case of a trailer drawn by a motor tractor or heavy motor car or motor car, if both are wheeled and it may be up to 32 tons if with special brakes and warning device for them Reg. 70).

Width.—The maximum width should not exceed 7½ feet (Reg. 54 and T. 35), but for exceptions, see " Width."

Wings.—These are necessary (Reg. 58 and T. 39), but for exceptions, see " Wings."

For other provisions affecting trailers, see " Dangerous Vehicle," " Lavatory," " Noise," " Obstruction," " Springs," " Tow-rope," and " Wheels".

Trailer Plate.—The back of the rearmost trailer drawn by a motor vehicle on a road shall display a trailer plate. This is a plate consisting of a white triangle bearing 8 red reflex lenses surrounding a smaller triangle in the centre. It shall be clean and unobscured, vertical, in the centre or off-side, and not more than 4 ft. from the ground. This will not apply to articulated vehicles, broken-down vehicles being towed in consequence of the break-down, trailers drawn by motor cycles, being passenger vehicles or by motor cars that are either passenger vehicles or dual purpose vehicles made for not more than seven passengers, trailers for carrying round timber, land implements (except living vans) and agricultural trailers and road rollers' water carts (Reg. 64 and T. 44 as amended by 1957 Regs.).

Trees and Round Timber.—When these are being hauled on trailers the following regulations as to trailers will not apply :—
9 and T. 7 (springs), 58 and T. 39 (wings), and 64 and T. 44 (trailer plate).

Rear wheels of a heavy motor car forming part of an articulated vehicle used for carrying round timber need not have wings (Regs. 41 and 33).

Tyres.—A pneumatic tyre is a collapsible continuous air-filled chamber round a wheel. It should comply with the following conditions :—

(1) A continuous closed chamber containing air at a pressure substantially exceeding atmospheric pressure when normally used but not subject to a load.

(2) Capable of being inflated and deflated without removal from the wheel or vehicle.

(3) When deflated and subject to a normal load the sides of the tyre collapse (Reg. 3 and T. 3).

A soft or elastic tyre is one of soft or elastic material which is continuous or in close-fitting sections round the circumference of the wheel and is of such thickness and design as to minimise so far as is possible vibration when the vehicle is in motion and is so constructed as to be free from any defect which might cause damage to the surface of a road (Reg. 3 and T. 3).

Locomotives should have (when used on a highway, Reg. 4) pneumatic, soft or elastic tyres on their wheels, except in the case of land locomotives which have smooth-soled tyres not less than 5 in. wide on their steering wheels (Reg. 30 and T. 27), and in the case of a wheeled vehicle tyres (smooth soled or with diagonal cross bars) not less than 12 in. wide on their driving wheels (Reg. 30). This does not apply to road rollers (Reg. 4).

Motor Tractors (when used on a highway, Reg. 4) should have pneumatic, soft or elastic tyres on their wheels. This does not apply to steering wheels of land tractors which have smooth-soled tyres not less than $2\frac{1}{2}$ in. wide on their steering wheels (Reg. 36 and T. 31) nor to land tractors with every driving wheel 6 in. wide if weight unladen exceeds 3 tons or 3 in. wide if weight unladen does not exceed 3 tons provided the tyres are either smooth-soled or have diagonal crossbars not more than 3 in. apart (Reg. 36). This does not apply to road rollers (Reg. 4 and T. 4).

Heavy Motor Cars (when used on highways, Reg. 4) should have pneumatic tyres on their wheels, but this does not apply to heavy motor cars over 4 tons weight unladen mainly used on rough ground or unmade roads ; or to vehicles of local authorities used for street cleansing or refuse disposal ; or to turntable fire escapes; or to tower wagons or works trucks if in each such case the vehicle, has soft or elastic tyres (Reg. 40 and T. 32).

This also does not apply to a heavy motor car first registered on or before 2 Jan., 1933, if it has soft or elastic tyres (Reg. 40 and T. 32).

Motor Cars (when used on a highway, Reg. 4), if unladen weight exceeds one ton, should have pneumatic tyres on their wheels, However, this does not apply to motor cars of unladen weight exceeding one ton which are works trucks, street cleansers, refuse collectors or were registered on or before 2 Jan. 1933 if they have soft or elastic tyres (Reg. 45 and T. 32).

Motor Cycles shall have pneumatic tyres but this does not apply to works trucks or pedestrian controlled vehicles if all the wheels have soft or elastic tyres (Reg. 48).

Trailers (when used on a highway, Reg. 4) should have pneumatic tyres or soft or elastic tyres on their wheels (Reg. 56 and T. 37). However, this does not apply :—

(1) to any land implement or agricultural trailer (Reg. 56 and T. 37) ;

(2) to any wheeled trailer made before 15 Jan., 1931, and specially designed for the conveyance of horses and cattle and used for that purpose or for agricultural purposes ;

(3) to any wheeled trailer made before 15 Jan., 1931, and specially designed and used for the conveyance of furniture ;

(4) to any trailer for the purpose of carrying water for a road roller used for roads (Reg. 56).

Every wheel of a trailer drawn by a heavy motor car or motor car and constructed after 1 Jan., 1933, shall (if used on a highway, Reg. 4) have a pneumatic tyre (Reg. 57 and T. 38). However, this does not apply to works trailers or to trailers for street cleansing or refuse disposal (Reg. 57), or to trailers drawn by heavy motor cars which are exempt from having pneumatic tyres (T. 38) or to trailers carrying water for road rollers used for roads (Reg. 57).

General.—All tyres of a motor vehicle or trailer, while it is used on a road, shall be kept in such condition as to be free from any defect which might cause damage to the road or danger to persons on the vehicle or using the road (Reg. 78 and T. 57).

Unfinished Vehicles.—Such motor vehicles or heavy motor vehicles proceeding to a works for completion need not have wings (Regs. 41 and 46).

A trailer which is a trolley vehicle in course of construction or delivery is not subject to the 22 ft. length limit for trailers (Reg. 53). Unfinished trailers proceeding to a works for completion need not have wings (Reg. 58 and T. 39).

View.—Every motor vehicle shall be so constructed that the driver, while controlling it, can at all times have a full view of the road and traffic ahead (Reg. 15 and T. 14). No person actually driving a motor vehicle shall be in such a position that he cannot have proper control over the vehicle or that he cannot retain a full view of the road and traffic ahead (Reg. 86 and T. 64).

Visiting Forces.—A vehicle in the service of a visiting force means a vehicle belonging to the service authorities of such a force and used for the purposes of such a force and any other vehicle when used as aforesaid by a person subject to the orders of any member of such a force (Reg. 3 and T. 3). See Visiting Forces Act, 1952, for meaning of " visiting force ". See Appendix V, Regs. 6 to 9 (length, height, load, springs), 11 to 13 (brakes, speed indicator, wheel diameter), 15 to 20 (view, mirror, glass, wiper, warning, silencer), 23 to 72 and 102 (width of loads) do not apply to such vehicles (Reg. 4).

Tracklaying Regs. 5 to 7, 9 to 12, 14 to 19, 22 to 50, 73 and 75 do not apply to such vehicles (T. 4).

Warning Instrument.—See " Horn, etc."

Weight.—*Locomotive.*—The unladen weight of a tracklayer shall not exceed 15¼ tons but may be 17½ tons if any wheels have soft or elastic tyres and resilient material is between the rims of the weight-carrying rollers and the road surface so as to support the weight of the vehicle. There may be 1½ tons extra if a permanent crane, dynamo or extra winding drum is fitted, and winding or windlass gear does not count in the weight of a cable ploughing engine (T. 26). The total laden weight of a tracklayer on a road shall not exceed the permitted unladen weight by more than 3 tons (T. 45).

The laden weight of a wheeled locomotive on a road shall not exceed 20¼ tons. If it has springs and pneumatic, soft or elastic tyres, it may be 22 tons if less than 6 wheels, 26 tons if 6 wheels, 30 tons if more than 6 wheels. The total weight on 2 transverse wheels shall not exceed 11 tons but this does not apply to a road roller or to a vehicle with not more than 4 wheels registered before 1st June, 1955 (Reg. 65). The total weight of all its trailers shall not exceed 40 tons (Reg. 66 and T. 46).

Except in the case of a road roller (Reg. 4), not more than three-fourths of the total weight of a wheeled locomotive having not more than 4 wheels and registered before 1st June, 1955 shall be transmitted to the road by any two wheels (Reg. 29).

Motor Tractor.—The unladen weight shall not exceed 7¼ tons (R.T. Act, 1930, s. 2). The total laden weight of a wheeled or tracklaying trailer with its motor tractor, heavy motor car or motor car shall not exceed 22 tons (T. 48). If all are wheeled the weight may be 24 tons and may be up to 32 tons if the trailer has power assisted brakes operable by the driver with warning to driver device. This Reg. does not apply to a trailer forming part of an articulated vehicle (Reg. 70).

Heavy Motor Car and Motor Car.—The total weight transmitted by a wheeled heavy motor car or motor car not a public service vehicle to the road (when on a highway, Reg. 4) shall not exceed:

14 tons—if not more than 4 wheels.
20 tons—if over 4 but not more than 6 wheels.
24 tons—if more than 6 wheels.

Weight on road by one wheel where no other wheel is in the same line transversely shall not exceed 4¼ tons, weight on two transverse wheels shall not exceed 9 tons (Reg. 68).

The weight shall be so distributed that the weight on each 2 feet of the road under the length of the vehicle does not exceed 11 tons or 10 tons if a tracklayer (Reg. 72 and T. 50). The total laden weight on the highway of a trailer wheeled or tracklaying and its heavy motor car or motor car shall not exceed 22 tons (Reg. 70 and T. 46) but if a wheeled trailer is drawn by a wheeled heavy motor car or wheeled motor tractor or motor car the weight may be 24 tons and it may be 32 tons if special brakes with warning device for them (Reg. 70).

Trailer.—The permissible weights of trailers depending on the types of vehicles drawing, are given under " Trailers."

Public service vehicles which are heavy motor cars or motor cars are allowed up to 9 tons weight on 2 wheels, and the sum of the weights on all wheels shall not exceed 14 tons (Reg. 67 as amended by 1956 Regs.).

Other Motor Vehicles.—The maximum unladen weights of motor cars, motor cycles and invalid carriages are given under " Classification of Vehicles," Chap. 24, and see also " Trailers."

General.—A highway or a bridge authority may grant a permit as regards its roads or bridges, allowing a trailer drawn by a locomotive to carry weights (as specified) in excess of what is prescribed by regulation (Road Traffic Act, 1930, s. 24). See also " Special Types of Motor Vehicles."

When s. 30 of the Road and Rail Traffic Act, 1933, has been put into operation (this can be done when Sched. 8 (32) of the R.T. Act, 1956 is put in force) a bridge authority may by notice prohibit the use of the bridge by motor vehicles exeeding a specified weight, either absolutely or at more than a specified speed. See " Regulation of Vehicular Traffic," Chap. 24.

Any damage done to a road by excessive weight passing along the road may be recovered from the person responsible (Road Traffic Act, 1930, s. 54). The owner of a locomotive, motor tractor or heavy motor car shall cause the unladen weight to be clearly marked on the left side of vehicle (Reg. 59 and T. 40 of 1957).

" Weight unladen " means the weight of the vehicle inclusive of the body and all parts necessary to or ordinarily used with the vehicle when working on a road, but exclusive of water, fuel, or accumulators used for its propulsion, and loose tools and loose equipment (Road Traffic Act, 1930, s. 26).

Any person authorised by a highway authority or any constable authorised on behalf of a highway authority, on production of his authority, may require the person in charge to allow a motor vehicle or its trailer to proceed to a weighbridge to be weighed. Refusal or neglect to comply is an offence.

However, such person or constable should not require such vehicle to be unloaded for the purpose of weighing it unladen.

When so weighed, a certificate of the weight must be given to the driver.

If the weight proves to be within the legal limit and the vehicle has had to travel more than a mile to the weighbridge, the highway authority shall pay for loss occasioned (Road Traffic Act, 1930, s. 27).

Wheels.—The " wheel " of a motor vehicle or trailer means a wheel the tyre or rim of which when the vehicle is in motion on a road is in contact with the ground (Reg. 3 and T. 3). " Wheeled " means that the whole weight of the vehicle is transmitted to the road surface by means of wheels (Reg. 3).

All the wheels of a motor vehicle or of a trailer which have not got pneumatic tyres (used on a highway, Reg. 4) shall have a rim diameter of not less than 670 mm. (26.38 inches). This does not apply to works trucks or works trailers; pedestrian controlled vehicles: vehicles for street cleansing or refuse collection. mobile cranes; and land implements. It does not apply to a wheel fitted to a motor car first registered on or before 1 July, 1936, if the diameter inclusive of tyre is not less than 670 mm. Motor vehicles first registered on or before 2 Jan., 1933, and trailers made before 1 Jan., 1933, do not come under this regulation (Reg. 13).

T. 12 deals similarly with the diameter of wheels used with a tracklaying motor vehicle of trailer and allows similar exemptions.

A wheeled motor vehicle or trailer with more than 4 wheels and a trailer with more than 2 wheels which is part of an articulated vehicle and a tracklaying vehicle or trailer with more than 2 wheels shall be made so as to ensure that all wheels will remain in contact with the road and will not be subjected to abnormal variations of load, but this will not apply to any steerable wheel if the load on it does not exceed $2\frac{1}{2}$ tons (Reg. 8 and T. 6). This does not apply to road rollers (Reg. 4 and T. 4).

Any two wheels shall be regarded as one wheel if the distance between the centres of the wheel tracks is less than 18 in. (Reg. 3 and T. 3).

Width.—The maximum allowable widths are :

9 ft.—for a locomotive (Reg. 28 and T. 25) ;

$7\frac{1}{2}$ ft.—for a motor tractor (Reg. 33 and T. 30), a heavy motor car (Reg. 37 and T. 30), a motor car (Reg. 42 and T. 30), and a trailer (Reg. 54 and T. 35).

7 ft. 2 in.—for an invalid carriage (Reg. 50).

However, a heavy motor car first registered on or before 1 July, 1932, and converted from use with solid tyres to use with pneumatic tyres, may be up to 8 ft. wide, and a heavy motor car if a public service vehicle or its chassis and a roadsweeper may be 8 ft. wide (Reg. 37 and T. 30), and a steam wheeled heavy motor car first registered before 1 Jan., 1939, may be 7 ft. 9 in. wide if the excess width of 3 in. is caused by the projection of the wheels or tyres and a heavy motor car 4 tons weight or more with pneumatic tyres on all wheels and which is a goods vehicle or part of an articulated vehicle may be 8 ft. wide (Reg. 37). A motor car which is a public service vehicle or its chassis or a road sweeper may be 8 ft. wide (Reg. 42). A trailer may be up to 8 ft. wide, if all its wheels have pneumatic tyres, if it is drawn by a vehicle over $7\frac{1}{2}$ ft. wide which is a locomotive or a heavy motor car which is a goods vehicle or an articulated vehicle weighing 4 tons or more and having pneumatic tyres on every wheel (Reg. 54). A travelling showman's trailer in use before 15 Jan., 1931, may be up to 8 ft. 9 in. wide, and a trailer made before 1 Jan., 1933, and converted from solid to pneumatic tyres, may be 8 ft. wide at the wheels (Reg. 54). " Width " does not include mirror, direction indicator, snowplough, tyre distortion due to weight of vehicle and if vehicle was registered before 2 Jan., 1939, a 4-inch projection of a swivelling window to allow hand signals (Reg. 3 and T. 3), and the trailer width limits do not apply to a land implement or to a trailer which is a trolley vehicle in the course of construction or delivery or to a broken-down vehicle being towed in consequence of breakdown (Reg. 54 and T. 35).

No load shall be carried on a motor vehicle or trailer if it projects more than one foot beyond the overall width or if the total width of the load exceeds $9\frac{1}{2}$ ft., but this will not apply to:

(a) an indivisible load if the prescribed notice is given to the chief officer of police of every district through which the load will pass (see " Special Types of Motor Vehicles " later) and

(b) the carriage of loose agricultural produce not baled or crated (Reg. 102 and T. 75).

Windscreen Wipers.—An efficient automatic windscreen wiper shall be fitted to every motor vehicle which is so constructed that the driver cannot, by opening the windscreen or otherwise obtain an adequate view to the front without looking through the windscreen (Reg. 18 and T. 17). While the vehicle is used on the road this wiper shall be kept in efficient working order and shall be properly adjusted (Reg. 76 and T. 54). See also " Glass."

Wings.—Wings or other similar fittings to catch, so far as practicable, mud or water thrown up by the wheels or tracks, shall be provided for motor cycles which are not works trucks (Reg. 49), invalid carriages (Reg. 52), heavy motor cars, and motor cars except rear wheels of articulated vehicles used for carrying round timber, works trucks, and unfinished vehicles proceeding to a works for completion (Regs. 41, 46 and T. 33).

Such fittings are necessary also for rear wheels of trailers unless adequate protection is afforded by the body (Reg. 58 and T. 39), except land implements, living vans, water carts, trailers for round timber, fire brigade pumps, trailers drawn by a vehicle restricted to 12 m.p.h. or less and unfinished trailers proceeding to a works for completion (Reg. 58 and T. 39).

Works Trucks and Trailers.—A works truck is a vehicle (not a straddle carrier) designed for use in private premises and used on a road for road works (1957 Regs.) or only in pasing from one part of such premises to another or to other private premises in the immediate neighbourhood (Reg. 3 and T. 3). See also Road Vehicles (Reg. and Lic.) Regs., 1955, Reg. 1, for similar definition.

A works trailer is a trailer designed for similar use and used on a road for similar purposes (Reg. 3 and T. 3).

The following regulations do not apply to works trucks— Reg. 9 and T. 7 (springs): 12 (speed indicator): 13 and T. 12 (diameter of wheels): 16 and T. 15 (mirror if driver has view to the rear): 19 and T. 18 (warning instrument): 40 and T. 32 (tyres if soft or elastic): 46 (wings): 48 (tyres if soft or elastic): 49 (wings).

The following Regulations do not apply to works trailers— Regs. 9 (springs): 13 (diameter of wheels): 57 (tyres): 105 (attendants if weight of works truck and trailer does not exceed 30 cwt.).

A works truck need have only one braking system with one means of operation (Regs. 39, 44, 47).

Special Types of Motor Vehicles.—The R.T. Act, 1930, s. 3, allows the Minister of Transport to authorise the use of special types of motor vehicles on roads and he has made the Motor Vehicles (Authorisation of Special Types) General Order, 1955, as amended 1956 and 1958, which revokes nearly all the previous similar Orders and authorises the use on roads of the following vehicles which do not comply in all respects with the requirements of the Construction and Use Regulations. The following authorisations are included in this Order.

Part I: The General Order, 1952, is revoked. Nothing of this Order relating to speed shall authorise any speed in excess of any other speed limit imposed by any other enactment (Art. 2).

Part II deals with miscellaneous vehicles not fully complying with the Regulations and authorises their use on roads as follows:—

Art. 3: Tracklaying vehicles and tracklaying trailers used on roads only for demonstration or for proceeding to railway stations for shipment and not carrying burden for hire or reward, provided that the written consent of the highway authorities concerned is first obtained.

Art. 4: Naval, Military, Air Force and Civil Aviation vehicles (which are for combative or training purposes, guns, stores, tanks, searchlights, aircraft, flying operations, drawing aircraft or constructed before 1 Jan., 1949. See First Schedule).

Art. 5: Lifeboat vehicles, viz. tracklayers also trailers used for drawing or launching lifeboats.

Art. 6: Grasscutting and hedge trimming machines not used for carrying any person, not exceeding 8 cwt. unladen and not more than $7\frac{1}{2}$ ft. wide except when actually engaged on their work.

A mechanically propelled grasscutting machine controlled by a pedestrian and not capable of being used or adapted for any other purpose shall be treated as not being a motor vehicle under the R.T. Acts, 1930–1956, and treated as a hand propelled vehicle (R.T. Act, 1956, s. 50).

Art. 7: Rotary ploughs—such a specially constructed land locomotive must not exceed 11 ft. 6 in. wide; weight unladen limit 26 tons; no trailer other than a living van or trailers carrying necessary equipment, etc.: if over 8 ft. wide and no trailer three persons to be in attendance inclusive of driver or drivers, one to proceed in front and one at the rear whenever necessary by reason of the width of the road or otherwise: and if over 8 ft. wide and drawing one or more trailers, 2 persons to drive or attend the vehicle and one person for each trailer, one of these attendants to follow on the road when necessary by reason of the width of the road or otherwise: if such vehicle is to be moved more than 5 miles on the road 4 days' notice should be given to the police and to the highway authorities concerned and the latter may postpone consent for good reason.

Art. 8: Vehicles for experiments or trials under s. 6, Roads Improvement Act, 1925.

Art. 9: Straddle carrier, provided it is used only for demonstration or on sale or for passing from premises to another premises in the immediate neighbourhood or for repair: no trailer: speed not to exceed 12 m.p.h.: length of vehicle and load or of vehicle or its load not to exceed 30 ft. except with the consent (on 2 days' notice) of the police: width not to exceed 9½ ft.

Art. 10: Reaper and thresher land tractors—provided any trailer drawn is two wheeled used solely for necessary equipment; width limit 14 ft. during July to Nov. and 10 ft. at any other time; one attendant necessary if width exceeds 8 ft. but not 11 ft. but 2 attendants if over 11 ft. wide, one in front and one at rear to warn traffic if necessary: if over 9½ ft. wide and it is to travel more than 5 miles, 24 hours' notice to be given to police who can prescribe route: if over 10 ft. wide speed limit is 5 m.p.h. but if under 10 ft. wide the speed limit is 10 m.p.h.

Art. 11: Hay and straw balers (motor tractors) provided width does not exceed 8 ft.: overhang does not exceed 8 ft.: speed limit 10 m.p.h.

Art. 12: Excavations carriers—viz. heavy motor car or trailer or articulated vehicle specially made for use in private premises for moving excavated material and fitted with tipping body or moving platform for discharging load. Provided that vehicle is used only for proceeding to and from private premises or between private premises and a port: no heavy motor car not part of an articulated vehicle shall draw a trailer: if a trailer is drawn by a motor vehicle no other trailer allowed: length of trailer not to exceed 28 ft. and length of articulated vehicle not to exceed 44 ft.: width not to exceed 11 ft.: speed limit 12 m.p.h. but if over 9½ ft. wide speed limit is 8 m.p.h.: all wheels must have pneumatic tyres: if width is over 8 but does not exceed 9½ ft. one attendant in addition to the driver but if width is over 9½ ft. 3 persons inclusive of driver must be in attendance. Heavy motor cars and articulated vehicles may not transmit more than 15 tons weight by any two wheels in line transversely or 25 tons overall.

Before using such vehicle over 8 ft. wide on a tramcar road or such a vehicle over 9½ ft. wide on any road the owner shall give 2 days' notice to the police who may prescribe the time or route. Highway and bridge authorities must also be similarly notified.

Part III deals with abnormal indivisible loads and engineering plant.

Art. 13: Abnormal indivisible load means a load which cannot without undue expense or risk of damage be divided into two or more loads for carriage on roads and cannot, owing to its dimensions or weight, be carried by a heavy motor car or trailer complying in all respects with the requirements of the Construction and Use Regs.

Art. 14: Heavy motor cars and trailers specially made for the carriage of such loads and locomotives and tractors specially made to draw such trailers are allowed by this Order to travel on roads, under the following conditions—

Every such vehicle shall be wheeled: overall width of such heavy motor car, trailer or locomotive shall not exceed 9½ ft. and of a trailer 9½ ft. except where a greater width (20 ft. limit) is necessary for the safe carriage of the load on the trailer; overall width of such a load or of the vehicle and load shall not exceed 20 ft.: all wheels shall have tyres pneumatic, soft or elastic: total weight on road shall not exceed 150 tons: a heavy motor car or trailer shall be used only for the carriage of such a load and a locomotive or tractor shall be used only for the drawing of trailers authorised by this Article, in both cases subject to the condition that no vehicle or combination of vehicles shall carry more than one such load at any one time provided that subject to the requirements of the Construction and Use Regs. as to the laden weights on road it shall be permissible for a vehicle and any vehicles used in combination to carry more than one such load of the same character and where such a load is carried articles of a similar character may be carried.

Art. 16: The speed limit is 5 m.p.h. but may be 12 m.p.h. if the total weight does not exceed 75 tons: if the overall width of all does not exceed 9½ ft.: if all wheels have pneumatic tyres: if the wheels have proper springs.

Art. 21: A vehicle carrying such a load must not enter upon any bridge whilst another such load is on the bridge and it must not remain stationary on any bridge except in circumstances beyond the drivers control.

Art. 13: Engineering plant means movable plant or equipment being a motor vehicle or trailer specially made for the special purposes of engineering operations or a mobile crane, both of which cannot comply in all respects with the requirements of the Construction and Use Regs.

Art. 15: This plant is allowed to be on roads provided that:— such a plant other than a mobile crane, is used on a road only in proceeding to and from the site of engineering operations or when actually engaged in such operations and carrying no load other than necessary equipment or necessary materials: no engineering plant other than a mobile crane shall draw a trailer other than one which is an engineering plant or a living van or office; no mobile crane shall draw a trailer: a mobile crane is to be used on a road only on journeys and not for lifting or carrying burden otherwise than when actually engaged in engineering operations: such a " plant " must be either wheeled or tracklaying: all wheels not having pneumatic soft or elastic tyres shall have smooth tyres with rounded edges (provided that gritting machines for use on ice-bound roads may have tyres shod with diagonal cross-bars): it should have an efficient brake or if steam-driven a reversing engine: a trailer should have an efficient brake or suitable scotches: no such motor vehicle over 26 ft. long shall draw a trailer but may draw a broken-down vehicle.

Art. 17: The speed limit for such a " plant " is 5 m.p.h. if it is wheeled and all tyres are pneumatic the speed limit is 8 m.p.h. It will be 12 m.p.h. if weight on road does not exceed 14 tons; if width does not exceed $9\frac{1}{4}$ ft; if all tyres are pneumatic; if length of a vehicle which is " plant " does not exceed 30 ft., and if length of motor vehicle and trailer " plant " does not exceed 60 ft.: if a trailer has efficient brake, and no " plant " shall draw a trailer.

General directions regarding such " loads " and " plant " are as follows—

Art. 18: Where width of vehicle or load or vehicle and load exceeds $9\frac{1}{4}$ ft. 3 persons inclusive of driver or drivers shall be in attendance while the vehicle is driven on the road. Provided that when a vehicle is actually engaged in engineering operations one person in addition to the driver or drivers will be sufficient. Where such width exceeds 8 ft. but does not exceed $9\frac{1}{4}$ ft. one person in addition to the driver or drivers will be sufficient while the vehicle is being driven.

Art. 19: Before using on a road any such " vehicle ", if the total width exceeds 8 ft. or if the total weight exceeds 75 tons, the owner shall give 2 days' notice (in the form specified in Part 1 of the 2nd Sched.) to the police of every district through which the vehicle is to pass and the police may vary the time, date or route.

Such notice is not necessary if the " vehicle " will not travel on tramcar roads and if the total width does not exceed $9\frac{1}{4}$ ft. and the total weight does not exceed 75 tons.

Art. 20: gives directions as to the notice (Part 2 of 2nd Sched.) to be given to the highway and bridge authorities but this Article does not apply to vehicles owned or under the control of the Admiralty, War Office or Air Force.

Under the Authorisation of Special Types Order (No. 3) 1941 the following motor vehicles were specially authorised:—Nos. FVP 920 to 923, HVP 816 to 822 and EAX 728, 729—thirteen in all. Under a similar Order, 1942, motor vehicles Nos. FVO 762, 763 were specially authorised. Under a similar Order (No. 2), 1951 the use on roads of Mack Type N.M. heavy artillery tractors for clearing snow or distribution of grit or salt on roads is allowed.

APPENDIX III

REGULATIONS AS TO THE PROSECUTION OF OFFENCES

The Prosecution of Offences Regulations, 1946, dated 23 August, 1946, made by the Attorney-General with the approval of the Lord Chancellor and the Secretary of State under the Prosecution of Offences Acts, 1879 to 1908, are as follows (summarised and with notes in brackets) :—

1. It shall be the duty of the Director of Public Prosecutions to institute, undertake or carry on criminal proceedings in the following cases :—

(*a*) Any offence punishable with death (these include murder, treason, arson of H.M. ships, dockyards, arsenals, etc., piracy with violence).

(*b*) Any case referred to him by a Government Department in which he considers criminal proceedings should be instituted.

(*c*) Any case which appears to him to be of importance or difficulty or which for any other reason requires his intervention.

2. The Director shall, on application or on his own initiative, give advice to Government Departments, clerks to justices, chief officers of police and such other persons as he may think right in any criminal matter which appears to him to be of importance or difficulty.

3. The Director may assist prosecutors by authorising special expenses.

4. The Director may employ a solicitor to act as his agent in a prosecution.

5. The Director shall in all matters be subject to the directions of the Attorney-General.

6. (1) The chief officer of every police district shall, as respects offences alleged to have been committed in his district, report to the Director :—

(*a*) Every offence punishable with death (see above).

(*b*) Every offence in respect of which the prosecution has by statute to be undertaken by or with the consent of the Director. These offences include :—

(1) Incitement to Disaffection Act, 1934, s. 3 ; consent necessary.

(2) Prevention of Fraud (Investments) Act, 1958, s. 1 : unlicensed dealer in securities, and s. 14 (distributing circulars inviting persons to invest in securities) ; consent of Board of Trade or Director necessary.

(3) Dangerous Drugs Act, 1951, s. 18, proceedings on indictment for any offence under the Act or Regulations can be instituted only by or with the consent of the Attorney-General or the Director.

(4) Firearms Act, 1937, s. 27 ; summary proceedings for an offence under the Act after six months and within four years after the commission of the offence can be instituted by or by direction of the Director.

(5) Betting and Lotteries Act, 1934, s. 22. The Director only can prosecute or direct prosecution of a newspaper, etc., for publishing inducement to take part in a lottery.

(c) Every indictable case in which the prosecution is wholly withdrawn or is not proceeded with within a reasonable time.

(d) Every case in which a request for information is made by the Director.

(e) Every case in which it appears to the chief officer of police that the advice or assistance of the Director is desirable.

(2) The chief officer of police shall also report, as respects offences alleged to have been committed within his district, to the Director :—

(a) Offences under the following Acts :—

(1) Sexual Offences Act, 1956 (incest).

(2) Official Secrets Acts, 1911 to 1939.

(3) Forgery Act, 1913, s. 2 (forgery, with intent to defraud, of many specified valuable documents) and s. 3 (forgery with intent to defraud or deceive, of certain documents, mainly official).

(4) Coinage Offences Act, 1936, and Gold and Silver (Export Control, etc.) Act, 1920, s. 2 (melting down, etc., current gold or silver coin).

(b) Offences of sedition (including seditious libel), conspiracies to pervert or defeat the course of justice, public mischief, libel on persons occupying judicial or public offices, bribery and corruption of or by a public official, fraudulent conversion by a public official, solicitor or trustee.

(c) Offences of manslaughter, attempted murder, rape, abortion, carnal knowledge of mental defectives, defilement of girls under thirteen years of age, indecent offences upon a number of children or young persons, sexual offences against a child or young person involving the communication of a venereal disease, and cases in which there has been a previous conviction for the same or a similar sexual offence and the offence charged is one that can be dealt with summarily.

(*d*) Cases of obscene or indecent libels, exhibitions or publications in which it appears to the chief officer of police that there is a *prima facie* case for prosecution ; and

(*e*) Cases under the Extradition Acts, 1870 to 1932, and the Fugitive Offenders Acts, 1881 and 1915.

7. When reporting an offence punishable with death the chief officer of police shall supply the Director with

(*a*) A full report on the circumstances ;

(*b*) copies of the statements of any witnesses ; and

(*c*) A report of any proceedings taken before a coroner or justice in connection with the offence.

8. A justice or coroner to whom the Director has sent notice that he is carrying on any criminal proceeding, shall, within three days of receipt of the notice, transmit to the Director all the documents and things connected with the case (see s. 5 of the Prosecution of Offences Act, 1879).

9. In any case in which the prosecution for an offence instituted before examining Justices or a Court of summary jurisdiction is wholly withdrawn or is not proceeded with within a reasonable time, the clerk to the Justices or to the Court shall send to the Director a report of the case and shall supply the Director with any further information or documents he may require (1879 Act, s. 5).

10. The Regulations dated 25 Jan., 1886, are revoked.

NOTE.—As regards the offences given above which are to be reported to the Director, it would seem that " undetected crime " need not be so reported, and that it would not be necessary to report any such offence unless there is a *prima facie* case against an alleged offender. Similarly it would not seem necessary to report when the police apply for the withdrawal of a summons or warrant.

Criminal Justice Act, 1925, s. 34, directs that any document purporting to be the consent, fiat or order for or to the institution of any criminal proceedings and to be signed by the Attorney-General, the Solicitor-General, the Director or an Assistant Director of Public Prosecutions shall be admissible as *prima facie* evidence without further proof.

APPENDIX IV

DEFENCE REGULATIONS

The Defence (General) Regulations 1939 were enacted in consequence of the emergency caused by the war in 1939 and were supplemented from time to time by various Statutory Orders.

Many of these Regulations (and Orders) have been revoked but a few remain some of which may concern police work and which are as follows:

Reg. 82.—Forgery of any document issued under the Regulations; using, lending or allowing use of such a document; making or having so similar a document as to be calculated to deceive or using a false document, return, etc. will be an offence. Knowingly or recklessly making false statement in supplying information for the purposes of the Regulations will be an offence.

Reg. 83.—It will be an offence to wilfully obstruct any person functioning under the Regulations and under Reg. 84 a person must not, without permission, disclose any information obtained under the Regulations.

Reg. 91.—If a body corporate is convicted of an offence under the Regulations every director or officer is guilty unless he proves the offence was committed without his knowledge or that he tried to prevent it.

Reg. 92.—Contravention of or non-compliance with any of the Regulations or any direction or requirement thereunder will be an offence punishable on summary conviction (up to 3 months prison or £100 fine or both) or on indictment (up to 2 years prison or £500 fine or both). There is no limit to the fine on a body corporate convicted on indictment.

Reg. 93.—Proceedings for an offence against the Regulations may be instituted by a constable or by or with the consent of the Director of Public Prosecutions. Notice may be served by post (Reg. 97).

N.B.—At the time of going to press it was expected that the Emergency Laws (Repeal) Bill would shortly receive the Royal Assent. If this expectation proves correct then the foregoing Regulations will be continued but with modifications in some instances.

APPENDIX V

VISITING FORCES

Under Visiting Forces Act, 1952, a " visiting force " means a force of a country to which the Act applies which is present in the United Kingdom on the invitation of H.M. Government (s. 12).

The provisions of the Act apply to Canada, Australia, New Zealand, the Union of South Africa, India, Pakistan and Ceylon (s. 1) and under the V.F. (Designation) Order, 1954, to Belgium, France, the Netherlands, Norway and the United States of America, and under the V.F. (Designation) Order, 1956, to Luxembourg, Turkey, Greece, Denmark, Portugal and Italy, also to Cyprus, Hongkong and Malta by the V.F. (Designation) (Colonies) Order, 1954.

The service courts (s. 12) of a sending country may exercise jurisdiction over the members of its visiting force and over persons who are not British citizens nor ordinarily resident in this country but who are subject to the service law of that country. On request of the appropriate authority of any such country British authorities may, by general or special orders, direct the British police to arrest any member of its visiting force and hand him over to the authority designated (s. 2).

N.B.—This does not exclude British courts from dealing with offences against British law, except in cases under s. 3.

A member of a visiting force or of its civilian component (as defined in s. 10) shall not be liable to be tried by a British court for an offence against British law if the offence arose out of and in the course of his duty, or if the offence (being one specified in the Schedule to the Act) was against a person having a relevant association (as defined in s. 12) with any visiting force of the same country or if the offence (being one in the Schedule) was against the property of the sending country, unless the appropriate authority (s. 17) of that country waives jurisdiction (s. 3).

British courts should not try offenders tried by such service courts (s. 4).

These sections 3 and 4 shall not affect any powers of arrest, search, entry, seizure, custody, recognizance or remand under British law exercisable with respect to offences against British laws. Where a constable arrests a person without warrant and it may be that he is subject to the jurisdiction of such a service court (see s. 2) such person may be kept in custody for up to 3 days but if not handed over within that period to his own authority he shall be released on bail or brought before a summary court as soon as practicable after the third day (s. 5).

S. 10 defines membership of a " civilian component " of a visiting force. It depends on the possession of a proper passport which is not a British one and is certified by the appropriate authority of the visiting force.

A certificate from the appropriate authority that a person is or is not a member of his " force " or was on duty at the time, etc., etc., shall be evidence of the fact unless the contrary is proved (see s. 11).

S. 12 defines " relevant association " with a visiting force as membership of that force or of its civilian component or of the dependants of same, being wives or husbands or being in their custody, charge or care.

S. 16 provides for the proof of facts by certificates from the appropriate authority of a visiting force or by admissions.

S. 17 states that the appropriate authority of a country is an authority appointed by the Government of that country for the purposes of the Act.

Generally speaking under s. 13, the Army Act, 1955, ss. 186 – 190, directing the arrest, etc., of deserters and absentees without leave applies as regards visiting forces. However the powers of arrest and surrender of such persons shall not be exercised unless on request (specific or general) from the appropriate authority of the sending country.

If a person surrenders as such to the police and on enquiry appears to be an absentee without leave or a deserter from a visiting force he can be delivered into the custody of his force.

The Visiting Forces (Application of Law) Orders, 1954 and 1956, apply to the visiting forces of the countries named above (Art. 3).

The Admiralty, Army Council or Air Council has power to nominate persons to be appointed special constables to act within certain places. They now can nominate persons to be appointed special constables in and within 15 miles of premises used by a visiting force and their own special constables can act within such premises and area (Art. 6).

The Road Traffic Acts, 1930 to 1956, and Part I of the Road and Rail Traffic Act, 1933, are not to apply to any vehicle in the service of a visiting force or to anything done or omitted in relation to any such vehicle by a member of such force acting in the course of his duty. However s. 121 (2) of the R. T. Act, 1930, (which allows certain exemptions to vehicles and persons in the public service of the Crown) shall apply to vehicles in the service of a visiting force, with some modifications as set out in this Article. Vehicles in the service of a visiting force have the same privileges as regards lights on vehicles as vehicles used for naval, military or air force purposes (Art. 8).

Under Art. 11 (1) any general Crown privilege which applies in respect to the numerous Acts specified in the 2nd Schedule to the Order, shall extend to the members or property of a visiting force as it does to the Home Forces.

Under Art. 11 (2) such provisions of the many enactments specified in the 3rd Schedule to the Order as confer privileges, etc., on the Home Forces, shall apply to visiting forces subject to any modifications given in the Schedule.

Art. 12 enables the provisions of the 4th Schedule to the Order to deal with civilian and service witnesses before service courts of visiting forces, and enables the 5th Schedule to deal with the custody, detention and treatment of persons sentenced by such courts. A person sentenced to imprisonment by such a service court who is unlawfully at large may be arrested by any constable without warrant and taken to any place where he may be legally detained. This place may be prison, naval, military or air force detention establishment or custody as arranged by the British authorities (5th Sched.). The Army Act, 1955, s. 192, provides for the punishment on summary conviction of persons who procure or persuade soldiers to desert or absent themselves without leave, etc., and by Art. 13 this applies as regards members of a visiting force.

Motor Vehicles (Construction and Use) Regs., 1955, provide by Reg. 4 that the Construction and Use Regs. 6 to 9 (length, height and springs), 11 to 13 (vacuum brakes, etc.), 15 to 20 (mirror, etc.), 23 to 72 (width, brakes, weight, etc.), and 102 (width of loads), do not apply to vehicles in the service of a visiting force. Similarly M.V.'s (c and u) (Track Laying Vehicles) Regs. 1955, by Reg. 4 direct that Regs. 5 to 7, 9 to 12, 14 to 19, 22 to 50 and 73 and 75 of the Tracklaying Regs. shall not apply to such vehicles.

M.V.s (Variation of Speed Limit) (Amendment) Regs., 1954, extend the exemptions from speed limits allowed by the Variation of Speed Limits Regs., 1947, to certain types of vehicles used for H.M. Forces, to vehicles in the service of a visiting force.

Public Health (Aircraft) (Amendment) Regs., 1954, and Public Health (Ships) (Amendment) Regs., 1954, exempt aircraft and ships of visiting forces from the provisions of the Public Health Aircraft and Ships Regs., of 1952. Air Navigation (Amendment) Order, 1954, provides that the principal Order does not apply to visiting forces, except the provisions that apply to aircraft of British Forces.

The Aliens Order, 1953, exempts aliens serving in visiting forces from the provisions of the Aliens Orders (see Art. 24).

The Control of Explosives Order, 1953, by a similar Order of 1954, does not apply to visiting forces.

TABLE OF REFERENCES TO STATUTES

PAGE

PAGE

PAGE

PAGE

TABLE OF REFERENCES TO CASES

TABLE OF ORDERS, REGULATIONS AND RULES

INDEX

M.P.L.